murach's
Python for Data Analysis

Scott McCoy

TRAINING & REFERENCE

murach's
Python for Data Analysis

Scott McCoy

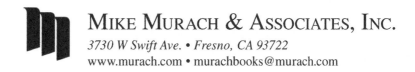

MIKE MURACH & ASSOCIATES, INC.
3730 W Swift Ave. • Fresno, CA 93722
www.murach.com • murachbooks@murach.com

Editorial team

Author:	Scott McCoy
Editors:	Mike Murach Anne Boehm
Contributor:	Joel Murach
Interior Design:	Erica Murach
Production:	Juliette Baylon

Books on programming languages

Murach's Python Programming

Murach's C#

Murach's C++ Programming

Murach's Java Programming

Books on SQL

Murach's MySQL

Murach's SQL Server for Developers

Murach's Oracle SQL and PL/SQL for Developers

Books on web development

Murach's HTML and CSS

Murach's JavaScript and jQuery

Murach's PHP and MySQL

Murach's Java Servlets and JSP

Murach's ASP.NET Core MVC

For more on Murach books, please visit us at www.murach.com

Printed in the United States of America

10 9 8 7 6 5 4 3 2 1
ISBN: 978-1-943872-76-3

Content

Expanded contents

Section 1 Get off to a fast start

Chapter 11 How to make predictions with a multiple regression model

Section 4 The case studies

Chapter 12 The Polling case study

Introduction

Today, data analysis is an essential skill in the fields of business, science, and social science, and Python has become the preferred language for doing that data analysis. That's why adding Python data analysis to your skillset can lead to new career opportunities.

The trouble is that mastering this skillset has been difficult because of the fragmented collection of books and training materials that have been available. But now, this book applies the proven Murach methods to Python data analysis so you can learn faster and better than ever. And after you've used this book to master the skills that you need on the job, you'll find that it will become your all-time favorite on-the-job reference.

What the four sections in this book do

- Section 1 consists of four chapters that get you off to a fast start. Here, you'll learn how to use JupyterLab and Jupyter Notebooks to organize and develop your analyses. You'll learn how to use a subset of the Pandas module for data analysis and visualization. And you'll learn how to use the Seaborn module to create professional data visualizations that can be used for presentations. When you're done with this section, you'll be able to start doing analyses of your own.
- Section 2 presents the critical skills for *descriptive analysis*, which is the analysis of past data. That includes how to read data into a Pandas DataFrame. How to clean the data by dropping unneeded rows and columns and fixing missing values, data types, and outliers. How to prepare the data by adding columns, modifying the data in columns, and combining DataFrames. How to analyze the data by grouping and aggregating the data, using pivot tables, and more. And how to analyze time-series data by reindexing, downsampling, and working with rolling windows and running totals.
- Although most analysis is descriptive analysis, *predictive analysis* takes data analysis to another level by using statistical models to predict unknown or future values. That's why section 3 presents a two-chapter introduction to

predictive analysis. This introduction includes how to find the correlations between variables, how to use Scikit-learn to work with linear regression models, and how to use Seaborn to create and plot linear regression models. It also shows you how to select the right variables and the right *number* of variables for multiple regressions...one of the critical skills for doing an effective job of making predictions.

- Section 4 presents four case studies that show you how the skills presented in the first three sections can be applied to real-world datasets. These datasets include polling data for the 2016 US presidential election, US Forest Service data for forest fires, US social survey data, and basketball shot location data for Stephen Curry of the Golden State Warriors. Frankly, you can't master on-the-job skills by working with toy datasets, so these in-depth case studies help make sure that you will master the professional skills you need.

Why you'll learn faster and better with this book

Like all our books, this one has features that you won't find in competing books. That's why you'll learn faster and better with our book than with any other. Here are a few of those features:

- As you page through this book, you'll see that all of the information is presented in what we call *paired pages*, with the essential syntax, guidelines, and examples on the right page and the perspective and extra explanation on the left page. This helps you learn faster by reading less... and this is the ideal reference format when you need to refresh your memory about how to do something.
- To show you how Python works for data analysis, the examples in this book are taken from eight analyses of real-world datasets…the four case studies that are presented in section 4 as well as four other analyses that provide additional examples. We believe that studying analyses like these is critical to the learning process...and yet you won't find anything like them in competing books or online courses.
- While section 4 gives you an in-depth look at four complete analyses, this book also provides hundreds of short examples that show you the details for tasks you want to do on your own. What's more, our paired-pages format always puts these examples on the righthand page. That makes it easier to find the example that you're looking for than it is with traditional books that embed the examples in the text.
- Like all our books, this one has exercises at the end of each chapter that give you hands-on experience. These exercises also encourage you to experiment and to apply what you've learned in new ways…just as you'll have to do on the job. And because our exercises start from Notebooks that provide the starting code for an analysis, you'll get more practice in less time.

The book prerequisites

Chapter 1 of this book reviews the Python skills that you should have before you start this book. The good news is that they're minimal. You need to know how to import modules; call and chain methods; code lists, slices, tuples, and dictionaries; and continue statements over two lines. That, plus a basic familiarity with the Python coding syntax, will get you going.

Occasionally, though, you'll see advanced Python coding in the examples in this book. That's why we recommend *Murach's Python Programming* as the perfect companion to this book. It presents the other Python skills that you might need, and like all our books, it doubles as a terrific on-the-job reference.

What software you need

To do data analysis with Python as shown in this book, you just need to download and install the Anaconda distribution of Python. It includes JupyterLab, Pandas, Seaborn, Scikit-learn, and more. To help you do that, appendixes A and B show how to install this distribution on both Windows and macOS systems. Then, chapter 1 shows you how to get started with JupyterLab.

How our downloadable files can help you learn

If you go to our website at www.murach.com, you can download all the files that you need for getting the most from this book. And here again, appendixes A and B show how to download and install these files on Windows and macOS systems. These files include:

- the Jupyter Notebooks for all the analyses that are presented in this book, including the four case studies
- the starting Notebooks for the exercises that are at the end of each chapter
- the Notebooks for the solutions to the exercises

After you download these Notebooks, you can run them and experiment with their code to understand that code better. In addition, you can copy code from these Notebooks to use in your own Notebooks.

Beyond that, if you have any problems with the exercises, you can study the solutions to help you over the learning blocks, which is an essential part of the learning process. And in some cases, the solutions will show you a more elegant way to handle a problem, even when you've come up with a solution that works.

Support materials for instructors and trainers

If you're a college instructor or corporate trainer who would like to use this book for a course, we offer the support materials that will help you set up and run the course as effectively as possible. That includes:

- instructional objectives that help your students focus on the skills that they need to develop

- test banks that let you measure how well your students have mastered those skills
- projects for each chapter that let your students get hands-on experience and prove how well they have mastered the skills of those chapters
- case studies that require the skills of several chapters so your students can get more hands-on experience and prove that they've mastered the skills in the context of a complete analysis
- a complete set of PowerPoint slides that you can use to review and reinforce the content of the book

To learn more about our instructor's materials, please go to our website at www.murachforinstructors.com if you're an instructor. Or, if you're a trainer, please go to www.murach.com and click on the *Courseware for Trainers* link, or contact Kelly at 1-800-221-5528 or kelly@murach.com.

One thing to keep in mind: Although all of these materials are useful in running a course, none of them will do you much good unless your students or trainees have this book. It's the primary component for a successful data analysis course.

Please let us know how this book works for you

From the start of this project, we had three primary goals. First, we wanted to present the data analysis skills that every Python data analyst should have. Second, we wanted to do that in a way that works for people with minimal programming experience as well as for those who are experienced programmers. And third, we wanted to make this the best on-the-job reference that you've ever used.

Now, we hope that we've succeeded. We thank you for buying this book. We wish you all the best with your data analysis projects. And if you have any comments, we would appreciate hearing from you.

Scott McCoy, Author
scott@murach.com

Mike Murach, Editor
mike@murach.com

Section 1

Get off to a fast start

This section will get you off to a fast start with Python for data analysis. In chapter 1, you will be introduced to Python for data analysis, and you'll learn how to use JupyterLab as your IDE. In chapter 2, you'll learn the Pandas essentials for data analysis. In chapter 3, you'll learn the Pandas essentials for data visualization. And in chapter 4, you'll learn the Seaborn essentials for enhanced data visualization.

When you complete those chapters, you'll have a subset of the skills that you need for doing analyses of your own. You'll also be able to skip to any chapter in section 2 whenever you need to learn more about a specific phase of data analysis.

Chapter 1

Introduction to Python for data analysis

This chapter starts by introducing you to data analysis with Python and by reviewing the Python coding skills that you'll need for data analysis. Then, it shows you how to use JupyterLab as your IDE. Last, this chapter introduces you to the case studies for this book because they are a critical part of the learning process.

When you finish this chapter, you'll have the background that you need for learning the essential skills for data analysis and visualization. And that's what you'll learn in chapters 2, 3, and 4 of this section.

Introduction to data analysis

Before you start learning how to analyze and visualize data, you should have some perspective on what data analysis is and isn't. So that's where this chapter begins.

What data analysis is

Figure 1-1 summarizes the components of *data analysis*. One of the key points here is that data analysis not only includes *data visualization* (or *data viz*), but also that data visualization often provides the best insights into the data. The goal of this book is to teach you a professional set of skills for data analysis and data viz.

Data modeling, or *predictive analysis*, is included within the context of data analysis. It involves the use of data for building models that can help predict what's going to happen in the future based on the data of the past.

Data analytics is often used as a synonym for data analysis and visualization. Similarly, *business analytics* refers to data analysis with the focus on business data, and *sports analytics* refers to data analysis with the focus on sports data. Of course, business and sports analytics are just applications of the skills that you'll learn in this book.

Data science is a field that starts with data analysis but also includes advanced skills like *data mining*, *machine learning*, *deep learning*, and *artificial intelligence* (*AI*). Although these advanced skills aren't included in this book, they all require a solid set of the essential skills for data analysis and data visualization. So that's where you need to start, and those are the skills that you'll learn from this book.

Data visualization often provides the best insights into the data

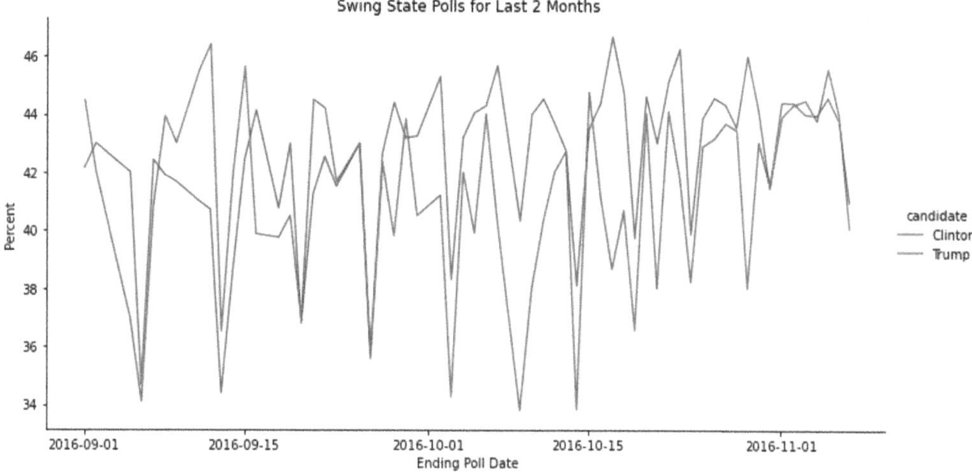

What data analysis includes

- Data analysis
- Data visualization (data viz)
- Data modeling (predictive analysis)

Related terms

- Data analytics
- Business analytics
- Sports analytics

Description

- In this book, you'll learn how to use Python for *data analysis* and *data visualization* (or *data viz*), and you'll be introduced to the skills for *predictive analysis*.
- *Data analytics* is often used as a synonym for data analysis. Similarly, *business analytics* refers to the analysis of business data, and *sports analytics* refers to the analysis of sports data.
- After you use this book to master data analysis and visualization, you'll be ready to learn advanced analytical skills like *data mining, machine learning, deep learning,* and *artificial intelligence* (*AI*).
- *Data science* is a term that includes both data analysis and advanced skills like data mining, machine learning, deep learning, and AI.

Figure 1-1 What data analysis is

The five phases of data analysis and visualization

To give you some idea of what you're getting into, figure 1-2 presents the five phases of a data analysis and visualization project. Note, however, that you don't just start into the five phases of analysis without any planning. Instead, you need to *set the goals* for your analysis project and *define the target audience*. Then, when you have a clear view of what you're going to do, you start the five phases of the project.

In phase 1, you *get the data* for the project. That can be from a third-party website or from one of your own company's databases or spreadsheets. In this phase, you read (or *import*) the data into a *DataFrame*, which is a data structure that consists of columns and rows. You'll learn more about DataFrames in the next chapter.

In phase 2, you *clean the data*. That includes removing unnecessary rows and columns, fixing invalid or missing data, and changing data types. As you will discover, most real-world data is surprisingly "dirty" so this is often a time-consuming phase of analysis. But if you don't clean the data, it will affect the accuracy of your analysis.

In phase 3, you *prepare the data*. That includes adding new columns that are calculated or derived from the original data and shaping the data into the forms that are needed for the analysis. It may also include doing some early visualizations that will help you understand the data.

In phase 4, you *analyze the data*. This includes getting new views of the data by grouping and aggregating the data. It includes doing data visualizations because they often provide insights and show relationships that you can't get from tabular data. And it may include predictive analysis that tries to predict future results based on past results.

In phase 5, you *visualize the data* in a way that's appropriate for your target audience. That means you enhance your visuals so they get their points across as clearly and quickly as possible...even to those with no technical or analytical background.

Of course, the divisions between these phases aren't nearly as clear as this figure might make them seem. In fact, there is usually some overlap between the phases. For instance, when you clean or prepare the data, you're already looking ahead to the analyze phase. And when you analyze the data, you may discover that you need to do more cleaning or preparation.

Nevertheless, these phases are a good guide to the work that you'll do for most analyses, and they provide a useful way to divide the chapters in this book. But note that data visualization is presented in chapters 3 and 4 because it is so critical to effective data analysis. Then, chapters 5 through 9 in section 2 show how to do each of the first four phases: get, clean, prepare, and analyze the data.

What you need to do before you start an analysis

Set your goals

- The *goals of analysis* can be well-defined, like trying to answer specific questions, or more general, like trying to extract useful information from large volumes of data.

Define your target audience

- If you're going to present your findings to other people like managers or clients, you also need to define your *target audience* before you start your analysis.

The five phases of data analysis and visualization

Get the data

- Find the data on a website or in one of your company's databases or spreadsheets.
- Read the data into a DataFrame or build a DataFrame from the data.

Clean the data

- Remove unnecessary rows and columns.
- Handle invalid or missing values.
- Change object data types to datetime or numeric data types.

Prepare the data

- Add columns that are derived from other columns.
- Shape the data into the forms that are needed for your analysis.
- Make preliminary visualizations to better understand the data.

Analyze the data

- Get new views of the data by grouping and aggregating the data.
- Make visualizations that provide insights and show relationships.
- Model the data as part of predictive analysis.

Visualize the data

- Enhance your visualizations so they're appropriate for your target audience.

Description

- Before you start any analysis, you need to *set your goals* and *define the target audience*.
- You can divide a typical data analysis project into five phases like those above. In practice, though, there's usually some overlap between the phases.

Figure 1-2 The five phases of data analysis and visualization

The IDEs for Python data analysis

In the appendixes for this book, you can learn how to install the *Anaconda distribution* of Python for both Windows and macOS. That distribution includes all the major components that you'll need for data analysis and visualization with Python, including the first two *Integrated Development Environments (IDEs)* in the table in figure 1-3. That's why we recommend that you install and use that distribution with this book.

We also recommend that you use *JupyterLab* as your IDE, which is an enhanced version of *Jupyter Notebook*. As you'll see later in this chapter, you start JupyterLab from the Anaconda Navigator, which is why JupyterLab isn't included in the menu shown in this figure.

JupyterLab lets you organize your analyses in *Notebooks* with one Notebook for each analysis. Within each Notebook, you write small blocks of code in cells that you can execute, one at a time. You can also include text within the Notebooks to document what the code in the cells is doing. As you'll see in a moment, these features make JupyterLab an excellent IDE, and that's especially true when you're learning.

Three of the IDEs you can use for Python data analysis

IDE	Description
Jupyter Notebook	A web-based IDE that organizes each project in a Notebook that can include text that describes the operations
JupyterLab	An enhanced IDE for using Jupyter Notebooks
VS Code	A Microsoft IDE with support for operations like debugging and version control

The programs that are installed by the Anaconda distribution

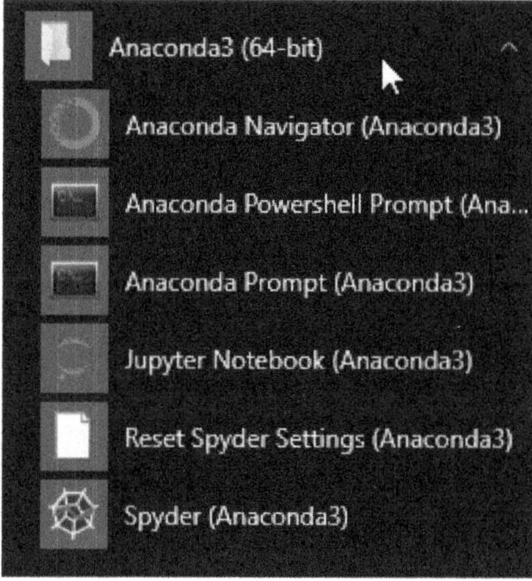

Our recommendations for Python distributions and IDEs

- Use the Anaconda distribution of Python.
- Use JupyterLab as your IDE.

Description

- *Jupyter Notebook* is an *Integrated Development Environment* (*IDE*) that helps you keep your code organized by dividing it into cells within *Notebooks*.
- *JupyterLab* is an enhanced version of Jupyter Notebook that provides features like split-screen editing of two different Notebooks.

Figure 1-3 The IDEs for Python data analysis

The Python skills that you need for data analysis

This book assumes that you have some programming experience with Python. So what follows is a quick refresher on the main Python skills that you'll need when you use Python for data analysis and visualization.

Since all of this is typical Python code, you shouldn't have any trouble with it. But if you do have trouble, by all means get the companion book to this one, *Murach's Python Programming*. It presents all of the Python skills that you will need, so this book can focus on the skills for data analysis and visualization.

How to install and import the Python modules for data analysis

When you use Python for data analysis, you use *modules* like the ones in the two tables in figure 1-4 for various aspects of your work. For instance, you'll use the Pandas module for much of the data analysis that you do. You'll use a module like Seaborn for data visualization.

Most of the modules that you will need for this book are included in the Anaconda distribution, so you won't need to install them. These modules are listed in the first table in this figure. However, you will need to install the modules that are listed in the second table.

To install a module, you can run a *conda command* from the *Anaconda Prompt*. This is illustrated by the first group of examples in this figure. Usually, the format for the first command will work. But sometimes, you will need to use the conda-forge channel as shown in the second command. This is because each channel holds different packages and not all packages are available from the default channel. For more information on how to display the Anaconda prompt and use the conda command to install the modules you need for this book, please see the appendixes.

After you install a module, you need to *import* it into your Notebook before you can use it. To do that, you use the *import statement* as shown in the second group of examples. Within those statements, it's best to use the standard abbreviations that are listed in the first table. For instance, pd is used to refer to the Pandas module, np is used for NumPy, and sns is used for Seaborn. You can also use the from clause in an import statement to import just one submodule or method from a module. In this figure, for example, the second import statement imports the request submodule of the urllib module.

Modules that are included with the Anaconda distribution

Module	Abbreviation	Provides methods for
pandas	pd	Data analysis and visualization
numpy	np	Numerical computing
seaborn	sns	Data visualization
datetime	dt	Working with datetime objects
urllib		Getting files from the web
zipfile		Working with zip files
sqlite3		Working with a SQLite database
json		Working with JSON data
sklearn		Regression analysis

The modules that you need to install for this book

Module	Chapter	Provides methods for
pyreadstat	5	Reading Stata files
geopandas	12	Plotting geographic data

Two ways to install a module

Use the conda command from the Anaconda Prompt

```
conda install pandas --yes
```

Use the conda command with a different channel

```
conda install --channel conda-forge pyreadstat --yes
```

How to import modules

How to import one module into the namespace specified by the as clause

```
import pandas as pd
```

How to import one submodule from a module

```
from urllib import request
```

Description

- Most of the *modules* that you need for this book are installed as part of the Anaconda distribution. But you still need to import them before you can use them.
- To *install* a module that isn't included in the Anaconda distribution, you can run a *!pip command* from a Notebook cell or a *conda command* from the Anaconda prompt.
- To *import* a module, you use the Python *import statement*. This statement lets you import an entire module or just the submodules or methods that you're going to use.
- See the appendixes for more on how to install the modules that you'll need for this book that aren't included in the Anaconda distribution.

Figure 1-4 How to install and import the Python modules for data analysis

How to call and chain methods

If you've used Python to develop applications, you already know how to call Python methods. But since this skill is so essential to using the modules for data analysis, figure 1-5 provides a quick review. In addition, it shows how to chain methods, which is another essential skill for data analysis.

After you import a module, you can *call* any of its methods, as shown by the first group of examples. Here, the first example shows how to call a method in a Pandas module. To do that, you code the abbreviation for the module (pd), a dot (period), the method name, and any *parameters* in parentheses. In this example, the read_csv() method is executed and its one parameter is the URL for a file on the FiveThirtyEight website. When this method is run, it reads the file into a Pandas DataFrame object named polls.

The second example in this group shows how to call a method from a Pandas object. To do that, you code the object name followed by a dot, the method name, and any parameters in parentheses. So in this case, the sort_values() method of the Pandas DataFrame object named polls is executed, and its one parameter specifies the column that the data should be sorted by.

The second group of examples in this figure shows how to use *dot notation* to *chain* methods. In the first statement, the head() method is chained to the sort_values() method. So after the data in the DataFrame named polls is sorted, the head() method displays the first five rows of the sorted data. This works because the sort_values() method returns a DataFrame object with the sorted data. Then, the head() method can be run on that object.

In the second statement in this group, the plot() method is chained to the query() method. So after the data is selected by the query() method, the plot() method plots the data for each poll.

When you code the parameters for a method, you need to recognize the difference between positional and keyword parameters. This is illustrated by the third group of examples in this figure. This starts with the *signature* for the sort_values() method. A signature is the part of the syntax for a method that lists its parameters.

Within a signature, the *positional parameters* are first and are identified by their position in the signature. In this case, the sort_values() method has one positional parameter named *by*. By contrast, each *keyword parameter* is followed by an equal sign and the default value for the parameter, if it has one. For instance, the sort_values() method has a keyword parameter named ascending that has a default value of True.

When you code the parameters for a method, you need to code the values for the positional parameters first and in the same sequence that the parameters are listed in the signature. This is illustrated by the statement after the signature. Here, the value of the positional parameter is the startdate column, and it's followed by the ascending and inplace keyword parameters. Because the other two keyword parameters aren't coded, their default values are used. As a result, the rows in the DataFrame will be sorted by the data in the startdate column in descending sequence, and the sorted result will replace the data in the polls DataFrame.

How to call methods

How to call a method in a module

```
import pandas as pd
polls_url = 'http://projects.fivethirtyeight.com/.../president_general_polls_2016.csv'
polls = pd.read_csv(poll_url)
```

How to call a method from a DataFrame object

```
polls.sort_values('startdate')
```

How to chain methods

How to chain the sort_values() and head() methods

```
polls.sort_values('startdate').head()
```

How to chain the query() and plot() methods

```
polls.query('state != "U.S."') \
    .plot(x='startdate', y=['Clinton_pct','Trump_pct'])
```

How to call a method with positional and keyword parameters

The signature for the sort_values() method

```
sort_values(by, axis=0, ascending=True, inplace=False,
                kind='quicksort', na_position='last')
```

The sort_values() method with positional and keyword parameters

```
polls.sort_values('startdate', ascending=False, inplace=True)
```

Description

- To *call* a *method* in a module, you code the module abbreviation, a dot, the method name, and the *parameters* (*arguments*) within parentheses. To call a method from an object, you code the object name, a dot, the method name, and the parameters within parentheses.
- To *chain methods*, you use *dot notation*.
- The *signature* of a method shows the parameters of the method. The parameters that have equal signs after them are *keyword parameters*; the others are *positional parameters*. The values after the equal signs in the keyword parameters are the default values.
- When methods accept both positional and keyword parameters, you need to code the positional parameters before the keyword parameters and in the sequence shown in the signature.

Figure 1-5 How to call and chain methods

The coding basics for Python data analysis

As you learn to use the modules and methods for data analysis and visualization, you'll see that you need to code some parameters as *lists*, some as *tuples*, some as *dictionary objects*, and some as *slices*. That's why figure 1-6 provides a quick review of the coding for these structures.

As you can see in the first group of examples, a *list* is a sequence of items that is coded within brackets. A *tuple* is a sequence of items coded within parentheses. A *dictionary object* (or *dict*) is a sequence of key/value pairs that are connected by colons and coded within braces. And a *slice* is coded as a start value, a stop value, and an optional step value with the values separated by colons.

In the second group of examples, you can see how these structures are used in Python statements for data analysis. In the first statement, a list of four values is coded for the columns parameter of a drop() method. In the second statement, a tuple is coded for the xlim parameter of a line() method. In the third statement, a dictionary is coded for the columns parameter of a rename() method.

In the fourth statement in this group of examples, two slices are coded in a loc[ ] accessor. Here, the first slice accesses every tenth row from 0 to 100, and the second slice accesses every column from the state column to the grade column.

The third group of examples shows how you can use a *list comprehension* to create a list. This is a shorthand way to create a for loop that populates a new list. To start, you code a set of brackets. Then, within the brackets, you code an expression, the word *for*, the name that will be used for each list member, and a function that returns the members for the list or a list that has already been defined.

In this case, the expression is x which represents one member. And the function is the range() function, which returns one member for each of the values specified by the start, stop, and step parameters. Note that when you use the range() function, the stop value isn't included in the generated list. As a result, this list comprehension returns the even numbers from 1900 through 1918.

In the next chapter, you'll start learning how to use the Pandas methods that require structures like lists, tuples, dictionaries, and slices. So for now, you just need to know how to code these structures.

But if you're new to Python, you also need to know the rules for continuing statements over more than one line. This is illustrated by the last group of examples in this figure. With *implicit continuation*, you divide a statement after separators like parentheses, brackets, braces, and commas and after operators like plus and minus signs. With *explicit continuation*, you code a backward slash to divide a statement anywhere and continue it on the next line.

When you use implicit continuation, you need to realize that dividing a statement at the wrong point or with the wrong amount of indentation will raise a syntax error. Then, the easiest way to fix that is to switch to explicit continuation. In this book, most of the examples are coded so they don't require explicit continuation.

The syntax for coding lists, slices, tuples, and dictionary objects

A list is a sequence of items within brackets

```
[item1,item2,...]
```

A tuple is coded like a list but in parentheses

```
(item1,item2,...)
```

A dictionary is a sequence of key/value pairs within braces

```
{key1:value1, key2:value2,...}
```

A slice sets the start and stop values and an optional step value

```
start:stop:step
```

How to use lists, slices, tuples, and dictionary objects

A list used as a keyword parameter

```
polls.drop(columns=['cycle','branch','matchup','forecastdate'], inplace=True)
```

A tuple used as a keyword parameter

```
polls.plot.line(xlim=('2016-06','2016-11'))
```

A dictionary used as a keyword parameter

```
polls.rename(columns={'adjpoll_clinton':'Clinton',
                      'adjpoll_trump':'Trump'})
```

Two slices used in a loc[ ] accessor

```
polls.loc[0:100:10,'state':'grade']
```

How to code a list comprehension

The syntax

```
[expression for member in iterable]
```

A list comprehension used to provide the list for a keyword parameter

```
xticks = [x for x in range(1900,1920,2)]
```

The resulting list

```
[1900, 1902, 1904, 1906, 1908, 1910, 1912, 1914, 1916, 1918]
```

Two ways to continue a statement over more than one line

With implicit continuation

```
polls.sort_values(
    ['state','startdate'],
    ascending=False,
    inplace=True)
```

With explicit continuation

```
polls.sort_values(['state','startdate'], \
                  ascending=False, \
                  inplace=True)
```

Figure 1-6 The coding basics for Python data analysis

How to use JupyterLab as your IDE

Remember that JupyterLab is the IDE that we recommend for doing your analysis and visualization. If you've used other IDEs for developing applications, you shouldn't have much trouble learning how to use JupyterLab. But the topics that follow will help you get started.

How to start JupyterLab and work with a Notebook

The first procedure in figure 1-7 shows how to start JupyterLab. To do that, you start Anaconda Navigator from the Start menu shown in figure 1-3. Then, you can click on the Launch button for JupyterLab in the Navigator. That starts a web server on your own computer and opens a browser tab for the JupyterLab IDE.

Within JupyterLab, you can use the other procedures in this figure to work with Notebooks. To start, you can open the File Browser by clicking on the File Browser icon in the upper left corner of the interface. This Browser makes it easy to find the Notebooks that you're looking for. So, to open a Notebook, you just browse to its file and double-click on it. That will display the Notebook in one tab within the Notebook panel.

Note that the first time you start JupyterLab, the File Browser will display the high-level folders that are available by default from your computer's file system. Then, if you've installed the Notebooks for this book in the Documents folder as described in the appendixes, you can open that folder and then the python_analysis subfolder to see the folders with the examples, exercises, and solutions.

To start a new Notebook, you select File→New Launcher to open a new tab in JupyterLab. Then, you click on the Python 3 icon. To perform other file operations, you can use the items in the File menu or the popup menu that's displayed when you right-click on a file in the Browser.

As the screenshots in this figure show, each open Notebook is displayed in a separate tab of JupyterLab. Then, to switch from one Notebook to another, you can click on its tab. You can also save the current version of a Notebook by clicking on the Save icon that's on the left side of the toolbar for the tab.

By default, JupyterLab also provides for *checkpoints*. That means that JupyterLab periodically saves a copy of each Notebook. Then, if something goes wrong and you want to restart from an earlier checkpoint, you can use File→Revert Notebook to Checkpoint to restore the DataFrame at that point.

One Notebook in JupyterLab with the File Browser open

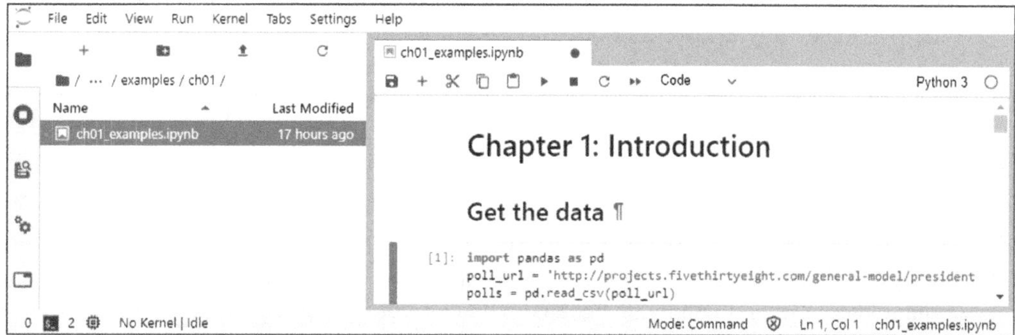

Two Notebooks in JupyterLab with the File Browser closed

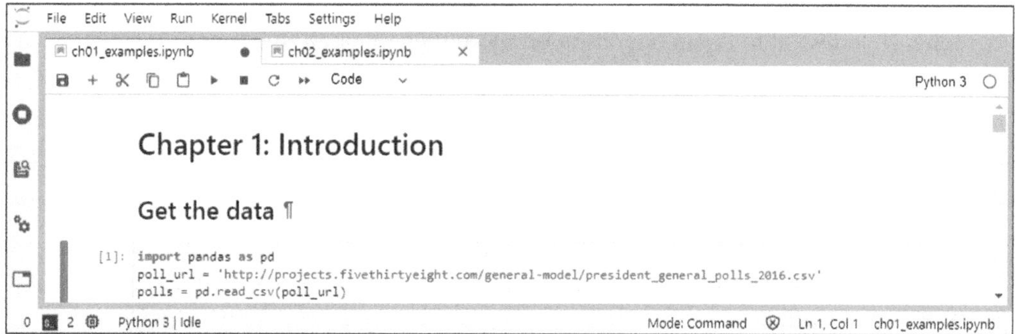

How to start JupyterLab

- Use the Start menu to start the Anaconda Navigator, and then launch JupyterLab.

How to work with Notebooks

- To open or close the File Browser, click the File Browser icon in the upper left corner.
- To open a Notebook, browse to the file you want to open and double-click on it.
- To start a new Notebook, select File→New Launcher to open a Launcher tab. Then, click the Python 3 icon.
- To save, close, or rename a Notebook, use the File menu. To save the active Notebook, click on the Save icon in the toolbar for the tab.
- To restore a Notebook to the last checkpoint, select File→Revert Notebook to Checkpoint.

Description

- JupyterLab runs as a web application on a web server that's installed on your computer.
- By default, JuptyerLab periodically saves each Notebook as a *checkpoint*. If necessary, then, you can use the File menu to restore a Notebook at a previous checkpoint.

Figure 1-7 How to start JupyterLab and work with a Notebook

How to edit and run the cells in a Notebook

When you use JupyterLab, each analysis is stored in a Notebook. In addition, each Notebook consists of *cells* that contain either one or more lines of code or the text for a heading that can be used to describe what the code in the cell or cells that follow are doing.

In figure 1-8, for example, the first cell contains text for the title of the Notebook, "Chapter 1: Introduction"; the second cell contains the text "Get the data"; and the third cell contains four lines of Python code. Then, when the code in that cell is run, the result is shown below the cell. This is an effective way to manage the code in an analysis because you can enter just a few lines of code in a cell, run the cell, and see the results right away. That's one reason why the Notebook approach has become so popular.

The procedures in this figure present the skills that you need to edit and run cells. If you want to do an operation on more than one cell, the first procedure shows how to select the cells. The key to this is to position the pointer to the left of a cell until it turns into a crosshair and then click. Then, the vertical blue line appears to show that the cell is selected.

Note that if you click when the cursor isn't a crosshair, the cell will still be selected but it will be collapsed so you can't see the code it contains. Then, you can click on the blue line to expand the cell. Once you've selected the cells, you can use the toolbar buttons or the items in the menus or popup menus to get the results you want.

When a cell is run, it's the Python interpreter, or *kernel*, that runs its statements. Then, to interrupt, restart, or shut down the kernel, you can use the items in the Kernel menu. For instance, one item lets you restart the kernel and clear all outputs. Another lets you restart the kernel and run all cells.

If you like to use the keyboard instead of the mouse to do operations, be sure to try Shift+Enter for running cells. This works when you want to run a cell right after you've entered its code. It also works when you want to step through the cells of a Notebook by running one cell at a time. Just be sure that the cursor is in a cell when you press Shift+Enter the first time.

A cell and its output when the cell is run

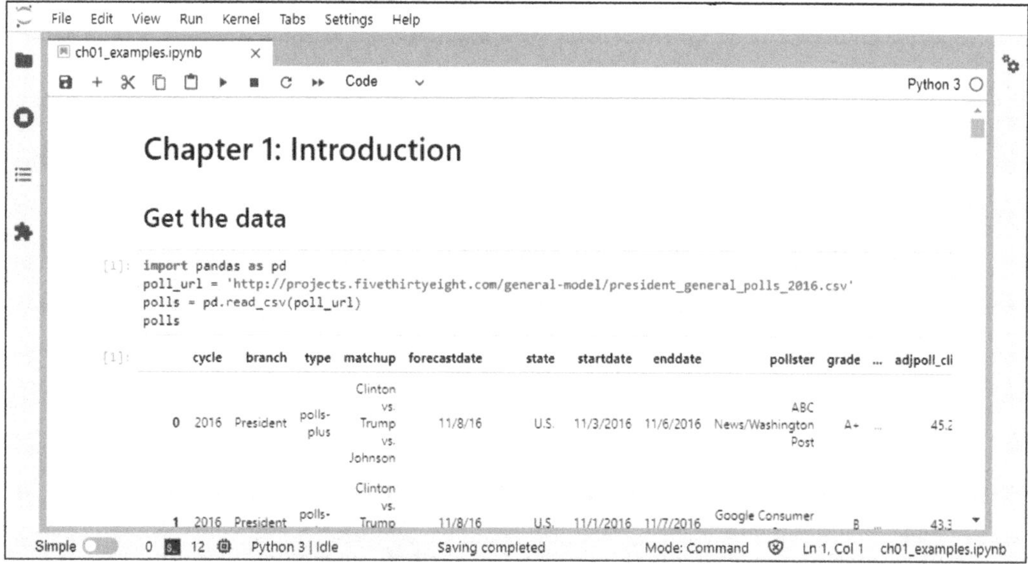

How to select one or more cells

- To select one cell, position the pointer in the left margin of the cell so it becomes a crosshair, and then click so a blue line is displayed.
- To select more than one cell, select the first cell, hold down the Shift key, and select the last cell.

How to copy, delete, merge, or move the selected cells

- Use the buttons in the toolbar or the items in the Edit or shortcut menu.

How to add a cell after the current cell

- Use the + button in the toolbar.

How to run the code in one cell

- Press Shift+Enter or click the Run button in the toolbar.

How to run the code in selected cells or all cells

- Use the Run button in the toolbar or the items in the Run menu.

How to interrupt, restart, or shutdown the kernel

- Use the items in the Kernel menu.

Description

- When you run a cell, any output is displayed below the cell.
- The *kernel* is the Python interpreter that runs the code in the cells. You can use the Kernel menu to restart the kernel and clear all output or to restart and run all cells.

Figure 1-8 How to edit and run the cells in a Notebook

How to use the Tab completion and tooltip features

As you enter or edit the code in a cell, JupyterLab provides two features that can help you work more productively. Both are illustrated in figure 1-9.

To activate the *Tab completion feature*, you press the Tab key after you enter an object name or an object name and a dot. Then, JupyterLab displays a drop-down list of all the attributes and methods that apply to the object. At that point, you can scroll down the list to find what you're looking for, or you can enter the first letter or two of the attribute or method that you're looking for to refine the entries in the list.

In the first example in this figure, you can see the two methods that start with the letters "so." They are the sort_index() and sort_values() methods. Then, you can click on the entry that you want. Or, you can scroll down to it and press the Enter key.

Be aware, however, that it may take several seconds for the drop-down list to appear if the method has many attributes and methods. So in some cases, you will want to enter the first letters of the attribute or method that you're looking for before you press the Tab key. That will speed up the display of the drop-down list.

To activate the *tooltip feature*, you press the Shift+Tab key after you enter an attribute or method name. This is illustrated by the second example in this figure. As you can see, this feature lets you scroll through the documentation for each attribute or method.

For each method, the documentation starts with the *signature*. As you have seen, the signature provides a list of the parameters for the method. This list starts with the positional parameters, which are indicated by keywords that aren't followed by equal signs. These positional parameters are followed by the keyword parameters, which are followed by equal signs and the default values.

After the signature, you can scroll down to get more information about each parameter in the signature. And after that, you can scroll down for even more information, like examples of how the method works and a summary of related methods. In short, this feature often provides all the information that you need so you don't have to go to other forms of documentation. That's especially true after you get used to working with the Pandas methods and accessors.

One shortcoming of the tooltips feature is that a tooltip disappears as soon as you type a character into the cell. However, you can get the tooltip back by pressing the Shift+Tab key again.

A more serious shortcoming is that you can't get tooltips for methods that are chained to other methods. You can only get a tooltip for the first method in a chain. In that case, though, you can get the information that you need by searching the Internet for the method.

The Tab completion feature is activated when you press the Tab key

```
polls.so
f sort_index   function
f sort_values  function
```

The tooltip feature is activated when you press the Shift+Tab key

The start of the tooltip for the sort_values() method

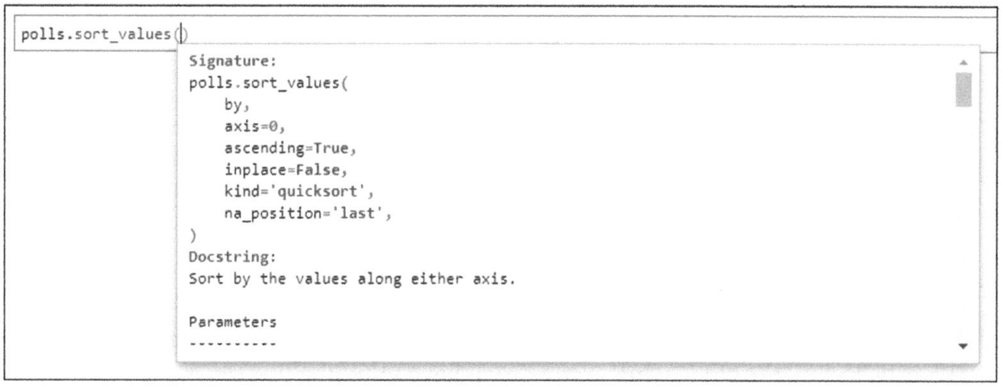

```
polls.sort_values()
Signature:
polls.sort_values(
    by,
    axis=0,
    ascending=True,
    inplace=False,
    kind='quicksort',
    na_position='last',
)
Docstring:
Sort by the values along either axis.

Parameters
----------
```

More of the tooltip after scrolling down to the start of the parameters

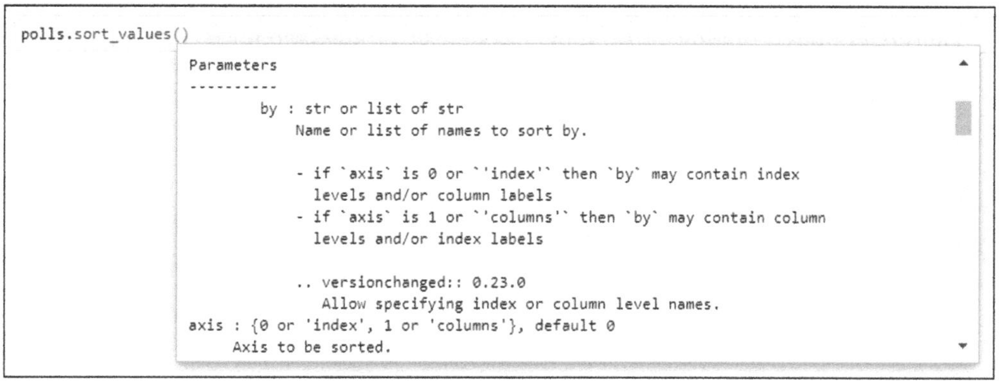

```
polls.sort_values()
Parameters
----------
        by : str or list of str
            Name or list of names to sort by.

            - if `axis` is 0 or `'index'` then `by` may contain index
              levels and/or column labels
            - if `axis` is 1 or `'columns'` then `by` may contain column
              levels and/or index labels

            .. versionchanged:: 0.23.0
               Allow specifying index or column level names.
axis : {0 or 'index', 1 or 'columns'}, default 0
     Axis to be sorted.
```

Description

- To activate the *Tab completion feature*, press the Tab key after you enter an object name, the dot after an object name, or the dot and one or more characters after an object name.
- The *tooltip feature* displays the *signature* for the method, a summary of the parameters for the method, and more.
- To activate the tooltip feature, press the Shift+Tab key with the cursor after a method name or anywhere within the parentheses for a method. However, this only works for the first method in a chain.

Figure 1-9 How to use the Tab completion and tooltip features

How syntax and runtime errors work

When you run one or more cells, either a syntax error or a runtime error may occur. A *syntax error* occurs when you enter a statement that doesn't have the proper syntax. A *runtime error* occurs when the Python interpreter can't run a statement even though its syntax is okay.

This is illustrated by figure 1-10. In the first example, the syntax error occurred because the right bracket is missing from what should be a pair of brackets. In this case, the error message is:

```
SyntaxError: closing parenthesis ')' does not match opening
parenthesis '['
```

In the second example, the error occurs because the name of the first column that the code refers to should be "startdate", not "stardate". As a result, the interpreter can't find the column that it is looking for. This time the message is:

```
KeyError: 'stardate'
```

This shows that unlike some IDEs that you may have used, JupyterLab doesn't identify syntax errors as you enter them. In fact, it doesn't find them until you run the code in the cell. And then, it only finds the first syntax error in the cell. To find the other syntax errors, you have to fix the first error and run the cell again.

Once the syntax errors have been fixed, you run the cell again. Then, if the interpreter finds a runtime error, it displays the error message for it. Here again, it finds only one runtime error at a time. So you need to fix each error and run the cell again until the code works.

If you run several cells at the same time, you should also know that the process will stop as soon as the first syntax or runtime error occurs. If, for example, you run the code for eight cells and a syntax error occurs in the third cell, the code in the last five cells won't be run.

A syntax error in a Notebook

```
[6]: polls.sort_values(['state','startdate')

       File "<ipython-input-6-fdb7f8ce318f>", line 1
         polls.sort_values(['state','startdate')
                                               ^
     SyntaxError: closing parenthesis ')' does not match opening parenthesis '['
```

A runtime error in a Notebook

```
[7]: polls.sort_values(['state','stardate'])

     ---------------------------------------------------------------------------
     KeyError                                  Traceback (most recent call last)
     <ipython-input-7-55333b88631d> in <module>
     ----> 1 polls.sort_values(['state','stardate'])

     ~\Anaconda3\lib\site-packages\pandas\core\frame.py in sort_values(self, by, axis, ascending,
     inplace, kind, na_position, ignore_index, key)
        5440         if len(by) > 1:
        5441
     -> 5442             keys = [self._get_label_or_level_values(x, axis=axis) for x in by]
        5443
        5444             # need to rewrap columns in Series to apply key function

     ~\Anaconda3\lib\site-packages\pandas\core\frame.py in <listcomp>(.0)
        5440         if len(by) > 1:
        5441
     -> 5442             keys = [self._get_label_or_level_values(x, axis=axis) for x in by]
        5443
        5444             # need to rewrap columns in Series to apply key function

     ~\Anaconda3\lib\site-packages\pandas\core\generic.py in _get_label_or_level_values(self, key,
     axis)
        1682             values = self.axes[axis].get_level_values(key)._values
        1683         else:
     -> 1684             raise KeyError(key)
        1685
        1686         # Check for duplicates

     KeyError: 'stardate'
```

Description

- A *syntax error* occurs when the code violates one of the rules of Python coding so the source code can't be interpreted.
- A *runtime error* occurs when a Python statement can't be executed.
- When you run the code in one or more cells, JupyterLab detects one syntax error at a time.
- When all syntax errors have been fixed, JupyterLab detects one runtime error at a time.

Figure 1-10 How syntax and runtime errors work

How to use Markdown language

To enter a heading into a cell, you use *Markdown language* as shown in figure 1-11. With the cursor in a cell, you use the drop-down menu in the toolbar to change from Code to Markdown. Then, you enter the text for the heading preceded by from one to five hash symbols (#). Those signs will determine what level of heading is used for the text. To display the text in the cell, you run the cell.

In the second screenshot, you can see that one # is used for the top heading and two are used for the next heading. That's why these headings appear the way they do in the first screenshot.

Later, if you want to change the text in a cell, you can use the second procedure in this figure. Just double-click in the cell, modify the markdown, and run the cell.

Although the examples in this book use Markdown language only for headings, you can also use it to apply boldface, italics, numbered lists, bulleted lists, and more. For instance, the text is boldfaced if it's preceded and followed by two asterisks (**). To find out more, you can select Markdown Reference from JupyterLab's Help menu. But for most Notebooks, you shouldn't need to use Markdown language other than for headings.

A Notebook with headings

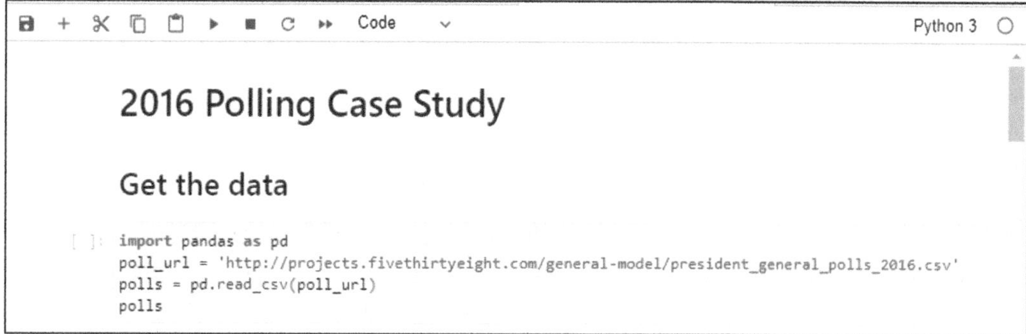

The Markdown language for the headings

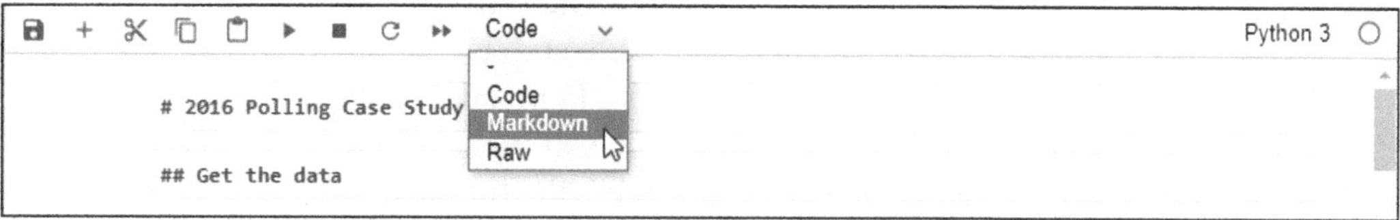

How to create a heading by using Markdown language

- With the cursor in a new cell, change the drop-down list from Code to Markdown.
- Type the text for a heading into the cell preceded by from one to five # signs. The number of signs determines the level of the heading.
- Run the cell to convert the Markdown language to the heading.

How to modify a heading in a Notebook cell

- Double-click in the cell to display the Markdown language, modify it, and run the cell.

Description

- You can use *Markdown language* to create cells that contain text that identifies the contents or purposes of the cells that follow.
- To create headings and subheadings, you precede the text by from one to five hash symbols (#).
- You can also use Markdown language to apply boldface, italics, numbered lists, bulleted lists and more, but for most analyses, you shouldn't need to do that.
- For more information about Markdown language, select Markdown Reference from JupyterLab's Help menu, which is shown in the next figure.

Figure 1-11 How to use Markdown language

How to get reference information

Figure 1-12 shows how to get the reference information that you need. Often, the fastest and best way to get that information is just to search the Internet for it. That way, you'll get links to all the official documentation for Pandas, Seaborn, and the other modules that you'll be using. But you'll also get links to a wider variety of information, including tutorials and videos. This is illustrated by the first screenshot in this figure.

However, you should also know that you can use the JupyterLab Help menu to get reference information. As you can see in the second example in this figure, that menu provides access to information about JupyterLab, Markdown language, Python, Pandas, and more. When you access any of this information, it's displayed in a new tab within JupyterLab.

Then, you can click on the links in the left sidebar or at the top of the tab to go to other information. You can also use the Search box at the top of the left sidebar (not shown) to search for information. For instance, the screenshot in this figure shows the result of a search for the sort_values() method, which is the same information that you can get by searching the Internet.

Remember too that tooltips provide much of the same information. For instance, the tooltip for the sort_values() method in figure 1-9 provides the same type of information that's shown in the second screenshot in this figure. That includes the signature for the method as well as a parameter summary. So, as you get more familiar with the methods for data analysis, you'll be able to use the tooltips more and reference information less.

A Google search for the Pandas sort_values() method

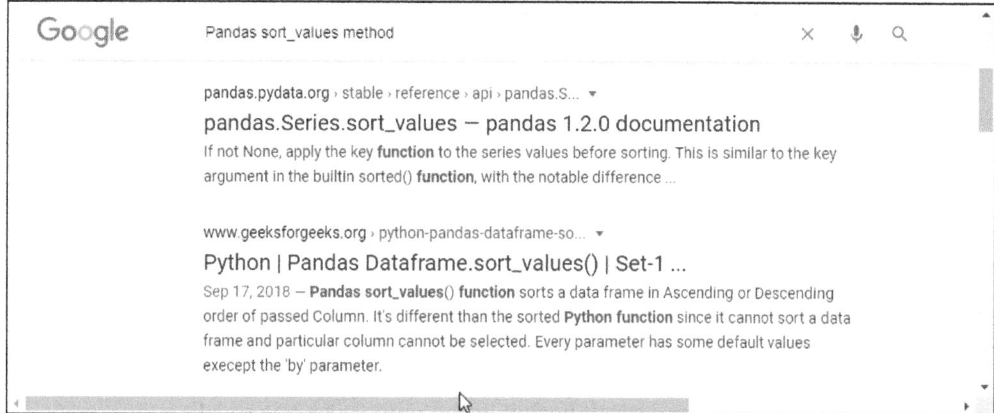

The JupyterLab Help menu and a page in the Pandas reference

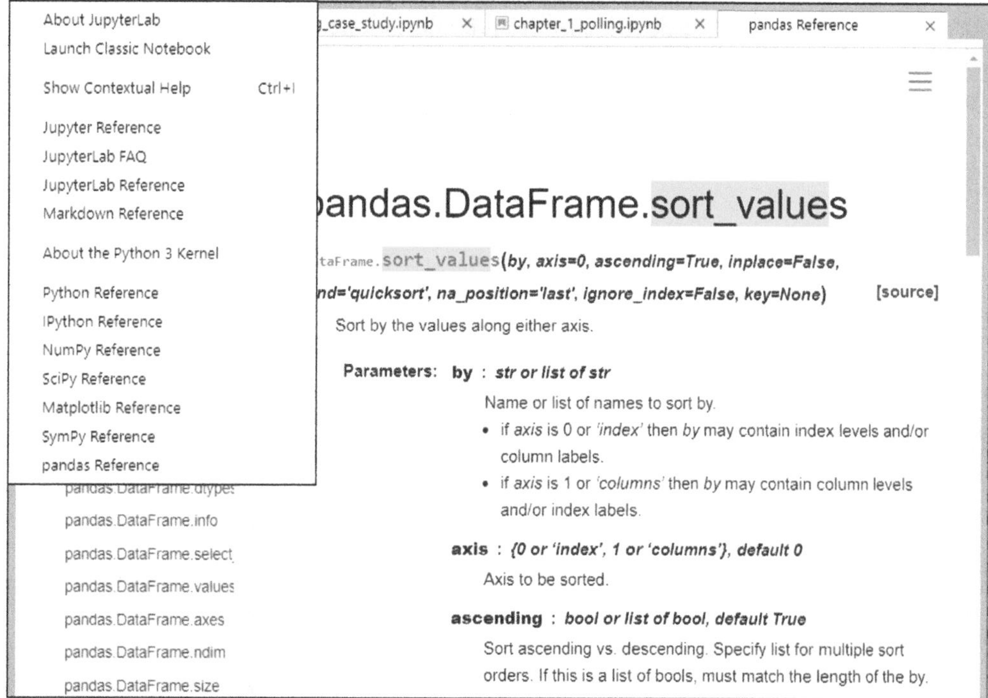

Description

- Often, the fastest way to get the reference information that you need is to search the Internet. That will lead you to the official Pandas and Seaborn documentation as well as to tutorials and more.
- You can also get reference information by using JupyterLab's Help menu. That will lead you to reference information for JupyterLab, Python, Pandas, and more.
- When you use JupyterLab, the reference information is displayed in a new tab.

Figure 1-12 How to get reference information

Two more skills for working with JupyterLab

At this point, you've learned the essential skills for entering and running the cells that contain your Python code as well as for the cells that contain Markdown language. Now, you'll learn two more skills that can come in handy from time to time...although you can easily get by without either of them.

How to split the screen between two Notebooks

Figure 1-13 shows how to split the JupyterLab screen between two Notebooks. In this example, the screen is split horizontally, but you can also split it vertically. The benefit of using split screens is that you can easily compare the code in two different Notebooks and copy code from one to the other.

To split the screen vertically, just drag the tab of one of the open Notebooks down and to the right. To split the screen horizontally, drag the tab down. To restore a tab, drag it back to the tab bar. It's that easy.

JupyterLab with two Notebooks in a horizontally split screen

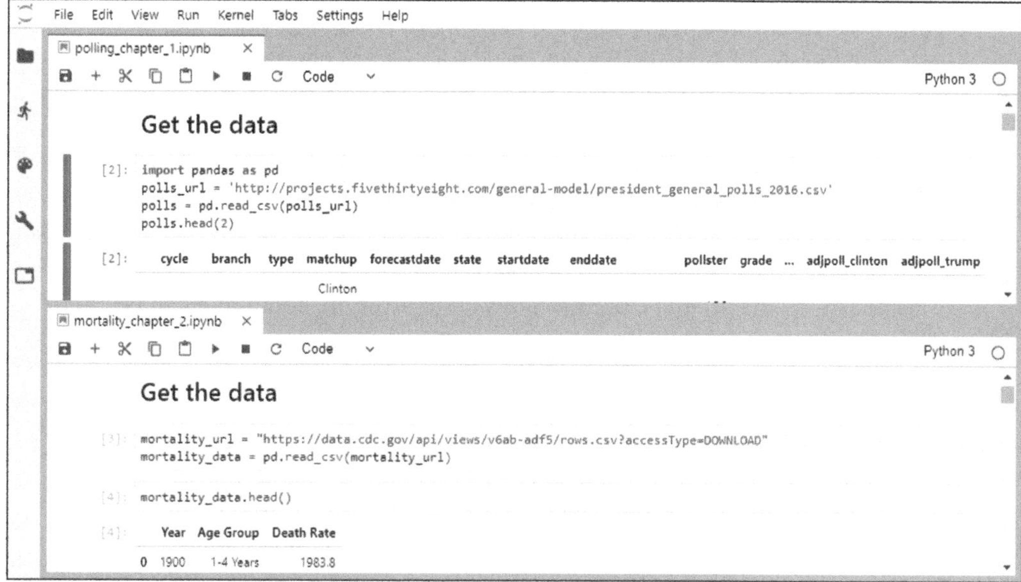

How to split the screen

- To split the screen vertically between two open Notebooks, drag the second tab down and to the right and drop it.
- To split the screen horizontally between two open Notebooks, drag the second tab down and drop it.

How to restore the screen

- Drag the tab of the bottom or right Notebook until it's next to the tab of the other Notebook and drop it.
- If you have trouble restoring the screen by dragging the split tab, you can close one of the Notebooks and then reopen it.

Description

- When you use JupyterLab, you can use split screen to make it easy to compare the code in two Notebooks and copy code from one Notebook to the other.
- By contrast, when you use Jupyter Notebook, each Notebook is in a separate browser tab. So to display two Notebooks at the same time, you need to open two browsers and arrange them side by side...a cumbersome process.

Figure 1-13 How to split the screen between two Notebooks

How to use Magic Commands

Figure 1-14 shows how to use *Magic Commands*. These are commands that aren't in the Python language. Instead, they are provided by the kernel. Although you may never need to use them, the table in this figure lists a few that can come in handy.

As the first example shows, the %time command returns the time that it takes to run a Python statement. In this case, it took the read_csv() method 7.37 seconds to import the code in the file. This command can be helpful when you're trying to improve the performance of your code.

Similarly, as the second example shows, the %%time command can be coded at the start of a cell that contains more than one statement. Then, the time to run all of the statements is displayed. This lets you time something like a for loop. In the example in this figure, it took 9.92 milliseconds to execute the two statements that follow the Magic Command.

In contrast to the timing commands, the %whos command returns a table of the active variables, plus the data type and some other information for each of the variables. This is illustrated by the third example in this figure. This information can be helpful when you're debugging because some methods can only be applied to specific data types. In this case, the command shows that only three variables have been created, and their data types are module, str (string), and DataFrame.

The fourth example shows that you can also use the Python type() function to get the data type of a variable. Here, the first type() function shows that the poll_url variable is of the str type. And the second type() function shows that the polls variable is a DataFrame. If you just want to find out what the data type of one variable is, this function is all that you need. But as you've seen, the %whos Magic Command displays the data types for all of the active variables in a single command.

The other useful Magic Command is the %magic command. But beware, it returns the documentation for all of the Magic commands, which can be overwhelming. Perhaps a better alternative is to search the Internet for something like "best Magic Commands for Python."

Four of the most useful Magic Commands

Command	Description
`%time`	Displays the time that it takes for a statement to run.
`%%time`	Displays the time that it takes for all the statements in a cell to run.
`%whos`	Displays the variables that are in the namespace along with their data types.
`%magic`	Displays a reference for all of the Magic commands.

How the %time command works

```
poll_url = 'http://projects.fivethirtyeight.com/general-model/president_general_polls_2016.csv'
%time polls = pd.read_csv(poll_url)
polls

Wall time: 7.37 s
```

How the %%time command works

```
%%time
polls = polls.sort_values('startdate', ascending=False)
polls

Wall time: 9.92 ms
```

How the %whos command works

```
%whos

Variable   Type         Data/Info
----------------------------------
pd         module       <module 'pandas' from 'C:<...>es\\pandas\\__init__.py'>
poll_url   str          http://projects.fivethirt<...>nt_general_polls_2016.csv
polls      DataFrame           cycle     branch  <...>[12624 rows x 27 columns]
```

How to use the Python type() function to check the data type of a variable

```
type(poll_url)

str


type(polls)

pandas.core.frame.DataFrame
```

Description

- Magic Commands provide some useful functions that aren't provided by the Python functions.
- In general, the commands that start with % apply to one statement, and the commands that start with %% apply to all the statements in the cell.

Figure 1-14 How to use Magic Commands

Introduction to the case studies

Section 4 of this book presents four case studies that show how the skills that you learn in this book are applied to real-world analyses. The next four figures introduce these case studies because the chapters in section 2 often present examples taken from them. Although those examples should be self-explanatory, this introduction should help you see the examples in a larger context.

Beyond that, this introduction is intended to encourage you to look through the case studies as you progress through this book. In fact, before you're through with this book, you should understand every line of code in each of the case studies. Since these are real-world analyses, that will show that you have mastered data analysis at a professional level.

The Polling case study

Figure 1-15 introduces the Polling case study. The data for this case study comes from the FiveThirtyEight.com website, a well-known analytical site for politics, economics, and sports. This data is for the polls that were taken for the 2016 presidential election in the United States. You may remember that most predictions were for Hillary Clinton to win, but somehow Donald Trump won.

As you can see in this figure, when the polling data is imported into a Pandas DataFrame, it consists of 12,624 rows. That's because there are three rows for each poll that was taken. The DataFrame also consists of 27 columns, but many of them aren't needed for the analysis. So, after the data is cleaned, the DataFrame is down to 4,116 rows and 10 columns.

When the data is prepared, voter_type, state_gap, and swing columns are added to the cleaned DataFrame. Then, a second DataFrame is prepared that shapes the data in a new way. This is illustrated by the third table in this figure. It consists of 8,232 rows and just 9 columns. In this DataFrame, there are two rows for each poll: one with the results for Clinton, the other with the results for Trump. Next, the month_bin and month_pct_avg columns are added to help improve the visualizations for this data.

The visualization in this figure is one of the several in this case study. In this case, the Seaborn relplot() method was used to plot the visualization from the data in the prepared DataFrame that's shown above it. This visualization shows the results of the polls for the swing states during the last 2 months before the election. This shows that those polls were always close but with some wide variations. And this shows that the polls got very close in the last few weeks before the election.

This complete case study in presented in chapter 12. There, you can see how the skills in this book are used to get, clean, prepare, analyze, and visualize the data. And that will give you the perspective that you need for applying those skills to your own analyses.

The URL for the Polling data

`http://projects.fivethirtyeight.com/general-model/president_general_polls_2016.csv`

The imported DataFrame (12,624 rows and 27 columns)

	cycle	branch	type	matchup	forecastdate	state	startdate	enddate	pollster	grade	...	adjpoll_clinton	adjpoll_tr
0	2016	President	polls-plus	Clinton vs. Trump vs. Johnson	11/8/16	U.S.	11/3/2016	11/6/2016	ABC News/Washington Post	A+	...	45.20163	41.7
1	2016	President	polls-plus	Clinton vs. Trump vs. Johnson	11/8/16	U.S.	11/1/2016	11/7/2016	Google Consumer Surveys	B	...	43.34557	41.2

The cleaned DataFrame (4,116 rows and 10 columns)

	state	startdate	enddate	pollster	grade	samplesize	population	poll_wt	clinton_pct	trump_pct
4208	U.S.	2016-11-03	2016-11-06	ABC News/Washington Post	A+	2220.0	lv	8.720654	47.00	43.00
4209	U.S.	2016-11-01	2016-11-07	Google Consumer Surveys	B	26574.0	lv	7.628472	38.03	35.69

The prepared DataFrame (8,232 rows and 9 columns)

	state	enddate	voter_type	state_gap	swing	candidate	percent	month_bin	month_pct_avg
0	U.S.	2016-11-06	likely	4.347514	False	Clinton	47.00	Nov 2016	45.067903
1	U.S.	2016-11-07	likely	4.347514	False	Clinton	38.03	Nov 2016	45.067903

A Seaborn plot of the swing state polls in the 2 months before the election

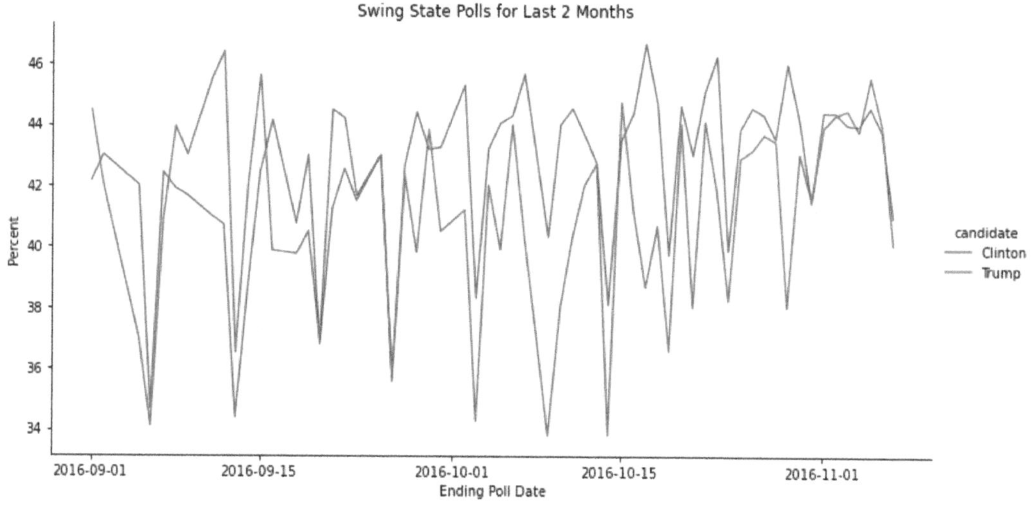

Figure 1-15 Introduction to the Polling case study

The Forest Fires case study

Figure 1-16 introduces the Forest Fires case study. This study analyzes the data for forest fires from 1992 through 2015. This study gets the data from the website for the US Forest Service, which is part of the US Department of Agriculture. The data is available in several forms, but this case study gets it as a SQLite database.

After the data is imported from the database, the DataFrame consists of just 8 columns but 1,880,465 rows. The first two rows of this DataFrame are shown in this figure. Since the SQL statement that's used to import this data selects the columns for the analysis, this DataFrame should require minimal cleaning.

In fact, the primary cleaning is to drop the rows for all fires that are less than 10 acres. But besides that, the column names are changed from upper to lowercase, and the fire names are changed to title case. That just makes it easier to work with the data.

Then, to prepare the DataFrame, just two columns are added: one for the month of the fire and one for the number of days that it took to contain the fire. So, the cleaned and prepared DataFrame consists of 247,123 rows and 10 columns.

The two visualizations in this figure illustrate the types of analysis that are done by this case study. The first one uses Pandas to plot the total number of acres that were burned in 2015 for the states with the top 10 totals. As you can see, Alaska had the most acres with more than 3,000,000 acres burned. And Idaho and California were second and third, both with more than 1,000,000 acres burned.

The second visualization uses Seaborn to plot the locations of the California fires in 2015 that were greater than or equal to 500 acres. Here, the size and darkness of each dot indicates the size of the fire: the larger and darker the dot, the larger the fire. To lay this plot on an outline of the state of California also required the installation and use of the GeoPandas module.

This complete case study is presented in chapter 13. There, you can see how the skills in this book are used to get, clean, prepare, analyze, and visualize the data. You'll also see how a module like GeoPandas can be used with Seaborn to create plots that are placed over the outlines of countries and states.

The URL for the Forest Fires data

```
https://www.fs.usda.gov/rds/archive/products/RDS-2013-0009.4/RDS-2013-0009.4_SQLITE.zip
```

The imported DataFrame (1,880,465 rows and 8 columns)

	FIRE_NAME	FIRE_SIZE	STATE	LATITUDE	LONGITUDE	FIRE_YEAR	DISCOVERY_DATE	CONTAIN_DATE
0	FOUNTAIN	0.10	CA	40.036944	-121.005833	2005	2005-02-02 00:00:00	2005-02-02 00:00:00
1	PIGEON	0.25	CA	38.933056	-120.404444	2004	2004-05-12 00:00:00	2004-05-12 00:00:00

The prepared DataFrame (247,123 rows and 10 columns)

	fire_name	acres_burned	state	latitude	longitude	fire_year	discovery_date	contain_date	fire_month	days_burning
16	Power	16823.0	CA	38.523333	-120.211667	2004	2004-10-06	2004-10-21	10	15.0
17	Freds	7700.0	CA	38.780000	-120.260000	2004	2004-10-13	2004-10-17	10	4.0

A Pandas plot of the total acres burned in the top 10 fire states in 2015

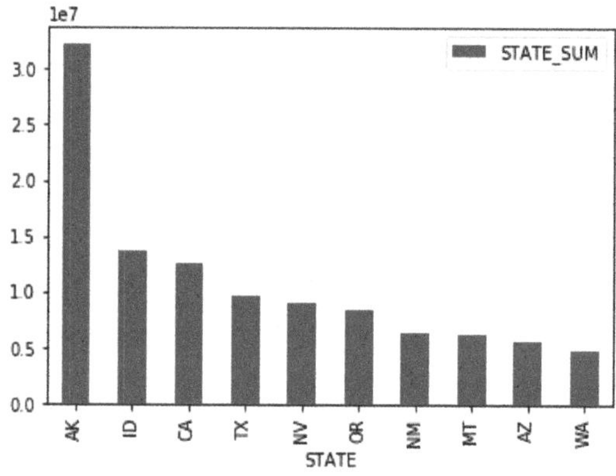

A GeoPandas and Seaborn plot of the California fires over 500 acres in 2015

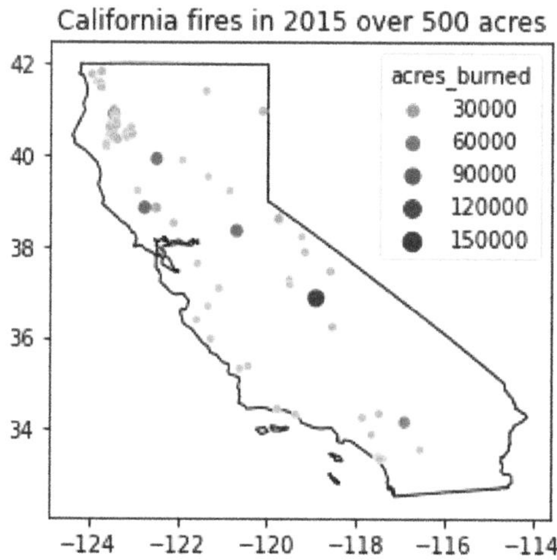

Figure 1-16 Introduction to the Forest Fires case study

The Social Survey case study

Figure 1-17 introduces the Social Survey case study. This study analyzes the data compiled by the National Opinion Research Center in Chicago. This data was compiled from 1972 to the present, and the questions varied from year to year. The result is that the data consists of 64,814 rows that represent the people who responded to the questions, and 6,110 columns that represent the questions that were asked.

This data is provided in a Stata file, which consists of two parts: metadata that provides information about the data, and the data itself. The trouble is that this dataset is so large that a computer needs about 3 gigabytes of memory to import it into a DataFrame. But that means that many computers won't be able to import the data.

For that reason, you need to use the metadata and the documentation that comes with the Stata file to figure out which portions of the data you want to import. For instance, this figure shows one of the DataFrames that this case study prepares for analysis. It consists of just 128 rows and 5 columns with the focus on the work status column (wrkstat) in the Stata file. Then, the plot that follows shows the changes in work status from 1972 to the present.

This example is typical of the approach that this case study takes to getting useful information from this dataset. First, you figure out which columns (questions) you want to work with. Then, you import and analyze those columns. As you will see when you read chapter 14, this data can lead the way to many insights about social behavior.

The URL for the Social Survey data

`http://gss.norc.org/Documents/stata/gss_stata_with_codebook.zip`

The starting dataset

- 64,814 rows and 6,110 columns
- This dataset is so large that importing it requires 3 gigabytes of memory. So instead of importing the entire file, you should import just the subsets of data that you need for your analyses.

One of the DataFrames that's prepared for analysis (128 rows, 5 columns)

	year	wrkstat	counts	countsTotal	percent
0	1972	working fulltime	750	1061	0.706880
1	1972	working parttime	121	1061	0.114043
2	1972	unempl, laid off	46	1061	0.043355
3	1972	retired	144	1061	0.135721
4	1973	working fulltime	651	974	0.668378

A Seaborn plot derived from the DataFrame

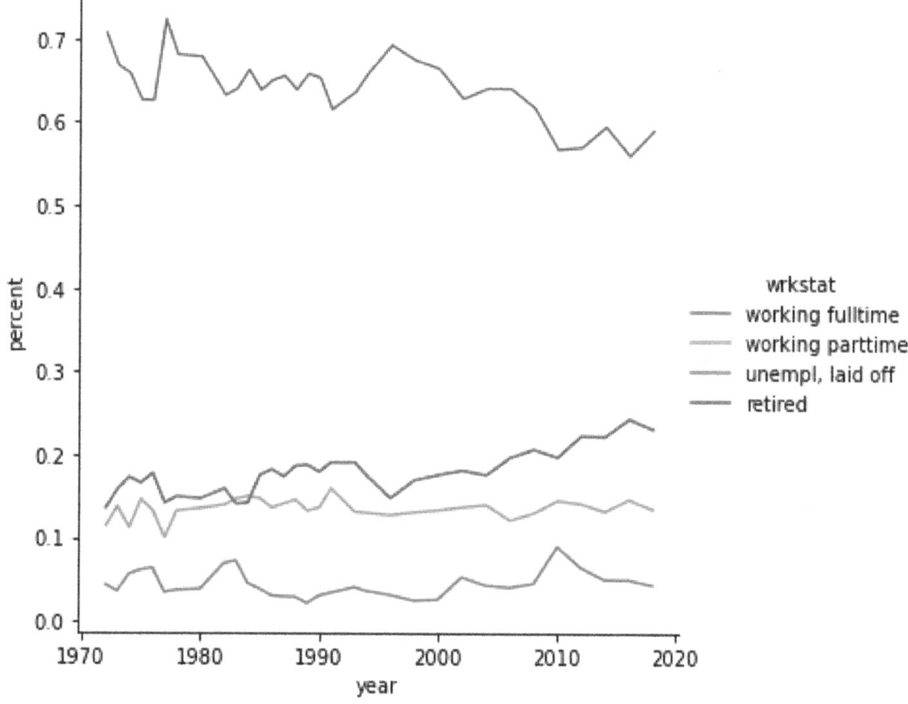

Figure 1-17 Introduction to the Social Survey case study

The Sports Analytics case study

Figure 1-18 introduces the Sports Analytics case study. This case study analyzes the shots that Stephen Curry of the Golden State Warriors took from 2009 through 2019. Since this data is provided in JSON format that's several levels deep, it can't just be imported into a DataFrame. Instead, you need to use the DataFrame() constructor to build the DataFrame from the available data.

After the DataFrame is constructed, it contains one row for every shot that Curry took during that time period with 24 columns of data. Since most of those columns aren't needed for the shot analysis, all but six are dropped when the data is cleaned. But then six summary columns are added when the data is prepared. These are the last six columns in the second DataFrame in this figure.

The analysis in this case study shows how Curry's statistics like shots and points per season changed as his career progressed. But beyond that, it focuses on how his shot selection changed from one year to the next. In this figure, for example, you can see a scatter plot of the shot locations for his missed and made shots in two different seasons: his rookie season and the first season in which he was the Most Valuable Player.

This complete case study is presented in chapter 15. There, you can see how the skills in this book are used to get, clean, prepare, analyze, and visualize the data. You can also see how the diagram of the basketball floor can be added to plots.

The URL for the Sports Analytics data

```
https://www.murach.com/python_analysis/shots.json
```

The imported DataFrame (11,846 rows and 24 columns)

	grid_type	game_id	game_event_id	player_id	player_name	team_id	team_name	period	minutes_remaining	seconds_remaining	...
0	Shot Chart Detail	0020900015	4	201939	Stephen Curry	1610612744	Golden State Warriors	1	11	25	...
1	Shot Chart Detail	0020900015	17	201939	Stephen Curry	1610612744	Golden State Warriors	1	9	31	...

2 rows × 24 columns

The prepared DataFrame (11,753 rows and 12 columns)

	shot_type	loc_x	loc_y	shot_made_flag	game_date	season	shot_result	points_made	shots_made	shots_attempted	points_made_game
game_id											
0020900015	3PT Field Goal	99	249	0	2009-10-28	2009-2010	Missed	0	7	12	14
0020900015	2PT Field Goal	-122	145	1	2009-10-28	2009-2010	Made	2	7	12	14
0020900015	2PT Field Goal	-60	129	0	2009-10-28	2009-2010	Missed	0	7	12	14
0020900015	2PT Field Goal	-172	82	0	2009-10-28	2009-2010	Missed	0	7	12	14
0020900015	2PT Field Goal	-68	148	0	2009-10-28	2009-2010	Missed	0	7	12	14
...	...	...	...	...	...	...	...	...	...	...	...

A Seaborn plot for how Curry's shot selection changed

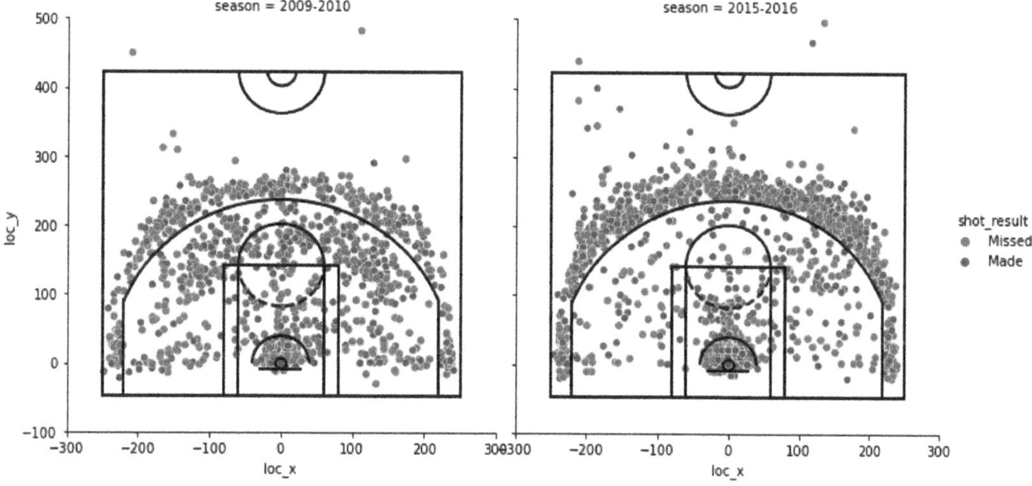

Figure 1-18 Introduction to the Sports Analytics case study

Perspective

Now that you've completed this chapter, you should be able to use JupyterLab to work with Notebooks. You should also realize that to master data analysis and visualization, you need to learn how to use the methods of modules like Pandas and Seaborn to get, clean, prepare, analyze, and visualize the data. With that as background, you're ready to learn the essential Pandas and Seaborn skills, and you'll start that in the next chapter.

Terms

data analysis
data visualization (data viz)
data modeling
predictive analysis
data analytics
business analytics
sports analytics
data science
get the data
import data
DataFrame
clean the data
prepare the data
analyze the data
visualize the data
Anaconda distribution
Integrated Development Environment (IDE)
JupyterLab
Jupyter Notebook
Notebook
module
install a module
!pip command
conda command
Anaconda Prompt
import a module
import statement
call a method
parameter
dot notation
chain methods
signature
positional parameter
keyword parameter
list
tuple
dictionary (dict)
slice
list comprehension
implicit continuation
explicit continuation
checkpoint
Notebook cell
kernel
Tab completion feature
tooltip feature
syntax error
runtime error
Markdown language
Magic Command

Summary

- The term *data analysis* (or *data analytics*) includes *data visualization* and *predictive analysis*. The term *data science* not only includes data analysis but also data mining, machine learning, deep learning, and artificial intelligence (AI).
- A data analysis project can be divided into five phases: *get*, *clean*, *prepare*, *analyze*, and *visualize* the data. Often, though, there's overlap between the phases.
- Three of the most popular IDEs for data analysis are *Jupyter Notebook*, *JupyterLab*, and *VS Code*. For this book, we recommend that you use JupyterLab as your IDE.
- The *Anaconda distribution* of Python includes JupyterLab as well as the Pandas and Seaborn *modules* that you'll use for data analysis and visualization.
- When you use Python for data analysis, you need to know how to *install* and *import* any *modules* that aren't included in your Python distribution. You need to know how to call and chain methods. And you need to know how to code *lists*, *tuples*, *dictionaries*, *slices*, and *list comprehensions*.
- A Jupyter Notebook consists of *cells* that contain either Python code or *Markdown language* that provides for five levels of headings. When you run a cell that contains code, any results are shown below the cell.
- The *kernel* for a Notebook is the Python interpreter that runs the code. You can use the Kernel menu in JupyterLab to restart the kernel and clear all output or run all of the cells.
- Two of the JupyterLab features that you'll want to use are the *Tab completion* and *tooltip features*.
- If a cell has a *syntax error* or a *runtime error*, an error message is displayed below the cell when you try to run it, but only one error is detected at a time.
- You can use the Help menu in JupyterLab to get reference information that is displayed in one tab of the IDE. Often, though, it's faster and easier to search for the information that you need on the Internet.
- JupyterLab lets you split the screen between two open Notebooks. That makes it easier to copy code from one Notebook to the other.
- You can code *Magic Commands* in the cells of a Notebook for special purposes like timing how long it takes to run a statement and displaying a table of the active variables and their data types.

Before you do the exercises for this chapter

Before you do any of the exercises in this book, you need to install the Anaconda distribution of Python. You also need to install the JupyterLab Notebooks for this book. For details, see the appendix for your operating system.

Exercise 1-1 Get started with JupyterLab

This exercise is designed to get you started with JupyterLab. It is not designed to teach you coding skills.

Start JupyterLab and set its theme

1. Start Anaconda Navigator. Then, use the Navigator to launch JupyterLab, and note that JupyterLab runs in your browser.
2. Use the Settings menu to determine if the theme for JupyterLab is set to Dark or Light. Then, change the theme to see if you like it better. If not, change it back. The screenshots in this book use JupyterLab Light, and that's the one we recommend.

Open the Polling Notebook and run the first three cells

3. Use the File Browser shown in figure 1-7 to open the Notebook named ex_1-1_polling that should be in this folder:
   `python_analysis/exercises/ch01`
4. Use the Kernel menu to restart the kernel and clear all outputs.
5. Click in the first cell that contains code and run the cell by clicking on the Run button in the toolbar. This code uses the Pandas read_csv() method to import polling data from the FiveThirtyEight website into a DataFrame named polls.
6. With the cursor in the next cell, press Shift+Enter to run the statement in that cell and see how it displays the data in the polls DataFrame. Next, change the code to:
   `polls.head()`

   Then, run the cell and note that the head() method displays just the first five rows in the DataFrame.
7. Run the sort_values() method in the third cell. Note that this method has one positional parameter (state) and one keyword parameter.

Fix syntax and runtime errors

8. Still in the third cell, delete the e in state to make it stat, and delete the right parenthesis at the end of the sort_values() method.
9. Run that cell and note that the error message says that a syntax error occurred. Fix that by replacing the right parentheses, and run the cell again.
10. This time, there's a runtime error because there's no column named "stat". Fix that, and run the cell again. Now, the sort should work.

Use Markdown language, Tab completion, and tooltips

11. Add a new cell after the one for the sort_values() method. Then, with figure 1-11 as a guide, use Markdown language to create a subheading that says: "Use Tab completion and tooltips".
12. Add a cell after the one you just created. Then, with figure 1-9 as a guide, enter:

    ```
    polls.s
    ```

    and press the Tab key. That should display a completion list, although it may take a while for it to be displayed. Then, type the letter *o* to refine the completion list, and select sort_values from the list.
13. Enter a set of parentheses after the sort_values method name, and with the cursor in the parentheses, press Shift+Tab to display the tooltip. Note that the signature lists one positional parameter (by) and five keyword parameters. Then, scroll through the tooltip to see all that it offers.
14. Finish the sort_value() method so it looks like this:

    ```
    sort_values('state', ascending=False)
    ```

    Next, run the statement to see how it displays the results. Then, chain a head() method to the sort_values() method, and run it to see the results.
15. Try the tooltip feature for the sort_values() method that you just coded, and see that it still works. But try it for the head() method, and you'll see that it only works for the first method in a chain.

Run the rest of the cells

16. Run the rest of the cells in the Notebook. To do that, press Shift+Enter for each cell or click on the Run button in the toolbar. (If the first cell for plotting doesn't display a plot when you run it, run it a second time.)
17. Review the code in each of the cells that you've just run. Note the use of a dictionary in the rename() method and the use of lists in some of the other statements. Note too that the plot() method in the last cell of this Notebook is chained to the query() method.

Use two Magic Commands and the Python type() function

18. Add the %%time Magic Command as the first line in the cell for the chained plot() method. Then, run the cell to see how long it takes.
19. In the new cell at the end of the Notebook, run the %whos command and note the data types for all the variables that have been created by this Notebook.
20. In the next cell, run the Python type() function for the polls DataFrame, which is another way to identify the data type for a variable.

Start a new Notebook, use a split screen, and copy code into it

21. Use File→New Launcher to open a new tab in JupyterLab, and click on the first Python 3 icon to start a new Notebook.
22. Right-click on the tab for the new file, which will say "Untitled.ipynb", select Rename in the popup menu, and change the name to ex_1-1_practice.
23. Select the first four cells in the chapter_1_exercise Notebook (the two heading cells and the two code cells), right-click on them, and select Copy Cells from the popup menu. Then, go to the tab for the new Notebook, right-click on the empty first cell, and select Paste Cells Below.
24. After you paste the cells into the new Notebook, the first cell in the notebook will be empty. To delete that cell, right-click on it and select Delete Cells from the popup menu.
25. With figure 1-13 as a guide, split the tabs for the two Notebooks vertically. Then, copy the next two or three cells from the first Notebook to the new Notebook.
26. Restore the split screens to a single screen.

Experiment on your own

27. If you have the time and interest, experiment with some of the other ways that JupyterLab provides for getting the results you want. Otherwise, close both Notebooks.

Chapter 2

The Pandas essentials for data analysis

The Pandas module is the primary module for Python data analysis, and it is installed as part of the Anaconda distribution. This module provides methods for getting the data into a DataFrame and for cleaning, preparing, analyzing, and visualizing that data. In this chapter, you'll learn the Pandas essentials that you'll use for almost every Python analysis that you undertake.

Introduction to the Pandas DataFrame

A *DataFrame* (or *DataFrame object*) is a Pandas object that stores the data for an analysis. This object also provides the attributes and methods for working with the data.

The DataFrame structure

Figure 2-1 shows the first five rows of the data in a DataFrame. This DataFrame contains child mortality data from 1900 to 2018.

As you can see, this data is stored as a table that consists of *rows* and *columns*. This table has a row *index* on the left that numbers the rows, starting with zero for the first row. And it has three columns named Year, Age Group, and Death Rate.

Using Pandas terminology, the data at the intersection of a column and row is an *element*, which is equivalent to a cell in a spreadsheet. And the data in each element is a *datapoint*.

But as the components table in this figure shows, a DataFrame is more than just a container for a table. Besides the data, a DataFrame object contains other information like the data types for each column as well as metadata that provides more information about the DataFrame. A DataFrame object also contains attributes and methods that let you work with the data in the DataFrame.

Within a DataFrame object, each column is a *Series object*. And Pandas provides methods for working with Series objects just as it does for working with DataFrame objects.

The first five rows of the Child Mortality data in a DataFrame

	Year	Age Group	Death Rate
0	1900	1-4 Years	1983.8
1	1901	1-4 Years	1695.0
2	1902	1-4 Years	1655.7
3	1903	1-4 Years	1542.1
4	1904	1-4 Years	1591.5

The components of a DataFrame

Component	Description
Column labels	The names at the tops of the columns.
Column data	The data in the columns. All of the data in a column typically has the same data type with one entry in each row.
Column data types	Each column has a defined data type. If all of the elements in a column don't have the same data type, the elements are stored with the object data type.
Index	Also known as a row label. If an index isn't defined, it is generated as a sequence of integers starting with zero.
Metadata	Attributes of the DataFrame that are generated by Pandas when the DataFrame is constructed or changed.

Description

- A *DataFrame* is a Pandas object that consists of *columns* and *rows*, much like a table. This object provides many attributes and methods for working with the data in the table.
- Each column in a DataFrame is a *Series object* that consists of an array of labeled values, plus attributes and methods for working with the object.
- The intersection of a column and row in a DataFrame is called an *element*, and each element can contain a value, which is called a *datapoint*.

Figure 2-1 The DataFrame structure

Two ways to get data into a DataFrame

You may remember from chapter 1 that the first phase of Python data analysis is to get the data from a website or database into a DataFrame. The easiest way to do that is to read, or *import*, the data into a DataFrame using one of the Pandas read methods.

Three of these methods are summarized in the first table in figure 2-2. For instance, the read_csv() method reads the data from a CSV (comma-separated values) file into a DataFrame. The read_excel() method reads the data from an Excel file into a DataFrame. And the read_sql_query() method reads the data from the results of a SQL query on a database into a DataFrame. As you'll see in chapter 5, Pandas also provides read methods for importing other types of files like Stata or JSON files.

In some cases, though, you can't read the data from a file directly into a DataFrame. Then, you have to use the second way to get data into a DataFrame. That is, you use the DataFrame() constructor to build a DataFrame from arrays of data, column labels, row labels, and data types.

This is illustrated by the simple example in this figure. Here, two Python arrays are used to provide the data and column names for the DataFrame. Then, when the DataFrame() constructor builds the DataFrame, the column names are used for the columns, the data is stored in those columns, and an index is generated that numbers the rows, starting with 0. Yes, this is a simple example, but you will see a real-world example that builds a DataFrame from a JSON file in chapter 5.

Three of the Pandas read() methods for importing data into a DataFrame

Method	Data format
`read_csv()`	CSV (comma-separated values)
`read_excel()`	Excel
`read_sql_query()`	SQL query

How to import a CSV file from a website into a DataFrame

```
import pandas as pd
url = "https://data.cdc.gov/api/views/v6ab-adf5/rows.csv?accessType=DOWNLOAD"
mortality_data = pd.read_csv(url)
```

The DataFrame() constructor

Constructor	Description
`DataFrame(params)`	Creates a DataFrame object.

Parameter	Description
`data`	Can be an array, dictionary, or other object that's shaped like a table.
`columns`	Column labels. If they aren't specified, they will be generated.
`index`	Row labels. If they aren't specified, they will be generated.

The data and columns arrays for a DataFrame

```
df_data=[[1900, '1-4 Years', 1983.8],[1901, '1-4 Years', 1695.0]]
df_columns=['Year', 'Age Group', 'Death Rate']
```

The code that creates the DataFrame

```
import pandas as pd
mortality_df = pd.DataFrame(
    data=df_data,
    columns=df_columns)
```

The DataFrame that's created

	Year	Age Group	Death Rate
0	1900	1-4 Years	1983.8
1	1901	1-4 Years	1695.0

Description

- You can use the Pandas read() methods to read (or *import*) a file into a DataFrame.
- You can use the DataFrame() constructor to build a DataFrame from the parameters that are passed to it.

Figure 2-2 Two ways to get data into a DataFrame

How to save and restore a DataFrame

Figure 2-3 shows how to save and restore a DataFrame. Although you can save a DataFrame in a CSV or Excel file, the attributes, data types, and methods of the DataFrame are lost in those formats. So, if you want to save and restore a DataFrame without losing anything, you need to save it and read it as a *pickle file*.

This is illustrated by the two coding examples. Here, the first one saves the DataFrame named mortality_data to a pickle file named mortality_data.pkl. Then, the second one reads that pickle file, which restores the data as a DataFrame.

Saving and restoring a DataFrame is a common practice when you work with a dataset that requires extensive cleaning and preparation. For instance, you may want to save a DataFrame as a pickle file after you prepare it. Later, if you want to restart your analysis from that point, you can restore the DataFrame from the pickle file. That saves you the time of having to run the cells that clean and prepare the data again.

Three of the Pandas methods for saving a DataFrame to disk

Method	Data format
`to_pickle()`	Pickle
`to_csv()`	CSV (comma-separated values)
`to_excel()`	Excel

How to save a DataFrame as a pickle file

```
mortality_data.to_pickle('mortality_data.pkl')
```

The Pandas read_pickle() method

Method	Data format
`read_pickle(filename)`	Pickle

How to read a pickle file to restore a DataFrame

```
mortality_data = pd.read_pickle('mortality_data.pkl')
```

The DataFrame that's restored

	Year	Age Group	Death Rate
0	1900	1-4 Years	1983.8
1	1901	1-4 Years	1695.0
2	1902	1-4 Years	1655.7
3	1903	1-4 Years	1542.1
4	1904	1-4 Years	1591.5

Description

- A *pickle file* is designed for saving Python objects, including DataFrames, on disk. This can be referred to as *pickling an object*.
- Although you can also save a DataFrame in other formats like CSV or Excel, that will only save the data, not all of the features of the DataFrame.
- In practice, you will often want to save a DataFrame at various points within a Notebook. Then, if you later want to perform additional operations after that point, you can restore the DataFrame that you saved. If you don't save the DataFrame, you'll need to run the cells from the beginning of the Notebook.

Figure 2-3 How to save and restore a DataFrame

How to examine the data

After you import the data into in a DataFrame, you examine the data to help you decide what needs to be done. For that, you can start by displaying the data. Then, you can use the attributes and methods of the DataFrame to get more information about it.

How to display the data in a DataFrame

The table in figure 2-4 presents two Pandas methods for displaying the data in a DataFrame. Beyond that, JupyterLab often displays the output of the *last* statement in a Notebook cell. So, if you code the name of a DataFrame as the last or only statement in a cell, the data in the DataFrame will be displayed as shown in the first example in this figure.

When you display an entire DataFrame, some of the columns and rows in the middle of the data are omitted as shown by the first example. Here, the first five rows and the last five rows are displayed with an ellipsis (…) in the middle to indicate that rows are omitted. This works the same way for columns if there are more columns than the Pandas options provide for. (JupyterLab displays up to ten rows as shown here, and up to 20 columns.)

In many cases, however, you will just want to look at the first or last rows in the DataFrame. For that, you can use the head() and tail() methods that are illustrated in the second set of examples. But these methods will also omit columns if there are more than the Pandas options provide for.

That's why the last example in this figure shows how to use the Pandas option_context() function to set the options that control the number of rows and columns that are displayed. Here, the display.max_rows parameter is set to 5 so a maximum of 5 rows will be displayed. But the display.max_columns parameter is set to None so all of the columns will be displayed. Note that you code the option_context() function in a with statement so the options it specifies apply to any statements coded within that statement.

With the mortality DataFrame, of course, setting these options has no value because the DataFrame has only three columns. But what if you want to look at the data in all of the columns of a DataFrame that has 27 columns? Then, this code will display all 27 columns so you can scroll through them.

You can also use this coding structure to display more rows. For example, you could set the maximum number of rows to None. Then, the code would display all 476 rows of the mortality DataFrame so you could scroll down through them. But be careful about setting the maximum number of rows to None. For some DataFrames, many thousands of rows will be displayed.

Two methods for displaying the data in a DataFrame

Method	Description
`head(rows)`	Displays the first 5 rows or the number of rows in the parameter.
`tail(rows)`	Displays the last 5 rows or the number of rows in the parameter.

JupyterLab automatically displays the contents of a named DataFrame

```
mortality_data
```

	Year	Age Group	Death Rate
0	1900	1-4 Years	1983.8
1	1901	1-4 Years	1695.0
2	1902	1-4 Years	1655.7
3	1903	1-4 Years	1542.1
4	1904	1-4 Years	1591.5
...	...	...	...
471	2014	15-19 Years	45.5
472	2015	15-19 Years	48.3
473	2016	15-19 Years	51.2
474	2017	15-19 Years	51.5
475	2018	15-19 Years	49.2

476 rows × 3 columns

How to use the head() and tail() methods

```
mortality_data.head()        # displays the first 5 rows
mortality_data.tail(3)       # displays the last 3 rows
```

How to display the data in 5 rows and all columns

```
with pd.option_context(
        'display.max_rows', 5,
        'display.max_columns', None):
    display(mortality_data)
```

Description

- If you run a statement that consists of just the name of a DataFrame, JupyterLab will display the DataFrame with missing rows or columns if they exceed the option settings.
- If necessary, you can set the options for the number of rows and columns that will be displayed before you run the display() function for the DataFrame.

Figure 2-4 How to display the data in a DataFrame

How to use the attributes of a DataFrame

Figure 2-5 presents five of the most useful attributes of a DataFrame. As you can see in the first example, the values attribute displays the data in a DataFrame as an array. Then, the second example uses the Python print() method to display the other four attributes. These attributes can give you a quick view of some of the aspects of a DataFrame.

The last example in this figure shows that you can use the columns attribute to modify the column names for a DataFrame. In this case, the spaces in the column names are removed by replacing the spaces with an empty string. This is a useful skill because it's easier to code some of the Pandas methods if the column names don't have spaces.

This code uses the Python replace() method to replace any spaces in the column names that are in the columns attribute with empty strings. It then assigns the result of the replacement to the columns attribute of the DataFrame. That in turn changes the column names for the DataFrame.

Note here that if you want to use a Python string method, you have to code the str accessor before coding the method. In Pandas, an *accessor* provides access to Python methods that you can execute on all or part of a DataFrame or Series object.

Some of the attributes of a DataFrame object

Attribute	Description
`values`	The values of the DataFrame in an array format
`index`	The row index
`columns`	The column names
`size`	The total number of elements
`shape`	The number of rows and columns

The values attribute

```
mortality_data.values
====================================================
array([[1900, '1-4 Years', 1983.8],
       [1901, '1-4 Years', 1695.0],
       [1902, '1-4 Years', 1655.7],
       ...,
       [2016, '15-19 Years', 51.2],
       [2017, '15-19 Years', 51.5],
       [2018, '15-19 Years', 49.2]], dtype=object)
```

The other four attributes

```
print("Index:   ", mortality_data.index)
print("Columns:", mortality_data.columns)
print("Size:    ", mortality_data.size)
print("Shape:   ", mortality_data.shape)
====================================================================
Index:    RangeIndex(start=0, stop=476, step=1)
Columns: Index(['Year', 'Age Group', 'Death Rate'], dtype='object')
Size:     1428
Shape:    (476, 3)
```

How to use the columns attribute to replace spaces with nothing

```
mortality_data.columns = mortality_data.columns.str.replace(" ", "")
```

The new column names

```
Index(['Year', 'AgeGroup', 'DeathRate'], dtype='object')
```

Description

- A DataFrame has attributes that include the five in the table above.
- It's a good practice to remove the spaces from column names because that will simplify some of your Pandas coding.

Figure 2-5 How to use the attributes of a DataFrame

How to use the info(), nunique(), and describe() methods

Figure 2-6 summarizes three methods that present more information about a DataFrame. The info() method summarizes the data for a DataFrame as shown by the first example. Here, you can see that the spaces in the column names have been removed, as in AgeGroup and DeathRate.

You can also see that each of the three columns contains 476 non-null values, which means these columns don't have any missing values. Each column also has an appropriate data type, like int64 for Year and float64 for DeathRate. As a result, this DataFrame probably isn't going to need much cleaning.

When you use this method, you don't have to code any parameters. But if you want the memory usage to be accurate, you should set the memory_usage parameter to "deep". Although you wouldn't think that you would need to do that, you can't be sure that the usage data is accurate if you don't. In this case, the usage is 11.3+ KB without this parameter and 38.7 KB when this parameter is coded.

In the second example, the nunique() method is used to summarize the number of unique values in each column. Here, you can see that the DataFrame contains the data for 119 years and for four age groups. This also shows that the DeathRate column has 430 unique values in the 476 rows. This means that a few of the values are duplicated, but that's just coincidence.

In the third example, the describe() method presents statistical information for each numeric column in the DataFrame. That includes the count, mean, standard deviation (std), minimum (min) value, the values that mark the first (25%), second (50%), and third (75%) quartiles, and the maximum (max) value.

If you study this data, it corroborates that the data is clean. Here, the Year ranges from 1900 to 2018, which shows the scope of the data. And the DeathRate ranges from 11.4 to 1983.8, which indicates major improvements in the death rate from 1900 to 2018.

In this third example, you can see that the T property is coded after the method name and its parentheses. This property is an accessor that provides access to the transpose() method, which transposes the data so the column names for the DataFrame are in the first column and the statistics are in the other columns. If you don't code this property, the statistic names are in the first column and the column names for the DataFrame are in the other columns.

When a DataFrame like this one has just a few numeric columns, transposing the describe() method can make the data easier to read. But when a DataFrame has many columns, you may find that it's better to code the describe() method without the T property.

The info(), nunique(), and describe() methods

Method	Description
`info(params)`	Returns information about the DataFrame and its columns.
`nunique()`	Returns the number of unique data items in each column.
`describe()`	Returns statistical information for each numeric column.

How to use the info() method

```
mortality_data.info()
=====================================
<class 'pandas.core.frame.DataFrame'>
RangeIndex: 476 entries, 0 to 475
Data columns (total 3 columns):
Year           476 non-null int64
AgeGroup       476 non-null object
DeathRate      476 non-null float64
dtypes: float64(1), int64(1), object(1)
memory usage: 11.3+ KB
```

The memory_usage parameter ensures a more accurate usage result

```
mortality_data.info(memory_usage='deep')
========================================
<class 'pandas.core.frame.DataFrame'>
...
memory usage: 38.7 KB
```

How to use the nunique() method

```
mortality_data.nunique()
========================
Year           119
AgeGroup         4
DeathRate      430
dtype: int64
```

How to use the describe() method

With the T property, the statistics are displayed in the columns

```
mortality_data.describe().T
```

	count	mean	std	min	25%	50%	75%	max
Year	476.0	1959.00000	34.387268	1900.0	1929.000	1959.0	1989.000	2018.0
DeathRate	476.0	192.92416	293.224216	11.4	40.575	89.5	222.575	1983.8

Without the T property, the statistics are displayed in the rows

```
mortality_data.describe()
```

Description

- These methods give you a quick view of the data that you're working with.

Figure 2-6 How to use the info(), nunique(), and describe() methods

How to access the columns and rows

As you work with the data in a DataFrame, you often have to access its columns and rows and sometimes a subset of its columns and rows. These are critical skills that can be done in several ways. The next four figures show how.

How to access columns

Figure 2-7 shows how to access columns. It starts by showing two ways to access one column. First, you can use *dot notation*. To do that, you code the name of the DataFrame, a dot (period), and the name of the column. This is the easiest way to access one column, but you can't use it if the column name contains a space.

The other way to access one column is to use brackets. To do that, you code the name of the DataFrame and a set of brackets, and you code the column name within quotation marks within those brackets. This coding is a little more work, but this does work with column names that contain spaces.

The last example in this figure shows how to access two or more columns. To do that, you code a list of column names within brackets, and you enclose that set of brackets within an outer set of brackets.

Because dot notation is easier to use and understand when you access one column, that notation is used in most of the examples in the rest of this chapter and book. However, as you have just seen, you can't use dot notation to access two or more columns. Beyond that, as you will soon see, some statements require bracket notation, even though you would think that dot notation would work.

You should also know that the way you access the columns changes the type of data that you get. If you use dot notation or a single set of brackets, the code returns a Series object. However, if you use two sets of brackets (regardless of how many columns you select), the code returns a DataFrame object. This can cause errors in code that looks correct, so it is important to be careful here.

The syntax for accessing columns

To access	With brackets	With dot notation
One column	`df[column_name]` `df[[column_name]]`	`df.column_name`
Two or more columns	`df[[col1,col2,...]]`	

Two ways to access one column

With dot notation

```
mortality_data.DeathRate.head(2)
================================
0    1983.8
1    1695.0
Name: DeathRate, dtype: float64
```

With brackets

```
mortality_data['DeathRate'].head(2)
===================================
0    1983.8
1    1695.0
Name: DeathRate, dtype: float64
```

How to use a list to access two or more columns

```
mortality_data[['Year','DeathRate']].head(2)
```

	Year	DeathRate
0	1900	1983.8
1	1901	1695.0

Description

- To access one column, you can use either *dot notation* or brackets. However, dot notation will simplify your code.
- When you use dot notation, the column names can't contain any spaces. That's why it's a common practice to remove the spaces in column names as part of the cleaning phase.
- To access more than one column, you code the column names in a list. That means that the names need to be coded within a set of brackets, which means that you code one set of brackets within another set of brackets.

Figure 2-7 How to access columns

How to access rows

Figure 2-8 shows how to use the query() method to access the rows in a DataFrame. When you use this method, the one parameter is a condition that you code between single quotation marks.

Within that condition, you use the Python operators for comparisons and compound conditions. And if you need to code a string literal within the condition, like "1-4 Years", you enclose it within double quotation marks since the entire condition is enclosed in single quotation marks.

This is illustrated by the three examples in this figure. The first one selects the rows for just the year 1900. The second one selects all the rows for the year 2000, except the row for the 1-4 age group. And the third one selects the rows for either the year 1900 or the year 2000.

The only complication when you code the query() method is referring to column names that contain spaces. Then, you need to enclose those column names within *backticks* (or *backquotes*), as shown by the last example in this figure. On most keyboards, the backtick key is the upper-left key. This complication is another reason why it's a common practice to remove the spaces from column names.

The query() method

Method	Description
`query(condition)`	Gets the data specified by the condition.

How to use the query() method to access rows

Based on a single column

```
mortality_data.query('Year == 1900')
```

	Year	AgeGroup	DeathRate
0	1900	1-4 Years	1983.8
119	1900	5-9 Years	466.1
238	1900	10-14 Years	298.3
357	1900	15-19 Years	484.8

Based on multiple columns with the *and* operator

```
mortality_data.query('Year == 2000 and AgeGroup != "1-4 Years"')
```

	Year	AgeGroup	DeathRate
219	2000	5-9 Years	15.8
338	2000	10-14 Years	20.3
457	2000	15-19 Years	67.1

Based on multiple columns with the *or* operator

```
mortality_data.query('Year == 1900 or Year == 2000').head()
```

	Year	AgeGroup	DeathRate
0	1900	1-4 Years	1983.8
100	2000	1-4 Years	32.4
119	1900	5-9 Years	466.1
219	2000	5-9 Years	15.8
238	1900	10-14 Years	298.3

With backticks for column names that contain spaces

```
mortality_data.query('Year == 2000 and `Age Group` != "1-4 Years"')
```

Description

- When you use the query() method to access rows, you code the condition between single quotation marks. However, to refer to column names that contain spaces, you need to enclose the names within *backticks*. That's another reason for removing the spaces from column names.

Figure 2-8 How to access rows

How to access a subset of rows and columns

In the last two figures, you saw how to access columns and rows from a DataFrame. In some cases, though, you'll need to access a subset of both rows and columns. Figure 2-9 shows you how.

To start, you use the query() method to access a subset of rows, just as you learned in the last figure. Then, you can use one of the techniques that you learned in figure 2-7 to access columns from the rows that are returned, as illustrated by the examples in this figure.

All four examples use the query() method to access the rows for the year 1900. Then, the first example uses dot notation to access the DeathRate column. The second example is similar, but it uses a single set of brackets to access the DeathRate column. Remember that both of these techniques return a Series object, as you can see by the output.

The third example uses a list with a single item to access the DeathRate column, and the fourth example uses a list to access both the AgeGroup and DeathRate columns. Both of these examples return a DataFrame object. As mentioned earlier, it's important to know whether the code you use returns a Series or a DataFrame object.

How to access one column from a subset of rows using dot notation

```
mortality_data.query('Year == 1900').DeathRate
==============================================
0       1983.8
119      466.1
238      298.3
357      484.8
Name: DeathRate, dtype: float64
```

How to access one column from a subset of rows using brackets

```
mortality_data.query('Year == 1900')['DeathRate']
=================================================
0       1983.8
119      466.1
238      298.3
357      484.8
Name: DeathRate, dtype: float64
```

How to access one column from a subset of rows using a list

```
mortality_data.query('Year == 1900')[['DeathRate']]
```

	DeathRate
0	1983.8
119	466.1
238	298.3
357	484.8

How to access two or more columns from a subset of rows using a list

```
mortality_data.query('Year == 1900')[['AgeGroup','DeathRate']]
```

	AgeGroup	DeathRate
0	1-4 Years	1983.8
119	5-9 Years	466.1
238	10-14 Years	298.3
357	15-19 Years	484.8

Description

- After you use the query() method to access a subset of rows, you can use dot notation or brackets to access one or more columns from that subset.
- In most cases, you'll use brackets with a list of the columns you want to access because this technique returns a DataFrame object rather than a Series object.

Figure 2-9 How to access a subset of rows and columns

Another way to access a subset of rows and columns

In the last figure, you saw how to combine the use of the query() method with the use of dot notation or brackets to access a subset of rows and columns. Another way to do that is to use the loc[ ] (location) or iloc[ ] (integer location) accessor as shown in figure 2-10.

With both accessors, you use one parameter to identify the rows for the subset and a second parameter to identify the columns. With the loc[ ] accessor, though, you use *labels* to identify the rows and columns, and with the iloc[ ] accessor, you use numeric *positions*. You can code these parameters as either a *list* or a *slice* of rows or columns.

If you've used slices with your Python code, you know that a slice has a starting value, an ending value, and an optional step value with the values separated by colons. If you're using positions instead of labels in your slices, those positions start from 0 and the ending position isn't included in the result. So, for example, 1:3 is a slice that refers to the second and third values, but not the fourth.

However, with the loc[] accessor, this works a little differently. When you use slices with DataFrames, the ending position is included. So, if you use 1:3 for a slice in the loc accessor, you get the rows where the index value is 1, 2, or 3.

The first group of examples in this figure shows how to access rows with the loc[ ] accessor. Here, the first statement uses a list to access rows 0, 5, and 10. The second statement uses a slice to access rows 4 through 6. The third statement uses a slice to access rows 0, 5, 10, 15, and 20. And the fourth statement shows that you can also use a conditional expression to access rows. In this case, the code accesses the rows for the year 1917.

The second group of examples shows how to access subsets of rows and columns with the loc[ ] accessor. Here, the first statement uses lists to access rows 0, 5, and 10, but only for the AgeGroup and DeathRate columns. Then, the second statement uses slices to access rows 4 through 6, but only for the AgeGroup and DeathRate columns.

The first two statements in the third group of examples get the same results, but they use the iloc[ ] accessor. Since this accessor uses normal python slicing, positions 4,5,6 in the list are equivalent to 4:7 in the slice because the ending position in the slice isn't included. Similarly, 1,2 is equivalent to 1:3.

The third statement in this group shows that you can also use a negative number with the iloc[ ] accessor to specify a position. In this case, the value -10 gets the last 10 rows in the DataFrame.

Since the mortality DataFrame in these examples has an integer index that ranges from 0 to 475, the loc[] and iloc[] accessors work the same. But some DataFrames have integer indexes that aren't in sequence because the DataFrame has been sorted. And some have a hierarchical index as shown later in this chapter. In those cases, the loc[] and iloc[] accessors work differently.

If you experiment with these accessors, you'll see how they work. But keep in mind that you probably won't need to use them much. That's because the techniques you saw in the last figure are easier to code and understand.

The loc[ ] and iloc[ ] accessors for accessing rows and columns

Accessor	Description
`loc[rows,columns]`	Accesses rows and columns by their labels.
`iloc[rows,columns]`	Accesses rows and columns by their positions.

How to access rows with the loc[ ] accessor

With a list to access the rows with labels 0, 5, and 10

```
mortality_data.loc[[0,5,10]]
```

With a slice to access the rows with labels 4 through 6

```
mortality_data.loc[4:6]
```

With a slice to access every 5th row from 0 through 20

```
mortality_data.loc[0:20:5]
```

With a conditional expression to access the rows for the year 1917

```
mortality_data.loc[mortality_data.Year == 1917]
```

How to access rows and columns with the loc[ ] accessor

With lists of row and column labels

```
mortality_data.loc[[0,5,10],['AgeGroup','DeathRate']]
```

With slices of row and column labels

```
mortality_data.loc[4:6,'AgeGroup':'DeathRate']
```

How to access rows and columns with the iloc[ ] accessor

With lists of row and column positions

```
mortality_data.iloc[[4,5,6],[1,2]]
```

With slices of row and column positions

```
mortality_data.iloc[4:7,1:3]
```

With a negative row position in a slice to access the last 10 rows

```
mortality_data.iloc[-10:]
```

Description

- You can use the loc[ ] and iloc[ ] accessors to access rows, columns, and subsets. However, you can usually get the same result in a way that's easier to understand.
- The loc[ ] accessor operates on the *labels* of rows and columns. By contrast, the iloc[ ] accessor operates on the *positions* of rows and columns, so a negative position is valid.
- To access rows or columns with the loc[ ] or iloc[ ] accessor, you can use values, lists, or slices. For rows, you can also use conditional expressions.
- When you use slices with the loc[ ] accessor, both the start and stop rows and columns are included. But with the iloc[ ] accessor, the stop row and stop column aren't included.

Figure 2-10 Another way to access a subset of rows and columns

How to work with the data

Now that you know how to examine and access the data in a DataFrame, you're ready to learn how to work with the data. The next four figures will get you started with that.

How to sort the data

To sort the data in a DataFrame, you can use the sort_values() method as shown in figure 2-11. By default, this sorts the data in ascending order based on the data in the columns that are specified in the first parameter. However, you can change the sort order by setting the ascending parameter to False.

This is illustrated by the three examples. The first example sorts by the values in the DeathRate column in descending order. The second example sorts by DeathRate within Year, both in ascending order. And the third example sorts first by Year in ascending order and then by DeathRate in descending order.

Note in the second and third examples that you need to code two or more sort columns within brackets. In other words, you're coding them as a Python list. However, you don't need the brackets if you're sorting by only one column.

Also note that the signature for the sort_values() method doesn't distinguish between positional and keyword parameters. That's because the examples make it clear that *columns* is a positional parameter and *ascending* is a keyword parameter.

The sort_values() method

Method	Description
`sort_values(columns, ascending)`	Sorts the DataFrame rows in ascending (the default) or descending order based on the data in the specified columns.

How to sort by one column in descending order

```
mortality_data.sort_values('DeathRate', ascending=False).head(3)
```

	Year	AgeGroup	DeathRate
0	1900	1-4 Years	1983.8
1	1901	1-4 Years	1695.0
2	1902	1-4 Years	1655.7

How to sort by multiple columns in ascending order

```
mortality_data.sort_values(['Year','DeathRate']).head(3)
```

	Year	AgeGroup	DeathRate
238	1900	10-14 Years	298.3
119	1900	5-9 Years	466.1
357	1900	15-19 Years	484.8

How to sort by multiple columns in mixed orders

```
mortality_data.sort_values(['Year','DeathRate'],
                           ascending=[True,False]).head()
```

	Year	AgeGroup	DeathRate
0	1900	1-4 Years	1983.8
357	1900	15-19 Years	484.8
119	1900	5-9 Years	466.1
238	1900	10-14 Years	298.3
1	1901	1-4 Years	1695.0

Description

- You can sort the data in a DataFrame in various sequences to help you understand the data.

Figure 2-11 How to sort the data

How to use the statistical methods

Figure 2-12 starts with a table that summarizes some of the Pandas methods for getting statistics. In fact, Pandas provides one set of these methods for Series objects and another set with the same names for DataFrame objects. That's why you don't have to worry about applying a DataFrame method to a Series object, or vice versa.

The first example in this figure shows how to apply the mean() method to one column. The second example shows how to apply the max() method to a list of two columns. And the third example shows how to apply the count() method to all the columns in a DataFrame.

In the second example, note that "5-9 Years" is given as the maximum value for the Age Group column. That's because it's based on the sort sequence for alphanumeric values. In that sequence, "5-9" comes before "1-4", "10-14", and "15-19" because 5 comes before 1.

The last example in this figure shows how to use the quantile() method. The parameter for this method specifies one or more decimal fractions that specify the cutoff point for the data. In this example, a list provides two fractions so the cutoff points are 10% and 90%. You can see how this works in the first two rows of data that are displayed for this method.

Here, the 10% mark is 1911.5 for the year and 21.50 for the death rate. That means that 10% of the death rates are less than 21.50. Similarly, the 90% mark is 2006.5 for the year and 430.85 for the death rate. That means that 90% of the rates are less than 430.85.

Some of the Pandas methods for both Series and DataFrame objects

Method	Returns
`count()`	Number of values not including null values
`mean()`	Mean (average)
`median()`	Median
`min()`	Minimum value
`max()`	Maximum value
`std()`	Standard deviation
`sum()`	Sum of the values
`cumsum()`	Cumulative sum of the values
`quantile(q)`	Quantile value specified as a decimal fraction like .25

How to apply a method to one column

```
mortality_data.DeathRate.mean()
=================================
192.92415966386568
```

How to apply a method to two columns

```
mortality_data[['AgeGroup','DeathRate']].max()
=================================================
AgeGroup     5-9 Years
DeathRate       1983.8
dtype: object
```

How to apply a method to all columns

```
mortality_data.count()
=======================
Year         476
AgeGroup     476
DeathRate    476
dtype: int64
```

How to apply the quantile() method to two different quantiles

```
mortality_data.quantile([.1,.9])
```

	Year	DeathRate
0.1	1911.5	21.50
0.9	2006.5	430.85

Description

- Pandas provides statistical methods for both Series and DataFrame objects.
- If you apply a method that requires numeric data to a DataFrame, it will be applied to just the numeric columns.

Figure 2-12 How to use the statistical methods

How to use Python for column arithmetic

Figure 2-13 shows how to use Python for column arithmetic. For that, you can use the standard Python arithmetic operators that are summarized in the table at the top of this figure. As you will see, you can use these operators to perform arithmetic on the data in entire columns. These are *vectorized operations* that run efficiently and don't require the use of for loops.

The first example in this figure shows how you can use column arithmetic to add a column to a DataFrame. In this case, a column named MeanCentered is added to the DataFrame by subtracting the mean of a series of values from each value in the series. Here, the mean for all the values in the DeathRate column is calculated by applying the mean() method to that column:

```
mortality_data.DeathRate.mean()
```

Then, this mean is subtracted from each value in the DeathRate column. The result is a value that shows how far from the mean each value is.

The second example in this figure shows how you can use column arithmetic to change the values in a column. In this case, the values in the DeathRate column are divided by 100,000. As a result, the new values represent the death rates for each of the rows, not the number of deaths per 100,000 children.

The Python operators for column arithmetic

Operator	Name	Description
+	Addition	Adds two operands.
-	Subtraction	Subtracts the right operand from the left.
*	Multiplication	Multiplies two operands.
/	Division	Divides the right operand into the left and returns a floating-point number.
//	Integer division	Divides the right operand into the left and drops the decimal portion of the result.
%	Modulo/Remainder	Divides the right operand into the left and returns the remainder as an integer.
**	Exponentiation	Raises the left operand to the power of the right operand.

How to add a column to a DataFrame

```
mortality_data['MeanCentered'] = \
    mortality_data.DeathRate - mortality_data.DeathRate.mean()
```

	Year	AgeGroup	DeathRate	MeanCentered
0	1900	1-4 Years	1983.8	1790.87584
1	1901	1-4 Years	1695.0	1502.07584
2	1902	1-4 Years	1655.7	1462.77584
3	1903	1-4 Years	1542.1	1349.17584

How to modify the data in an existing column

```
mortality_data['DeathRate'] = mortality_data.DeathRate / 100000
```

	Year	AgeGroup	DeathRate	MeanCentered
0	1900	01-04 Years	0.019838	1790.87584
1	1901	01-04 Years	0.016950	1502.07584
2	1902	01-04 Years	0.016557	1462.77584
3	1903	01-04 Years	0.015421	1349.17584

Description

- Pandas lets you use the Python arithmetic operators to perform arithmetic operations on the data in columns. These are *vectorized operations* that run efficiently and don't require the use of for loops.

Figure 2-13 How to use Python for column arithmetic

How to modify the string data in columns

In some cases, you will want to improve the string data in the columns of a DataFrame. To do that, you can use Pandas or Python string methods. Figure 2-14 shows how.

In the first example, the Pandas replace() method is used to add leading zeros to the year values for the 1-4 and 5-9 age groups. That will keep the age groups in the right sequence when you work with them later on. To do that, you code a list of the strings to be replaced in the to_replace parameter and another list for the values to replace them with in the value parameter. You also set the inplace parameter to True so the values are replaced in the DataFrame.

Another way to accomplish this is to use code like this:

```
mortality_data = mortality_data.AgeGroup.replace(
    to_replace = ['1-4 Years','5-9 Years'],
    value = ['01-04 Years','05-09 Years'])
```

Here, the inplace parameter is omitted, so the default value of False is used. Then, the DataFrame that's returned by the replace() method is assigned to the variable that contained the original DataFrame. As you'll see, some Pandas methods provide for modifying a DataFrame in place, and others don't. So, you'll need to be familiar with both of these techniques.

The second example also uses the Pandas replace() method. But this time, a dictionary is used to specify the old and the new values. This is another way to get the same result as the first example.

In the third example, the Python replace() method is used to get the same result. To use one of the Python string methods, though, you need to code the str accessor after the column name and before you code the Python method. In this case, one Python replace() method is coded for each string that's replaced.

Of course, you can also use many of the other Python methods for working with strings. In most cases, though, you will only need to replace strings or portions of strings when you're modifying the string data in columns.

The Pandas replace() method

Method	Description
`replace(to_replace,value, inplace)`	Replaces the strings in the to_replace parameter with the strings in the value parameter or replaces the old values in a dictionary with the new values.

The Python replace() method

Method	Description
`replace(old,new)`	Replaces the string in the old parameter with the string in the new parameter.

How to modify the string data in a column

With the Pandas replace() method with three parameters

```
mortality_data.AgeGroup.replace(
    to_replace = ['1-4 Years','5-9 Years'],
    value = ['01-04 Years','05-09 Years'],
    inplace = True)
```

With the Pandas replace() method and a dictionary of old and new values

```
mortality_data.AgeGroup.replace(
    {'1-4 Years':'01-04 Years','5-9 Years':'05-09 Years'},
    inplace = True)
```

Wth the Python replace() method

```
mortality_data['AgeGroup'] =
    mortality_data.AgeGroup.str.replace('1-4 Years', '01-04 Years')
mortality_data['AgeGroup'] =
    mortality_data.AgeGroup.str.replace('5-9 Years', '05-09 Years')
```

The result for all three of the examples

	Year	AgeGroup	DeathRate	MeanCentered
0	1900	01-04 Years	0.019838	1790.87584
1	1901	01-04 Years	0.016950	1502.07584
2	1902	01-04 Years	0.016557	1462.77584
3	1903	01-04 Years	0.015421	1349.17584

Description

- When you clean the data for a DataFrame, you may need to modify the string data in a column. To do that, you can use Pandas methods or Python methods.
- To use Python string methods, you code the str accessor followed by the string method.

Figure 2-14 How to modify the string data in columns

How to shape the data

When you prepare the data in a DataFrame, you often shape the data so it's appropriate for analysis. To do that, you can create indexes that refer to the rows in the DataFrame. You can create wide data by pivoting the data. And you can create long data by melting the data. The next three figures show how.

How to use indexes

By default, the *index* for a DataFrame identifies each row by an index value starting with zero. So, the last index value is one less than the number of rows in the DataFrame. In some cases, though, it's better to set an index for a DataFrame that is based on the data in one or more columns. That DataFrame can make it easier to do operations like plotting the data.

As figure 2-15 shows, you can use the set_index() method to set the index for a DataFrame. In the first example, the index is set to a single column, the year column. Here, you can see that the column name for the index is shown at a lower level than the other columns.

Although the set_index() method doesn't require that the index for each row be unique, you may sometimes want it to be. To check that, you can set the verify_integrity parameter to True. Then, if each index value isn't unique, an error is raised. This is illustrated by the second example, which says that the index has duplicate keys.

The third example shows how to set the index to the combination of the Year and AgeGroup columns. Because each combination of Year and AgeGroup refers to only one row, this passes the integrity test. Here again, you can see that the column names for the index are displayed at one level, and the column names for the other columns are displayed at a higher level. When an index consists of two or more columns, as it does in this example, the index can be referred to as a *multi-level index*, or a *multi-index*.

When you set an index for a DataFrame, you need to know that you won't be able to use the columns in the index as parameters in other methods. That's why you may need to reset an index, as illustrated by the fourth example in this figure. This returns the DataFrame to its original form. But note that this method includes an inplace parameter like the replace() method shown in the previous figure. Because of that, you have to either set this parameter to True to reset the index or assign the DataFrame returned by the reset_index() method to the original DataFrame.

You should also know that other Pandas methods set indexes. For instance, the pivot() method that you'll learn about in the next figure sets an index. That's why you need to understand how indexes work.

The set_index() and reset_index() methods

Method	Description
`set_index(columns, verify_integrity)`	Sets an index based on the columns that are specified and verifies the integrity of that index if verify_integrity is set to True.
`reset_index(inplace)`	Resets the index to the original index for the DataFrame.

How to set a one-column index

```
mortality_data = mortality_data.set_index('Year')
mortality_data.head(2)
```

	AgeGroup	DeathRate	MeanCentered
Year			
1900	01-04 Years	0.019838	1790.87584
1901	01-04 Years	0.016950	1502.07584

How to verify the integrity of a one-column index

```
mortality_data = mortality_data.set_index('Year', verify_integrity=True)
mortality_data.head(2)
==========================================================================
ValueError: Index has duplicate keys: Int64Index([1900, 1901, ....
```

How to set a two-column index

```
mortality_data.set_index(['Year','AgeGroup'], verify_integrity=True)
mortality_data.head(2)
```

		DeathRate	MeanCentered
Year	**AgeGroup**		
1900	01-04 Years	0.019838	1790.87584
1901	01-04 Years	0.016950	1502.07584

How to reset an index

```
mortality_data.reset_index(inplace=True)
mortality_data.head(2)
```

	Year	AgeGroup	DeathRate	MeanCentered
0	1900	01-04 Years	0.019838	1790.87584
1	1901	01-04 Years	0.016950	1502.07584

Description

- When you set an *index*, the index doesn't have to be unique for each row.
- Because you can't uses index columns as parameters, you often need to reset the index.

Figure 2-15 How to use indexes

How to pivot the data

Figure 2-16 shows how to use the pivot() method to *pivot* the data in a DataFrame based on an index column. This changes the data from *long form* to *wide form* (or from *long data* to *wide data*). Keep in mind, though, that neither form is better than the other. It's just that some methods work better with long data, and some work better with wide data. That's why you need to be able to shape the data into either form.

When you use the pivot() method to create wide data, you use the index parameter to set the index and the columns parameter to specify the column or columns to be pivoted. You can also use the values parameter to specify the columns that supply the data for the pivoted columns.

This is illustrated by the examples in this figure. In both examples, the DataFrame named mortality_data has four columns. And in both examples, the pivoted data is assigned to a new DataFrame named mortality_wide. In the resulting DataFrames, the formatting shows that the Year column is the index and the pivoted column is the AgeGroup column.

In the first example, the AgeGroup column is pivoted on the Year column, but only for the DeathRate column. As a result, the AgeGroup column has been pivoted into four columns (01-04 Years, 05-09 Years, 10-14 Years, and 15-19 Years), and these columns contain the death rates for the age groups.

The second example is the same as the first example, except that the values parameter isn't coded. As a result, the AgeGroup column is pivoted for all of the other columns. In this case, that's just the DeathRate and MeanCentered columns. But you can imagine what the result would be if there were many other columns.

The pivot() method of a DataFrame

Method	Description
`pivot(index,columns,values)`	Pivots the data on the index parameter, gets the columns to be pivoted from the columns parameter, and gets the values for the new columns from the values parameter.

How to pivot the AgeGroup column for the death rate

```
mortality_wide = mortality_data.pivot(
    index='Year', columns='AgeGroup', values='DeathRate')
mortality_wide.head(3)
```

AgeGroup	01-04 Years	05-09 Years	10-14 Years	15-19 Years
Year				
1900	0.019838	0.004661	0.002983	0.004848
1901	0.016950	0.004276	0.002736	0.004544
1902	0.016557	0.004033	0.002525	0.004215

How to pivot the AgeGroup column for all other data

```
mortality_wide = mortality_data.pivot(
    index='Year', columns='AgeGroup')
mortality_wide.head(3)
```

	DeathRate				MeanCentered			
AgeGroup	01-04 Years	05-09 Years	10-14 Years	15-19 Years	01-04 Years	05-09 Years	10-14 Years	15-19 Years
Year								
1900	0.019838	0.004661	0.002983	0.004848	1790.87584	273.17584	105.37584	291.87584
1901	0.016950	0.004276	0.002736	0.004544	1502.07584	234.67584	80.67584	261.47584
1902	0.016557	0.004033	0.002525	0.004215	1462.77584	210.37584	59.57584	228.57584

Description

- When you *pivot* the data in a DataFrame, you spread the values in one or more columns over two or more new columns. In other words, you create *wide data.*
- The pivot() method uses the index parameter to set an index for the data.
- If you don't specify the values parameter, all of the other columns are included.

Figure 2-16 How to pivot the data

How to melt the data

When you *melt* the data in a DataFrame, you convert some of the columns from wide form to long form. To do that, you use the melt() method to combine two or more columns into just two new columns: one that contains the names of the melted columns, and one that contains the related values. This is illustrated by the example in figure 2-17.

In this case, the starting DataFrame is in wide form. That is, the death rates for each year are spread over four columns: 01-04 Years, 05-09 Years, 10-14 Years, and 15-19 Years.

To convert that data to long form, the melt() method sets all four of the parameters. Here, the id_vars parameter says that the Year column will be used to identify each row in the result. The value_vars parameter says that just the columns named "01-04 Years" and "05-09 Years" should be melted. The var_name parameter says that a new column named AgeGroup should be used to identify the data in each of the melted rows. And the value_name parameter says that a new column named DeathRate should be used to store the values for each row.

You can see how this works in the resulting DataFrame. Here, the column names for just the 01-04 and 05-09 columns are stored in the AgeGroup column, and the death rates for those columns are stored in the DeathRate column. This means that the new DataFrame has twice as many rows as the starting DataFrame. In short, the wide data has been converted to long data.

Note, however, that if you don't code the value_vars parameter, all of the columns except the Year column will be melted. That means that the new DataFrame will be four times as long as the starting DataFrame.

The melt() method of a DataFrame

Method	Description
`melt(params)`	Melts the data in two or more columns into two columns: one for the column names and one for the values.

Parameter	Description
`id_vars`	The column or columns that identify each row.
`value_vars`	The columns to melt. If none are specified, all other columns will be melted.
`var_name`	The name of the column that will contain the melted column names, or "variable" by default.
`value_name`	The name of the column that will contain the values, or "value" by default.

The starting DataFrame in wide form

	Year	01-04 Years	05-09 Years	10-14 Years	15-19 Years
0	1900	0.019838	0.004661	0.002983	0.004848
1	1901	0.016950	0.004276	0.002736	0.004544
2	1902	0.016557	0.004033	0.002525	0.004215
3	1903	0.015421	0.004147	0.002682	0.004341

How to melt the data for just the 01-04 and 05-09 columns

```
mortality_long = mortality_wide.melt(
    id_vars = 'Year',
    value_vars=['01-04 Years','05-09 Years'],
    var_name ='AgeGroup',
    value_name='DeathRate')
```

	Year	AgeGroup	DeathRate
0	1900	01-04 Years	0.019838
1	1901	01-04 Years	0.016950
...	...	...	...
236	2017	05-09 Years	0.000116
237	2018	05-09 Years	0.000115

Description

- When you *melt* the data in a DataFrame, you combine two or more columns into just two columns: one that contains the names of the combined columns as variables and one that contains the related values. In other words, you create *long data.*

Figure 2-17 How to melt the data

How to analyze the data

This chapter finishes by presenting three of the methods that you'll use the most when you analyze the data in a DataFrame. They are the groupby(), agg(), and plot() methods.

How to group the data

When you analyze data, you frequently need to *group* the data. To do that, you use the groupby() method.

Figure 2-18 shows how to use this method. In the first example, the groupby() method is used to group the mortality data by age group. To do that, the one parameter specifies just the AgeGroup column. Then, the mean() method is chained to the groupby() method so the mean for each age group is displayed for the DeathRate and MeanCentered columns in the resulting DataFrame. Note here that the AgeGroup column becomes the index, and there are only four rows in the result.

The second example shows how to group the data by the Year column and chain the median() method to it. This time, the Year column becomes the index, and there is one row for each year. In addition, the AgeGroup column isn't included in the resulting DataFrame because it contains string data.

The third example shows how to group the data on multiple columns. In this case, these are the Year and AgeGroup columns. Then, the count() method is chained to the groupby() method. This shows that there is only one row for each of the resulting groups. As a result, it makes no sense to group the data this way, but this would make sense if there were multiple rows for each group.

The groupby() method

Method	Description
`groupby(columns)`	Groups the data based on the columns that are specified.

How to group the data on the AgeGroup column

```
mortality_data.groupby('AgeGroup').mean().head(4)
```

AgeGroup	Year	DeathRate	MeanCentered
01-04 Years	1959	0.003832	190.301891
05-09 Years	1959	0.001173	-75.598109
10-14 Years	1959	0.000938	-99.154412
15-19 Years	1959	0.001774	-15.549370

How to group the data on the Year column

```
mortality_data.groupby('Year').median().head(4)
```

Year	DeathRate	MeanCentered
1900	0.004755	282.52584
1901	0.004410	248.07584
1902	0.004124	219.47584
1903	0.004244	231.47584

How to group the data on multiple columns

```
mortality_data.groupby(['Year','AgeGroup']).count().head()
```

Year	AgeGroup	DeathRate	MeanCentered
1900	01-04 Years	1	1
	05-09 Years	1	1
	10-14 Years	1	1
	15-19 Years	1	1
1901	01-04 Years	1	1

Description

- The groupby() method lets you group the data and apply one method to the group. This method uses the grouping column or columns as its index.

Figure 2-18 How to group the data

How to aggregate the data

In the last figure, you saw how one statistical method can be chained to a groupby() method. However, you can use the agg() method to apply more than one method to a group, which can be referred to as *aggregating* the data. This is illustrated in figure 2-19.

In the first example, you can see how the agg() method is used to apply the mean and median methods to each age group. Here, the two statistical methods are coded within a list. In the resulting DataFrame, you can see that the results of the two methods are displayed for each of the three columns in each group.

In the second example, you can see how four statistical methods are applied to each age group. But this time, the DeathRate column is accessed from the resulting DataFrame, so the statistics are only applied to that column.

In the third example, you can see how the rows are grouped by the Year column. As in the second example, the DeathRate column is accessed from the resulting DataFrame. Then, the agg() method is used to apply seven statistical methods to that column for each of the year groups.

The agg() method

Method	Description
agg(methods)	Aggregates the grouped data using the methods that are specified.

How to aggregate the data for all columns in each age group

```
mortality_data.groupby('AgeGroup').agg(['mean','median'])
```

	Year		DeathRate		MeanCentered	
	mean	median	mean	median	mean	median
AgeGroup						
01-04 Years	1959	1959	0.003832	0.001091	190.301891	-83.82416
05-09 Years	1959	1959	0.001173	0.000484	-75.598109	-144.52416
10-14 Years	1959	1959	0.000938	0.000446	-99.154412	-148.32416
15-19 Years	1959	1959	0.001774	0.001069	-15.549370	-86.02416

How to aggregate the data for just the death rate in each age group

```
mortality_data.groupby('AgeGroup')['DeathRate'] \
    .agg(['mean','median','std','nunique'])
```

	mean	median	std	nunique
AgeGroup				
01-04 Years	0.003832	0.001091	0.005005	117
05-09 Years	0.001173	0.000484	0.001275	115
10-14 Years	0.000938	0.000446	0.000884	115
15-19 Years	0.001774	0.001069	0.001384	117

How to aggregate the data for just the death rate in each year group

```
mortality_data.groupby('Year')['DeathRate'] \
    .agg(['mean','median','std','min','max','var','nunique'])
```

	mean	median	std	min	max	var	nunique
Year							
1900	0.008082	0.004755	0.007882	0.002983	0.019838	6.212178e-05	4
1901	0.007127	0.004410	0.006597	0.002736	0.016950	4.352410e-05	4
1902	0.006832	0.004124	0.006527	0.002525	0.016557	4.260299e-05	4

Description

- The agg() method lets you apply one or more methods to the grouped data.

Figure 2-19 How to aggregate the data

How to plot the data

Of course, *data visualization* is a critical component of data analysis. So, to help get you started with that, figure 2-20 introduces the Pandas plot() method, which is the method that you use to *plot* the data.

When you use this method without any parameters, it plots the index on the x-axis and all numeric columns on the y-axis. So if you prepare the data properly, you don't have to code any parameters.

This is illustrated by the two examples in this figure. In the first one, the pivot() method is used to create the wide data that is needed for this plot. Then, the plot() method is chained to it without any parameters. In the result, you can see that the years are used for the x-axis and the death rates for the age groups are plotted on the y-axis.

In the second example, the groupby() and agg() methods are used to apply the mean, median, and std methods to the death rate column for each age group. Then, the plot.barh() method is chained to these methods. As a result, a horizontal bar chart is created for the grouped data.

Note in the first example that the plot() method works on the wide data that has been created by the pivot() method. And note in the second example that the plot() method works on long data that has been grouped. That shows how important it is to be able to shape the data into either wide or long form.

Of course, there's a lot more to data visualization than this. That's why chapter 3 presents the Pandas essentials for data visualization. And chapter 4 presents the Seaborn essentials for enhanced data visualization.

How to chain the pivot() and plot() methods

```
mortality_data.pivot(index='Year', columns='AgeGroup')['DeathRate'].plot()
```

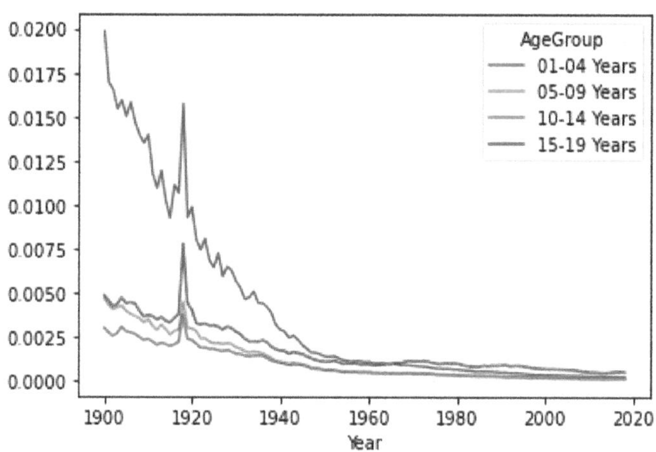

How to chain the groupby(), agg(), and plot() methods

```
mortality_data.groupby('AgeGroup')['DeathRate'] \
    .agg(['mean','median','std']).plot.barh()
```

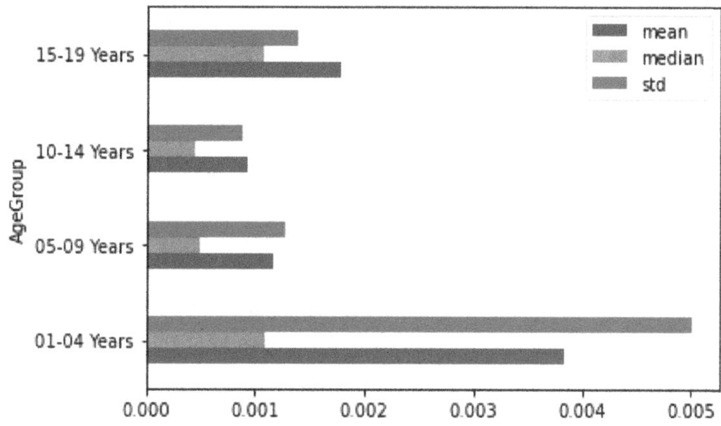

Description

- By default, the plot() method plots the index values on the x-axis and all numeric columns on the y-axis.
- To prepare the data for plotting, you will often use the pivot() or groupby() method and then chain the plot method to it.

Figure 2-20 How to plot the data

Perspective

This chapter has presented the essential Pandas skills that you'll use in almost every analysis that you undertake. This is a powerful subset of the skills that you need for data analysis, which means that you can get started with your own analyses right now.

Of course, there's a lot more to learn. That's why the chapters in section 2 present the specific skills that you need for getting, cleaning, preparing, and analyzing the data. In those chapters, you'll review some of the skills in this chapter, and you'll see them applied in new ways. You'll also learn all the other skills that you need for data analysis.

Before you go on to the chapters in section 2, though, chapter 3 presents the Pandas skills for data visualization. And chapter 4 presents the Seaborn skills for enhanced data visualization. That's because data visualization is such an essential part of data analysis. Once you learn those skills, you'll be ready to learn all of the other skills that are presented in this book.

Terms

DataFrame
DataFrame object
row
column
element
datapoint
Series object
import data
pickle file
pickling
accessor
dot notation
backtick
backquote
vectorized operation
index
multi-level index (multi-index)
pivot the data
long form (long data)
wide form (wide data)
melt the data
group the data
aggregate the data
data visualization
plot the data

Summary

- A *DataFrame*, or *DataFrame object*, is a Pandas object that stores data in *columns* and *rows*. A DataFrame also provides attributes and methods for working with the data that it contains.
- The columns in a DataFrame are *Series objects*, and Pandas provides attributes and methods for working with Series objects.
- The intersection of a column and row in a DataFrame is an *element*, and the value of each element is a *datapoint*.
- To get data into a DataFrame, you can (1) import data from a file or database or (2) use the DataFrame() constructor to build a DataFrame from the data and column labels that are passed to it.
- To examine the data in a DataFrame, you can display the data, review the values of its attributes, or use its info(), nunique(), and describe() methods.
- To access one column in a DataFrame, you can use *dot notation* or brackets. To access more than one column, you use a list.
- To access rows in a DataFrame, you can use the query() method.
- To access a subset of rows and columns in a DataFrame, you can use the query() method along with dot notation or brackets. You can also use the loc[ ] or iloc[ ] *accessor* to access a subset of rows and columns.
- To sort the values in a DataFrame, you can use the sort_values() method.
- Pandas provides statistical methods for both DataFrame and Series objects. You can also use Python operators to perform *vectorized* arithmetic operations on the data in columns.
- You can use the Pandas replace() method or the Python replace() method to modify the string data in a column.
- You can use the set_index() method to set an *index* that consists of one or more columns in a DataFrame. But because you can't use index columns as parameters in other methods, you will often need to use the reset_index() method to reset an index.
- You can use the pivot() method to convert *long data* to *wide data*. And you can use the melt() method to convert wide data to long data.
- After you use the groupby() method to *group* the data in a DataFrame, you can use the agg() method to *aggregate* the data by applying statistical methods to each group.
- The plot() method is the Pandas method for *data visualization* that lets you *plot* the data in a DataFrame.

Exercise 2-1 Review the Mortality Notebook

In this exercise, you'll run the cells in the Mortality Notebook. This Notebook includes all the examples that are in this chapter, plus a few variations. As you run each cell, be sure that you understand what it does. To help you understand it, you may want to change some of the parameters to see how that changes the results.

Open the Notebook and run the cells that get the data

1. Start JupyterLab and open the Notebook named ex_2-1_mortality that should be in this folder:
   `python_analysis/exercises/ch02`
2. Use the Kernel menu to restart the kernel and clear all outputs.
3. Run the cells that import the Pandas module and get the data.
4. Run the cells that save and restore the DataFrame.

Run the cells that examine and clean the data

5. Run the cells that use various techniques to display the data in the DataFrame.
6. Run the cells that display the DataFrame attributes.
7. Run the cells that change and display the column names.
8. Run the cells that use the info() and nunique() method, and note how the changes to the column names are reflected in the results.
9. Run the cells that use the describe() method, and note how the T attribute changes the display.
10. Run the cells that save and restore the cleaned DataFrame.

Run the cells that access the data

11. Run the cells that access columns, and note the difference in the output when you use dot notation or brackets to access a single column and a list to access multiple columns.
12. Run the cells that access rows and note the use of the query() method.
13. Run the cells that access rows and columns using the query() method along with dot notation or brackets, and note the difference in the output between the first two cells and the next two cells.
14. Run all the cells that use the loc[ ] and iloc[ ] accessors to access subsets of rows and columns, and note the use of lists and slices.

Run the cells that prepare the data

15. Run the cells that sort the data, and note the difference in the sequence of the data for the last three cells.
16. Run the cells that apply statistical methods, and note the use of dot notation and brackets for accessing columns.
17. Run the cells that uses column arithmetic to add a column named MeanCentered to a DataFrame, modify the data in the DeathRate column, and display the results.

18. Run the cell that modifies the string data in the AgeGroup column. Then, run the cells that save and restore the prepared data.

Run the cells that shape the data

19. Run the cells that set different indexes for the DataFrame, and note that the index must be reset before a new one can be set.
20. Run the cells that pivot the data, and note that both of these create a new DataFrame named mortality_wide. As a result, the second DataFrame replaces the first one. Note too that all of the other columns are pivoted if you don't specify a values parameter.
21. In the cells that melt the wide DataFrame, note that the first cell saves the wide DataFrame as an Excel file, and the second one imports the Excel file back into the DataFrame. That's just an easy way to create a wide DataFrame that can be used to demonstrate the use of the melt() method.
22. In the cell that contains the melt() method, note that this method creates a new DataFrame named mortality_long, but it melts just two of the wide columns into the AgeGroup and DeathRate columns. To melt all four, you can delete the value_vars parameter and run the cell again.
23. Run the cells that melt the data and then the cells that save and restore the wide DataFrame.

Run the cells that analyze the data

24. Run the cells that group and aggregate the data, and note how the functions are applied to the columns in each group.
25. Run the cells that visualize the data, and note how the plot() method is chained to the preceding methods.

Exercise 2-2 Write your own code for the Mortality Notebook

In this exercise, you'll write and test your own code for a Mortality dataset that's slightly different from the one for exercise 2-1. When you write your code, you can create it from scratch using this book as a guide. Or, you can copy something similar from the Mortality Notebook for exercise 2-1 and modify it to suit your purposes.

Open and run the cells in the Mortality Notebook

1. Start JupyterLab and open the Notebook named ex_2-2_mortality that should be in this folder:

   `python_analysis/exercises/ch02`

2. Use the Kernel menu to restart the kernel and clear all outputs.
3. Run the cells that import the Pandas module and get the data from the file named mortality_data.pkl.
4. Run the cell that gets the data from the file named mortality_wide.pkl.

Work with the data in the long DataFrame

For each of the following steps, add a cell that performs the required task.

5. Display the first five rows of the DataFrame.
6. Change the name of the "DeathRate" column to "Deaths/100K", since that's a more accurate description of the data in that column.
7. Access and display the first five rows of the Year and MeanCentered columns.
8. Access and display the last six rows of data from 1915 through 1920.
9. Access and display the Year and Deaths/100K columns for the age group 01-04 Years.
10. Sort the DataFrame by the Deaths/100K column in descending sequence, and display the results. Then, modify the cell so it displays the first and last three rows of the results.
11. Calculate the median of all of the values in the Deaths/100K column.
12. Group the data by year, and calculate the sum of the Deaths/100K column.

Work with the data in the wide DataFrame

13. Display the first five rows of the DataFrame.
14. Display the index information for the DataFrame.
15. Use the describe() method to display statistical information for the numeric columns in the DataFrame. Start by coding this statement without the T property. Then, add the T property to see how the display changes.
16. Access and display just the Year and 01-04 Years columns.
17. Access and display just the rows for the years from 1915 through 1920.
18. Combine steps 16 and 17 into a single cell that accesses and displays the Year and 01-04 Years columns for the years from 1915 through 1920.
19. Aggregate the data for all numeric columns in each year, and display the mean, median, and sum for those columns.
20. Add a new column to the DataFrame named TotalDeaths. The value of this column should be the sum of the values in each of the year range columns. Display the DataFrame with the new column.
21. Create a line plot that shows the total death rates by year.

Chapter 3

The Pandas essentials for data visualization

In chapter 2, you learned the Pandas essentials for getting, cleaning, preparing, and analyzing data. Now, in this chapter, you'll learn the Pandas essentials for data visualization.

As you will see, Pandas works okay for getting quick visualizations as you prepare and analyze the data. But it has some quirks that can make it difficult to use. And it doesn't provide all the features that you need for refining your visualizations so they're suitable for presentation. To get around those limitations, you need to use a module that's specifically designed for data visualization, like the Seaborn module that's presented in the next chapter.

Introduction to data visualization

To start, this chapter introduces you to the Python libraries for data visualization. Next, it shows how long or wide data affects the way you code your visualizations. Then, it introduces you to the Pandas plot() method, which is the method you use for creating your visualizations.

The Python libraries for data visualization

Data visualization, also known as *data viz* or *data plotting*, is the graphic presentation of data with the goal of making the data easier to understand. It does that by showing relationships that are hard to see otherwise. Data viz can also make it easier to spot outliers, which are datapoints that are far outside the rest of the data.

Figure 3-1 summarizes some of the popular libraries, or modules, for data visualization with Python. Although Matplotlib was the original library for that purpose, the other libraries are easier to use. That's why this book shows how to use Pandas and Seaborn for data visualization. Even though Matplotlib generates the plots for both of these modules, Pandas and Seaborn provide an interface that hides the Matplotlib details.

Once you've mastered data viz with Pandas and Seaborn, you may be interested in some of the other libraries for Python data viz. For instance, Altair is a popular alternative to Seaborn that is relatively easy to use and provides some extra features, including interactive visualizations. And ggplot is the Python version of the ggplot2 package for the R language. So, if you already know how to use R and ggplot2, this should be an easy adjustment for you.

Nevertheless, it makes sense to start by learning how to use Pandas and Seaborn. They are included in the Anaconda distribution of Python, so you already have them. They are widely used, so knowing how to use them is a valuable job skill. And they provide the background you need for learning how to use any other data viz package.

Data visualization libraries for Python

Library	Description
`matplotlib`	The original matrix plotting library for Python and NumPy. Provides a low-level API that gives you a lot of control over the plots. Can be difficult to learn when compared with more modern libraries.
`pandas`	Provides a plot() method for its DataFrame and Series objects. Uses Matplotlib to generate its plots. Is easier to use than Matplotlib but doesn't provide as much functionality.
`seaborn`	Provides a high-level API for plotting data. Uses Matplotlib to generate its plots. Makes it easier to create attractive plots than it is when you're using Maplotlib or Pandas.
`altair`	Provides a high-level, declarative API that lets you create plots with a minimal amount of code.
`ggplot`	The Python version of the ggplot2 package for the R language.

Data visualization can help you...

- Understand your data more easily.
- See the relationships between variables.
- Spot unusual datapoints like outliers.

Description

- *Data visualization*, also known as *data viz* or *data plotting*, is the graphic presentation of data with the goal of making it easier to understand.
- *Matplotlib* is a visualization library that's based on MATLAB, a numerical computing environment that provides for plotting with the proprietary MATLAB language. It is the underlying library for the Pandas plot() method and the Seaborn library.
- Instead of using Matplotlib directly, we recommend the use of the higher-level APIs provided by Pandas and Seaborn.

Figure 3-1 The Python libraries for data visualization

Long vs. wide data for data visualization

As you learned in chapter 2, the source data that you import into a DataFrame may be in long form or wide form. Then, if the original data is in long form, you may want to prepare another version of the DataFrame in wide form, or vice versa.

These forms are illustrated by the two examples in figure 3-2. In the first DataFrame, the data is in long form. In the second DataFrame, the data is in wide form after the pivot() method was used to prepare the new DataFrame from the long data. Note that the first DataFrame has a MeanCentered column that isn't in the second DataFrame because it was dropped by the pivot() method.

In terms of data analysis, there's nothing wrong with either form. It's just that some operations are easier to do with long data, and some are easier to do with wide data. This is illustrated by the examples in this figure. Here, the first example uses the Pandas plot() method to create a scatter plot from the long data, which couldn't be done with the wide data. And the second example uses the plot() method without any parameters to create a line plot for the death rates in the four age groups in the wide data.

As you will see, the Pandas plot() method often works better with wide data. As a result, you will sometimes work with long data and sometimes with wide data. By contrast, a data visualization library like Seaborn typically works with long data so you won't need to shape the data into wide form.

The mortality data in long form (mortality_data)

	Year	AgeGroup	DeathRate	MeanCentered
0	1900	01-04 Years	1983.8	1790.87584
1	1901	01-04 Years	1695.0	1502.07584

A scatter plot derived from the long data

```
mortality_data.query('AgeGroup == "01-04 Years"') \
    .plot.scatter(x='Year', y='DeathRate')
```

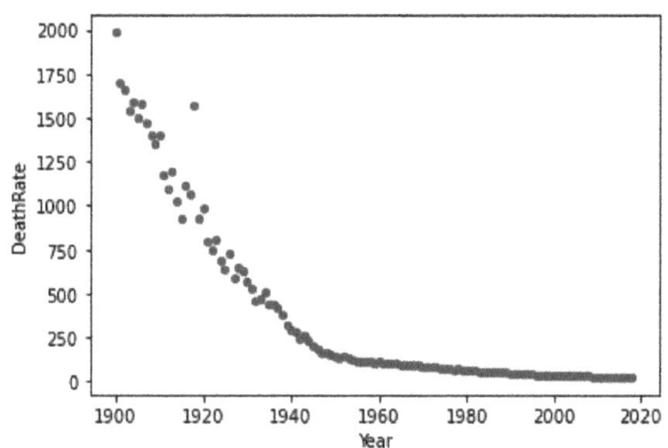

The mortality data in wide form with Year as the index (mortality_wide)

Age_Group	01-04 Years	05-09 Years	10-14 Years	15-19 Years
Year				
1900	1983.8	466.1	298.3	484.8
1901	1695.0	427.6	273.6	454.4

A line plot derived from the wide data

```
mortality_wide.plot()
```

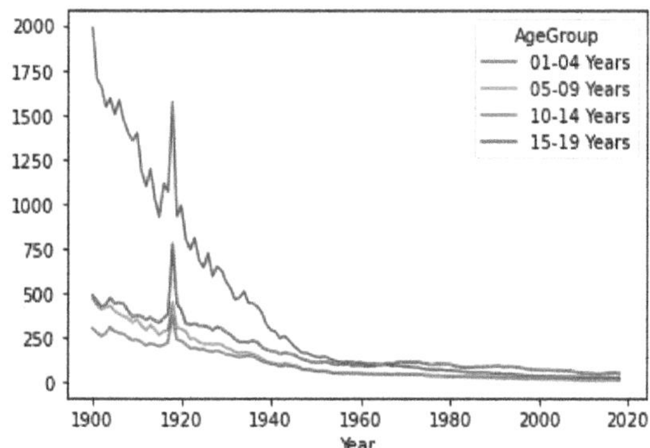

Description

- Neither long nor wide data is best for plotting. What's important is to prepare the data so it will work for the plotting library and the plotting methods that you're going to use.

Figure 3-2 Long vs. wide data for data visualization

How the Pandas plot() method works by default

Figure 3-3 shows how the Pandas plot() method works when no parameters are coded for it. Then, by default, this method creates a line plot with the values of the index column on the x-axis and all of the numeric columns on the y-axis. This is illustrated by the two examples in this figure.

In the first example, the long data shown in the previous figure is plotted. Since the index consists of the numbers from 0 through 475, those are the numbers that are plotted on the x-axis. Then, since the Year, DeathRate, and MeanCentered columns are numeric, they are plotted on the y-axis. In this case, the result shows that the default settings can lead to some strange and confusing plots.

By contrast, the second example works with the wide data shown in the previous figure. For that DataFrame, the index is the Year column and the four numeric columns contain the death rates for the age groups. As a result, the defaults deliver a line plot that shows the death rates in each of the four age groups. This illustrates how important indexes and shaping can be when you're using the Pandas plot() method.

A plot() method that plots the long data with no parameters

```
mortality_data.plot()
```

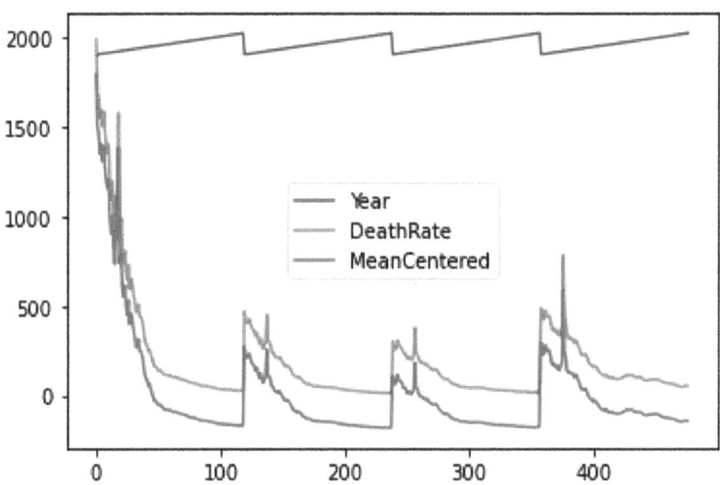

A plot() method that plots the wide data with no parameters

```
mortality_wide.plot()
```

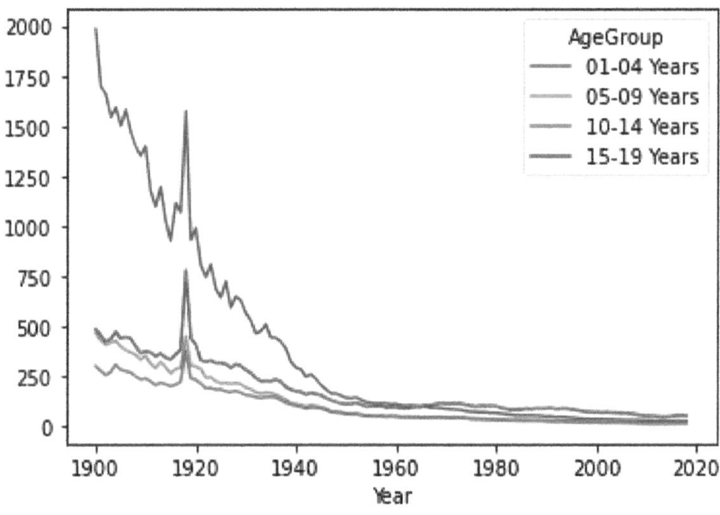

Description

- By default, the plot() method creates a line plot with the index value on the x-axis and the values in any numeric columns on the y-axis.
- This can work well if you set the index and shape the data so the defaults work the way you want them to. But if you don't do that, the defaults can lead to some confusing results.
- In the second example, the index is the Year column and the DeathRate column is the only other numeric columns, so it's plotted by age group.

Figure 3-3 How the Pandas plot() method works

The three basic parameters for the Pandas plot() method

Figure 3-4 shows how the three basic parameters of the Pandas plot() work. As you can see, the x parameter specifies the column to be plotted on the x-axis. The y parameter specifies the column or columns to be plotted on the y-axis. And the kind parameter specifies the kind of plot, which includes line, scatter, bar, and more.

However, as the first set of examples in this figure shows, you can also specify the type of plot without coding the kind parameter. To do that, you just code "plot", a dot (period), and the kind of plot. Since this is easier to code and understand, all of the plot() methods in this chapter are coded that way.

The two examples that follow show how the x and y parameters work. In the first example, both the x and y parameters are set. As a result, a scatter plot is created from the long data with Year on the x-axis and DeathRate on the y-axis. As you will see in a moment, a scatter plot requires that you code both the x and the y parameters.

Then, the last example shows how the y parameter works with wide data that has the index set to the Year column. Remember that by default, this method plots all of the numeric columns on the y-axis. In this case, though, the y parameter is set to a list of just two of the columns. As a result, only the data for the 01-04 and 15-19 age groups is plotted.

The three basic parameters for the Pandas plot() method

Parameter	Description
`x`	The column to be plotted on the x-axis. This column can't be in an index.
`y`	The column or list of columns to be plotted on the y-axis.
`kind`	The kind of plot to be displayed. By default, this is set to 'line', but other values are: scatter, bar, barh, hist, box, density (or kde), area, pie, and hexbin.

How to code the plot() method without using the kind parameter

```
mortality_data.plot.scatter()   # same as plot(kind='scatter')
mortality_data.plot.bar()       # same as plot(kind='bar')
```

How to create a scatter plot from the long data

```
mortality_data.query('AgeGroup == "01-04 Years"') \
    .plot.scatter(x='Year', y='DeathRate')
```

How to create a line plot from the wide data for just two of the columns

```
mortality_wide.plot.line(y=['01-04 Years','15-19 Years'])
```

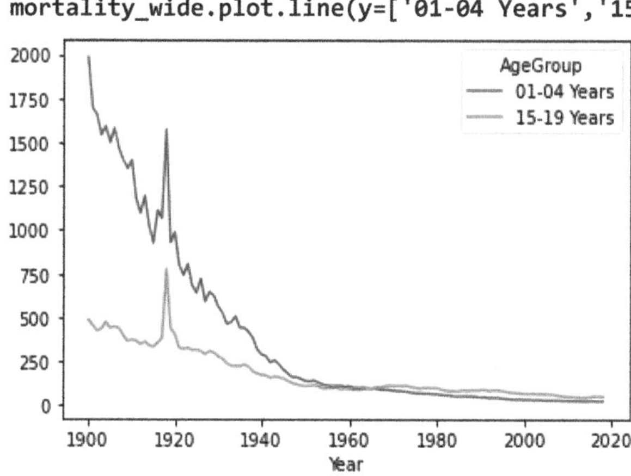

Figure 3-4 The three basic parameters for the Pandas plot() method

How to create 8 types of plots

The next five figures show how to use Pandas to create 8 of the 9 types of plots that it's designed for. These are the types of plots that you're most likely to need. As you will see, some of these plots use wide data and some use long data.

How to create a line plot or an area plot

Figure 3-5 shows how to create a *line plot* or an *area plot*. These plots are useful for seeing how data changes over time.

The two examples in this figure are plotted from the wide version of the DataFrame. As you can see in figure 3-2, that DataFrame has the Year column as its index and the other four columns contain the data that you want to plot.

In the first example, you can see how the plot() method is used to create a *line plot* using just the defaults. In the second example, you can see how that method is used to create an area plot with just the defaults.

In contrast to the line plot, the *area plot* stacks the data for the four Age Group columns, one on top of the other, and it colors the area for each age group with a different color. Here, for example, you can see that the total number of deaths in 1900 was over 3000, and the number of deaths for the 01-04 age group was just short of 2000.

How to create a line plot from wide data

```
mortality_wide.plot.line()
```

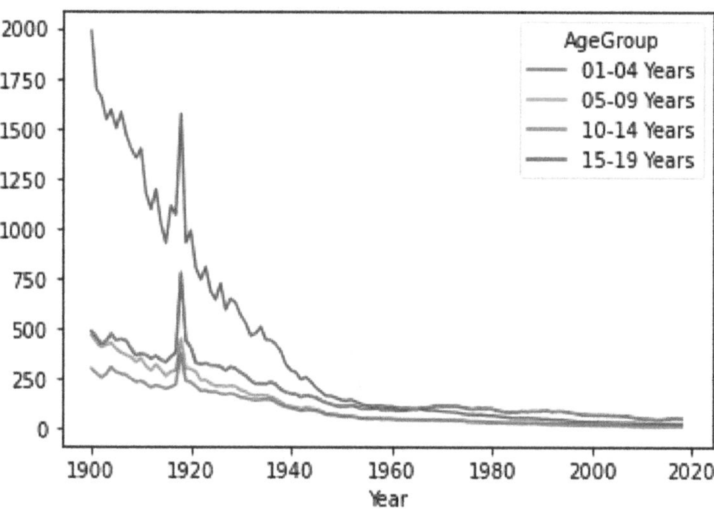

How to create an area plot from wide data

```
mortality_wide.plot.area()
```

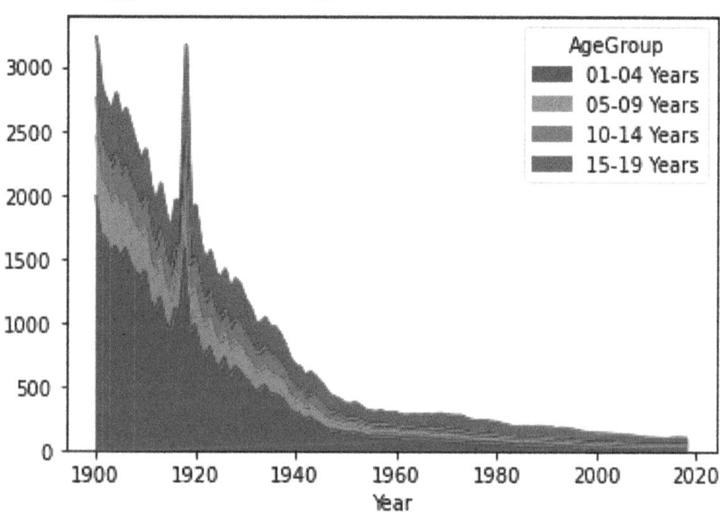

Description

- A *line plot* shows the relationship between two or more columns of data, often with the x-axis used to plot changes over time.
- An *area plot* is similar to a line plot, but the data in each column is added to the data in the previous columns.

Figure 3-5 How to create a line plot or an area plot

How to create a scatter plot

Figure 3-6 shows how to create a *scatter plot*. This type of plot is useful for showing the relationship between two columns of data.

The first example in this figure shows how to use the plot() method to create a scatter plot from the long mortality data. For this type of plot, both the x and y parameters are required. But note in the plot that you can't tell which dots represent which age groups, even though the death rates are plotted for all four age groups.

To get around that, you would think you could use wide data. But the next group of examples shows two of the error messages that result from trying to do that.

First, you need to code both the x and y parameters. Second, the column for the x parameter can't be an index, but the Year column is the index. You can get around that by resetting the index so the Year column isn't in the index. But you still can only plot one column on the y-axis at a time.

One easy way to solve these problems is to use Seaborn to plot the data as shown by the last example in this figure. Here, the scatterplot() method is used to plot the long data. This method uses the x and y parameters to specify the columns to be plotted. And it uses the hue parameter to specify that the values in the AgeGroup column should be used to set the colors for the datapoints in each age group.

This shows that there's a time for the Pandas plot() method and there's a time when it's better to use Seaborn to get the results that you want. That's why chapter 4 presents the essentials for Seaborn visualization. There, you'll see that Seaborn is also better for enhancing plots so they're ready for reports and presentations.

How to create a scatter plot from long data

```
mortality_data.plot.scatter(x='Year', y='DeathRate')
```

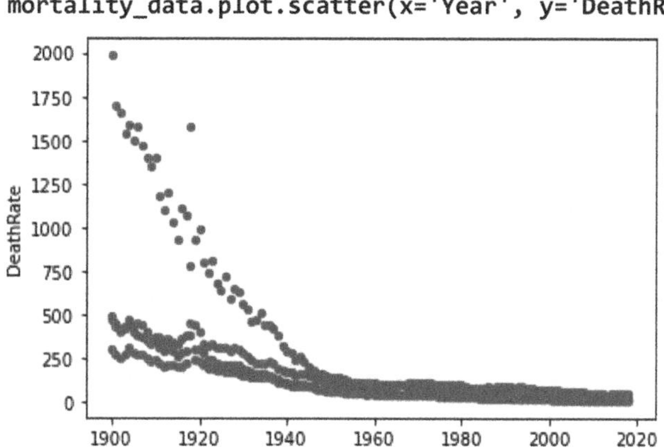

Common problems with scatter plots based on wide data

You have to code both x and y parameters

```
mortality_wide.plot.scatter()
==============================
TypeError: scatter() missing 2 required positional arguments: 'x' and 'y'
```

The x parameter can't be in an index

```
mortality_wide.plot.scatter(x='Year', y='DeathRate')
=================================================
KeyError: 'Year'
```

How Seaborn improves on Pandas

```
import seaborn as sns
sns.scatterplot(data=mortality_data, x='Year', y='DeathRate', hue='AgeGroup')
```

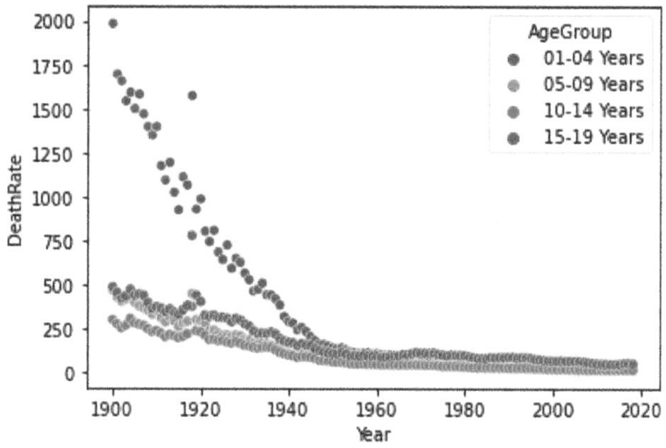

Description

- A *scatter plot* shows the relationships between two columns of numeric data. As a result, it requires both x and y parameters.

Figure 3-6 How to create a scatter plot

How to create a bar plot

Figure 3-7 shows how to use Pandas to create a *bar plot* (*bar chart*) or *horizontal bar plot (bar chart*). These plots can be used to plot the data in different categories.

In this figure, both types of bar plots are derived from the wide data shown in figure 3-2. So, in the first example, the code starts with a query() method that selects the data for the years 1900 and 2000. Then, a chained plot() method creates the chart.

The second example is almost the same, but it creates a horizontal bar plot. In some cases like this one, a horizontal plot is easier to interpret than a vertical plot. The only difference in the coding is that you use the barh attribute of the plot() method instead of the bar attribute.

How to create a vertical bar plot from the wide data

```
mortality_wide.query('Year in (1900,2000)').plot.bar()
```

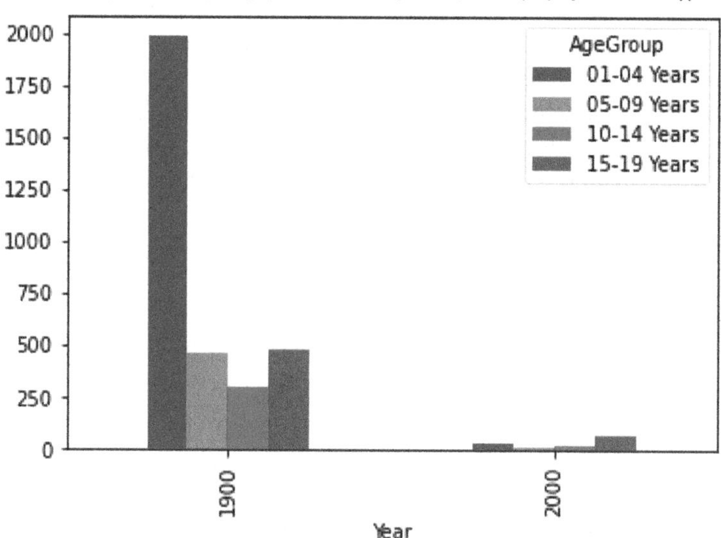

How to create a horizontal bar plot from the wide data

```
mortality_wide.query('Year in (1900,2000)').plot.barh()
```

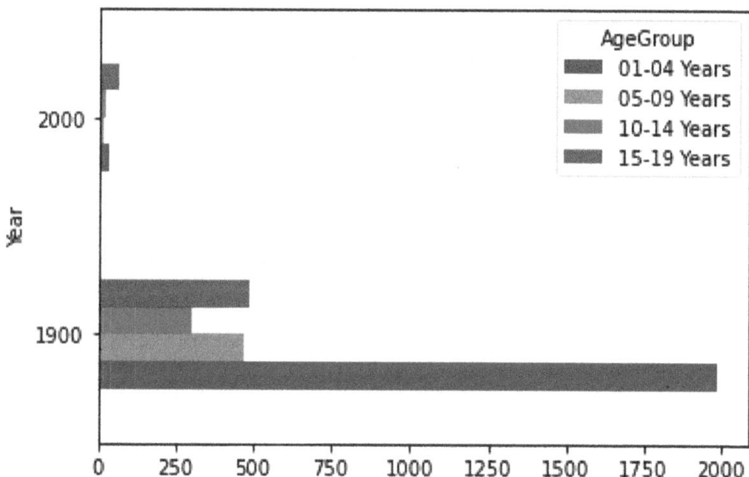

Description

- A *bar plot* or a *horizontal bar plot* is used to chart the data for different categories.

Figure 3-7 How to create a bar plot

How to create a histogram or a density plot

The first example in figure 3-8 shows how to create a histogram from the long data. A *histogram* shows the frequency of the datapoints in a numeric column by dividing the data on the x-axis into *bins*.

In this example, the bins parameter has been used to divide the death rates into 8 bins, instead of using the default of 10 bins. As a result, each bin in the histogram is 250 units wide (from 0 through 2000 divided by 8). Then, you can see from the bar for the first bin that more than 350 of the death rate values are less than 250. Similarly, you can see from the bars for the other bins that very few of the death rates are over 500.

Often, a histogram will give you a quick view of the range of data that you're dealing with. If, for example, you're examining the data for forest fires, a histogram might tell you that the majority of fires (over 95 percent) are less than 10 acres and only a few are greater than 100,000 acres. That in turn can help you decide how to clean and prepare the data.

The second example in this figure shows how to create a *density plot* (or *KDE plot*). Like a histogram, a density plot shows the distribution of data in a numeric column. However, it uses a *kernel density estimate* (*KDE*) to smooth the data.

Unlike a histogram, though, the y-axis in a density plot represents the probability of a datapoint occurring, and that value is derived from the KDE. For instance, the density plot in this figure shows that the probability of the next death rate being 2000 is close to zero. The probability of the next death rate being 500 is somewhere between .0000 and .0005. And the greatest probability is that the next death rate will be less than 100.

The KDE is calculated by weighting the distances of the datapoints for each location on the density line. So, the more datapoints there are in a location, the higher the KDE. And that indicates that the probability of seeing a datapoint in that location is higher.

Note here that some negative values are assigned to the plot line, even though there aren't any negative values in the data. That's because the way the data is sampled in the KDE calculations includes some negative values.

How to create a histogram

```
mortality_data.plot.hist(y='DeathRate', bins=8)
```

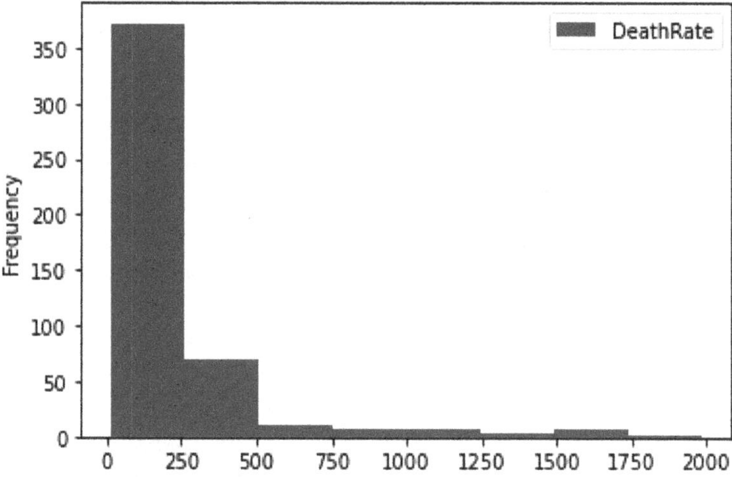

How to create a density plot

```
mortality_data.plot.density(y='DeathRate')
```

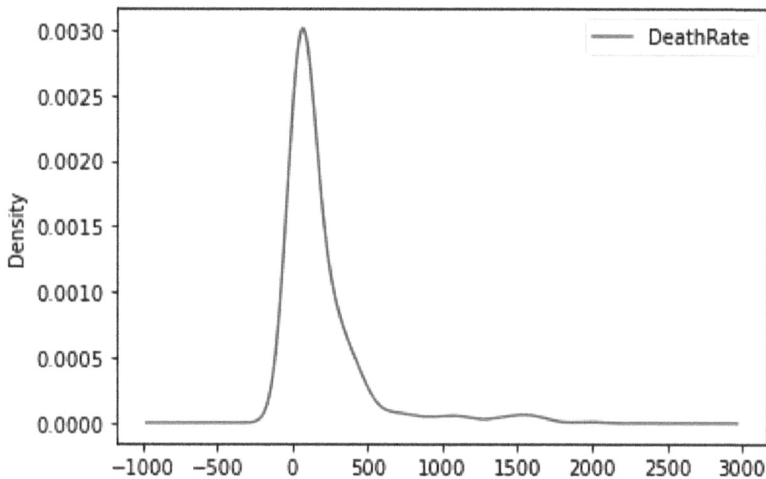

Description

- A *histogram* shows the *frequency* of the datapoints in a numeric column by dividing the data on the x-axis into segments called *bins*. By default, the Pandas plot method() uses 10 bins, but you can use the bins parameter to change that.
- A *density plot*, like a histogram, shows the distribution of the data in a numeric column. However, it uses a *kernel density estimate* (*KDE*) to smooth the data in the histogram. And its y-axis represents the probability of a datapoint that's derived from the KDE.

Figure 3-8 How to create a histogram or a density plot

How to create a box plot or a pie plot

The first example in figure 3-9 shows how to use Pandas to create a *box plot* (also known as a *box and whisker plot*). This type of plot provides a quick way to get a five-number summary of the data that's being plotted.

In a box plot, the box represents the first and third quartiles, and the horizontal line through the box represents the median or second quartile. Then, the whisker at the bottom of the box goes down to the minimum, the whisker at the top goes up to the maximum, and any circles below the minimum or above the maximum represent outliers.

Of course, the minimum and maximum represented by the whiskers aren't the actual minimum and maximum. The outliers are. To separate the minimum and maximum from the outliers, though, Pandas uses a complex formula based on the first and third quartiles.

In this example, the box plot gives a quick view of the data for each of the four age groups in the mortality data. In contrast to the 01-04 age group, the other age groups have far less variation and fewer outliers. But you can also see that the data for the 15-19 group has a higher death rate than the data for the 05-09 and 10-14 groups.

The second example creates a *pie plot* (or *pie chart*) that shows the sum of the death rates in each age group. Note here that it uses the groupby() method to group the data in the long DataFrame by AgeGroup. Then, it uses the sum() method to get the sum for each age group. Last, it uses the default settings to plot that data in a pie chart.

How to create a box plot from the wide data

```
mortality_wide.plot.box()
```

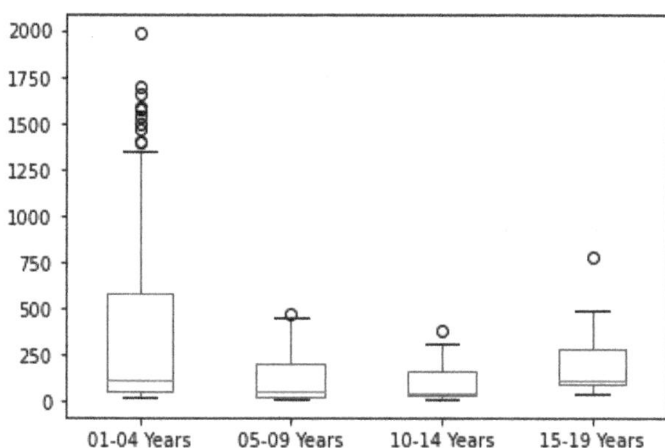

How to create a pie plot from the long data

```
mortality_data.groupby('AgeGroup')['DeathRate'].sum().plot.pie()
```

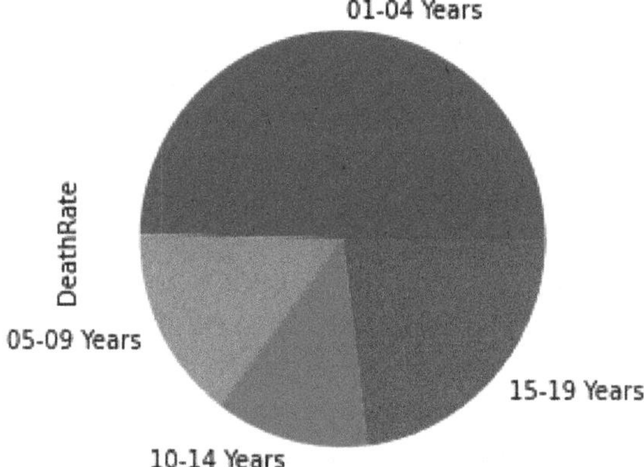

Description

- A *box plot* provides a quick way to get a five-number summary of the data that's plotted. A box plot is sometimes called a *box and whisker plot*.
- The box in a box plot represents the second and third quartiles, and the horizontal line through the box represents the median. Then, the whisker at the bottom of the box goes down to the minimum, and the whisker at the top goes up to the maximum.
- If there are any outliers in the data for a box plot, they are shown as circles below the minimum value and above the maximum value. In that case, the minimum and maximum values don't include the outliers.
- A *pie plot* is used to show the proportions of the categories that make up the whole.

Figure 3-9 How to create a box plot or a pie plot

How to enhance a plot

The plots that you've seen so far work well for your own use. But if you're going to present your plots to others or use them in reports, you should try to make them as self-explanatory as possible. You may also want to create plots that contain subplots. So that's what you'll learn next.

How to improve the appearance of a plot

Figure 3-10 presents the parameters that you need for improving the appearance of your plots with the goal of making them easier to understand. For instance, the first example in this figure uses the title parameter to add a title, the ylabel parameter to add a label for the y-axis, the grid parameter to add grid lines, and the rot parameter to rotate the tick values that identify the data on the x-axis.

This makes the plot easier to understand. The title, for example, makes it clear that the data runs from 1900 through 2018. The label on the y-axis shows that the chart is plotting the number of deaths per 100,000. And the grid lines make it easier to tell what the value at any datapoint is. For instance, you can easily tell that the death rate for 15-19 year-olds in 1918 was just over 750.

The second example shows the use of the figsize, xlim, and ylim parameters. Here, the xlim parameter is used to show the data for just the years 2000 to 2018. That gives this data a modern perspective. In particular, it shows that the death rate for the 15-19 age group is higher than the rate for the 01-04 age group, which is quite a change from the early 1900s. Yes, you could get the same result by querying the data before you plot it, but the xlim parameter makes this easier.

Similarly, the ylim parameter decreases the range of the values from the default to 100. This parameter is important when the default values don't accurately represent the data. If, for example, the ylim values weren't set in this example, the upper limit would be over 2000, as shown by the first plot. In that case, though, the data would be difficult to interpret.

Note that both of these plots include a legend that shows the color of the line used for each age group. In most cases, you'll want to include the legend to identify the data that's being plotted. If appropriate, however, you can remove the legend by setting the legend parameter to False, and you can reverse the order of the items in the legend by setting this parameter to 'reverse'.

If you experiment with the parameters in this figure, you'll quickly see how they work. Just keep in mind that you will usually want to keep your Pandas visualizations simple and use Seaborn for your presentation graphics.

Some of the parameters for the Pandas plot() method

Parameter	Description
`title`	The title of the plot.
`legend`	If False, the legend isn't displayed. If 'reverse', the legend items are displayed in reverse order.
`grid`	If True, displays gridlines.
`rot`	The rotation of the tick labels from 0 (the default) to 360.
`xlabel, ylabel`	The label for the x- or y-axis.
`xlim, ylim`	Tuples that set the range for the x- or y-axis.
`figsize`	A tuple that sets the width and height of the plot in inches.

A plot with a title and a grid

```
mortality_wide.plot.line(title='Child Mortality: 1900-2018',
                         ylabel='Deaths per 100,000', grid=True, rot=45)
```

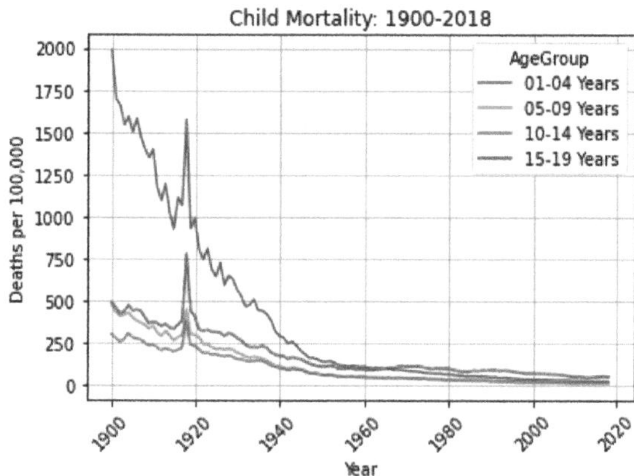

A plot with x and y limits

```
mortality_wide.plot.line(title='Child Mortality: 2000-2018',
     ylabel='Deaths per 100,000', figsize=(8,4), grid=True, rot=45,
     xlim=(2000,2018), ylim=(0,100))
```

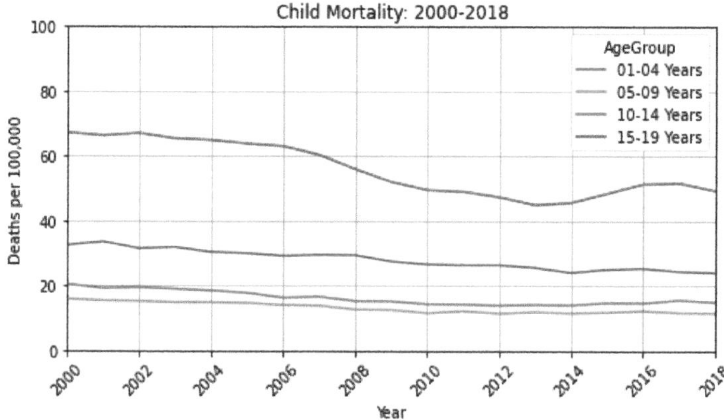

Figure 3-10 How to improve the appearance of a plot

How to work with subplots

Figure 3-11 shows how to work with *subplots*. Here, you can see the parameters for creating subplots, as well as the code that produces the four subplots, one for each of the four age groups in the wide mortality data. This makes it easier to see the variations in the data for each of the groups.

In the code for this plot, you can see how a list is used in the title parameter to provide a title for each of the four subplots. When you do that, you also want to set the legend parameter to False. Otherwise, a legend that specifies the age group will be displayed in each subplot.

Then, to create the subplots, you set the subplots parameter to True, and you use the layout parameter to specify the number of rows and columns you want to include in the subplot. You can also set the sharey parameter to True to share the label for the y-axis across the subplots, and you can set the sharex parameter to False to stop sharing the labels for the x-axis. Here again, if you experiment with these parameters, you'll quickly see how they work.

One caution when you provide a separate title for each subplot: Be sure that your subtitles match the data in the subplots. To do that, you can test your titles with the legend parameter set to True. That will display a legend in each subplot. Then, when you're sure that your subtitles match the legends, you can change the legend parameter to False.

The Pandas parameters for working with subplots

Parameter	Description
`title`	A string for the plot title or a list of strings for the subplot titles.
`subplots`	If True, creates subplots if the y-axis plots more than one Series.
`layout`	A tuple that sets the number of rows and columns for the subplots.
`sharex, sharey`	If True, shares the label for the x- or y-axis so it won't be repeated for each subplot. By default, sharex is True, sharey is False.

A plot with four subplots

```
mortality_wide.plot.line(
    title=['Child Mortality: 01-04','Child Mortality: 05-09',
           'Child Mortality: 10-14','Child Mortality: 15-19'],
    ylabel='Deaths per 100,000', sharey=True,
    grid=True, rot=45, xlim=(1900,1950), legend=False,
    subplots=True, layout=(2,2), figsize=(10,10))
```

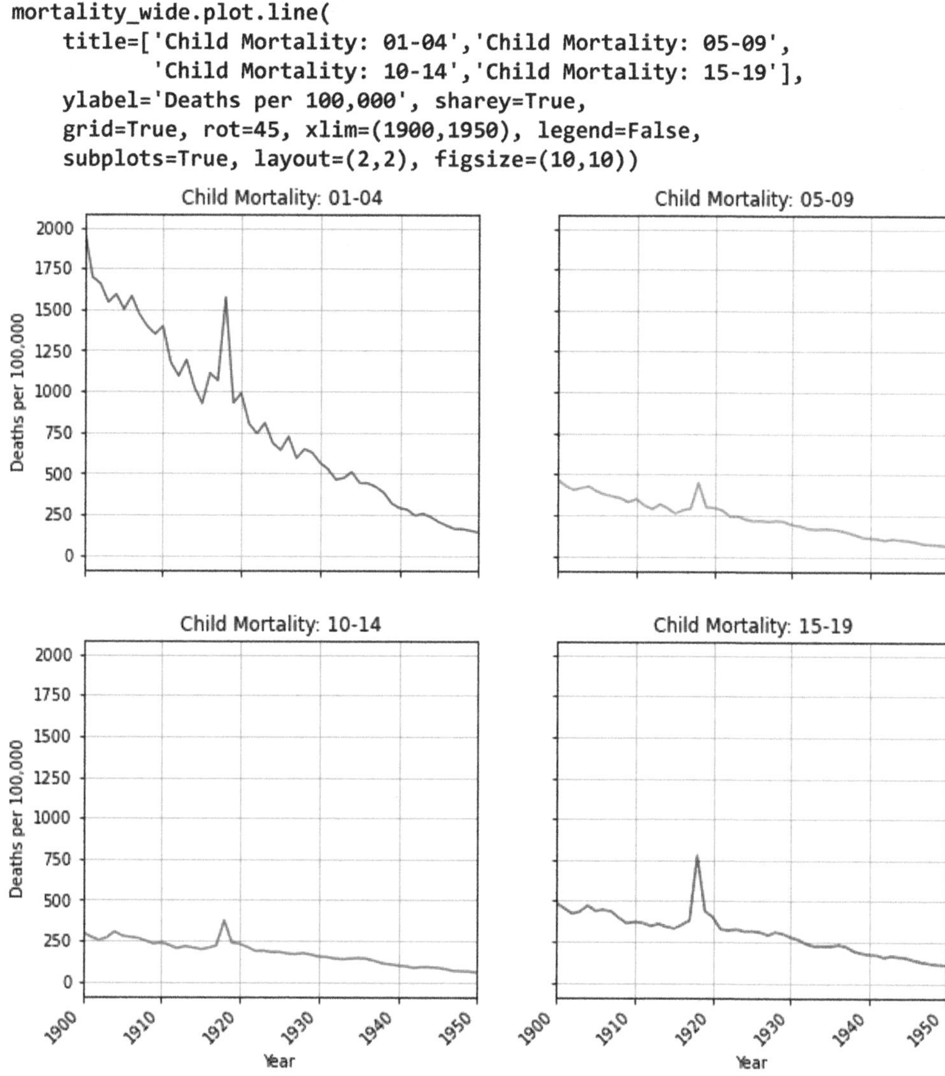

Description

- *Subplots* can sometimes make the data easier to understand.

Figure 3-11 How to work with subplots

How to use chaining to get the plots you want

The first example in figure 3-12 shows that you don't need to create a wide DataFrame when you want to plot wide data. Instead, you can code a pivot() method to create the wide data and then chain a plot() method to it. Here, the chained statement not only does that, but it starts with a query() method that gets the data for just two of the years.

This is typical of the code you might use as you plot the data during an analysis. Often, in fact, chaining the methods makes the code easier to understand because it's all there in one statement. By contrast, if you break the chaining down into separate statements, it can be hard to see what's going on.

The second example shows how the groupby() method can be used when you're plotting data. Here, the long mortality data is grouped by year and the chained agg() method calculates the mean, median, and standard deviation for each year. Then, a chained plot() method plots the three aggregate values.

This again shows how chaining can make the code easier to follow. And this again shows that you don't have to create separate DataFrames for your plots. In fact, this is the type of coding that you're likely to use on the job.

How to use chaining to create a bar plot from long data

```
mortality_data.query('Year in (1900,2018)') \
    .pivot(index='AgeGroup', columns='Year', values='DeathRate') \
    .plot.barh()
```

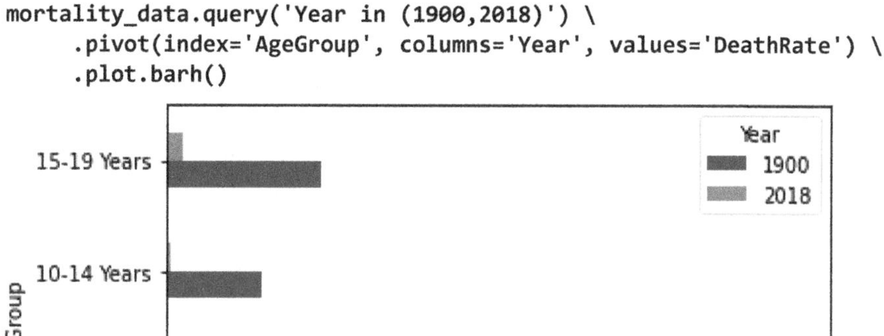

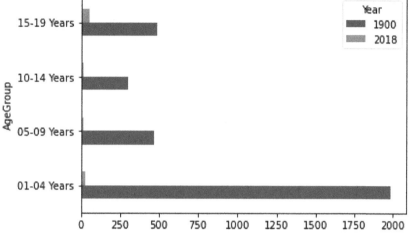

How to use the groupby() method and chaining to create a plot

```
mortality_data.groupby('Year')['DeathRate'] \
   .agg(['mean','median','std']).plot(ylabel='Deaths per 100,000')
```

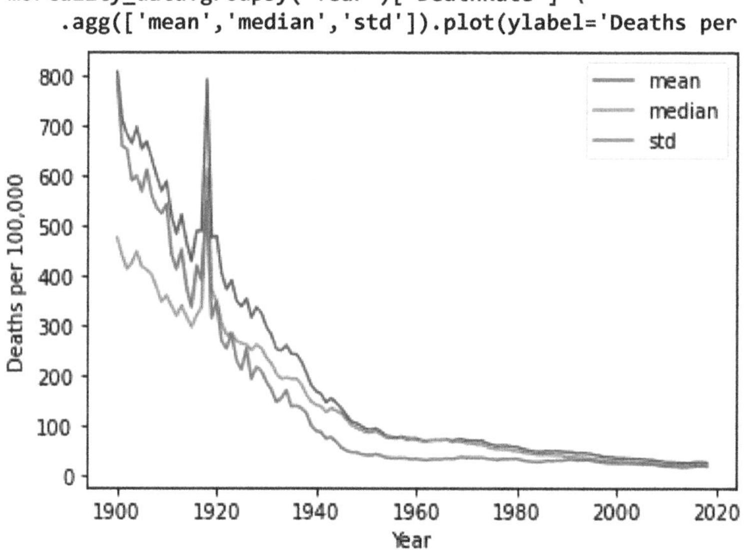

Description

- Chaining will often make the code easier to understand. Chaining also means that you will create fewer variables.
- When you combine chaining with the groupby() method, you can summarize data before you plot it.

Figure 3-12 How to use chaining to get the plots you want

Perspective

As you clean, prepare, and analyze the data in a DataFrame, you can use the Pandas plot() method to get the quick plots that you need. In general, this method is easy to use, and it provides for the basic types of plots.

When compared to a visualization library like Seaborn, though, the Pandas plot() method has several shortcomings. That's why chapter 4 shows you how to use Seaborn. There, you'll see that Seaborn not only provides for more types of plots, but it also has better features for enhancing plots. Seaborn also makes it easier to create some types of plots.

Terms

data visualization
data viz
data plotting
line plot
area plot
scatter plot
bar plot (bar chart)
horizontal bar plot (bar chart)
histogram
bin
density plot (KDE plot)
kernel density estimate (KDE)
box plot (box and whisker plot)
pie plot (pie chart)
subplot

Summary

- *Data visualization* (also known as *data viz* or *data plotting*) is a critical part of data analysis because it helps you see the relationships between the data.
- Neither long data nor wide data is better for data visualization. What's important is that you prepare your data so it works for the types of plots that you want to create and the methods that you want to use.
- By default, the Pandas plot() method plots the index values on the x-axis and the values for all numeric columns on the y-axis. You can modify that by coding the x and y parameters, but the column for the x parameter can't be an index.
- The Pandas plot() method can be used to create these types of plots: *line*, *area*, *scatter*, *bar*, *histogram*, *density* (or *KDE*), *box*, and *pie*.
- Pandas provides parameters for the plot() method that can be used to enhance a plot and to create *subplots*.
- In practice, you often use chaining to improve the readability of your code and to eliminate the need for preparing separate DataFrames.

Exercise 3-1 Create some plots

In this exercise, you'll create some of your own plots from the long and wide DataFrames for the mortality data.

Open the Notebook and create the DataFrames

1. Start JupyterLab and open the Notebook named ex_3-1_mortality that should be in this folder:

   `python_analysis/exercises/ch03`

2. Use the Kernel menu to restart the kernel and clear all outputs. Then, run all of the cells in this Notebook. That will import the long and wide data from pickle files and create the DataFrames that you need for plotting. It will also create two plots.

Add some visualizations to the Notebook

As you create the visualizations described in the steps that follow, you shouldn't create any new DataFrames. Instead, you should use chaining to get the results that you want.

3. Use the wide data to create a line plot for just the data in the 15-19 age group. Include an appropriate title on the plot and remove the legend.
4. Use the wide data to create an area plot for all age groups, and reverse the order of the items in the legend to see how that looks.
5. Use the wide data to create a bar plot for all age groups that shows the mortality rates for just the year 1900, and note the values on the y-axis.
6. Change the bar plot you created in step 5 to show the mortality rates for the year 2000, and note how the values on the y-axis change. Then, add an appropriate title to the plot and remove the label for the x-axis.
7. Use the long data to create a bar plot like the one in step 6. To do that, you'll need to chain the pivot() method to the query() method. Compare the two bar charts, and then make improvements so the plot that uses the long data is easier to read.
8. Use the long data to create a histogram that shows the frequency of the death rates in the default number of bins. Then, change the number of bins to 15 to see how this changes the histogram. Does this make it easier to determine the frequency at various datapoints?
9. Use the long data to create a density plot that shows the distribution of the death rates in the year 1900. Include a title and grids in the plot to make the data easier to read.
10. Use the long data to create a pie plot that shows the sum of the death rates for the years 1900, 1925, 1950, 1975, and 2000.
11. Create a plot with four subplots in two rows and two columns. The subplots should be horizontal bar charts that show the child mortality rates for each age group for the years 1900, 1925, 1950, 1975, and 2000. Format the subplots so they're easy to read.

Chapter 4

The Seaborn essentials for data visualization

As chapter 3 pointed out, the Pandas plot() method is okay for creating quick plots as you clean, prepare, and analyze the data. But you're going to want to use a data visualization library like Seaborn for most of your plots. As you will learn in this chapter, Seaborn not only makes it easier to prepare a wider variety of plots, but it also lets you enhance those plots so they're suitable for presentation.

Introduction to Seaborn

This chapter starts by introducing you to the Seaborn methods for plotting. Then, it shows you how to use the basic parameters for those methods.

The Seaborn methods for plotting

Figure 4-1 summarizes the methods for three types of Seaborn plots. As you can see, each of these types includes one general and two or more specific methods. You'll learn more about that in the next figure.

The first type of plot is the *relational plot*, which includes scatter plots and line plots. Scatter plots are best used to show the relationships between numeric variables, while line plots are best used to identify trends in data and show change over time.

The second type of plot is the *categorical plot*. As this figure shows, there are eight types of categorical plots, but all of them break the data into different categories and then compare those categories. That's why categorical plots are best used when you want to compare the data in different categories.

The third type of plot is the *distribution plot*. The three types of distribution plots are the histogram, the kernel density estimate (KDE) plot, and the empirical cumulative distribution function (ECDF) plot. These plots are best used to examine how numeric data is distributed across a range of values.

As you will see in section 3 of this book, Seaborn also provides plots that are designed for predictive analysis, such as plots for linear regression models. But the plots that are presented in this figure and in this chapter are the ones that you'll use most of the time.

The tables in this figure also show that the general methods return a *FacetGrid* (or just *Grid*) *object* and the specific methods return an *Axes object*. As you will soon see, you can use these objects to enhance and save your plots.

Relational plots

General method	Object returned	Plot type
`relplot(params)`	FacetGrid	Relational
Specific method	**Object returned**	**Plot type**
`scatterplot(params)`	Axes	Scatter plot
`lineplot(params)`	Axes	Line plot

Categorical plots

General method	Object returned	Plot type
`catplot(params)`	FacetGrid	Categorical
Specific method	**Object returned**	**Plot type**
`barplot(params)`	Axes	Bar plot (or bar chart)
`boxplot(params)`	Axes	Box plot
`stripplot(params)`	Axes	Strip plot
`swarmplot(params)`	Axes	Swarm plot
`pointplot(params)`	Axes	Point plot
`boxenplot(params)`	Axes	Boxen plot
`violinplot(params)`	Axes	Violin plot
`countplot(params)`	Axes	Count plot

Distribution plots

General method	Object returned	Plot type
`displot(params)`	FacetGrid	Distribution
Specific method	**Object returned**	**Plot type**
`histplot(params)`	Axes	Histogram
`kdeplot(params)`	Axes	Kernel density estimate
`ecdfplot(params)`	Axes	Empirical cumulative distribution function

Description

- Seaborn provides both general and specific methods for creating plots.
- The general methods return FacetGrid objects that contain one or more Axes objects, and the specific methods return Axes objects. Either way, you can use the methods of the Axes objects to enhance and save your plots.
- The plots in these tables are the ones you'll use the most. But you'll also learn how to use the plots for predictive analysis in chapters 10 and 11.

Figure 4-1 The Seaborn methods for plotting

The general methods vs. the specific methods

When you use Seaborn, you can create each type of plot by using a general or a specific method. To illustrate, figure 4-2 shows how to create a line plot using both the general and the specific method for that. In these examples, the data in the mortality DataFrame is plotted with the Year on the x-axis and the DeathRate on the y-axis.

In the first example, the general relplot() method is used to create the plot. As a result, the kind parameter is required. So the kind parameter is set to 'line', and the x and y parameters are set to the Year and DeathRate columns. Then, the hue parameter is set to the AgeGroup column so the data is broken into the four age groups. This shows that you usually pass a categorical data column to the hue parameter.

The second example in this figure shows how to create the same plot with the specific lineplot() method. Here, you can see that the only difference in the parameters is that the kind parameter isn't required.

But you'll also note that there are some differences in the resulting plots. In general, charts that are created by the specific methods are wider and shorter than those created by the general methods. There is also a border for the specific plots and the legend is placed within that border.

As you will see in a moment, the general methods let you create plots that contain subplots, but the specific methods don't. Otherwise, you can get the same results with either type of method. In this chapter, most of the examples use the general methods, but it's easy to convert those examples to specific methods.

How to use the relplot() method to create a line plot

```
import seaborn as sns
sns.relplot(data=mortality_data, kind='line',
            x='Year', y='DeathRate', hue='AgeGroup')
```

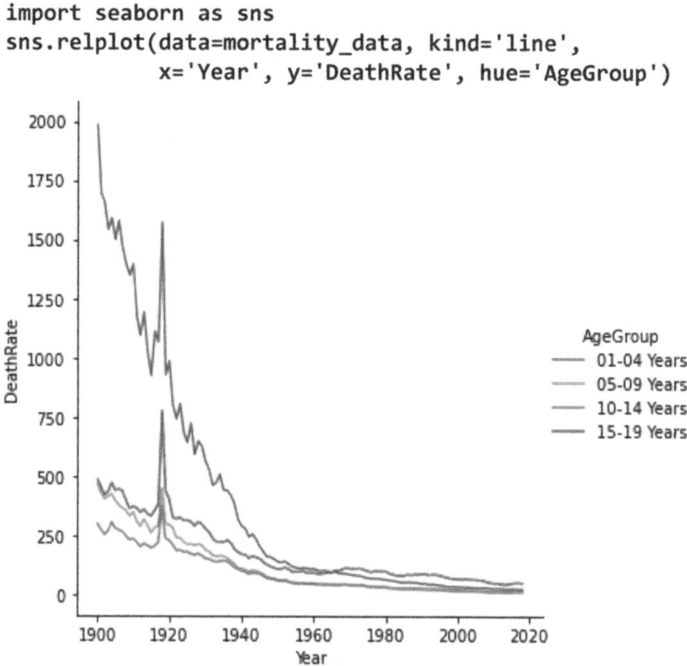

How to use the lineplot() method to create a line plot

```
sns.lineplot(data=mortality_data,
             x='Year', y='DeathRate', hue='AgeGroup')
```

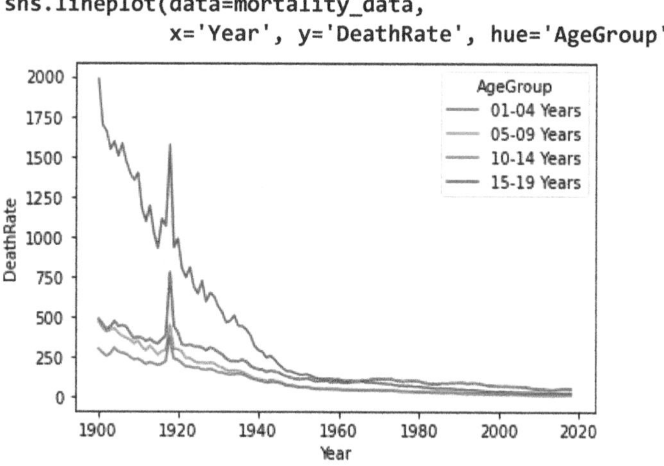

The differences between the general and specific methods

- The general methods require the kind parameter; the specific methods don't.
- You can't use the specific methods to create plots that contain more than one subplot.
- The general methods return a Grid object that contains an Axes object for each subplot. The specific methods return an Axes object.

Figure 4-2 The general methods vs. the specific methods

How to use the basic Seaborn parameters

Seaborn provides several parameters that you can use with nearly every type of Seaborn plot. These parameters are listed in the table in figure 4-3. They control factors like the columns to be plotted, the column that determines the categories to be displayed, the color palette to be used, the height of the plot, the ratio of the width of the plot to the height, and how the legend is displayed.

In the example in this figure, you can see how all of these parameters except for legend can be used with the relplot() method. In most cases, you'll leave the legend parameter at its default value of auto so the legend that's displayed is determined by the plot. In the next figure, though, you'll see one case where you'll want to remove the legend.

In this example, a line plot is created with the year on the x-axis and the death rate on the y-axis. Next, the hue parameter is set to the AgeGroup column so each of the four age groups will be plotted separately using a different color for each group. And the palette parameter is set to bright, so bright colors are used.

Last, the height parameter is set to 4 inches and the aspect parameter is set to 1.5, which means that the width of the plot will be 1.5 times the height. When you set the aspect ratio, you should try to make the slope of the plot lines reflect the data. If, for example, you look at the first plot in the previous figure, it looks like the death rate came down rapidly. But the major part of that decline actually took 60 years, from 1900 to 1960. By contrast, the plot with the 1.5 aspect ratio stretches out the x-axis so the slope of the plot lines isn't as steep.

Note in this example that the label for the x-axis is "Year" because that's the name of the column that's set by the x parameter. And the label for the y-axis is DeathRate because that's the name of the column that's set by the y parameter. In some cases, the defaults are okay, but you will often want to change them so they're more specific. In this case, for example, a better label for the y-axis would be "Deaths per 100,000" because that's what the numbers on that axis represent. That's why you'll soon learn how to change the default labels for the axes.

The basic Seaborn parameters

Parameter	Description
`data`	The DataFrame that provides the data.
`kind`	The type of plot.
`x, y`	The columns for the x- and y-axis.
`hue`	The column that determines the categories to plot using a different color for each category.
`palette`	The color palette for the plot. Can be set to colorblind, pastel, flare, or bright (the default is None). The palette can also be set in other ways (see figure 4-19).
`height`	The height of the plot in inches with a default of 5. Only for general plots.
`aspect`	The ratio of the width to the height so: width = aspect * height. Only for general plots.
`legend`	Four options that determine how the legend will be drawn: auto (the default), brief, full, and False. Only for general plots.

How to create a line plot

```
import seaborn as sns
sns.relplot(data=mortality_data, kind='line',
            x='Year', y='DeathRate', hue='AgeGroup', palette='bright',
            height=4, aspect=1.5)
```

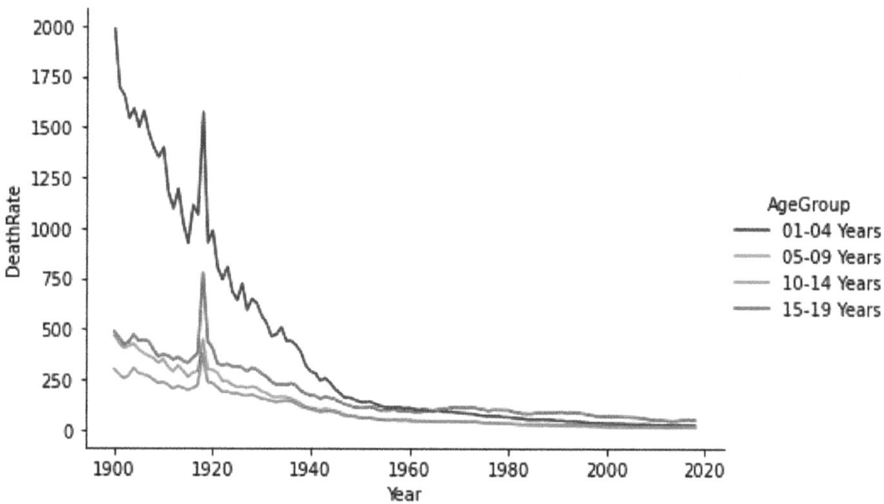

Description

- The basic Seaborn parameters are usually all that you need for the plots you develop for your own analyses.

Figure 4-3 How to use the basic Seaborn parameters

How to use the Seaborn parameters for working with subplots

The table in figure 4-4 summarizes two of the parameters that you need for working with subplots. Here, the example creates a plot with four subplots. As you can see, the data, kind, x, y, hue, and height parameters are the same as in the previous example, but the aspect parameter has been set to 1.25 instead of 1.5. These parameters are followed by the ones that create the subplots.

The col parameter is the one that causes the chart to be broken into subplots. Since it is set to the AgeGroup column, a subplot is created for each of the four age groups. Then, since the col_wrap parameter is set to 2, two subplots are displayed in each row.

In this example, the legend parameter is set to False so the legend won't be displayed. Instead, the title for each of the subplots is generated automatically. For instance, the title for first subplot is: AgeGroup = 01-04 Years; the title for the second subplot is: AgeGroup = 05-09 Years; and so on.

Note too in this example that the default labels for the x-axis and y-axis are the same as in the previous figure. But also note that these labels are shared by default. In this case, the DeathRate label is shown just once for each row, and the Year label is shown just once for each column. And that's usually the way you will want them.

The Seaborn parameters for working with subplots

Parameter	Description
`col`	The column that determines the subplots.
`col_wrap`	The number of subplots in each row.

How to create a plot with four subplots

```
sns.relplot(data=mortality_data, kind='line',
            x='Year', y='DeathRate', hue='AgeGroup',
            height=4, aspect=1.25,
            col='AgeGroup', col_wrap=2, legend=False)
```

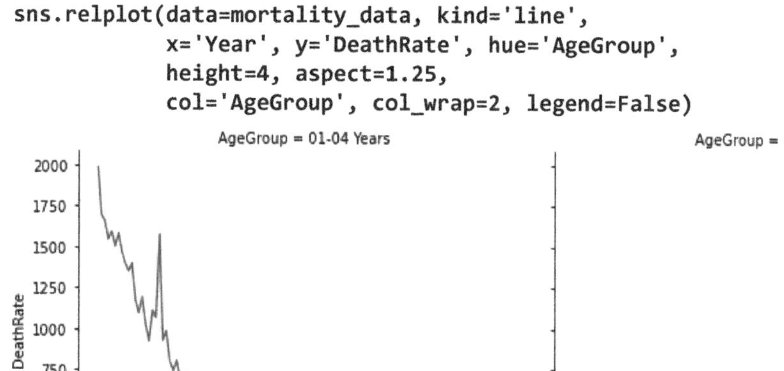

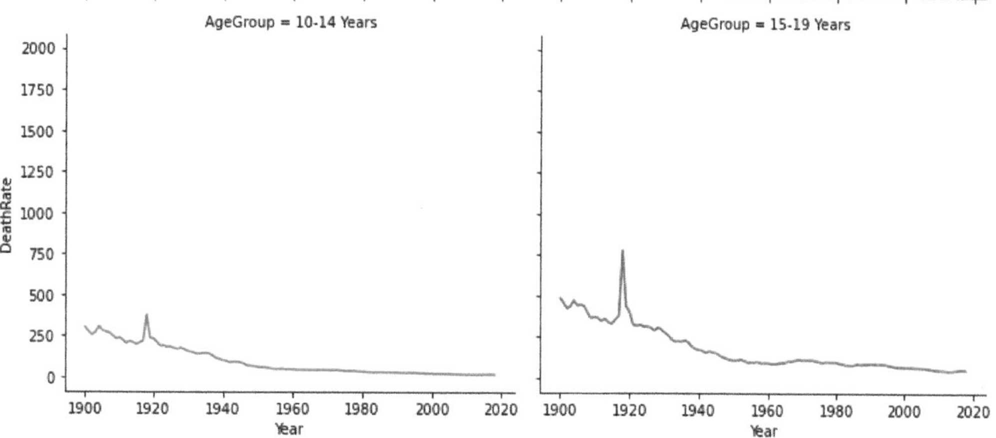

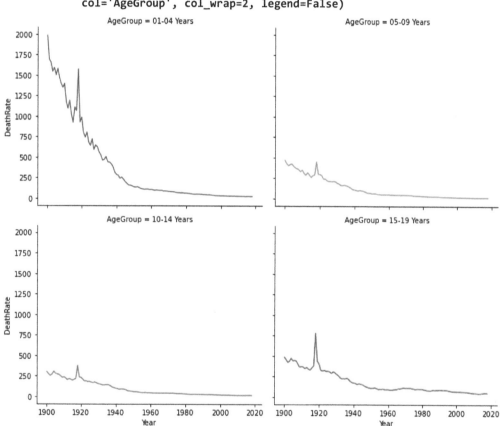

Description

- The Seaborn parameters above are usually all that you need for creating subplots for your own analyses.
- Note that the x and y labels are automatically shared by the subplots.

Figure 4-4 How to use the Seaborn parameters for working with subplots

How to enhance and save plots

When you use a specific method to create a plot, it returns an Axes object. And when you use a general method to create a plot, it returns a FacetGrid object that contains one or more Axes objects. Either way, you can use the methods of the Axes objects to enhance and save plots.

How to set the title, x label, and y label

To give you a better idea of how the Axes methods work, figure 4-5 shows how to use the set() method to add a title and y label to a plot. Here, the first example shows how to do that when you use the lineplot() method to create the plot. The second example shows how when you use the relplot() method.

When you use a specific method like the lineplot() method, it always returns an Axes object that provides methods for enhancing a plot. To use this object, you can assign it to a variable as shown by the first example in this figure. Here, the Axes object that's returned by the lineplot() method is assigned to a variable named *ax*, which is a common naming convention.

Once the Axes object is assigned to a variable, you can use its methods to enhance the plot. In this first example, the set() method is used to set the title and ylabel parameters. You can see the results in the plot that's displayed. But note that "Year" is used by default for the x label since that's the name of column that's set by the x parameter. Of course, you could override that default by coding the xlabel parameter.

In the second example, a general method is used so it returns a FacetGrid object, and that object is assigned to a variable named *g* (also a common naming convention). Then, the code loops through the Axes objects contained in the FacetGrid object. To do that, it uses the axes attribute to get the array of Axes objects from the grid, and it uses the flat attribute to get an iterator that can be used to loop through this array. In this case, though, there's only one Axes object in the array. Inside the loop, you can use the set() method just as you would with specific plots.

If you're going to present your plots to others, you should always try to include titles, x labels, and y labels that accurately identify what's being plotted. In these examples, the title describes the data that's being plotted, and the y label describes what the y axis represents: "Deaths per 100,000". By default, the y label would be "DeathRate" and that would be misleading.

The title and label parameters for the set() method of an Axes object

Parameter	Description
`title`	The title
`xlabel, ylabel`	The labels for the x- and y-axis

How to use the set() method to enhance a specific plot

```
ax = sns.lineplot(data=mortality_data,
                  x='Year', y='DeathRate', hue='AgeGroup')
ax.set(title='Deaths by Age Group', ylabel='Deaths per 100,000')
```

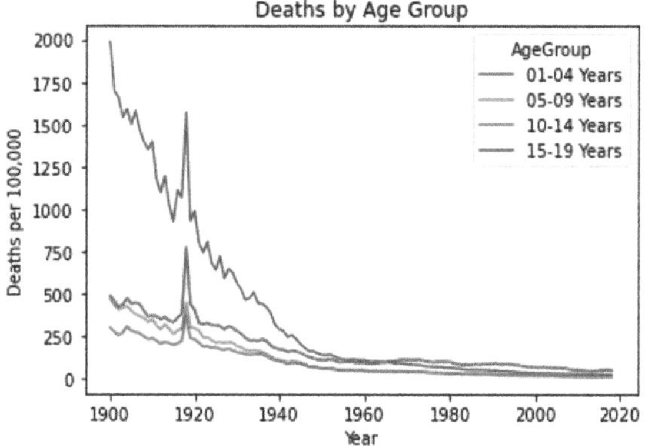

How to use the set() method to enhance a general plot

```
g = sns.relplot(data=mortality_data, kind='line',
    x='Year', y='DeathRate', hue='AgeGroup', aspect=1.5)
for ax in g.axes.flat:
    ax.set(title='Deaths by Age Group', ylabel='Deaths per 100,000')
```

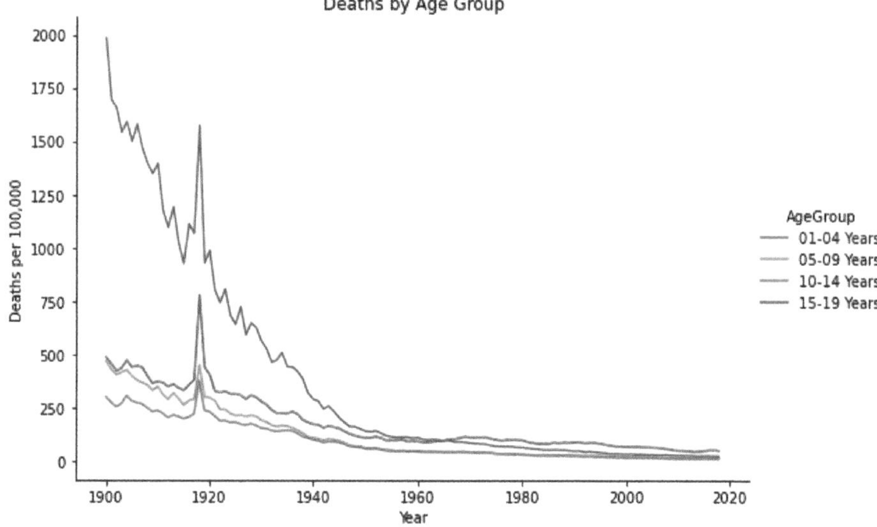

Figure 4-5 How to set the title and the x and y labels

How to set the ticks, x limits, and y limits

The first table in figure 4-6 presents four more parameters for the set() method that can help you enhance a plot. First, you can use the xticks and yticks parameters to set specific tick values for your plots. Second, you can use the xlim and ylim parameters to limit the data that's presented in your plots.

The second table presents the tick_params() method of an Axes object. You can use this method to rotate the tick labels so they don't run together.

The first example in this figure shows how this works. Since this is a general method, you need to use the g.axes.flat accessor to loop through the Axes objects, even if there's only one. In the loop, the xticks parameter of the set() method uses a Python list comprehension to generate a list that includes every other year from 1910 to 1931. So those are the values used for the ticks on the x-axis.

Then, the xlim parameter limits the data to the years from 1910 through 1930, and the ylim parameter limits the data to the values from 0 through 1750. The last statement in the loop uses the tick_params() method to rotate the xtick labels by 30 degrees.

You can see the results in the plot for this method. Here, only the data for the years from 1910 through 1930 is plotted, and the tick labels range from 1910 through 1930. To make this work, of course, the xlim and xticks parameters have to be closely coordinated. Otherwise, errors will be raised.

In this example, the ylim parameter is used to limit the height of the y-axis. If it weren't coded, the y-axis would accommodate the largest y value in the entire DataFrame, not just the largest value within the years specified by the xlim parameter. As a result, the y-axis would range from 0 through 2000.

The second example in this figure shows how to get the same results with a specific plot. The main difference is that you use the Axes object instead of the Grid object to access the set() and tick_params() methods. You also don't need to code the aspect parameter because the default value is okay.

The ticks and limit parameters for the set() method of an Axes object

Parameter	Description
`xticks, yticks`	The locations and values for the xticks and yticks.
`xlim, ylim`	Tuples that set the upper and lower limits of the x- and y-axis.

The tick_params() method of an Axes object

Method	Description
`tick_params()`	Sets tick parameters like the label rotation for the xticks or yticks.

How to use the set() and tick_params() methods to enhance a general plot

```
g = sns.relplot(data=mortality_data, kind='line',
    x='Year', y='DeathRate', hue='AgeGroup', aspect=1.25)
for ax in g.axes.flat:
    ax.set(title='Deaths by Age Group (1910-1930)', ylabel='Deaths per 100,000',
        xticks=[x for x in range(1910, 1931, 2)],
        xlim=(1910,1930), ylim=(0,1750)),
    ax.tick_params('x', labelrotation=30)
```

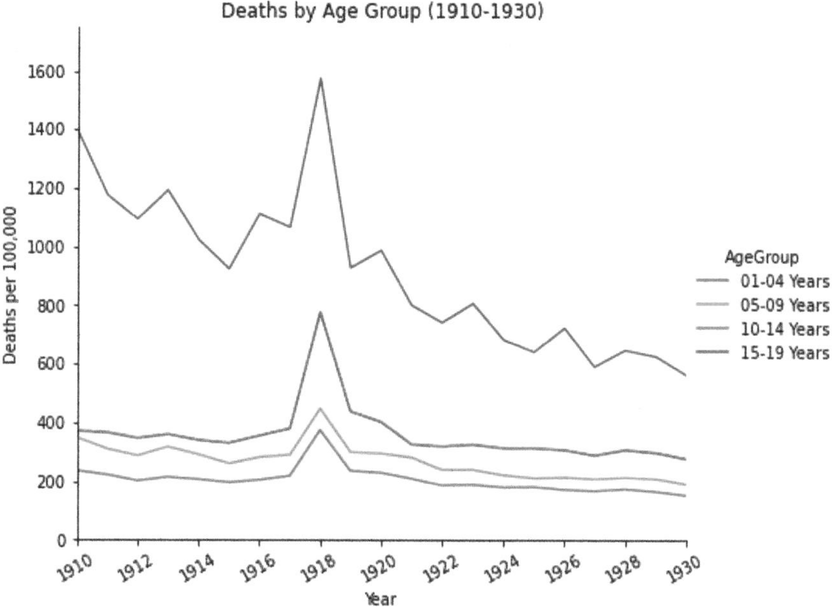

How to enhance a specific plot in the same way

```
ax = sns.lineplot(data=mortality_data,
                  x='Year', y='DeathRate', hue='AgeGroup')
ax.set(title='Deaths by Age Group (1910-1930)',
       ylabel='Deaths per 100,000',
       xticks=[x for x in range(1910, 1931, 2)],
       xlim=(1910,1930), ylim=(0,1750))
ax.tick_params('x', labelrotation=30)
```

Figure 4-6 How to set the ticks, x limits, and y limits for a plot

How to set the background style

To set the background style for a plot, you use the set_style() method that's summarized in figure 4-7. Its one parameter is used to select one of the five preset styles.

The default style is ticks, which has a plain white background and tick marks for each of the ticks on the axes. The white style provides a plain white background but without the tick marks. The dark style is the same as the white style but the background is dark rather than white. And the whitegrid and darkgrid styles add grid lines to each tick for the dark and white styles.

The whitegrid and darkgrid styles are illustrated in this figure. As you can see, gridlines are displayed for each tick mark. In some cases, the gridlines make it easier to interpret your data. In most cases, though, they just clutter the plot and make the data more difficult to interpret. Because of that, they aren't used in this book.

Once a style is set, it will stay in effect until it is changed. So, to return the style to its default, you need to run the set_style() method again with the parameter to 'ticks'. This is illustrated by the last example in this figure.

Incidentally, these examples illustrate why you sometimes need to set your own tick marks and labels. As you can see, the default values for the year tick labels have one decimal place. That's because, by default, Seaborn set a tick mark on the x axis every 2.5 years. As a result, it needs the decimal place to represent half years. However, that's probably not what you want. To fix this, you can use the xticks parameter of the set() method to set the x ticks so they're displayed every 2 years as shown in the previous figure.

The Seaborn set_style() method

Method	Description
`set_style(style)`	Sets the background style with one of these values: darkgrid, whitegrid, dark, white, and ticks (the default). This style stays in effect until it is changed by another set_style() method.

How to set the background style

```
sns.set_style('whitegrid')
sns.relplot(data=mortality_data.query('Year >= 1910 and Year <= 1930'),
    kind='line', x='Year', y='DeathRate', hue='AgeGroup', aspect=1.25)
```

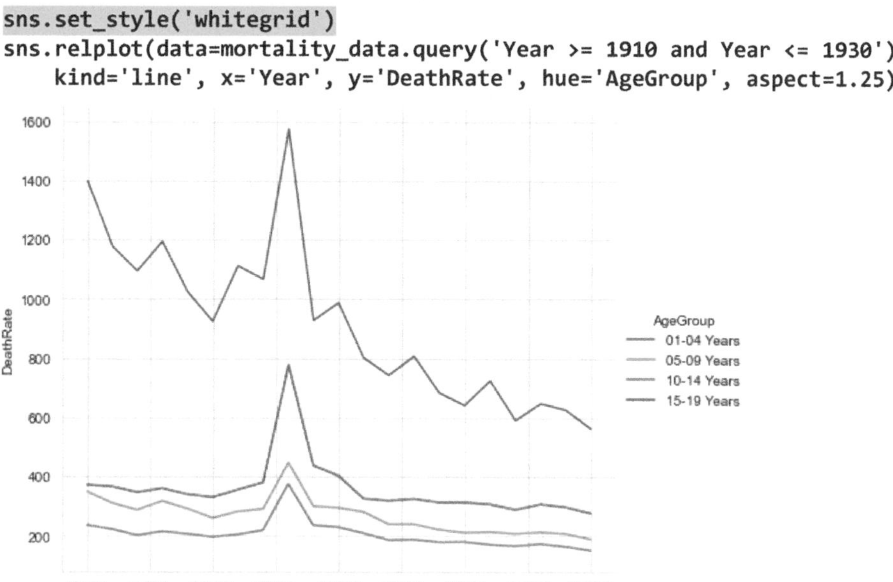

The same plot but with the darkgrid style

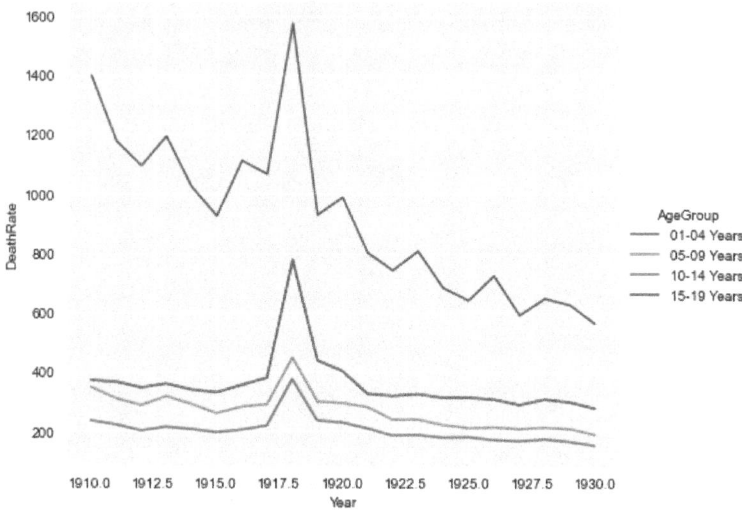

How to restore the default background style

```
sns.set_style('ticks')
```

Figure 4-7 How to use the set_style() method to set the background style

How to work with subplots

Figure 4-8 shows how to use the skills you've just learned with a plot that has subplots. The only difference is that the col parameter is set to AgeGroup so there's one plot for each of the four age groups. And the col_wrap parameter is set to 2 so there are two subplots in each row.

Here, as before, the x label and y label are shared by the subplots, which is usually what you want. You can also see that the default titles for the subplots accurately describe the age group for each subplot.

In addition, this code uses the fig attribute of the FacetGrid object to access the *Figure object* that contains the FacetGrid object. Then, it uses the suptitle() method of the Figure object to add a top-level title (a super title) to the plot. subplots.

To set the vertical location of the top-level title, this code sets the y parameter of the suptitle() method to a coordinate of 1.025. This displays the title slightly above the grid of Axes objects whose top is at a y coordinate of 1. If you didn't set the y parameter in this way, the top-level title would display on top of the titles for the two Axes objects that are displayed in the top row of the grid.

The parameters of the suptitle() method of the Figure object

Parameter	Description
t	Sets the text for the title.
y	Sets the y location of the title in figure coordinates where 1 is the top of the figure and 0 is the bottom of the figure.

How to use the set() and suptitle() methods with subplots

```
g = sns.relplot(data=mortality_data.query('Year >= 1910 and Year <= 1930'),
    kind='line', x='Year', y='DeathRate', hue='AgeGroup', legend=False,
    col='AgeGroup', col_wrap=2, height=4)
g.fig.suptitle('Deaths by Age Group (1910-1930)', y=1.025)
for ax in g.axes.flat:
    ax.set(ylabel='Deaths per 100,000',
           xticks=[x for x in range(1910,1931,2)],
           ylim=(0,1750))
```

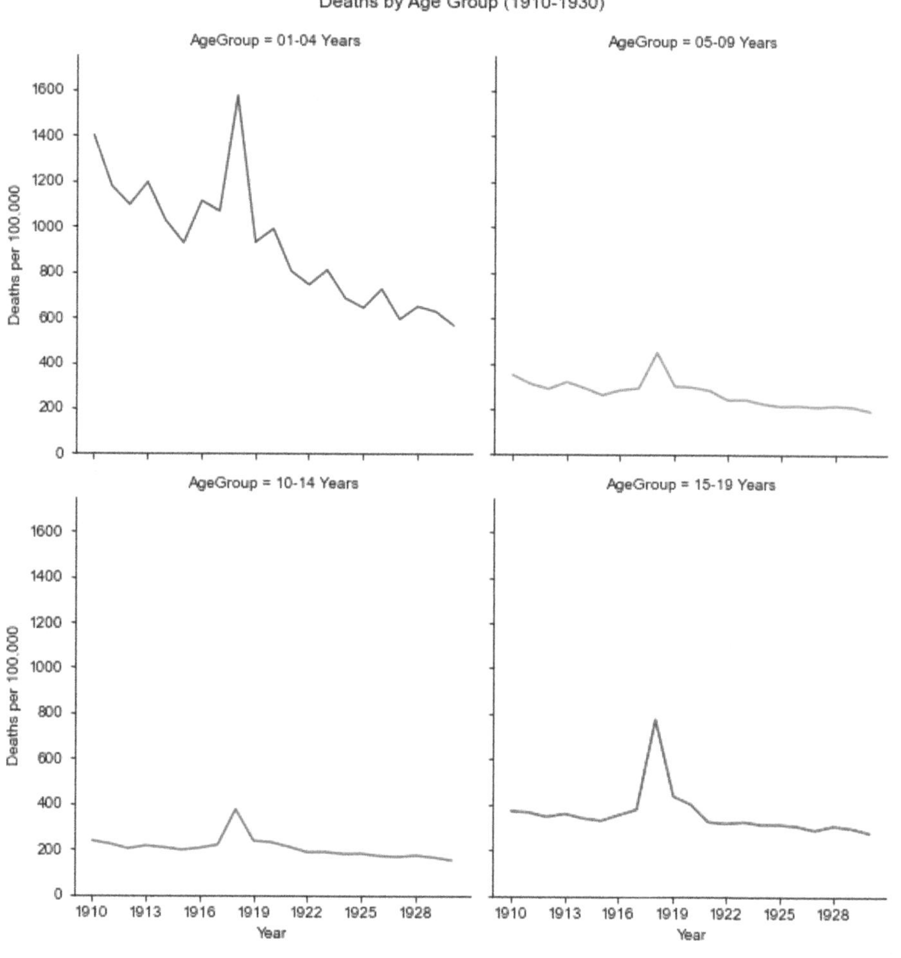

Figure 4-8 How to use the set() and suptitle() methods with subplots

How to save a plot

When you want to use a plot in a report or presentation, you need to save it in a file. Figure 4-9 shows how.

The first example shows how to save a plot with a general method. To do that, you start by assigning the FacetGrid object for the plot to a variable named g. Then, you use the savefig() method of the FacetGrid object to save the file. The filename parameter of that method provides the name for the file, and the extension of the filename determines the format in which it is saved.

The second example shows how this works with a plot created by a specific method. To start, you call the getfigure() method from the Axes object that's returned by the lineplot() method to get the Figure object for the plot. Then, you chain the savefig() method to the getfigure() method to save the plot.

If you want to save a file in the same folder as the Notebook, you just specify the filename, as in the first two savefig() methods in each of the examples. If you want to save the file in another folder, though, you can also specify the path. This is illustrated by the last statement in each of the examples. Here, the files are saved in the figures subfolder of the folder for the Notebook. For this to work, the path has to exist before the statements are executed. In other words, specifying the path doesn't create the folder. If the folders in the path don't exist when the statement is executed, it causes an error.

After you save a plot in a graphics format, you can view it by opening it with the appropriate software. For example, you can open a PNG file with image editing software, and you can open a PDF file with Acrobat Reader. Then, you can make sure the plot is ready for presentation.

In some cases, you may want to make adjustments to the saved plot. If, for example, there's too much empty space around the image, you can use your image editing software to crop the image. And if the title or labels for the figure are truncated, you can use the subplots_adjust() method of the Figure object to adjust the amount of space that's allocated for the top, bottom, and sides of the figure. For instance, the first example in this figure shows how you can use this method to adjust the bottom of a plot so the labels won't get truncated. However, you should know this method doesn't work with Axes objects.

If your plot doesn't have a high enough resolution, you can increase the size of the plot. For a general plot method like relplot(), you do that by using the height and aspect parameters described earlier in this chapter. For a specific plot method like lineplot(), you do that by using the technique presented at the end of this chapter in figure 4-22.

A few of the supported file formats

File extension	File format
.png	PNG (Portable Network Graphics)
.svg	SVG (Scalable Vector Graphics)
.pdf	PDF (Portable Document Format)

The savefig() method of a FacetGrid object or a Figure object

Method	Description
savefig(filename)	Saves the figure to a file.

The get_figure() method of the Axes object

Method	Description
get_figure()	Gets the Figure object for the plot.

The subplots_adjust() method of the Figure object

Method	Description
subplots_adjust()	Adjusts the position of the subplots.

How to save a general plot

```
g = sns.relplot(data=mortality_data, kind='line',
                x='Year', y='DeathRate', hue='AgeGroup')
g.fig.subplots_adjust(bottom=0.35)  # adjust the bottom to fix the y labels
g.savefig('lineChart.png')
g.savefig('lineChart.svg')
g.savefig('figures/lineChart.pdf')
```

How to save a specific plot

```
ax = sns.lineplot(data=mortality_data,
                  x='Year', y='DeathRate', hue='AgeGroup')
ax.get_figure().savefig('lineChart.png')
ax.get_figure().savefig('lineChart.svg')
ax.get_figure().savefig('figures/lineChart.pdf')
```

Description

- To save a plot that is created by a general method, you use the savefig() method of its FacetGrid object.
- To save a plot that is created by a specific method, you use the get_figure() method of its Axes object to get the Figure object that contains the Axes object. Then, you call the savefig() method from the Figure object. An easy way to do that is to chain the calls to these two methods.
- If you want, you can include a path with the filename. However, if the path doesn't already exist, the savefig() method throws an error.

Figure 4-9 How to save a plot to a file

How to create relational plots

The two types of *relational plots* that you can create with Seaborn are the line plot and the scatter plot. In the examples that follow, the Seaborn general methods are used to create these plots, but remember that you can also create these plots by using the specific methods.

How to create a line plot

To create a *line plot* with a general method, you need to use the Seaborn relplot() method with the kind parameter set to line. This is illustrated by the two examples in figure 4-10.

In the first example, you can see how to create a line plot for the mortality data where x is the year that the measurement was taken and y is the number of deaths per 100,000 people. Here, the hue parameter is coded, so a line is plotted for each of the four age groups.

By contrast, the second example shows what will happen if you don't code the hue parameter. This time, the one line plots the average death rate for the four age groups. In addition, a *confidence interval* is generated for the plot. This is indicated by the shaded areas above and below the plot line.

By default, the confidence interval is 95%. That means that if you collected new data, there would be a 95% chance that the average of that data would fall within the high and low marks for the interval. However, you can modify the size of this interval by using the ci parameter. In a moment, you'll see that this parameter can also be used with other types of plots.

In the case of the mortality data, of course, the data is for years in the past so new data can't be collected. In other words, the confidence interval doesn't apply if the data is time-dependent. It only applies if new samples of the data can be collected.

The ci parameter for line plots

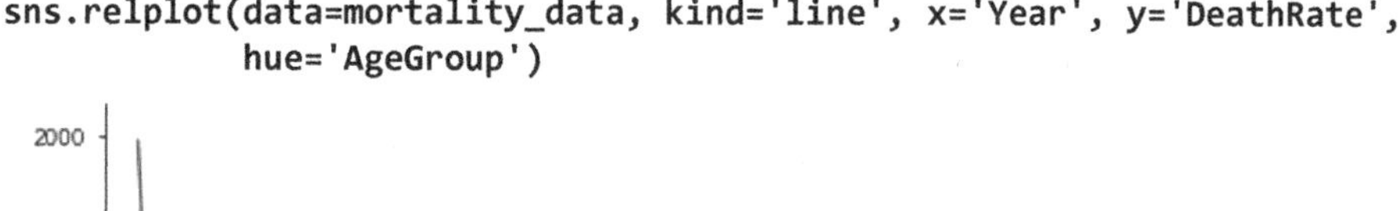

Parameter	Description
`ci`	The size of the confidence interval from 0 to 100. The default is 95. If None, the interval isn't shown. If 'sd', the interval is the standard deviation.

How to create a line plot

```
sns.relplot(data=mortality_data, kind='line', x='Year', y='DeathRate',
            hue='AgeGroup')
```

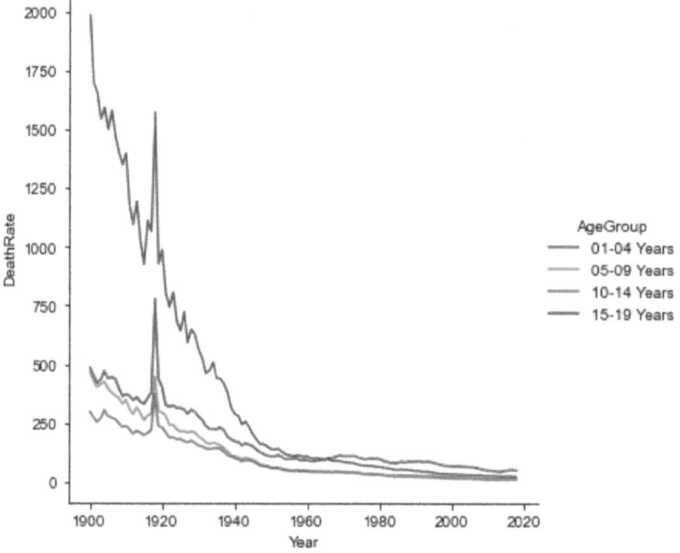

How to create a line plot with a confidence interval

```
sns.relplot(data=mortality_data, kind='line', x='Year', y='DeathRate')
```

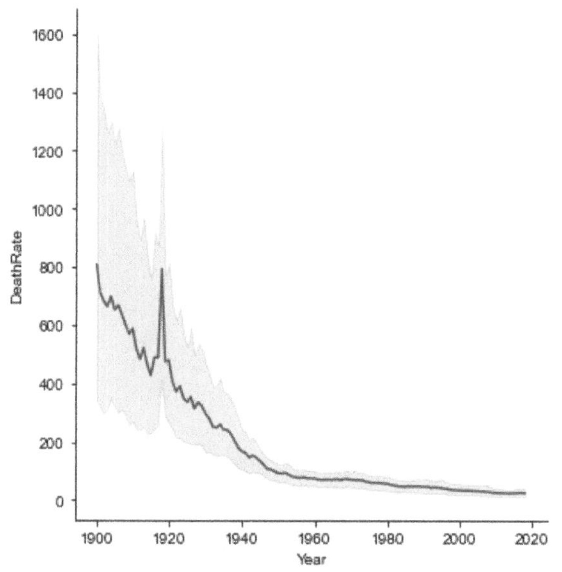

Figure 4-10 How to create a line plot

How to create a scatter plot

The second type of relational plot is the *scatter plot*. A scatter plot can be created by calling the relplot() method with the kind parameter set to scatter. This is illustrated by the two examples in figure 4-11.

In the first example, you can see that the code for a scatter plot is like the code for a line plot, except that the kind parameter is set to scatter. In fact, the difference between those plots is that the line plot shows the datapoints in a continuous line, while the scatter plot shows the datapoints as dots so the variations are easier to identify.

The second example in this figure shows how to plot the data for a smaller date range. Here, a query() method selects the data for the years 1910 through 1930. Then, the set() method uses a list comprehension to provide the tick values for the plot. This example shows that there's much more variation in the data for the 01-04 age than there is for the other age groups.

In this second example, the size parameter is used to set the size of the dots based on the values in the DeathRate column. As a result, Seaborn divides the death rates into six groups, and the sizes of the dots correspond to the death rates in those groups. That's why the dots at the top of the plot are larger than the ones near the bottom.

If you want to provide more or less variance in the sizes of the dots, you can also use the sizes parameter as shown in the second example. Here, the tuple for this parameter says that the dots should range in size from 10 through 100, so the largest dots are ten times larger than the smallest dots. Then, you can adjust the tuple until you get the size variations that you want.

In a plot like this, of course, the dot sizes don't make the plot any more meaningful. But the size and sizes parameters can come in handy when you're plotting something like the location of forest fires on a map. Then, the dot sizes can be based on the fire sizes. You can see this illustrated in the Forest Fires case study.

The size and sizes parameters for a scatter plot

Parameter	Description
`size`	A numeric column that determines the size of the dots.
`sizes`	A tuple that sets the smallest and largest size of the dots.

How to create a scatter plot

```
sns.relplot(data=mortality_data,
    kind='scatter', x='Year', y='DeathRate', hue='AgeGroup')
```

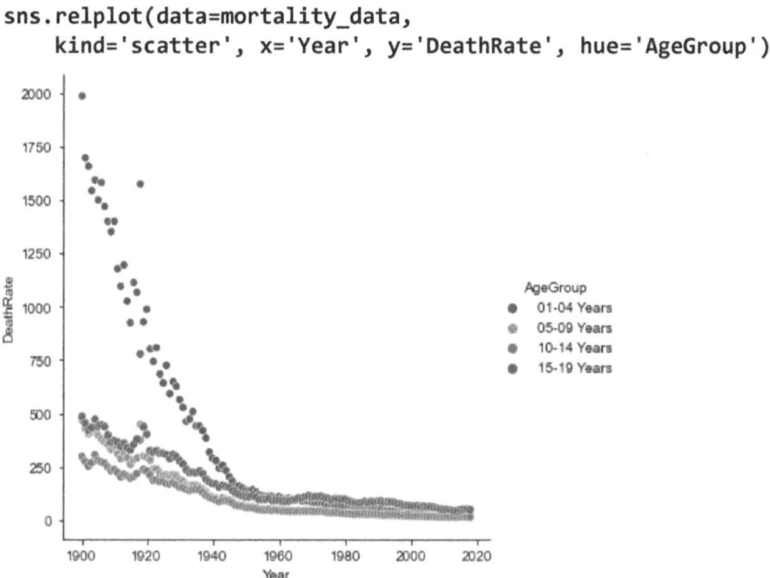

How to create a scatter plot for a smaller date range

```
g = sns.relplot(data=mortality_data.query('Year >= 1910 and Year <= 1930'),
    kind='scatter', x='Year', y='DeathRate', hue='AgeGroup',
    size='DeathRate', sizes=(10,100))
for ax in g.axes.flat:
    ax.set(xticks=[x for x in range(1910,1931,2)])
```

Figure 4-11 How to create a scatter plot

How to create categorical plots

Seaborn provides for the eight different types of *categorical plots* shown in figure 4-1. In practice, though, you're only likely to need two of them: the bar plot and the box plot. So, the topics that follow show you how to create those plots by using the general catplot() method. Remember, though, that you can also use specific methods to create them.

How to create a bar plot

In the table at the top of figure 4-12, you can see some of the parameters that are specific to the catplot() method. Then, the two examples show how these parameters can be used to create *bar plots*.

In the first example, a query() method is used to select data for the years 1950 and 2000. Then, the death rate is plotted for both of those years. But since the hue parameter isn't coded, the bars represent the average death rate for the four age groups in each of those two years. And since the ci parameter is set to None, no confidence interval is displayed for this plot.

The second example in this figure shows how to create a horizontal bar plot. This time, the hue parameter is coded, so there's one bar for each age group within each year, and there's no line for the confidence interval so you don't have to disable it.

Note here that the x and y parameters in this example are the opposite of what they are in the first example. That's why this bar chart is horizontal. Although the orient parameter is coded, it isn't necessary. In some cases, though, you will need to code this parameter.

The basic parameters for categorical plots

Parameter	Description
`kind`	The kind of plot: bar, box, strip, point, swarm, boxen, violin, or count.
`orient`	The orientation of the plot: v for vertical (the default) and h for horizontal. But this is inferred if only one dimension is numeric.
`ci`	The size of the confidence interval.

How to create a vertical bar plot

```
sns.catplot(data=mortality_data.query('Year in (1950,2000)'),
            kind='bar', x='Year', y='DeathRate', ci=None)
```

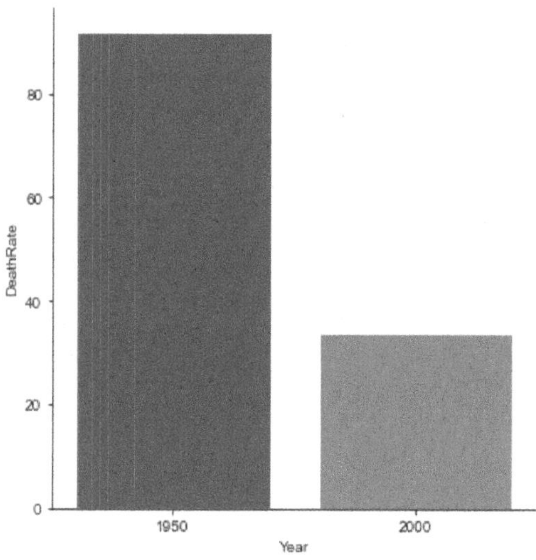

How to create a horizontal bar plot

```
sns.catplot(data=mortality_data.query('Year in (1950,2000)'), kind='bar',
            x='DeathRate', y='Year', hue='AgeGroup', orient='h')
```

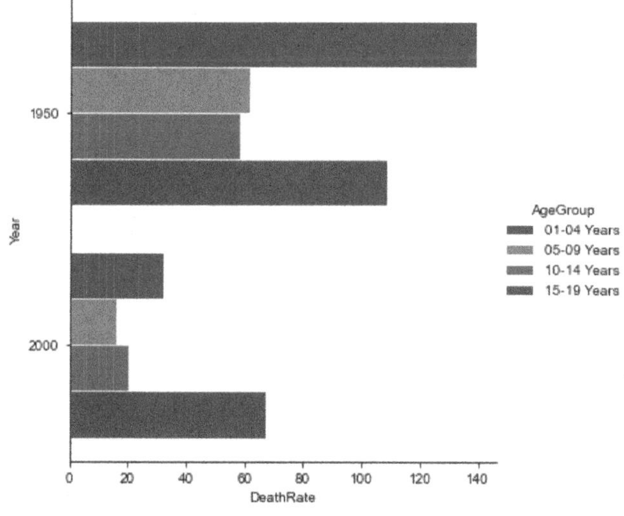

Figure 4-12 How to create a bar plot

How to create a box plot

Figure 4-13 shows how to create a *box plot* (also known as a *box and whisker plot*). This type of plot provides a quick way to get a five-number summary of the data that's plotted.

As you learned in chapter 3, the box in a box plot represents the first and third quartiles of the data that's being plotted, and the horizontal line through the box represents the median. Then, the whisker at the bottom of the box goes down to the minimum, and the whisker at the top goes up to the maximum. And any diamonds below the minimum or above the maximum whiskers represent outliers.

In the first example in this figure, you can see a box plot for the six years from 1915 through 1920. Here, the box for each year represents the values for all four age groups. So, for example, the maximum value for all four age groups in 1918 was almost 1600, and the median value was just over 600.

In the second example, each box represents the values for each age group for all years. Here, the DeathRate values that are being plotted have moved from the y-axis in the first example to the x-axis in the second example, and the orient parameter has been set to 'h'. As a result, the plot is horizontal, not vertical. This plot clearly shows that the 01-04 age group had the highest death rate.

How to create a box plot

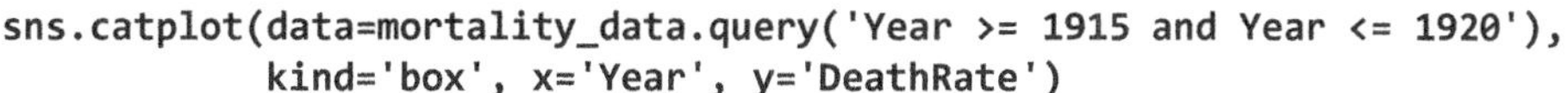

```
sns.catplot(data=mortality_data.query('Year >= 1915 and Year <= 1920'),
            kind='box', x='Year', y='DeathRate')
```

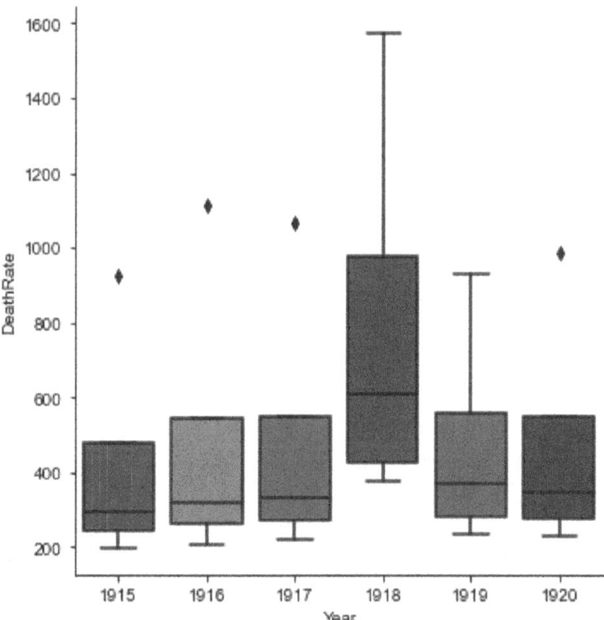

How to create a horizontal box plot

```
sns.catplot(data=mortality_data,
            kind='box', x='DeathRate', y='AgeGroup', orient='h')
```

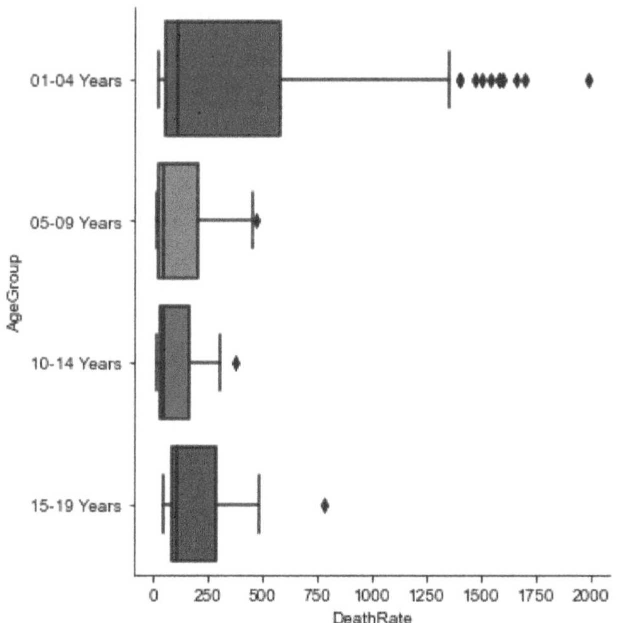

Figure 4-13 How to create a box plot

How to create distribution plots

Seaborn provides for three types of *distribution plots*: histograms, KDE plots, and ECDF plots. In the figures that follow, you'll learn how to create these plots by using the general displot() method. But here again, remember that you can also use specific methods to create them.

How to create a histogram

The table at the top of figure 4-14 presents the three parameters that you're likely to need for distribution plots. Then, the two examples show how to use them to create *histograms*. In both examples, note that a y parameter isn't coded. That's because a histogram shows the frequency of the occurrences for the x values. That's why "Count" is used as the default label for the y-axis.

The first example shows how to create a histogram. In this case, since the bins parameter isn't coded, the default is used, and the death rates are divided into many *bins*. As a result, it's difficult to interpret the results, other than to say that almost all of the death rates are under 500.

In the second example, though, the bins parameter has been used to divide the death rates into 8 bins. As a result, each bin in the histogram is 250 units wide (from 0 through 2000 divided by 8). That way, it's easy to see that more than 350 of the death rate values are less than 250, while very few are over 500.

This shows that it's important to pick a bin size that's appropriate for your data. In general, if there are too many bins, the histogram becomes hard to interpret. And if there are too few bins, the histogram begins to lose precision.

Also, if you can split the data into bins that line up well with your tick marks, the data will be easier to read. The other alternative is to use Axes methods to adjust the ticks to your bins, but that can take more time.

The basic parameters for distribution plots

Parameter	Description
`kind`	Any of these: histplot, kdeplot, or ecdfplot.
`bins`	The number of bins on the x-axis. Only used with histplots.
`fill`	Fills the interior of the plot. Not used with ECDF plots.

How to create a histogram with the default settings

```
sns.displot(data=mortality_data, kind='hist', x='DeathRate')
```

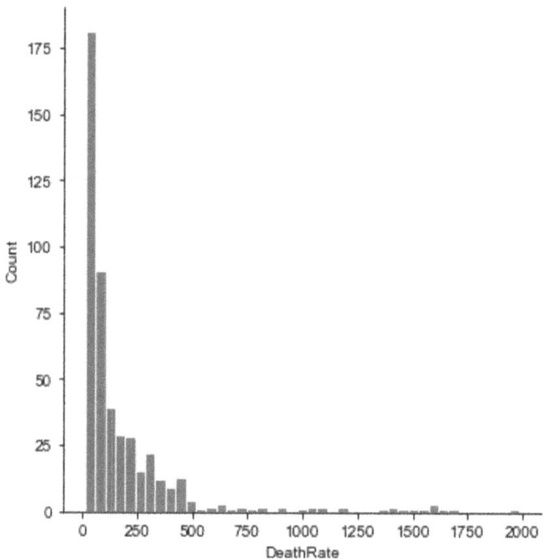

How to create a histogram with 8 bins

```
sns.displot(data=mortality_data, kind='hist', x='DeathRate', bins=8)
```

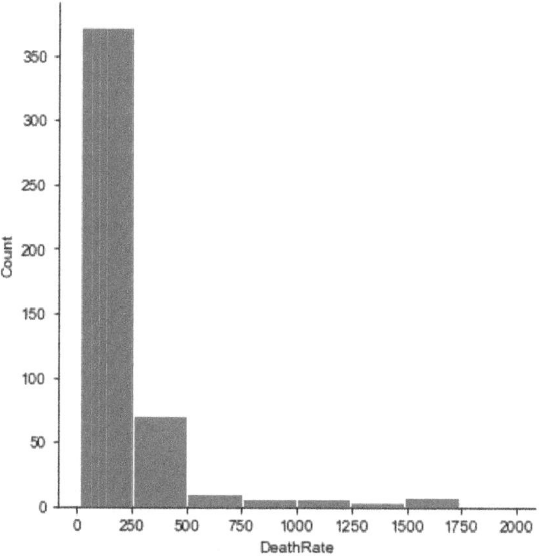

Figure 4-14 How to create a histogram

How to create a KDE or ECDF plot

The first example in figure 4-15 shows how to create a *density plot* (or *KDE plot*). Like a histogram, a density plot shows the distribution of data in a numeric column. However, it uses a *kernel density estimate* (*KDE*) to smooth the data.

Unlike a histogram, the y-axis in a density plot represents the probability of a datapoint occurring, and that value is derived from the KDE. For instance, the density plot in this figure shows that the probability of the next death rate being 2000 is close to zero. The probability of the next death rate being 500 is a little bit higher. And the probability of the next death rate being 100 is considerably higher than that. Keep in mind though that to get the actual probability you have to get the area under the curve (the integral) for the line.

The KDE is calculated by weighting the distances of the datapoints for each location on the density line. So, the more datapoints there are in a location, the higher the KDE. And that indicates that the probability of seeing a datapoint in that location is higher.

Also note in this first example that the plot line assigns some probability to negative values, even though there aren't any negative values in the data. That's because the way the data is sampled in the KDE calculations includes some negative values.

In contrast to a KDE plot, an *ECDF* (*Empirical Cumulative Distribution Function*) *plot* shows what percent of the data falls at or below a plotted x value. So, in the plot in the second example in this figure, you can see that roughly 80% of the death rates in the 01-04 age group are below 750 per 100,000. You can also see that 100% of the death rates in the other three age groups are below 500.

In the code for these examples, note that the code for the KDE plot doesn't have a hue parameter, but the code for the ECDF plot does. That's why there is one plot line for the KDE plot and four plot lines for the ECDF plot.

How to create a KDE (or density) plot

```
sns.displot(data=mortality_data, kind='kde', x='DeathRate')
```

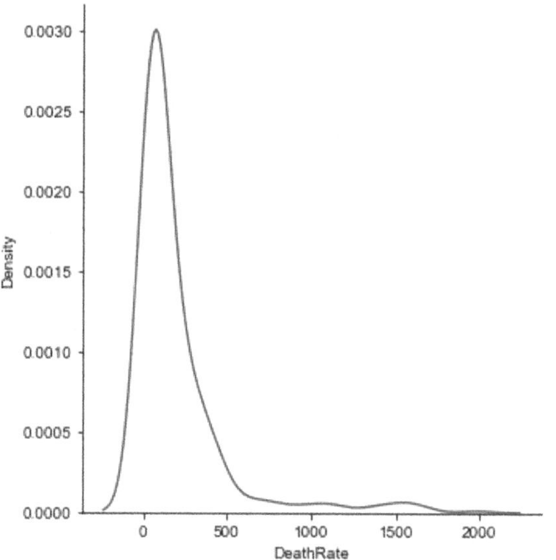

How to create an ECDF plot

```
sns.displot(data=mortality_data, kind='ecdf', x='DeathRate', hue='AgeGroup')
```

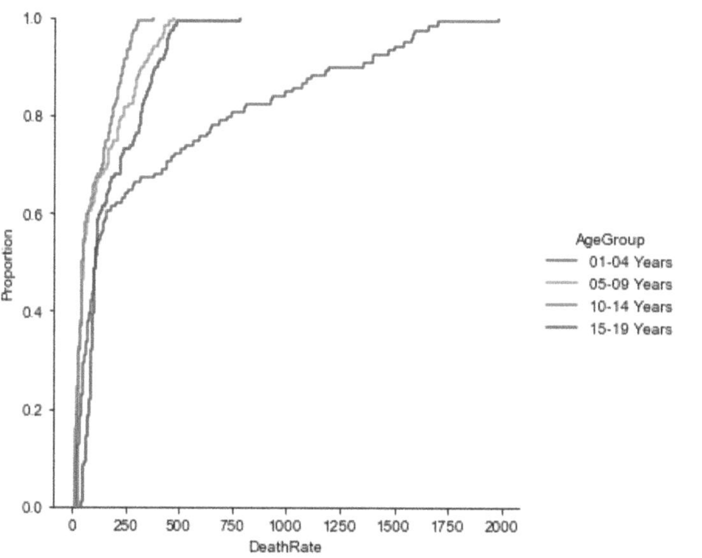

Description

- A *density plot* (or *KDE plot*) shows the distribution of the data in a numeric column. However, it uses a *kernel density estimate* (*KDE*) to smooth the data in the histogram.
- An *ECDF* plot shows the proportion of the datapoints that fall at or below the values on the x-axis.

Figure 4-15 How to create a KDE plot or an ECDF plot

How to enhance a distribution plot

Figure 4-16 presents two of the ways that distribution plots can be enhanced so the data is easier to interpret. In the first example, a histogram is enhanced by laying a KDE curve over the histogram. That's done by setting the kde parameter to True. The alternative is to create separate histogram and KDE plots. But when you overlay them, you know that they will be scaled the same way.

The second example in this figure shows how a KDE plot can be split into subplots to show each density curve more clearly. That way, it's easier to examine each of the plot lines individually and to compare them to each other. In this example, the fill parameter is set to True, which also makes the data easier to interpret.

How to combine a histogram with a KDE plot

```
sns.displot(data=mortality_data, kind='hist', x='DeathRate', kde=True, bins=8)
```

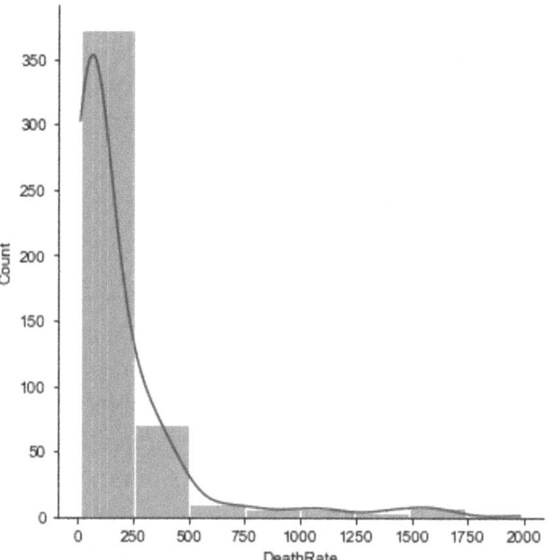

How to create a KDE plot with filled subplots

```
sns.displot(data=mortality_data, kind='kde', x='DeathRate', hue='AgeGroup',
            fill=True, col='AgeGroup', col_wrap=2, height=3, legend=False)
```

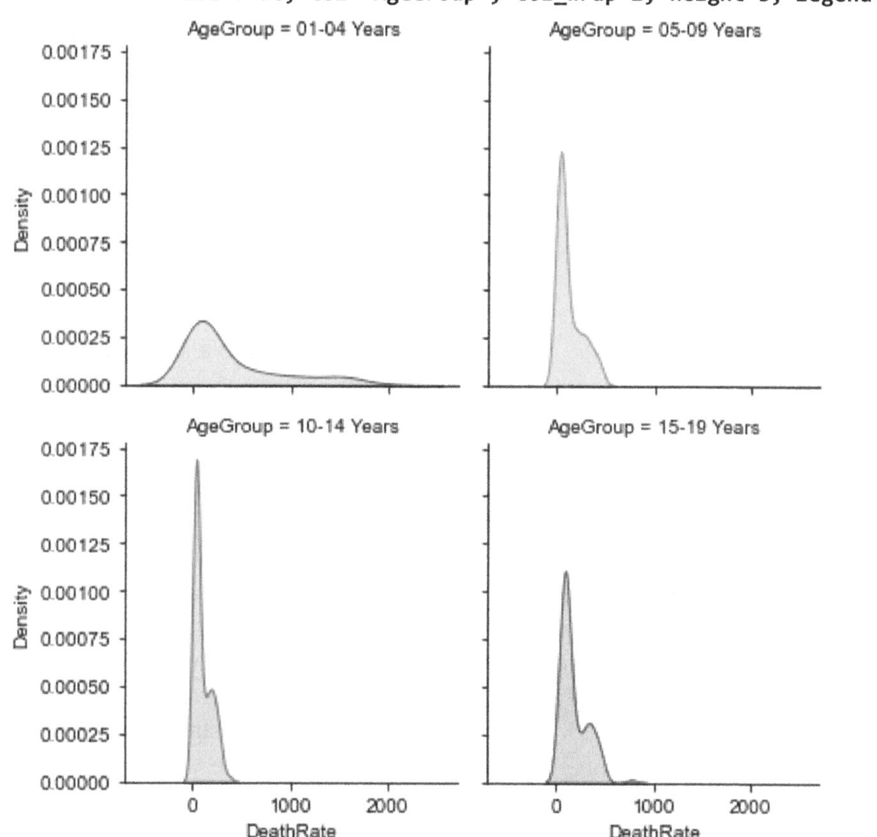

Figure 4-16 How to enhance a distribution plot

Other techniques for enhancing a plot

At this point, you should know how to create the types of plots that you'll use the most. You should also know how to use two of the Axes methods to enhance your plots, the set() and tick_params() methods. Now, in the last six figures in this chapter, you'll learn how to use some other methods and techniques for enhancing your plots.

How to use other Axes methods to enhance a plot

The Axes methods in the table in figure 4-17 can be used to modify plots in a way that's similar to using the set() method. Just like the set() method, you'll need to use the g.axes.flat accessor to loop through and access the Axes objects.

In the example, the relplot() method creates a line plot using the parameters for that method. Then, the FacetGrid object (or just Grid object) that's returned by the relplot() method is assigned to a variable named g. Next, the loop iterates through the Axes objects with the g.axes.flat attribute, and the one Axes object that's in the Grid object is stored in a variable named *ax*. At that point, eight of the Axes methods are used to enhance the plot.

The first of these methods just sets the title for the plot. Then, the next three methods show how you can set up custom tick labels for a plot. First, the set_xlabel() method turns off the default label for the x-axis by setting it to an empty string. Next, the set_xticks() method uses a list comprehension to set the tick marks to the even years from 2000 through 2016. Note that this is coordinated with the set_xlim() method that's coded later on.

After that, the set_xticklabels() method uses a list comprehension to set the tick labels to these strings: Year 0, Year 2, and so on. This shows how you can set custom tick labels instead of using the default labels of 2000, 2002, and so on. In the list comprehension, you can see how the parameters for the Python range() method are coordinated with the one for the range() method in the preceding method. Then, each value that's returned is converted to a string and concatenated to a string that contains 'Year' followed by one space.

The next Axes method for this plot is the tick_params() method. It can be used to set the rotation of the tick labels for the x- or y-axis. This comes in handy when your labels are too long to fit properly. In this case, the rotation for the custom tick labels for the x-axis are set to 30 degrees.

This is followed by the set_ylabel() method, which changes the default label to: 'Deaths per 100,000'. Then, the last two methods set the limits for the x- and y-axis. Here, the set_xlim() method limits the data to the years from 2000 through 2016, which of course has to be coordinated with the tick locations and values for the x-axis. And the set_ylim() method limits the height of the y-axis to the death rates from 0 through 80. Otherwise, the y-axis would range from 0 through 2000 because that's the range of the data in the DataFrame.

Some of the other Axes methods

Method	Description
`set_title()`	Sets the title.
`set_xlabel()`	Sets the x-axis label.
`set_xticks()`	Sets the values of the xticks.
`set_xticklabels()`	Sets xtick labels that are different than the values of the xticks.
`set_ylabel()`	Sets the y-axis label.
`set_yticks()`	Sets the values of the yticks.
`set_yticklabels()`	Sets ytick labels that are different than the values of the yticks.
`tick_params()`	Sets tick parameters like the label rotation for the xticks or yticks.
`set_xlim()`	Uses a tuple to set the upper and lower limits of the x-axis.
`set_ylim()`	Uses a tuple to set the upper and lower limits of the y-axis.

How to enhance a general plot with the Axes methods

```
g = sns.relplot(data=mortality_data, kind='line',
                x='Year', y='DeathRate', hue='AgeGroup', aspect=1.25)
for ax in g.axes.flat:
    ax.set_title('Deaths by Age Group (2000-2016)')
    ax.set_xlabel('')
    ax.set_xticks([x for x in range(2000,2017,2)])
    ax.set_xticklabels(['Year ' + str(x) for x in range(0,17,2)])
    ax.tick_params('x', labelrotation=30)
    ax.set_ylabel('Deaths per 100,000')
    ax.set_xlim(2000,2016)
    ax.set_ylim(0,80)
```

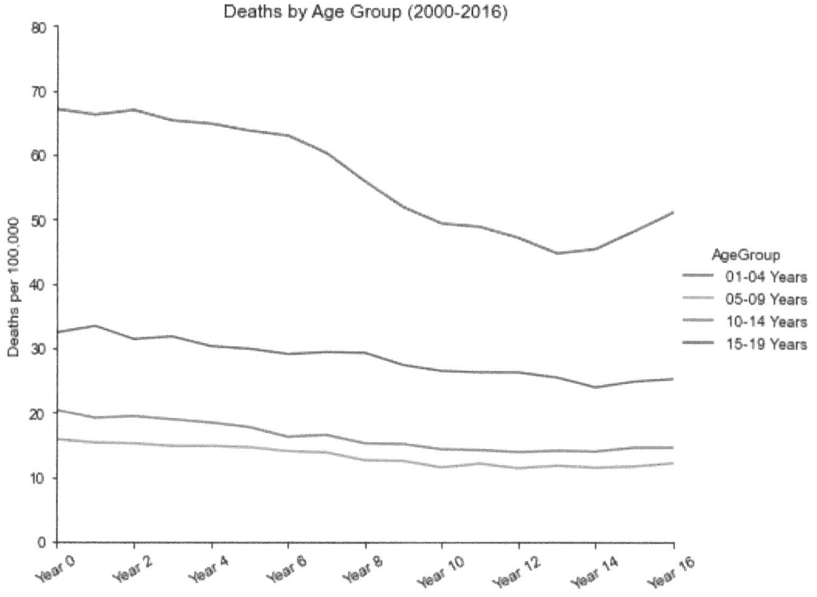

Figure 4-17 How to use other Axes methods to enhance a plot

How to annotate a plot

For some plots, you may want to annotate one or two of the key datapoints. To do that, you can use the annotate() method that's shown in figure 4-18. Here, a specific method is used for the plot so you don't need to use a for loop to access the Axes object.

In this example, the text parameter of the annotate() method sets the text for the annotation. The xytext parameter provides the x and y coordinates for the start of the text. And the xy parameter provides the coordinates for the tip of the arrow. You can see that these coordinates are based on the year and death rates that are in this plot. So, for example, the tip of the arrow is located at the intersection of the year 1918 and the death rate 1650.

Last, the arrowsprops parameter is set to a dictionary that provides the values for four keys. The facecolor key sets the color of the arrow to red. The width key sets the width of the arrow. And the headwidth and headlength keys set the width and length of the arrowhead.

The annotate() method of the Axes object

Method	Description
`annotate(params)`	Adds an annotation to the Axes object.
Parameter	**Description**
`text`	The string for the annotation.
`xy`	The x and y coordinates for the point to annotate.
`xytext`	The x and y coordinates for the start of the text for the annotation.
`arrowprops`	The properties of the arrow with measurements in points: facecolor (the color of the arrow), width (the width of the arrow), headwidth (the width of the arrowhead), and headlength (the length of the arrowhead).

How to add an annotation to a plot

```
ax = sns.lineplot(data=mortality_data,
                  x='Year', y='DeathRate', hue='AgeGroup')
ax.set_title('Deaths by Age Group')
ax.set_ylabel('Deaths per 100,000')
ax.annotate(text='Spanish Flu Pandemic',
    xy=(1918, 1650), xytext=(1925, 1900),
    arrowprops=dict(facecolor='red', width=3, headwidth=12, headlength=6))
```

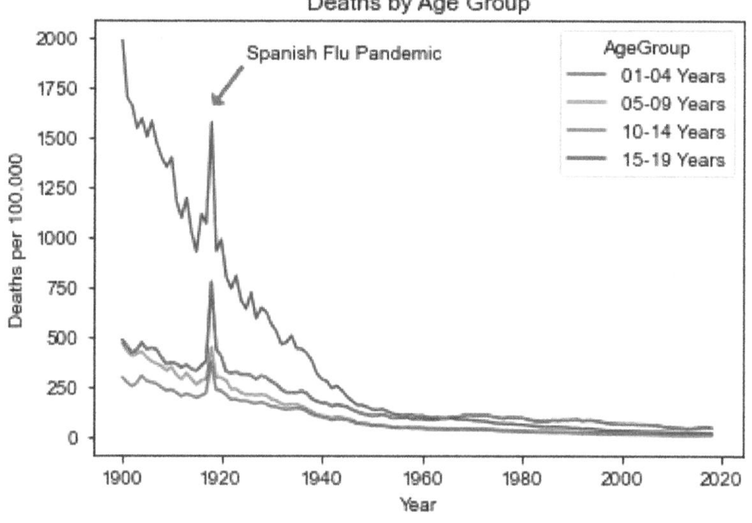

Figure 4-18 How to annotate a plot

How to set the color palette

For most plots, the default color palette is all that you need. But sometimes, a plot is easier to understand if you change the color palette. In the Polling case study, for example, some of the plots will be easier to understand if you use blue for Democratic values and red for Republican values, because those are the colors that are commonly used for the two parties. Similarly, it makes sense to use red for plotting the fires in the Fires case study on a map.

When you use Seaborn, you can change the color palette in several different ways. But one of the easiest is shown in figure 4-19. In this case, you change the palette so it stays in effect until you reset it to the default palette or change it to another palette. That's often what you will want to do.

The first example in this figure shows how to change the palette. Here, the color_palette() method sets the colors for the palette, and the set_palette() method sets the palette to the palette with those colors.

In this example, HTML color names are used for the new colors: black, red, orange, and blue. But you can also use hex or decimal codes for those values. To find the names or values that you need, you can search the Internet for the HTML color codes.

When you code the list of colors, you need to provide one color for each group that's specified by the hue parameter. You should also provide the colors in the sequence that you want them applied. In this example, black is applied to the first age group (01-04), red to the second age group (05-09), and so on. Often, you will need to experiment with the color sequence to get the result that you want.

When you want to change back to the default palette, you can use the code in the second example in this figure. Here, the parameter for the color_palette() method is 'tab10', which refers to the default Matplotlib palette. This palette is similar to the default for Seaborn, but it's a little brighter.

The color_palette() and set_palette()methods

Method	Description
`color_palette(colors)`	Sets the colors for a palette.
`set_palette(palette)`	Sets the palette for the plots that follow.

How to change the palette for the plots that follow

```
colors = ['black','red','orange','blue']
sns.set_palette(sns.color_palette(colors))
sns.relplot(data=mortality_data, kind='line',
            x='Year', y='DeathRate', hue='AgeGroup')
```

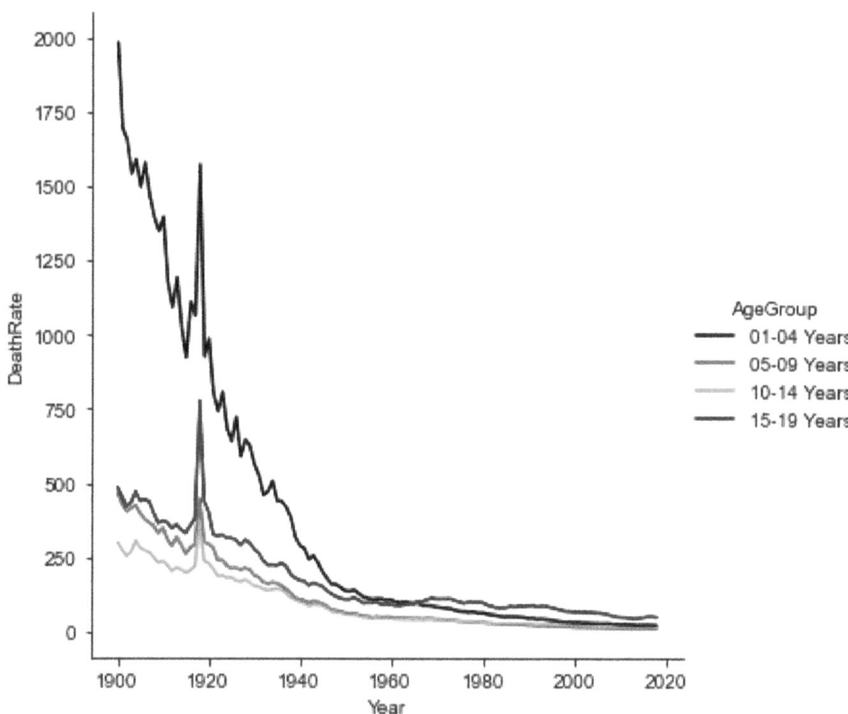

How to reset the color palette to the default palette

```
sns.set_palette(sns.color_palette('tab10'))
```

Description

- When you set the colors for a palette, you can use the HTML color names, hex codes, or decimal codes.
- When you run the set_palette() method, the color palette stays in effect until it is changed by another set_palette() method.

Figure 4-19 How to set the color palette for your plots

How to enhance a plot that has subplots

The example in figure 4-20 shows that you can also use the Axes methods to enhance a plot that contains subplots. To start, the fig.suptitle() method is used to provide a top-level title for the plot. Then, three of the Axes methods are used to set the y label, the xticks, and the rotation of the xtick labels. The result is a plot that is easy to interpret.

In this case, the titles for the subplots are the default titles, and they work okay. But sometimes, you may want to customize the titles for the subplots so they more accurately describe what's in each subplot. Or, you may want to customize the titles to reduce duplication. In this figure, for example, the top-level title already indicates that the plots are for each age group, so there's no need to include "Age Group = " in the subplot titles. Either way, you can learn how to customize the titles for each subplot in the next figure.

How to enhance a plot that has subplots

```
g = sns.relplot(
    data=mortality_data.query('Year >= 1910 and Year <= 1930'), kind='line',
    x='Year', y='DeathRate', hue='AgeGroup', legend=False,
    col='AgeGroup', col_wrap=2, height=3, aspect=1.2)
g.fig.suptitle('Deaths by Age Group (1910-1930)', y=1.025)
for ax in g.axes.flat:
    ax.set_ylabel('Deaths per 100,000')
    ax.set_xticks([x for x in range(1910, 1931, 2)])
    ax.tick_params('x', labelrotation=45)
```

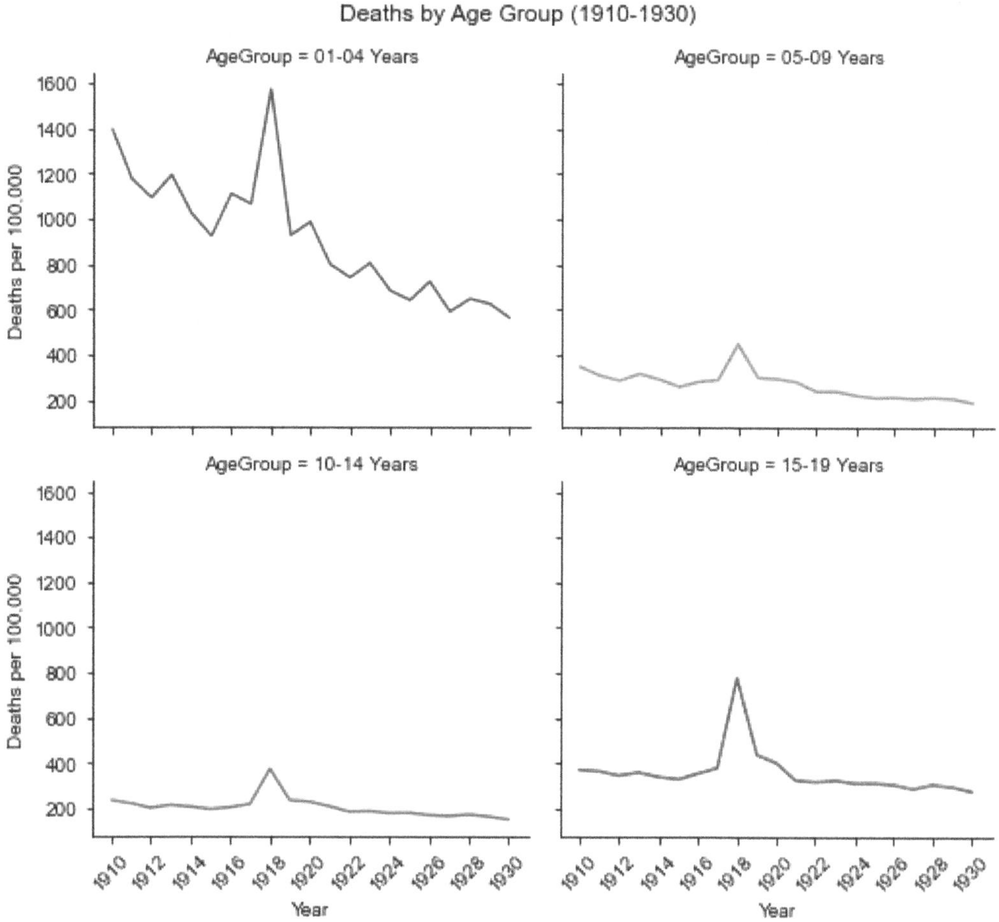

Description

- By default, the subplots share the x and y labels, which is usually what you want when the x and y labels are the same for all of the subplots.

Figure 4-20 How to use other Axes methods to enhance a plot that has subplots

How to customize the titles for subplots

The first example in figure 4-21 shows how to customize the titles for the subplots within a plot. After the plot is created by the relplot() method, a list of the four different age groups is created and assigned to a variable named ageGroups.

This list is created by running the drop_duplicates() method and then chaining the to_list() method to it. You'll learn more about these methods in section 2. For now, you just need to know that the drop_duplicates() method drops all of the duplicate values in the AgeGroup column so only four values are left: 01-04 Years, 05-09 Years, 10-14 Years, and 15-19 Years. Then, the tolist() method converts these four values to a list.

After the list is created, a for statement is used to loop through the Axes objects. In this case, though, the loop also needs to access the index of each Axes object so it can set the title for each subplot. To make that possible, this code uses the enumerate() function to create a list of tuples where the first value in each tuple is the index of the Axes object and the second value is the Axes object.

Within the for loop, the set_title() method uses the index to get the related age group from the ageGroups list. You can see the results in the plot that has been created. Here, each subplot has a title that identifies the age group that it is for.

How to create specific titles for subplots

```
g = sns.relplot(
    data=mortality_data.query('Year >= 1910 and Year <= 1930'),
    kind='line', x='Year', y='DeathRate', hue='AgeGroup', legend=False,
    col='AgeGroup', col_wrap=2, height=3, aspect=1.2)
g.fig.suptitle('Deaths by Age Group (1910-1930)', y=1.025)
ageGroups = mortality_data['AgeGroup'].drop_duplicates().tolist()
for index, ax in enumerate(g.axes.flat):
    ax.set_title(ageGroups[index])
    ax.set_ylabel('Deaths per 100,000')
    ax.set_xticks([x for x in range(1910, 1931, 2)])
    ax.tick_params('x', labelrotation=45)
```

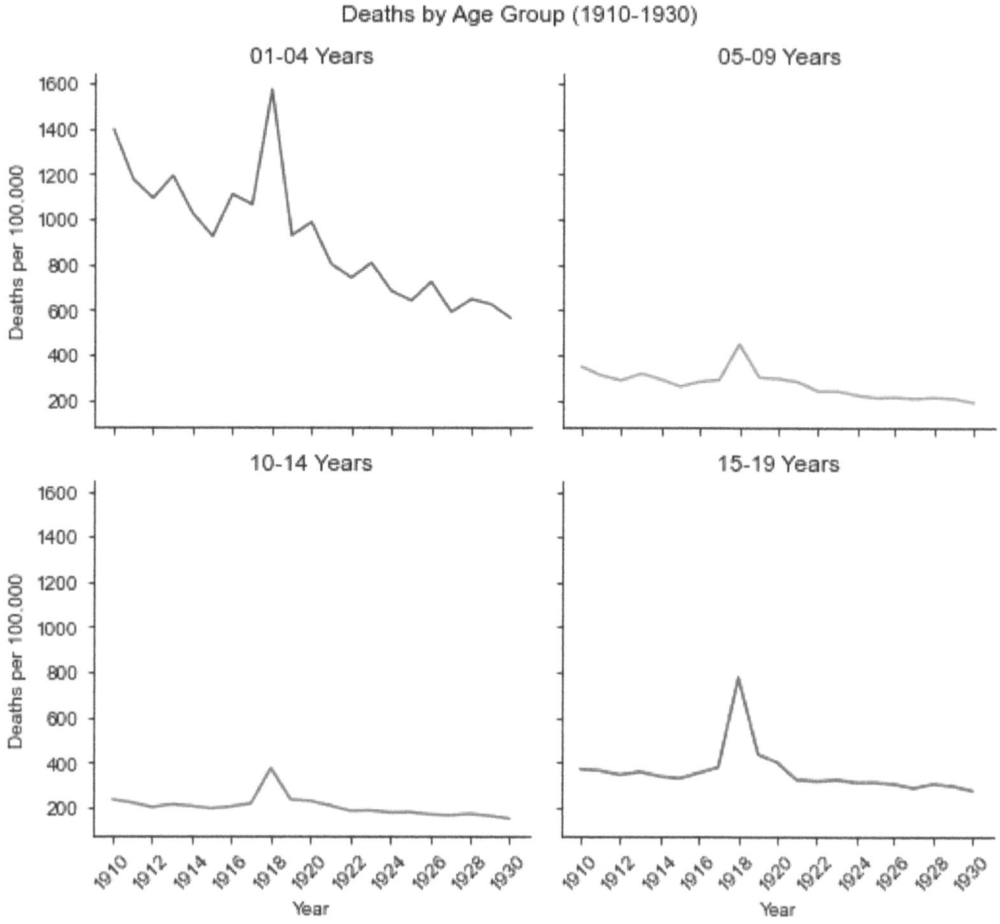

Figure 4-21 How to set custom titles for the subplots

How to set the size of a specific plot

When you use a general plot method like relplot(), you can use the height and aspect parameters to set the height and width of the plot. To do this, Seaborn sets the height and width of the Figure object that's used by Matplotlib. This Figure object contains one or more Axes objects for the plot as well as the title of the plot.

However, specific plot methods like lineplot() don't provide the height and aspect parameters. So, how can you set the size of the plot when you use a specific method? The most common way is to access Matplotlib directly, as shown in figure 4-22.

To start, you import Matplotlib's pyplot module. Then, you can call the subplots() method from this module and use its figsize parameter to set the size of the figure. To do that, you set the figsize parameter to a tuple that contains the width and height of the figure in inches. This sets the size of the current Figure and Axes objects and returns these objects. Remember, there's only one Axes object for a specific plot method like lineplot().

Then, if you use a specific method to create a plot, the plot uses the current Figure and Axes objects. In this figure, for example, the lineplot() method uses a Figure object that's 10 inches wide by 7.5 inches tall. This makes the figure larger than the default size when displayed in JupyterLab, but still not as large as its actual size.

To view the actual size of the figure, you need to save the Figure object in a graphics format and open it with image editing software. In this figure, for instance, the code saves the Figure object as a PNG file. Since Matplotlib uses 72 DPI (dots per inch) when saving PNG files, this results in an image that's 720 pixels wide by 540 pixels tall. You can check this by opening the PNG file with image editing software.

As you review this code, note that it uses the Axes object that's returned by the subplots() method to enhance the formatting of the plot. That way, you don't have to assign the Axes object that's returned by the lineplot() method to a variable like some of the examples shown earlier in this chapter.

The figsize parameter of Matplotlib's subplots() method

Parameter	Description
`figsize`	Uses a tuple to set the width and height of the figure in inches.

How to set the figure size of the plot and save the plot

```
# import Matplotlib's pyplot module and set the figure size
import matplotlib.pyplot as plt
fig, ax = plt.subplots(figsize=(10,7.5))

# create the line plot
sns.lineplot(data=mortality_data, x='Year', y='DeathRate', hue='AgeGroup')

# use the ax and fig objects to enhance and save the plot
ax.set(title='Deaths by Age Group (1910-1930)',
    ylabel='Deaths per 100,000',
    xticks=[x for x in range(1910, 1931, 2)],
    xlim=(1910,1930), ylim=(0,1750)),
ax.tick_params('x', labelrotation=45)
fig.savefig('deaths_by_age_group_line.png')
```

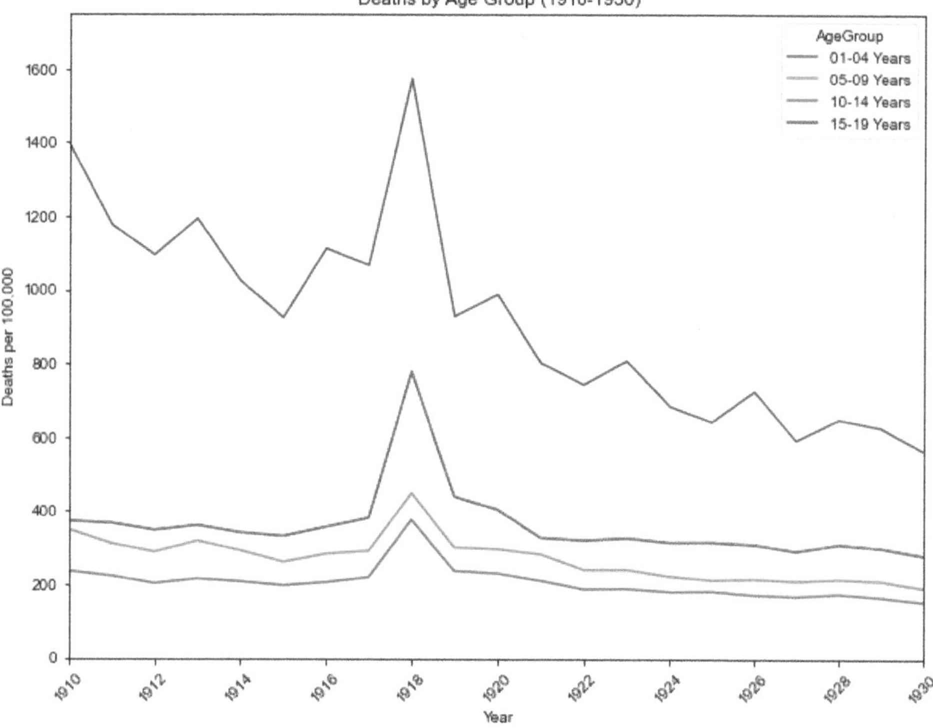

Description

- If you use a specific method like lineplot(), you can't use the height and aspect parameters to set the size of the plot like you can when you use a general plot method like relplot(). Instead, you can access Matplotlib directly and use the subplots() method to set the size of the plot.

Figure 4-22 How to set the size of a specific plot

Perspective

Now that you've completed this chapter, you should be able to create and enhance the types of plots that you're going to need for most of your analyses. You should also know how to save your plots so you can use them for presentations.

As you will see in section 3, though, Seaborn also provides for the types of plots that you need for predictive analysis. In particular, Seaborn provides for plots that do linear regressions. So, in chapters 10 and 11, you'll learn the other plotting skills that you need for Python data analysis.

Terms

relational plot
categorical plot
distribution plot
FacetGrid (Grid) object
Axes object
Figure object
line plot
confidence interval
scatter plot
bar plot
box plot (box and whisker plot)
histogram
bin
KDE (kernel density estimate)
KDE plot (density plot)
ECDF (Empirical Cumulative Distribution Function)
ECDF plot

Summary

- The three types of plots that you'll use the most are: *relational*, *categorical*, and *distribution*.
- Seaborn provides both specific and general methods for creating plots. The general methods can create plots that contain subplots; the specific methods can't.
- The general methods for plotting return Grid objects that contain one Axes object for each subplot. The specific methods return one Axes object. Either way, you can use the Axes objects to enhance a plot.
- You can use the set() method of an Axes object or a Grid object to set the title, x label, y label, and tick labels of a plot. These settings help make a plot self-explanatory.
- You can use the set_style() method to set the background for a plot.
- To save a plot created by a general method, you use the savefig() method of the Grid object for the plot. To save a plot created by a specific method, you chain the savefig() method of a Figure object to the get_figure() method of the Axes object for the plot.
- *Line plots* and *scatter plots* show the relationships between the variables that are being plotted.

- *Bar plots* and *box plots* (also known as *box and whisker plots*) summarize the data for the categories within a DataFrame.
- *Histograms*, *KDE* (or *density*) *plots*, and *ECDF plots* show the distribution of data within a DataFrame.
- You can use other methods of the Axes object to further enhance a plot. For instance, the set_xticklabels() and set_yticklabels() methods let you create custom tick labels. And the annotate() method lets you add an annotation to a plot.
- You can use the set_palette() method in combination with the color_palette() method to change the color palette for your plots and to change that palette back to the default palette.
- To enhance a plot with subplots, you code a for loop that accesses the Axes objects that are in the Grid object for the plot. Then, you can execute the Axes methods from within the loop.
- When you use a specific method to create a plot, you can't use parameters of the method to set the size of the plot. Instead, you can access Matplotlib directly and use the subplots() method to set the size of the plot.

Exercise 4-1 Create some Seaborn plots

In this exercise, you'll examine the Notebook for this chapter. Then, you'll modify some of the plots and create some new plots.

Open the Notebook and run the cells that create the DataFrame

1. Start JupyterLab and open the Notebook named ex_4-1_mortality that should be in this folder:

   python_analysis/exercises/ch04

2. Use the Kernel menu to restart the kernel and run all cells. That will import the data from a pickle file and create a DataFrame named mortality_data. It will also prepare the plots that are illustrated in this chapter.

Experiment with the cells that create the plots

For the steps that follow, change the existing cells as indicated to see how that changes the plots.

3. Change the aspect parameter for the plot in cell 6 to 2.
4. Change cell 10 so every fifth year is displayed on the x-axis for the plot and so the labels on the x-axis are displayed at their default rotation.
5. Change cell 17 so the confidence interval for the plot shows the standard deviation.
6. Change cell 19 so it uses a specific method to create the scatter plot.
7. Change cell 20 so it uses a specific method to create the bar plot, and change the confidence interval to 75.
8. Change cell 25 so the histogram uses twice as many bins as it currently does.

Prepare some plots of your own

As you create the plots in the steps that follow, don't create new DataFrames, but note that you may need to chain some of the methods.

9. Create a vertical bar plot that shows the deaths rates for the four age groups for the years 1900, 1950, and 2000, and note that the bars represent the average death rates for the three years. Now, modify the plot so it shows the death rates for each of the three years, and increase the width of the plot so it's 1.8 times the height of the plot.
10. Create another plot that displays the same data as the plot you created in step 9, but this time, create a subplot for each of the three years. Display all three subplots in one row.
11. Use a specific method to draw a line plot for just the data in the 15-19 age group, and note the values on the y-axis. Modify the plot to include an appropriate title, and change the y-axis label to "Deaths per 100,000".
12. Create a line plot that shows the death rates by age group for the years from 1950 to 2000.
13. Create a scatter plot that displays the same data as the line plot you created in step 12. Set the size and sizes parameters so the plot is easy to read.
14. Create a plot that contains four bar subplots that display the death rates by age group for the years 1900, 1925, 1950, 1975, and 2000. Display two subplots in each row, and set the height of the plot to an appropriate size. Add a title to the plot, and set the label for the y-axis to "Deaths per 100,000". Note the position of the title, and then fix it so it's displayed above the titles for the subplots. Save the plot to a file named barCharts.png in the same folder as the Notebook.

Section 2

The critical skills for success on the job

In section 1, you learned a subset of the skills that you need for Python data analysis. You also learned most of the data visualization skills that you will need for your analyses. Now, this section presents five chapters that focus on how to get, clean, prepare, and analyze the data. When you combine these skills with the data visualization skills of section 1, you will be able to do professional analyses of your own.

Although the chapters in this section are in the sequence of the normal workflow for an analysis, you don't have to read them in sequence. With the skills you learned in section 1, you're prepared for any of the chapters in this section. So, for example, if you're more interested in analyzing the data than you are in getting the data, you can go right to chapter 8.

Eventually, though, you'll want to read all five chapters because they all present critical skills for success on the job. And if you don't have a compelling reason for skipping chapters, it also makes sense to read the chapters in sequence. Just remember that they are written as independent modules, which is why they work so well for reference.

Chapter 5

How to get the data

This chapters shows you how to get the data that you're going to analyze. That not only includes finding the data on a website, but also importing it into a Pandas DataFrame. Once the data is in a DataFrame, you can use the methods of the DataFrame to clean, prepare, analyze, and plot the data.

For some readers, this chapter may present more than you need to know. That's because it not only shows you how to get the data from simple files like CSV or Excel files, but also how to get the data from zip files, databases, Stata files, and JSON files. If that's more than you need, you can read just the portions of this chapter that apply to the types of data that you will be importing.

How to find the data that you want to analyze

Before you can get the data for an analysis, you need to find the data that you want to analyze. So, this chapter starts by presenting some general ideas for finding that data.

Common data sources

Figure 5-1 starts by summarizing some common data sources. That starts with the databases and spreadsheets in your own company. Often, though, you will want to analyze data that's available from third-party websites. That's why this figure lists three websites that will help you find the data that you're looking for.

This figure also lists the websites that provide the data used in the case studies in this book. They include the websites for the Center for Disease Control and the U.S. Forest Service, as well as the FiveThirtyEight website, which is well-known for providing the data for political polls.

How to find and select the data that you want

As you look for data on third-party websites, you'll quickly discover that finding and importing the data that you want can be frustrating. In some cases, you'll need to use an *API* (*Application Programming Interface*) to get the data. You may also need to get permission to use the API, download the data, or both.

Worse, it may be difficult or impossible to find useful documentation for the data. In fact, some sites, like the NBA Stats website, don't provide any public documentation. To work with these stats, you have to use an API that's provided by a third-party website.

This often means that you won't be sure that you have the data that you want until after you import it. Then, you can use Pandas to display and summarize the data as you try to understand it.

In short, there's no easy procedure for finding the data that you want and figuring out what the data in the columns represents. Each website is different, and you usually have to figure out how it works on your own. That's why the rest of this chapter focuses on the Pandas methods that you use for importing data, not on how you find and select the data that you want to import.

The download page for the Childhood Mortality data

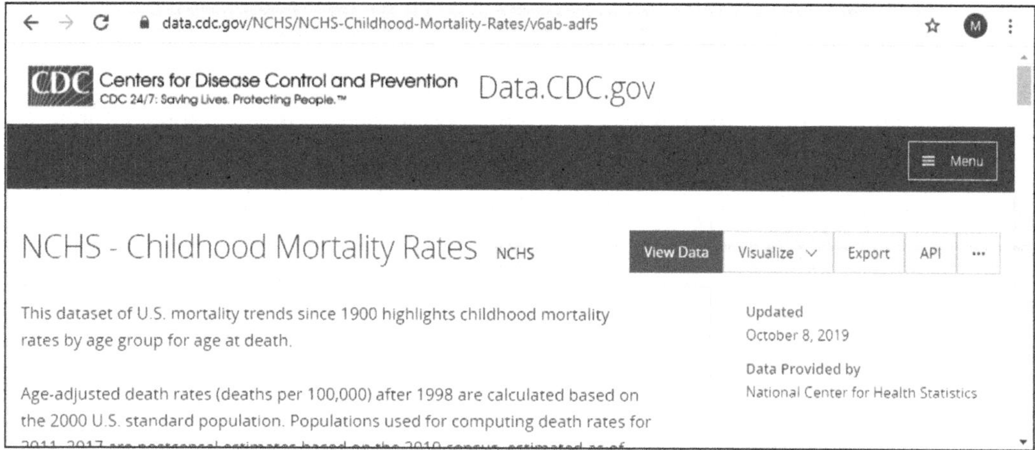

Common sources of data

Internal datasets and databases

This can include everything from departmental spreadsheets to any of the databases used by a corporation.

Third-party websites

This includes the hundreds of websites that let you download data for your own analysis.

Good places to look for external datasets

Google Dataset Search: https://toolbox.google.com/datasetsearch

Kaggle: https://www.kaggle.com/datasets

Registry of Open Data on AWS: https://registry.opendata.aws

The websites for the case studies in this book

- **Child Mortality**: Centers for Disease Control (data.cdc.gov)
- **2016 Polling**: FiveThirtyEight (fivethirtyeight.com)
- **Forest Fires**: U.S. Forest Service (fs.fed.us)
- **Social Survey**: General Social Survey (gss.norc.org)
- **Sports Analytics**: NBA stats (stats.nba.com)

Description

- On some sites, you will need to use an *API* (*Application Programming Interface*) to get the data that you want. An API is a set of methods, functions, or other tools for interacting with a resource.

Figure 5-1 Introduction to getting the data

How to import data into a DataFrame

In many cases, you will be able to import data from a website directly into a DataFrame. But sometimes, you will have to download the data to your computer or unzip a file before you can import the data. In the next three figures, you'll learn the three most common ways to get data into a DataFrame.

How to import data directly into a DataFrame

Figure 5-2 shows how to read (or *import*) data directly into a DataFrame. Here, the first table lists the several types of files that you might be working with. Then, the second table lists the Pandas read methods that you're most likely to use when you import data.

Note, however, that these methods only work when the data is in a tabular form. If the data isn't tabular, the read method will throw an error. As a result, these methods work the best on tabular files like CSV (comma-separated values) and Excel files. But they will fail on files with complex or nested data. For instance, the read_JSON() method will fail if the JSON file has more than one level of nesting.

The first example in this figure shows how to import data that's in CSV format from a website. This is the statement that imports the mortality data from the website for the Center of Disease Control. Here, the only parameter of the read_csv() method is the URL for the file.

By contrast, the second example imports a file after it has been downloaded to your computer. In this case, the parameter of the read_excel() method is the path to the file on your computer.

Some of the file formats for data found on websites

Type	Extension	Description	Contents
CSV	`.csv`	Comma-separated values	One table
TSV	`.tsv`	Tab-separated values	One table
Excel	`.xlsx`, `.xls`	Excel spreadsheet	One or more sheets
Stata	`.dta`	Stata statistical package	Complex data
JSON	`.json`	JavaScript Object Notation	Nested data
XML	`.xml`	Extensible Markup Language	Nested data
SAS	`.sd7`, `.sd6`	SAS statistical package	Complex data
SPSS	`.sav`	SPSS statistical package	Complex data
HDF5	`.h5`	Structured format for large datasets	Complex data
Zip	`.zip`	Archive format	One or more files

Some of the Pandas methods for importing data into a DataFrame

Method	Data format
`read_csv(file)`	CSV
`read_excel(file)`	Excel
`read_stata(file,columns)`	Stata
`read_json(file)`	JSON
`read_hdf(file,columns)`	HDF5
`read_sas(file)`	SAS
`read_sql_query(query,con)`	Database

How to import a CSV file from a website

```
mortality_url = "https://data.cdc.gov/.../rows.csv?accessType=DOWNLOAD"
mortality_data = pd.read_csv(mortality_url)
```

How to import the first sheet of an Excel file that has been downloaded to your computer

```
jobs = pd.read_excel("oesm18all/all_data_M_2018.xlsx")
```

Description

- The Pandas read methods *import* files directly into a DataFrame if the data is in the shape of a table. Otherwise, the operation will fail.
- If the file that's being imported is on a website, the parameter provides the URL that identifies the file on the website.
- If the file that's being imported is on a local disk or server, the parameter provides the path to the file on disk.

Figure 5-2 How to use the read methods to import data

How to download a file to disk before importing it

In some cases, you will want to download a file and save it on disk before you import it into a DataFrame. For instance, you may want to download a CSV or Excel file to your computer so you can open it and review its data before you import it. Figure 5-3 shows how.

Here, the urlretrieve() method of the urllib.request module is used to download the file to your computer and save it with the name in the filename parameter. Once the file is on your computer, you can use the read method for that type of file to import the data into a DataFrame.

If you download a file in a format like CSV or Excel, you can open it in Excel or JupyterLab. Then, you can examine the data before you import it into a DataFrame. In this example, the data is downloaded to a file named president_polls_2016.csv so it can be opened in either Excel or JupyterLab.

The urlretrieve() method of the urllib.request module

Method	Description
`urlretrieve(url,filename)`	Reads the file at the URL and saves it in the named file.

How to download a file to disk before importing it

How to download the file to disk

```
from urllib import request
polls_url = \
    'http://projects.fivethirtyeight.com/.../president_general_polls_2016.csv'
request.urlretrieve(polls_url, filename='president_polls_2016.csv')
```

How to import the file into a DataFrame

```
polls = pd.read_csv('president_polls_2016.csv')
polls.head(2)
```

	cycle	branch	type	matchup	forecastdate	state	startdate	enddate	pollster	grade	...	adjpoll_clinton	adjp
0	2016	President	polls-plus	Clinton vs. Trump vs. Johnson	11/8/16	U.S.	11/3/2016	11/6/2016	ABC News/Washington Post	A+	...	45.20163	
1	2016	President	polls-plus	Clinton vs. Trump vs. Johnson	11/8/16	U.S.	11/1/2016	11/7/2016	Google Consumer Surveys	B	...	43.34557	

2 rows × 27 columns

Description

- On some third-party websites, you can download the file to your computer by clicking on a link or button, so no programming is required. Then, you can use Pandas to import the file into a DataFrame.
- To automate the process, you can use the urlretrieve() method to download the file to your computer. Then, you can use a read method to import the downloaded file into a DataFrame. That makes it easy to update the DataFrame whenever the data changes.
- If you download a file that can be opened by Excel, such as a CSV or Excel file, you can examine the data in Excel before you import it.

Figure 5-3 How to download a file to disk before importing it

How to work with a zip file on disk

In some cases, you'll be working with a *zip file*. That's a file that consists of one or more files in compressed format so they require less storage. In that case, you usually download the zip file to disk, extract the files from the zip file, and read the file that contains the data into a DataFrame. Figure 5-4 shows how.

This figure starts by summarizing the two methods of the ZipFile class that you can use to get the file you want. Then, the first example shows how this works. To download the zip file to disk, you use the urlretrive() method shown in the previous figure. This downloads the file and saves it with the name in the filename parameter.

Next, you use the ZipFile class within a with statement to create an object from the class and assign it to a variable named zip. Then, you can use the extractall() method to extract all the files from the zip file. In addition, you can use a for loop to process the files in the list that's created by the infolist() method. In this case, the loop appends the filenames of those files to the list named file_names, and the print function displays the filename, compressed size, and file size for each file.

In the output for this statement, you can see that this zip file contained only one file and it's in Excel format (xlsx). At that point, you can import the Excel file into a DataFrame in two different ways. The first way is to specify the path and filename that has been displayed, as in:

```
pd.read_excel('oesm18all/all_data_M_2018.xlsx')
```

This works well unless the filename changes when the data is updated. Then, you have to change the filename in the read_excel() method.

The second way to import the file is to specify the position of the filename in the file_names list as in:

```
pd.read_excel(file_names[0])
```

Then, if the filename changes but the position doesn't, the code will still work.

Two methods of the ZipFile module

Method	Description
`extractall()`	Extracts all of the files from the zip file and saves them in the default directory.
`infolist()`	Reads the zip file and returns the file information as a list.

How to download a zip file, extract its files, and list their names

Download the zip file to disk

```
from urllib import request
zip_url = 'https://www.bls.gov/oes/special.requests/oesm18all.zip'
request.urlretrieve(zip_url, filename='oesm18all.zip')
```

Extract the files and list their names

```
from zipfile import ZipFile
file_names = list()
with ZipFile('oesm18all.zip', mode='r') as zip:
    zip.extractall()
    for file in zip.infolist():
        file_names.append(file.filename)
        print(file.filename, file.compress_size, file.file_size)
=================================================================
oesm18all/all_data_M_2018.xlsx 70296790 71834374
```

Two ways to read an extracted file into a DataFrame

By specifying the filename

```
jobs = pd.read_excel("oesm18all/all_data_M_2018.xlsx")
```

By specifying the position of the file in the file_names list

```
jobs = pd.read_excel(file_names[0])
```

Description

- If the data that you download is in a *zip file*, you need to unzip the file before you can access the files that it contains. To do that, you can use the methods of the ZipFile class that is imported from the zipfile package.
- After you use the extractall() method to extract the files from the zip file, you can use the infolist() method to get the file information.
- After you get the file information, you can use it to import the right file into a DataFrame.
- If you want to be sure that your Python code will work even if the data is updated and the filename in the zip file has changed, you can save the filenames in a list. Then, you can refer to the location in that list instead of using the current filename.

Figure 5-4 How to work with a zip file on disk

How to get database data into a DataFrame

If you work with your company's data, that data is likely to be in a database. But that's also true for some of the data that you get from third-party websites. Either way, the next two figures show how to get the data into a DataFrame. This assumes that you have a basic knowledge of how databases and SQL queries work.

How to run queries against a database

The table at the top of figure 5-5 summarizes some of the types of databases that you can use with Python. That includes the three most popular databases: MySQL, Oracle, and SQL Server. It also includes SQLite, which is a popular, open-source, relational database that can be embedded into programs.

In this figure and the next, SQLite is used as the database because it's easy to set up and because Python has built-in support for working with it. However, the concepts are the same for whatever database you're going to use. You just need to find out the details for connecting to the type of database that you're using.

To import data from a database into a DataFrame, you need to run a query that gets the data you want to import. To run any query, you use the connect() method to create a *connection object*. You use the cursor() method of the connection object to return a *cursor object*. And you use the execute() and fetchall() methods of the cursor object to execute a query and fetch all the rows in the result set. Although this figure shows how to run queries with SQLite, this works the same for most databases.

The example in this figure shows how this works. Here, the first group of statements creates a connection object for a database that has been downloaded to disk, and it creates a cursor object from that connection object. Then, the second group of statements chains the fetchall() method to an execute() method that runs a query that gets the names of all of tables in the master table for the database. In the partial results, you can see that "Fires" is one of the tables in that database.

Packages for connecting to databases in Python

Package name	Database	Availability
`sqlite3`	SQLite	Built-in
`pymysql`	MySQL	Needs to be installed
`psycopg2`	PostgreSQL	Needs to be installed
`cx_oracle`	Oracle	Needs to be installed
`pymssql`	SQL Server	Needs to be installed

The connect() method of the SQLite module

Method	Description
`connect(path)`	Returns a connection object for the database identified by the path.

The cursor() method of a connection object

Method	Description
`cursor()`	Returns a cursor object.

Two methods of a cursor object

Method	Description
`execute(sql)`	Executes the SQL statement.
`fetchall()`	Returns a list containing all the rows in the result set.

How to run queries on a SQLite database that has been downloaded to disk

Create a connection object and a cursor object

```
import sqlite3
fires_con = sqlite3.connect('Data/FPA_FOD_20170508.sqlite')
fires_cur = fires_con.cursor()
```

Run a query that lists the tables in the database

```
fires_cur.execute(
    'SELECT name FROM sqlite_master WHERE type="table"').fetchall()
==================================================================
[('spatial_ref_sys',),
 ('spatialite_history',),
 ...
 ('Fires',),
 ...
 ('NWCG_UnitIDActive_20170109',)]
```

Description

- To execute a SELECT statement, you use the cursor() method of the *connection object* to create a *cursor object*. Then, you chain the execute() and fetchall() methods of the cursor object to execute the SQL statement and fetch all of its rows.

Figure 5-5 How to run queries against a database

How to use a SQL query to import data into a DataFrame

To import the data from a SQL query into a DataFrame, you use the read_sql_query() method that's shown in figure 5-6. Before you can do that, though, you need to decide what the SQL query should include.

One way to do that is shown by the first example in this figure. This is a query that runs a PRAGMA statement that gets the table information for the Fires table. As the partial results show, this lists the names of the columns as well as the datatype for each column. That in turn provides the basis for selecting the columns that will be imported into the DataFrame.

In case you aren't familiar with *PRAGMA statements*, they are SQL extensions to SQLite that can be used to query the SQLite library for internal data. In this example, the statement gets the internal information for the Fires table.

Once you know what you want to import, you can pass a SQL query to the read_sql_query() method to import the data from the query into a DataFrame, as shown by the second example in this figure. Here, the SQL query selects seven columns from the Fires table. It also converts the dates in the DISCOVERY_DATE column to datetime objects. This limits the data that's imported so the DataFrame will require little or no cleaning.

Of course, you can also use your DBMS (Database Management System) to explore the data and create the query that you want to use for importing the data. For instance, you can use DB Browser to do that with a SQLite database. Then, when you're sure that you've created the right query, you can use it to import the data.

After you examine the data with your DBMS, you may want to improve the query. For instance, you could change the query in this example so it only imports rows in which the FIRE_SIZE is over 10 acres. Because this database contains more than 1.8 million rows, that could make everything work more efficiently.

The read_sql_query() method of the Pandas module

Method	Description
`read_sql_query(SQL,connection)`	Imports the query data into a DataFrame.

How to get information about a table

```
fires_cur.execute('PRAGMA table_info(Fires)').fetchall()
========================================================
[(0, 'OBJECTID', 'integer', 1, None, 1),
 (1, 'FOD_ID', 'int32', 0, None, 0),
 (2, 'FPA_ID', 'text(100)', 0, None, 0),
 ...
 (12, 'FIRE_CODE', 'text(10)', 0, None, 0),
 (13, 'FIRE_NAME', 'text(255)', 0, None, 0),
 ...
 (19, 'FIRE_YEAR', 'int16', 0, None, 0),
 (20, 'DISCOVERY_DATE', 'realdate', 0, None, 0),
 ...
 (28, 'FIRE_SIZE', 'float64', 0, None, 0),
 (29, 'FIRE_SIZE_CLASS', 'text(1)', 0, None, 0),
 (30, 'LATITUDE', 'float64', 0, None, 0),
 (31, 'LONGITUDE', 'float64', 0, None, 0),
 ...
 (34, 'STATE', 'text(255)', 0, None, 0),
 ...
 (38, 'Shape', 'POINT', 1, None, 0)]
```

How to import the data from a query into a DataFrame

```
fires = pd.read_sql_query(
    '''SELECT STATE, FIRE_YEAR, DATETIME(DISCOVERY_DATE) AS DISCOVERY_DATE,
       FIRE_NAME, FIRE_SIZE, LATITUDE, LONGITUDE
       FROM Fires''', fires_con)
```

	STATE	FIRE_YEAR	DISCOVERY_DATE	FIRE_NAME	FIRE_SIZE	LATITUDE	LONGITUDE
0	CA	2005	2005-02-02 00:00:00	FOUNTAIN	0.10	40.036944	-121.005833
1	CA	2004	2004-05-12 00:00:00	PIGEON	0.25	38.933056	-120.404444
2	CA	2004	2004-05-31 00:00:00	SLACK	0.10	38.984167	-120.735556
3	CA	2004	2004-06-28 00:00:00	DEER	0.10	38.559167	-119.913333
4	CA	2004	2004-06-28 00:00:00	STEVENOT	0.10	38.559167	-119.933056

Description

- To import data from a SQL query into a DataFrame, you call the read_sql_query() method and pass it two parameters: a SQL query and a connection object.
- Before you create the SQL query for importing the data, you need to run queries that help you decide what to import. When you're using a SQLite database, those queries can include *PRAGMA statements* that return information about a table.

Figure 5-6 How to use a SQL query to import data into a DataFrame

How to work with a Stata file

A *Stata file* consists of a data file and a *metadata container*. This container is an object that provides information about the data file. With that information, you can use the data in the data file to build a Pandas DataFrame. The next two figures show how.

Of course, if you aren't going to be working with Stata files, you can skip this topic. Just know that it's here whenever you need it.

How to get and explore the metadata of a Stata file

Figure 5-7 shows how to use the read_dta() method of the pyreadstat module to read just the metadata of a Stata file into a DataFrame. Since the pyreadstat module isn't included in the Anaconda distribution, you may need to install it, as shown by the first example in this figure.

The second example shows how to read a Stata file. This example assumes that the data has already been downloaded to disk, so the file is read from disk. Then, to read just the metadata, you set the metadataonly parameter to True, which means that the data file won't be read. You also assign the result of the read_dta() method to two variables: one for an empty data file, and one for the metadata file. In this example, these files are named gss_empty and gss_meta.

At that point, you can use the attributes of the metadata container to get more information about the data in the data file. So in the third example, the number_columns attribute shows that the data file has 6,110 columns! The number_rows attribute shows that the data file has 64,814 rows. The column_names attribute shows the column names for those 6,110 columns. And if this example included the column_labels attribute, you would see the descriptions of the data in the columns.

The read_dta() method of the pyreadstat package

Method	Description
`read_dta(filename,columns, metadataonly)`	Reads a Stata file and returns two objects: A DataFrame for the data and a metadata container. If metadataonly is set to True, the DataFrame is empty.

Some of the attributes for a metadata container

Attribute	Description
`column_names`	The names of the columns in the dataset.
`column_labels`	Descriptions of the data in the columns of the dataset.
`number_columns`	The number of columns in the dataset.
`number_rows`	The number of rows in the dataset.

How to install the pyreadstat module with a conda command

```
conda install --channel conda-forge pyreadstat --yes
```

How to get the metadata from a Stata file that has been downloaded to disk

```
import pyreadstat
gss_stata_filename = 'GSS7218_R3.DTA'

gss_empty, gss_meta = pyreadstat.read_dta(
    gss_stata_filename,
    metadataonly=True)
type(gss_meta)
==================================================
<pyreadstat._readstat_parser.metadata_container
```

What the attributes of the metadata container can tell you

```
print("Number of columns:", gss_meta.number_columns)
print("Number of rows:", gss_meta.number_rows)
print("Column names:", gss_meta.column_names)
==============================================================================
Number of columns: 6110
Number of rows: 64814
Column names: ['year', 'id', 'wrkstat', 'hrs1', 'hrs2', 'evwork', 'occ',
'prestige', 'wrkslf', 'wrkgovt', 'commute', 'industry', 'occ80', 'prestg80',
'indus80', 'indus07', 'occonet', 'found', 'occ10', 'occindv', 'occstatus',
'occtag', 'prestg10', 'prestg105plus', 'indus10', 'indstatus', 'indtag',
...
```

Description

- A *Stata file* consists of a data file and a *metadata container.*
- The metadata container provides information about the data, including the column names that identify the columns and the column labels that describe the data in the columns.
- The pyreadstat package provides methods for working with Stata, SAS, and SPSS files.

Figure 5-7 How to get and explore the metadata of a Stata file

How to build DataFrames for the metadata and the data

The first example in figure 5-8 shows how to use the DataFrame() constructor to build a DataFrame from the metadata. Here, the column labels are used as the data for the DataFrame. The column names are used as the index. And the constructor assigns the name "description" to the column that contains the data. The result is a DataFrame that shows the column name and description for each of the 6,110 columns in the data file. This information can then be used to create a DataFrame that contains the data that you want to analyze.

This is illustrated by the second example in this figure. This time, the read_stata() method is used to import the data of the Stata file, and the columns parameter specifies the eight columns that should be imported into the DataFrame. Although you could use the read_dta() method without the metadataonly parameter to import the data, this also imports the metadata, which isn't needed. In addition, the read_stata() method is easier to use because it's available from the Pandas library. As a result, you don't need to import the pyreadstat module to call it.

In practice, of course, you would study the documentation for the columns and make sure that you import all the ones that you're interested in. You will see how that works in the case study for the Social Survey.

For now, though, please notice the number of NaN values that are in the 5 rows that are displayed. Those represent missing values, and missing values are something that you'll have to deal with when you clean the data. You'll learn how to do that in the next chapter.

The DataFrame() constructor

Method	Description
`DataFrame(params)`	Constructs a DataFrame.

Parameter	Description
`data`	Can be an array, dictionary, or other object that's shaped like a table.
`columns`	Column labels. If they aren't specified, they will be generated.
`index`	Row labels. If they aren't specified, they will be generated.

How to build a DataFrame for the column descriptions in the metadata

```
import pandas as pd
meta_cols=pd.DataFrame(
    data=gss_meta.column_labels,
    index=gss_meta.column_names,
    columns=['description'])
meta_cols.head(5)
```

	description
year	gss year for this respondent
id	respondent id number
wrkstat	labor force status
hrs1	number of hours worked last week
hrs2	number of hours usually work a week

How to import seven columns of the data into a DataFrame

```
gss_data = pd.read_stata('GSS7218_R3.DTA',
    columns=['year','id','wrkstat','hrs1','hrs2','evwork','wrkslf','wrkgovt'])
gss_data.tail()
```

	year	id	wrkstat	hrs1	hrs2	evwork	wrkslf	wrkgovt
64809	2018	2344	working fulltime	36	NaN	NaN	someone else	government
64810	2018	2345	working parttime	36	NaN	NaN	someone else	private
64811	2018	2346	retired	NaN	NaN	yes	someone else	private
64812	2018	2347	retired	NaN	NaN	yes	someone else	private
64813	2018	2348	keeping house	NaN	NaN	yes	someone else	government

Description

- To help you understand the data in the columns of a Stata file, you can build a DataFrame that consists of the column names and the column labels in the metadata.
- Once you understand the data for a dataset, you can use the read_stata() method to read the specified columns into a DataFrame.

Figure 5-8 How to build DataFrames for the metadata and the data

How to work with a JSON file

If a *JSON file* has just one level of nesting, it is tabular so it can be imported by the Pandas read_json() method. Most of the time, though, a JSON file has two or more levels of nesting so it isn't tabular. Then, the data has to be downloaded to disk and read into a Python dictionary before it can be used to build a DataFrame object. The next three figures show how this works.

Of course, you can skip this topic if you aren't going to be working with JSON files. Just know that it's here whenever you need it.

How to download a JSON file to disk

To download a JSON file to disk, you use the urlretrieve() method of the request module in the urllib package. Figure 5-3 showed how to use this method to download a CSV file, and the first example in figure 5-9 shows how to use it to download a JSON file.

Here, the first parameter of the urlretrieve() method is the URL for the file, and the second parameter is the filename that will be used for the saved JSON file. In this case, the file is saved in the same directory as the Notebook.

In this example, the JSON file is named shots.json where json is the extension to the filename. You should know, however, that the URL for this data gets only the shots data for Stephen Curry of the Golden State Warriors.

How to open a JSON file in JupyterLab

Once the JSON file is on your disk, you can use JupyterLab to open it. To do that, you just double-click on the filename in the File Browser. Then, the file is opened in a new tab, as shown in the first screenshot in this figure. As you can see, it shows the root level of the JSON file.

In this case, the root level consists of three sublevels: resource, parameters, and resultSets. Then, you can click on the triangles in front of these levels to drill down into them, as shown in the next figure.

How to download a JSON file to disk

```
import json
from urllib import request
shots_url = 'https://www.murach.com/python_analysis/shots.json'
request.urlretrieve(shots_url, filename='shots.json')
```

Double-click on the JSON file in JupyterLab to open it

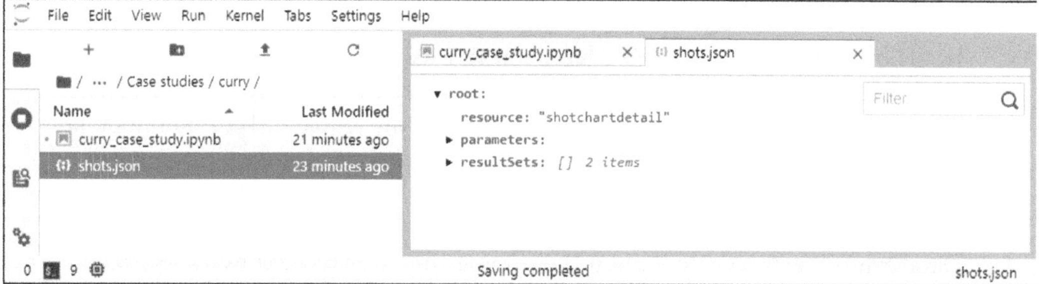

The root level of the JSON file

```
▾ root:
    resource: "shotchartdetail"
  ▸ parameters:
  ▸ resultSets: [] 2 items
```

Description

- When a JSON file has more than two levels of data, it can't be read by the Pandas read_json() method. Then, you need to convert it to a dictionary object and figure out how to build a DataFrame from the data.
- After you download a JSON file with JupyterLab, you can double-click on it in the File Browser to open the file in a new tab. Then, you can *drill down* into the data by clicking on the triangles that precede each of the levels, as shown in the next figure.

Figure 5-9 How to download and open a JSON file

How to drill down into the data

Figure 5-10 shows how you can use JupyterLab to *drill down* into the JSON data as you try to find the data that you want to work with. In the first screenshot, you can see the first two levels of the resultSets data. This helps you decide that you want to work with the Shot_Chart_Detail data, not the LeagueAverages data, and that you want to work with the resultSets[0] data.

Then, the next two screenshots show the data in the headers and rowSet levels of the resultSets[0] data. Here, you can see that the headers data provides the names for the columns and the rowSet data provides the data for the rows. You can also see the data for the first row in the rowSet data. But if you look at the notation for the rowSet data, you can see that it provides for 11,846 items (one for each shot that Stephen Curry took in each game that he played).

Once you locate the data that you want to work with, you can use the DataFrame constructor to build a DataFrame from it. The next figure shows how.

The first two levels of the resultSets data


```
▼ root:
    resource: "shotchartdetail"
  ▶ parameters:
  ▼ resultSets: [] 2 items
    ▼ 0:
        name: "Shot_Chart_Detail"
      ▶ headers: [] 24 items
      ▶ rowSet: [] 11846 items
    ▼ 1:
        name: "LeagueAverages"
      ▶ headers: [] 7 items
      ▶ rowSet: [] 20 items
```


The headers and rowSet levels of the resultSets[0] data


```
▼ root:
    resource: "shotchartdetail"
  ▶ parameters:
  ▼ resultSets: [] 2 items
    ▼ 0:
        name: "Shot_Chart_Detail"
      ▼ headers: [] 24 items
          0: "GRID_TYPE"
          1: "GAME_ID"
          2: "GAME_EVENT_ID"
          3: "PLAYER_ID"
          4: "PLAYER_NAME"
          5: "TEAM_ID"
          6: "TEAM_NAME"
          7: "PERIOD"
          8: "MINUTES_REMAINING"
          9: "SECONDS_REMAINING"
          10: "EVENT_TYPE"
          11: "ACTION_TYPE"
          12: "SHOT_TYPE"
          13: "SHOT_ZONE_BASIC"
          14: "SHOT_ZONE_AREA"
          15: "SHOT_ZONE_RANGE"
          16: "SHOT_DISTANCE"
          17: "LOC_X"
          18: "LOC_Y"
          19: "SHOT_ATTEMPTED_FLAG"
          20: "SHOT_MADE_FLAG"
          21: "GAME_DATE"
          22: "HTM"
          23: "VTM"
```

```
▼ root:
    resource: "shotchartdetail"
  ▶ parameters:
  ▼ resultSets: [] 2 items
    ▼ 0:
        name: "Shot_Chart_Detail"
      ▶ headers: [] 24 items
      ▼ rowSet: [] 11846 items
        ▼ 0: [] 24 items
            0: "Shot Chart Detail"
            1: "0020900015"
            2: 4
            3: 201939
            4: "Stephen Curry"
            5: 1610612744
            6: "Golden State Warriors"
            7: 1
            8: 11
            9: 25
            10: "Missed Shot"
            11: "Jump Shot"
            12: "3PT Field Goal"
            13: "Above the Break 3"
            14: "Right Side Center(RC)"
            15: "24+ ft."
            16: 26
            17: 99
            18: 249
            19: 1
            20: 0
            21: "20091028"
            22: "GSW"
            23: "HOU"
```


Figure 5-10 How to drill down into the JSON data

How to build a DataFrame for the data

Before you can use the DataFrame constructor to build a DataFrame for JSON data, you need to convert it to a dictionary. To do that, you can use the json.load() method as shown in the first example in figure 5-11. This code opens the JSON file, and then it converts it to a dictionary,

After you create the dictionary, you can use the DataFrame() constructor to build the DataFrame for the data. But first, you need to isolate the headers and data that you're going to use to construct the DataFrame.

This is illustrated by the first two statements in the second example. First, the shot data that you identified by drilling down into the data is stored in the allRows variable. Then, the headers that you identified are stored in the columnHeaders variable.

At that point, you can use the DataFrame constructor to build the DataFrame. In this example, the data parameter is set to allRows, and the columns parameter is set to columnHeaders. The result is a DataFrame with 11,846 rows and 24 columns.

You may have noticed that a list comprehension is used in the statement that creates the columnHeaders variable. This list comprehension uses the Python lower() method to change the strings for the headers to lowercase. You can see the results in the display of the data in the shots DataFrame.

The load() method of a JSON object

Method	Description
`load()`	Converts the data in a JSON file to a dictionary.

How to convert a JSON file to a dictionary object

```
with open('shots.json') as json_data:
    shots = json.load(json_data)
```

The DataFrame() constructor

Method	Description
`DataFrame(params)`	Constructs a DataFrame.
Parameter	**Description**
`data`	Can be an array, dictionary, or other object that's shaped like a table.
`columns`	Column labels. If they aren't specified, they will be generated.
`index`	Row labels. If they aren't specified, they will be generated.

How to use the DataFrame() constructor to build a DataFrame for the shots

```
allRows = shots['resultSets'][0]['rowSet']
columnHeaders = [x.lower() for x in shots['resultSets'][0]['headers']]
shots = pd.DataFrame(data=allRows, columns=columnHeaders)
shots.head()
```

	grid_type	game_id	game_event_id	player_id	player_name	team_id	team_name	period	minutes_remaining	seconds_remainin
0	Shot Chart Detail	0020900015	4	201939	Stephen Curry	1610612744	Golden State Warriors	1	11	2
1	Shot Chart Detail	0020900015	17	201939	Stephen Curry	1610612744	Golden State Warriors	1	9	3
2	Shot Chart Detail	0020900015	53	201939	Stephen Curry	1610612744	Golden State Warriors	1	6	
3	Shot Chart Detail	0020900015	141	201939	Stephen Curry	1610612744	Golden State Warriors	2	9	4
4	Shot Chart Detail	0020900015	249	201939	Stephen Curry	1610612744	Golden State Warriors	2	2	1

5 rows × 24 columns

Description

- Before you can use the DataFrame constructor to build the DataFrame, you need to convert the JSON data to a dictionary.
- When you build the DataFrame, the rowSet variable in the first result set (resultSets[0]) provides the shot data and the headers variable in that result set provides the headers.

Figure 5-11 How to build a DataFrame for the data

Perspective

Now that you've completed this chapter, you should have the skills that you need for importing data from the most common file types into a DataFrame: CSV, Excel, Stata, and JSON. You should also be able to import data from a database into a DataFrame, and you should be able to get the data you need from zip files.

Often, though, importing the data is the easy part of getting the data. The hard part is finding the data that you want to analyze, getting access to that data, and figuring out what portions of the data you want to import. Although this chapter has given you a few ideas for how to go about that, there's no one right way to find and access what you're after. And to compound the problem, these websites keep changing.

Terms

API (Application Programming Interface)
import data
zip file
connection object
cursor object
PRAGMA statement
Stata file
metadata container
JSON file
drill down

Summary

- Finding and accessing the data on a third-party website is often the hardest part of getting the data. To do that, you may have to use an *API* (*Application Programming Interface*) that provides the information that you will need.
- When you use a Pandas read method to get the data for an analysis, you *import* the data from its source into a DataFrame. But if the data isn't in tabular form, the method will fail.
- If you download a CSV or Excel file to your computer, you can use Excel or JupyterLab to examine the data before you import it.
- You can use the methods of the ZipFile class to work with a *zip file* that has been downloaded to your computer. These methods let you extract the files from the zip file and get information about each file.
- You can use the read_sql_query() method to import the data from a database query into a DataFrame.
- A *Stata file* consists of a data file and a *metadata container* that provides information about the data in the data file. You can use the metadata to figure out which columns to use when you build a DataFrame from the data.
- When a *JSON file* has more than one level of nesting, you need to download the file to disk, use JupyterLab to drill down into the data, and use the DataFrame() constructor to build a DataFrame from the data.

About the exercises for this chapter

The exercises that follow give you a chance to experiment with the techniques for getting the data from a website into a DataFrame. For now, you only need to do the ones that apply to the types of files that you'll be working with.

Exercise 5-1 Get data from a CSV file

In this exercise, you'll get polling data about the 2016 presidential election in the US. To do that, you'll download a CSV file, save it to your disk, and read that CSV file into a DataFrame.

1. Open the Notebook named ex_5-1 that should be in this folder:

   `/exercises/ch05/ex1`

   Note that this file includes one cell that imports the Pandas library and another cell that specifies the URL for the CSV file.
2. With figure 5-3 as a guide, add a cell that downloads the CSV file for the Polling data and saves it to your local disk.
3. Find the CSV on your disk and open it. This is an easy way to examine the data in a dataset.
4. Add a cell that uses the read_csv() method to read the downloaded CSV file into a DataFrame.
5. Add a cell that calls the info() method of the DataFrame to display some information about its columns.

Exercise 5-2 Get data from an Excel file in a zip file

In this exercise, you'll get data about jobs in the US. To do that, you'll download a zip file that contains an Excel file, save it to your disk, unzip the Excel file, and read it into a DataFrame.

1. Open the Notebook named ex_5-2 that should be in this folder:

   `/exercises/ch05/ex2`

   Note that this file includes one cell that imports the Pandas library and another cell that specifies the URL for the zip file.
2. With figure 5-3 as a guide, add a cell that downloads the zip file and saves it in the same folder as the Notebook. This may take a while because the Excel file that it contains has over 400,000 rows.
3. With figure 5-4 as a guide, add another cell to extract the files from the zip file and display the names of those files.
4. Find the Excel file on your disk and open it. Note that this file contains two tabs: one for the data and one for documentation.

5. Review the documentation tab to determine whether it's useful.
6. Add a cell that reads the data from the Excel file into a DataFrame and displays its first five rows.

Exercise 5-3 Get data from a database

In this exercise, you'll get data about forest fires in the US. To do that, you'll download a zip file that contains a SQLite database file, unzip the database file, and read selected data from the database into a DataFrame.

1. Open the Notebook named ex_5-3 that should be in this folder:

   `/exercises/ch05/ex3`

   Note that this file includes one cell that imports the Pandas library and another cell that specifies the URL for a zip file that contains a database.
2. With figure 5-3 as a guide, add a cell that downloads the zip file and saves it in the same folder as the Notebook. It may take more than a minute for this cell to run because the database is large.
3. With figure 5-4 as a guide, add a cell that extracts the files from the zip file and prints the filenames that are in the zip file. Then, note that the first file is a SQLite file in the Data folder, and the fourth one is a PDF file in the Supplements folder.
4. Find the PDF file, open it, and see whether it provides any useful documentation.

Run queries against the database

5. With figure 5-5 as a guide, add a cell that creates a connection object and a cursor object for the database file. Then, run a query that lists the names of the tables in the database. Note that one of the tables is named Fires.
6. With figure 5-6 as a guide, run a query that lists information about the columns in the Fires table.

Read the results of a SQL query into a DataFrame

7. With figure 5-6 as a guide, add a cell that uses the read_sql_query() method to read the query data into a DataFrame. This retrieves thousands of rows, so it may take a long time for the query to execute.
8. Add a cell that displays the first 5 rows of the DataFrame.
9. Add a cell that calls the info() method of the DataFrame. Note that it has more than 1,880,000 rows and uses 114.8+ MB of memory.

Exercise 5-4 Get data from a Stata file

In this exercise, you'll get data about social surveys that are conducted by NORC at the University of Chicago. To do that, you'll get data from a Stata file that's stored in a zip file.

1. Open the Notebook named ex_5-4 that should be in this folder:

   `/exercises/ch05/ex4`

   Note that this Notebook includes cells that import the Pandas library, download a zip file that contains a Stata file, and unzip that file.
2. Run the cells in the Notebook. Note that the downloaded zip file unzips into three files: a PDF for release notes, the data file, and a PDF file named GSS_Codebook.
3. Find the GSS_Codebook PDF and open it. Go to page 1 (after the front matter) and note that it lists the column names and descriptions. That is useful information.

Build a DataFrame for the metadata

4. Add a cell that gets the metadata container for the Stata file.
5. Use the attributes shown in figure 5-7 to display information about the metadata. Note that this dataset has 6,110 columns! To clear the output for the cell, you can right-click on it and select Clear Outputs.
6. Use the first procedure in figure 5-8 to build a DataFrame for the metadata. Then, display all of its rows and scroll through them to see the type of data that this metadata includes. Note that this is the same information that's in the GSS_Codebook PDF.

Read the data into a DataFrame

7. Use the second procedure in figure 5-8 to read the data from at least five columns in the Stata data file into a DataFrame, and display the results.

Exercise 5-5 Get data from a JSON file

In this exercise, you'll get data from a JSON file that contains data about the shots taken by basketball superstar Stephen Curry.

1. Open the Notebook named ex_5-5 that should be in this folder:

   `/exercises/ch05/ex5`
2. Run the first two cells to import the Pandas library, download the JSON file, and save it on disk in a file named shots.json.
3. Find the shots.json file in the File Browser, open it by double-clicking on it, and then drill down into the data as shown in figure 5-10.
4. With figure 5-11 as a guide, convert the JSON file to a dictionary object. Then, build the DataFrame for the shot data, and display the results.

Chapter 6

How to clean the data

Like it or not, most of the data that you work with will have data problems that need to be fixed before you can analyze the data. That's true whether you get the data from a third-party website or you're using data from your own company's databases or spreadsheets. In fact, some estimates say that cleaning the data takes from 20 to 25 percent of the time in a typical analysis project.

What's worse is that if you don't clean the data, the results of your analysis are likely to be misleading or inaccurate. That's why this chapter presents the skills that you'll need for cleaning the various types of data that you'll be working with.

Introduction to data cleaning

When you clean the data for an analysis, you should have a general idea of how to get started and what to look for. So that's how this chapter begins.

A general plan for cleaning the data

In figure 6-1, you can see the basic workflow for cleaning the data in a dataset. Of course, you won't have to do all of these tasks for every dataset. But for some datasets, you will.

As the procedure in this figure shows, you start by identifying the problems that need to be fixed. If there's any documentation for the dataset, it makes sense to start with that. For instance, the Excel spreadsheet in this figure documents some of the data issues for a Jobs dataset. Note that this is in one tab of the spreadsheet while the data is in the other tab.

Then, after you've reviewed the documentation, you can examine the data, as shown in the next three figures. At that point, you can plan the cleaning that needs to be done.

To simplify the data, you usually start by dropping unnecessary rows and columns. That may include rows and columns that don't present useful information, duplicate rows, and rows that aren't within the scope of your analysis. After that, you may want to rename columns so it's easier to tell what they contain.

After you've simplified the data, you're ready to fix any data problems. That includes finding and fixing missing data. It includes applying the right data types to data that has been imported as objects. And that may include handling *outliers* that are datapoints so far off the mean that they either represent invalid data or valid values that are likely to skew the results.

Before you start cleaning the data, though, you should make sure that you've set the goals for your analysis. That will help you decide which rows and which columns are okay to drop. In fact, those goals should guide your actions throughout the cleaning process. Above all, be sure that you aren't dropping rows or columns that will affect the results of your analysis.

A general plan for cleaning a DataFrame

Identify the problems

1. Review whatever documentation is available to help you understand the data.
2. Examine the data after you import it into a DataFrame.
3. Plan the cleaning that needs to be done.

Simplify the data

4. Drop duplicate rows.
5. Drop rows that aren't needed for the analysis.
6. Drop columns that aren't needed for the analysis.
7. Rename columns so the names are easier to understand.

Fix data problems

8. Find and fix missing values.
9. Fix data type problems like dates or numbers that are imported as strings.
10. Find and fix outliers.

But before you start cleaning...

- Be sure that you've set the goals for your analysis. That will help you decide what cleaning needs to be done.

Documentation that identifies some data problems in the Jobs data

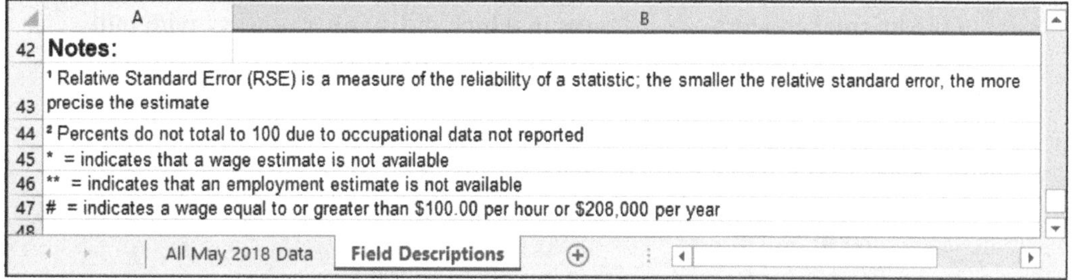

	A	B
42	**Notes:**	
43	[1] Relative Standard Error (RSE) is a measure of the reliability of a statistic; the smaller the relative standard error, the more precise the estimate	
44	[2] Percents do not total to 100 due to occupational data not reported	
45	* = indicates that a wage estimate is not available	
46	** = indicates that an employment estimate is not available	
47	# = indicates a wage equal to or greater than $100.00 per hour or $208,000 per year	

All May 2018 Data | Field Descriptions

Descriptions

- Most datasets aren't clean when you import them. So to get accurate results, you need to clean them before you analyze and visualize the data.
- Data cleaning typically takes as much as 20 to 25 percent of the total time for an analysis.
- When you drop rows or columns, you need to be sure that you aren't dropping data that will affect your analysis.

Figure 6-1 A general plan for cleaning the data

What the info() method can tell you

After you review the documentation for a dataset, you can do your own analysis of potential data problems. To start, you can run the info() method of a DataFrame as shown in figure 6-2. Here, the verbose=True parameter ensures that the method will return all the information rather than an abridged version. The memory_usage='deep' parameter ensures that the memory usage will be accurate. And the show_counts=True parameter ensures that the method will return the non-null counts for each column.

Depending on how your system is set up, you may not need to code the verbose and show_counts parameters. To see whether you need them, you can run the method with and without those parameters. But as strange as it sounds, you do need to code the memory_usage parameter to get an accurate value for memory usage.

When the info() method displays the information, you look for potential problems. First, you should look for object (or string) columns that look like they contain numbers or dates. For instance, columns with names like "total", "mean", and "pct" should probably be numeric data types. And columns with names that include "date" or "time" should probably be datetime objects.

Second, you should analyze the columns that have non-null counts that are less than the number of rows in the DataFrame. For instance, the "rawpoll_mcmullin" and "adjpoll_mcmullin" columns have only 90 non-null values. What's going on there?

Of particular concern are columns in which the number of rows with null or non-null values is extremely small because those rows are likely to contain errors. In the polling data, for example, the "samplessize" column must have just 3 null values because it has 3 fewer non-null values than there are rows. As a result, those rows are likely to contain errors.

Three parameters of the info() method

Parameter	Description
`verbose=True`	Ensures that the method returns info for all of the columns.
`memory_usage='deep'`	Ensures that the memory usage information is accurate.
`show_counts=True`	Ensures that the non-null counts for each column will be displayed.

Partial results for the info() method when run on the Polls data

```
polls.info(verbose=True, memory_usage='deep', show_counts=True)
================================================================
<class 'pandas.core.frame.DataFrame'>
RangeIndex: 12624 entries, 0 to 12623
Data columns (total 27 columns):
forecastdate        12624 non-null object
startdate           12624 non-null object
enddate             12624 non-null object
samplesize          12621 non-null float64
rawpoll_mcmullin    90 non-null float64
adjpoll_mcmullin    90 non-null float64
dtypes: float64(10), int64(3), object(14)
memory usage: 12.9 MB
```

Likely dates stored as strings

3 rows have null values: Why?

Mostly null values: Why?

Partial results for the info() method when run on the Jobs data

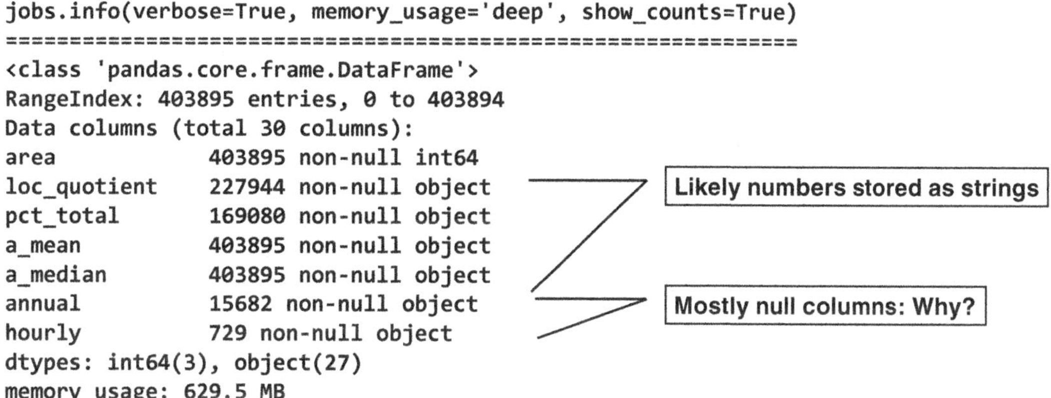

```
jobs.info(verbose=True, memory_usage='deep', show_counts=True)
================================================================
<class 'pandas.core.frame.DataFrame'>
RangeIndex: 403895 entries, 0 to 403894
Data columns (total 30 columns):
area            403895 non-null int64
loc_quotient    227944 non-null object
pct_total       169080 non-null object
a_mean          403895 non-null object
a_median        403895 non-null object
annual          15682 non-null object
hourly          729 non-null object
dtypes: int64(3), object(27)
memory usage: 629.5 MB
```


What you should be looking for

- Object or string variables that look like they should be dates or numbers.
- Non-null counts that are lower than the non-null counts of other columns may indicate missing data.
- Small numbers of non-nulls or nulls may indicate problems with related columns or rows.

Figure 6-2 What the info() method can tell you

What the unique values can tell you

The first example in figure 6-3 shows how to use the nunique() method to display the number of unique values there are in each column of a DataFrame. Then, the second example shows how to use a lambda expression that uses the unique() method to display the unique values in each column. The resulting information can help you understand the data.

First, you should look for columns with just one unique value. For instance, the “cycle”, “branch”, “matchup”, and “forecastdate” columns have only one unique value, and the four columns together identify the poll. Since these columns won’t have anything to do with your analysis, you can drop them from the DataFrame.

Second, you should look for columns with a small number of unique values, especially strings or objects. These columns often provide values that identify groups of data. As a result, you may want to use one of these columns to filter the rows of data and limit the scope of the project.

For instance, the “type” column in this figure has just three values: “polls-plus”, “now-cast”, and “polls-only”. As it turns out, the “now-cast” values identify the actual values of the votes that were cast in the poll, while the other two values represent calculated values that were based on the actual values. As a result, you may want to drop the “polls-plus” and “polls-only” rows, and base your analysis on just the “now-cast” rows.

Third, you should look for columns with as many unique values as rows in the DataFrame. These are likely to be ID or index columns that identify each row in the database with a unique value like a reference number. If no columns have as many unique values as rows in the DataFrame, it may mean that two or more columns are used to identify unique rows.

Last, you should look for ID or index columns with fewer rows than the number of rows in the DataFrame. In the Polls data, for example, the “poll_id” and “question_id” columns have exactly one-third the number of unique values as the DataFrame has rows. As it turns out, these columns do identify each poll, but there are three versions of the results for each poll that are specified by the “type” column: “polls-plus”, “now-cast”, and “polls-only”.

The nunique() and unique() methods

Method	Description
`nunique(dropna=False)`	Returns the number of unique values in each column.
`unique()`	Returns the unique values in each column.

Partial results for the nunique() method when run on the Polls data

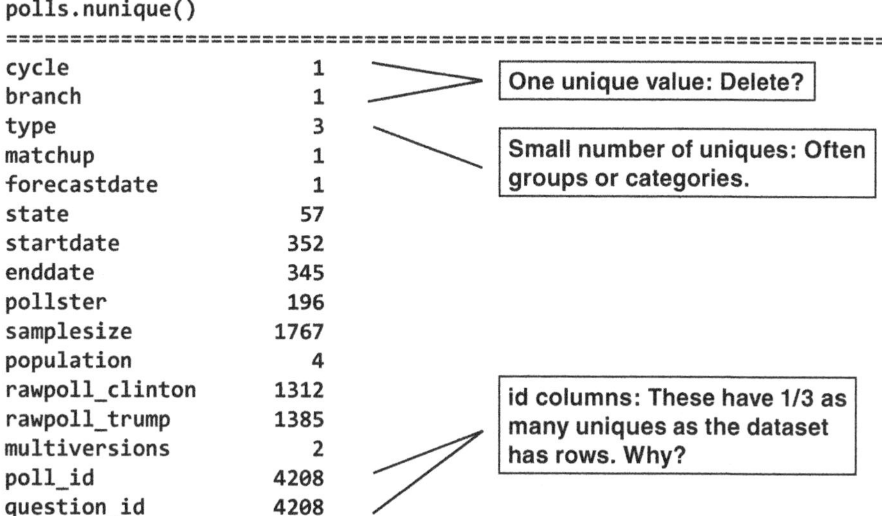
One unique value: Delete?
Small number of uniques: Often groups or categories.
id columns: These have 1/3 as many uniques as the dataset has rows. Why?

```
polls.nunique()
======================================================================
cycle                    1
branch                   1
type                     3
matchup                  1
forecastdate             1
state                   57
startdate              352
enddate                345
pollster               196
samplesize            1767
population               4
rawpoll_clinton       1312
rawpoll_trump         1385
multiversions            2
poll_id               4208
question_id           4208
```

Partial results for a unique() method that gets the unique values

```
polls.apply(pd.unique)
======================================================================
cycle                                                         [2016]
branch                                                 ['President']
type                         ['polls-plus' 'now-cast' 'polls-only']
matchup                          ['Clinton vs. Trump vs. Johnson']
forecastdate                                            ['11/8/16']
state              ['U.S.' 'New Mexico' 'Virginia' 'Iowa' 'Wiscon...
startdate          ['11/3/2016' '11/1/2016' '11/2/2016' '11/4/201...
enddate            ['11/6/2016' '11/7/2016' '11/5/2016' '11/4/201...
pollster           ['ABC News/Washington Post' 'Google Consumer S...
samplesize           [2220.0 26574.0 2195.0 ... 2422.0 1576.0 950.0]
population                                      ['lv' 'rv' 'a' 'v']
rawpoll_clinton              [47.0 38.03 42.0 ... 46.54 21.33 46.46]
rawpoll_trump                [43.0 35.69 39.0 ... 40.04 35.05 37.41]
multiversions                                           [nan '*']
poll_id                    [48630 48847 48922 ... 48838 48248 44180]
question_id                [76192 76443 76636 ... 76427 75549 66128]
```

Description

- Examining the number of unique values in a column and the unique values themselves can help you understand the data and identify problems that need to be fixed.
- You need to use the apply() method to apply the unique() method to more than one column, because the unique() method operates on a Series object, not a DataFrame.

Figure 6-3 What the unique values can tell you

What the value counts can tell you

Figure 6-4 presents the value_counts() method. It returns each unique value in a column, as well as the number of times each non-null value occurs. This is illustrated by the first example. Here, the value_counts() method is applied to the state column in the polls DataFrame. As you can see, the "U.S." value occurred 3318 times in that column, and "North Carolina" occurred just 375 times. Here, just the first four rows are shown, but the last few states occur fewer than 90 times.

The second example works like the first example, but this time the normalize parameter is set to True. As a result, the count for each unique value is displayed as a percentage of the total. So, for example, the U.S. value occurs in more than 26% of the rows.

The third example shows how the dropna parameter can be used. When it is set to False, the null values are counted too. This shows that almost all the rows in the multiversions column are NaN values and 36 have the value "*".

The fourth example shows how the value_counts() method can be applied to more than one column. Then, the counts are displayed for all combinations of the columns. This is similar to the way that the groupby() method behaves when it groups data on more than one column.

Note, however, that the dropna parameter can't be used when you apply this method to two or more columns. That's because the DataFrame version of this method is applied to the columns, not the Series version, and the DataFrame version doesn't have a dropna parameter.

The value_counts() method

Method	Description
`value_counts(params)`	Returns the count for each of the unique values in a series.
Parameter	**Description**
`normalize`	If True, returns the counts as a percent of the total rather than the actual counts.
`dropna`	If True (the default), it ignores null values. Can only be used with Series objects.

How to use the value_counts() method

```
polls.state.value_counts().head(4)
==================================
U.S.                3318
Florida              444
Pennsylvania         375
North Carolina       375
Name: state, dtype: int64
```

How to use the normalize parameter

```
polls.state.value_counts(normalize=True).head(4)
================================================
U.S.                0.262833
Florida             0.035171
Pennsylvania        0.029705
North Carolina      0.029705
Name: state, dtype: float64
```

How to use the dropna parameter

```
polls.multiversions.value_counts(dropna=False)
==============================================
NaN    12588
*         36
Name: multiversions, dtype: int64
```

How to use the value_counts() method with multiple columns

```
polls[['state','grade']].value_counts()
=======================================
state     grade
U.S.      A-        1215
          C+         546
          B          162
          C-         126
          A+         114
                    ...
Oregon    B+           3
          A            3
Kentucky  B-           3
Texas     B+           3
Illinois  A            3
Length: 321, dtype: int64
```

Figure 6-4 What the value counts can tell you

How to simplify the data

After you've analyzed the data in a DataFrame, you're ready to clean it. And the best way to start is to simplify the data by dropping the rows and columns that you don't need. After that, you may want to rename the remaining columns so the names are easier to understand and remember. The topics that follow present these skills.

How to drop rows based on conditions

In most cases, you drop rows based on conditions. This is illustrated by the examples in figure 6-5. Here, the first example assigns all of the rows that have a value of "now-cast" in the type column to the polls DataFrame. That means that all of the rows that don't have "now-cast" in the type column are dropped.

The second example gets the same result by using the query() method to select the rows with "now-cast" in the type column. Here again, those rows are assigned to the polls DataFrame so all other rows are dropped.

If you look at the examples in the previous figure, you can see that the original DataFrame has just three unique values in the type column: polls-plus, now-cast, and polls-only. These represent three different types of results for each poll. In this case, the analyst decided to work with the "now-cast" rows, which drops the other two-thirds of the rows.

How to drop duplicate rows

When data comes from several sources, *duplicate rows* are possible. In that case, you're going to want to remove all but one of the rows in each set of duplicates. To do that, you can use the duplicated() method to find the duplicate rows and the drop_duplicates() method to drop the duplicates. This is illustrated by the second part of figure 6-5.

Although you can use the subset parameter of these methods to identify duplicates based on the values of selected columns, you usually want to base the duplicates on the values of all columns. So, you don't code that parameter for either the duplicated() or drop_duplicates() method.

However, you probably will want to code the keep parameter. In the example that finds duplicate rows, this parameter is set to False so all duplicate rows will be marked. But in the example that drops duplicate rows, this parameter is set to 'first' so the first duplicate in each set of duplicates will be kept.

These examples are taken from the Fires case study, which did get data from many sources. So even after the DataFrame had been reduced to 274,170 rows, the duplicated() method returned 94 rows. Then, the drop_duplicates() method dropped 47 of them.

How to drop rows based on conditions

By directly accessing a column

```
polls = polls[polls.type == 'now-cast']
```

With the query() method

```
polls = polls.query('type == "now-cast"')
```

How to drop duplicate rows

The duplicated() method

Method	Description
`duplicated(params)`	Identifies duplicated rows.

Parameter	Description
`subset`	List of columns to be used for identifying duplicates; otherwise, all columns are used.
`keep`	If 'first' (the default), all duplicates are marked as True except for the first occurrence in each set. If 'last', all duplicates are marked as True except for the last occurrence. If False, all duplicates are marked as True.

The drop_duplicates() method

Method	Description
`drop_duplicates(params)`	Returns the DataFrame with duplicate rows removed.

Parameter	Description
`subset`	Same as for the duplicated() method.
`keep`	Same as for the duplicated() method except that the duplicate rows are dropped, not marked.
`inplace`	True makes the changes directly to the DataFrame; False (the default) returns a copy of the DataFrame with the duplicates dropped.

How to find duplicate rows

```
fires[fires.duplicated(keep=False)]
```

How to drop duplicate rows

```
fires.drop_duplicates(keep='first', inplace=True)
```

Description

- To simplify the data, you can start by dropping the rows that you won't need. That way, you will have less data to clean. Just make sure that you won't need those rows later on.
- When data is compiled from more than one source, *duplicate rows* may enter the dataset. That's why you should check for duplicates and remove all but one of the rows in each set of duplicates. Just make sure that they are really duplicates.

Figure 6-5 How to drop rows

How to drop columns

When you drop columns, you first identify the columns that you want to drop and then use the drop() method to drop them. To help identify those columns, you can use the nunique() method as in the first example in figure 6-6. This shows the results after two-thirds of the rows were dropped by the example in the previous figure. As a result, the DataFrame has 4208 rows.

At this point, the nunique() method shows that the first four columns in the DataFrame each contain just one value. As a result, they aren't going to contribute to the analysis. Similarly, the last two columns contain one unique value for each of the rows in the DataFrame, which probably means that they are columns that identify the rows. As a result, they aren't going to contribute to the analysis either. In either case, it's safe to drop the columns.

Then, to drop the columns, you can use the drop() method. This is illustrated by the second group of examples in this figure. Here, the first example drops the "cycle" and "forecastdate" columns. But note that the result is assigned to the polls DataFrame. Otherwise, the DataFrame wouldn't be changed.

By contrast, the second example in this group sets the inplace parameter of the drop() method to True. As a result, the polls DataFrame is changed without assigning the result to it. In addition, since the errors parameter is set to "raise", the statement won't work if an error is raised.

The drop() method

Method	Description
`drop(params)`	Drops the columns that are specified by the columns parameter.
Parameter	**Description**
`columns`	List of columns to be dropped.
`errors`	What to do if a specified column doesn't exist: 'ignore' (the default) or 'raise'.
`inplace`	True makes the changes directly to the DataFrame.

How the nunique() method helps you identify columns that you may want to drop

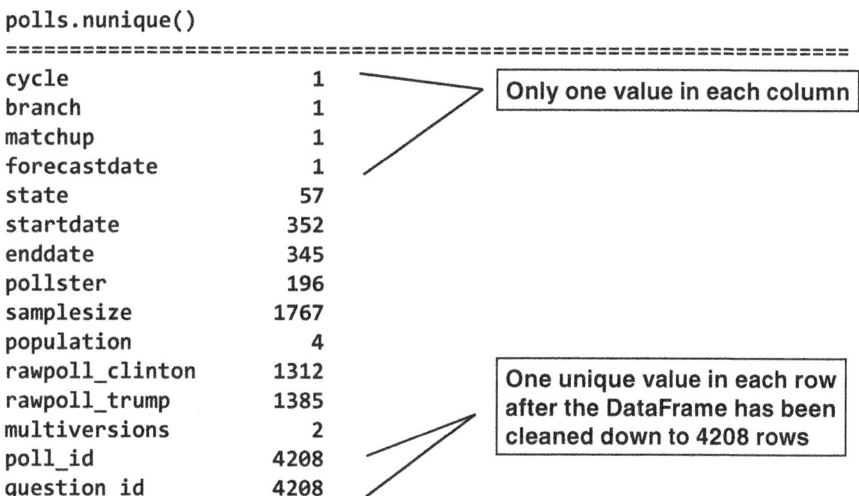

polls.nunique()
==
cycle 1
branch 1
matchup 1
forecastdate 1
state 57
startdate 352
enddate 345
pollster 196
samplesize 1767
population 4
rawpoll_clinton 1312
rawpoll_trump 1385
multiversions 2
poll_id 4208
question_id 4208
Only one value in each column
One unique value in each row after the DataFrame has been cleaned down to 4208 rows

How to use the drop() method to drop columns

With inplace=False

```
polls = polls.drop(columns=['cycle','forecastdate'])
```

With inplace=True

```
polls.drop(columns=['cycle','forecastdate'], errors='raise', inplace=True)
```

Description

- Most datasets have more columns than you need for your analysis, so it makes sense to drop the ones that you don't need.
- Columns that have only one unique value are commonly used to identify the entire dataset, so they usually aren't needed for the analysis.
- Columns that have a unique value in each row are commonly used to identify the rows, so they usually aren't needed for the analysis either.

Figure 6-6 How to drop columns

How to rename columns

When you get a new dataset, it's often hard to tell what the columns in a dataset contain based on their column names. In fact, you often have to study the documentation or the data itself to figure out what the columns contain.

For that reason, you may want to change the column names so they're more descriptive and easier to remember. That's always okay if you're working on your own, but if you're working with a group, you may need to get everyone in your group to agree to the changes.

Once you decide what name changes you want to make, you can use the rename() method to change them as shown in figure 6-7. With this method, the columns parameter is coded as a dictionary with the current column name and the new column name in each dictionary item. This is illustrated by the first group of examples in this figure.

In the first example, the dictionary of original names and new names is coded within the rename() method. In the second example, the dictionary is coded separately. Both examples show how easy renaming can be...once you figure out what each column contains.

Another way to change column names is to use the Python replace() method to change the names in the columns attribute of a DataFrame, which changes the names of the columns. This is illustrated by the second group of examples in this figure. In both of these examples, note that the replace() method has to be preceded by the str accessor of the DataFrame.

The first example of the replace() method changes the characters "_pct" to an empty string, which in effect deletes those characters. This will change all of the column names that include those characters.

The second example uses three replace() methods to replace strings in the column names. The first two methods use the regular expressions "^a_" and "^h_" to change the characters "a_" and "h_" to "annual" and "hourly", but only when the "a_" and "h_" are the first characters in the column name. To specify that these methods use regular expressions, this code sets the regex parameter for these methods to True. The third method changes "_pct" to "_percent" no matter where "_pct" is within a column name. Since this code doesn't use a regular expression, it doesn't need to set the regex parameter to True.

As these examples show, you can use regular expressions in your replace() methods if you know how to use them. But if you don't, you can usually get by with simple string expressions like the one in the first example in this group. Or, you can use the rename() method to specify the exact name changes that you want to make.

The rename() method for columns

Method	Description
`rename(params)`	Renames the columns of a DataFrame.
Parameter	**Description**
`columns`	A dictionary that contains the columns to be renamed and the new names for those columns.
`inplace`	Whether to make changes directly to the DataFrame. The default is False.

How to rename columns with the rename() method

How to rename columns with an embedded dictionary

```
polls = polls.rename(columns={
    'rawpoll_clinton':'clinton_pct',
    'rawpoll_trump':'trump_pct'})
```

How to rename columns with a separate dictionary and inplace set to True

```
polls_names_dict = {'rawpoll_clinton':'clinton_pct',
                    'rawpoll_trump':'trump_pct'}
polls.rename(columns = polls_names_dict, inplace = True)
```

How to rename columns with the Python replace() method

How to use a simple expression with the replace() method

```
polls.columns = polls.columns.str.replace('_pct','')
```

How to use regular expressions with the replace() method

```
jobs.columns = jobs.columns \
    .str.replace('^a_','annual_', regex=True) \
    .str.replace('^h_','hourly_', regex=True) \
    .str.replace('_pct','_percent')
```

Description

- When the column names are difficult to understand and remember, it makes sense to change the names so they will be easier to work with.
- One way to rename columns is to use the Pandas rename() method.
- Another way to rename columns is to use the Python replace() method to replace the values in the columns attribute of a DataFrame. To use this method, though, you need to first code the str accessor.

Figure 6-7 How to rename columns

How to find and fix missing values

NA values (or *NAs*) are Not Available. That means they are *missing values*. These values include NA, None, NaN (not a number), and NaT (not a datetime).

How to find missing values

The key point here is that the NA values are usually missing for a reason. So you can't just fill them with zeros or estimated values and hide the fact that the data was missing. Instead, you need to figure out what the reasons are for the missing data and then decide how to handle them.

So to start, you need to find the missing values. To do that, you can use the methods in figure 6-8. To illustrate these methods, this figure works with a ten-row version of the mortality DataFrame. But this time, the data has been modified so the Year and DeathRate columns have some missing values that are identified by NaN.

Since most datasets are likely to have some missing values, you can start by seeing whether any of the columns in the DataFrame have some. This is illustrated by the first example in this figure. Here, the code uses the count() method of the DataFrame to count all of the values that aren't missing in each column. Then, it subtracts that value from the number of rows in each column. To do that, it gets the first value from the tuple for the shape attribute of the DataFrame. Then, the print() method prints the number of missing values for each column.

When you discover that some of the columns in the DataFrame do have missing values, you can take a closer look at them by using the technique in the second example. Here, the any() method is chained to the isnull() method, and the axis parameter of the any() method is set to 1. As a result, this statement displays any rows with at least one column that contains a missing value.

The next example shows how to display the rows that have missing values in just one column, in this case, the DeathRate column. When you're working with a large DataFrame, this helps you focus on the missing values in that column, which can help you decide how you're going to handle those values.

The last example shows how you can use the notnull() method to display all the rows that don't have missing values in the DeathRate column. That lets you see what the valid rows look like.

The isnull(), notnull(), and any() methods

Method	Description
`isnull()`	Returns a Boolean same-sized object indicating whether the values are NA.
`notnull()`	Returns a Boolean same-sized object indicating whether the values are not NA.
`any(axis=1)`	Returns True if any column in a row contains a missing value.

A ten-row DataFrame named mortality_data that has some missing values

	Year	AgeGroup	DeathRate
0	1900.0	01-04 Years	1983.8
1	NaN	01-04 Years	1695.0
2	1902.0	01-04 Years	NaN
3	1903.0	01-04 Years	1542.1
4	NaN	01-04 Years	NaN

	Year	AgeGroup	DeathRate
5	1905.0	01-04 Years	1498.9
6	NaN	01-04 Years	NaN
7	1907.0	01-04 Years	NaN
8	1908.0	01-04 Years	1396.8
9	1909.0	01-04 Years	1348.9

How to display the count of the missing values in the DataFrame

```
missing_count = mortality_data.shape[0] - mortality_data.count()
print(missing_count)
=================================================================
Year          3
AgeGroup      0
DeathRate     4
```

How to display all rows that contain NA values

```
mortality_data[mortality_data.isnull().any(axis=1)]
```

	Year	AgeGroup	DeathRate
1	NaN	01-04 Years	1695.0
2	1902.0	01-04 Years	NaN
4	NaN	01-04 Years	NaN
6	NaN	01-04 Years	NaN
7	1907.0	01-04 Years	NaN

How to display all rows with NA values in the DeathRate column

```
mortality_data[mortality_data.DeathRate.isnull()]
```

How to display all rows that don't have NA values in the DeathRate column

```
mortality_data[mortality_data.DeathRate.notnull()]
```

Description

- When data is imported into a DataFrame, *missing values* are set to NaN (Not a Number) for numeric and object columns and to NaT (Not a Time) for datetime columns. Missing values, also known as *NA (*Not Available*) values*, include NaN, NaT, None, and NA.

Figure 6-8 How to find missing values

How to drop rows with missing values

One way to handle rows with missing values is to drop them. However, you should only do that if the rows represent invalid cases so dropping them won't skew the results of your analysis. If you do decide to drop rows with missing values, figure 6-9 shows how.

To drop rows with missing values, you use the dropna() method. By setting its parameters, you can delete all rows that contain a missing value or drop only the rows that contain more than a specific number of missing values. You can also drop only the rows that have missing values in specific columns.

This is illustrated by the three examples in this figure. Here, the first example drops all rows that contain a missing value in any column. The second example drops only the rows that have two or more missing values. And the third example drops only the rows that have missing values in the DeathRate column.

The dropna() method

Method	Description
`dropna(params)`	Drops the rows that are specified by the parameters.

Parameter	Description
`subset`	A list of the columns that the drop should be based on.
`how`	If 'any' (the default), a row is dropped if any column contains an NA value. If 'all', a row is dropped only if all columns contain NA values.
`thresh`	An integer that specifies how many columns need to contain NA values before the row is dropped.
`inplace`	Whether to make changes directly to the DataFrame. The default is False.

A ten-row DataFrame named mortality_data that has some missing values

	Year	AgeGroup	DeathRate
0	1900.0	01-04 Years	1983.8
1	NaN	01-04 Years	1695.0
2	1902.0	01-04 Years	NaN
3	1903.0	01-04 Years	1542.1
4	NaN	01-04 Years	NaN

	Year	AgeGroup	DeathRate
5	1905.0	01-04 Years	1498.9
6	NaN	01-04 Years	NaN
7	1907.0	01-04 Years	NaN
8	1908.0	01-04 Years	1396.8
9	1909.0	01-04 Years	1348.9

How to drop all rows that contain an NA value

```
mortality_data = mortality_data.dropna()
```

	Year	AgeGroup	DeathRate
0	1900.0	01-04 Years	1983.8
3	1903.0	01-04 Years	1542.1
5	1905.0	01-04 Years	1498.9
8	1908.0	01-04 Years	1396.8
9	1909.0	01-04 Years	1348.9

How to drop only the rows that have two or more NA values

```
mortality_data.dropna(thresh=2, inplace=True)
```

How to drop only the rows that have NAs in the DeathRate column

```
mortality_data.dropna(subset=['DeathRate'], inplace=True)
```

Description

- In general, you should only drop rows when the NAs represent invalid cases. Otherwise, you should fill the NAs with reasonable values, as shown in the next figure.

Figure 6-9 How to drop rows with missing values

How to fill missing values

If only a couple of columns in a row have missing values and the other columns contain values that represent a reasonable case, you probably shouldn't drop the row. In that case, you can fill the missing values as shown in figure 6-10.

Here, the first example uses the fillna() method to fill the missing values in the DeathRate column with the mean value of the data in that column. That will make sense for some DataFrames, but that won't work well for the mortality DataFrame because the range of values is too large.

The second example is more reasonable for the mortality DataFrame because it forward fills the missing values with the data from the first row before the missing values. You can see this in the Year column, which has forward filled the value for the year 1900 into the second row of data. You can also see this in the DeathRate column, which has forward filled the rate 1695.0 from the second row of data into the third row.

In this example, though, the limit parameter is set to 2, so this method will only fill two missing values. As a result, if a column contains three missing values in a row, only two will be filled and one missing value will remain.

By contrast, the third example shows how to use the interpolate() method to smooth out the missing values. This means that it calculates the new values by finding the midpoint between the cells before and after the missing values. As a result, the missing value in the Year column of the second row becomes 1901.0, which is the right year for that row. And the missing DeathRate value for the year 1902 is converted to 1618.55.

Note that when you code the interpolate() method without parameters, it uses linear interpolation. As just described, that means it gets the midpoint between the values of the cells before and after any missing values. If you want to use a different type of interpolation, you code the method parameter. In most cases, though, linear interpolation is all you need.

The fillna() method

Method	Description
`fillna(params)`	Fills the NA values in a DataFrame.
Parameter	**Description**
`value`	The value that will replace the NAs or a dict with the column name and value for each column that will be filled.
`method`	The method to use for replacing the NAs: 'pad' or 'ffill' to forward fill and 'backfill' or 'bfill' to backward fill.
`limit`	The maximum number of consecutive NAs in a column to fill.
`inplace`	Whether to make changes directly to the DataFrame. The default is False.

How to replace the NAs in a column with the mean value of the column

```
mortality_data.DeathRate.fillna(
    value=mortality_data.DeathRate.mean(), inplace=True)
```

How to forward fill NA values with a limit of 2 consecutive fills

```
mortality_data.fillna(method='ffill', limit=2, inplace=True)
mortality_data.head(4)
```

	Year	AgeGroup	DeathRate
0	1900.0	01-04 Years	1983.8
1	1900.0	01-04 Years	1695.0
2	1902.0	01-04 Years	1695.0
3	1903.0	01-04 Years	1542.1

The interpolate() method

Method	Description
`interpolate()`	Uses linear interpolation to fill the missing values in a DataFrame.

How to fill NA values with linear interpolation

```
mortality_data = mortality_data.interpolate()
mortality_data.head(4)
```

	Year	AgeGroup	DeathRate
0	1900.0	01-04 Years	1983.80
1	1901.0	01-04 Years	1695.00
2	1902.0	01-04 Years	1618.55
3	1903.0	01-04 Years	1542.10

Description

- If all the other values in a row are reasonable, it may make sense to use the fillna() or interpolate() method to fill in the missing values.

Figure 6-10 How to fill missing values

How to fix data type problems

When you import data into a DataFrame, dates and numbers are often imported as object data types instead of datetime and numeric data types. So, before you can use any of the methods that work with datetime and numeric data types, you need to convert the object types to the right data types. The next six figures show how.

How to find dates and numbers that are imported as objects

Figure 6-11 starts with a table that lists the data types that Pandas applies when data is imported into a DataFrame. When a column consists entirely of numbers and NA values, Pandas applies either the int64 or the float64 data type to the column. And when a column consists entirely of True and False values, Pandas applies the bool data type to the column.

For all other columns, Pandas applies the object data type. That includes columns that contain strings, columns that contain dates and times, columns that contain some but not all Boolean values, and columns that contain mostly numeric data but with some non-numeric data.

When the data in a column isn't imported with the right data type, you will need to change the data type if you want to use methods that require a specific data type. For instance, you'll need to change date and time columns to the datetime data type if you want to use methods that work with that data type. Similarly, you'll want to change columns that contain integers to the int64 data type and columns that contain decimal numbers to the float64 data type.

Before you can change the data types, of course, you need to know which columns need to be changed. To do that, you can use the select_dtypes() method to identify the columns that have been imported with the object data type, as shown in this figure. Then, you can display and inspect the columns to see whether they contain dates and times, integers, floating-point numbers, or Boolean values.

For example, the "startdate" and "enddate" columns in the Polls data look like they contain dates. As a result, you should probably convert them to the datetime data type. Similarly, all but three columns in the Jobs data appear to be numbers, so you should probably convert them to integer or floating-point data types. And perhaps the columns named "annual" and "hourly" in the Jobs data should be converted to the bool data type because they contain True values for True and NaN values for False.

Remember, though, that Pandas imports columns that contain all numeric values or all bool values with the right data types. So when that doesn't happen, you need to figure out what went wrong. If, for example, you scroll through the Jobs data, you'll see some hashtags (#) and some asterisks (*) in what look like they should be numeric columns. Similarly, you'll find just NaN values and True values in the annual and hourly columns. That's why the object data type was applied to those columns instead of the bool data type.

The data types that Pandas applies to imported columns

Data type	When the column contains...
`int64`	Only integers or NAs
`float64`	Only floating-point numbers or NAs
`bool`	Only Boolean values (True or False)
`object`	Strings or data that doesn't import as another data type

The select_dtypes() method of a DataFrame

Method	Description
`select_dtypes(type)`	Selects all columns with the specified data type.

Polls data: Dates stored as objects

```
polls.select_dtypes('object').head(2)
```

	startdate	enddate	pollster	grade	population	multiversions	url	create
4208	11/3/2016	11/6/2016	ABC News/Washington Post	A+	lv	NaN	https://www.washingtonpost.com/news/the-fix/wp...	1
4209	11/1/2016	11/7/2016	Google Consumer Surveys	B	lv	NaN	https://datastudio.google.com/u/0/#/org//repor...	1

Jobs data: Numeric and Boolean values stored as objects

```
jobs.select_dtypes('object').head(2)
```

tot_emp	emp_prse	jobs_1000	...	h_median	h_pct75	h_pct90	a_pct10	a_pct25	a_median	a_pct75	a_pct90	annual	hourly
144733270	0.1	NaN	...	18.58	30.06	47.31	20690	25740	38640	62510	98410	NaN	NaN
7616650	0.2	NaN	...	50.11	72.93	#	49260	70880	104240	151700	#	NaN	NaN

How Pandas applies data types to imported columns

- If a column consists entirely of numbers and NA values, Pandas imports the column with either the int64 or float64 data type.
- If a column consists entirely of True and False values, Pandas imports the column with the bool data type.
- Pandas imports all other columns with the object data type.

Description

- If a column appears to be numeric or Boolean but is imported with the object data type, you need to find out why.
- The recent releases of Pandas have added a string data type to the data types that Pandas supports. At this writing, though, Pandas still imports strings as object data types.

Figure 6-11 How to find date and number columns that are imported as objects

How to convert date and time strings to the datetime data type

Figure 6-12 shows how to convert date and time strings to datetime objects. To do that, you use the Pandas to_datetime() method. Note, however, that this method operates on Series objects (columns), not DataFrames. As a result, if you want to apply this method to more than one column, you need to use the apply() method.

This is illustrated by the first example in this figure. In this case, no parameters are coded for the datetime() method, so Pandas infers the formats that it applies to the dates and times. Since Pandas does a good job of that, that should be all that you need.

Later, if you want to convert the datetime objects to strings with specific formats so they're better for display, you can use the Python strftime() method. This is illustrated by the second example in this figure. Here, just a few of the standard formatting codes are used to do the conversions, but you can look online or refer to *Murach's Python Programming* for more information about these codes.

The Pandas to_datetime() method

Method	Description
`to_datetime()`	Converts columns that contain date strings to datetime objects.

A few of the formatting codes for the Python strftime() method

Code	Description
%m	The month of the year as an integer
%d	The day of the month as an integer
%y	A 2-digit year
%Y	A 4-digit year

Four of the date columns in the polls DataFrame

```
date_cols = ['startdate','enddate','createddate','timestamp']
```

	startdate	enddate	createddate	timestamp
4208	11/3/2016	11/6/2016	11/7/16	09:24:53 8 Nov 2016
4209	11/1/2016	11/7/2016	11/7/16	09:24:53 8 Nov 2016

How to convert dates to datetime objects with inferred formatting

```
polls[date_cols].apply(pd.to_datetime)
```

	startdate	enddate	createddate	timestamp
4208	2016-11-03	2016-11-06	2016-11-07	2016-11-08 09:24:53
4209	2016-11-01	2016-11-07	2016-11-07	2016-11-08 09:24:53

How to use the Python strftime() method to format dates as strings

```
polls['startdate'] = polls.startdate.dt.strftime("%m/%d/%Y")
polls['enddate'] = polls.enddate.dt.strftime("%m-%d-%y")
```

	startdate	enddate	createddate	timestamp
4208	11/03/2016	11-06-16	2016-11-07	2016-11-08 09:24:53
4209	11/01/2016	11-07-16	2016-11-07	2016-11-08 09:24:53

Description

- You can convert date and time strings to datetime objects with the Pandas to_datetime() method. Then, you can use the methods of the datetime objects to work with the dates.
- You need to use the apply() method to apply the to_datetime() method to more than one column, because the to_datetime() method operates on a Series object, not a DataFrame.
- To convert a datetime object to a string that can be displayed, you can use the Python strftime() method. To do that, you code the dt accessor followed by the strftime() method.

Figure 6-12 How to convert date and time strings to the datetime data type

How to convert object columns to numeric data types

The first example in figure 6-13 shows how to use the to_numeric() method to convert columns that contain numeric strings to integer or float data types. When you use this method, though, you must remember that only numbers and NAs are valid in a numeric field. As a result, before you use this method, you may need to fix any non-numeric data in a column. Otherwise, this method will raise an error. You'll learn more about fixing the data in the next figure.

An alternative that should be used with caution is to set the errors parameter to "coerce" so any non-numeric values in a column are converted to NA values. This is illustrated by the second example in this figure. Here, the column in the original data has some values that contain non-numeric data like asterisks (**). Then, when the statement is run without an errors parameter, an error is raised. But when the statement is run with the errors parameter set to "coerce", the non-numeric data is converted to NaN values.

Of course, you should only use coercion if you're sure that the conversions will be okay. In most cases, though, you should fix any data problems before you convert the columns to numeric data types. Then, if the to_numeric() method raises an error, you know that you haven't fixed all of the problems.

The to_numeric() method

Method	Description
`to_numeric(columns,errors)`	Tries to convert the data in a column to a numeric type.

Three options for the errors parameter

Option	Description
`raise`	Raises an error if there is any non-numeric data in a column except for NA values. This is the default.
`ignore`	Ignores the error and doesn't change the column at all.
`coerce`	Converts non-numeric values to NaN.

How to convert columns with valid numeric strings to numeric data types

```
pd.to_numeric(jobs.tot_emp)
```

How to coerce columns with invalid strings into numeric data types

The original data

```
jobs.tot_nemp.tail(3)
==========================================================
403892    170
403893    130
403894     **
Name: tot_emp, dtype: object
```

Without an errors parameter, an error is raised

```
pd.to_numeric(jobs.tot_emp)
==========================================================
ValueError: Unable to parse string "**" at position 1906
```

With the errors parameter set to coerce

```
pd.to_numeric(jobs.tot_emp, errors='coerce').tail(3)
==========================================================
403892    170.0
403893    130.0
403894      NaN
Name: tot_emp, dtype: float64
```

Description

- Remember that only numbers and NAs are valid in a numeric column. By default, anything else will raise an error.
- Although you can use the coerce value in the errors parameter to convert invalid data into NaNs, you need to find out what data is raising the error before you do that. Otherwise, it may cause problems later on.

Figure 6-13 How to convert object columns to numeric data types

How to work with the category data type

The *category data type* consists of index numbers in a column that point to a table of text entries. To illustrate, remember that each row in the AgeGroup column of the mortality dataset consisted of one of these entries: 1-4 Years, 5-9 Years, 10-14 Years, and 15-19 Years. That means that each of these values is repeated many times.

By contrast, if that column were converted to the category data type, each of the four values would be put into a table just once. Then, each row in the column would consist of an index number that points to the right entry in the table. You can imagine how that could save memory in a dataset with thousands of rows.

With that as background, figure 6-14 starts by showing how to use the astype() method to convert object columns to the category data type. Here, the object data in the state column of the fires DataFrame is converted to the category data type. After that, the state column will contain integers that point to the 51 state codes or names in the table.

For some columns, converting object columns to the category type can save considerable memory. As you'll see in a minute, though, this can also create some problems. As a result, it usually isn't worth converting object columns to the category data type.

But even if you don't convert object columns to the category type, you may need to know how to work with that data type. That's because the columns in some datasets have columns that are imported with the category data type. That's the case with the Social Survey case study, for example.

One of the problems that can occur when working with the category data type is illustrated by the second set of examples in this figure. In this case, the wrkstat column of a DataFrame named filteredStatCounts has the category data type, and that column consists of 8 categories. But when a new DataFrame that uses just 3 of those categories is extracted from the first DataFrame, the value_counts() method shows that the new DataFrame still has all 8 categories, even though 5 of the categories aren't used. And that can cause problems with some operations.

To fix that, though, you can remove the unused categories by using the cat accessor to run the remove_unused_categories() method. That of course removes the unused categories, as the value_counts() method in this example illustrates.

The astype() method for converting data types

Method	Description
`astype(type,errors)`	Tries to convert the data to the specified data type. Errors are raised by default, but they can be ignored by setting the errors parameter to 'ignore'.

How to convert object columns to the category data type

```
fires.state = fires.state.astype('category')
```

The remove_unused_categories() method

Method	Description
`remove_unused_categories()`	Removes unused categories from a table.

How to drop rows for specific categories

Drop the rows for the categories that aren't in the query

```
filteredStatCounts = statCounts.query(
    'wrkstat in ["working fulltime","working parttime","retired"]')
filteredStatCounts.wrkstat.value_counts()
===================================================================
retired             31892
working parttime     9121
working fulltime     6719
other                   0
keeping house           0
school                  0
unempl, laid off        0
temp not working        0
Name: wrkstat, dtype: int64
```

Drop the unused categories

```
filteredStatCounts['wrkstat'] = \
    filteredStatCounts.wrkstat.cat.remove_unused_categories()
filteredStatCounts.wrkstat.value_counts()
=============================================================
retired             31892
working parttime     9121
working fulltime     6719
Name: wrkstat, dtype: int64
```

Description

- A column with the *category data type* consists of index numbers that point to a table of text entries with just one instance of each entry.
- Because the data in some files is imported with the category data type, you need to know how to work with that data type. In some cases, it also makes sense to save memory by converting object columns to the category data type.
- If you drop all the rows for a specific category, the category still remains in the table, and that can cause problems. To solve the problem, though, you can remove the unused categories from the table.

Figure 6-14 How to work with the category data type

How to replace invalid values and convert a column's data type

After you analyze the non-numeric values in what should be numeric columns, you can decide how to handle them. Then, if you decide to replace the non-numeric values, you can use the replace() method as shown in figure 6-15.

The examples in this figure work with the data in a jobs DataFrame that was imported from an Excel spreadsheet. In this case, the second tab in the spreadsheet documented some of the data problems. Specifically, * or ** means that a value is missing, and # indicates an hourly wage greater than $100 or an annual wage greater than $208,000.

The first example in this figure shows how to use the replace() method to replace the * and ** values in a single column. In this case, those values are replaced with NaN. To do that, this code starts by importing a module named NumPy as np. Then, it uses np.nan as the replacement values, which is NumPy's floating-point representation of NaN (Not a Number). Note that the to_replace parameter is coded with two values, so the value parameter must also be coded with two values.

The second example shows how to replace the same values as in the first example, but it uses a dictionary to specify the old and new values. And the third example shows how to replace # values in the hourly_median column with a value of 100.

The fourth example shows how you can use the replace() method with the data in what should be a Boolean column. In this case, the hourly column is imported with True values for the rows that are hourly and NaN values for rows that aren't. Then, the replace() method converts the NaN values to False. That makes all the data in the column Boolean.

After you replace the invalid values in a numeric column with valid values, you can use the to_numeric() method to convert the column to a numeric data type. By contrast, when you convert all of the values in what should be a Boolean column to either True or False, Pandas automatically converts the column to the bool data type.

Note that to use np.nan in these examples, you have to import NumPy as np. That's required even though Pandas uses NumPy under the hood for many of its mathematical operations. Also note that if you code np.nan as np.NaN, the code will still work. However, np.nan is the way that the NumPy documentation says to code it.

The Pandas replace() method

Method	Description
`replace(to_replace,value, inplace)`	Replaces the strings in the to_replace parameter with the strings in the value parameter or replaces the old values in a dictionary with the new values.

Documentation that identifies some data problems in the Jobs data

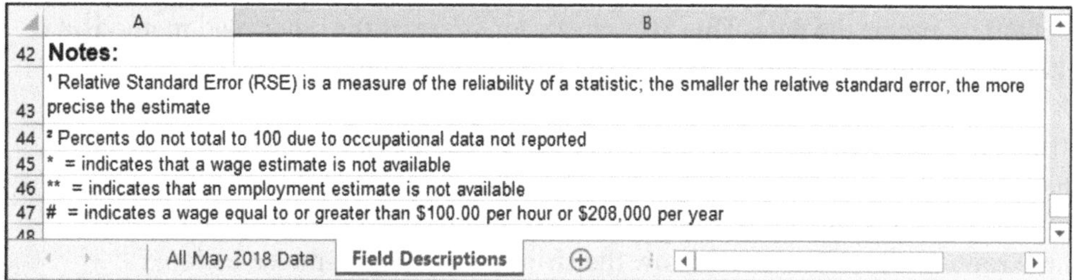

	A	B
42	**Notes:**	
43	[1] Relative Standard Error (RSE) is a measure of the reliability of a statistic; the smaller the relative standard error, the more precise the estimate	
44	[2] Percents do not total to 100 due to occupational data not reported	
45	* = indicates that a wage estimate is not available	
46	** = indicates that an employment estimate is not available	
47	# = indicates a wage equal to or greater than $100.00 per hour or $208,000 per year	

How to replace * or ** values in a single column with NaN

```
import numpy as np
jobs.tot_emp.replace(to_replace=['*','**'], value=[np.nan,np.nan], inplace=True)
```

How to use a dictionary to replace * or ** values in a single column with NaN

```
jobs.tot_emp.replace({'*':np.nan, '**':np.nan}, inplace=True)
```

How to replace # values with a numeric value

```
jobs.hourly_median = jobs.hourly_median.replace(
    to_replace='#', value=100)
```

How to replace NaN values with False in what should be a Boolean column

```
jobs.hourly.replace(to_replace=np.nan, value=False, inplace=True)
```

Description

- After you replace the invalid numeric values in a column, you can use the to_numeric() method to convert the column to a numeric data type.
- After you replace the invalid values in what should be a Boolean column, the data type of the column is automatically changed to the bool data type.
- The NumPy module provides a constant named nan that represents a floating-point representation of NaN (or Not a Number). But before you can use that constant, you need to import NumPy.

Figure 6-15 How to replace invalid values and convert a column's data type

How to fix data problems when you import the data

Now that you know how to fix data problems, you should know that you can fix some types of problems when you import the data. That way, you don't have to fix them later on. This is useful when you're going to import a dataset every time you use it to make sure that it's up-to-date.

To illustrate, figure 6-16 shows how to do that when you use the read_csv() method to import the data. This also works for some of the other read methods, although the import options may not be exactly the same.

This figure shows how to use the parse_dates parameter to convert date strings to datetime objects. To start, it creates a list that includes the names of the five date columns to be converted. Then, it gets the URL for the Polls data, imports that data into a DataFrame, and displays the date columns for the first three rows of data. This shows how the strings that contain the dates look.

Next, this figure shows what happens if you set the parse_dates parameter of the read_csv() method to the list of column names. From the results, you can see how the formats of the dates have changed after they're converted to datetime objects.

Although this figure only shows how to use the parse_dates parameter, some of the other parameters are also useful. For instance, you can use the header parameter to specify the row and column where the data starts. That's useful when there is more than one header row at the top of the data or one or more columns on the left side of the dataset that don't need to be imported.

The usecols and nrows parameters are useful when the dataset is so large that you don't want to import it all before examining it. For example, you could import just the first 1000 rows by using nrows=1000 as a parameter. Then, after you examine the data, you could set the usecols parameter to list just the column names that you want to use for your analysis.

Last, the na_values, true_values, and false_values parameters are useful when you want to convert some values to NaN, True, or False during the import. For instance, you could set the na_values parameter to "**" if you want two asterisks converted to NaN. Or, you could set the false_values parameter to NaN, if you want NaN values converted to False. If these changes fix the problems in the columns, the right data types will be applied to the columns when they're imported.

Of course, you need to understand the data before you can decide how the parameters should be set when you import the data. But once you get the import parameters set up right, they should work each time you import an updated version of the data.

Some useful parameters of the read_csv() method

Parameter	Description
`header`	The row and column names where the import should start.
`usecols`	The columns to be imported.
`nrows`	The number of rows to import.
`parse_dates`	The columns that the to_datetime() method should try to convert.
`na_values`	The strings that should be treated as NAs.
`true_values`	The values that the dataset uses for True.
`false_values`	The values that the dataset uses for False.

How to parse object columns that contain dates and times

The date columns to be parsed

```
date_cols = ['forecastdate','startdate','enddate','createddate','timestamp']
```

The url for the file

```
polls_url = \
   'http://projects.fivethirtyeight.com/.../president_general_polls_2016.csv'
```

An import with no changes

```
polls = pd.read_csv(polls_url)
polls[date_cols].head(3)
```

	forecastdate	startdate	enddate	createddate	timestamp
0	11/8/16	11/3/2016	11/6/2016	11/7/16	09:35:33 8 Nov 2016
1	11/8/16	11/1/2016	11/7/2016	11/7/16	09:35:33 8 Nov 2016
2	11/8/16	11/2/2016	11/6/2016	11/8/16	09:35:33 8 Nov 2016

An import with parsed dates

```
polls_new = pd.read_csv(polls_url, parse_dates=date_cols)
polls_new[date_cols].head(3)
```

	forecastdate	startdate	enddate	createddate	timestamp
0	2016-11-08	2016-11-03	2016-11-06	2016-11-07	2016-11-08 09:35:33
1	2016-11-08	2016-11-01	2016-11-07	2016-11-07	2016-11-08 09:35:33
2	2016-11-08	2016-11-02	2016-11-06	2016-11-08	2016-11-08 09:35:33

Description

- If you're going to import a file every time you work with it to make sure it is the latest version, you may want to set some of the parameters for the read method that you're using. That way, some data problems will be fixed when the file is imported.

Figure 6-16 How to fix data problems when you import the data

How find and fix outliers

Outliers are values that are far outside the normal range of values in a column. For instance, the year 1918 is an outlier for the mortality data, because that was the year of the Spanish flu epidemic. As a result, far more children died that year than in the preceding or following year.

In general, there are two types of outliers: mistakes in the data and true outliers like the death rates in the year 1918. Either way, the outliers can affect the results of your analysis. So, when you clean the data for an analysis, you need to find the outliers and decide whether you need to fix them.

How to find outliers

Figure 6-17 shows a few of the ways to find outliers. The data for these examples is the morality data for just the children from 15 through 19 years of age. This data is saved in a DataFrame named mortality_group, and the first three rows of this DataFrame are shown in this figure.

Then, the first example shows how to use the describe() method to find outliers. In the results, you can see that the maximum value for the death rate is 777.4, which is far more than the death rate at the 75th percentile (283.65) or the mean death rate (177.37479). As a result, that value is probably an outlier.

The second example in this figure shows how to use the Pandas plot() method to find outliers. Here, it's easy to tell that the death rate for one of the years around 1920 is far greater than the death rates for the other years.

The third example shows how to display the death rates that are greater than 500. In this case, only one year is listed: 1918. As a result, it is clearly an outlier.

The mortality data for the 15-19 age group

```
mortality_group = mortality_data.query('AgeGroup == "15-19 Years"')
mortality_group.head(3)
```

	Year	AgeGroup	DeathRate
357	1900	15-19 Years	484.8
358	1901	15-19 Years	454.4
359	1902	15-19 Years	421.5

How to use the describe() method to find outliers

```
mortality_group.describe().T
```

	count	mean	std	min	25%	50%	75%	max
Year	119.0	1959.00000	34.496377	1900.0	1929.50	1959.0	1988.50	2018.0
DeathRate	119.0	177.37479	138.362290	44.8	85.45	106.9	283.65	777.4

How to use the plot() method to find outliers

```
mortality_group.plot(x='Year', y='DeathRate')
```

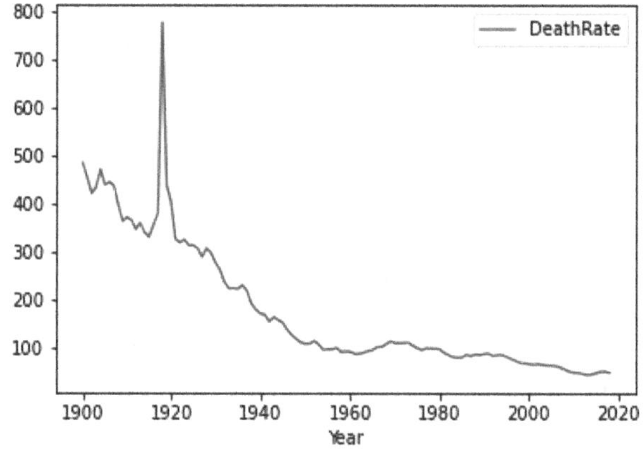

How to review the outliers in the Death Rate column

```
mortality_group.query('DeathRate > 500')
```

	Year	AgeGroup	DeathRate
375	1918	15-19 Years	777.4

Description

- An *outlier* is a value that is far outside the normal range for the values in that column.
- In general, an outlier belongs to one of two categories: a mistake in the data or a true outlier.

Figure 6-17 How to find outliers

How to fix outliers

Once you find the outliers, you need to decide how you're going to handle them. If, for example, you decide that the data for an outlier is invalid, you can drop its row. That's an easy decision.

On the other hand, what if the data for the outliers is valid but you don't want the outliers to skew your results? In that case, you can consider one of the three solutions in figure 6-18.

First, you can drop the rows for the outliers as shown by the first example in this figure. Here, the query() method is used to get just the rows in the mortality_group DataFrame where the DeathRate column is less than or equal to 500. This eliminates the outlier with a death rate greater than 500 so it won't skew your results. But in this case, you'll be missing the data for one of the years, which isn't good either.

Second, you can cap the values of the outliers. This is illustrated by the second example, which caps the outliers at 450. This will make the data for 1918 more consistent with the data for the other years.

Third, you can assign new values to the outliers like the mean of the column or the value derived from a linear interpolation. This is illustrated by the third and fourth examples. In the third example, though, the line plot shows that assigning the mean value for the DeathRate column to death rates greater than or equal to 500 isn't a good solution. On the contrary, it skews the data even more.

By contrast, the fourth example shows how the interpolate() method can be used to smooth the data. As a result, the changed data more accurately reflects the declining death rates than the data that includes the outlier. But note that you need to set the death rate values for the years that are going to be interpolated to None before the interpolate() method can be used to replace those values with interpolated values.

In this case, the plot that's prepared after the values are interpolated gives an accurate view of how the death rates have declined from 1900 to 2018, when you exclude the effect of the outliers. As a result, interpolation is the best way to handle the outliers for the mortality data, although it may not be the best way to handle other types of outliers.

Three ways to handle outliers that are valid

- Drop the outliers.
- Cap the outliers at values that won't skew the results.
- Assign new values to the outliers like the mean of the column or a linear interpolation.

How to drop the rows for the outliers

```
mortality_group = mortality_group.query('DeathRate <= 500')
```

How to cap the values of the outliers at 450

```
mortality_group.loc[mortality_group.DeathRate > 500,'DeathRate'] = 450
```

How to assign the mean of the column to the outliers

```
mortality_group.loc[mortality_group.DeathRate > 500,'DeathRate'] \
    = mortality_group.DeathRate.mean()
mortality_group.plot(x='Year', y='DeathRate')
```

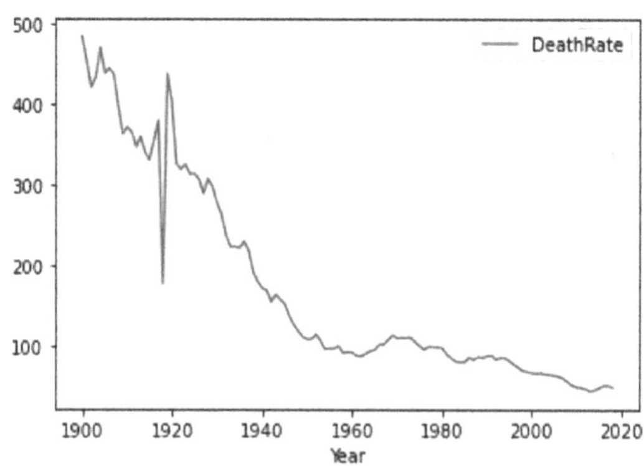

How to use interpolation to smooth the outliers

```
mortality_group.loc[mortality_group.Year.isin([1917,1918,1919,1920]),
                    'DeathRate'] = None
mortality_group = mortality_group.interpolate()
mortality_group.plot(x='Year', y='DeathRate')
```

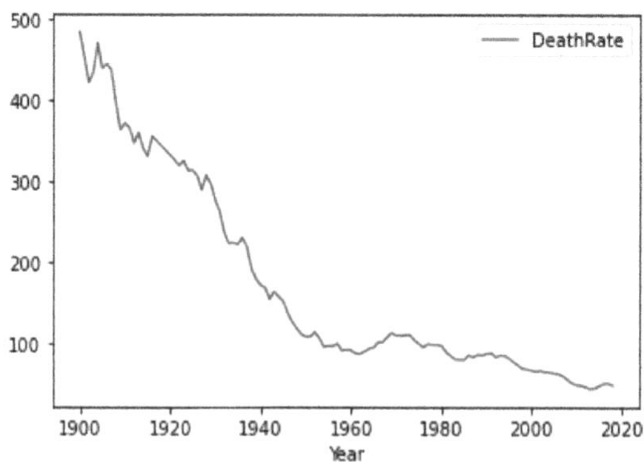

Figure 6-18 How to fix outliers

Perspective

Now that you've finished this chapter, you should realize how time-consuming it can be to clean the data and how important it is. In fact, if the data isn't clean, it will not only be hard to analyze, but your results are likely to be inaccurate or misleading.

Terms

duplicate rows
missing value
NA value (NA)
category data type
outlier

Summary

- When you clean the data in a DataFrame, you identify and fix any data problems. That can include dropping unneeded rows and columns, renaming columns, and finding and fixing *missing values*, data type problems, and *outliers*.
- To decide what cleaning needs to be done, you can analyze the non-null counts, the data types, the unique values, and the counts of the values that are in each column.
- To drop rows based on conditions, you first use the conditions to find the rows that you want to keep. Then, you drop all of the other rows by assigning just the rows that you want to keep to the DataFrame.
- When the data for a DataFrame comes from many sources, *duplicate rows* are likely. Then, you can use the duplicated() method to find those rows and the drop_duplicates() method to drop the duplicate rows from the DataFrame.
- You can use the nunique() method to help identify the columns that you want to drop. Then, you can use the drop() method to drop them.
- If the column names for a DataFrame are hard to read and understand, you can use the rename() method to rename the columns. Or, you can use Python string methods to change the names in the columns attribute of the DataFrame.
- Missing values are also known as *NA values* (or *NAs*) because they are Not Available. They include values like NaN (not a number), NaT (not a datetime), None, and NA. After you find these values, you can drop or fill the rows that contain them.
- When data is imported into a DataFrame, columns that contain only numeric data or NA values get the int64 or float64 data type. Similarly, columns that contain only True or False values get the bool data type. All others get the object data type.

- You can use the select_dtypes() method to select columns with the object data type. Then, if a column contains valid dates and times, you can use the to_datetime() method to convert the column to the datetime data type.
- If a column contains only numeric or NaN values, you can use the to_numeric() method to convert it to a numeric data type. In some cases, though, you will need to use the replace() method to fix the data before you can convert it.
- A column with the *category data type* consists of index numbers that point to a table of text entries. Because some columns are imported with this data type, you need to know how to work with it. In some cases, you may also want to save memory by using the astype() method to convert object columns to this data type.
- After you use the replace() method to fix the data in a numeric column, you can use the to_numeric() method to convert the column to a numeric data type. By contrast, when you fix the data in a Boolean column, Pandas automatically converts it to the bool data type.
- You can fix some types of data problems when you import the data. To do that, you set the parameters of the read method that you're using.
- An *outlier* is a value that is far outside the normal range for the values in that column. You can use the describe() and plot() methods to help find them.
- Three ways to fix outliers are: drop them, cap them at values that won't skew the results, or assign new values to them like the mean value of the column or a linear interpolation.

Exercise 6-1 Clean the Polling data

This exercise will guide you through the process of cleaning the Polling data for the 2016 election for president of the United States. As you clean that data, you'll use most of the procedures and methods presented in this chapter.

Read the data

1. Start JupyterLab and open the Notebook named ex_6-1_polls that should be in this folder:
   `/exercises/ch06`
2. If necessary, run the Kernel→Restart Kernel and Clear All Outputs command.
3. Run the first two cells to read the data into the DataFrame named polls.

Examine the data

4. Run the info() method on the DataFrame. Make a note of the columns that have missing values.
5. Run the nunique() method on the DataFrame. Make a note of the columns with only one value.

Drop columns and rows

6. Drop all rows except where the type column contains a value of "now-cast".
7. Run the nunique() method again to make sure the rows have been dropped. This should show that the adjpoll columns have about one third as many rows as they did before.
8. Drop all columns with a single value.
9. Drop all rows where the state column has a value of "U.S.".
10. Run the nunique() method one more time to see how the values have changed.

Rename columns

11. Rename each rawpoll_*name* column to *name*_pct where *name* is the candidate's name. For example, rename the rawpoll_clinton column to clinton_pct.

Fix data types

12. Run the info() method on the data.
13. Create a list of columns that should use the datetime type.
14. Apply the Pandas to_datetime() method to the columns in the list of datetime columns to convert these columns to the datetime type.
15. Convert the state and population columns to the category type.
16. Run the info() method one more time to see the new data types.
17. Display the Polls data to see how it looks.

Exercise 6-2 Clean the Cars data

This exercise will guide you through the process of cleaning data on various makes and models of cars.

Read the data

1. Start JupyterLab and open the Notebook named ex_6-2_cars that should be in this folder:

   `/exercises/ch06`

2. If necessary, run the Kernel→Restart Kernel and Clear All Outputs command.
3. Run the first two cells to read the data into the DataFrame named cars.
4. Display the first five rows.

Examine the data

5. Examine the data with the info() method. Note that none of the columns seem to have missing data.
6. Examine the fueltype column with the value_counts() method. Note that this column stores string values of "gas" and "diesel" that put a car into a category.
7. Examine the CarName column with the unique() method. Note that this data contains some spelling errors and inconsistent capitalization.

Fix spelling and capitalization problems in the data

8. Run the cell that adds the brand and name columns. Note that the two statements in this cell use lambda expressions, which you'll learn about in chapter 7.
9. Display each unique value in the brand column. This should help you identify spelling mistakes and inconsistent capitalization.
10. Use the replace() method to fix misspelling and inconsistent capitalization in the brand column.
11. Store the corrected data in the CarName column. To do that, you need to combine the data in the brand and name columns.
12. Display the first five rows again to see how the data has been fixed.

Rename and drop columns

13. Use the rename() method to rename the CarName column to brandname and the car_ID column to carid. That way, these columns use a naming convention that's consistent with the rest of the column names.
14. Display the first five rows. Note that the carid and symboling columns don't contain useful data for an analysis.
15. Drop the carid and symboling columns, and display the first five rows again.

Chapter 7

How to prepare the data

This chapter shows how to prepare a DataFrame for analysis. To do that, you may add and modify columns; apply functions and lambda expressions; set, unstack, and reset indexes; and combine the data in two or more DataFrames. So those are the skills that you'll learn in this chapter. But you'll also learn how to handle the SettingWithCopyWarning, which you've probably been getting from time to time.

How to add and modify columns

When you prepare your data, you often need to add columns to a DataFrame or modify the data within one of the columns. You may also want to add a column that provides summary data for groups of rows. So that's what you'll learn first in this chapter.

How to work with datetime columns

When dates and times are stored as datetime objects, you can extract parts of the object such as the year or month. Once you've done that, you can add it to the DataFrame as a new column or use it to replace the data in the original column. You can also perform calculations with datetime objects, like calculating the elapsed time between two datetime objects.

To illustrate, the first example in figure 7-1 shows the first five rows of the fires DataFrame that's used for the next two figures. This DataFrame contains six columns of data on wildfires in the United States.

Then, the second example adds a new column named fire_month that stores the month that the fire was discovered. To do that, it uses dot notation to access the discovery_date column. Then, it calls the dt accessor and accesses the month property of the discovery date. This returns the month as an integer, which is assigned to the new column.

Besides the month property, the dt accessor provides access to many other properties including the properties in the table at the top of this figure. These properties are similar to the properties that are available from Python datetime and timedelta objects, but the dt accessor doesn't provide access to all of those properties. It just provides access to the most important ones for data analysis.

The third example shows how you can use datetime objects in calculations. First, it subtracts the discovery_date column from the contain_date column. This calculation is coded in parentheses because it needs to be done before it uses the dt accessor. When it's done, this calculation returns a timedelta64 object that represents the elapsed time between the two datetime objects. Next, the code calls the dt accessor and its days property, which returns the number of days between the two datetime objects. Then, that number is assigned to the days_burning column of the DataFrame.

The DataFrame in the third example shows the new columns that have been added to it. In the next chapter, you'll see how these columns can be used to group and analyze the data.

Some of the properties that are available from the dt accessor

Property	Description
year	The year from a datetime object.
month	The month from a datetime object.
day	The day from a datetime object.
quarter	The quarter from a datetime object.
days	The number of days in a timedelta object
seconds	The number of seconds between two datetime objects.

The fires DataFrame

```
fires.head()
```

	fire_name	fire_year	state	discovery_date	contain_date	acres_burned
16	POWER	2004	CA	2004-10-06	2004-10-21	16823.0
17	FREDS	2004	CA	2004-10-13	2004-10-17	7700.0
25	BACHELOR	2004	NM	2004-07-20	2004-07-20	10.0
37	HOWARD GAP	2005	NC	2005-01-27	2005-01-28	50.3
39	AUSTIN CREEK	2005	NC	2005-02-12	2005-02-13	125.0

How to add a numeric column derived from a datetime column

```
fires['fire_month'] = fires.discovery_date.dt.month
```

How to add a numeric column derived from a datetime calculation

```
fires['days_burning'] = (fires.contain_date - fires.discovery_date).dt.days
```

	fire_name	fire_year	state	discovery_date	contain_date	acres_burned	fire_month	days_burning
16	POWER	2004	CA	2004-10-06	2004-10-21	16823.0	10	15.0
17	FREDS	2004	CA	2004-10-13	2004-10-17	7700.0	10	4.0
25	BACHELOR	2004	NM	2004-07-20	2004-07-20	10.0	7	0.0
37	HOWARD GAP	2005	NC	2005-01-27	2005-01-28	50.3	1	1.0
39	AUSTIN CREEK	2005	NC	2005-02-12	2005-02-13	125.0	2	1.0

Description

- For datetime data, you can use the dt accessor to access a subset of properties that are available from Python's datetime and timedelta objects.

Figure 7-1 How to work with datetime columns

How to work with string columns

The first example in figure 7-2 shows how you can use the str accessor to modify the fire_name column so it uses title case instead of all caps. This accessor lets you use vectorized versions of most of the Python string methods, and the most useful methods are summarized in the table in this figure. If you want to use a method that isn't in this table, though, you can check the documentation for the Series.str accessor.

The second example shows how to add a new column that contains a more elaborate string. It combines data from the fire_name and fire_year columns to create a new column named full_name. It uses Python techniques to concatenate string literals with the fire name and fire year. It also uses the astype() method to convert the fire year to a string.

You can see the results in the DataFrame in the fourth example. It shows that the fire names in the fire_name column have been converted to title case. It also shows that the names in the new full_name column include the year of the fire.

How to work with numeric columns

The third example in figure 7-2 shows how you can add a numeric column named acres_per_day to a DataFrame. It computes the average number of acres that a fire burned per day. To do that, it divides the number of acres burned by the number of days the fire was burning and assigns the result to the new column.

In this example, the two dropna() methods drop all rows that contain NA values before accessing the acres_burned and days_burning columns. That's done because NA values in these columns will cause errors if you use them as operands in the division.

You can see the results in the fourth example. But note that the third row contains an inf value for acres per day. That's because the number of acres burned was divided by 0, which results in an infinite value. Of course, you could fix that by replacing each inf value with a value that makes more sense such as 0 or the value from the acres_burned column.

Some of the methods that are available from the str accessor

Method	Description
`count(str)`	Returns a count of the number of times the substring occurs.
`lower(str)`	Converts the string to lowercase.
`upper(str)`	Converts the string to uppercase.
`title(str)`	Converts the string to title case.
`lstrip(str)`	Strips whitespace from the left side of the string.
`rstrip(str)`	Strips whitespace from the right side of the string.
`strip(str)`	Strips whitespace from both sides of the string.
`startswith(str)`	True if the string starts with the specified string. Otherwise, False.
`endswith(str)`	True if the string ends with the specified string. Otherwise, False.
`find(str)`	Searches for the specified substring and returns the index of the first occurrence or -1 if the string isn't found.
`replace(old,new)`	Replaces occurrences of the old substring with the new substring.
`join(sequence)`	Joins the elements of a sequence into a string that uses the current string as the delimiter.

How to modify a column derived from string data

```
fires['fire_name'] = fires.fire_name.str.title()
```

How to add a column derived from string data

```
fires['full_name'] = 'The ' + fires.fire_name + ' Fire ' \
                   + '(' + fires.fire_year.astype(str) + ')'
```

How to add a column derived from numeric computations

```
fires['acres_per_day'] =
    fires.dropna().acres_burned / fires.dropna().days_burning
```

The new and modified columns

```
fires[['fire_name','full_name','acres_burned','days_burning','acres_per_day']].head()
```

	fire_name	full_name	acres_burned	days_burning	acres_per_day
16	Power	The Power Fire (2004)	16823.0	15.0	1121.533333
17	Freds	The Freds Fire (2004)	7700.0	4.0	1925.000000
25	Bachelor	The Bachelor Fire (2004)	10.0	0.0	inf
37	Howard Gap	The Howard Gap Fire (2005)	50.3	1.0	50.300000
39	Austin Creek	The Austin Creek Fire (2005)	125.0	1.0	125.000000

Description

- For string data, you can use the str accessor to access a subset of methods that are available from a Python string.

Figure 7-2 How to work with string and numeric columns

How to add a summary column to a DataFrame

Figure 7-3 shows how to use the transform() method to add a summary column to a DataFrame. To illustrate, the first example shows the fires data that will be used for this operation. It contains two columns: one for the state and one for the number of days each fire burned.

Then, the second example shows how to add a new column called mean_days to the DataFrame. It will contain the mean number of days that the fires in each state burned. To do that, the groupby() method groups the data by state. Then, the transform() method calculates the average number of days that the fires burned in each state, and it puts that average in each of the rows for each state.

You can see how this works in the DataFrame for the second example. Here, the average number of burn days for each fire in California is in each row of the mean_days column for California. This works the same for North Carolina, as well as all the other states. Of course, that average is for all the fires in each state, not just the ones in the first five rows.

The transform() method

Method	Description
transform(params)	Adds summary values to each row.
Parameter	**Description**
func	The function to apply.
axis	0 (the default) for rows; 1 for columns.

The fires data

```
fires[['state','days_burning']].head()
```

	state	days_burning
16	CA	15.0
17	CA	4.0
25	NM	0.0
37	NC	1.0
39	NC	1.0

How to add a summary column to a DataFrame

```
fires['mean_days'] = fires.groupby('state')['days_burning']. \
    transform(func='mean')
fires[['state','days_burning','mean_days']].head()
```

	state	days_burning	mean_days
16	CA	15.0	5.387197
17	CA	4.0	5.387197
25	NM	0.0	6.085806
37	NC	1.0	1.015474
39	NC	1.0	1.015474

Description

- The transform() method can be used to get the summary data for groups and add it to each row in a DataFrame.

Figure 7-3 How to add a summary column to a DataFrame

How to apply functions and lambda expressions

Sometimes, the techniques you've just learned don't provide all the functionality that you need to add or modify a column. In that case, you can use the apply() method to apply a function or a lambda expression to a column or row.

How to apply functions to rows or columns

Figure 7-4 shows how to use the apply() method to apply a function to each of the rows or columns of a DataFrame. As the examples show, you can use this method to apply a built-in Pandas function or a function from another library like NumPy. And as the next three figures show, you can also use this method to apply a user-defined function or a lambda expression.

To illustrate how the apply() method works, the first example in this figure shows the first three rows of the DataFrame that's used in the next few figures. This DataFrame has seven columns that contain data from a survey about work.

Then, the second example shows how to apply the built-in Pandas mean() function to all numeric columns in that DataFrame. And the third example shows how to apply the NumPy mean() function to two of the numeric columns in the DataFrame. Since the axis parameter isn't specified, the default value is used, which applies these functions to the columns, not the rows.

The last example shows how the NumPy mean() function can be applied to rows rather than columns. To do that, the axis parameter is set to 1. As a result, this code returns a Series object that contains the average of the three columns for each row. Then, it assigns this Series object to a new column named avg_rating.

In practice, though, you usually won't use the apply() method to apply an aggregate function like the mean() function. Instead, you would call the mean() function directly from the DataFrame or Series object that you're working with. That's why the apply() method is normally used to apply user-defined functions and lambda expressions as shown in the next three figures.

The apply() method

Method	Description
`apply(params)`	Applies a function to the data in a row or a column and returns a Series.
Parameter	**Description**
`function`	The function that's applied to each row or column. It can be a built-in function, a NumPy function, a user-defined function, or a lambda expression.
`axis`	The axis that the function is applied to: axis=0 (the default) for columns and axis=1 for rows.

The workData DataFrame

```
workData.head(3)
```

	sex	region	wrkstat	hrs1	wkcontct	talkspvs	effctsup
id							
2	2	1	1.0	40.0	3.0	4.0	4.0
4	2	1	2.0	20.0	1.0	4.0	4.0
14	2	2	1.0	37.0	1.0	4.0	3.0

How to apply a built-in Pandas function to all numeric columns

```
workData.apply('mean')
```

How to apply a NumPy function to two columns

```
import numpy as np
workData[['sex','hrs1']].apply(np.mean)
========================================
sex      1.529897
hrs1    42.083505
```

How to apply a function to row data

```
workData['avg_rating'] = workData[
    ['wkcontct','talkspvs','effctsup']].apply(np.mean, axis=1)
workData.head(3)
```

	sex	region	wrkstat	hrs1	wkcontct	talkspvs	effctsup	avg_rating
id								
2	2	1	1.0	40.0	3.0	4.0	4.0	3.666667
4	2	1	2.0	20.0	1.0	4.0	4.0	3.000000
14	2	2	1.0	37.0	1.0	4.0	3.0	2.666667

Description

- Although you can use the apply() method to apply functions like the mean function, the apply() method is normally used to apply user-defined functions and lambda expressions.

Figure 7-4 How to apply functions to rows or columns

How to apply user-defined functions

Figure 7-5 shows how to use a user-defined function to modify the data in a column or to add a new column to a DataFrame. Here, the first example presents a user-defined function named convert_sex that modifies the data in a column. It changes the integer codes 1 and 2 to "male" and "female". And if the code isn't either 1 or 2, it puts "non-binary" in the row.

After this function is defined, the apply() method applies it to the column named sex in the DataFrame. Because this method also sets the axis parameter to 1, the convert_sex() function is applied to each row in the DataFrame. Because of that, this function defines a parameter for a row. Then, within the function, the code uses this parameter to access the value of the sex column and return the correct string.

Note, however, that since this function is designed to process rows, it only works correctly if you set the axis parameter to 1. Although you could also code the function so it works with a column rather than a row, it typically makes sense to work with rows. That way, the function has access to any column it needs.

The second example uses a DataFrame that consists of a subset of the shot data for Stephen Curry. Specifically, it includes just the game_id and game_date columns with all duplicates dropped. That way, the DataFrame includes just one row for each game.

This example applies a user-defined function named get_season() to the DataFrame. Like the first function, this function also defines a parameter for a row. Then, it uses this parameter to access the game_date column to determine what season the game belongs to. Since basketball season starts in the late fall and ends in the late spring, this code uses June as a safe point at which to divide the games up into seasons. However, any month after May and before December should work.

So, within this function, the if statement checks whether the month that's stored in the game_date column is greater than 6. If so, the season must have started in the year that's stored in the game_date column. As a result, this function returns a string that consists of that year, a dash, and the next year. Otherwise, it returns a string that consists of the previous year, a dash, and the current year.

To do that, this code uses a Python *formatted string literal*, also known as an *f-string*. This string begins with an f followed by a string literal that uses braces to identify the data to be inserted into the string literal. After the string is built, the function returns it and the code assigns it to a new column named season.

How to apply a user-defined function to a column

```
def convert_sex(row):
    if row.sex == 1:
        return 'male'
    elif row.sex == 2:
        return 'female'
    else:
        return 'non-binary'

workData['sex'] = workData.apply(convert_sex, axis=1)
workData.head()
```

	sex	region	wrkstat	hrs1	wkcontct	talkspvs	effctsup
id							
2	female	1	1.0	40.0	3.0	4.0	4.0
4	female	1	2.0	20.0	1.0	4.0	4.0
14	female	2	1.0	37.0	1.0	4.0	3.0
19	male	1	1.0	50.0	1.0	3.0	4.0
21	female	1	1.0	38.0	1.0	4.0	4.0

How to apply another user-defined function to a column

```
def get_season(row):
    if row.game_date.month > 6:
        season = f'{row.game_date.year}-{row.game_date.year + 1}'
    else:
        season = f'{row.game_date.year - 1}-{row.game_date.year}'
    return season

gameData['season'] = gameData.apply(get_season, axis=1)
with pd.option_context('display.max_rows', 6, 'display.max_columns', None):
    display(gameData)
```

	game_id	game_date	season
0	0020900015	2009-10-28	2009-2010
12	0020900030	2009-10-30	2009-2010
21	0020900069	2009-11-04	2009-2010
...	...	...	...
11801	0021801191	2019-04-05	2018-2019
11822	0021801205	2019-04-07	2018-2019
11842	0021801215	2019-04-09	2018-2019

Description

- When you code a user-defined function, make sure it defines a parameter for the row or column that it will be applied to.

Figure 7-5 How to apply user-defined functions

How lambda expressions work with DataFrames

You can also use the apply() method to apply *lambda expressions*, or *lambdas*, These expressions are more concise than user-defined functions and they are commonly used for short functions that are only used once.

The only problem with lambdas is that the coding syntax can be confusing. That's why figure 7-6 starts by presenting the syntax of lambda expressions. Here, the italicized parts of the syntax are the parts that you code.

One difference between a normal if statement and an if statement in a lambda expression is that the return value if True comes before the conditional statement. Despite this, the return value for the else branch in the if-else syntax comes last.

Similarly, the if-elif-else syntax is unusual. Here again, the return value if True is coded before the if condition. Then, a second if-else structure is coded in parentheses. It covers the elif-else portion of the if-elif-else structure.

To illustrate how this syntax works, the first example in this figure shows a simple DataFrame that has three columns and two rows. Then, the second example uses a lambda to apply the sum() method to each column and then multiply the result by 2. And the third example does the same operation as the second one, but it uses 1 for the axis parameter so the operation is applied to each row.

One thing you may realize here is that you can get the same result by performing the operations directly on the column. So, to do that for the first column, you could use this code:

```
df.col1.sum() * 2
```

For this reason, lambdas are typically used to modify row data rather than column data.

The syntax of a lambda expression

The if syntax

```
lambda arguments: return-value-if-true if condition
```

The if-else syntax

```
lambda arguments: return-value-if-true if condition else
    return_value-if-false
```

The if-elif-else syntax

```
lambda arguments: return_value-if-condition1-true if condition1 else
    (return-value-if-condition-2-true if condition-2 else
     return_value-if-condition-2-false)
```

The example data

```
df
```

	col1	col2	col3
0	0	1	2
1	3	4	5

A lambda expression that sums and then doubles the value in each column

```
df.apply(lambda x: x.sum() * 2, axis=0)
========================================
col1     6
col2    10
col3    14
dtype: int64
```

A lambda expression that sums and then doubles the value in each row

```
df.apply(lambda x: x.sum() * 2, axis=1)
========================================
0     6
1    24
dtype: int64
```

Description

- A *lambda expression*, or just *lambda*, is a concise way to write a short function. In most cases, lambdas are used when a function is only going to be needed once in the analysis.
- A lambda can have any number of arguments but only one expression.

Figure 7-6 How lambda expressions work with DataFrames

How to apply lambda expressions

Figure 7-7 presents two examples that apply lambda expressions to rows. Here, the first example applies a lambda expression that converts the values 1.0 and 2.0 that are in the wrkstat column into strings that say “full-time” or “part-time”. Here, the lambda uses its row parameter to access the wrkstat column.

Although x is commonly used for the argument in a lambda, this example shows that you can name the argument just as would any other variable. In this case, since the lambda operates on row data, the use of “row” can make the code easier to follow.

The second example shows how to extract the brand of a car from its full name. Here, the car name consists of the brand followed by a space and the rest of the car name. This time, the lambda expression uses x as the argument. Then, the expression accesses the CarName column with dot notation, and it uses the Python split() method to split the string at its spaces. Next, it uses the 0 index value to get the first string in the list of strings, and it assigns that string to a new column named Brand.

These examples give you a quick idea of how lambdas work and how useful they can be, especially if the lambda expressions are short and will only be used once. However, lambda expressions do have a syntax that can be hard to code and hard to read. So if you code a lambda that gets too complicated, remember that you can replace it with a user-defined function.

How to apply a lambda expression to a column

```
workData['wrkstat'] = workData.apply(
    lambda row: 'full-time' if row.wrkstat == 1.0 else 'part-time', axis=1)
workData.head()
```

id	sex	region	wrkstat	hrs1	wkcontct	talkspvs	effctsup
2	female	1	full-time	40.0	3.0	4.0	4.0
4	female	1	part-time	20.0	1.0	4.0	4.0
14	female	2	full-time	37.0	1.0	4.0	3.0
19	male	1	full-time	50.0	1.0	3.0	4.0
21	female	1	full-time	38.0	1.0	4.0	4.0

How to use a lambda expression to add a new column

```
carsData['Brand'] = carsData.apply(lambda x: x.CarName.split()[0], axis=1)
carsData[['CarName','Brand']].head()
```

	CarName	Brand
0	alfa-romero giulia	alfa-romero
1	alfa-romero stelvio	alfa-romero
2	alfa-romero Quadrifoglio	alfa-romero
3	audi 100 ls	audi
4	audi 100ls	audi

Description

- In most cases, you'll apply lambda expressions to rows rather than columns. That's because using a lambda to apply a method to a column is the same as using dot notation to access the column and then calling the method directly.

Figure 7-7 How to apply lambda expressions

How to work with indexes

In chapter 2, you were introduced to indexes. There, you learned that you can use the set_index() method to set an *index* that can be used to access each row in a DataFrame. You also learned that some methods like the pivot() and groupby() methods also set an index. Now, you'll learn more about working with indexes.

How to set and remove an index

The first table in figure 7-8 summarizes the set_index() method and a few of its most useful parameters. Then, the first example shows how to set an index on the state column of the fires data. Here, the inplace parameter is set to True so the index is added to the DataFrame.

The second example shows how to set a *multi-level index* (or *hierarchical index*). That is an index that's set on more than one column. In this case, it's set on the state, fire_year, and fire_month columns. As you can see in the results, the names for these index columns are displayed on the left of the DataFrame at a lower level than the names for the other columns.

The second table in this figure summarizes the reset_index() method, which provides a way to remove an index. This is illustrated by the last example. Here, the results show that the reset_index() method returns the index columns to normal columns. That's essential when you're working with Seaborn, because you can't use Seaborn to plot the data in index columns.

By contrast, the Pandas plot() method is designed to work with indexed data. That's also true for some other Pandas methods like the join() and concat() methods, which you'll learn about later in this chapter.

When you reset all indexes as shown in the third example, the index resets to a numeric index that starts with 0 and continues with an ordered sequence of integers that identifies each row. However, this sequence of integers can get gaps in it if you later remove rows from the DataFrame. In that case, you may want or need to reset the index so it uses an ordered sequence of integers.

To do that, you can call the reset_index() method and set the drop parameter to True. That way, the old index that isn't in an ordered sequence is dropped, which is usually what you want. Otherwise, this index would be stored as a column in the DataFrame, which isn't usually what you want.

When you use a hierarchical index, the repeating index values aren't displayed. That's why the second example only displays AK and 1992 once instead of displaying them three times. In this case, these values aren't repeated because this DataFrame happened to be sorted by its index before the set_index() method was called. However, you can always sort a DataFrame by its index by calling its sort_index() method. Since this method works much like the reset_index() method, you shouldn't have much trouble using it if you ever need it.

The set_index() method

Method	Description
`set_index(params)`	Sets an index for the specified column or list of columns.

Parameter	Description
`keys`	The column or list of columns to be used for the index.
`inplace`	If set to True, modifies the DataFrame in place.
`verify_integrity`	If set to True, throws an error if the specified index contains any duplicates.

How to set an index

```
fires_by_month.set_index('state', inplace=True)
```

How to set an index on multiple columns

```
fires_by_month.set_index(['state','fire_year','fire_month'], inplace=True)
fires_by_month.head(3)
```

			acres_burned	days_burning	fire_count
state	fire_year	fire_month			
AK	1992	5	4202.0	135.0	14
		6	86401.0	417.0	23
		7	48516.7	500.0	26

The reset_index() method

Method	Description
`reset_index(params)`	Resets the index to an auto-generated list of integers.

Parameter	Description
`inplace`	If set to True, modifies the DataFrame in place.
`level`	The level of index to reset. By default, all indexes are reset.
`drop`	If set to True, drops the index columns instead of converting them to DataFrame columns.

How to remove an index

```
fires_by_month.reset_index(inplace=True)
fires_by_month.head(3)
```

	state	fire_year	fire_month	acres_burned	days_burning	fire_count
0	AK	1992	5	4202.0	135.0	14
1	AK	1992	6	86401.0	417.0	23
2	AK	1992	7	48516.7	500.0	26

Figure 7-8 How to set and remove an index

How to unstack indexed data

After you set an index for a DataFrame, you can use the unstack() method to *unstack* the data based on the index. This is illustrated in figure 7-9. Here, the first example sets a two-level index for a DataFrame that contains the data for the 5 largest fires in each state in each year.

Then, the second example unstacks the values in the state column of the index so they're displayed as columns below the days_burning and fire_count columns. This creates wide data with five columns for the original days_burning column and five more for the original fire_count column. When wide data is indexed like this, it can be easily plotted by the Pandas plot() method.

The next three examples are like the second one, but the third example unstacks the state column for all three columns (acres_burned, days_burning, and fire_count). The fourth example unstacks the state column for just the fire_count column. And the fifth example works like the second example, but it uses an integer to specify the index level instead of using a column name.

You can also unstack the rightmost index column without specifying the index level. This is illustrated by the last example in this figure. Here, the level parameter is omitted, so the fire_year column will be unstacked. This is simpler than specifying the column name or index level.

Although the fill_value parameter isn't used in these examples, you can use it to replace any NaN values that are generated by the unstack() method. If, for example, you set the fill_value parameter to 0, any NaN values in the resulting DataFrame are replaced with 0.

The unstack() method

Method	Description
unstack(params)	Unstacks the data in an indexed DataFrame.

Parameter	Description
level	The index column or list of index columns to unstack.
fill_value	A value that replaces any NA values.

The top_states DataFrame in long form

```
top5_states.set_index(['state','fire_year'], inplace=True)
top5_states.head(3)
```

		acres_burned	days_burning	fire_count
state	fire_year			
AK	1992	142444.7	1145.0	68.0
	1993	686630.5	3373.0	144.0
	1994	261604.7	2517.0	126.0

How to unstack two of the columns at the state level

```
top_wide = top5_states[['days_burning','fire_count']].unstack(level='state')
top_wide.head(3)
```

	days_burning					fire_count				
state	AK	ID	CA	TX	NV	AK	ID	CA	TX	NV
fire_year										
1992	1145.0	1375.0	434.0	11.0	88.0	68.0	192.0	819.0	22.0	65.0
1993	3373.0	130.0	302.0	39.0	83.0	144.0	33.0	726.0	42.0	62.0
1994	2517.0	3039.0	727.0	35.0	235.0	126.0	245.0	720.0	54.0	109.0

How to unstack all columns at the state level

```
top_wide = top5_states.unstack(level='state')
```

How to unstack a single column at the state level

```
top_wide = top5_states.fire_count.unstack(level='state')
```

How to use an integer to specify the state level

```
top_wide = top5_states[['days_burning','fire_count']].unstack(level=0')
```

How to unstack the rightmost index column

```
top_wide = top5_states.unstack()
```

Figure 7-9 How to unstack indexed data

How to combine DataFrames

When you prepare your data, you may need to combine data that's stored in two or more DataFrame or Series objects into a single DataFrame. To do that with Pandas, you can use the join(), merge(), or concat() methods. The next four figures show how to use them.

How to join DataFrames with an inner join

Figure 7-10 presents the join() method that you can use to *join* two DataFrames based on their index values. If you're familiar with database joins, you'll see that the join() method works the same way. You'll also see that it provides for inner, left, right, and outer joins.

To illustrate, the first two examples in this figure present the two DataFrames to be joined. Here, the shots DataFrames has just 4 rows, and the points_by_game DataFrame has just 3 rows. That will make it easier for you to see how the join() method works.

As you can see, both of these DataFrames are indexed by the game_id column. Since there are multiple shots (rows) for each game, the first DataFrame has two rows with the same index value. But since there's only one total score for each game, the rows in the second DataFrame have unique index values.

The third example joins the two DataFrames with an *inner join* that's specified by the how parameter. That means that rows in the left DataFrame will only be joined with rows that have matching index values in the right DataFrame. As a result, this join() method will join the data in the total_score column in the second DataFrame to the matching rows in the first DataFrame.

Notice that that the last row in each of the joined DataFrames isn't included in the result. That's because the second DataFrame doesn't include a row for the game in the last row of the first DataFrame. Similarly, the first DataFrame doesn't include a row for the game in the last row of the second DataFrame. Although this may not be realistic, it should help you understand how inner joins work.

By default, the join() method joins the DataFrames on the index columns. But if the index for the left DataFrame hasn't been set, you can use the on parameter to specify the column to join on. However, the right DataFrame always uses the index that has been set for it. In the next figure, you'll see how the lsuffix and rsuffix parameters work.

The join() method

Method	Description
`join(params)`	Joins the columns in the left DataFrame with the columns in the right DataFrame based on an index.

Parameter	Description
`df`	The DataFrame or list of DataFrames to join with the calling DataFrame.
`on`	The column to be used for the index in the left DataFrame.
`how`	The type of join to use: left (the default), right, inner, or outer.
`lsuffix`	The suffix to append to any overlapping columns in the left DataFrame.
`rsuffix`	The suffix to append to any overlapping columns in the right DataFrame.

The shots DataFrame (just 4 rows)

game_id	player_name	event_type	shot_type	shot_distance
0020900015	Stephen Curry	Missed Shot	3PT Field Goal	26
0020900015	Stephen Curry	Made Shot	2PT Field Goal	18
0020900030	Stephen Curry	Missed Shot	3PT Field Goal	24
0020900069	Stephen Curry	Made Shot	3PT Field Goal	25

The points_by_game DataFrame (just 3 rows)

game_id	total_score
0020900015	14
0020900030	12
0020900082	2

How to inner join the two DataFrames

```
shots_joined = shots.join(points_by_game, how='inner')
shots_joined
```

game_id	player_name	event_type	shot_type	shot_distance	total_score
0020900015	Stephen Curry	Missed Shot	3PT Field Goal	26	14
0020900015	Stephen Curry	Made Shot	2PT Field Goal	18	14
0020900030	Stephen Curry	Missed Shot	3PT Field Goal	24	12

Figure 7-10 How to join DataFrames with an inner join

How to join DataFrames with a left or outer join

Figure 7-11 shows how to join DataFrames with left and outer joins. In a *left join*, all rows in the left DataFrame are joined with the matching indexes in the right DataFrame, but rows in the right DataFrame that don't match are dropped. In an *outer join*, all rows in both DataFrames are included in the resulting DataFrame whether or not the indexes match.

The first two examples in this figure show the two DataFrames that will be joined. Here again, the first DataFrame has just 4 rows and the second DataFrame has just 3 rows. But note that both of these DataFrames also have a column named player_name, and that will cause problems when the DataFrames are joined.

To deal with that, though, you can use the rsuffix and lsuffix parameters as shown by the third example. This appends the strings in the parameters to any conflicting column names. As a result, a string of "_1" is appended to the player_name column in the left table, and a string of "_2" is appended to the player_name column in the right table.

This shows how both suffix parameters work, but you only need to specify one suffix to fix the problem. For example, you could specify a string of "_dup" for the rsuffix parameter to create a column named player_name_dup. Then, once you are sure that this column doesn't contain data that you want to keep, you can drop the column.

The fourth example in this figure is for an outer join, so all rows in both DataFrames will be joined. But since the points_by_game DataFrame doesn't have the same columns as the shots DataFrame, any rows in the right DataFrame that don't match rows in the left DataFrame will have missing values for the columns in the left DataFrame. Similarly, any rows in the left DataFrame that don't match rows in the right DataFrame will have missing values for the right DataFrame.

What about right joins? You don't ever need to use them because you can get the same results with a left join. You just need to reverse the sequence of the DataFrames that are joined.

The shots DataFrame (just 4 rows)

game_id	player_name	event_type	shot_type	shot_distance
0020900015	Stephen Curry	Missed Shot	3PT Field Goal	26
0020900015	Stephen Curry	Made Shot	2PT Field Goal	18
0020900030	Stephen Curry	Missed Shot	3PT Field Goal	24
0020900069	Stephen Curry	Made Shot	3PT Field Goal	25

The points_by_game DataFrame (just 3 rows)

game_id	total_score	player_name
0020900015	14	Steph Curry
0020900030	12	Steph Curry
0020900082	2	Steph Curry

How to left join the two DataFrames

```
shots_joined = shots.join(points_by_game, lsuffix='_1', rsuffix='_2',
                          how='left')
shots_joined
```

game_id	player_name_1	event_type	shot_type	shot_distance	total_score	player_name_2
0020900015	Stephen Curry	Missed Shot	3PT Field Goal	26	14.0	Steph Curry
0020900015	Stephen Curry	Made Shot	2PT Field Goal	18	14.0	Steph Curry
0020900030	Stephen Curry	Missed Shot	3PT Field Goal	24	12.0	Steph Curry
0020900069	Stephen Curry	Made Shot	3PT Field Goal	25	NaN	NaN

How to outer join the two DataFrames

```
shots_joined_outer = shots.join(points_by_game, lsuffix='_1',
                                rsuffix='_2', how='outer')
shots_joined_outer
```

game_id	player_name_1	event_type	shot_type	shot_distance	total_score	player_name_2
0020900015	Stephen Curry	Missed Shot	3PT Field Goal	26.0	14.0	Steph Curry
0020900015	Stephen Curry	Made Shot	2PT Field Goal	18.0	14.0	Steph Curry
0020900030	Stephen Curry	Missed Shot	3PT Field Goal	24.0	12.0	Steph Curry
0020900069	Stephen Curry	Made Shot	3PT Field Goal	25.0	NaN	NaN
0020900082	NaN	NaN	NaN	NaN	2.0	Steph Curry

Figure 7-11 How to join DataFrames with a left or outer join

How to merge DataFrames

The merge() method is like the join() method but it *merges* the data in two DataFrames based on the data in one or more columns that aren't indexed. This method is summarized in figure 7-12. Here, you can see that the on, how, and suffixes parameters work like those for the join() method. However, the suffixes parameter takes a tuple that provides the values to append to columns with the same names.

The examples in this figure show how this works. Here, the first two examples present the DataFrames to be merged. Note that these DataFrames don't use the game_id column as an index. Instead, they use the default numeric index.

Then, the third example shows how to merge the DataFrames based on the game_id column. To do that, this example uses the on parameter to specify the game_id column. In this case, since the how parameter is set to left, the result is similar to the result for the left join in the previous figure. The main difference is that game_id is an index in the previous figure, but it's a column in this figure.

The merge() method

Method	Description
`merge(params)`	Merges the columns in the left DataFrame with the columns in the right DataFrame based on the data in one or more columns that aren't indexed.
Parameter	**Description**
`right`	The DataFrame to merge with the current DataFrame.
`on`	The column or list of columns to merge on. By default, it uses the column names that are the same in both DataFrames.
`how`	Works like the join() method but uses 'inner' by default.
`suffixes`	A tuple that provides the values to append to columns with the same name in the left and right DataFrames.

The shots DataFrame (just 4 rows)

	game_id	player_name	event_type	shot_type	shot_distance
0	0020900015	Stephen Curry	Missed Shot	3PT Field Goal	26
1	0020900015	Stephen Curry	Made Shot	2PT Field Goal	18
2	0020900030	Stephen Curry	Missed Shot	3PT Field Goal	24
3	0020900069	Stephen Curry	Made Shot	3PT Field Goal	25

The points_by_game DataFrame (just 3 rows)

	game_id	total_score
0	0020900015	14
1	0020900030	12
2	0020900082	2

How to merge the two DataFrames

```
shots_merged = shots.merge(points_by_game, on='game_id', how='left')
shots_merged
```

	game_id	player_name	event_type	shot_type	shot_distance	total_score
0	0020900015	Stephen Curry	Missed Shot	3PT Field Goal	26	14.0
1	0020900015	Stephen Curry	Made Shot	2PT Field Goal	18	14.0
2	0020900030	Stephen Curry	Missed Shot	3PT Field Goal	24	12.0
3	0020900069	Stephen Curry	Made Shot	3PT Field Goal	25	NaN

Description

- You can use the merge() method to *merge* DataFrames based on the data in one or more columns that aren't indexed.

Figure 7-12 How to merge DataFrames

How to concatenate DataFrames

The third way to combine DataFrames is to *concatenate* them. To do that, you use the concat() method that's summarized in figure 7-13. This method lets you add rows from the second DataFrame in this figure to the bottom of the first DataFrame. Or, it lets you add columns from the second DataFrame to the right of the first DataFrame.

To illustrate, the first DataFrame in this figure contains just three rows and the second DataFrame contains two rows. Although both DataFrames contain data about fires, the first DataFrame contains two more columns than the second.

Then, the third example concatenates the DataFrames in the first two examples. To do that, it calls the concat() method from the Pandas library, not from the first DataFrame. It lists the two DataFrames to be concatenated as the first parameter. And it sets the ignore_index parameter to True so the old index values are dropped and the index is reset.

In the DataFrame that results from this method, you can see that the two rows in the second DataFrame have been concatenated to the bottom of the first DataFrame. That's because the default value for the axis parameter is 0. But since the second DataFrame doesn't have the fire_month and days_burning columns, the added rows have null values in those columns.

If the axis parameter was set to 1, columns would be added to the right side of the DataFrame instead of rows to the bottom. In this example, the five columns in the second DataFrame would be added to the first DataFrame, duplicating those columns. Because that's not usually what you want, you would typically only concatenate columns that contain different data.

In that case, though, the concat() method would work more like the join() method. But since the join() method works better for joining columns than the concat() method, you usually use the concat() method to add rows, not columns.

Now that you've seen the three methods for combining data, here's a quick summary. If you want to combine the columns in two or more DataFrames based on indexes, use the join() method. If you want to combine columns in two DataFrames based on columns, use the merge() method. And if you want to combine the rows for two DataFrames, use the concat() method.

The concat() method

Method	Description
`concat(params)`	Concatenates (adds) the data in one DataFrame to another DataFrame.
Parameter	**Description**
`objs`	A list of the DataFrames that you want to concatenate.
`axis`	The default of 0 adds rows to the bottom of the first DataFrame. Setting it to 1 adds columns to the right side of the first DataFrame.
`ignore_index`	If True, don't keep the index values along the concatenation axis. Instead, reset the index on that axis.
`join`	If 'inner', use an inner join. Otherwise, use an outer join.

The fires_1 DataFrame (just 3 rows)

	fire_name	fire_year	state	discovery_date	acres_burned	fire_month	days_burning
0	Inowak	1997	AK	1997-06-25	606945.0	6	76.0
1	Long Draw	2012	OR	2012-07-08	558198.3	7	22.0
2	Wallow	2011	AZ	2011-05-29	538049.0	5	44.0

The fires_2 DataFrame (just 2 rows)

	fire_name	fire_year	state	discovery_date	acres_burned
0	Boundary	2004	AK	2004-06-13	537627.0
1	Minto Flats South	2009	AK	2009-06-21	517078.0

The concatenated DataFrame

```
fires_concat = pd.concat([fires_1,fires_2], ignore_index=True)
fires_concat
```

	fire_name	fire_year	state	discovery_date	acres_burned	fire_month	days_burning
0	Inowak	1997	AK	1997-06-25	606945.0	6.0	76.0
1	Long Draw	2012	OR	2012-07-08	558198.3	7.0	22.0
2	Wallow	2011	AZ	2011-05-29	538049.0	5.0	44.0
3	Boundary	2004	AK	2004-06-13	537627.0	NaN	NaN
4	Minto Flats South	2009	AK	2009-06-21	517078.0	NaN	NaN

Description

- You normally use the concat() method to *concatenate* (add) rows, not columns, to a DataFrame

Figure 7-13 How to concatenate DataFrames

How to handle the SettingWithCopyWarning

By this time, you've probably encountered the SettingWithCopyWarning that's sometimes displayed by JupyterLab after you run a cell. You probably also noticed that the code runs even though the warning is displayed. If you haven't yet encountered this warning, you probably will before long. It's shown in figure 7-14.

What the warning is telling you

The SettingWithCopyWarning tells you that some unexpected behavior *might* happen when your code is run. This is illustrated by the example in figure 7-14. Here, the first statement in the code creates a slice of the DataFrame named df that consists of just the rows for game 0020900015 and saves it in a new DataFrame named dfSlice. Then, the data in the player_name column of the dfSlice DataFrame is changed from "Stephen Curry" to "Curry".

This generates the warning message, but the code still runs. In the results of the code, though, you can see that the data in the player_name column has been changed in both the df and dfSlice DataFrames, which isn't what you would expect. Although this is a trivial error because the data involved is a string, this could cause serious errors if the changed data was critical to the results.

What's happening here is that the first statement in the code doesn't generate a new DataFrame named dfSlice. Instead, it generates a *reference*, or pointer, to the data in the original DataFrame. In other words, the dfSlice DataFrame is a *view* of the original DataFrame. As a result, any change to the dfSlice DataFrame will also be made to the df DataFrame, which usually isn't what you want.

To compound the problem, you can't be sure whether Pandas is going to create a view or a *copy* of the original DataFrame. That depends on how the statement is handled internally. But that means that sometimes there is a problem that needs to be fixed and sometimes there isn't. Besides that, using the loc accessor doesn't always fix the problem, even though that's what the warning suggests.

The SettingWithCopyWarning

```
df.head()
```

	player_name	event_type	shot_type	shot_distance
game_id				
0020900015	Stephen Curry	Missed Shot	3PT Field Goal	26
0020900015	Stephen Curry	Made Shot	2PT Field Goal	18
0020900015	Stephen Curry	Missed Shot	2PT Field Goal	14

Code that generates the warning and corrupts the data

```
dfSlice = df.loc['0020900015',:]           # creates the slice (view)
dfSlice.loc[:,'player_name'] = 'Curry'     # modifies the slice
```

The warning

```
<ipython-input-93-57fca793a825>:1: SettingWithCopyWarning:
A value is trying to be set on a copy of a slice from a DataFrame.
Try using .loc[row_indexer,col_indexer] = value instead

See the caveats in the documentation: https://pandas.pydata.org/pandas-
docs/stable/user_guide/indexing.html#returning-a-view-versus-a-copy
  self[name] = value
```

The data after modification...but both DataFrames have been modified!

```
df.head(3)
```

	player_name	shot_type	shot_distance
game_id			
0020900015	Curry	3PT Field Goal	26
0020900015	Curry	2PT Field Goal	18
0020900015	Curry	2PT Field Goal	14

```
dfSlice.head(3)
```

	player_name	shot_type	shot_distance
game_id			
0020900015	Curry	3PT Field Goal	26
0020900015	Curry	2PT Field Goal	18
0020900015	Curry	2PT Field Goal	14

Description

- The SettingWithCopyWarning warns that your code might modify a *view* (also called a *reference*) of a DataFrame instead of a *copy* of the DataFrame. So, if you modify the view, the original DataFrame may also be modified.
- The trouble is that some Pandas methods return a view, and some return a copy, but you can't be sure which is returned.

Figure 7-14 What the SettingWithCopyWarning is telling you

What to do when the warning is displayed

Figure 7-15 presents two examples that illustrate code that generates the warning. The first example generates the warning but works correctly. The second generates the warning but doesn't work correctly. Instead, it corrupts the data in the original DataFrame.

In the first example, the query() method creates a new DataFrame named dfSlice that's a slice of the df DataFrame. Then, the player_name column is modified in the new DataFrame. This works correctly and doesn't corrupt the data in the df DataFrame, even though the warning message is displayed. That's because the query returned a copy instead of a reference.

In the second example, the code uses the loc[ ] accessor to get the same slice of the original DataFrame and create a new DataFrame for it. Once again, the player_name column is modified in the new DataFrame. But this time, the data in both DataFrames is modified. This corrupts the data in the original DataFrame.

The trouble is that you can't be sure whether Pandas is going to return a view or a copy when a new DataFrame is created. That depends on what's going on internally. So how do you handle the warning message?

First, if you are assigning the new DataFrame to the same variable as the original DataFrame, you can ignore the warning message since it's clear that you're no longer using that variable to refer to the original DataFrame. Second, if you know that you aren't going to use the original DataFrame again, you can be sure that there won't be a problem. In either case, you can ignore the warning.

Another way to handle the warning is to use the copy() method to guarantee that a copy is returned rather than a reference. You can see how to do that in the code at the end of each example in this figure. That will both remove the warning and protect you from the unpredictable behavior. However, the copy will take up more memory so you shouldn't use this technique more than necessary, especially if you are working with large DataFrames.

What to watch for when the warning isn't displayed

Now that you're aware of the potential problem with a reference to a DataFrame instead of a copy of a DataFrame, you need to know that this type of problem can occur even when a warning isn't displayed. Suppose, for example, that you write code like this:

```
dfSlice = df
dfSlice.loc[:,'player_name'] = 'Curry'
```

It might corrupt the data in the df DataFrame just as in the second example in this figure. However, the warning won't be displayed.

Here again, that won't cause a problem if you don't use the original DataFrame again. And, you can make a copy of it if you do want to use the original DataFrame again. But what's most important right now is that you understand the potential problems that references can cause because it can sometimes help you debug some mysterious problems with DataFrames.

Code that generates the warning and doesn't corrupt the data

```
dfSlice = df.query('game_id == "0020900015"')
dfSlice.loc[:,'player_name'] = 'Curry'
df.head(2)
```

	player_name	shot_type	shot_distance
game_id			
0020900015	Stephen Curry	3PT Field Goal	26
0020900015	Stephen Curry	2PT Field Goal	18

```
dfSlice.head(2)
```

	player_name	shot_type	shot_distance
game_id			
0020900015	Curry	3PT Field Goal	26
0020900015	Curry	2PT Field Goal	18

How to use the copy() method to stop the warning message

```
dfFixed = df.query('game_id == "0020900015"').copy()
dfFixed.loc[:,'player_name'] = 'Curry'
```

Code that generates the warning and does corrupt the data

```
dfSlice = df.loc['0020900015',:]
dfSlice.loc[:,'player_name'] = 'Curry'
df.head(2)
```

	player_name	shot_type	shot_distance
game_id			
0020900015	Curry	3PT Field Goal	26
0020900015	Curry	2PT Field Goal	18

```
dfSlice.head(2)
```

	player_name	shot_type	shot_distance
game_id			
0020900015	Curry	3PT Field Goal	26
0020900015	Curry	2PT Field Goal	18

How to use the copy() method to fix this code

```
dfFixed = df.loc['0020900015',:].copy()
dfFixed.loc[:,'player_name'] = 'Curry'
```

Description

- Contrary to what the warning suggests, using the loc[] accessor doesn't always protect the data or stop the warning.

Figure 7-15 What to do when the SettingWithCopyWarning is displayed

Perspective

This chapter has presented the essential skills for preparing data for analysis, and the next chapter presents the essential skills for analyzing data. As you will see, however, you often continue to prepare the data as you analyze it. That's because, in many cases, you don't know what you need to do to prepare the data until you start trying to analyze it.

Terms

formatted string literal
f-string
lambda expression
lambda
index
multi-level index
hierarchical index
unstack indexed data
join data
inner join
left join
outer join
merge data
concatenate data
reference
view
copy

Summary

- You can use the dt and str accessors to work with data that's stored in datetime and string columns. And you can use arithmetic operations to work with numeric data. This lets you add new columns based on the data in other columns or modify the data in those columns.
- You can use the transform() method to add summary data to each row in a DataFrame.
- You can use the apply() method to apply a user-defined function or lambda expression to rows or columns.
- A *lambda expression*, also known as a *lambda*, is a concise way to write a function that will only be used once.
- An *index* provides a way to access the rows in a DataFrame. A *multi-level index* (or *hierarchical index*) is an index that's based on two or more columns.
- You can use the unstack() method to *unstack* the values in an index column of a DataFrame.
- You can use the join() method to *join* the columns in two or more DataFrames based on the indexes of the DataFrames.
- An *inner join* returns only the rows in which the indexes in both DataFrames match. A *left join* returns all rows from the left DataFrame, but only the rows in the right DataFrame with matching indexes. An *outer join* returns all rows from both DataFrames.
- You can use the merge() method to *merge* the columns in two DataFrames based on the data in one or more columns in the DataFrames.

- You can use the concat() method to *concatenate* the data in two DataFrames by adding columns or rows from the second DataFrame to the first DataFrame.
- The SettingWithCopyWarning can mean that your code has created a *reference* (or *view*) of the data in another DataFrame instead of a *copy* of that data. Then, if you modify the data in the reference, you can corrupt the data in the original DataFrame.

Exercise 7-1 Prepare the Forest Fires data

This exercise will guide you through the process of preparing the Forest Fires data.

Read the data

1. Open the Notebook named ex_7-1_fires that should be in this folder: `/exercises/ch07`
2. If necessary, run the Kernel→Restart Kernel and Clear All Outputs command.
3. Run the first two cells to read the data into the DataFrame named fires_by_month.
4. Display the first five rows.

Add and modify columns

5. Add a column for the mean number of acres burned per day for each row.
6. Add a column for the mean number of acres burned per day for each row by applying a lambda expression. Use an if-else structure to handle the division by 0 error.
7. Write a function that accepts a row and converts the numeric value in the fire_month column to a string value such as Jan, Feb, or Mar.
8. Apply the function you wrote in the previous step to every row in the DataFrame.

Work with indexes

9. Set an index on the state, fire_year, and, fire_month columns.
10. Unstack the fire_month column and store the result in a DataFrame named fires_by_month_wide.
11. Reset the index for the fires_by_month DataFrame, but don't drop any columns. This should add a numeric index from 0 to 9299 to the DataFrame.

Add a row of data

12. Run the cell that creates and displays the DataFrame named new_fire.
13. Add the row in the new_fire DataFrame to the original DataFrame. When you do that, don't use the ignore_index parameter.
14. Display the last five rows of the original DataFrame. The last row should include the new fire, but the index label for this row shouldn't be correct.

15. Use the reset_index() command to reset the index, and use the drop parameter to drop the old numeric index, which is no longer needed.
16. Display the last five rows of the original DataFrame again. This time, the index for the last row should be correct.

Fix the SettingWithCopyWarning

17. Run the cell that causes the warning. Note that it successfully rounds the values in the mean_acres_per_day column of the fires_ak DataFrame.
18. Run the cell that displays the fires_by_month DataFrame. Note that the values in the mean_acres_per_day column aren't rounded. This shows that you can ignore the warning if you want.
19. Fix the warning by adding the copy() method to the statement that creates the fires_ak DataFrame.

Exercise 7-2 Prepare the Cars data

This exercise will guide you through the process of preparing the Cars data.

Read the data

1. Open the Notebook named ex_7-2_cars that should be in this folder:
   `/exercises/ch07`
2. If necessary, run the Kernel→Restart Kernel and Clear All Outputs command.
3. Run the first two cells to read the data into the DataFrame named cars.
4. Display the first five rows.

Add and drop columns

5. Display the unique values for the CarName column.
6. Add a column named brand that stores the brand of the car. To do that, use a lambda that calls the split() method to access portions of the strings in the CarName column.
7. Add a column named model that stores the car name without the brand. To do that, apply a user-defined function to each row.
8. Drop the CarName column and the car_ID column.

Set an index and unstack the data

9. Filter the cars DataFrame by getting the rows for the Volkswagen brand and the columns named model, horsepower, carbody, and doornumber. Assign the new DataFrame to a variable named cars_filtered, and display the first five rows.
10. Set an index on the model, carbody, and doornumber columns of the cars_filtered DataFrame, assign the new DataFrame to a variable named cars_indexed, and display that DataFrame.
11. Unstack the carbody column of the index. Note how this unstacks the carbody values (sedan and wagon) so they become columns and how it adds NaN values to the wagon column where appropriate.

Chapter 8

How to analyze the data

In the previous chapter, you learned how to prepare the data for analysis. Now, in this chapter, you'll learn how to analyze the data that you've prepared. As you will see, however, there's a lot of overlap between preparation and analysis. That's why this chapter presents some of the preparation skills that are closely related to the analytical skills.

How to create and plot long data

Before you can plot your data with Seaborn, you often need to create long data by combining columns. To do that, you *melt* the columns that you want to plot into just two columns.

How to melt columns to create long data

To melt columns, you use the Pandas melt() method that's summarized in figure 8-1. For this method, the id_vars parameter specifies the column or columns that won't be melted, and this parameter is required. By contrast, the value_vars parameter specifies the columns that contain the values that will be melted. Or, if you omit this parameter, this method melts all of the columns that aren't specified by the id_vars parameter.

When the melt() method is executed, it melts all of the columns in the value_vars parameter into just two columns. Then, each row in the first column contains the original column name for each of the melted columns, and the rows in the second column contain the values that correspond to the original column names. By default, these two columns are named "variable" and "value", but you can use the var_name and value_name parameters to change these default names.

To illustrate, the first example in this figure shows the first five rows of a cars dataset. Then, the second example shows how to use the melt() method to melt the enginesize and curbweight columns into the feature and featureValue columns.

Here, the first parameter specifies the DataFrame that contains the cars data. Then, the id_vars parameter sets the price column as the column that won't be melted. The value_vars parameter sets the columns that will be melted to the enginesize and curbweight columns. The var_name parameter sets the name of the column that contains the column names for the melted columns to "feature". And the value_name parameter sets the column that contains the melted column values to "featureValue".

The screenshot in the second example shows the results of this method. Here, the names for the enginesize and the curbweight columns are in the feature column, and the values that were in those columns are now in the featureValue column. This causes the price column, which wasn't melted, to be in each row of the melted data. In other words, melting the data reduced the number of columns to 3, but it doubled the number of rows.

The melt() method

Method	Description
`melt(params)`	Melts the data in two or more columns into two columns.

Parameter	Description
`id_vars`	The column or columns that won't be melted.
`value_vars`	The columns to melt. If none are specified, all will be melted.
`var_name`	The name of the column that will contain the melted column names, or "variable" by default.
`value_name`	The name of the column that will contain the melted column values, or "value" by default.

The cars DataFrame

```
cars.head()
```

	aspiration	carbody	enginesize	curbweight	price
0	std	convertible	130	2548	13495.0
1	std	convertible	130	2548	16500.0
2	std	hatchback	152	2823	16500.0
3	std	sedan	109	2337	13950.0
4	std	sedan	136	2824	17450.0

How to use the melt() method

```
cars_melted = pd.melt(cars, id_vars='price',
                      value_vars=['enginesize','curbweight'],
                      var_name='feature', value_name='featureValue')
cars_melted
```

	price	feature	featureValue
0	13495.0	enginesize	130
1	16500.0	enginesize	130
2	16500.0	enginesize	152
3	13950.0	enginesize	109
4	17450.0	enginesize	136
...	...	...	...
405	16845.0	curbweight	2952
406	19045.0	curbweight	3049
407	21485.0	curbweight	3012
408	22470.0	curbweight	3217
409	22625.0	curbweight	3062

Figure 8-1 How to melt columns to create long data

How to plot melted columns

Figure 8-2 shows how to use Seaborn to plot the melted data in the previous figure. Here, the first example plots the melted data in a single plot. It sets the hue parameter to the feature column so a different color is applied to each of the original columns.

The second example shows another way to plot the melted columns. It uses the col parameter to make a subplot for each of the columns that were melted into the feature column. But note here that the facet_kws parameter is set so the x axes for the subplots aren't shared. If they were, the x-axis for each subplot would range from 50 to 4000, which would make the data hard to interpret.

Although these examples use just two melted columns, the same technique can be used to create plots with more than two columns. Consider, for example, a cars DataFrame that contains data about other features such as horsepower, miles per gallon, car width, and so on. In that case, you might want to melt all of those columns into feature and featureValue columns.

How to plot melted data with the hue parameter

```
sns.relplot(data=cars_melted, x='featureValue', y='price',
            hue='feature')
```

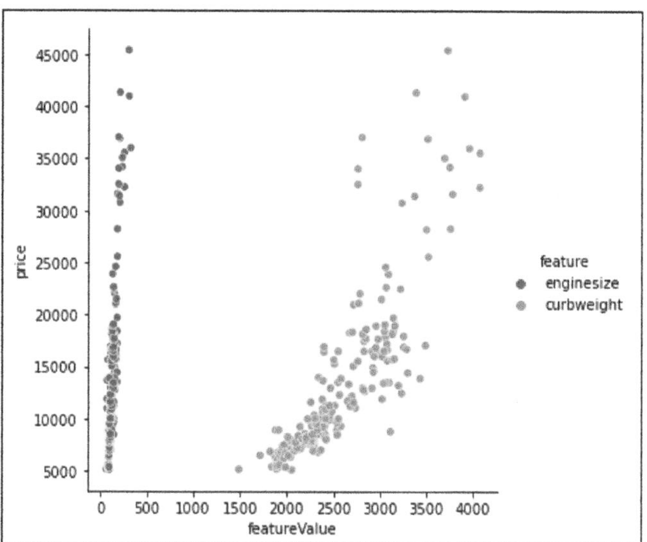

How to plot melted data with the col parameter

```
sns.relplot(data=cars_melted, x='featureValue', y='price',
            col='feature', facet_kws={'sharex':False})
```

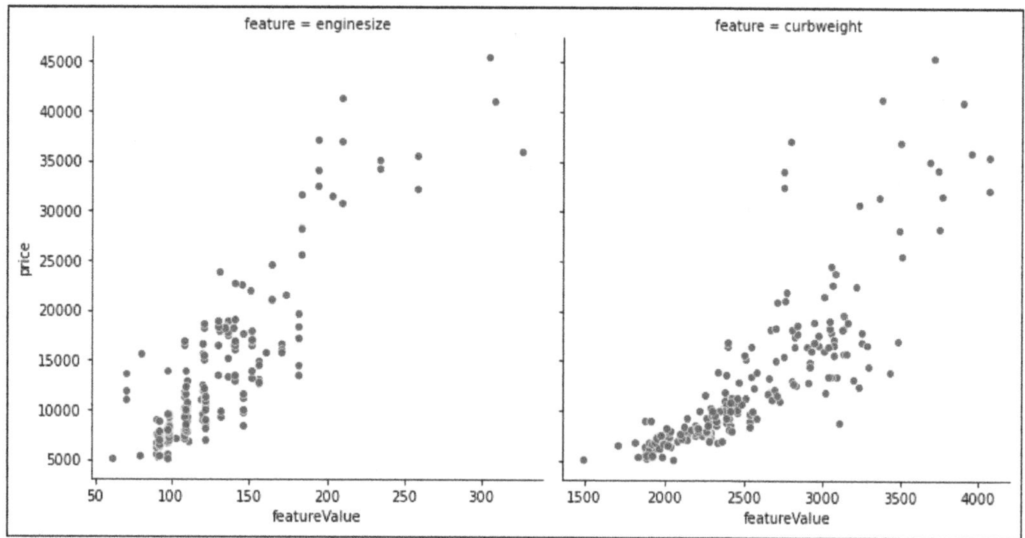

Description

- After you melt data, you can use Seaborn to plot the data in the melted columns.

Figure 8-2 How to plot melted columns

How to group and aggregate the data

When you analyze data, you will often want to get summary statistics for different groups of data. For example, you may want to calculate summary statistics for each state in the fires dataset or each brand in the cars dataset. To do that, you use the groupby() method to *group* the data and aggregate methods to *aggregate* the data.

How to group and apply a single aggregate method

The table in figure 8-3 presents some of the aggregate methods that are optimized to work with grouped data. Note, however, that Pandas also provides other methods to work with grouped data such as var(), prod(), first(), and last(). You can also use any aggregate method that works on a Series object such as quantile(), which was introduced in chapter 2. You can even define your own aggregate methods, although this chapter will focus on methods that have already been defined.

The first example in this figure shows the first three rows of a DataFrame named fires. Then, the second example groups the data by the state column and uses the mean() method to calculate the averages for all numeric columns for each state.

The third example groups the data by state, fire_year, and fire_month and uses the max() method to get the maximum value for each column. Since this method works on datetime values as well as numeric values, it returns both numeric and datetime columns.

The third example also illustrates the use of the dropna() method. Here, this method drops all rows that contain an NA value. Since Alaska didn't have any fires in months 1 through 4, those rows have been dropped in the resulting DataFrame.

Some of the aggregate methods that are optimized for grouping

Method	Description
`sum()`	Sum of all non-NA values.
`mean()`	Average of all non-NA values.
`median()`	Median value of all non-NA values.
`count()`	Count of all non-NA values.
`std()`	Unbiased standard deviation.
`min()`	Minimum non-NA value.
`max()`	Maximum non-NA value.

The fires DataFrame

```
fires.head(3)
```

	fire_name	acres_burned	state	fire_year	discovery_date	fire_month	days_burning
0	Power	16823.0	CA	2004	2004-10-06	10	15.0
1	Freds	7700.0	CA	2004	2004-10-13	10	4.0
2	Bachelor	10.0	NM	2004	2004-07-20	7	0.0

How to get the average for each numeric column in each state

```
fires.groupby('state').mean().head(3)
```

	acres_burned	fire_year	fire_month	days_burning
state				
AK	11367.199362	2004.742504	6.264198	32.081535
AL	42.348169	2003.885422	5.022529	0.272676
AR	50.281673	2005.850793	5.581081	0.400992

How to get the maximum value for each month in each state

```
fires.groupby(['state','fire_year','fire_month']).max().dropna().head(3)
```

			acres_burned	discovery_date	days_burning
state	**fire_year**	**fire_month**			
AK	**1992**	**5**	1410.0	1992-05-31	50.0
		6	48087.0	1992-06-29	82.0
		7	35090.0	1992-07-30	77.0

Figure 8-3 How to group and apply a single aggregate method

How to work with a DataFrameGroupBy object

Instead of chaining an aggregate method to the groupby() method, you can assign the DataFrameGroupBy object that's returned by the groupby() method to a variable. Then, you can call the aggregate method from that object. This is a good practice if you plan to use the GroupBy object several times.

To illustrate, the second example in figure 8-4 shows how you can group the fires data in the first example by the fire_year column and assign the GroupBy object that's returned to a variable named yearly_group. Then, you can call the sum() method from the GroupBy object and the resulting DataFrame is assigned to the variable named yearly_sums.

Note here that this summarizes the three numeric columns because they're the only ones that the sum() method works for. The other columns are sometimes referred to as *nuisance columns* because they can't be aggregated. But note that the fire_month column is also aggregated by the sum() method, even though the result makes no sense.

Incidentally, since this example summarizes the data in more than one column, it returns a DataFrame. However, if the sum() method is applied to just one column, it returns a Series object.

The third example in this figure shows how to use the as_index parameter. If set to False, this parameter causes the column that you are grouping on to not be converted into an index. This can be useful if you plan to plot or further process the data after the grouping operation.

The groupby() method

Method	Description
`groupby(params)`	Returns a GroupBy object that supports aggregate methods such as sum().

Parameter	Description
`by`	The column or list of columns to group by.
`as_index`	If False, doesn't create an index based on the groupby columns. If True (the default), it does.

The fires DataFrame

```
fires.head(3)
```

	fire_name	acres_burned	state	fire_year	discovery_date	fire_month	days_burning
0	Power	16823.0	CA	2004	2004-10-06	10	15.0
1	Freds	7700.0	CA	2004	2004-10-13	10	4.0
2	Bachelor	10.0	NM	2004	2004-07-20	7	0.0

A GroupBy object with the fire_year column as the index

```
yearly_group = fires.groupby('fire_year')
yearly_sums = yearly_group.sum()
yearly_sums.head(3)
```

	acres_burned	fire_month	days_burning
fire_year			
1992	2123889.91	45643	6230.0
1993	2118394.10	52880	7283.0
1994	4033880.06	57669	20158.0

A GroupBy object without indexes

```
yearly_group = fires.groupby('fire_year', as_index=False)
yearly_sums = yearly_group.sum()
yearly_sums.head(3)
```

	fire_year	acres_burned	fire_month	days_burning
0	1992	2123889.91	45643	6230.0
1	1993	2118394.10	52880	7283.0
2	1994	4033880.06	57669	20158.0

Description

- By default, the groupby() method excludes any columns that don't work with the specified aggregate method. Since it doesn't make sense to aggregate those columns, they're sometimes referred to as *nuisance columns*.

Figure 8-4 How to work with a DataFrameGroupBy object

How to apply multiple aggregate methods

The agg() method can be used to apply several aggregate methods to a DataFrameGroupBy object at the same time. The table in figure 8-5 summarizes this method, and the examples illustrate its use.

Here, the first example creates a GroupBy object and assigns it to a variable named monthly_group. Then, the second example uses the agg() method to apply three aggregate methods to this GroupBy object. To do that, the parameter for the agg() method is set to a list of method names. This creates a hierarchical index for the columns where the first level displays the columns and the second level displays the aggregate method for each of the columns. Because the dropna() method is chained to the agg() method, the rows that contain NA values are dropped from the results.

The third example shows how to apply several aggregate methods to a single column. Since this only returns one column, it doesn't create a two-level hierarchical index. Instead, it displays the aggregate results for the specified column.

The fourth example applies a variety of aggregate methods to specific columns. To do that, it passes a dictionary to the agg() method. Here, each key is a string that specifies the column name and each value is a string or list of strings that specifies the aggregate methods to apply to that column. When you use this technique, you don't need to apply the same aggregate methods or even the same number of aggregate methods to each column.

The agg() method

Method	Description
agg()	Applies an aggregate method or list of methods to a Series or DataFrame object.

The GroupBy object

```
monthly_group = fires.groupby(['state','fire_year','fire_month'])
```

How to apply aggregate methods to all numeric columns

```
monthly_group.agg(['sum','count','mean']).dropna().head(3)
```

			acres_burned			days_burning		
			sum	count	mean	sum	count	mean
state	fire_year	fire_month						
AK	1992	5	4202.0	15	280.133333	135.0	14	9.642857
		6	86401.0	26	3323.115385	417.0	25	16.680000
		7	48516.7	26	1866.026923	500.0	22	22.727273

How to apply aggregate methods to a single column

```
monthly_group.days_burning.agg(['sum','count','mean']).dropna().head(3)
```

			sum	count	mean
state	fire_year	fire_month			
AK	1992	5	135.0	14	9.642857
		6	417.0	25	16.680000
		7	500.0	22	22.727273

How to apply varied aggregate methods to numeric columns

```
df = monthly_group.agg({'acres_burned':['sum','max','min'],
                        'days_burning':['sum','mean'],
                        'fire_name':'count'}).dropna()
df.head(3)
```

			acres_burned			days_burning		fire_name
			sum	max	min	sum	mean	count
state	fire_year	fire_month						
AK	1992	5	4202.0	1410.0	10.0	135.0	9.642857	14
		6	86401.0	48087.0	10.0	417.0	16.680000	23
		7	48516.7	35090.0	10.0	500.0	22.727273	26

Figure 8-5 How to apply multiple aggregate methods

How to create and use pivot tables

In chapter 7, you learned how to use the unstack() method to convert an index level into a column. Now, you will learn how to use the pivot() and pivot_table() methods to *pivot* the data, which is similar to unstacking it.

How to use the pivot() method

The pivot() method provides a way to create wide data by creating an index and unstacking data in a single operation. In other words, instead of using the set_index() method to set the index and the unstack() method to unstack an index level, you can use the pivot() method to do both in a single operation. This method is summarized in figure 8-6.

Here, the index parameter specifies the column or columns that become the row index in the pivoted table. The columns parameter specifies the column or columns whose values become the new columns in the pivoted table. And the values parameter specifies the column or columns that provide the values for the DataFrame.

The first example in this figure shows the first two rows of a DataFrame named top_states that are used by the other examples in this figure. This DataFrame is created by a groupby() method that groups the data by state and fire year. Since the as_index parameter is set to False when the GroupBy object is created, this DataFrame has a simple numeric index. Then, a query() method selects just four of the states in the DataFrame, the ones with the most acres burned. To do that, it refers to the list of states that's created at the beginning of this example in the query condition using the @ symbol followed by the variable name for the list.

The second example shows how to use the pivot() method to convert this data to wide form. Here, the index parameter is set to the fire_year column and the columns parameter is set to the state column. As a result, the fire_year column becomes the index for the DataFrame and the state column is pivoted. Then, since the values parameter is set to the acres_burned column, the resulting DataFrame only contains the values for each state for that column. Otherwise, the resulting DataFrame would contain the values for each state for all of its columns.

The third example is like the second example, but the Pandas plot() method is chained to the pivot() method. As a result, the acres_burned column is plotted in a line plot. In fact, one of the reasons for pivoting data is that the Pandas plot() method works with wide data. The other reason is that wide data makes it easier to interpret some data. For instance, the table in the second example makes it easy to compare the total acres burned for each of the four states by year.

Before going on, you should notice the "1e6" above the upper left corner of the plot. This is standard scientific notation, and in this case, it indicates that the values along the y-axis should be multiplied by a factor of 6. So, for example, the 6 on the y-axis represents 6 x 10^6, or 6,000,000.

When you use the pivot() method, you should know that there can't be any duplicates in the index for the resulting DataFrame. If, for example, the column

The pivot() method

Method	Description
`pivot(params)`	Pivots the data based on the index, columns, and values parameters.
Parameter	**Description**
`index`	The column or list of columns to use as the row index (no duplicates).
`columns`	The column or list of columns to use as the column index.
`values`	The column or list of columns to use to populate the new DataFrame. By default, all remaining columns are used.

The top_states DataFrame

```
states = ['AK','CA','ID','TX']
top_states = fires.groupby(['state','fire_year'], as_index=False).sum()
top_states = top_states.query('state in @states')
top_states.head(2)
```

	state	fire_year	acres_burned	fire_month	days_burning
0	AK	1992	142444.7	454	1145.0
1	AK	1993	686630.5	961	3373.0

How to pivot the data

```
top_states.pivot(index='fire_year', columns='state', values='acres_burned').head(2)
```

state	AK	CA	ID	TX
fire_year				
1992	142444.7	289254.9	683495.2	31500.3
1993	686630.5	315011.1	7658.5	114265.5

How to plot the data with the Pandas plot() method

```
top_states.pivot(index='fire_year', columns='state', values='acres_burned').plot()
```

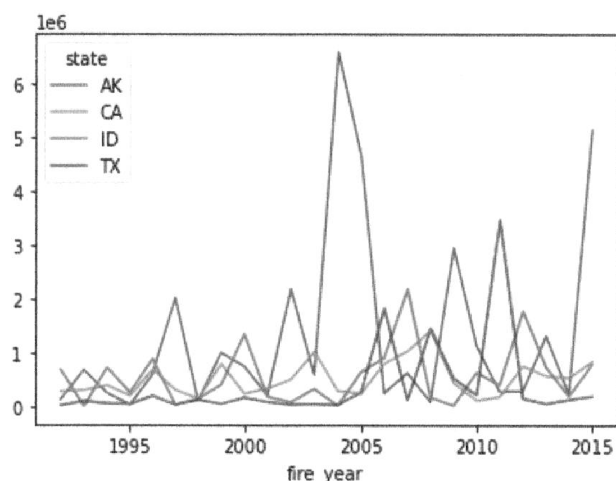

Figure 8-6 How to use the pivot() method

or combination of columns specified by the index parameter has duplicates, the pivot() method won't work. Instead, it will return an error message that says, "Index contains duplicate entries, cannot reshape". In these examples, though, the data has been grouped before the pivot() methods are run, and the grouped data doesn't have any duplicates.

How to use the pivot_table() method

The pivot_table() method is similar to the pivot() method, but it takes the pivot operation a step further. The main differences are that the pivot_table() method applies an aggregate method when it pivots the data, and it lets you specify index columns that contain duplicate values. The result is a *pivot table* that summarizes the data.

In other words, the pivot_table() method works much like a call to the groupby() method followed by a call to the pivot() method and then a call to the agg() method. This makes the pivot_table() method easier to use than the pivot() method, which displays an error if the index contains duplicate values.

The table in figure 8-7 summarizes the pivot_table() method. Here, you can see that the index, columns, and values parameters work the same as they do for the pivot() method. And the aggfunc parameter works like the agg() method.

The first example in this figure shows how you can use the pivot_table() method to group, pivot, and aggregate data. After the data for the top four states has been selected from the fires DataFrame, the pivot_table() method sets the index parameter to the fire_year column and the columns parameter to the state column. Then, it sets the values parameter to the acres_burned column, so that's the column that will be aggregated. Last, it sets the aggregate method to sum.

The second example shows how to use the Pandas plot() method to plot the data in the pivot table. Here again, one of the reasons for creating pivot tables is so they can be plotted by the Pandas plot() method.

The pivot_table() method

Method	Description
`pivot_table(params)`	Produces a pivot table with an applied aggregate method.

Parameter	Description
`index`	The column or list of columns to use as the row index (allows duplicates).
`columns`	The column or list of columns to use as the column index.
`values`	The column or list of columns that contain the values to be aggregated. By default, all non-nuisance columns are aggregated.
`aggfunc`	The aggregate method or list of methods to be applied to each column in the values parameter.
`fill_value`	The value to replace any missing values with in the resulting pivot table.

How to use the pivot_table() method to create a DataFrame

```
states = ['AK','CA','ID','TX']
fires_top_4 = fires.query('state in @states')
fires_top_4 = fires_top_4.pivot_table(index='fire_year', columns='state',
    values='acres_burned', aggfunc='sum')
fires_top_4.head(2)
```

state	AK	CA	ID	TX
fire_year				
1992	142444.7	289254.9	683495.2	31500.3
1993	686630.5	315011.1	7658.5	114265.5

How to plot the data with the Pandas plot() method

```
fires_top_4.plot()
```

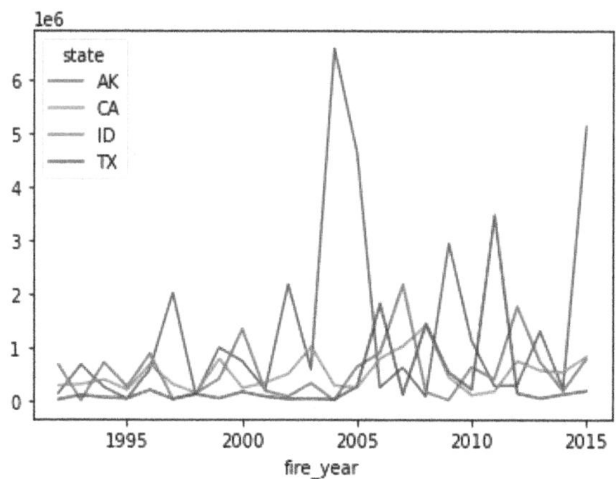

Figure 8-7 How to use the pivot_table() method

How to work with bins

For some analyses, you may want to prepare the data by converting continuous data such as a range of numbers into categories. This process is called *binning* because you divide the data into *bins*.

With Pandas, you can use the cut() and qcut() methods to bin data. These methods are similar, but each creates its bins in a different way. As you will see, the cut() method creates equal-sized bins based on the range of the values, and the qcut() method creates bins with equal numbers of values. Both methods operate on a single column.

How to create bins of equal size

The first example in figure 8-8 creates the fires_filtered DataFrame that's used by the examples in this figure and the next. This DataFrame contains data about all fires in the year 2010 that burned for at least one day.

The second example shows how to use the cut() method to put the data in the acres_burned column into 4 bins. This returns a Series object in which each row is represented by an interval, not a discrete value. The bottom of the output for this method shows the interval for each bin and how those bins are ordered. Note that each bin has two *bin edges*: one for the first value in the interval and one for the last value.

To create the intervals for each bin, the total range of the values is divided by the number of bins. For example, the largest value in the acres_burned column is 306,113 and the smallest value is 10, so the range is 306,103. If you divide that number by the number of bins, in this case, 4, each interval should have a width of 76,525.75. To check that, you can subtract the beginning value for the interval from the ending value for the interval.

Note, however, that the beginning value for the first interval is a negative number. And, if you subtract this value from the ending value for the interval, you'll find that the interval is larger than what it should be. However, as long as the beginning value is less than 10, this will work because the smallest value in the acres_burned column is 10.

Also notice that each interval is enclosed in a left parenthesis and a right bracket. The left parenthesis indicates that the left bin edge isn't included in the interval, and the right bracket indicates that the right bin edge is included in the interval. Because the right bin edge of an interval is the same as the left bin edge of the interval that follows, that ensures that the two intervals don't overlap. If you set the right parameter to False, however, the left bin edges are included in the intervals and the right bin edges aren't.

Although the bin intervals in the second example are useful, they aren't easy to read and don't work well with plots. To fix this, you can specify labels for each of the bins by passing a list of names for the bins as shown by the third example. The output for this example shows how each of the intervals for the bins has been replaced with the label for each bin. In addition, the bottom of the output shows that the bins are ordered correctly.

The cut() method

Method	Description
`cut(params)`	Bins the data into equal-sized bins.
Parameter	**Description**
`x`	The column that contains the data to be binned.
`bins`	The number of bins to create, or a list of values for the bin edges.
`labels`	The labels to use for the bins.
`right`	If set to False, the right edges are not included in the bins.

The fires_filtered DataFrame

```
fires_filtered = fires.query('fire_year == 2010 and days_burning > 0').dropna()
```

How to create four bins for the data

```
pd.cut(fires_filtered.acres_burned, bins=4)
==============================================
1145154    (-296.103, 76535.75]
1145175    (-296.103, 76535.75]
                    ...
1879725    (-296.103, 76535.75]
1880370    (-296.103, 76535.75]
Name: acres_burned, Length: 1858, dtype: category
Categories (4, interval[float64]): [(-296.103, 76535.75] < (76535.75, 153061.5] <
(153061.5, 229587.25] < (229587.25, 306113.0]]
```

How to add labels to the bins

```
pd.cut(fires_filtered.acres_burned, bins=[0,100000,200000,300000,400000],
    labels=['small','medium','large','very large'])
=======================================================
1145154    small
1145175    small
           ...
1879725    small
1880370    small
Name: acres_burned, Length: 1858, dtype: category
Categories (4, object): ['small' < 'medium' < 'large' < 'very large']
```

The distribution of values in the bins

```
pd.cut(fires_filtered.acres_burned, bins=[0,100000,200000,300000,400000],
    labels=['small','medium','large','very large']).value_counts()
=======================================================================
small         1855
medium           2
very large       1
large            0
Name: acres_burned, dtype: int64
```

Description

- *Binning* is a way to put data that is continuous into *bins*.

Figure 8-8 How to create bins of equal size

Notice in this example that the bins parameter specifies the exact bin intervals rather than the number of bins. In this case, then, the interval for the first bin is 0 to 100,000.00, the interval for the second bin is 100,000.01 to 200,000.00, and so on.

The fourth example in figure 8-8 uses the value_counts() method to show how many values there are in each bin. In this case, almost all the values are in the first bin, which probably isn't what you want. That's because the cut() method doesn't consider distribution when creating bins.

How to create bins with equal numbers of values

In contrast to the cut() method, the qcut() method creates bins with equal numbers of unique values, called *quantiles*. This is illustrated by the first example in figure 8-9. Here, the data and the labels work the same as with the cut() method. However, the qcut() method uses the q parameter to specify the number of quantiles that the data should be divided into.

In the first example, the q parameter is set to 4, so the data is divided into four bins. In addition, this example sets the labels for the four bins to small, medium, large, and very large, just as in the third example in figure 8-8. If you compare the output with that example, though, you'll see that the qcut() method has assigned some of the values to different bins.

The second example uses the value_counts() method to show the distribution of the values from the first example. As you can see, each bin now contains almost the same number of values.

The third example shows how to assign bin labels to a new column named fire_size in the DataFrame. Here, the qcut() method bins the data into four bins as in the first two examples. You'll see the result of this statement in the next figure.

Now that you've seen how the qcut() method works, you should know that it sometimes generates two or more bins with the same bin edges. That can happen if a large number of the values in the column of data being binned fall into a small range. This is illustrated by the last example in this figure. Here, the data is binned by the days_burning column, and many of the values in that column are equal to 1. So, if you divided these values into four bins, the first two bins would be for the values .999 to 2, the third bin would be for the values from 2.1 to 7, and the fourth bin would be for the values from 7.1 to 378. In this case, because there are duplicate bins, a ValueError would occur.

To prevent this error, you can set the duplicates parameter to drop as shown here. Then, the duplicate bin will be dropped and the data will be divided into the three remaining bins. Note that when that happens, though, the values are no longer equally divided among the bins because the values in the first two bins have been combined into a single bin.

The qcut() method

Method	Description
qcut(params)	Bins the data into quantiles with the same number of values in each bin.

Parameter	Description
x	The column that contains the data to be binned.
q	The number of quantiles to create.
labels	The labels to use for the bins.
duplicates	What to do with bins that have the same edges. The default is raise, which raises a ValueError. If set to drop, the non-unique bins are dropped.

How to use four quantiles to bin the data

```
pd.qcut(fires_filtered.acres_burned, q=4,
        labels=['small','medium','large','very large'])
==========================================================
1145154        medium
1145175    very large
                ...
1880209         small
1880370         large
Name: acres_burned, Length: 4882, dtype: category
Categories (4, object): ['small' < 'medium' < 'large' < 'very large']
```

The distribution of the values in each bin

```
pd.qcut(fires_filtered.acres_burned, q=4,
        labels=['small','medium','large','very large']).value_counts()
======================================================================
medium        1227
small         1221
very large    1220
large         1214
Name: acres_burned, dtype: int64
```

How to assign bin labels to a new column

```
fires_filtered['fire_size'] = pd.qcut(fires_filtered.acres_burned, q=4,
    labels=['small','medium','large','very large'])
```

A qcut() method that drops duplicate bins

```
pd.qcut(fires_filtered.days_burning, q=4,
        labels=['short','medium','long'], duplicates='drop').value_counts()
===========================================================================
short     1018
long       433
medium     407
Name: days_burning, dtype: int64
```

Description

- When you bin data using the qcut() method, each bin, or *quantile*, contains approximately the same number of values.

Figure 8-9 How to create bins with equal numbers of values

How to plot binned data

Once you add the bins to your data, you can use them to help you create plots. This is illustrated by figure 8-10. Here, the first example shows the results of the third example in figure 8-9, which adds the fire_size column by using the qcut() method to bin the data into four quantiles.

Then, the second example uses the Seaborn catplot() method to create a count plot. This plot creates a bar chart that shows a count of the number of fires for each fire_size bin for each month. To do that, it specifies that the fire_month column should be displayed on the x-axis and that the fire_size column should be used to determine the color of each bar. Then, the y-axis displays the count for each bar.

The DataFrame with a fire_size column that bins the data

```
fires_filtered.head()
```

	fire_name	fire_year	state	discovery_date	contain_date	acres_burned	fire_month	days_burning	fire_size
1145154	Fourmile Trail	2010	AK	2010-04-28	2010-05-05	16.8	4	7.0	small
1145175	Granite Tors	2010	AK	2010-05-27	2010-08-11	7880.0	5	76.0	very large
1145187	Goldbug Creek	2010	AK	2010-06-23	2010-06-28	2777.0	6	5.0	very large
1145198	Broken Tree	2010	AK	2010-05-24	2010-07-08	112.0	5	45.0	large
1145208	Folger Creek	2010	AK	2010-07-01	2010-07-16	90.0	7	15.0	medium

How to plot the binned data

```
sns.catplot(data=fires_filtered, kind='count', x='fire_month', hue='fire_size')
```

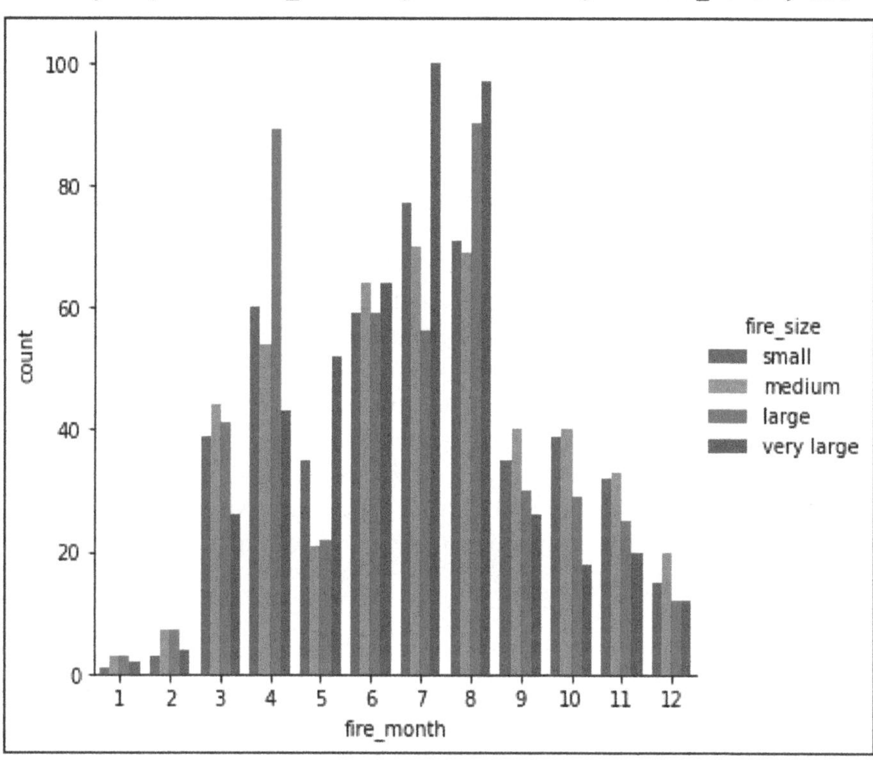

Description

- After you bin the data in a DataFrame, you can create a plot that shows a count of the number of items in each bin based on another column in the DataFrame.

Figure 8-10 How to plot binned data

More skills for data analysis

The goal of this book is to present the 20% of the Pandas methods that you'll use 90% of the time. You should know, however, that there are dozens of other methods that you can use for special purposes. The figures that follow present just a few, plus some insight into when and how to look for other methods.

How to select the rows with the largest values

Figure 8-11 presents the nlargest() method. It returns the specified number of rows that have the largest values in the specified columns of a DataFrame. In the first example, you can see how to use this method to select the 6 rows with the largest values in the enginesize column of the cars DataFrame. Here, the n parameter determines how many rows to return, and the columns parameter specifies the column that the largest values are drawn from.

When you select the largest values from a single column, you can use the keep parameter to determine which rows to keep when the values in the columns are the same. In this example, for instance, the rows with index values 47 and 48 have the same value in the enginesize column. So, if you retrieved just the rows with the four largest values, the row with index 47 would be returned by default. If you specified last for the keep parameter, though, the row with index 48 would be returned. And if you specified all for the keep parameter, both rows would be returned, even though that would result in a total of five rows.

In the second example, the same parameters are used except that the price column is also specified for the columns parameter. So, when the nlargest() method selects the columns, it first looks at the enginesize. Then, if there is a tie in enginesize, the price column is used to break the tie. That's why the fourth and fifth rows have swapped places in the results of the two examples and the sixth row is completely different.

The nlargest() method

Method	Description
`nlargest(params)`	Returns the first n rows with the largest values in the specified columns.
Parameter	**Description**
`n`	The number of rows to return.
`columns`	The columns that determine which rows to keep.
`keep`	The rows to keep in the event of a tie. Possible values: first, last, and all. The default is first.

How to use the nlargest() method

```
cars.nlargest(n=6, columns='enginesize')
```

	aspiration	carbody	enginesize	curbweight	price
49	std	sedan	326	3950	36000.0
73	std	sedan	308	3900	40960.0
74	std	hardtop	304	3715	45400.0
47	std	sedan	258	4066	32250.0
48	std	sedan	258	4066	35550.0
71	std	sedan	234	3740	34184.0

Another nlargest() example

```
cars.nlargest(n=6, columns=['enginesize','price'])
```

	aspiration	carbody	enginesize	curbweight	price
49	std	sedan	326	3950	36000.0
73	std	sedan	308	3900	40960.0
74	std	hardtop	304	3715	45400.0
48	std	sedan	258	4066	35550.0
47	std	sedan	258	4066	32250.0
72	std	convertible	234	3685	35056.0

Description

- The nlargest() method selects the rows that contain the specified number of largest values.
- The first column that's specified is used to determine what is kept. Then, if there is a tie, the second column that's specified is used to break the tie, and so on.
- The nsmallest() method works the same way but it selects the smallest values.

Figure 8-11 How to select the rows with the largest values

How to calculate the percent change

Figure 8-12 presents the pct_change() method. It is used to calculate the percent change from one row to the next for a DataFrame or Series object. To illustrate, the first example creates a DataFrame for the grouped fires data that summarizes how many acres were burned each year in each state. Then, the second example shows how to use the pct_change() method.

In the results for the second example, you can see that the first row is NaN because there is no row before it to compare it with. After that, you can see the percent change from one row to the next. Note, however, that the percent is in decimal format, so you will need to multiply it by 100 to display it properly. For example, the percent change for Alaska in 1993 should be 382%, not 3.82%.

To understand how the pct_change() method works, you need to understand how the percent change is calculated. To illustrate, consider the percent change from 1992 to 1993 for the state of Alaska. In the first example, if you subtract the acres_burned value for 1992 from the value for 1993, you get the difference between the two years. In this case, the acres burned increased by 544,185.8. Then, to get the percent change, you divide that value by the acres burned for 1992, which results in the value shown in the second example for 1993.

The pct_change() method

Method	Description
`pct_change()`	Calculates the percent change from the previous row to the current row for a DataFrame or Series object.

The fires data

```
df = fires[['state','fire_year','acres_burned']] \
    .groupby(['state','fire_year']).sum()
df.head()
```

		acres_burned
state	fire_year	
AK	1992	142444.7
	1993	686630.5
	1994	261604.7
	1995	43762.6
	1996	598407.2

How to use the pct_change() method

```
df.pct_change()
```

		acres_burned
state	fire_year	
AK	1992	NaN
	1993	3.820330
	1994	-0.619002
	1995	-0.832715
	1996	12.673941
...	...	...
WY	2011	0.552941
	2012	2.582104
	2013	-0.888021
	2014	-0.866764
	2015	4.046849

Description

- The first value will always be null because there is nothing to compare the first value with.

Figure 8-12 How to calculate the percent change

How to rank rows

Figure 8-13 presents the rank() method. It is used to compute a numerical rank based on the values in the specified column. To illustrate, the first example presents the DataFrame that will be used. It holds the sum of the values for each of the three named columns by state.

Then, the second example shows how to rank each state in descending order by total acres burned and then store that rank in a new column named acres_rank. In this case, since the ascending parameter is set to False, the states with the most acres burned will be given the lower rank numbers. So, since Alaska has the most acres burned, it is ranked number 1.

Before going on, you might wonder why Alaska is ranked before Alabama, which is ranked before Arkansas. What you might miss when you look at the values in the acres_burned column is that the value for Alaska is multiplied by a factor of 7 and is equal to 32,226,010. By contrast, the values for Alabama and Arkansas are multiplied by a factor of 5 and are equal to 810,162.8 and 450,222.1 respectively. So, it's important to pay attention to the notation that's used for large values like these.

The third example shows how to use the method parameter with the rank() method. This parameter comes into effect if two or more of the values that are used to rank the rows are the same. Then, this parameter determines how to rank the values that are the same. In other words, it determines how ties are ranked.

By default, the method parameter is set to average. As a result, the rank() method assigns the average rank for tied values. If, for example, two states are tied for second, both states are assigned a rank of 2.5 since that's the average of 2 and 3. In most cases, this default setting is adequate for what you're trying to do.

But if you want to fine tune the rankings, you can use the method parameter. In the third example, max is used to assign the maximum rank to any states with tied ranks. As you can see, that causes the states that are ranked second and third—Vermont and Connecticut—to both be assigned a rank of 3. A value of min does the opposite by assigning the minimum rank to any states with tied ranks. A value of first assigns the tied rank to the first row and the next rank to the second row. Finally, a value of dense works like min, but it doesn't skip ranks when there's a tie. If, for example, you use min for the method parameter on a DataFrame with four rows and there is a tie for second and third place, the ranks will be [1,2,2,4]. But if you use dense, the ranks will be [1,2,2,3].

Since this example omits the ascending parameter, the values are ranked in ascending order. As a result, Rhode Island (RI) has a rank of 1 in its days_rank column. However, it has a rank of 51 in its acres_burned column. To make these rankings consistent, with big and long fires having a low rank, you could set the ascending parameter to False for the days_rank column. Then, Rhode Island would have a rank of 51 for both its days_rank and acres_rank columns.

The rank() method

Method	Description
`rank(params)`	Computes numerical data ranks (1 through n) along an axis. By default, equal values are assigned a rank that is the average of the ranks of those values.
Parameter	**Description**
`ascending`	If False, ranks in descending order. If True (the default), ranks in ascending order.
`method`	How to rank the group of records that have ties. Possible values include average (the default), min, max, first, and dense.
`pct`	If True, displays the rankings in percentile form. False is the default.

The state totals

```
df = fires.groupby('state').sum() \
    [['acres_burned','fire_year','days_burning']]
df.head(3)
```

	acres_burned	fire_year	days_burning
state			
AK	3.222601e+07	5683445	80268.0
AL	8.101628e+05	38336332	2886.0
AR	4.502221e+05	17960388	1132.0

How to add an acres_rank column based on acres burned

```
df[acres_rank'] = df.acres_burned.rank(ascending=False)
df.head(3)
```

	acres_burned	fire_year	days_burning	acres_rank
state				
AK	3.222601e+07	5683445	80268.0	1.0
AL	8.101628e+05	38336332	2886.0	23.0
AR	4.502221e+05	17960388	1132.0	27.0

How to add a days_rank column based on days burning

```
df['days_rank'] = df.days_burning.rank(method='max')
df.sort_values('days_burning').head(4)
```

	acres_burned	fire_year	days_burning	acres_rank	days_rank
state					
RI	147.45	22092	0.0	51.0	1.0
VT	985.70	46240	6.0	50.0	3.0
CT	7358.20	364159	6.0	46.0	3.0
NH	1232.23	82240	9.0	49.0	4.0

Figure 8-13 How to rank rows

How to find other methods for analysis

The last three figures have shown just a few of the special-purpose methods that Pandas provides. But remember that Pandas provides dozens of others. So when you want to do something, Pandas probably has a method for that.

In many cases, the best way to find the methods for special purposes is to search the Internet. When you do that, you need to include the keywords for the library that you're using (like Pandas or Seaborn) and the object type that you're working with (like a DataFrame or Series object), followed by the keywords for what you're trying to do. This is illustrated by the example in figure 8-14. Here, a search for "pandas dataframe count of unique values," returns a number of links that will help you find what you're looking for, including a link to the value_counts() method.

The other way to find the methods that you need is to study the official documentation. If, for example, you go to the Pandas website, you can use its API reference to learn about all the objects and methods that Pandas provides and to see some simple usage examples. You can also do that for other libraries like Seaborn. In fact, it's important that you get used to reading the documentation since no book or website explains every method and parameter the way the documentation does.

The trouble with the official documentation is that it can be hard to navigate, especially if you don't know what you're looking for. That's why it's often better to do a keyword search for what you want to do. Since Pandas provides such a wide variety of methods, the chances are good that you'll find a method that does just what you want.

A Google search for a way to count the unique values in a column

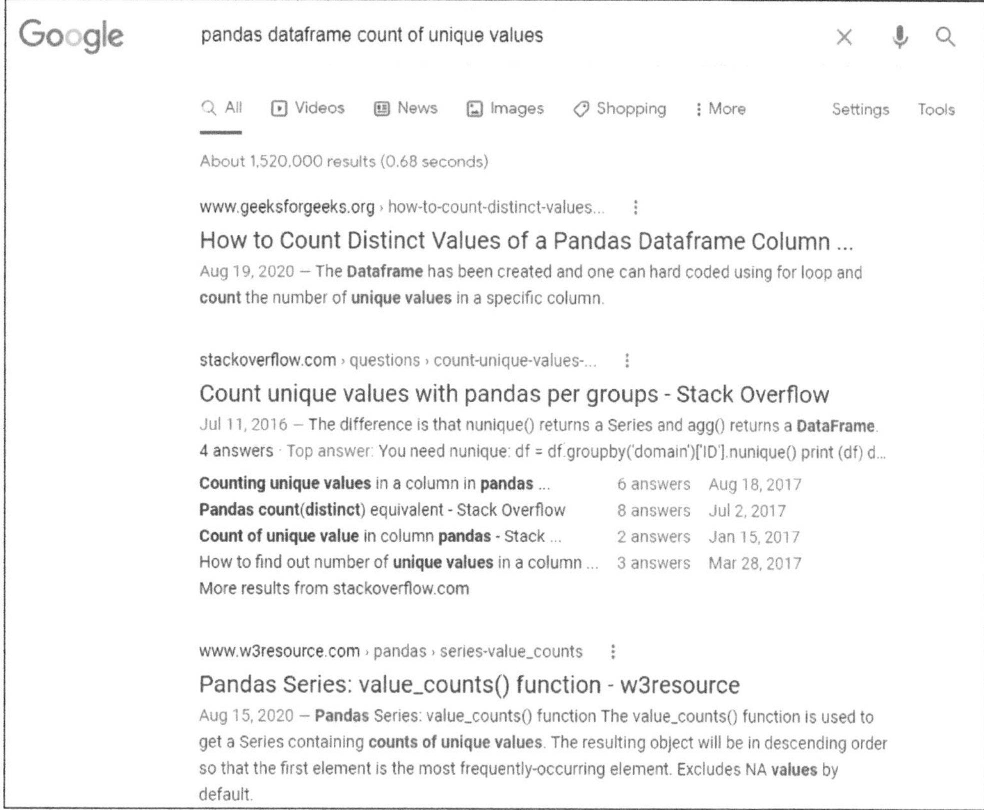

Description

- Pandas provides dozens of methods for analyzing data. So when you find the need for a specific method, you should start by seeing whether Pandas has a method that does what you want to do.
- Although the official Pandas documentation is excellent, it can be difficult to find the methods that you're looking for in it. Besides that, this documentation often lacks the concrete examples that help you apply the methods that you find.
- That's why it's usually better to search the Internet for the methods that you need. When you do that, be sure to include the library that you're using (like Pandas or Seaborn), the object that you're working with (like Series or DataFrame), and a description of what you're trying to do.

Figure 8-14 How to find other methods for analysis

Perspective

This chapter has presented the methods and parameters that you'll use most of the time when you analyze data. Remember, though, that Pandas provides dozens of other methods, like the n_largest() and rank() methods, that come in handy for occasional use. So if you have a specific need as you analyze data, be sure to check the Internet to see whether there's already a method that does what you want.

Terms

melt columns
group data
aggregate data
nuisance column
pivot data
pivot table
bin
quantile
bin edge

Summary

- The melt() method lets you *melt* two or more columns into a variable column that contains the melted column names and a value column that contains the related values. This lets you create the long data that Seaborn uses for plotting.
- You use the groupby() method to *group* data, and aggregate methods to *aggregate* data.
- When aggregating data, columns that can't be aggregated are sometimes referred to as *nuisance columns*.
- Both the pivot() and pivot_table() methods provide a way to *pivot* data based on an index. This lets you group and aggregate data into a *pivot table*.
- The cut() and qcut() methods let you divide the data in a column into *bins* of equal size or bins with equal numbers of unique values. Then, you can plot the data in the bins.
- Pandas provides dozens of methods for special purposes like the n_largest(), pct_change(), and the rank() methods. So when you have a special purpose and wonder if there's a method for it, you should search the Internet with keywords that describe the library, object, and method that you're looking for.

Exercise 8-1 Analyze the Forest Fires data

This exercise guides you through the process of analyzing the Forest Fires data.

Read the data

1. Start JupyterLab and open the Notebook named ex_8-1_fires that should be in this folder:

   `exercises/ch08`

2. If necessary, run the Kernel→Restart Kernel and Clear All Outputs command.
3. Run the first two cells to read the data into the DataFrame named fires_by_month.
4. Display the first five rows of the DataFrame.

Group and aggregate the data

5. Group the data by state and year and assign it to a variable called fires_grouped.
6. Sum the grouped data and assign the DataFrame that's returned to the variable named fires_by_year.
7. Drop the fire_month column because it doesn't make sense anymore.

Use pivot tables

8. Use the query() method to select all the data for the years 2013 and later. Then, reset the index for the DataFrame that's returned and assign the DataFrame to a variable named fires_recent.
9. Use the pivot() method to pivot the data so the state column provides the values for the row labels, the fire_year column provides the values for the column labels, and the acres_burned column provides the data for the table.
10. Use the pivot_table() method with the fires_by_month DataFrame to get the same result as the previous step. Note how this saves you several steps.

Work with bins

11. Reset the index for the DataFrame named fires_by_year.
12. Use the cut() method to bin the rows by decade and store the results in a new column named decade.
13. Double-check the values on the edge of each bin to make sure that they are binned properly. To do that, you can display the first 25 or so rows of the DataFrame.
14. Drop the fire_year column and assign the DataFrame that's returned to a variable named fires_by_decade.
15. Group the DataFrame by the state and decade columns and sum the data.

Exercise 8-2 Analyze the Cars data

This exercise guides you through the process of analyzing the Cars data.

Read the data

1. Open the Notebook named ex_8-2_cars that should be in this folder: `exercises/ch08`
2. If necessary, run the Kernel→Restart Kernel and Clear All Outputs command.
3. Run the first two cells to read the data into the DataFrame named cars.
4. Display the first five rows of the DataFrame.

Melt the data

5. Use the melt() method to combine the enginesize and curbweight columns. Name the new variable column feature and use the default name of value for the value column.
6. Use the relplot() method to create a scatterplot for the feature and price data. Use the col parameter to create a different plot for each feature. Use the facet_kws parameter to give each subplot an independent x-axis.

Rank the data by price

7. Use the rank() method to add a priceRank column that ranks each row by the price value.
8. Display the ten rows with the lowest price in ascending order from lowest price to highest, and note that the ranks in row 8 and 9 have been averaged.

Bin the data with quantiles

9. Use the qcut() method to create three price bins for the data: low, medium, and high. Store these bins in a new column named priceGrade.
10. Use the value_counts() method to display the number of values for each bin in the priceGrade column.

Group and aggregate the data

11. Group the cars data by the priceGrade column. Use the agg() method to aggregate the price data with the min() and max() methods. This should display the highest and lowest prices for each bin.
12. Group the data by the carbody and aspiration columns, and get the average price for each group. This returns a Series object with an index that's created from the carbody and aspiration columns.
13. Unstack the aspiration column of the index so the aspiration values are displayed as columns.
14. Use the pivot_table() method to accomplish the same task as steps 12 and 13.
15. Use the Pandas plot() method to create a bar chart from the DataFrame returned by the pivot_table() method.

Chapter 9

How to analyze time-series data

In the previous chapter, you learned the critical skills for analyzing data. Now, this chapter expands on that by showing you how to analyze data that is indexed by dates and times. Although the general analysis techniques stay the same, many of the operations that you do with time-series data are unique.

How to reindex time-series data

When you work with time-series data, you'll often want to index the data based on time periods like weeks, months, or quarters. To do that, you first generate the time periods that you want. Then, you reindex the data based on those periods. Once that's done, it's easy to summarize or plot the data based on those time periods.

How to generate time periods

Figure 9-1 shows how to use the date_range() method to generate the time periods that you want to use. To do that, you specify the start date and the end date for the time period. Then, you use the freq parameter to set the frequency of the dates within that period. The result is a DatetimeIndex object that contains those dates.

To illustrate, the first example shows how to generate the first date in each month from January 1, 2020, through December 31, 2020. The output for this method shows that this works the way you would expect it to. So the DatetimeIndex contains January 1, February 1, and so on, ending with December 1, 2020.

The other examples show the use of other frequencies. The second example shows how to get all the business days (Monday through Friday) in the date range. However, that doesn't take any holidays into account, even when you use the business frequencies.

The third example shows how to generate all of the Mondays in the date range. To do that, you use the W frequency followed by a dash and the three-letter abbreviation for the day that you want.

The fourth example shows how to use an integer to change the frequency. In this example, 12 is used to change the frequency from every hour to every 12 hours. And if you change the freq parameter for the third example from W-MON to 2W-MON, the dates for every other Monday will be generated.

For some frequencies, you can also use decimal numbers to change the frequency. If, for example, you change the freq parameter for the fourth example to 0.5H, you get the time periods for every 30 minutes. Note, however, that this decimal frequency isn't valid for days (D). So, if you need a frequency that isn't provided by one of the freq values, you will probably have to experiment to find out what works and what doesn't.

The date_range() method

Method	Description
`date_range(params)`	Generates a list of datetime periods and returns a DatetimeIndex that contains them.
Parameter	**Description**
`start`	The start of the generated datetime values.
`end`	The end of the generated datetime values.
`freq`	The frequency of the generated datetime values.

Some of the aliases for the freq parameter

Alias	Frequency	Alias	Frequency
B	business day	Q	quarter end
D	calendar day	QS	quarter start
W	weekly	Y	year end
M	month end	YS	year start
SM	semi-month end (15th and last day)	H	hourly
MS	month start	T	minutely
SMS	semi-month start (1st and 15th)	S	secondly

How to generate a DatetimeIndex for the first date of each month

```
pd.date_range('01/01/2020', '12/31/2020', freq='MS')
==========================================================================
DatetimeIndex(['2020-01-01', '2020-02-01', '2020-03-01', '2020-04-01',
               '2020-05-01', '2020-06-01', '2020-07-01', '2020-08-01',
               '2020-09-01', '2020-10-01', '2020-11-01', '2020-12-01'],
              dtype='datetime64[ns]', freq='MS')
```

How to generate a DatetimeIndex for all Monday-Friday dates

```
pd.date_range('01/01/2020', '01/31/2020', freq='B')
```

How to generate a DatetimeIndex for all Mondays

```
pd.date_range('12/01/2020', '12/31/2020', freq='W-MON')
```

How to generate a DatetimeIndex for every 12 hours

```
pd.date_range('01/01/2020', '01/31/2020', freq='12H')
```

Description

- You can add a B before most frequency aliases to convert it to its business equivalent. For example, BM specifies business month end.
- You can also code an integer before most of the frequency aliases to change the frequencies. For example, 12H is every 12 hours.

Figure 9-1 How to generate time periods

How to reindex with datetime indexes

After you create a DatetimeIndex object that contains the date range that you want, you can use it to *reindex* a DataFrame as shown in figure 9-2. Here, the first example shows the first five rows of a DataFrame for one stock on the stock market during the year 2020. As you can see, this data is already indexed on a datetime column called Date, which is important because the reindex() method only operates on indexes.

Then, the second example shows how to use the date_range() method to generate a DatetimeIndex object for just the Fridays in the year 2020 and store it in a variable named fridays. And the third example shows how you can use that DatetimeIndex object to reindex the stock data. When the data is reindexed, only the rows for Fridays remain in the DataFrame.

Note, however, that there will be some missing values in the reindexed data because the stock market isn't open on holidays and some of them fall on Friday. In 2020, that included Good Friday, Independence Day (taken on July 3), and Christmas. In some cases, you can use the fill_value parameter or the method parameter of the reindex() method to fill the missing values, but often that won't be adequate. To deal with this issue, you can apply a user-defined function as shown later in this chapter.

Although this figure shows how to reindex with DatetimeIndexes, you should know that you can also use the reindex() method with other types of indexes. If, for example, you're analyzing fires data with state as the index, you could reindex with a list of just the states that you want to analyze or plot.

The reindex() method

Method	Description
`reindex(params)`	Replaces the old index with a new one, keeping the rows where the indexes match.
Parameter	**Description**
`index`	The new index.
`fill_value`	The value that's used for missing values in the index. The default is NaN.
`method`	A method that determines how gaps in an index with increasing or decreasing values are filled.

The stock market data

```
stockData.set_index('Date', inplace=True)
stockData.head(3)
```

Date	Open	High	Low	Close
2020-01-02	74.059998	75.150002	73.797501	75.087502
2020-01-03	74.287498	75.144997	74.125000	74.357498
2020-01-06	73.447502	74.989998	73.187500	74.949997

How to generate a DataTimeIndex for all Fridays in a year

```
fridays = pd.date_range('01/01/2020', '12/31/2020', freq='W-FRI')
fridays
=================================================================
DatetimeIndex(['2020-01-03', '2020-01-10', '2020-01-17', '2020-01-24',
               '2020-01-31', '2020-02-07', '2020-02-14', '2020-02-21',
               ...
               '2020-11-06', '2020-11-13', '2020-11-20', '2020-11-27',
               '2020-12-04', '2020-12-11', '2020-12-18', '2020-12-25'],
              dtype='datetime64[ns]', freq='W-FRI')
```

How to reindex the data

```
stockData.reindex(fridays).head(3)
```

	Open	High	Low	Close
2020-01-03	74.287498	75.144997	74.1250	74.357498
2020-01-10	77.650002	78.167503	77.0625	77.582497
2020-01-17	79.067497	79.684998	78.7500	79.682503

Description

- You can select stock data for only the generated dates by setting an index on the Date column and then reindexing on the DatetimeIndex object.
- Since the stock market only trades on business days, the reindexed stock data for 2020 won't have values for holidays like Good Friday and Christmas.

Figure 9-2 How to reindex with datetime indexes

How to reindex with a semi-month index

The first example in figure 9-3 shows how you can use SMS for the freq parameter to generate all the semi-month starting dates for the year. Of the two dates, the first one is always the 1st of the month and the second one is always the 15th. But because of this, the dates often land on the weekends, and that creates missing values.

The second example shows how this frequency looks in a DataFrame. Here, you can see the missing value for January 1, which is a holiday. But you can also see missing values when the 1st or the 15th falls on a weekend.

These missing values are easy to see in the plot in the third example. In fact, these missing values occur more often than you might think. So in the next figure, you'll learn how a user-defined function can fix these missing values.

How to generate all the semi-month dates in a year

```
semiMonths = pd.date_range('01/01/2020', '12/31/2020', freq='SMS')
semiMonths
===================================================================
DatetimeIndex(['2020-01-01', '2020-01-15', '2020-02-01', '2020-02-15',
               '2020-03-01', '2020-03-15', '2020-04-01', '2020-04-15',
               '2020-05-01', '2020-05-15', '2020-06-01', '2020-06-15',
               '2020-07-01', '2020-07-15', '2020-08-01', '2020-08-15',
               '2020-09-01', '2020-09-15', '2020-10-01', '2020-10-15',
               '2020-11-01', '2020-11-15', '2020-12-01', '2020-12-15'],
              dtype='datetime64[ns]', freq='SMS-15')
```

How to reindex the stock data with the semi-month index

```
stockData.reindex(semiMonths).head()
```

	Open	High	Low	Close
2020-01-01	NaN	NaN	NaN	NaN
2020-01-15	77.962502	78.875	77.387497	77.834999
2020-02-01	NaN	NaN	NaN	NaN
2020-02-15	NaN	NaN	NaN	NaN
2020-03-01	NaN	NaN	NaN	NaN

How to plot the semi-month data

```
stockData.reindex(semiMonths).plot()
```

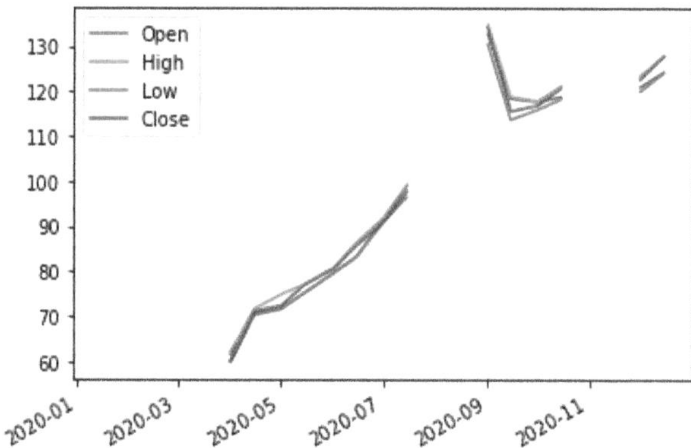

Description

- When you reindex and plot the data for a range of dates, you may be surprised to see the number of missing values.

Figure 9-3 How to reindex with a semi-month index

How a user-defined function can improve a datetime index

The first example in figure 9-4 presents a user-defined function that you can use to improve a datetime index. Its basic logic is this: If the date is a weekday, do nothing. If the date is a Saturday, move it back a day so it will be a Friday. And if the date is a Sunday, move it forward a day so it will be a Monday.

In case you aren't familiar with the methods that are used within this function, the weekday() method returns an integer that corresponds to the day of the week for a datetime object. And the timedelta() method creates objects that can be used for datetime arithmetic. In this case, the days parameter is set to 1 so the timedelta object functions as a single day when it is added or subtracted from a datetime object.

After you write the function, you need to generate a DatetimeIndex and apply the user-defined function to it, as shown by the second example. For this to work, you must convert the DatetimeIndex to a Series object. To do that, you can use the to_series() method. That way, you can use the apply() method to apply the user-defined function to each datetime object in the Series.

In the results that are shown for this example, you can see that the weekend dates have been replaced by the adjusted dates. Here, the first column shows the index value generated by the date_range() method, and the second column shows the adjusted date value.

After the third example reindexes on the adjusted dates, you can see that the index for the DataFrame uses the adjusted dates. Although that fills most of the missing values, it still doesn't handle holidays. That's why the first row still contains missing values. In some cases, that will be good enough. Otherwise, you can apply similar logic to extend the user-defined function so it fixes the dates for the holidays.

A user-defined function that converts weekend dates to weekdays

```
import datetime as dt

def adjustDate(date):
    if date.weekday() < 5:
        return date
    elif date.weekday() == 5:
        return date - dt.timedelta(days=1)
    else:
        return date + dt.timedelta(days=1)
```

How to apply the user-defined function

```
semiMonths = pd.date_range('01/01/2020', '12/31/2020', freq='SMS')
semiMonthsAdjusted = semiMonths.to_series().apply(adjustDate)
semiMonthsAdjusted.head()
=============================================================
2020-01-01   2020-01-01
2020-01-15   2020-01-15
2020-02-01   2020-01-31
2020-02-15   2020-02-14
2020-03-01   2020-03-02
```

How to reindex on the adjusted dates

```
stockData.reindex(semiMonthsAdjusted).head()
```

	Open	High	Low	Close
2020-01-01	NaN	NaN	NaN	NaN
2020-01-15	77.962502	78.875000	77.387497	77.834999
2020-01-31	80.232498	80.669998	77.072502	77.377502
2020-02-14	81.184998	81.495003	80.712502	81.237503
2020-03-02	70.570000	75.360001	69.430000	74.702499

Description

- If the freq parameter for the date_range() method doesn't return the results you want, you can define your own function to adjust the dates before you use them to reindex the data.
- The adjustDate() function above converts a weekend value to a Friday or Monday, but it doesn't provide for holidays.

Figure 9-4 How a user-defined function can improve a datetime index

How reindexing with an improved index can improve plots

The last figure showed how a user-defined function can improve an index. Now, the first two examples in figure 9-5 show how the data in the index has been improved. Then, the third example shows how using the improved index improves the plot for the data.

As you can see, there are four rows of missing values in the first five rows of the first DataFrame, but there is only one such row when the index is improved. This shows in the plot of the data with the improved index. If you compare this plot with the one in figure 9-3, you can see how much the user-defined function has improved the plot.

The semiMonths data before adjustment

```
stockData.reindex(semiMonths).head()
```

	Open	High	Low	Close
2020-01-01	NaN	NaN	NaN	NaN
2020-01-15	77.962502	78.875	77.387497	77.834999
2020-02-01	NaN	NaN	NaN	NaN
2020-02-15	NaN	NaN	NaN	NaN
2020-03-01	NaN	NaN	NaN	NaN

The semiMonthsAdjusted data

```
stockData.reindex(semiMonthsAdjusted).head()
```

	Open	High	Low	Close
2020-01-01	NaN	NaN	NaN	NaN
2020-01-15	77.962502	78.875000	77.387497	77.834999
2020-01-31	80.232498	80.669998	77.072502	77.377502
2020-02-14	81.184998	81.495003	80.712502	81.237503
2020-03-02	70.570000	75.360001	69.430000	74.702499

The plotted semiMonthsAdjusted data

```
stockData.reindex(semiMonthsAdjusted).plot()
```

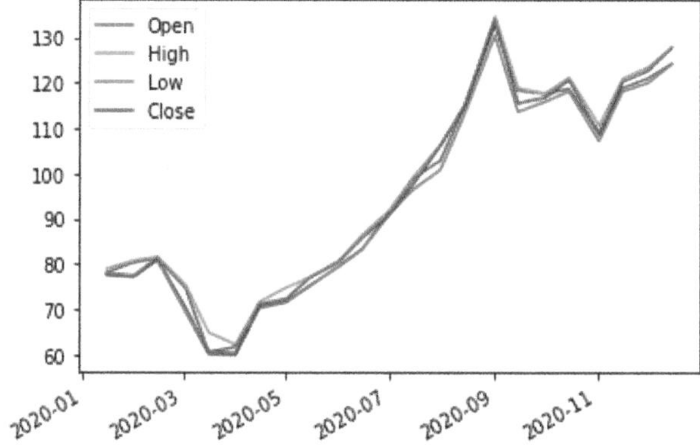

Figure 9-5 How reindexing with an improved index can improve plots

How to resample time-series data

When you work with datetime indexes, you will sometimes want to adjust the frequency of the data. This is known as *resampling*. When you move the data from a higher to a lower frequency (daily to monthly, for example), it's called *downsampling*. When you move the data from a lower frequency to a higher frequency (daily to hourly, for example), it's called *upsampling*.

How to use the resample() method

To resample data, you use the resample() method, as shown in figure 9-6. Here, the first example shows a DataFrame that's indexed by the discovery date for each fire, and the acres_burned column represents the total number of acres burned each day.

Then, the second example shows how to *downsample* this data to a monthly frequency by specifying M for the rule parameter. When you downsample, though, you must call an aggregate method that aggregates the values so they're appropriate for the new index. In this example, the sum() method sums the acres burned for each month.

The third example shows how to *upsample* (or *interpolate*) this data from daily to every 12 hours. But note that this means that every other row will have 0.00 for the acres_burned column. That's why upsampling isn't appropriate for most types of analysis, even though you can use the fillna() method to fill the missing values. However, upsampling is useful for a narrow range of applications like digital signal processing.

The resample() method

Method	Description
`resample(params)`	Converts time-series data from one frequency to another.
Parameter	**Description**
`rule`	The new frequency. Uses the same values as the freq parameter in figure 9-1.

The acresBurned data

```
acresBurned.head(3)
```

	acres_burned
discovery_date	
1992-01-01	1280.76
1992-01-02	122.50
1992-01-03	526.00

How to downsample the data

```
acresBurned.resample(rule='M').sum().head(3)
```

	acres_burned
discovery_date	
1992-01-31	26779.35
1992-02-29	73605.86
1992-03-31	115644.53

How to upsample the data

```
acresBurned.resample(rule='12H').sum().head(4)
```

	acres_burned
discovery_date	
1992-01-01 00:00:00	1280.76
1992-01-01 12:00:00	0.00
1992-01-02 00:00:00	122.50
1992-01-02 12:00:00	0.00

Description

- When you *downsample*, you change the time series to a less frequent interval. When you *upsample*, you change the time series to a more frequent interval.

Figure 9-6 How to use the resample() method

How to use the label and closed parameters when you downsample

Figure 9-7 shows how to use the label and closed parameters when you downsample a time series. Here, the first example shows the starting DataFrame.

Then, the second example downsamples the data in the DataFrame from a daily frequency to a quarterly frequency. Here, the label parameter is set to right, which means that the right bin edge is used as the index, and the closed parameter is set to right, which means that the values that fall on the right bin edge will be included in the aggregate calculation.

As a result, the bin edges are 12/31/1991 to 03/31/1992, 03/31/1992 to 06/30/1992, and so on. But, since the bins are closed on the right, the left bin edge will not be used in the calculation. So, the sum() operation is applied to these date ranges: 01/01/1992 to 03/31/1992, 04/01/1992 to 06/30/1992, and so on.

The third example also downsamples the data, but this time the label and closed parameters are set to left. As a result, the sum() method is applied to these date ranges: 12/31/1991 to 03/30/1992, 03/31/1992 to 06/29/1992, and so on.

This shows that it makes sense to close the bin edge on the same side as the label. That way, the data for the labels date will be included in the calculations for that label. That's why both of the examples in this figure do that.

The label and closed parameters of the resample() method

Parameter	Description
`label`	Which bin edge will be used as the label: right or left. The default depends on the rule parameter.
`closed`	Which bin edge will be closed: right or left. The closed edge is included in the aggregated data.

The acresBurned data

```
acresBurned.head(3)
```

discovery_date	acres_burned
1992-01-01	1280.76
1992-01-02	122.50
1992-01-03	526.00

How to downsample with right labels and a closed right edge

```
acresBurned.resample(rule='Q', label='right', closed='right').sum().head()
```

discovery_date	acres_burned
1992-03-31	216029.74
1992-06-30	485118.67
1992-09-30	1293714.71
1992-12-31	129026.79
1993-03-31	141047.95

How to downsample with left labels and a closed left edge

```
acresBurned.resample(rule='Q', label='left', closed='left').sum().head()
```

discovery_date	acres_burned
1991-12-31	213086.74
1992-03-31	487341.67
1992-06-30	1290628.71
1992-09-30	132765.79
1992-12-31	139471.71

Description

- In general, you should set the label and closed parameters the same way: both left or both right. That way, the data for the label date is included in the aggregation.

Figure 9-7 How to use the label and closed parameters when you downsample

How downsampling can improve plots

Figure 9-8 demonstrates how downsampling can improve plots. Here, the first example shows the data before downsampling, and the second one shows a plot derived from that data. As you can see, the daily variations in the stock price can make it hard to interpret the data.

By contrast, the third example shows a plot of the same data after it has been downsampled to the average value for each week. Here, the trends are easier to see because most of the noise has been removed from the plot.

The data before downsampling

```
stockData.head(2)
```

	Open	High	Low	Close
Date				
2020-01-02	74.059998	75.150002	73.797501	75.087502
2020-01-03	74.287498	75.144997	74.125000	74.357498

A line plot before downsampling

```
stockData.plot(y='Close')
```

A line plot after downsampling

```
stockData.resample(rule='W').mean().plot(y='Close')
```

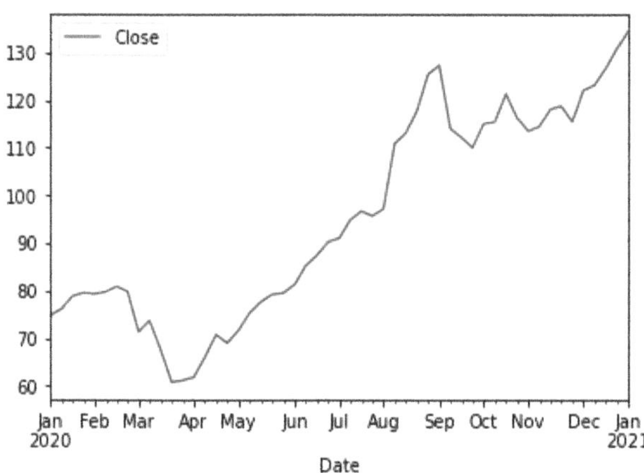

Description

- Downsampling can make your plots easier to read by reducing the noise in the data.

Figure 9-8 How downsampling can improve plots

How to work with rolling windows

Rolling windows, also known as *moving windows*, provide another way to smooth the trendlines in noisy data. Instead of plotting the actual value for each day, you plot an aggregation of values over a set number of days. In the figures that follow, you'll learn how to create and plot rolling windows.

The concept of rolling windows

Figure 9-9 presents the concept of rolling windows. In the first example, you can see a plot of the original stock market data for the month of January 2020. This shows some large fluctuations in the last third of the month. It also shows that only values for working days are included in the plot because these are the only days that data is provided for.

The second example shows a plot of the same data, but this time it plots the data that's in moving windows. Here, the windows consist of the average of the stock price over 7 working days. Because January 1 is a holiday, and because January 4 and January 5 are weekend days, the first window consists of the average stock price from January 2 through January 10. That's why the first value is plotted for January 10. The second window moves up one working day, so it consists of the average stock price from January 3 through January 13. And so on.

The data in these moving windows can be referred to as a *rolling average, moving average*, *rolling mean*, or *moving mean*. However, you can also use other types of aggregations in rolling windows.

Now, look at the differences in the two plots in this figure. Here, the second plot not only removes some of the noise from the data, but also gives a more accurate picture of what the trends are.

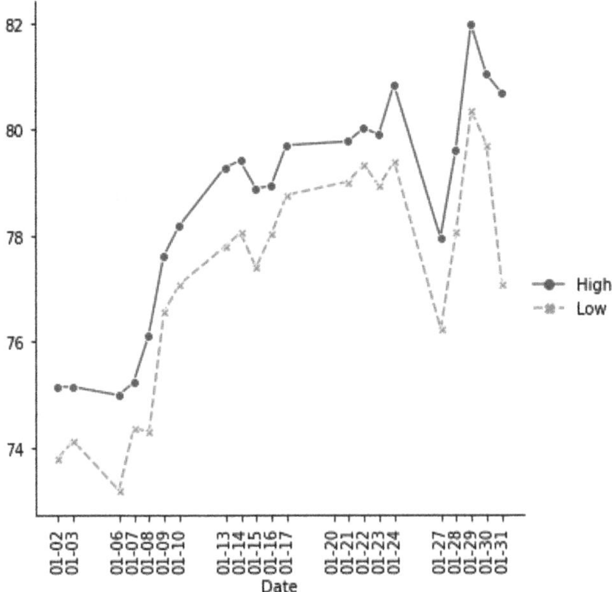

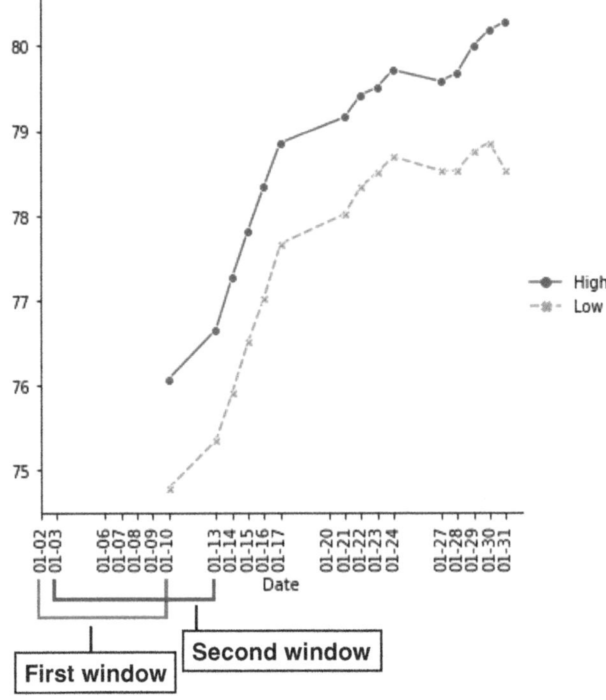

Figure 9-9 The concept of rolling windows

How to create rolling windows

To create rolling windows, you use the Pandas rolling() method, as shown in figure 9-10. Here, the first example shows how to create windows like the ones in the previous figure with the average of the data in 7 rows in each window. In the results, you can see that the first six rows have missing values. That's because the window size is set to 7 and the min_periods parameter isn't set, which prevents the aggregation from happening until there are 7 consecutive non-missing values.

In the second example, the min_periods parameter is set to 1 so the mean will be computed for the window as long as there is at least one valid value in the window. As you can see in the results, there are no longer any missing values. So, if you know that there aren't any missing values in the DataFrame, this can be a good way to prevent missing values from being created for the rows at the start of the DataFrame. But remember, if you have more consecutive missing values than the min_periods parameter anywhere in the DataFrame, there will be missing values in the results for that window.

Also note that when you code the min_periods parameter as in the second example, you won't get a true rolling average until the seventh row is reached. Instead, the values in the first row will be the same as the values in the original DataFrame. The values in the second row will be the average of the values in the first two rows. The values in the third row will be the average of the values in the first three rows. And so on.

The rolling() method

Method	Description
`rolling(params)`	Creates a moving window (bin) that can be used for performing aggregations.

Parameter	Description
`window`	The size in number of rows or columns of the window.
`min_periods`	The minimum number of consecutive values required for a window value. The default is the size of the window.

How to use the rolling() method

```
df = stockData[['High','Low']]. \
    query('Date <= "01/31/2020"').rolling(window=7).mean()
df.head(8)
```

Date	High	Low
2020-01-02	NaN	NaN
2020-01-03	NaN	NaN
2020-01-06	NaN	NaN
2020-01-07	NaN	NaN
2020-01-08	NaN	NaN
2020-01-09	NaN	NaN
2020-01-10	76.056428	74.768930
2020-01-13	76.644642	75.338929

Another example of the rolling() method

```
df = stockData[['High','Low']]. \
    query('Date <= "01/31/2020"').rolling(window=7, min_periods=1).mean()
df.head(8)
```

Date	High	Low
2020-01-02	75.150002	73.797501
2020-01-03	75.147500	73.961251
2020-01-06	75.094999	73.703334
2020-01-07	75.127499	73.870001
2020-01-08	75.323999	73.954001
2020-01-09	75.704582	74.386668
2020-01-10	76.056428	74.768930
2020-01-13	76.644642	75.338929

Figure 9-10 How to create rolling windows

How to plot rolling window data

After you create rolling windows, you can plot the data in them. Because this type of data is continuous, line plots usually work the best for plotting it. This is illustrated by the plot in figure 9-11. Because the window size for this data is set to 7 and the min_periods parameter isn't set, the first rolling average will be for the seventh row. That's why this plot starts on January 10, not January 1.

But also note how the ticks and tick labels for the x-axis are coordinated with the rolling averages. Here, the set_xticks() method uses the date_range() method with a freq parameter of B to create the range of dates that determine where the tick marks are. Then, the set_xticklabels() method uses the same date_range() method to set the dates for the tick labels, and the strftime() method formats those dates with this format: YYYY-MM-DD.

How to plot rolling windows

```
df = stockData[['High','Low']]. \
    query('Date <= "01/31/2020"').rolling(window=7).mean()

g = sns.relplot(data=df, kind='line', markers=True)
for ax in g.axes.flat:
    ax.tick_params('x', labelrotation=90)
    ax.set_xticks(pd.date_range(start='01/10/2020', end='01/31/2020',
        freq='B'))
    ax.set_xticklabels(pd.date_range(start='01/10/2020', end='01/31/2020',
        freq='B').strftime('%Y-%m-%d'))
```

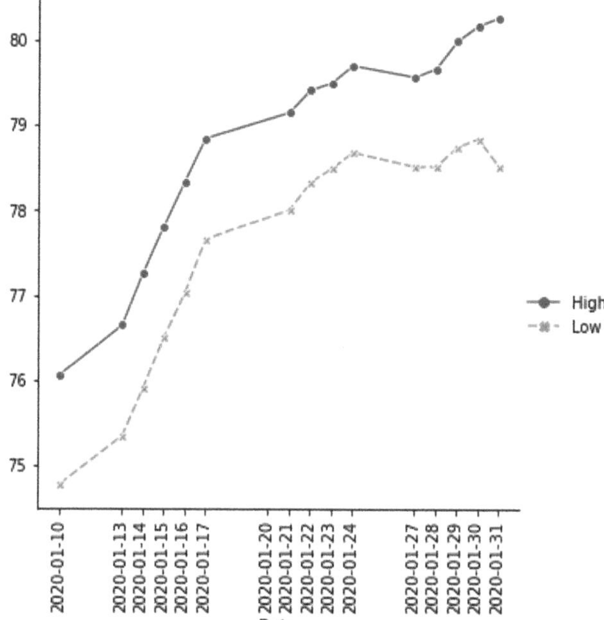

Description

- When you plot rolling window data, it makes sense to adjust the x labels so they're coordinated with the data that's being plotted.

Figure 9-11 How to plot rolling window data

How to work with running totals

Running totals provide yet another way to smooth the trendlines in noisy data. A *running total* is the sum of a sequence of numbers that's updated each time a new number is added to the sequence. This is also known as a *cumulative sum*. In the figures that follow, you'll learn how to create and plot running totals.

How to create running totals

To create a running total, you can use the expanding() method as shown in figure 9-12. This method creates a running aggregation of the data in a DataFrame. Unlike a rolling window where the front and back edge of the window move, an expanding window only moves the back edge. As a result, the size of the aggregation window expands until it includes the entire DataFrame. Like the rolling() method, the expanding() method also uses the min_periods parameter.

The first example in this figure shows the data for a DataFrame named acresBurned. Then, the second example shows how to use the expanding() method to create a running total for each row in the DataFrame and store it in a new column named running_total. Since the sum() method is used as the aggregate method, the data in each row is added to the sum of the data in all of the previous rows.

Although this example uses the sum() method, you should know that you can also use the expanding() method with other aggregate methods. For example, you can chain the mean() method to the expanding() method to get a running average of the data in the rows.

The expanding() method

Method	Description
`expanding(params)`	Creates a running aggregation for the DataFrame.
Parameter	**Description**
`min_periods`	Minimum number of observations required to have a value.

The acresBurned DataFrame

```
acresBurned.head()
```

discovery_date	acres_burned
1992-01-01	1280.76
1992-01-02	122.50
1992-01-03	526.00
1992-01-04	1150.13
1992-01-05	408.00

How to use the expanding() method

```
acresBurned['running_total'] = acresBurned.expanding().sum()
acresBurned.head()
```

discovery_date	acres_burned	running_total
1992-01-01	1280.76	1280.76
1992-01-02	122.50	1403.26
1992-01-03	526.00	1929.26
1992-01-04	1150.13	3079.39
1992-01-05	408.00	3487.39

Description

- The expanding() method iterates through the DataFrame and applies the aggregate method up to and including the current row or column.
- When the expanding() method is used with the sum() method, it generates *running totals* for the DataFrame.

Figure 9-12 How create running totals

How to plot running totals

Figure 9-13 gives you an idea for how you can plot the data in running totals. Here, the first example shows a DataFrame for the first 10 days of 1992. As you can see, it has a running_total column. Note, however, that the index for this DataFrame has been reset so the discovery_date column can be used by Seaborn when the data is plotted.

The second example shows how to melt the data in the acres_burned and running_total columns. That way, Seaborn can plot them in the same plot. The result is that the names for those two columns are in the value_type column and the related values are in the value column.

Then, the third example uses Seaborn to plot both the acres burned each day and the running total for the first 10 days of the year. Here, the plot is a bar plot, and the hue parameter is used to distinguish the daily total from the running total. As a result, this plot makes it easy to see how the running total builds over time and how each day contributes to that total.

Here again, the set_xticklabels() method is used to set the tick labels for the x-axis. But this time, the dates in the discovery_date column are used for the labels. Then, the drop_duplicates() method drops the duplicates from this column so only one date appears on the x-axis. (Remember that when the acres_burned and running_total columns are melted, the DataFrame will contain two rows with the same date but different value types and values.) Then, the astype() method converts the remaining dates to strings.

The acresBurned data for the first 10 days of 1992

```
acresBurned.reset_index(inplace=True)
acresBurned.head(3)
```

	discovery_date	acres_burned	running_total
0	1992-01-01	1280.76	1280.76
1	1992-01-02	122.50	1403.26
2	1992-01-03	526.00	1929.26

The prepared data

```
acresMelted = pd.melt(acresBurned, id_vars='discovery_date',
              value_vars=['acres_burned','running_total'], var_name='value_type')
acresMelted.head(3)
```

	discovery_date	value_type	value
0	1992-01-01	acres_burned	1280.76
1	1992-01-02	acres_burned	122.50
2	1992-01-03	acres_burned	526.00

How to plot the running totals

```
g = sns.catplot(data=acresMelted, kind='bar',
              x='discovery_date', y='value', hue='value_type', aspect=1.5)
for ax in g.axes.flat:
    ax.tick_params('x', labelrotation=90)
    ax.set_xticklabels(acresMelted.discovery_date.drop_duplicates().astype(str))
```

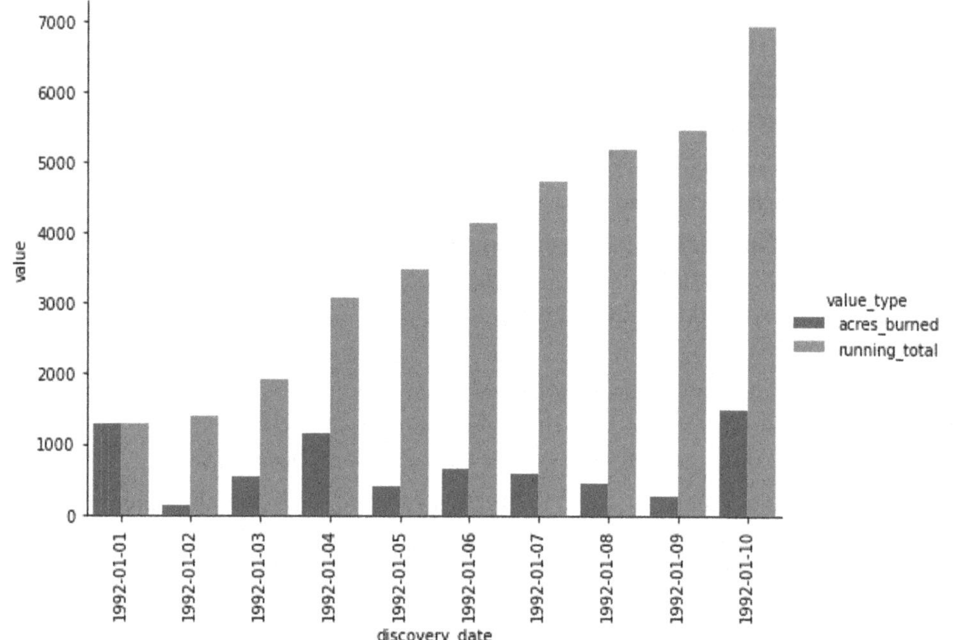

Figure 9-13 How to plot running totals

Perspective

Now that you've finished this chapter, you should have the essential skills for working with time-series data. As a result, you should be able to reindex data, downsample data, and use rolling windows and running totals. When you combine these skills with the skills that you learned in the other chapters in this section, you have a solid set of skills for data analysis.

Terms

reindex
resample
downsample
upsample
interpolate
rolling window
moving window
rolling average
moving average
rolling mean
moving mean
running total
cumulative sum

Summary

- After you use the date_range() method to generate a DatetimeIndex object for the dates in a range, you can use the reindex() method to *reindex* a DataFrame with the DatetimeIndex. This replaces the old index with a new one, keeping the rows where the indexes match.
- If necessary, you can apply a user-defined function to adjust the datetime values stored in a DatetimeIndex.
- You can use the resample() method to adjust the frequency of the data in a DataFrame. This is known as *resampling*.
- When you move the data from a higher frequency to a lower frequency (daily to monthly, for example), it's called *downsampling*.
- When you move the data from a lower frequency to a higher frequency (daily to hourly, for example), it's called *upsampling* or *interpolating*. Since this creates rows that contain NaN values, it isn't used for most types of data analysis.
- *Rolling windows,* also known as *moving windows*, provide a way to smooth the trendlines in noisy data. Instead of plotting the actual value for each day, you plot an aggregation of values over a set number of days.
- You can use the expanding() method to create a *running total*, which is the sum of a sequence of numbers that's updated each time a new number is added to the sequence. This is also known as a *cumulative sum*.

Exercise 9-1 Analyze time-series data

This exercise guides you through the process of analyzing the time-series data that's available from some of the stock market data.

Read the data

1. Open the Notebook named ex_9-1_stocks that should be in this folder:
   `exercises/ch09`
2. If necessary, run the Kernel→Restart Kernel and Clear All Outputs command.
3. Run the first two cells to read the data into the DataFrame named stockData.
4. Display the first five rows of the DataFrame.

Generate date ranges

5. Use the date_range() method to generate a date range for every other day in the year 2020.
6. Use the date_range() method to generate a date range for every three hours in the year 2020.
7. Use the date_range() method to generate a date range for every other Friday in the year 2020.

Reindex the data

8. Set an index on the Date column for the stockData DataFrame, and display the first five rows of the result.
9. Reindex the data so it contains only Fridays, assign the result to a variable named stockDataFridays, and display the first five rows.
10. Use Pandas to plot the Close column of the stockDataFridays DataFrame.

Resample the data

11. Downsample the stockData DataFrame to a monthly frequency. When you do, use the mean() method to aggregate the data and assign the DataFrame that's returned to a variable named stockDataDown.
12. Use Pandas to plot the Close column of the stockDataDown DataFrame.

Compute a rolling window

13. Compute a 2-week rolling average for the Close column. Set the min_periods parameter to 1, and assign the DataFrame that's returned to a variable named stocksRolling.
14. Use Pandas to plot the Close column of the stocksRolling DataFrame.

Section 3

An introduction to predictive analysis

So far in this book, you've learned how to use the Pandas and Seaborn libraries for descriptive analysis. Now, this section introduces a solid set of skills for predictive analysis.

To start, chapter 10 shows you how to use the Pandas, Scikit-learn, and Seaborn libraries to create statistical models that you can use to make predictions about an unknown or future value based on a single variable. Then, chapter 11 expands on those skills by showing how to make predictions based on multiple variables.

Chapter 10

How to make predictions with a linear regression model

This chapter begins by showing you how to use the Pandas and Seaborn libraries to find correlations between variables. Then, it shows how to use the Scikit-learn library to create a linear regression model and use it to make predictions. Finally, it shows how to use Seaborn to automatically create and plot a linear regression model.

Introduction to predictive analysis

Descriptive analysis analyzes historical data to understand the past and to gain insights that can be used to make decisions. However, it isn't designed to predict unknown or future values. That's the job of *predictive analysis*.

Types of predictive models

The first table in figure 10-1 presents five types of predictive models that are used in predictive analysis. This isn't a complete list, but it gives you an idea of what predictive analysis can be used for. This book focuses on the forecast and time series models because these models are used in a wide variety of industries and they're relatively easy to understand.

The second table lists some of the ways different industries use predictive analysis. For example, the healthcare industry uses it to predict the odds of a patient being readmitted after a hospital stay. And the marketing industry uses it to provide product recommendations and to predict customer satisfaction.

Introduction to regression analysis

To make a prediction, you use one or more *independent variables* to predict the value of a variable that is called the *dependent variable*. For instance, some of the variables for predicting whether a patient will be readmitted may focus on the patient's current condition, such as their blood pressure or hemoglobin count. Others may focus on the conditions of their initial admission, such as whether the initial admission involved a surgery and whether the surgery was planned or due to an emergency.

Regression analysis is one of the main tools used in predictive analysis. It involves creating and using regression models to make predictions. A *linear regression model* is a conceptual model that is used to predict the value of a dependent variable based on the values of one or more independent variables.

When a regression model uses only one independent variable to predict the value of a dependent variable, it is called a *simple linear regression*. When a regression model uses more than one independent variable to predict the value of a dependent variable, it is called a *multiple linear regression*. In this chapter, you will learn how to use a simple linear regression, and you will learn how to use a multiple linear regression in the next chapter.

To put this in context, this figure lists some real-world examples of regression models. These listings use DV to identify each dependent variable and IV to identify each independent variable. These are the types of predictive analysis that a data analyst is likely to face when on the job.

Types of predictive models

Model	Description
Classification model	Categorizes data into predefined groups based on historic data.
Clustering model	Identifies similarities in data and creates groups based on these similarities.
Outliers model	Identifies anomalies relative to historic data.
Forecast model	Makes predictions about numeric data based on historic data.
Time series model	Makes predictions about numeric data based on historic data with time as a factor.

Real-world applications of predictive analysis

Industry	Usage
Finance	Credit scores, loan applications, risk analysis, fraud detection.
Healthcare	Personalized healthcare, patient deterioration detection, readmission prevention.
Manufacturing	Maintenance prediction, product quality prediction.
Marketing	Product recommendation, customer satisfaction analysis.
Sports	Individual performance prediction, team performance prediction.
Entertainment	Content curation, content adoption prediction.

An introduction to regression analysis

- A *linear regression model* is a conceptual model that uses an equation to predict an unknown value called a *dependent variable* based on the values of one or more known values called *independent variables.*
- A *simple linear regression* uses only one independent variable, and a *multiple linear regression* uses two or more independent variables.

Real-world linear regression examples

- Predict revenue (DV) based on advertising budget (IV).
- Predict patient readmission rate (DV) given factors like hemoglobin count (IV), prior admissions (IV), blood pressure (IV), current medications (IV), and age (IV).
- Predict household energy consumption (DV) given factors like the number of people living there (IV), the size of the house (IV), the energy consumption of surrounding houses (IV), and past energy consumption (IV).
- Predict the odds of a sports team winning a game (DV) given factors like who they are playing (IV), the current season record (IV), any injured players (IV), and where the game is played (IV).

Figure 10-1 Introduction to predictive analysis

How to find correlations between variables

If two or more variables are related in a linear way, they are said to be *correlated*. In a moment, you'll learn several techniques for identifying those *correlations*. But first, you'll be introduced to the dataset that will be used throughout this chapter.

The Housing dataset

Figure 10-2 presents the Housing dataset that will be used to illustrate the skills for predictive analysis that are presented in this chapter. This dataset contains information on the housing market over the course of several months in the state of Washington in the USA.

As you can see, this dataset includes data for each house sale like the price, number of bedrooms, and square footage. All but one of these columns contains either floating-point or integer data, but the has_basement column stores a Boolean value of True or False.

Beyond that, though, some of these integer variables are numeric while others are categorical. *Numeric variables* represent measurements such as price or square footage. But *categorical variables* try to put a feature like its view or condition into categories that are identified by integers.

You should also know this dataset has already been cleaned and prepared for predictive analysis. That's why it has only 10 columns. For example, since this analysis doesn't focus on how prices change over time, the date column was dropped. And since this dataset had only 4600 rows and spanned several zip codes, it was unlikely that there would be enough clustering of house sales by street to derive any meaningful information from the street column. So that column was dropped.

Although meaningful information could be found by examining house prices by city and zip code, this analysis doesn't use this data, so those columns were dropped too. Also, since the square footage in the basement can be calculated by subtracting the sqft_above value from the sqft_living value, the sqft_basement column was dropped. Finally, since the country for every row is USA, the country column was dropped.

The columns of the Housing dataset

```
housing.info()
```

```
<class 'pandas.core.frame.DataFrame'>
Int64Index: 4207 entries, 0 to 4599
Data columns (total 11 columns):
 #   Column        Non-Null Count  Dtype
---  ------        --------------  -----
 0   price         4207 non-null   float64
 1   bedrooms      4207 non-null   float64
 2   bathrooms     4207 non-null   float64
 3   sqft_living   4207 non-null   int64
 4   floors        4207 non-null   float64
 5   waterfront    4207 non-null   int64
 6   view          4207 non-null   int64
 7   condition     4207 non-null   int64
 8   sqft_above    4207 non-null   int64
 9   yr_built      4207 non-null   int64
 10  has_basement  4207 non-null   bool
dtypes: bool(1), float64(4), int64(6)
memory usage: 365.6 KB
```

The first five rows of the Housing dataset

```
housing.head()
```

	price	bedrooms	bathrooms	sqft_living	floors	waterfront	view	condition	sqft_above	yr_built	has_basement
0	313000.0	3.0	1.50	1340	1.5	0	0	3	1340	1955	False
2	342000.0	3.0	2.00	1930	1.0	0	0	4	1930	1966	False
3	420000.0	3.0	2.25	2000	1.0	0	0	4	1000	1963	True
4	550000.0	4.0	2.50	1940	1.0	0	0	4	1140	1976	True
5	490000.0	2.0	1.00	880	1.0	0	0	3	880	1938	False

Description

- This Housing data consists of data collected over several months in the state of Washington in the USA.
- The data that's shown above is a cleaned and prepared version of the original dataset.

Figure 10-2 The Housing dataset

How to identify correlations with a scatter plot

One of the easiest ways to find a correlation between two variables is to plot the data with a scatter plot. To find correlations in scatter plot data, you look for a pattern in the distribution of the data. Sometimes this pattern is a straight line, such as when x increases y also increases or when x increases y decreases. But the correlation may also be a curved line, such as when you plot a sine or cosine function.

Figure 10-3 presents two scatter plots. The first shows the relationship between the price variable and the sqft_living variable. This shows that there is a weak positive linear relationship between the variables. So in general, as x increases, y also increases.

The second scatter plot shows the relationship between the price variable and the yr_built variable. But this plot shows that there isn't a clear linear relationship between the two variables. Nevertheless, it's still possible that there is a correlation. That's because when data is densely clustered like it is in this scatter plot, the trends and data clusters may be hidden.

When you use scatter plots to identify correlations, you should ask yourself this question: If I want to draw a line through this dataset where the line would be as close as possible to as many datapoints as possible, is there a clear way for me to do that? If you can answer, yes, the data is probably correlated.

Of course, there are a couple disadvantages to using scatter plots to identify correlations. First, when there is a high density of datapoints, the overlapping dots on the plot make it difficult to determine if there is a correlation. Second, it can be time consuming to create a scatter plot for every pair of datapoints that you want to compare. That's why the next figure shows a technique for speeding up the way that you create scatter plots.

A scatter plot that shows two variables that have a correlation

```
sns.relplot(data=housing, x='sqft_living', y='price')
```

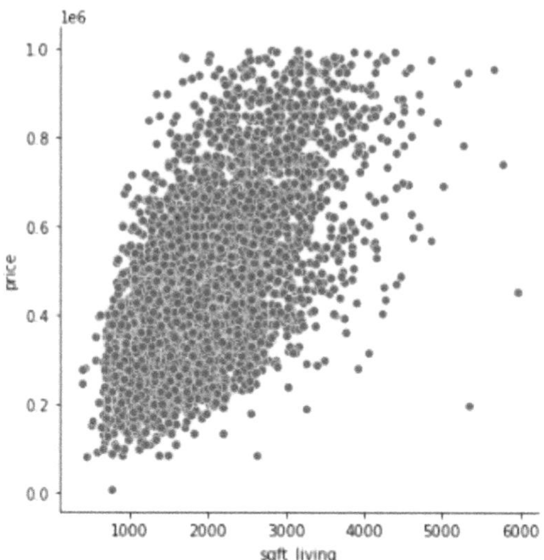

A scatter plot that shows two variables that don't have a correlation

```
sns.relplot(data=housing, x='yr_built', y='price')
```

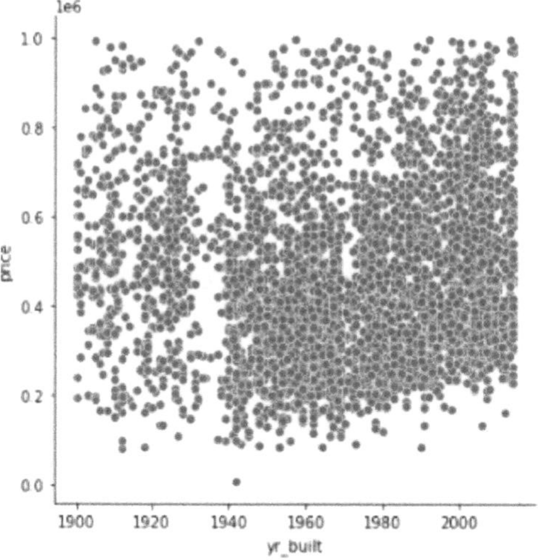

Description

- You can use scatter plots to visually identify correlations.
- If you can see a clear pattern in the data, there is a correlation. If not, there is probably no correlation, though it's still possible that a correlation exists.

Figure 10-3 How to identify correlations with a scatter plot

How to identify correlations with a grid of scatter plots

One way to speed up the creation of scatter plots for multiple pairs of datapoints is to use the Seaborn pairplot() method. This method creates a grid of plots where each cell is the plot for the corresponding x and y variables. By default, this method uses scatter plots for most of the cells. However, it uses a histogram or KDE plot when a variable is paired with itself because it wouldn't make sense to show a scatter plot for this relationship. These histograms appear on the diagonal from the upper left plot to the lower right plot.

Figure 10-4 describes the pairplot() method and a few of its parameters. Then, the example shows how to use this method to create a grid of scatter plots. Here, the data parameter specifies the DataFrame that contains the housing data, and the y_vars and x_vars parameters specify the variables to be plotted. In this case, both the y-axis and the x-axis plot the price, sqft_living, and sqft_above variables. Then, the diag_kind parameter specifies that kde (kernel density estimate) plots should be used for the plots on the diagonal.

In the resulting plots, note that each pairwise relationship is plotted twice and that the plots with the same variables are the same except that the x and y variables have been switched. For example, the top right and bottom left scatter plots represent the same variables but with swapped x and y values. Another example is the plot in the top row, middle column and the plot in the middle row, left column. To remove these redundant plots, you can set the corner parameter to True. Then, the pairplot() method won't generate the plots to the right of the diagonal.

If you study these plots, you can see that they show a weak positive correlation between the sqft_living and price variables as well as between the sqft_above and price variables. There's also a strong positive correlation between the sqft_living and sqft_above variables. However, that correlation is so obvious that it doesn't provide any insight into the data.

The Seaborn pairplot() method for generating a grid of plots

Method	Description
`pairplot(params)`	Creates a grid of plots for all possible pairs of the specified variables.
Parameter	**Description**
`kind`	The default is scatter. Other values include 'kde', 'hist', or 'reg'.
`diag_kind`	The type of plot for the diagonal. Possible values include 'hist', 'kde', or None. The default is 'hist'.
`x_vars, y_vars`	The x or y variables to use. By default, it uses all variables.
`corner`	If False (the default), show all plots. If True, don't show the plots to the right of the diagonal.

How to use the pairplot() method

```
sns.pairplot(data=housing,
             y_vars=['price','sqft_living','sqft_above'],
             x_vars=['price','sqft_living','sqft_above'],
             diag_kind='kde')
```

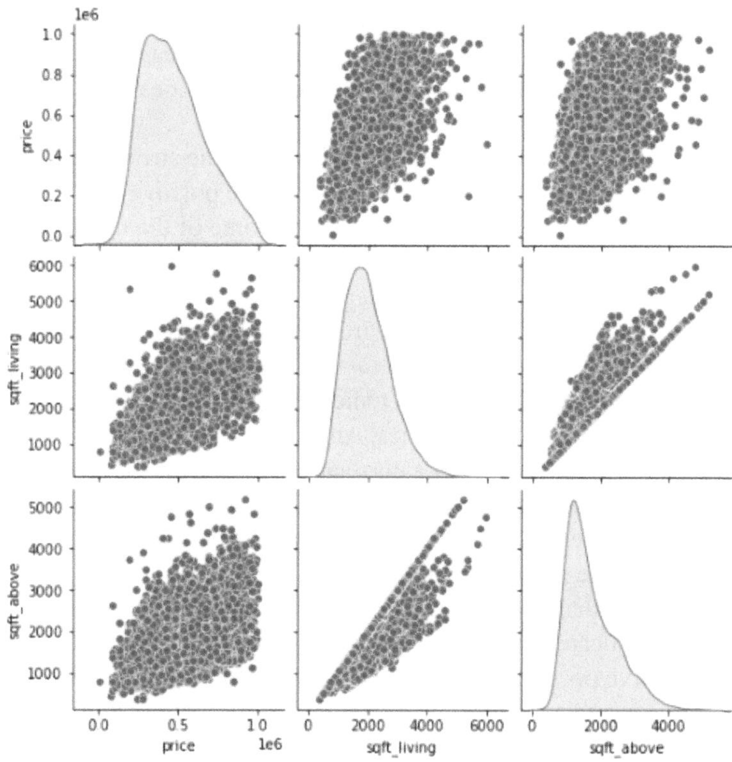

Description

- You can use the Seaborn pairplot() method to generate a grid of plots that allows you to quickly identify correlations.

Figure 10-4 How to identify correlations with a grid of scatter plots

How to identify correlations with r-values

Another way to identify correlations is to get the *Pearson correlation coefficient*, or *r-value*, for the correlation between each pair of numeric variables in a DataFrame. As the table in figure 10-5 shows, the r-value is a number between 1.0 and -1.0 that measures the type and strength of the linear correlation between two variables. When the r-value is close to 1.0, it indicates a strong positive correlation. When the r-value is close to -1.0, it indicates a strong negative correlation.

Note, however, that the r-value only detects linear relationships. So if the data has some other type of correlation, you could miss that correlation by depending on r-values alone. That's why it's a good practice to use both scatter plots and r-values to identify correlations.

To show the r-values for the relationships between each pair of numeric variables in a DataFrame, you can use the Pandas corr() method, as shown by the first example in this figure. Here, you can see that when a variable is paired with itself, the r-value is 1.0. You can also see the range of r-values that you get from the pairing of the variables in the Housing dataset.

To make this data easier to read, you can filter the data by the price column after calling the corr() method as shown in the second example. You can also sort the values in the price column in descending sequence to make it easy to identify the variables with the strongest correlations.

This second example shows that the sqft_living variable has the strongest correlation with price. Although an r-value of 0.60 is a moderate positive correlation, that's stronger than the correlations provided by some of the other numeric variables such as yr_built. If more than one independent variable provides a moderate or stronger correlation with a dependent variable, though, you might want to consider using multiple linear regression as shown in the next chapter.

When you use the corr() method, you need to remember that some categorical variables use integers for the categories. And since this method operates on all numeric variables, you will get a correlation for these variables, whether or not it is valid. For instance, *dichotomous variables* are categorical variables that only have two values, like the waterfront and has_basement variables. For those variables, the r-value is valid.

However, if there are more than two categories, the r-value isn't valid. For instance, the view variable is a categorical variable that stores an integer value from 0 to 4. Because it has five possible values, it isn't dichotomous and its r-value isn't valid.

How to interpret the r-value

r-value	Correlation type	r-value	Correlation type
`1.00`	Perfect positive	`-1.00`	Perfect negative
`.90 to .99`	Very strong positive	`-.90 to -.99`	Very strong negative
`.70 to .89`	Strong positive	`-.70 to -.89`	Strong negative
`.50 to .69`	Moderate positive	`-.50 to -.69`	Moderate negative
`.30 to .49`	Weak positive	`-.30 to -.49`	Weak negative
`.01 to .30`	Negligible positive	`-.01 to -.30`	Negligible negative
`0.00`	No correlation	`0.00`	No correlation

How to use the Pandas corr() method

```
housing.corr().head()
```

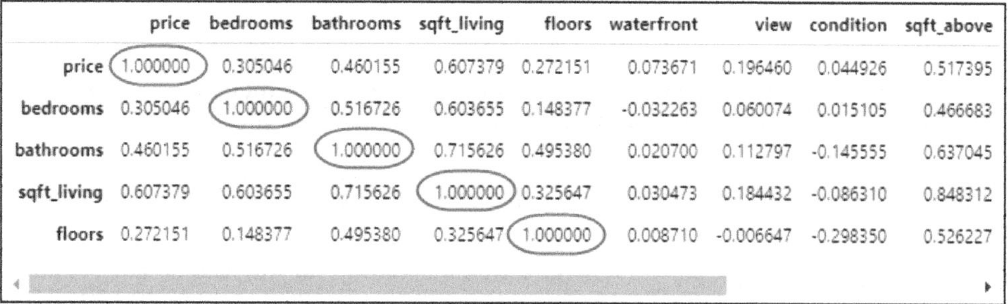

	price	bedrooms	bathrooms	sqft_living	floors	waterfront	view	condition	sqft_above
price	1.000000	0.305046	0.460155	0.607379	0.272151	0.073671	0.196460	0.044926	0.517395
bedrooms	0.305046	1.000000	0.516726	0.603655	0.148377	-0.032263	0.060074	0.015105	0.466683
bathrooms	0.460155	0.516726	1.000000	0.715626	0.495380	0.020700	0.112797	-0.145555	0.637045
sqft_living	0.607379	0.603655	0.715626	1.000000	0.325647	0.030473	0.184432	-0.086310	0.848312
floors	0.272151	0.148377	0.495380	0.325647	1.000000	0.008710	-0.006647	-0.298350	0.526227

How to filter the results of the Pandas corr() method

```
housing.corr()[['price']].sort_values(by='price', ascending=False)
```

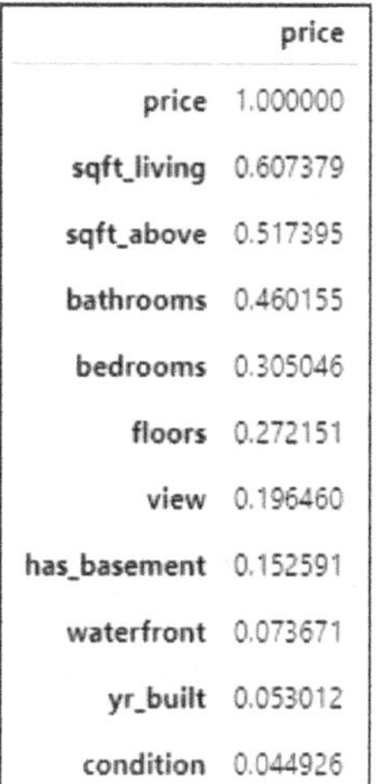

	price
price	1.000000
sqft_living	0.607379
sqft_above	0.517395
bathrooms	0.460155
bedrooms	0.305046
floors	0.272151
view	0.196460
has_basement	0.152591
waterfront	0.073671
yr_built	0.053012
condition	0.044926

Figure 10-5 How to identify correlations with r-values

How to identify correlations with a heatmap

A *heatmap*, or *heat map*, is a graphical representation of data where values are depicted by shades of color. To create a heatmap for the correlation data that's calculated by the Pandas corr() method, you can use the Seaborn heatmap() method. This method creates a grid and applies shades of a color to the cells of the grid based on the values of the cells.

Figure 10-6 shows how this works. Here, the first example uses the heatmap() method to create a heatmap for the correlation data. To do that, the data parameter is set to the DatFrame that's returned by the corr() method. Then, the cmap parameter specifies the built-in color map named 'Blues', which colors each cell a shade of blue from that color map.

Last, since the r-values from the corr() method lie between -1.0 and 1.0, this example uses the vmin and vmax parameters to set the minimum and maximum values to those values. Then, since the lowest actual value in the range is 0.045, this results in a light blue color (but not white) to be used for the lower values.

If you tighten the range between the vmin and vmax parameters, you can make the color contrast between the cells more obvious. And if you don't set these parameters, the min and max values in the data will be used as the boundaries for the color map. That way, the lowest value will be displayed in white and the highest value in dark blue.

The second example shows how to create a heatmap for the filtered and sorted correlation data. Here, the annot parameter is set to True so the r-value is displayed in each cell in the heatmap. Also, since this example doesn't use the vmin and vmax parameters, the heatmap() method automatically determines the minimum and maximum values from the data. This provides greater color contrasts between the r-values. For instance, the condition variable has the minimum r-value, so it's displayed in near-white, not light blue as it was in the first example.

Since the heatmap in the first example doesn't display the r-values, the color bar that's displayed on the right side of the heat map provides useful information about how the colors are mapped to the r-values. But since the second heatmap displays the r-values, the color bar isn't as useful. That's why the bar is hidden by setting the cbar parameter to False.

Finally, if the numeric values that are displayed in each cell aren't in the format that you want, you can use the fmt parameter to specify another format. That's also illustrated by the second example, which sets the format to a Python f-string that specifies a two-digit, floating-point number (.2f). For more information about using f-strings, you can refer to *Murach's Python Programming*.

The Seaborn heatmap() method

Method	Description
`heatmap(params)`	Creates a heat map.
Parameter	**Description**
`cmap`	The color map to use. Possible values include the built-in color maps named 'Reds', 'Greens', 'Blues', and so on.
`vmin, vmax`	The minimum and maximum value used to determine the color shading.
`annot`	If set to True, each cell is annotated with its numeric value.
`cbar`	If set to False, the color bar isn't displayed.
`fmt`	The format string to apply to numbers when they're annotated.

How to plot correlation data with a heatmap

```
sns.heatmap(data=housing.corr(), cmap='Blues', vmin=-1.0, vmax=1.0)
```

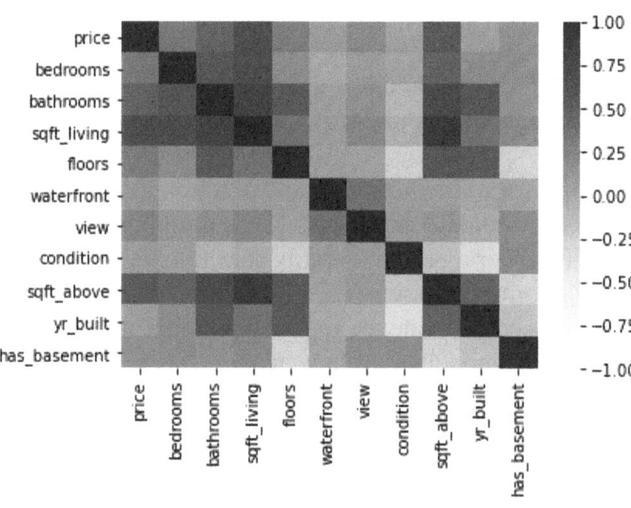

How to condense a heatmap

```
sns.heatmap(data=housing.corr()[['price']].sort_values(by='price', ascending=False),
            annot=True, cmap='Blues', cbar=False, fmt=f'.2f')
```

	price
price	1.00
sqft_living	0.61
sqft_above	0.52
bathrooms	0.46
bedrooms	0.31
floors	0.27
view	0.20
has_basement	0.15
waterfront	0.07
yr_built	0.05
condition	0.04

Figure 10-6 How to identify correlations with a heatmap

How to use Scikit-learn to work with a linear regression

As you learned earlier in this chapter, a regression model is a conceptual model that is used to predict the value of a dependent variable based on the values in one more independent variables. To create and use a model like that, you can use a library that provides those capabilities. One such library for Python is called *Scikit-learn*, or just *sklearn*, and you'll learn how to use it now.

However, sklearn isn't the only Python library that you can use to create a regression model. In fact, many other libraries are available. So, if sklearn doesn't provide the features that you need, you can look for another library that does.

A procedure for creating and using a regression model

Figure 10-7 diagrams a procedure for creating and using a regression model. This procedure provides the conceptual background that you need for using any modeling library, including sklearn.

In step 1, the dataset is split into a *training dataset* that's used to train the model and a *test dataset* that's used to validate the model. These training and test datasets can be created with specific criteria or by randomly selecting values and assigning them to either the training or test dataset.

In step 2, the training dataset is used to create the regression model. And in step 3, the test dataset is run against the model to see how accurate the results of the model are. If the values that are generated by the model are close to the actual values, the model is considered to be valid.

In step 4, if the model is valid, you can use it to predict the dependent variable based on the independent variables. That of course is the purpose of a regression model.

The procedure for creating, testing, and using a regression model

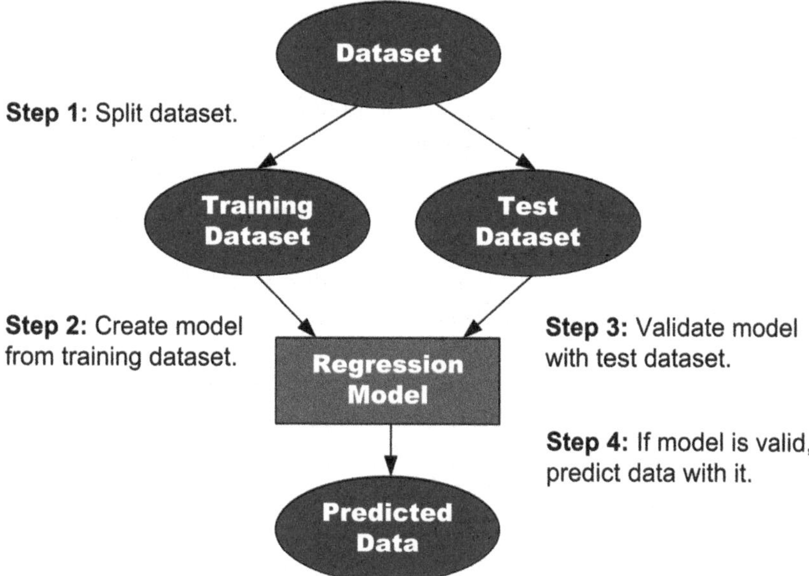
Dataset
Step 1: Split dataset.
Training Dataset
Test Dataset
Step 2: Create model from training dataset.
Regression Model
Step 3: Validate model with test dataset.
Step 4: If model is valid, predict data with it.
Predicted Data

Description

- The procedure above is used by most Python libraries that support regression models, including the Scikit-learn library that you'll learn how to use in this chapter.
- After you use the *training dataset* to train the model and the *test dataset* to validate the model, you can use the model to predict the value of a dependent variable based on the value of an independent variable.

Figure 10-7 A procedure for creating and using a regression model

The function and methods for linear regression models

Figure 10-8 presents the Scikit-learn function and methods for working with a linear regression model. To work with this type of model, you start by using the train_test_split() function to split a dataset into a training and a test dataset. Then, you use three methods of the LinearRegression class to fit the model, score the predictions of the model, and predict y values given a set of x values.

When you import and use the train_test_split() function, you start by coding one or more positional parameters. You'll see examples of that in the next figure and in chapter 11. Then, the test_size and train_size parameters determine the size of the training and testing datasets. If you only set one of these parameters, the other parameter takes the remainder of the dataset. If, for example, you set the test_size parameter to 0.15 (15%) and don't set the train_size parameter, the training dataset will be set to 0.85 (85%).

The shuffle and random_state parameters determine how the function shuffles the data before it splits the data. By default, the shuffle parameter is set to True, which shuffles the data before splitting it. If you don't set the random_state parameter, this shuffling will be done differently each time the method is run. But if you set the random-state parameter to an integer like 42, this function will do the same shuffle every time you use that integer value.

After you use the test_train_split() function to generate the training and testing datasets, you import the LinearRegression class and create a LinearRegression object from it. Then, you call the three methods of this object that are summarized in this figure to create a linear regression model and use it to make predictions.

The fit() method accepts a training dataset and fits the regression line to the dataset. This is what creates the regression equation for the LinearRegression object. The score() method accepts a test dataset and returns the R^2 value for the regression. This *R^2 value* is the percent of the change in the dependent variable that can be attributed to the independent variable or variables. And the predict() method accepts x values from the test dataset and returns predicted y values.

How to import sklearn's train_test_split() function

```
from sklearn.model_selection import train_test_split
```

The train_test_split() function

Function	Description
`train_test_split(params)`	Splits a dataset into training and test datasets. Must include one or more positional parameters that identify the data, followed by any optional named parameters.

Parameter	Description
`test_size`	The percentage of the dataset that will make up the test dataset. Should be a float between 0.0 and 1.0. The default is 0.25.
`train_size`	The percentage of the dataset that will make up the training dataset. Should be a float between 0.0 and 1.0.
`shuffle`	If True (the default), the data is shuffled before splitting.
`random_state`	If set to an integer value, the shuffling can be reproduced. Otherwise, the shuffling is random.

How to import sklearn's LinearRegression class

```
from sklearn.linear_model import LinearRegression
```

Methods of the LinearRegression object

Method	Description
`fit(x,y)`	Fits the linear regression model using a sample of x and y values.
`score(x,y)`	Returns the R^2 value for the prediction.
`predict(x)`	Predicts the y values given a set of x values.

Description

- *Scikit-learn*, also known as *sklearn*, is a free library for the Python programming language that includes support for linear regression analysis.
- The train_test_learn() function is in the sklearn.model_selection module. You use it to split a dataset into training and test datasets.
- The LinearRegression class is in the sklearn.linear_model module. You use it to create a LinearRegression object that provides the methods that fit and score a model as well as a method that can be used to predict values based on the model.

Figure 10-8 The function and methods for linear regression models

How to create, validate, and use a linear regression model

Figure 10-9 shows how to use SkiKit-learn to create, validate, and use a linear regression model. To start, it imports the function and class that you need from Scikit-learn. Then, the four steps that follow create and use the model.

In step 1, the test_train_split() function is used to create the training and test datasets. Here, the first parameter specifies the sqft_living column, which provides the data for the x_train and x_test variables. Then, the second parameter specifies the price column, which provides the data for the y_train and y_test columns.

Next, the test_size parameter specifies that the test dataset should be 0.33, or 33% of the total dataset. As a result, the other 67% will be in the training dataset. Also, since the random_state parameter is set to an integer value of 42, the shuffling that is done will be the same every time that integer value is used. That way, you will get the same results shown here if you run this code. Of course, you can go back to random shuffling by deleting this parameter.

In step 2, a LinearRegression object named linearModel is created from the LinearRegression() constructor. Then, the fit() method is called from that object, which passes the x_train and y_train variables of the training dataset to the model. The fit() method uses these variables to create the model.

In step 3, the score() method passes the x_test and y_test variables of the test dataset to the model, which returns an R^2 value that scores the model. You can use this value to judge the performance of the regression model. Here, an R^2 value of 0.35 indicates that about 35% of the change in the dependent variable can be attributed to the independent variable. But this is only part of the process for judging the regression. The other part requires that you plot the regression results as shown in the next figure.

You should also know that R^2 values aren't additive. This means that if the R^2 value for another predictor is 25%, together the two predictors don't explain 60% of the variance; it would be less than that. In other words, the sum of the parts is less than the whole.

In step 4, the predict() method is used to predict the y values based on the x values in the test dataset. As a result, this method returns the predicted price values for the same values that were used to validate the model in step 3.

After step 4, you can see a DataFrame that shows the predicted prices that were returned by step 4 as well as the sqft_living and price variables in the test dataset. Then, you can compare the predicted prices with the actual prices in the test dataset. As you can see, they're not that close, which is consistent with the R^2 value returned in step 3.

Import the function and class that you need from Scikit-learn

```
from sklearn.model_selection import train_test_split
from sklearn.linear_model import LinearRegression
```

Step 1: Split the data into the training and test datasets

```
x_train, x_test, y_train, y_test = train_test_split(
    housing[['sqft_living']], housing[['price']],
    test_size=0.33, random_state=42)
```

Step 2: Create the model from the training dataset

```
linearModel = LinearRegression()
linearModel.fit(x_train, y_train)
```

Step 3: Validate the model with the test dataset

```
linearModel.score(x_test, y_test)
=================================
0.35072654653322344
```

Step 4: Use the model to make predictions

```
y_predicted = linearModel.predict(x_test)
y_predicted
=========================================
array([[355333.11742787],
       [545363.47687159],
       [466838.5349527 ],
       ...,
       [325493.63949869],
       [415012.07328623],
       [394595.58838732]])
```

The predicted prices vs. the test prices

	price_predicted	sqft_living	price
0	364756.110458	1300	425000.0
1	383602.096519	1420	510000.0
2	688278.871164	3360	455000.0
3	416582.572125	1630	339950.0
4	327064.138337	1060	461000.0
...	...	...	...
1384	432287.560508	1730	535500.0
1385	421294.068640	1660	220000.0
1386	534369.985003	2380	330000.0
1387	342769.126721	1160	390000.0
1388	298795.159246	880	312500.0

1389 rows × 3 columns

Figure 10-9 How to create, validate, and use a linear regression model

How to plot the predicted data

Once you have the predicted data, you can plot it to view its regression line as shown in figure 10-10. Here, the first set of examples prepares the data for plotting. In step 1, the y_predicted values that were created in the last figure are put into a DataFrame named predicted that contains a single column named price_predicted. To do that, the DataFrame() constructor is used.

In step 2, the x_test and y_test columns of the previous figure are joined with the predicted DataFrame. At this point, the DataFrame has a column named sqft_living and two columns named price and price_predicted that contain data about the price, as in the DataFrame that's shown in the previous figure.

In step 3, the melt() method melts the two price columns into a single column. At this point, you can see that the DataFrame has a price_type column that indicates whether the price is an actual price or a predicted price, a price_value column that contains the values for the actual and predicted prices, and a sqft_living column for the independent variable. You need to melt the data in this way so you can plot both types of prices in a single plot.

After the data is prepared, the second example plots the data. To do that, it uses the hue parameter to distinguish between the actual values and the predicted values. The resulting plot shows that the predicted price data forms a straight line through the scatter plot data. It also shows that the regression line is drawn down the middle of the actual values, which is what you would hope for with a simple linear regression. In this situation, though, the regression line serves more as a trendline than a predictor because of the variation in the data.

How to prepare the data for plotting

Step 1: Put the predicted values in a DataFrame

```
predicted = pd.DataFrame(y_predicted, columns=['price_predicted'])
```

Step 2: Combine the test data and the predicted data

```
combined = predicted.join([x_test.reset_index(drop=True),
                           y_test.reset_index(drop=True)])
```

Step 3: Melt the price and price_predicted columns into a single column

```
melted = pd.melt(combined, id_vars=['sqft_living'],
                 value_vars=['price','price_predicted'],
                 var_name='price_type', value_name='price_value')
```

The resulting DataFrame

```
melted.head()
```

	sqft_living	price_type	price_value
0	1240	price	390000.0
1	2450	price	345000.0
2	1950	price	375000.0
3	2280	price	500324.0
4	2410	price	600000.0

How to plot the test and training data

```
sns.relplot(data=melted, x='sqft_living', y='price_value',
            hue='price_type')
```

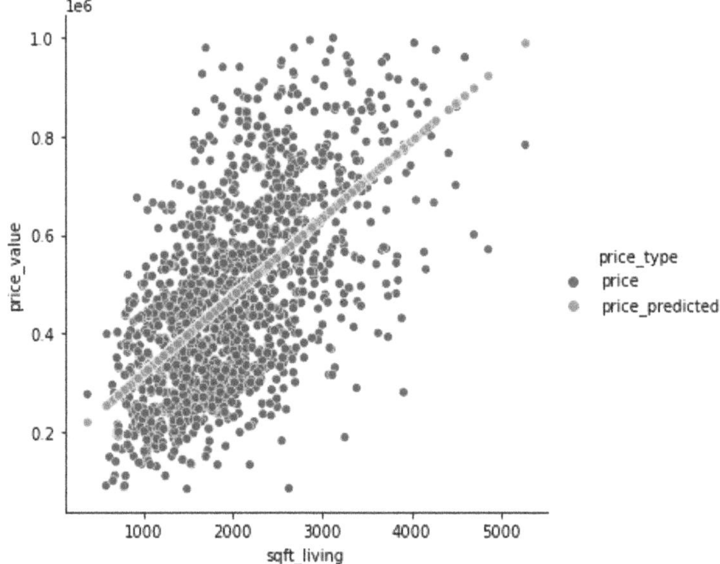

Figure 10-10 How to plot the predicted data

How to plot the residuals

Earlier in this chapter, you learned that one way to evaluate a regression model is to use the score() method to return the R^2 value for model. Another way to evaluate the model is to plot the regression residuals.

A *regression residual* (or just *residual*) is the difference between the actual value for a dependent variable and the predicted value. As a result, the residuals show how far off the predictions are.

Before you can plot the residuals, you need to calculate the residual values and add them to your DataFrame as shown by the first example in figure 10-11. This code works with the DataFrame named combined that was created by the first two steps in the previous figure. Here, the code calculates the residuals by subtracting the predicted price from the price. Then, it stores the residuals in a new column named residual in the combined DataFrame

The second example in this figure shows how to use the Seaborn relplot() method to create a scatter plot of the residuals where the x parameter specifies the independent variable and the y parameter specifies the residuals. On the plot, if a point has a y value of 0, the prediction was exactly correct. For incorrect predictions, a positive y value indicates that the prediction was too low, and a negative y value indicates that the prediction was too high.

After it calls the relplot() method, the second example loops through the one Axes object in the grid that's returned by the relplot() method. Within that loop, the axhline() method of the Axes object adds a horizontal line at the 0 value of the y-axis. This method also uses the ls parameter to specify a dashed ('--') line style. Although this line isn't necessary, it makes it easier to see how far the residuals are from 0.

How to calculate residuals

```
combined['residual'] = combined.price - combined.price_predicted
combined.head()
```

	price_predicted	sqft_living	price	residual
0	355333.117428	1240	390000.0	34666.882572
1	545363.476872	2450	345000.0	-200363.476872
2	466838.534953	1950	375000.0	-91838.534953
3	518664.996619	2280	500324.0	-18340.996619
4	539081.481518	2410	600000.0	60918.518482

How to plot the residuals

```
g = sns.relplot(data=combined, x='sqft_living', y='residual')

# draw a horizontal line where the y axis is 0
for ax in g.axes.flat:
    ax.axhline(0, ls='--')    # use dashed line style
```

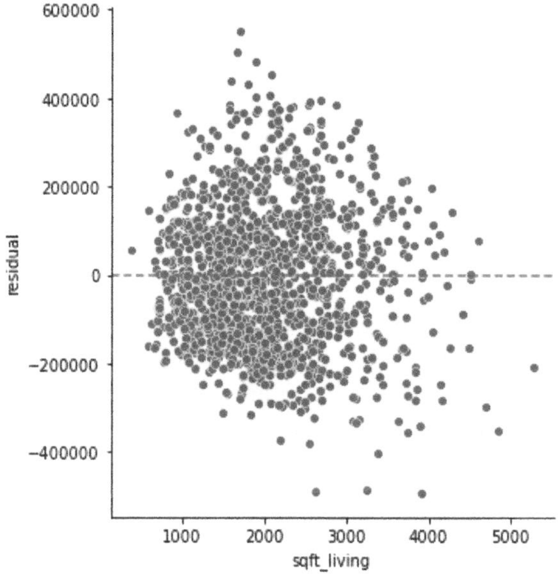

Description

- A *regression residual* is the difference between the actual value and the predicted value.
- You can use the axhline() method of the Axes object to draw a horizontal line at the specified y value.

Figure 10-11 How to plot the residuals

How to plot regression models with Seaborn

Another way to work with regression models is to use Seaborn to create the regression models and plot the *regression lines* that fit the data. The downside is that you don't have access to or control of the regression model, so you can't use it to make predictions. But if you're just trying to find a trend and don't need to make predictions, Seaborn provides a quick way to plot a regression.

The lmplot() method and some of its parameters

The first table in figure 10-12 summarizes six types of regressions that you can plot with the Seaborn lmplot() method. As you have already learned, a *simple linear regression* uses a single independent variable to predict the value of the dependent variable. And a *multiple linear regression* uses two or more independent variables.

By contrast, a *logistic regression* measures the probability of the state of a dichotomous (two state) variable based on the value of a predictor variable. A *robust regression* is a type of linear regression that is designed to minimize the influence of outliers on the regression line. And a *polynomial regression* is a type of linear regression where the relationship between the independent variable or variables and the dependent variable is calculated by a polynomial equation. As a result, a polynomial regression can be used to fit regression lines to data that can't be represented with a straight line.

Last, a *lowess (locally weighted scatterplot smoothing) regression* uses moving averages to fit the regression line of a polynomial regression to the scatter plot. This is useful when your data is time-sensitive. If, for example, you plot temperature throughout the year, the predicted temperature should take the temperatures for the last two weeks into account more than the temperatures from several months ago.

The second table in this figure summarizes the Seaborn lmplot() method. Here, the *lm* in lmplot() stands for *linear model*, which makes sense because this method provides a way to plot linear regressions.

With this method, the scatter and fit_reg parameters control whether the scatter plot and regression line are displayed in the plot. The parameters named line_kws and scatter_kws (*kws* stands for *keywords*) can be used to change the appearance of the regression line or scatter plot. The markers parameter can be used to change the type of marker that's used by the scatter plot. And the x_bins parameter provides a way to group the data on the x-axis in bins.

The next three parameters in the table (logistic, robust, and lowess) can be used to change the type of regression. Similarly, the order parameter lets you specify the degree of the polynomial equation that's used for a polynomial regression. In the figures that follow, you'll see how to use most of these parameters.

Types of linear regressions

Type	Description
simple	Fits a straight line to a dataset using one variable as a predictor as shown earlier in this chapter.
multiple	Fits a line to a dataset using several variables as predictors as shown in the next chapter.
logistic	Measures the probability of a dichotomous variable based on a predictor variable.
robust	Reduces the effect of outliers.
polynomial	Uses a polynomial equation to model the relationship for the predictor variable.
lowess	Uses the *locally weighted scatterplot smoothing* (*lowess*) technique to create a polynomial regression. This works well when there is noisy data, sparse data points, or weak interrelationships between data points.

A Seaborn method for plotting linear regression models

Method	Description
`lmplot(params)`	Uses a linear regression model to create a scatter plot with a regression line fitted to it.
Parameter	**Description**
`scatter`	If True (the default), displays the scatter plot.
`fit_reg`	If True (the default), displays the regression line.
`line_kws`	A dictionary of parameters for the regression line.
`scatter_kws`	A dictionary of parameters for the display of the scatter plot.
`markers`	The type of marker that's used by the scatter plot. Possible values include c for circle, s for square, and d for diamond.
`x_bins`	The number of bins for datapoints on the x-axis.
`logistic`	If True, creates a logistic regression.
`robust`	If True, creates a robust regression.
`lowess`	If True, creates a lowess regression.
`order`	The degree of the polynomial equation to use when fitting the line. This creates a polynomial regression.

Description

- You can use the lmplot() method to create a linear regression model and use that model to plot its *regression line*. The *lm* in lmplot() stands for *linear model*.

Figure 10-12 The lmplot() method and some of its parameters

How to plot a simple linear regression

Figure 10-13 shows how to plot a simple linear regression for the Housing dataset. This plot looks much like the plot in figure 10-10 that was created by using the sklearn library. That's because this example automatically creates and uses a linear regression model that's similar to the one used by figure 10-10.

To change the color of the regression line to red, this example uses the line_kws parameter. This makes it easier to see the regression line that's displayed across the blue dots on the scatter plot. Similarly, this example uses the scatter_kws parameter to change the size of the dots to a smaller size. This makes it easier to see the individual dots on the scatter plot because they don't overlap as much. The confidence interval has also been removed from the regression line.

This example shows that plotting linear regressions with Seaborn is easier and faster than when using the sklearn library. You can also use Seaborn to plot other types of linear regressions, as shown in the next few figures.

How to plot a logistic regression

The second example in figure 10-13 shows how you can use the logistic parameter to plot a logistic regression. Here, the y-axis plots the has_basement column, which is a dichotomous variable that represents whether a house has a basement. Then, the x-axis plots the house price. This creates a regression line that shows a positive correlation between having a basement and the price of the house.

In a logistic plot, the y-axis represents a probability. In this example, a house at the top of the price range on the chart is predicted to have a basement roughly 60% of the time, and a house at the bottom of the price range is predicted to have a basement just under 25% of the time.

Note that the markers on the scatter plot all have values of 1 or 0 to indicate if the houses do or don't have basements. Since these markers are so tightly clustered, it's hard to read them. However, you can see that the low end of the price range doesn't have as many markers for the 1 value. In other words, not many houses at the low end of the price range have a basement.

A simple linear regression

```
sns.lmplot(data=housing, x='sqft_living', y='price', ci=None,
           scatter_kws={'s':5}, line_kws={'color':'red'})
```

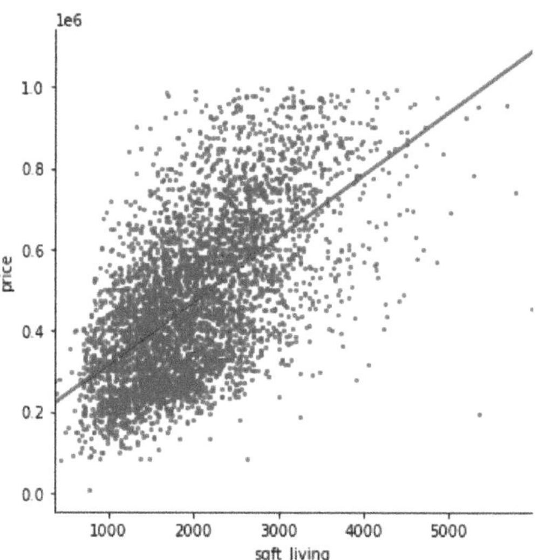

A logistic regression

```
sns.lmplot(data=housing, x='price', y='has_basement', ci=None,
           scatter_kws={'s':1}, line_kws={'color':'red'},
           logistic=True)
```

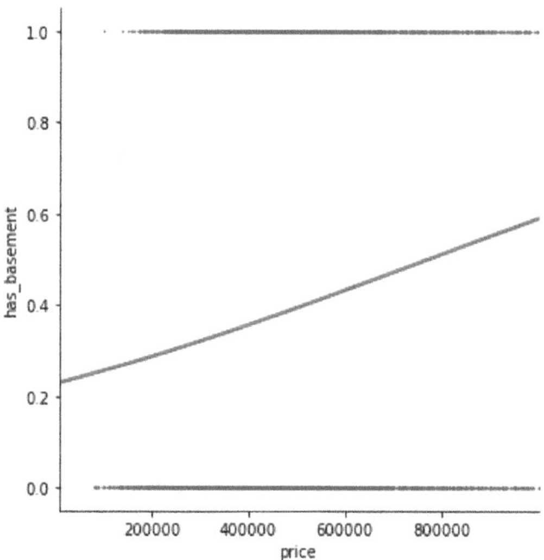

Description

- A *logistic regression* represents the probability of a dichotomous variable being in one or two states.

Figure 10-13 How to plot a simple or logistic regression

How to plot a polynomial regression

The first example in figure 10-14 shows how to create and plot a polynomial regression. Here, since the order parameter is set to 3, Seaborn uses a third-degree polynomial equation to fit the regression line to the dataset. For this dataset, that does a good job of fitting the regression line to the scatter plot.

In practice, though, you typically experiment with different integers until you find a value for the model parameter that generates a line that fits the data. If you choose an integer that's too low or too high, the line will either overfit or underfit the data. *Overfitting* is when the line fits the data too closely, which can cause strange spikes or dips in the line. *Underfitting* is when the line doesn't fit the data very well or at all.

This example also illustrates the use of the markers and x_bins parameters. Here, the markers are set to the diamond shape instead of the default circle shape. But more important, 20 bins are set for the x-axis. That means that the data is consolidated into 20 bins and the markers show the means of those bins. If you experiment with these settings, you'll see that using bins can make the plot easier to read.

How to plot a lowess regression

The second example in this figure shows how to create and plot a lowess regression. To do that, the lowess parameter is set to True. Here again, the markers are set to diamonds and the data is consolidated into 20 bins. But note that the smoothing isn't as accurate as you might expect. That's because the regression for each point is based on the datapoints that are near the original datapoint. This is in contrast to the polynomial regression, which works by fitting the line to the entire dataset.

So for this dataset, the polynomial regression fits the data better than the lowess regression. Keep in mind, though, that a lowess regression can work better for data that has trends that change over time. It can also work better when the data is noisy, sparse, or weakly related. In practice, then, you need to experiment with the different types of regressions until you find the one that best fits the data that you're working with.

A polynomial regression

```
sns.lmplot(data=mortality_data, x='Year', y='DeathRate', hue='AgeGroup',
           ci=None, markers='d', x_bins=20, order=3)
```

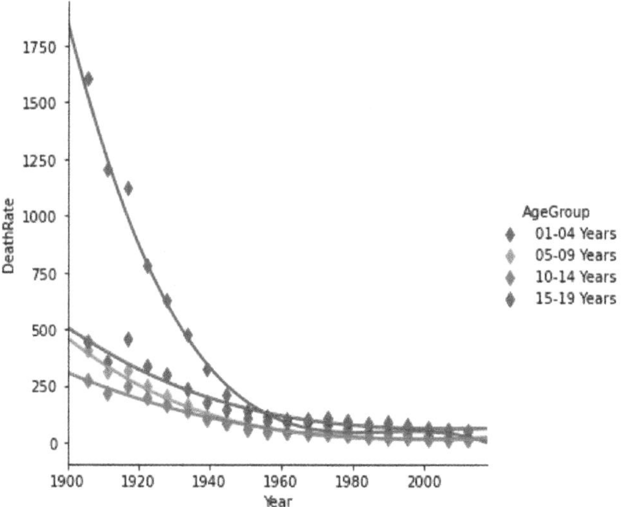

A lowess regression

```
sns.lmplot(data=mortality_data, x='Year', y='DeathRate', hue='AgeGroup',
           ci=None, markers='d', x_bins=20, lowess=True)
```

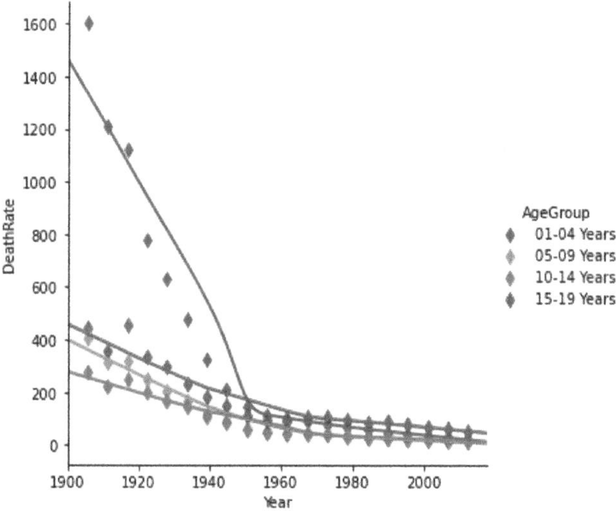

Description

- A *polynomial regression* uses a polynomial equation to create the regression line.
- A *lowess (locally weighted scatterplot smoothing) regression* fits a curved regression line to the data.

Figure 10-14 How to plot a polynomial or lowess regression

How to use the residplot() method to plot the residuals

If you use the lmplot() method to create a regression, you can use the Seaborn residplot() method to plot the residuals. Figure 10-15 shows how. Here, the table summarizes the residplot() method and some of its parameters. This shows that the residplot() method shares the lowess, order, and robust parameters with the lmplot() method.

Then, the first example shows how you can use this method to plot the residuals for the simple linear regression in figure 10-13. In both examples, the data, x, and y parameters are the same. The difference is that the lmplot() method plots a simple linear regression, and the residplot() method plots the residuals for that regression.

If you compare the plot in this figure with the one in figure 10-11 that plots the sklearn residuals, you can see that they are similar. But if you look closely, you can see that the plot in this figure shows some outliers on the upper end of the price and sqft_living range that aren't in the earlier plot. That's because the residuals in figure 10-11 were only calculated for the test data, not the training data. By contrast, the residuals calculated by the residplot() method are for the entire dataset.

The second example in this figure shows how to use the residplot() method to plot the residuals for the polynomial regression shown in figure 10-14. Here again, the data, x, y, and order parameters are the same. The resulting plot shows that the polynomial regression fits the data fairly well, especially in the later years.

The Seaborn residplot() method for plotting residuals

Method	Description
`residplot(params)`	Creates a plot of the residuals of a regression. Returns an Axes object.
Parameter	**Description**
`lowess`	If True, create the residuals for a lowess regression.
`order`	The order of the polynomial equation that's used to create the residuals.
`robust`	If True, create the residuals for a robust regression.

The residuals for a simple linear regression

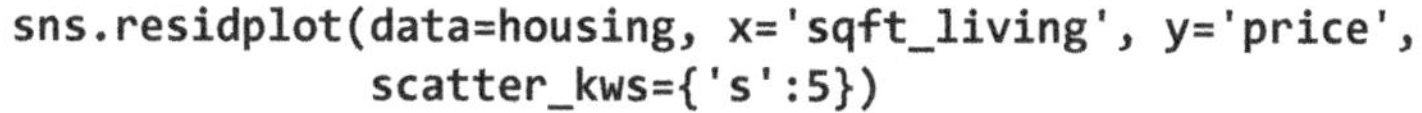

```
sns.residplot(data=housing, x='sqft_living', y='price',
              scatter_kws={'s':5})
```

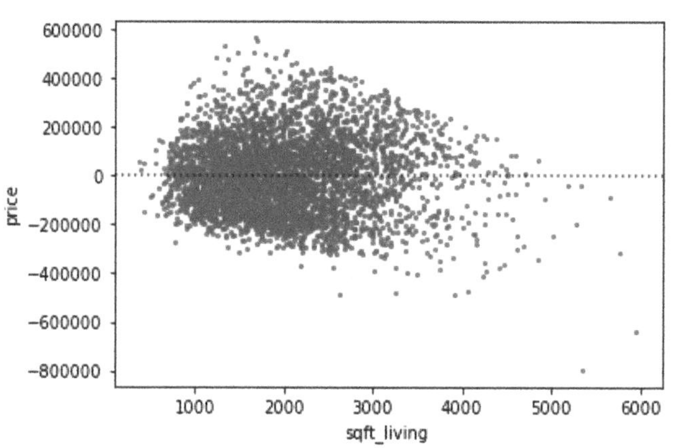

The residuals for a polynomial regression

```
sns.residplot(data=mortality_data, x='Year', y='DeathRate',
              order=3, scatter_kws={'s':5})
```

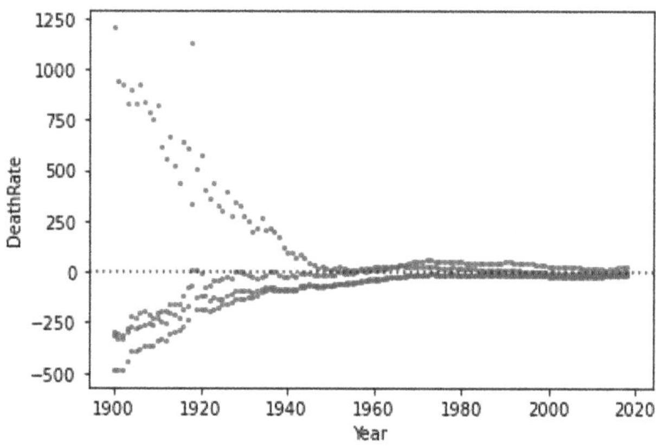

Figure 10-15 How to use the Seaborn residplot() method to plot the residuals

Perspective

Now that you've completed this chapter, you should be off to a good start with predictive analysis. You should be able to find correlations between the variables in a dataset. You should be able to use Scikit-learn to create and use a linear regression model. And you should be able to use Seaborn to plot linear regressions.

Terms

descriptive analysis
predictive analysis
independent variable
dependent variable
linear regression model
simple linear regression
multiple linear regression
correlation
numeric variable
categorical variable
dichotomous variable
Pearson correlation coefficient
r-value
heatmap (heat map)
training dataset
test dataset
R2 value
regression residual (residual)
regression line
logistic regression
polynomial regression
lowess (locally weighted scatterplot smoothing) regression
overfitting
underfitting

Summary

- *Descriptive analysis* uses historical data to provide insights about the past that can be used to make decisions. *Predictive analysis* tries to predict future values.
- A *linear regression model* is a conceptual model that uses an equation to predict an unknown value called a *dependent variable* based on the values of one or more known values called *independent variables.*
- A *simple linear regression* uses only one independent variable, and a *multiple linear regression* uses two or more independent variables.
- A *numeric variable* represents a measurement. A *categorical variable* represents a category. And a *dichotomous variable* is a type of categorical variable that only has two values such as 0 and 1.
- The *Pearson correlation coefficient*, also known as the *r-value*, is a number between 1.0 and -1.0 that measures the type and strength of the linear correlation between two variables.

- You can identify correlations by using scatter plots, a grid of scatter plots, or the Pandas corr() method.
- A *heatmap*, or *heat map*, is a graphical representation of data where values are depicted by shades of a color. It provides another way to identify correlations.
- A *training dataset* is used to train a regression model, and a *test dataset* is used to validate the model. Once validated, the model can be used to predict unknown values based on the values of independent variables.
- In a regression model, the *R^2 value* is the percent of change in the dependent variable that can be attributed to the independent variable or variables.
- You can use the train_test_split() function of the *Scikit-learn* (or *sklearn*) library to split the data into training and test datasets. Then, you can use the fit(), score(), and predict() methods of the LinearRegression object to fit the model, validate it, and use it to make predictions.
- A *regression residual* (or just *residual*) is the difference between the actual value of a dependent variable and the predicted value. You can plot these values to see how well a model works.
- You can use the Seaborn lmplot() method to plot several types of linear regressions, including *simple*, *logistic*, *polynomial*, and *lowess regressions*. You can use the Seaborn residplot() method to plot the residuals of these regressions.
- *Overfitting* is when a regression line fits the data too closely, which can cause strange spikes or dips in the line. *Underfitting* is when a regression line doesn't fit the data very well or at all.

Exercise 10-1 Create a linear regression

This exercise guides you through the process of using predictive analysis for data about a fish market.

Get the data

1. Start JupyterLab and open the Notebook named ex_10-1_fish that should be in this folder:
   `exercises/ch10`
2. If necessary, run the Kernel→Restart Kernel and Clear All Outputs command.
3. Run the first three cells to read the data into the DataFrame named fish.

Clean the data

4. Use a text editor to open the info.txt file that's in the same folder as the Notebook and read the description of each column.
5. Rename the Length1 column to VerticalLength, the Length2 column to DiagonalLength, and the Length3 column to CrossLength.

Identify a correlation

6. Use the corr() method to view how other columns correlate with the Weight column.
7. Create a heatmap that shows how other columns correlate with the Weight column.
8. Create a scatter plot that shows the relationship between the Weight and VerticalLength columns for all fish.
9. Create the same scatter plot as the previous step, but use color to identify the data for each species.
10. Create the same scatter plot as the previous step, but only plot the data for the species named Bream.

Create a linear model

11. Use the correlation data to choose an independent variable.
12. Filter the DataFrame so it only contains the values for the Bream species, and assign the resulting DataFrame to a variable named bream.
13. Use the train_test_split() method to split the training and testing data for the Bream species data.
14. Create the model and fit the training data.
15. Score the testing data.
16. Make the predictions and store the results in a DataFrame.

Plot the regression line

17. Join the column for the predicted data with the columns for the original data, and assign the resulting DataFrame to a variable named final.
18. Melt the actual and predicted values into columns named Variable and Value, and assign the resulting DataFrame to a variable named finalMelt.
19. Use the relplot() method to create a scatter plot that plots the actual and predicted values. Make sure to use a different color for actual and predicted values.
20. Use the lmplot() method to produce a similar plot.

Plot the residuals

21. Calculate the residuals and add them as a new column in the DataFrame named final.
22. Use relplot() to create a scatter plot that plots the residuals, and use the axhline() method to improve your plot.
23. Use the residplot() method to produce a similar plot.

Chapter 11

How to make predictions with a multiple regression model

In the previous chapter, you learned how to make predictions with a simple regression model. In the real world, though, the dependent variable is usually affected by more than one independent variable. That's why this chapter shows how to create a multiple regression model and use it to make predictions. That should lead to more accurate predictions.

A simple regression model for a Cars dataset

To get started, this chapter reviews the skills for working with a simple regression model. This will also give you a chance to become familiar with the Cars dataset that is used in this chapter.

The Cars dataset

Figure 11-1 presents the Cars dataset that is used in this chapter. This dataset contains data on a variety of features for 205 types of cars. For example, it contains data about the price, body type, engine size, and horsepower for each type of car.

The info() method shows that this dataset has 26 columns. Some of these columns store their values as integers, some as floating-point numbers, and some as strings (objects). But note that some of the data that's in string format is *categorical data*. For example, the carbody column stores string data that puts the car body into a category such as convertible, hatchback, or sedan. As you will see, those columns may also be important in a regression model.

The heatmap in this figure shows the correlations with price for the numeric columns in the Cars dataset. This shows that variables like enginesize and curbweight have a high positive correlation with price. Variables like citympg and highwaympg have a high negative correlation. And some variables have essentially no correlation. When you choose the independent variables for a regression, you focus on the variables that have a strong correlation.

In this chapter, you will use this dataset to predict the price of a product (in this case, a car) based on a set of independent variables. That type of prediction can be useful in many industries. For example, imagine that you work for a car company that's planning to introduce a new car model or to move into a foreign market. In either case, you can use regression analysis to help predict (or set) the price for the car.

The columns of the Cars dataset

```
carsData.info()
```

```
<class 'pandas.core.frame.DataFrame'>
RangeIndex: 205 entries, 0 to 204
Data columns (total 26 columns):
 #   Column            Non-Null Count  Dtype
---  ------            --------------  -----
 0   car_ID            205 non-null    int64
 1   symboling         205 non-null    int64
 2   CarName           205 non-null    object
 3   fueltype          205 non-null    object
 4   aspiration        205 non-null    object
 5   doornumber        205 non-null    object
 6   carbody           205 non-null    object
 7   drivewheel        205 non-null    object
 8   enginelocation    205 non-null    object
 9   wheelbase         205 non-null    float64
 10  carlength         205 non-null    float64
 11  carwidth          205 non-null    float64
 12  carheight         205 non-null    float64
 13  curbweight        205 non-null    int64
 14  enginetype        205 non-null    object
 15  cylindernumber    205 non-null    object
 16  enginesize        205 non-null    int64
 17  fuelsystem        205 non-null    object
 18  boreratio         205 non-null    float64
 19  stroke            205 non-null    float64
 20  compressionratio  205 non-null    float64
 21  horsepower        205 non-null    int64
 22  peakrpm           205 non-null    int64
 23  citympg           205 non-null    int64
 24  highwaympg        205 non-null    int64
 25  price             205 non-null    float64
dtypes: float64(8), int64(8), object(10)
memory usage: 41.8+ KB
```

A heatmap for the correlations with price

```
sns.heatmap(data=carsData.corr()[['price']].sort_values('price', ascending=False),
            annot=True, cmap='Blues', vmin=-1.0, vmax=1.0, cbar=False, fmt='.2f')
```

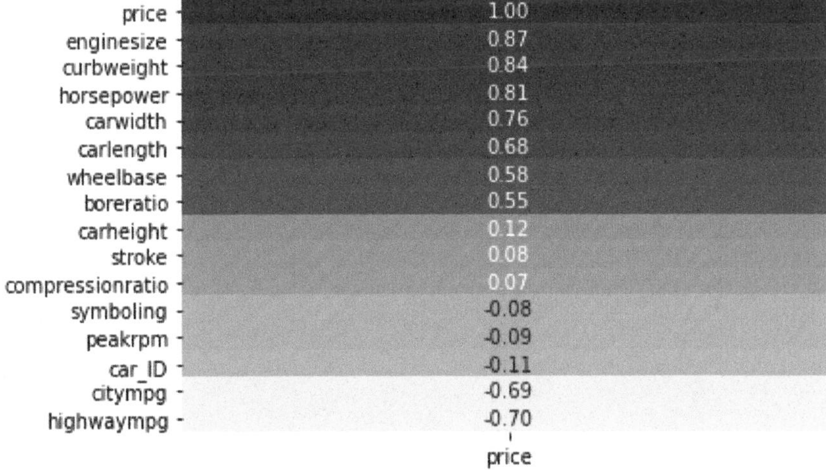

Figure 11-1 The Cars dataset

How to create a simple regression model

Figure 11-2 shows how use Scikit-learn (sklearn) to create a simple regression model that can be used to predict the price of a car. Since you learned how to do that with the Housing dataset in the previous chapter, this should all be review. The only difference is the dataset and the variable used for the simple regression.

Here, the enginesize variable has been chosen as the independent variable because the heatmap in the previous figure shows that it has the highest correlation with price. Then, after the training and test datasets are created, the fit() method creates the regression model and the score() method scores the model with the test dataset. Based on the R^2 value returned by the score() method, the enginesize column seems to be a good choice for the independent variable.

After the score() method is used to score the model with the test dataset, this method is used to score the model with the training dataset. As you can see, the R^2 value for the training dataset is higher than the one for the test dataset. That is almost always true because the regression model was developed by using the data in the training dataset.

After you validate the model by scoring it, you can use the model to make predictions for the data in the test dataset. Then, you can create a DataFrame that includes the data for the engine size, predicted price, and actual price. The resulting DataFrame shows how closely the predicted prices and actual prices are...or aren't.

How to create a linear regression model

Import the LinearRegression class and the train_ test_split() function

```
from sklearn.linear_model import LinearRegression
from sklearn.model_selection import train_test_split
```

Step 1: Split the data into the training and test datasets

```
x_train, x_test, y_train, y_test =
    train_test_split(carsData[['enginesize']], carsData[['price']],
    test_size=0.20, random_state=20)
```

Step 2: Create the model from the training dataset

```
model = LinearRegression()
model.fit(x_train, y_train)
```

Step 3: Score the model with the test dataset

```
model.score(x_test, y_test)
===========================
0.7063964117029844
```

Step 4: Score the model with the training dataset

```
model.score(x_train, y_train)
=============================
0.766524123801206
```

How to use the model to make predictions for the test dataset

```
y_predicted = model.predict(x_test)
```

How to create a DataFrame for the predicted and actual prices

Create the DataFrame for the price predictions

```
predicted = pd.DataFrame(y_predicted, columns=['predictedPrice'])
```

Combine the test data and the predicted data into a DataFrame

```
final = predicted.join([x_test.reset_index(drop=True),
                        y_test.reset_index(drop=True)])
final[['enginesize','price','predictedPrice']].head()
```

	enginesize	price	predictedPrice
0	136	15250.0	14905.920686
1	90	8916.5	7164.387613
2	92	8778.0	7500.976007
3	203	31400.5	26181.631901
4	92	6488.0	7500.976007

Description

- You can use the same techniques to create a simple regression for the Cars dataset that you used for the Housing dataset in the previous chapter.

Figure 11-2 How to create a simple regression model

How to plot the residuals of a simple regression

Although the R^2 value returned by the score() method for the test dataset gives a good indication of how well a regression model is working, you can also plot the residuals to see how well the model has worked. This is illustrated by the first two examples in figure 11-3.

As you learned in the previous chapter, a residual is the difference between the test value for the dependent variable and the predicted value. As a result, plotting the residuals shows how far off your predictions are. The horizontal line at zero on the y-axis is where the predicted price and the actual price are the same.

Another way to evaluate a regression model is to plot the distribution of the residuals with a KDE plot as in the third example in this figure. Then, if the distribution of the residuals forms a bell-shaped curve across the x-axis, and a majority of the datapoints are relatively close to where x equals 0, your regression is a good fit. Otherwise, your regression isn't a good fit, and your predictions won't be good.

In this case, most of the residuals are within +5000 and -5000 of zero, but there is a wider range on the negative side of the bell curve. This indicates that the model is overestimating what the price should be. This could be caused by a few cars with much higher prices. Also, the scatter plot shows the outliers that are more than 5000 dollars away from zero. This indicates that you may be able to improve the model by dropping some outliers.

How to calculate the residuals

```
final['residual'] = final.price - final.predictedPrice
final.head(2)
```

	predictedPrice	enginesize	price	residual
0	14905.920686	136	15250.0	344.079314
1	7164.387613	90	8916.5	1752.112387

How to plot the residuals with a scatter plot

```
g = sns.relplot(data=final, x='enginesize', y='residual')
for ax in g.axes.flat:
    ax.axhline(0, ls='--')
```

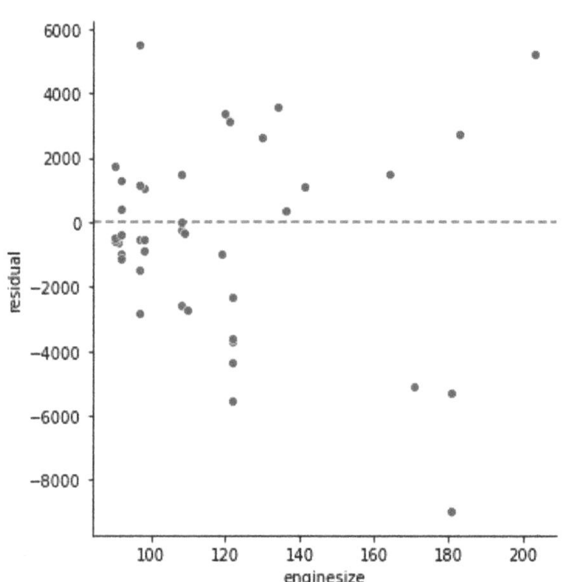

How to plot the distribution of the residuals

```
sns.kdeplot(data=final, x='residual')
```

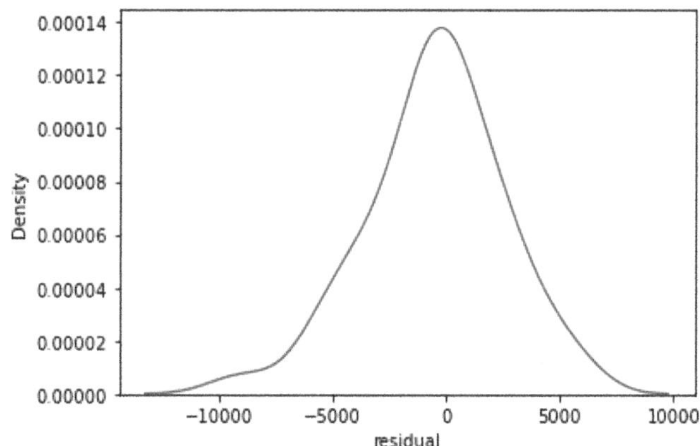

Figure 11-3 How to plot the residuals of a simple regression

How to work with a multiple regression model

Multiple regressions are similar to simple regressions, but instead of using one independent variable they use two or more. As you might expect, that can improve the model and lead to better predictions.

How to create a multiple regression model

Figure 11-4 shows how to create a multiple regression model. As you can see, this works like creating a simple regression model. The only difference is that you specify two or more columns for the independent variables in the first parameter of the train_test_split() function instead of only one.

In this example, that parameter specifies the enginesize and curbweight columns of the DataFrame named carsData. This regression uses those columns because they have the two highest correlations with the price column (see figure 11-1).

After the model is fitted, this code scores the model by passing the test dataset to the score() method. Here, you can see that the R^2 value has gone up from 70% for the simple regression to 75% for this multiple regression. This indicates that using the enginesize and curbweight columns creates a better model for predicting the price.

Here again, the score for the training dataset is higher than the one for the test dataset, but now the difference between the two is smaller. That's good because you want the gap between the score for the test and training datasets to be as small as possible.

After validating the model, you can use the model to predict price values by passing the x values of the test dataset to the predict() method. Then, you can create a DataFrame for the predicted and actual prices.

How to create a multiple regression model with two variables

Step 1: Split the data into the training and test datasets

```
x_train, x_test, y_train, y_test = train_test_split(
    carsData[['enginesize','curbweight']], carsData[['price']],
    test_size=0.20, random_state=20)
```

Step 2: Create the model from the training dataset

```
model = LinearRegression()
model.fit(x_train, y_train)
```

Step 3: Score the model with the test dataset

```
model.score(x_test, y_test)
===========================
0.758107274867953
```

Step 4: Score the model with the training dataset

```
model.score(x_train, y_train)
=============================
0.7950435284247739
```

How to use the model to make predictions for the test dataset

```
y_predicted = model.predict(x_test)
```

How to create a DataFrame for the predicted and actual prices

Create the DataFrame for the price predictions

```
predicted = pd.DataFrame(y_predicted, columns=['predictedPrice'])
```

Combine the test data and the predicted data into a DataFrame

```
final = predicted.join([x_test.reset_index(drop=True),
                        y_test.reset_index(drop=True)])
final.head()[['enginesize','curbweight','price','predictedPrice']]
```

	enginesize	curbweight	price	predictedPrice
0	136	2507	15250.0	14186.974331
1	90	1874	8916.5	5681.243299
2	92	3110	8778.0	12256.116157
3	203	3366	31400.5	26252.387995
4	92	2015	6488.0	6633.723732

Description

- To create a multiple regression model, you use the same procedure that you use for a simple regression model. The only difference is that you set the first parameter in the train_test_split() function to two or more columns of the DataFrame.

Figure 11-4 How to create a multiple regression model

How to plot the residuals of a multiple regression

Figure 11-5 shows how to plot the residuals for a multiple regression. This works the same as it does for a simple regression. First, you calculate the residuals and add them to a new column in the DataFrame. Then, you use the Seaborn kdeplot() method to create a KDE plot.

Here again, most of the residuals are within +5000 and -5000 of zero and they are centered on zero. Besides that, the plot indicates that the outliers are still affecting the regression on the negative side of the curve. However, the curve has also compressed inward, which indicates that the predictions improved even though they were already fairly accurate.

How to calculate the residuals

```
final['residual'] = final.price - final.predictedPrice
final.head()
```

	predictedPrice	enginesize	curbweight	price	residual
0	14186.974331	136	2507	15250.0	1063.025669
1	5681.243299	90	1874	8916.5	3235.256701
2	12256.116157	92	3110	8778.0	-3478.116157
3	26252.387995	203	3366	31400.5	5148.112005
4	6633.723732	92	2015	6488.0	-145.723732

How to plot the residuals

```
sns.kdeplot(data=final, x='residual')
```

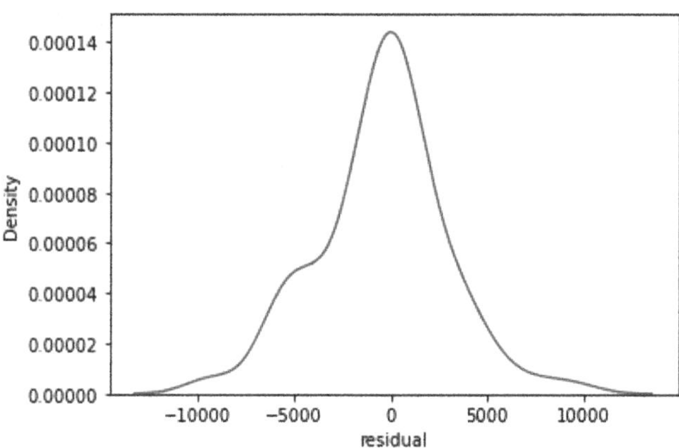

Description

- What you want to see in the KDE plot for the residuals is a bell-shaped curve centered over 0 on the x-axis and with most of the datapoints close to 0.

Figure 11-5 How to plot the residuals of a multiple regression

How to work with categorical variables

Earlier in this chapter, you learned that some of the columns in a dataset that have a string format may contain *categorical data*. In other words, the data may be divided into a distinct number of categories. Categorical data can also be stored in columns with integer values. You can use this data to create *categorical variables* that can be used as independent variables for your models.

Before you can use categorical variables as independent variables, you need to prepare them. That includes identifying them, reviewing them to see whether it makes sense to include them when you fit a model, converting them to dummy variables if you decide to use them, and then rescaling the other data so it will work with the dummy variables.

How to identify categorical variables

The table in figure 11-6 lists the three types of categorical variables. *Nominal variables* have values like "red", "yellow", and "blue", so they can't be ordered in a meaningful way. *Ordinal variables* have values like 0, 1, 2, and 3, so they can be ordered in a meaningful way. And *dichotomous variables* have just two values, like 0 and 1 or "front" and "rear".

To identify the categorical variables in a dataset, you can use the nunique() method as shown in this figure. It displays the number of unique values for each column in the dataset. Then, to identify the variables, you look for a low number of unique values.

If a variable has only two unique values, it is almost certainly a dichotomous variable. For example, the fueltype, aspiration, and doornumber variables are most likely dichotomous variables. Similarly, the carbody variable has five unique values, so it probably stores categorical data. Once you know which variables are likely to be categorical variables, you can use the value_counts() method to be sure, as shown in the next figure.

Types of categorical variables

Type	Description
nominal	Categorical data that can't be ordered in a meaningful way
ordinal	Categorical data that can be ordered in a meaningful way
dichotomous	Categorical data that can fall into only two categories

How to identify different types of categorical data

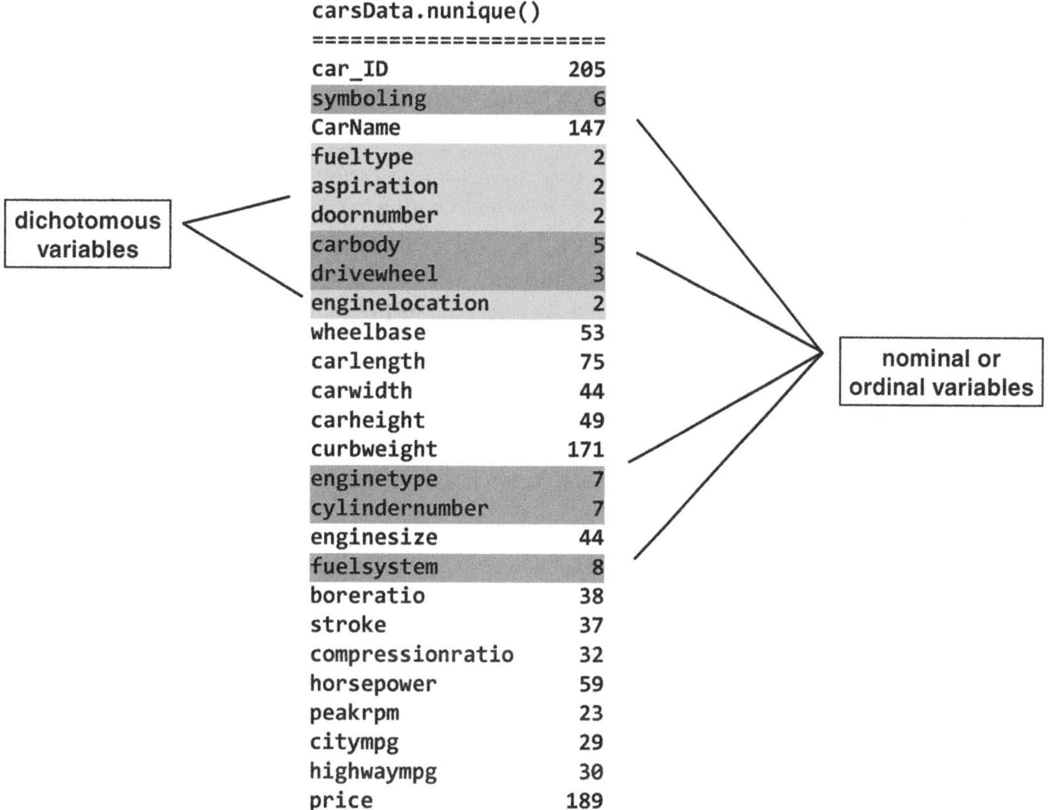

carsData.nunique()
========================
car_ID 205
symboling 6
CarName 147
fueltype 2
aspiration 2
doornumber 2
carbody 5
drivewheel 3
enginelocation 2
wheelbase 53
carlength 75
carwidth 44
carheight 49
curbweight 171
enginetype 7
cylindernumber 7
enginesize 44
fuelsystem 8
boreratio 38
stroke 37
compressionratio 32
horsepower 59
peakrpm 23
citympg 29
highwaympg 30
price 189
dichotomous variables
nominal or ordinal variables

Description

- To identify categorical data, you can use the nunique() method to find columns that have a low number of unique values.
- Categorical data can be stored as string or integer values.

Figure 11-6 How to identify categorical variables

How to review categorical variables

Figure 11-7 shows how to use the value_counts() method to review the variables that you think might be categorical. This method lists each unique value in a column along with the number of times it occurs. That makes it easy to spot the categorical variables. In this case, the DataFrame contains dichotomous and nominal variables but no ordinal variables.

When you choose categorical variables for a regression analysis, you try to choose variables that are well balanced. That means that each category value has a similar number of entries. For instance, the fuelsystem and carbody columns are fairly well balanced. But the enginelocation column is poorly balanced with just 3 values in one category and 202 in the other.

Why does being well balanced matter? Suppose that you decide to use the enginelocation column as one of the independent variables for creating a model. Then, if you call the train_test_split() function with a 20% test dataset size, there is a strong possibility that all three of the "rear" values will end up in the training dataset, and none will be in the test dataset.

You should know, however, that balance doesn't equate to correlation. In other words, just because a column is well balanced doesn't mean that it has a high R^2 value. That's why balance is just one of the characteristics that you use for selecting the independent variables.

How to review the dichotomous variables

```
carsData.enginelocation.value_counts()
=======================================
front    202
rear       3
```

```
carsData.aspiration.value_counts()
===================================
std      168
turbo     37
```

```
carsData.fueltype.value_counts()
=================================
gas       185
diesel     20
```

```
carsData.doornumber.value_counts()
===================================
four    115
two      90
```

How to review the nominal variables

```
carsData.fuelsystem.value_counts()
===================================
mpfi    94
2bbl    66
idi     20
1bbl    11
spdi     9
4bbl     3
spfi     1
mfi      1
```

```
carsData.enginetype.value_counts()
===================================
ohc      148
ohcf      15
ohcv      13
l         12
dohc      12
rotor      4
dohcv      1
```

```
carsData.carbody.value_counts()
===============================
sedan          96
hatchback      70
wagon          25
hardtop         8
convertible     6
```

```
carsData.cylindernumber.value_counts()
=======================================
four      159
six        24
five       11
eight       5
two         4
three       1
twelve      1
```

```
carsData.drivewheel.value_counts()
==================================
fwd    120
rwd     76
4wd      9
```

Description

- You can use the value_counts() method to review categorical variables and to determine which ones are well balanced.
- Categorical variables with well-balanced values often yield better results in regressions.

Figure 11-7 How to review categorical variables

How to create dummy variables

Figure 11-8 shows how to use the Pandas get_dummies() method to create *dummy variables*. This method creates a new column for each unique value of the original column.

For example, since the aspiration column has just two unique values, "turbo" and "std", the get_dummies() method creates two columns named aspiration_turbo and aspiration_std. Then, if the car is in the "std" category, 1 is the value for that row in the aspiration_std column. And if the car is in the "turbo" category, 1 is the value for that row in the aspiration_turbo column. Otherwise, the values are 0.

In this first example, the get_dummies() method creates dummy variables for the four columns that are passed to it and puts the dummy columns into a DataFrame named dummies. As the results of the info() method show, the four original columns have been expanded into 12 dummy columns.

After you create the dummy columns, you need to combine them with the original DataFrame as shown in the second example in this figure. Here, the first statement drops the original categorical columns from the DataFrame and assigns the result to a new DataFrame named carsDummies. Then, the DataFrames named carsDummies and dummies are combined by the join() method.

At this point, the carsDummies DataFrame consists of all the numeric variables along with the dummy variables for the categorical data. You can see this in the results of the info() method.

How to create dummy variables for the categorical columns

```
catColumns = ['aspiration','doornumber','carbody','drivewheel']
dummies = pd.get_dummies(carsData[catColumns])
dummies.info()
===============================================
Data columns (total 12 columns):
 #   Column               Non-Null Count  Dtype
---  ------               --------------  -----
 0   aspiration_std       205 non-null    uint8
 1   aspiration_turbo     205 non-null    uint8
 2   doornumber_four      205 non-null    uint8
 3   doornumber_two       205 non-null    uint8
 4   carbody_convertible  205 non-null    uint8
 5   carbody_hardtop      205 non-null    uint8
 6   carbody_hatchback    205 non-null    uint8
 7   carbody_sedan        205 non-null    uint8
 8   carbody_wagon        205 non-null    uint8
 9   drivewheel_4wd       205 non-null    uint8
 10  drivewheel_fwd       205 non-null    uint8
 11  drivewheel_rwd       205 non-null    uint8
dtypes: uint8(12)
memory usage: 2.5 KB
```

How to combine the numeric data with the dummy variables

```
carsDummies = carsData.drop(columns=catColumns)
carsDummies = carsDummies.join(dummies)
carsDummies.info()
=================================================
RangeIndex: 205 entries, 0 to 204
Data columns (total 26 columns):
#    Column               Non-Null Count  Dtype
---  ------               --------------  -----
 0   car_ID               205 non-null    int64
 1   symboling            205 non-null    int64
 2   CarName              205 non-null    object
 3   fueltype             205 non-null    object
 4   enginelocation       205 non-null    object
 5   wheelbase            205 non-null    float64
 6   carlength            205 non-null    float64
 ...
 28  carbody_hatchback    205 non-null    uint8
 29  carbody_sedan        205 non-null    uint8
 30  carbody_wagon        205 non-null    uint8
 31  drivewheel_4wd       205 non-null    uint8
 32  drivewheel_fwd       205 non-null    uint8
 33  drivewheel_rwd       205 non-null    uint8
dtypes: float64(8), int64(8), object(6), uint8(12)
memory usage: 37.8+ KB
```

Description

- After you create the dummy columns, you need to replace the original categorical columns with the dummy columns.

Figure 11-8 How to create dummy variables

How to rescale the data and check the correlations

After the numeric columns are joined with the dummy columns, the DataFrame named carsDummies has data on two different scales: the scale for the numeric columns and the scale for the dummy columns. For example, the curbweight variable has values that range from roughly 2000 to roughly 4000, but the dummy variables have values of either 0 or 1. As a result, the curbweight variable will always outweigh a dummy variable when creating the regression.

Before you create a multiple regression model from that data, then, you need to *rescale* the data. That's important because if data is on different scales, the data on the larger scale will outweigh the data on the smaller scale and reduce the accuracy of your predictions.

To rescale the data, you can use the StandardScaler object in the sklearn library as shown in the first example in figure 11-9. To start, this code imports the StandardScaler class and creates an object from it named scaler. Then, the code stores the numeric columns in a list called numCols. But note that this list doesn't include the dependent variable (price) or the dummy columns because you don't want to rescale them.

After it creates the list of columns, this code calls the fit_transform() method and passes it the numeric columns. This replaces the original values of the numeric columns with the rescaled values that are on the same scale as the dummy columns. The result is that each of the numeric columns has a much smaller value.

The second example in this figure shows the correlations of the rescaled columns with the price column. Here, you can see that some of the dummy columns like the drivewheel_rwd and the drivewheel_fwd have relatively high positive and negative correlations. You can also see that the top correlations are still with numeric columns like enginesize, curbweight, and horsepower. In fact, those correlations are close to the correlations shown in figure 11-1 that were taken before the data was rescaled. This shows that the rescaling has worked.

How to rescale the data

```
from sklearn.preprocessing import StandardScaler

scaler = StandardScaler()
numCols = ['wheelbase','carlength','carwidth','carheight','curbweight',
           'enginesize','boreratio','stroke','compressionratio',
           'horsepower','peakrpm','citympg','highwaympg']
carsDummies[numCols] = scaler.fit_transform(carsDummies[numCols])
carsDummies.head()
```

fueltype	enginelocation	wheelbase	carlength	carwidth	carheight	curbweight	...	doornumber_four	doornumber_two
gas	front	-1.690772	-0.426521	-0.844782	-2.020417	-0.014566	...	0	1
gas	front	-1.690772	-0.426521	-0.844782	-2.020417	-0.014566	...	0	1
gas	front	-0.708596	-0.231513	-0.190566	-0.543527	0.514882	...	0	1
gas	front	0.173698	0.207256	0.136542	0.235942	-0.420797	...	1	0
gas	front	0.107110	0.207256	0.230001	0.235942	0.516807	...	1	0

How to check the correlations in the rescaled data

```
carsDummies.corr()[['price']].sort_values(by='price', ascending=False)
=======================================================================
                     price
                     -----
price                1.000000
enginesize           0.874145
curbweight           0.835305
horsepower           0.808139
carwidth             0.759325
carlength            0.682920
drivewheel_rwd       0.638957
wheelbase            0.577816
boreratio            0.553173
carbody_hardtop      0.225824
...
aspiration_std      -0.177926
carbody_hatchback -0.262039
drivewheel_fwd      -0.601950
citympg             -0.685751
highwaympg          -0.697599
```

Description

- You only need to rescale the numeric columns for the independent variables, and you shouldn't rescale the column for the dependent variable.
- When you rescale numeric columns, you change them to use the same proportions as the scale for the dummy variables so they can be used together.

Figure 11-9 How to rescale the data and check the correlations

How to create a multiple regression that includes dummy variables

Figure 11-10 shows how to create and use a regression model from the rescaled DataFrame named carsDummies that includes the dummy variables. This is similar to what you've done before, but it uses a different technique for splitting and using the training and test datasets. This technique makes it easier to experiment with different groups of independent variables.

In step 1 of the procedure for creating the regression model, this code only passes one positional argument (the DataFrame named carsDummies) to the train_test_split() function. As a result, this method returns only two datasets: one for the training dataset (carsTrain) and one for the test dataset (carsTest).

Then, in step 2, the fit() method creates the model. Here, since the training dataset hasn't been split into x and y DataFrames, this code splits this data when it calls the fit() method.

To do that, it first creates a list of the five independent variables to use for the regression and assigns this list to a variable named xCols. Then, it passes these columns to the fit() method as the first (or x) parameter, and it passes the column for the dependent variable (price) as the second (or y) parameter. Because the columns for the independent variables are passed as a list, this makes it easy to adjust the list of variables without changing any of the other code.

After the model has been created, you can score the test and training datasets as shown in steps 3 and 4. If you compare these scores with the ones in figure 11-4, you can see that the training score is better but the test score is worse. That means that you may want to try different combinations of the independent variables as you create other models. To do that, of course, you just need to change the list of columns that's assigned to the xCols variable.

Once the model has been created, you can use the model to make predictions as shown in the second example in this figure. Then, you can create a DataFrame for the predicted and actual prices as shown in the third example. Here again, you can see that some of the prices and predicted prices are close...but some aren't. The question then is: how can you improve this multiple regression model?

How to create a multiple regression model that includes dummy variables

Step 1: Split the data into the training and test datasets

```
carsTrain, carsTest = train_test_split(carsDummies, test_size=0.2,
    random_state=20)
```

Step 2: Create the multiple regression model

```
model = LinearRegression()
xCols = ['enginesize','horsepower','carwidth',
         'drivewheel_rwd','highwaympg']
model.fit(carsTrain[xCols], carsTrain['price'])
```

Step 3: Score the model with the test dataset

```
model.score(carsTest[xCols], carsTest['price'])
===============================================
0.6910912856235985
```

Step 4: Score the model with the training dataset

```
model.score(carsTrain[xCols], carsTrain['price'])
=================================================
0.8507491647131596
```

Use the model to make predictions

```
y_predicted = model.predict(carsTest[xCols])
```

Create a DataFrame for the predicted and actual prices

```
predicted = pd.DataFrame(y_predicted, columns=['predictedPrice'])

final = predicted.join([carsTest[xCols].reset_index(drop=True),
                        carsTest['price'].reset_index(drop=True)])

final[['enginesize','horsepower','carwidth','drivewheel_rwd',
       'highwaympg','price','predictedPrice']].head()
```

	enginesize	horsepower	carwidth	drivewheel_rwd	highwaympg	price	predictedPrice
0	0.218885	0.149133	0.183272	0	-0.837195	15250.0	13517.858822
1	-0.888455	-0.864871	-1.078431	0	1.783034	8916.5	5968.304606
2	-0.840310	-1.067671	-1.078431	0	0.181783	8778.0	4984.725918
3	1.831749	4.661448	2.987056	1	-0.400490	31400.5	37778.843127
4	-0.840310	-1.067671	-1.078431	0	1.055193	6488.0	5347.966676

Description

- Once you create a model that includes dummy variables, you can use the model to make predictions, and you can create a DataFrame for the predicted and actual values.

Figure 11-10 How to create a multiple regression that includes dummy variables

How to improve a multiple regression model

Now that you know how to create and use a multiple regression model, you need to know how to improve it so it does the best job of predicting the value of a dependent variable. That starts with knowing how to choose the independent variables.

How to select the independent variables

To create the best model for predicting the values of a dependent variable, you need to select the right independent variables. To help you make those selections, you can start by preparing a heatmap like the one in figure 11-11 for all the independent variables in the training dataset. Note that this plot shows the correlation between nine of the variables and each of the numeric and dummy variables.

When you select the variables for a model, you start by looking for the variables that have the highest correlations with the dependent variable (price). But it doesn't matter whether the correlations are positive or negative. For instance, the enginesize and curbweight variables have high positive correlations with price (.88 and .84), and the citympg and highwaympg variables have high negative correlations (-0.69 and -0.71). But both should be considered when you select the variables for a model.

You should also be aware that some independent variables are correlated with each other as well as the dependent variable. For example, the enginesize and the curbweight variables have a .86 correlation with each other, and the citympg and highwaympg variables have a .97 correlation. Variables with a high correlation like that can be referred to as *collinear*, which means that both variables will have the same or similar effect on the dependent variable. As a result, the statistical significance of either variable is decreased.

In general, though, collinearity doesn't affect the overall fit of a model, its R^2 value, or the predictions that it produces. That's why it is often okay to include collinear variables in your selections. Nevertheless, this is something you should be aware of as you try to improve your models.

A heatmap for the independent variables

```
sns.heatmap(carsTrain.corr()[['enginesize','curbweight','horsepower','carwidth',
                              'drivewheel_rwd','highwaympg','citympg','boreratio',
                              'price']].sort_values(by='price', ascending=False),
        cmap='Blues', annot=True)
```

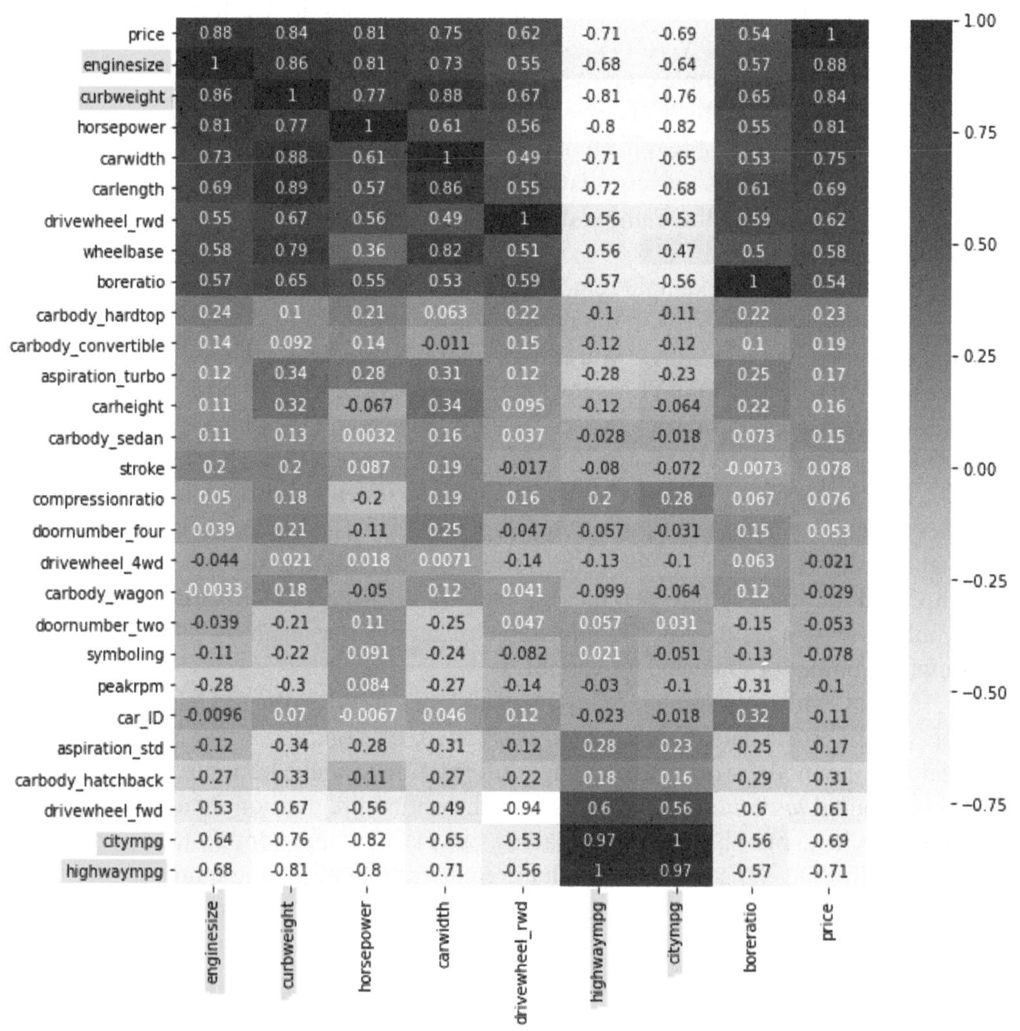

Description

- The independent variables that you select should have a high correlation with the dependent variable, but it doesn't matter whether that correlation is positive or negative.
- When two independent variables have a high correlation with each other, they are said to be *collinear*. That means that their effects on the dependent variable will be similar, which decreases the statistical significance of either collinear variable.

Figure 11-11 How to select the independent variables

How to test different combinations of variables

To find the combination of independent variables that produces an optimal regression model, you need to experiment with different combinations of variables. Then, you can compare the scores of the models to determine which one will perform better. To illustrate, figure 11-12 shows three different models and their test and training scores.

Here, the first example creates an initial model that's fitted to the eight columns that have the highest correlations with price. The first six have positive correlations and the last two have negative correlations. Note too that one of the columns with a positive correlation is the drivewheel_rwd dummy variable. Here, the R^2 value for the training dataset is .85 and the R^2 value for the test dataset is .68.

Then, the second example removes just the citympg column, which has a strong collinearity (0.97) with the highwaympg variable. But if you look closely at the training and test scores, you can see that they're almost the same as the ones for the first example. This shows that dropping a collinear variable from the selection doesn't improve the scores. Or conversely, including collinear variables doesn't hurt the scores.

The third example shows the scores when the independent variables include every column but the one for the dependent variable. That includes the columns that have low correlations with price. Here, both the training and test scores have improved, but the gap between the test and training scores is still larger than you would like. As a result, you should be able to get a better result by selecting a smaller number of independent variables.

In fact, when you use too many independent variables, the model becomes too specific to the data. This is called *overfitting*. By contrast, if you use too few features, the model won't have enough information to make accurate predictions. This is called *underfitting*. So, to produce the optimal regression model, you need to select not only the right variables, but the right number of variables.

The trouble is that going through different combinations and numbers of variables is slow and tedious when you use the methods in this figure. That's why the next figure shows how you can use Scikit-learn to simplify this process.

An initial model that's fitted to eight independent variables

```
model = LinearRegression()
xCols = ['enginesize','curbweight','horsepower','carwidth', 'carlength',
    'drivewheel_rwd','highwaympg','citympg']
model.fit(carsTrain[xCols], carsTrain['price'])
model.score(carsTest[xCols], carsTest['price'])
==========================================================================
0.684810264257876

model.score(carsTrain[xCols], carsTrain['price'])
==========================================================================
0.851624608739667
```

The initial model without the citympg column

```
model = LinearRegression()
xCols = ['enginesize','curbweight','horsepower','carwidth', 'carlength',
    'drivewheel_rwd','highwaympg']
model.fit(carsTrain[xCols], carsTrain['price'])
model.score(carsTest[xCols], carsTest['price'])
==========================================================================
0.6892190640435765

model.score(carsTrain[xCols], carsTrain['price'])
==========================================================================
0.851100492829518
```

A model that's fitted to all the numeric and dummy variables

```
model = LinearRegression()
xCols = carsTrain.corr().drop(columns=['price']).columns.tolist()
model.fit(carsTrain[xCols], carsTrain['price'])
model.score(carsTest[xCols], carsTest['price'])
==========================================================================
0.7668904310536844

model.score(carsTrain[xCols], carsTrain['price'])
==========================================================================
0.9031423149672445
```

Description

- The basic strategy for selecting variables is to add variables with high correlations to the selection as long as both the training and test scores keep going up.
- But you need to stop adding variables when the training score continues to increase but the test score stays the same or drops. At that point, you are *overfitting* the model to the variables.

Figure 11-12 How to test different combinations of variables

How to use Scikit-learn to select the variables

Selecting the right independent variables (or *features*) and the right number of independent variables can be referred to as the *feature selection problem.* Fortunately, Scikit-learn provides *feature selection models* that help you select the right features. That means you only have to figure out how many of these features you should use.

The first example in figure 11-13 shows how this works. In step 1, the train_test_split() function splits the data into training and test datasets as before. Here, the non-numeric columns are dropped because the fit() method of the feature selection object only works with numeric columns.

In step 2, the SelectKBest() method creates a feature selection object named fs. Then, the fit() method of that object fits the data in the training dataset to the feature selection model. The SelectKBest() method lets you specify the number of features (columns) that you want to use as well as the scoring function that's used to select them. This scoring function assigns each feature a score that indicates how important it is and thus whether it should be selected.

In this case, the 20 features with numeric values will be selected and the mutual_info_regression function will be used as the scoring function. This function does an effective job of scoring collinear variables, but you can use other scoring functions if your dataset has other characteristics. As usual, you can study the documentation to determine which function is best for your data.

In step 3, the transform() method of the feature selector transforms the training and test datasets based on the results of the fit() method. Finally, in step 4, the fit() method of the LinearRegression object uses the transformed training dataset to create a new multiple regression model. Then, the score() method scores the results of the test and training datasets just as in earlier examples. Here, you can see that the scores are about the same as those in the third example in the last figure, which probably means that this model has been overfitted because it used too many variables.

However, since you've used the sklearn feature selector, you no longer have to worry about which independent variables to use. You just need to figure out how many to use. And to find that out, you can try different values for the k parameter of the SelectKBest() method in step 2. Or, you can put the code for steps 2 through 4 into a for loop and check the results for each k value, as shown in the next figure.

In case you're interested, the second example in this figure shows how you can display the importance values that the feature selection model has assigned to each feature. Here, the importance scores are concatenated with the DataFrame for the variables by using the scores_ attribute of the feature selector. This attribute consists of an array of the importance scores. Then, the column names in the resulting DataFrame are changed to "feature" and "importance", and the DataFrame is sorted in descending sequence by the "importance" column.

If you compare the results with the correlations in figure 11-11, you can see that the feature selection model determined that the horsepower feature is more important than the enginesize feature even though the enginesize feature has a higher correlation with price. You can see that the highwaympg and citympg features are ranked third and fifth even though they have a negative correlation with price. And you can see that all five of these features are in the top 5 even though some of them have a high degree of collinearity.

The SelectKBest() method

Method	Description
SelectKBest(params)	Selects the top k features based on the values returned by the scoring function. Returns a feature selection object that has fit() and transform() methods.

Parameter	Description
score_func	The scoring function that selects the variables.
k	The number of independent variables to use. Use 'all' for all variables.

How to select the right features

Import the SelectKBest() method and the mutual_info_regression function

```
from sklearn.feature_selection import SelectKBest
from sklearn.feature_selection import mutual_info_regression
```

Step 1: Split the data and drop non-numeric columns

```
carsTrain, carsTest = train_test_split(carsDummies.drop(
    columns=['CarName','fueltype','enginelocation','cylindernumber',
             'fuelsystem','enginetype']), test_size=0.2, random_state=20)
```

Step 2: Create the feature selector and fit the data to it

```
fs = SelectKBest(score_func=mutual_info_regression, k=20)
fs.fit(carsTrain.drop(columns=['price']), carsTrain['price'])
```

Step 3: Transform the training and test data

```
x_train_fs = fs.transform(carsTrain.drop(columns=['price']))
x_test_fs = fs.transform(carsTest.drop(columns=['price']))
```

Step 4: Use the transformed data in the regression

```
model = LinearRegression()
model.fit(x_train_fs, carsTrain['price'])
model.score(x_test_fs, carsTest['price'])
=========================================
0.7672356288280073

model.score(x_train_fs, carsTrain['price'])
===========================================
0.8916022232056895
```

How to display the importance of each feature

```
df1 = pd.DataFrame(carsTrain.drop(columns=['price']).columns, columns=['feature'])
df2 = pd.DataFrame(fs.scores_, columns=['importance'])
importance = df1.join(df2)
importance.sort_values('importance', ascending=False).head()
```

	feature	importance
6	curbweight	0.901491
11	horsepower	0.896991
14	highwaympg	0.876316
7	enginesize	0.865330
13	citympg	0.734691

Figure 11-13 How to use Scikit-learn to select the independent variables

How to select the right number of variables

Now that you know how to use sklearn to select the right features for a model, figure 11-14 shows how to select the right *number* of features. Here, the first example uses a for loop to score the model for varying numbers of features. But before it runs the for loop, it creates a LinearRegression object named model and two empty lists. The first list will hold the test scores for each of the models that is created, and the second list will hold the training scores for each of the models.

Then, the for loop creates and scores the models with the number of features ranging from 1 to one less than the number of columns in the carsTrain dataset. That's because the range() function stops one short of the second parameter passed to it. Although you might think that you could just add one to the second parameter to include all the features, that doesn't work because you have to pass "all" to the SelectKBest() method to do that. But because the last feature will have the lowest importance score, it's okay for the loop to stop before it reaches that feature.

Within the loop, the code starts by creating and fitting the feature selector. The main difference between this code and the code in the previous figure is that the k parameter is set to the counter value for the loop so that each iteration of the loop will use one more feature.

Still within the loop, the transform() method of the feature selector creates the training and test datasets with the number of features specified by the k parameter. Then, the fit() method of the LinearRegression model fits the regression model to the training data, and the score() method scores both the test and training datasets. This is like the code in the previous figure. Last, the test and training scores are appended to the testScores and trainScores lists so these lists can be used to plot the scores.

The second example in this figure shows how to plot the scores. To start, the testScores and trainScores lists are used to build a DataFrame for the results. Then, the index is reset, renamed to numFeatures, and incremented by one. This results in a column that ranges from 1 to the number of features so it can be used as the x-axis in a line plot. At that point, the Pandas plot() method plots the test and training scores.

In the line plot, you can see that the test scores start to decrease after the model reaches four features. Then, the scores start to increase again around 15 features, ending at a score that's slightly higher than the score at four features. You can also see that the gap between the test and training scores keeps getting larger after you reach four features.

The data in a plot like this usually makes it relatively easy to select the right number of features for the optimal model. What you're looking for is the highest training score, the smallest gap between the test and training scores, and the fewest features. Based on those criteria, the right number of features for this regression model is 4.

In fact, this plot indicates that the model is overfitted as soon as the number of features gets beyond 4. That's because the test scores start to go down even as the training scores continue to go up. Although overfitting won't always be so obvious, remember that overfitting is indicated whenever the gap between the test and training scores increases at the same time that the training score stagnates or decreases.

How use a for loop to score the model for varying numbers of features

```
model = LinearRegression()
testScores = []
trainScores = []

for i in range(1, len(carsTrain.columns)):
    fs = SelectKBest(score_func=mutual_info_regression, k=i)
    fs.fit(carsTrain.drop(columns=['price']), carsTrain['price'])

    x_train_fs = fs.transform(carsTrain.drop(columns=['price']))
    x_test_fs = fs.transform(carsTest.drop(columns=['price']))

    model.fit(x_train_fs, carsTrain['price'])

    testScore = model.score(x_test_fs, carsTest['price'])
    trainScore = model.score(x_train_fs, carsTrain['price'])
    testScores.append(testScore)
    trainScores.append(trainScore)
```

How to plot the test and training scores

```
df = pd.DataFrame(data={'testScores':testScores, 'trainScores':trainScores})
df.reset_index(inplace=True)
df.rename(columns={'index':'numFeatures'}, inplace=True)
df.numFeatures = df.numFeatures + 1
df.plot(x='numFeatures', y=['testScores','trainScores'])
```

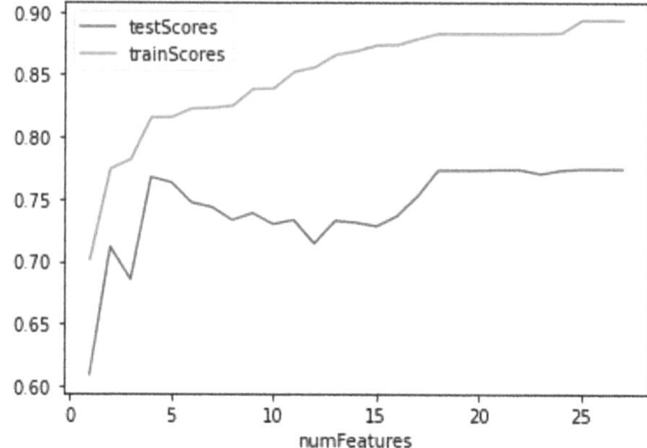

Description

- To select the right number of independent variables, you try to identify the lowest number of features that delivers the highest training score with the smallest gap between the training and test scores.

Figure 11-14 How to select the right number of independent variables

Perspective

Now that you've completed this chapter, you should be able to create and use a multiple regression model. As part of that, you should be able to create dummy variables, rescale the data, and select the independent variables for a model. You should be able to use Scikit-learn to automate the process of selecting the right independent variables. And you should know how to use a for loop to help you select the right number of independent variables.

Although the two chapters in this section are just an introduction to predictive analysis, they have presented the essential concepts and skills that you need for making predictions with simple and multiple regression models. Linear models like the ones in these chapters are used in a wide variety of predictive analyses. Although Scikit-learn also provides other models, the process of preparing, fitting, and testing a model is similar no matter which model you use.

Of course, there is still much more to learn about Scikit-learn. For instance, one of the things that these chapters don't present is cross-validation, which can improve the performance of a model by avoiding overfitting. You can learn about cross-validation and other features of Scikit-learn on your own.

Terms

multiple regression
categorical data
categorical variable
nominal variable
ordinal variable
dichotomous variable
dummy variables
rescale data
collinear
overfitting
underfitting
feature
feature selection problem
feature selection model

Summary

- *Categorical data* consists of string or integer values that are divided into a distinct number of categories. You can use this data to create *categorical variables* that can be used as independent variables for your models.
- A *nominal variable* contains categorical data that can't be ordered in a meaningful way. An *ordinal variable* contains categorical data that can be ordered in a meaningful way. And a *dichotomous variable* contains categorical data that has just two categories.

- A *dummy variable* represents one category in a categorical variable. If its value in a row is 1, it belongs to that category. If 0, it doesn't.
- When you *rescale* data, you change the scale of the numeric columns to the scale of the dummy columns. That way, both types of columns can be used as the independent variables for a multiple regression model.
- When two independent variables have a high correlation with each other, they are said to be *collinear*. That means that their effects on the dependent variable will be similar, which decreases the statistical significance of either collinear variable.
- When a regression model is created from too many independent variables, it is said to be *overfitted*. When it's created from too few, it is said to be *underfitted*.
- The *feature selection problem* is trying to select the independent variables (*features*) that lead to the optimal regression model.
- Scikit-learn provides *feature selection models* that help you select the features that will produce the optimal regression model.
- To determine the right number of features to use for an optimal model, you can run a loop that creates and scores the models for varying numbers of features. Then, you can plot the scores to find the number that has the best combination of high training score, low gap between test and training score, and low number of features.

Exercise 11-1 Create a multiple regression

This exercise will guide you through the process of creating a multiple regression for data about a fish market. If you already did exercise 10-1, you can use much of the same code in the exercises, especially to clean the data and identify the correlations.

Read the data

1. Start JupyterLab and open the Notebook named ex_11-1_fish that should be in this folder:

   `exercises/ch11`

2. If necessary, run the Kernel→Restart Kernel and Clear All Outputs command.
3. Run the first three cells to read the data into the DataFrame named fish.

Clean the data

4. Open the info.txt file and read the info for each column.
5. Rename the Length1 column to VerticalLength, Length2 to DiagonalLength, and Length3 to CrossLength.

Identify correlations

6. Use the corr() method to look at the correlation data for the Weight column.
7. Create a heatmap for the correlation data

Create a multiple regression model

8. Use the correlation data to choose three independent variables. The first two should be the Height and Width columns. The third should be one of the length columns.
9. Filter the DataFrame so it only contains the values for the Bream species and assign the resulting DataFrame to a variable named bream.
10. Use the train_test_split() method to split the training and testing data for the Bream species data.
11. Create the model and fit the training data.
12. Score the testing data.
13. Make the predictions and store the results in a DataFrame.
14. Join the column for the predicted data with the columns for the actual data and assign the resulting DataFrame to a variable named final.

Plot the residuals

15. Calculate the residuals and store them in a new column in the DataFrame.
16. Use the kdeplot() method to create a KDE plot that plots the residuals. Note whether this provides a bell-shaped curve centered over 0.

Section 4

The case studies

This section presents four real-world case studies that illustrate the skills that are presented in the first three sections of this book. These case studies not only show how these skills can be applied in the context of a complete analysis, they also demonstrate the thought processes that you use when you analyze data.

Since the Notebooks for these case studies are included in the download for this book, you can open the Notebooks and run the code as you read the descriptions of the code in the chapters. That way, you can experiment with the code as you work your way through the chapters. You can also copy snippets of the case study code into your own Notebooks and modify them for your analyses.

Chapter 12

The Polling case study

The Polling case study analyzes the data for the polls that preceded the 2016 presidential election for the United States. This study gets the data from the FiveThirtyEight website, which is a statistical site that focuses on opinion polls, politics, economics, and sports.

To get the most from this case study, you can open the case study Notebook that's in the download for this book. Then, as you read this chapter, you can run the code in each cell to see exactly what it does. Or, if you prefer, you can read this chapter first and run the code later.

Get and display the data

In all analyses, the first step is to get the data. For this case study, the data is available as a CSV (comma-separated values) file that you can download from the FiveThirtyEight website.

Import the modules that you will need

Figure 12-1 starts by importing the Pandas and Seaborn modules that you'll need for this case study.

Get the data

This figure then shows how to get the data for this case study. First, the path and filename for the file on the FiveThirtyEight website are set. Next, the request object from the urllib module is imported and used to retrieve the CSV file and download it to a file on disk. Last, the read_csv() method reads the CSV file into a DataFrame named polls.

Display the data

After you get the data, you're going to want to look at it. To do that, you can display the data by coding the variable name of the DataFrame or by calling the head() or tail() method of the DataFrame. However, when you use these techniques and there are more columns than will fit on the screen, some of the columns in the middle aren't displayed.

Then, if you want to review the data in all of the columns, you can use the option_context() method as shown in the last example in this figure. This displays all of the columns, but only the first and last rows. That way, you can scroll through the columns to get an idea of what they contain. In this case, the DataFrame has 12,624 rows and 27 columns.

Import Pandas and Seaborn

```
import pandas as pd
import seaborn as sns
```

Get the data

Set the path and the filename

```
poll_path = 'http://projects.fivethirtyeight.com/general-model/'
filename = 'president_general_polls_2016.csv'
```

Download the CSV file

```
from urllib import request
request.urlretrieve(poll_path+filename, filename=filename)
```

Read the CSV file into a DataFrame

```
polls = pd.read_csv(filename)
```

Display the data

Display the DataFrame

```
polls
```

Display the first five rows

```
polls.head()
```

Display the last five rows

```
polls.tail()
```

Display all columns but just the first and last row

```
with pd.option_context(
        'display.max_rows', 2,
        'display.max_columns', None):
    display(polls)
```

	cycle	branch	type	matchup	forecastdate	state	startdate	enddate	pollster	grade	samplesize
0	2016	President	polls-plus	Clinton vs. Trump vs. Johnson	11/8/16	U.S.	11/3/2016	11/6/2016	ABC News/Washington Post	A+	2220.0
...	...	...	...	...	...	...	...	...	...	...	...
12623	2016	President	polls-only	Clinton vs. Trump vs. Johnson	11/8/16	Wisconsin	6/9/2016	6/12/2016	Marquette University	A	666.0

12624 rows × 27 columns

Figure 12-1 Get and display the data

Clean the data

The four parts of figure 12-2 show how to clean the data for the polling analysis. To start, you examine the data.

Examine the data

Part 1 of this figure shows how to use the info() method to examine the data. Here, the first three highlighted columns contain dates, but they are object data types instead of datetime data types. So, before you can use them as dates, you need to convert them to datetime objects.

The next four highlighted columns show that there are two columns for Clinton and two for Trump that contain numbers that are float64 (floating-point) data types. For analysis, though, you probably only need to use one set of columns. So, you can drop the other set of columns. That's why this case study drops the columns with the adjusted data.

As you can see, most of the columns have as many non-null values as there are rows in the DataFrame. However, the columns for Johnson and McMullin have many fewer non-null values. That means those candidates weren't included in all of the polls. Similarly, the multiversions column has only 36 non-null values.

Examine the data

With the info() method

```
polls.info(memory_usage='deep')
==========================================
<class 'pandas.core.frame.DataFrame'>
RangeIndex: 12624 entries, 0 to 12623
Data columns (total 27 columns):
cycle                 12624 non-null int64
branch                12624 non-null object
type                  12624 non-null object
matchup               12624 non-null object
forecastdate          12624 non-null object
state                 12624 non-null object
startdate             12624 non-null object
enddate               12624 non-null object
pollster              12624 non-null object
grade                 11337 non-null object
samplesize            12621 non-null float64
population            12624 non-null object
poll_wt               12624 non-null float64
rawpoll_clinton       12624 non-null float64
rawpoll_trump         12624 non-null float64
rawpoll_johnson       8397 non-null float64
rawpoll_mcmullin      90 non-null float64
adjpoll_clinton       12624 non-null float64
adjpoll_trump         12624 non-null float64
adjpoll_johnson       8397 non-null float64
adjpoll_mcmullin      90 non-null float64
multiversions         36 non-null object
url                   12621 non-null object
poll_id               12624 non-null int64
question_id           12624 non-null int64
createddate           12624 non-null object
timestamp             12624 non-null object
dtypes: float64(10), int64(3), object(14)
memory usage: 12.9 MB
```

Figure 12-2 Clean the data (part 1)

Part 2 of figure 11-2 shows the results for the nunique() method that counts the number of unique values in each column. Here, each of the first four highlighted columns has only one unique value, which means that these columns aren't going to be useful for the analysis. By contrast, the state column has 57 unique values, but the United States has only 50 states. So, that's something that needs to be looked into.

Similarly, several other columns have a small number of unique values. For example, the population column has just four unique values. The multiversions column has just two unique values. And the poll_id and question_id columns have 4208 values, which is one-third of the number of rows in the DataFrame. All of these results raise questions that need to be answered.

The second example shows how to list the unique values in each column. To do that, you apply the unique() method to each column. Here, you can see that the type column has three values that indicate the type of data in the row, which explains why there are only 4208 poll ids. Specifically, there are three different types of rows for each poll, but you only need one of them for your analysis.

For the state column, note that "U.S." is one of the unique values. In other words, there are polls for the entire country and polls for individual states. As a result, you need to decide whether your analysis is going to focus on the polls for the entire country, the polls for states, or both.

For the population column, the unique values show that there are just four values for the population column: "lv" for likely voter, "rv" for registered voter, "a", and "v". Since this case study focuses on the likely and registered voters, you can drop the rows that contain "a" or "v".

Finally, you can see that the multiversions column contains only two values, "nan" and "*". So, you need to figure out what's going on there too.

Examine the data (continued)

With the nunique() method

```
polls.nunique(dropna=False)
====================================
cycle                    1
branch                   1
type                     3
matchup                  1
forecastdate             1
state                   57
startdate              352
enddate                345
pollster               196
grade                   11
samplesize            1767
population               4
poll_wt               4399
rawpoll_clinton       1312
rawpoll_trump         1385
rawpoll_johnson        585
rawpoll_mcmullin        17
adjpoll_clinton      12569
adjpoll_trump        12582
adjpoll_johnson       6630
adjpoll_mcmullin        58
multiversions            2
url                   1305
poll_id               4208
question_id           4208
createddate            222
timestamp                3
dtype: int64
```

With the unique() method (partial results)

```
polls.apply(pd.unique)
======================================================================
cycle                                                           [2016]
branch                                                     [President]
type                                [polls-plus, now-cast, polls-only]
matchup                                [Clinton vs. Trump vs. Johnson]
forecastdate                                                 [11/8/16]
state                [U.S., New Mexico, Virginia, Iowa, Wisconsin, ...
...
population                                               [lv, rv, a, v]
multiversions                                              [nan, *]
```

Figure 12-2 Clean the data (part 2)

Drop columns and rows

Part 3 of figure 12-2 shows the code for dropping unnecessary columns and rows. Then, it shows the DataFrame after all of the operations have been completed. In practice, though, you might want to display the DataFrame after each step to make sure each operation was successful.

To start, the first statement drops the four columns that contain just one value. Then, the second block of code keeps only the rows that have "now-cast" in the type column. To do that, it uses the query() method to select those rows, and it assigns the result to the polls DataFrame. After that, it uses the drop() method with the inplace parameter to drop the type column.

The third block of code uses the query() method to select the rows that don't have "lv" or "rv" in the population column. This shows that there are only 63 of them. Then, it drops those rows by assigning the rows that do contain "lv" or "rv" to the polls DataFrame.

The fourth block of code uses the loc accessor and the nunique() method to find the columns that have the same number of unique values as there are rows. To do that, it compares the number of unique values to the first value in the shape attribute of the DataFrame, which is the number of rows. For this DataFrame, this statement returns the poll_id and question_id columns. That's why the second statement drops those columns.

The fifth block finds the columns that start with "adjpoll" and drops them. To do that, it uses the str accessor and the startswith() method with a loc accessor to find the column names in the columns attribute of the DataFrame that start with "adjpoll". Then, to drop those columns, it assigns the reverse (~ operator) of that loc accessor to the polls DataFrame.

Of course, you can drop those columns in a simpler way by specifying a list of column names in the drop() method as shown by the sixth block of code. Here, the code drops the columns for Johnson and McMullin.

The seventh block of code checks the multiversions column by looking for rows that aren't null. Remember from part 2 of this figure that this column contains only two values, nan and *. As a result, this code displays the rows with asterisks (*) in them. Since the data in the 10 rows that are displayed looks legitimate, this analysis keeps them. However, it drops the multiversions column.

To further reduce the data, the eighth block of code drops three more columns that aren't needed for this analysis. Of course, if you want to be able to go to the URL for a specific poll, you wouldn't drop the url column.

If you review the code in this figure, you can see that there are many ways you could get the same results. To start, the operations could be done in different sequences. However, it makes sense to drop the unnecessary rows early in the process because that makes it easier for you to focus on the rows that are important to your analysis.

There are also other ways in which these operations can be coded. For instance, to drop columns, you can select the columns that you want to keep and assign them to the DataFrame. Or, you can use the drop() method to specify the columns that you want to drop.

Drop unnecessary columns and rows

1. Drop columns with only one value

```
polls.drop(columns=['cycle','branch','matchup','forecastdate'],inplace=True)
```

2. Keep only the rows with "now-cast" in the type column and drop that column

```
polls = polls.query('type == "now-cast"')
polls.drop(columns='type', inplace=True)
```

3. Keep only the rows that have 'lv' or 'rv' in the population column

```
polls.query('population !="lv" & population != "rv"')     # just 63 rows
polls = polls.query('population in ["lv","rv"]')
```

4. Find unnecessary index columns and then drop them

```
polls.loc[:, polls.nunique() == polls.shape[0]]  # display columns
polls.drop(columns=['poll_id','question_id'], inplace=True)
```

5. Find columns that start with 'adjpoll' and then drop them

```
polls.loc[:, polls.columns.str.startswith('adjpoll')]
polls = polls.loc[:, ~polls.columns.str.startswith('adjpoll')]
```

6. Drop the columns for Johnson and McMullen

```
polls.drop(columns=['rawpoll_johnson','rawpoll_mcmullin'], inplace=True)
```

7. Check the non-null rows in the multiversions column and drop that column

```
polls.loc[polls.multiversions.notnull()]
polls.drop(columns='multiversions')
```

8. Drop 3 more columns

```
polls.drop(columns=['createddate','timestamp','url'], inplace=True)
polls.head()
```

The resulting DataFrame

	state	startdate	enddate	pollster	grade	samplesize	population	poll_wt	rawpoll_clinton	rawpoll_trump
4208	U.S.	11/3/2016	11/6/2016	ABC News/Washington Post	A+	2220.0	lv	8.720654	47.00	43.00
4209	U.S.	11/1/2016	11/7/2016	Google Consumer Surveys	B	26574.0	lv	7.628472	38.03	35.69
4210	U.S.	11/2/2016	11/6/2016	Ipsos	A-	2195.0	lv	6.424334	42.00	39.00
4211	U.S.	11/4/2016	11/7/2016	YouGov	B	3677.0	lv	6.087135	45.00	41.00
4212	U.S.	11/3/2016	11/6/2016	Gravis Marketing	B-	16639.0	rv	5.316449	47.00	43.00

Description

- Although you could do these operations in other sequences, it makes sense to drop the unnecessary rows early in the process. This makes it easier to work with the rows that are important to your analysis.
- You could also code most of these operations in other ways.

Figure 12-2 Clean the data (part 3)

Rename columns

Part 4 of figure 12-2 starts by renaming two of the columns. To do that, it uses the rename() method with a columns parameter that's coded as a dictionary. Here, the dictionary specifies the name of each column to be replaced and the replacement name. The new column names make it easier to remember what these columns contain.

Similarly, you could change the names for other columns to make them more meaningful. For instance, you could rename the population column to something like voter_type.

Fix object types

The second example fixes the data types for columns of the object type that should be datetime or numeric types. Here, the select_dtypes() method displays the six columns that have the object type, but two of them contain dates. As a result, those columns should be converted to the datetime data type.

The second block of code performs this conversion. To do that, it creates a list that identifies the columns. Then, it applies the to_datetime() method to the columns in that list. Of course, you also could do this without creating a list by coding the column names directly in the statement that applies the to_datetime() method.

Fix data

The next block of code starts by listing the unique values in the state column. That uncovers the fact that some state names have suffixes like CD-1 or CD-2 where CD refers to Congressional District. So, the next statement lists all the state values that contain CD- just to make sure it's okay to drop those rows. Then, the last statement uses the reverse operator (~) to drop those rows by assigning all the other rows to the DataFrame.

Take an early plot with Pandas

Now that the data has been cleaned, why not use Pandas to take an early plot of the data to see what it looks like? In the plot in this figure, you can see that the number of polls increases as the election day nears. You can also see that the results not only have a wider range as election day nears, but also more overlap.

Save the DataFrame

At this point, you've done a lot of work. So this is a good time to save the DataFrame in a pickle file. That way, you won't have to run the preceding cells again if you want to start over from that point. Instead, you can use the read_pickle() method to read the cleaned data into a DataFrame.

Rename voting columns

```
polls.rename(columns={'rawpoll_clinton':'clinton_pct',
                      'rawpoll_trump':'trump_pct'}, inplace=True)
```

Fix object types that should be numeric or datetime objects

List the object types

```
polls.select_dtypes('object').head(2)
```

	state	startdate	enddate	pollster	grade	population
4208	U.S.	11/3/2016	11/6/2016	ABC News/Washington Post	A+	lv
4209	U.S.	11/1/2016	11/7/2016	Google Consumer Surveys	B	lv

Convert the object types that are dates to datetime objects

```
date_cols = ['startdate','enddate']
polls[date_cols] = polls[date_cols].apply(pd.to_datetime)
```

Fix the data for the state column

List the unique values in the state column

```
polls.state.unique()  # this lists values like "Maine CD-1" and "Maine CD-2"
```

List all the state values that contain “CD-”

```
polls[polls.state.str.contains('CD-')]['state']
```

Drop those rows after you find out that CD stands for Congressional District

```
polls = polls.loc[~polls.state.str.contains('CD-')]
```

Take an early plot with Pandas

```
polls.plot.line(x='enddate', y=['clinton_pct','trump_pct'])
```

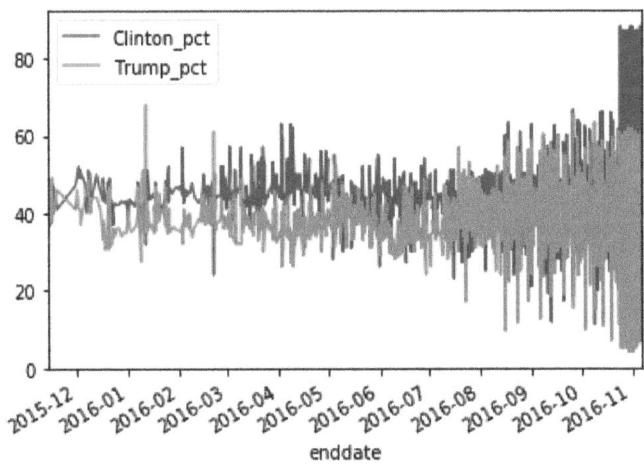

Save the DataFrame as a pickle file

```
polls.to_pickle('polls_clean.pkl')
```

Figure 12-2 Clean the data (part 4)

Prepare the data

The three parts of figure 12-3 show how to prepare the polling data. As you will see, this code adds four new columns of data that can be used to filter and group the data. It creates a long version of the wide data and takes an early Seaborn plot of that data. Then, it adds monthly bins for the polling data as well as a monthly percent column for each bin.

Add columns for grouping and filtering

The first block of code in part 1 adds a voter_type column that's derived from the population column. To do that, it uses the replace() method to replace "lv" with "likely" and "rv" with "registered", and it assigns the changed data to a new column named voter_type. Then, it drops the original population column.

The second block of code adds a gap column to the DataFrame. This column subtracts the Trump percent from the Clinton percent and assigns the result to the new column.

The third block of code uses a transform() method that's chained to a groupby() method to create a new column named state_gap. Here, the groupby() method groups the polls by state. Then, the transform() method gets the mean value of the gap column for each state group, and it puts that mean value in each row within the group.

The fourth block of code adds a swing column to the DataFrame. To do that, it selects the rows that don't have "U.S." in the state column and do have a state_gap value that is less than 7. However, since this value could be negative, the abs() method is used to get the absolute value of the state gap before it's compared to 7. The result is a new swing column that contains either True or False.

After you add the swing column, you can easily select the swing states. To do that, you can use the query() method as shown by the first statement in the second group of examples. Or, you can use the loc accessor as shown by the second statement.

Add columns for grouping and filtering

1. Add a voter_type column and drop the population column

```
polls['voter_type'] = polls.population.replace(
    {'lv':'likely','rv':'registered'})
polls.drop(columns='population', inplace=True)
```

2. Add a gap column for the gap between the Clinton and Trump percents

```
polls['gap'] = polls.clinton_pct - polls.trump_pct
```

3. Add a state_gap summary column that contains the gap for each state

```
polls['state_gap'] = polls.groupby('state').gap.transform(func='mean')
```

4. Add a swing column that identifies states with a less than a 7 percent gap

```
polls['swing'] = (polls.state != "U.S.") & (abs(polls.state_gap) < 7)
```

The resulting DataFrame

	state	startdate	enddate	pollster	grade	samplesize	poll_wt	clinton_pct	trump_pct	voter_type	gap	state_gap	swing
4208	U.S.	2016-11-03	2016-11-06	ABC News/Washington Post	A+	2220.0	8.720654	47.00	43.00	likely	4.00	4.347514	False
4209	U.S.	2016-11-01	2016-11-07	Google Consumer Surveys	B	26574.0	7.628472	38.03	35.69	likely	2.34	4.347514	False
4210	U.S.	2016-11-02	2016-11-06	Ipsos	A-	2195.0	6.424334	42.00	39.00	likely	3.00	4.347514	False
4211	U.S.	2016-11-04	2016-11-07	YouGov	B	3677.0	6.087135	45.00	41.00	likely	4.00	4.347514	False
4212	U.S.	2016-11-03	2016-11-06	Gravis Marketing	B-	16639.0	5.316449	47.00	43.00	registered	4.00	4.347514	False

Two ways to display the rows for swing states

With the query() method

```
polls.query('swing == True')
```

With the loc accessor

```
polls.loc[polls.swing == True]
```

Description

- When you prepare the data, you often add columns for grouping and filtering the data.

Figure 12-3 Prepare the data (part 1)

Create a new DataFrame in long form

Since the percentages for Clinton and Trump are in separate columns named clinton_pct and trump_pct, this data is in wide form, not long form. However, if you want to use Seaborn to plot this data, you typically want the data to be in long form. That's because Seaborn works best with data in long form, which you may remember from chapter 4.

To convert data from wide form to long form, you use the melt() method as shown by the first example in part 2 of this figure. Here, the code melts the clinton_pct and trump_pct columns into columns named candidate and percent.

After you melt the data, you can clean up the data in the new columns. Here, the code begins by dropping the "_pct" suffix from the data in the candidate column. As a result, "clinton_pct" and "trump_pct" become "clinton" and "trump". Then, the code converts this data to title case. As a result, "clinton" and "trump" become "Clinton" and "Trump".

Take an early plot of the long data with Seaborn

Now that the data is in long form, why not take an early plot with Seaborn. To do that, you can use the Seaborn lineplot() method as shown by the second example. This shows how the percentages for Clinton and Trump changed over the dates leading up to the election.

Before calling the lineplot() method, though, this code defines a custom color palette of blue and red and sets it as the current palette. These colors make sense because Clinton was the candidate of the Democratic Party, which is typically represented by blue, and Trump was the candidate of the Republican Party, which is typically represented by red. These color changes should make this plot easier to understand for anyone who is familiar with these color associations. These colors will also stay set until they are changed.

Once the colors are set, the next statement draws the line plot for the polls in the swing states. In this case, the ci parameter is set to None, so a shadowed confidence interval isn't shown on the plot. Here, you can see that Clinton had an early lead, but the polls got much tighter as election day neared.

In contrast to the Pandas plot in figure 12-2, part 4, this plot shows that Seaborn automatically averages the percentages (or y values) for each day. This makes the line plot easier to understand. To get a similar result with the Pandas plot() method, you would need to calculate the average percentage for each day and then plot those averages.

Create a new DataFrame in long form

Melt the data to add two columns

```
polls_long = polls.melt(
    id_vars=['state','enddate','voter_type','state_gap','swing'],
    value_vars=['clinton_pct','trump_pct'],
    var_name='candidate',
    value_name='percent')
```

Clean up the strings in the candidate column

```
polls_long['candidate'] = polls_long.candidate.str.replace('_pct','').str.title()
```

	state	enddate	voter_type	state_gap	swing	candidate	percent
0	U.S.	2016-11-06	likely	4.347514	False	Clinton	47.00
1	U.S.	2016-11-07	likely	4.347514	False	Clinton	38.03
2	U.S.	2016-11-06	likely	4.347514	False	Clinton	42.00

Take an early plot of the long data with Seaborn

```
colors = ['#2281c4','#d75c5d']                # blue and red
sns.set_palette(sns.color_palette(colors))  # change color palette

sns.lineplot(data=polls_long, x='enddate', y='percent',
             hue='candidate', ci=None)
```

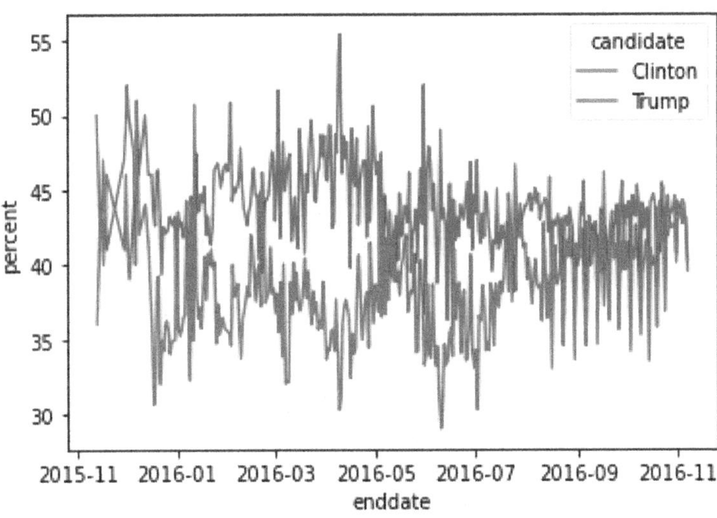

Description

- Because Clinton was the candidate of the Democrat party whose color is blue, and Trump was the candidate of the Republican party whose color is red, a custom color palette is used to apply those colors to the plot lines. In the palette, blue is specified first because the first row to be plotted is for the Democrat.

Figure 12-3 Prepare the data (part 2)

Add monthly bins to the DataFrame

Although the Seaborn plot that you've just seen is easier to understand than the Pandas plot shown earlier, it's still hard to interpret because the plot lines are so close together. So, one way to make the data easier to interpret is to create monthly bins for the polls as shown by the first example in part 3 of figure 12-3. That way, you can plot the average for each month instead of plotting the average for each day.

In this example, the code adds a month_bins column that contains monthly bins with labels that range from "Nov 2015" through "Nov 2016". To do that, this code uses the Pandas date_range() method to create a range of monthly dates from October 1, 2015 to December 1, 2016.

The code then uses a list comprehension with the datetime method named strftime()to create the labels for each monthly bin. Here, the "%b %Y" formatting code creates labels that consist of a 3-letter month and a 4-digit year. But since the first date is the starting bin edge, the list comprehension slices the dates so the labels start at the second date (index 1), which is "Nov 2015" instead of "Oct 2015".

At that point, this code uses the Pandas cut() method to create the bins from the dates and labels, and it assigns the bins to a new column named month_bin. You can see the results in the DataFrame that's displayed. Later in the analysis, if you decide that the monthly bins are too large, you can use the same technique to create bi-monthly or weekly bins.

Add an average percent column for each month

After the monthly bins are created, you can add a new column that contains the average voting percent for each of the bins. That's illustrated by the second example in this figure. Here, the rows are grouped by the candidate, state, and month_bin columns, and the transform() method gets the average percent for each group and puts it in the month_pct_avg column for each group.

Save the wide and long DataFrames

Here again, you've done a lot of work as you prepared the data. So it makes sense to save both the wide and long DataFrames as pickle files. That way, you can easily recover the prepared data if you mess up the DataFrame later in your analysis.

Add monthly bins to the DataFrame

```
import datetime as dt
dates = pd.date_range('10/01/2015', '12/01/2016', freq='M')
bin_labels = [dt.datetime.strftime(x, '%b %Y') for x in dates[1:]]
monthly_bins = pd.cut(x=polls_long.enddate, bins=dates, labels=bin_labels)
polls_long['month_bin'] = monthly_bins
polls_long.head()
```

	state	enddate	voter_type	state_gap	swing	candidate	percent	month_bin
0	U.S.	2016-11-06	likely	4.347514	False	Clinton	47.00	Nov 2016
1	U.S.	2016-11-07	likely	4.347514	False	Clinton	38.03	Nov 2016
2	U.S.	2016-11-06	likely	4.347514	False	Clinton	42.00	Nov 2016
3	U.S.	2016-11-07	likely	4.347514	False	Clinton	45.00	Nov 2016
4	U.S.	2016-11-06	registered	4.347514	False	Clinton	47.00	Nov 2016

Add an average percent column for each month

```
polls_long['month_pct_avg'] = polls_long.groupby(
    ['candidate','state','month_bin']).percent.transform(func='mean')
polls_long.head()
```

	state	enddate	voter_type	state_gap	swing	candidate	percent	month_bin	month_pct_avg
0	U.S.	2016-11-06	likely	4.347514	False	Clinton	47.00	Nov 2016	45.067903
1	U.S.	2016-11-07	likely	4.347514	False	Clinton	38.03	Nov 2016	45.067903
2	U.S.	2016-11-06	likely	4.347514	False	Clinton	42.00	Nov 2016	45.067903
3	U.S.	2016-11-07	likely	4.347514	False	Clinton	45.00	Nov 2016	45.067903
4	U.S.	2016-11-06	registered	4.347514	False	Clinton	47.00	Nov 2016	45.067903

Save the wide and long DataFrames as pickle files

```
polls.to_pickle('polls_prepared.pkl')
polls_long.to_pickle('polls_long.pkl')
```

Description

- If the plot lines for the dates in your plots are hard to read because they're so close together, you can put the data in monthly, bi-monthly, or weekly bins and then plot the data in the bins.

Figure 12-3 Prepare the data (part 3)

Analyze the data

The four parts of figure 12-4 show how to analyze the data. As you will see, a large part of that analysis is plotting the data so you can better understand the relationships between the data items.

Plot the national and swing state polls

Part 1 shows how to use plots to analyze the trends in the polling data. Here, the first plot is for the national polls, and the second one is for the swing states. Both use the month_bin column for the x-axis, the month_pct_avg column for the y-axis, and the candidate column for the color.

The only difference in the code for these plots is in the query() method that selects the data for the plot. In the first example, the plot only includes rows where the state column is equal to "U.S." In the second example, the plot only includes rows where the swing column is True. Remember that this column contains True or False based on whether the absolute value of the state_gap column is less than 7 *and* the state column isn't equal to "U.S.".

If you look at the plots, you can see the differences in the results. This shows that Clinton was leading in the national polls in the early months, but these polls tightened as the election date neared. Similarly, Clinton was leading in the early polls for just the swing states, but these polls became extremely close as the election date neared with Trump taking a brief lead in August.

Plots like these should help you determine what you might want to look at more closely. For instance, you might want to look at the results for the swing states when the state_gap is less than 5 instead of less than 7. To do that, you could adjust the query() method like this:

```
polls_long.query(
    'state != "U.S." & state_gap < 5 & state_gap > -5')
```

This gets the rows for the swing states and selects only the ones with the smaller state gap. However, if you find yourself consistently using the smaller gap to define swing states, you can go back to the prepare step that creates the swing column and change the gap from 7 to 5.

When you decide that you want to use a plot for presentation, you should enhance the plot with the goal of making it as self-explanatory as possible. This is illustrated by both of these examples. To start, these examples get the Axes object that is returned by the lineplot() method. Then, they use the set() method of the Axes object to set the text for the title of the plot as well as the labels for the x and y axes. They also use the tick_params() method to rotate the labels on the x-axis by 45 degrees.

Plot the national and swing state polls

The national polls

```
ax = sns.lineplot(data=polls_long.query('state == "U.S."'),
    x='month_bin', y='month_pct_avg', hue='candidate', ci=None)

ax.set(title='U.S. Polls', xlabel='Month', ylabel='Average Percent')
ax.tick_params('x', labelrotation=45)
```

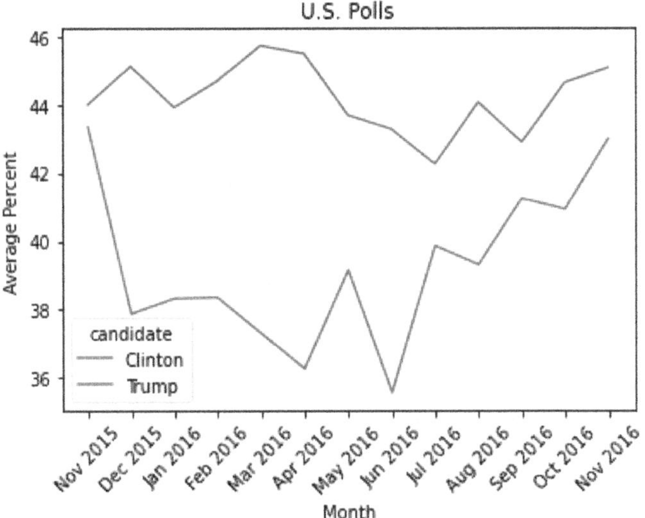

The swing state polls

```
ax = sns.lineplot(data=polls_long.query('swing == True'),
    x='month_bin', y='month_pct_avg', hue='candidate', ci=None)

ax.set(title='Swing State Polls', xlabel='Month', ylabel='Average Percent')
ax.tick_params('x', labelrotation=45)
```

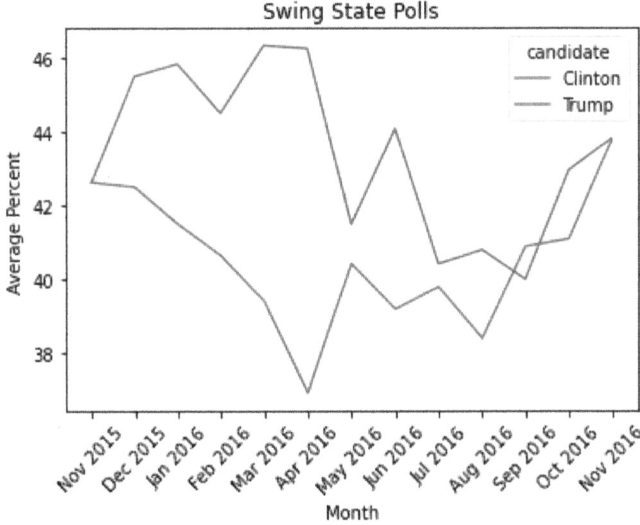

Figure 12-4 Analyze the data (part 1)

Plot the voter types

Because of the way the voting system is set up in the United States, the swing states typically determine who will win. Based on that, and on what you've learned by the previous plots in this chapter, let's focus on the swing states. To do that, you can use techniques like those in part 2 of figure 12-4.

Here, the first example uses the query() and groupby() methods to group the swing state data based on the voter_type and candidate columns. Then, the second example uses the agg() method to get the mean and standard deviation of the percent column. Next, it unstacks the candidate level. This creates hierarchical column indexes that make it easier to view the mean and standard deviation for each candidate.

The resulting DataFrame shows that the mean values for the percent column for Clinton and Trump are so close for both the likely and registered voters that it's hard to draw any conclusions. If you look at the mean, Clinton seems to have a small lead among registered voters but that lead is even smaller among likely voters. In addition, the standard deviation for likely voters is almost 5% for Clinton and over 5% for Trump. This indicates that it's going to be hard to predict the winner.

To make this data easier to interpret, you can plot it as shown in the third example. This time, the Seaborn catplot() method creates a bar plot from the polling data that's in long form. Here again, this example uses a query() method to select the data for the swing states. But this time, it specifies the voter_type column for the x-axis. It also sets the ci parameter to "sd" so a black whisker shows the standard deviation for those polls. Once again, this shows how close the polling results are.

Plot the swing state results by voter type

Group the data by voter_type and candidate

```
polls_grouped = polls_long.query('swing == True') \
                .groupby(['voter_type','candidate'])
```

Look at the mean and standard deviation of the percent column

```
polls_grouped.percent.agg(['mean','std']).unstack(level='candidate').head()
```

	mean		std	
candidate	Clinton	Trump	Clinton	Trump
voter_type				
likely	42.339206	41.223044	4.672971	5.497081
registered	42.771795	40.431624	4.433704	4.564361

Plot the mean and standard deviation of the percent column for each candidate

```
sns.catplot(data=polls_long.query('swing == True'), kind='bar',
    x='voter_type', y='percent', hue='candidate', ci='sd')
```

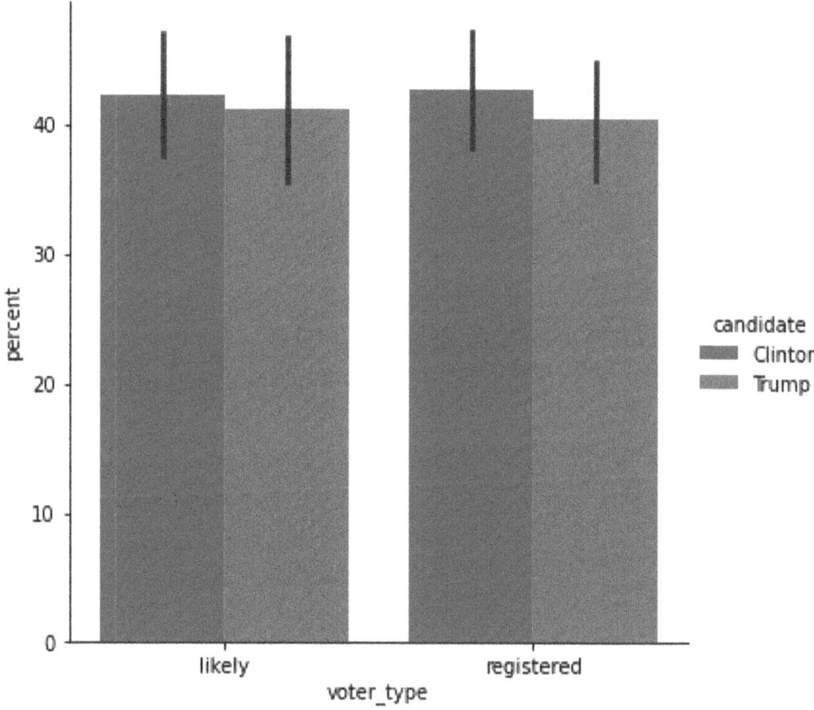

Figure 12-4 Analyze the data (part 2)

Plot the last two months of polling

The closer the polls are to the election date, the more significant they are. Because of that, it makes sense to look at the results for just the last 2 months before the election date, which was November 8, 2016. This is illustrated by part 3 of figure 12-4.

The first example in this figure uses the query() method to select the likely voters in the swing states, but only when the enddate is greater than September 2016. It also sets the aspect parameter to 2 to make the plot twice as wide as it would be otherwise. This makes it easier to see how the percents for each candidate change over time. The resulting plot shows that the percents get much closer as the election day nears.

The second example is much like the first one. But instead of using the swing column to select all the swing states, it uses the query() method to select just Michigan and Florida. That's because those states played a big role in deciding the 2016 election. In the first subplot, Trump takes the lead on the last day of the plot. In the second one, Clinton holds the lead on the last day, but barely.

Plot the last two months of polling for likely voters in all swing states

```
g = sns.relplot(data=polls_long.query('voter_type == "likely" \
        & swing == True & enddate >= "2016-09"'),
    kind='line', x='enddate', y='percent', hue='candidate', ci=None, aspect=2)
```

Plot the last two months of polling for likely voters in selected states

```
sns.relplot(data=polls_long.query('state in ["Michigan","Florida"] \
        & voter_type == "likely" & enddate >= "2016-09"'),
    kind='line', x='enddate', y='percent', hue='candidate', ci=None,
    col='state', col_wrap=1, aspect=2)
```

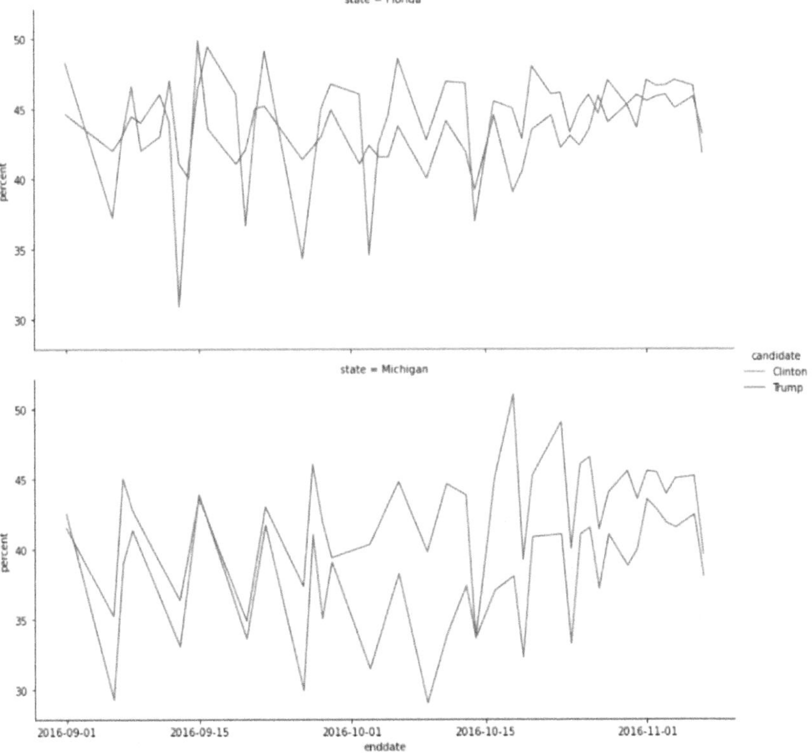

Figure 12-4 Analyze the data (part 3)

Plot the gap changes in selected states

The example in part 4 works much like the example in part 3. In fact, it uses the same rows of data. However, instead of plotting the average percent for both candidates, it plots the average percent gap between the two candidates. This makes it easier to determine which candidate was leading in the polls at each point in time.

Since this plot doesn't need to use the blue and red colors for each candidate, this example begins by restoring Seaborn's default color palette. To do that, it uses the set_palette() method to set the palette to a built-in palette named tab10.

Then, the relplot() method is used to plot the data with the y parameter set to the gap column so it plots the gaps between the voting percents for Clinton and the percents for Trump. Here, the col and col_wrap parameters are also set so the data for each state is in a subplot.

To enhance the formatting for this plot, the code gets the FacetGrid object that's returned by the relplot() method and uses its suptitle() method to set the title for the entire plot and its set() method to set the x and y labels. Then, it uses a for loop to run the tick_params() and axhline() methods for each subplot. As a result, the tick labels for the x-axis are rotated 45 degrees, and a horizontal red line is drawn at the point where the y value is zero.

Since the gap values were calculated by subtracting the Trump percent from the Clinton percent, a positive value favors Clinton and a negative value favors Trump. As a result, the red line makes it easy to see that Florida wavered between Clinton and Trump during the last two months of the election. It's also easy to see that Clinton was ahead in Michigan for most of the time, although that gap got smaller as election day neared.

Plot the gap changes in selected states

```
# restore the default color palette
sns.set_palette(sns.color_palette('tab10'))

# create the plot
g = sns.relplot(data=polls.query('state==["Michigan", "Florida"] \
        & enddate > "2016-09"'),
    kind="line", x='enddate', y='gap', ci=None,
    col='state', col_wrap=2)

# format the plot
g.fig.suptitle('Percent Gap for Key Swing States', y=1.025)
g.set(xlabel="Polling End Date",
      ylabel="Percent Gap: Clinton - Trump")
for ax in g.axes.flat:
    ax.tick_params('x', labelrotation=45)
    ax.axhline(0, color='red')
```

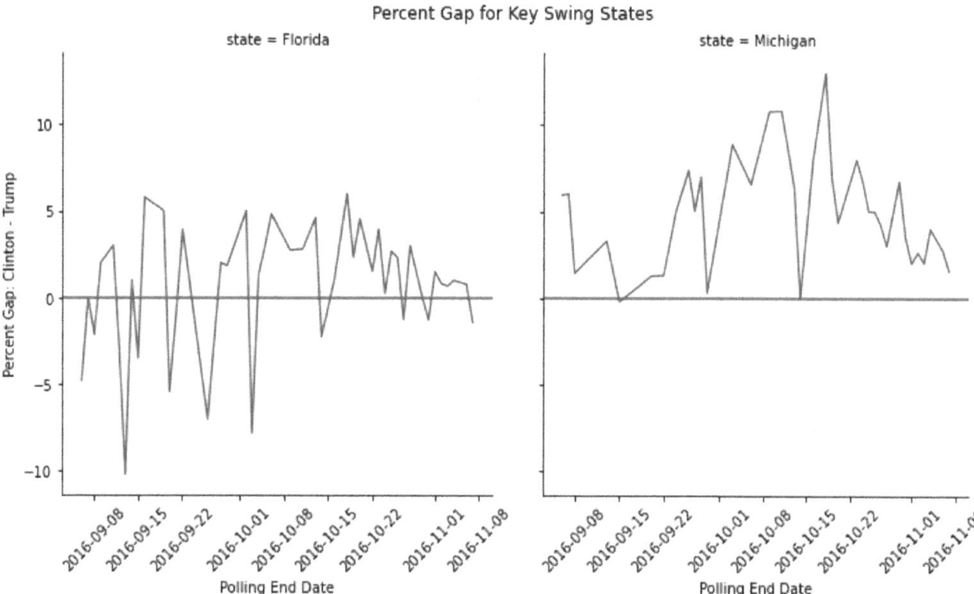

Figure 12-4 Analyze the data (part 4)

More preparation and analysis

At this point, you've done enough analysis to get some ideas for further analysis. For example, you might want to look at the polling gap in the last week of the election in key swing states. Or, you might want to look at how the polling gap changed each week in the swing states over the last two months leading up to the election.

The four parts of figure 12-5 show that ideas like these require more preparation and further analysis. That's to be expected because data analysis is a process that often requires going back and forth between the preparation and analysis phases.

Prepare the gap data for the last week of polling

Part 1 of figure 12-5 shows the code that prepares a DataFrame named polls_gap that contains the data needed to create a bar plot of the percent gap for eight key swing states. To start, this code uses the query() method to get the state and gap columns for the last week of the election for the eight swing states. Then, it groups the data by the state and gets the average of the gap column. This works because the gap column is the only remaining column in the DataFrame.

After getting the average gap for each state, this code adds a column named advantage that contains the name of the candidate that is leading in the polls at that time. To do that, the code checks whether the gap is greater than 0. If so, Clinton is leading. Otherwise, Trump is leading.

After the advantage column has been created, there's no need to use negative numbers for Trump. That's why the code uses the abs() function to convert all numbers in the gap column to positive numbers. Then, to make it so Seaborn can use the state data, the code resets the index.

Prepare the gap data for the last week of polling

```
polls_gap = polls.query('state==["Wisconsin", "Arizona", \
    "Pennsylvania","Nevada","Iowa","Florida","North Carolina","Ohio"] \
    & enddate > "2016-11-01"')[['state','gap']]
polls_gap = polls_gap.groupby('state').mean()
polls_gap
```

state	gap
Arizona	-1.376923
Florida	0.573500
Iowa	-4.243846
Nevada	0.413529
North Carolina	2.471176
Ohio	-1.652632
Pennsylvania	2.608571
Wisconsin	4.712308

```
polls_gap['advantage'] = polls_gap.apply(
    lambda row: 'Clinton' if row.gap > 0 else 'Trump', axis=1)
polls_gap['gap'] = abs(polls_gap.gap)
polls_gap = polls_gap.reset_index()
polls_gap
```

	state	gap	advantage
0	Arizona	1.376923	Trump
1	Florida	0.573500	Clinton
2	Iowa	4.243846	Trump
3	Nevada	0.413529	Clinton
4	North Carolina	2.471176	Clinton
5	Ohio	1.652632	Trump
6	Pennsylvania	2.608571	Clinton
7	Wisconsin	4.712308	Clinton

Description

- After you prepare the gap data for the eight swing states for the week before the election, you can use it to create a bar plot that makes it easy to see who is leading in the polls.

Figure 12-5 More preparation and analysis (part 1)

Plot the gap data for the last week of polling

Part 2 of figure 12-5 shows how to plot the data from the DataFrame in part 1. To start, it sets a custom color palette that uses the same red and blue colors defined earlier in this analysis. But for this plot, the colors are reversed because the first row that's plotted is for Trump. If the colors weren't reversed, the Trump bars would be blue and the Clinton bars would be red.

After setting the color palette, the Seaborn catplot() method creates a bar chart with the state on the x-axis, the gap on the y-axis, and the leading candidate as the color for each bar. But also note that this method uses the dodge parameter, which isn't presented elsewhere in this book. It is used to fix a formatting problem that causes the bars to be spaced unevenly. This parameter isn't presented earlier in the book because it's rarely needed.

The shows that you will sometimes need to find solutions to problems that aren't addressed in this book. In those cases, you can usually use the Internet to find the solutions that you need. If, for example, you search the Internet for information about fixing the uneven spacing in a Seaborn bar plot, you'll find information about how you can use the dodge parameter to do that.

After creating the plot, this example uses the FacetGrid object that's returned by the catplot() method to enhance the formatting of the plot. To start, it loops through all Axes objects in the FacetGrid object, although in this case there's only one of them. Then, it rotates the tick labels for the x-axis by 45 degrees, it sets the title for the Axes object, and it sets the labels for its x and y axes.

After enhancing the plot, this code saves the plot as a PNG file. But first, it uses the subplots_adjust() method to adjust the areas at the top and bottom of the figure so it allocates 10% for the title at the top of the figure and 35% for the labels at the bottom of the figure. This was needed to prevent the title and labels from being truncated in the PNG file that's saved.

Interestingly, JupyterLabs displays the plot correctly even if you don't adjust the areas at the top and bottom of the figure. However, if you open the PNG file that's saved, the title and labels will be truncated if you don't adjust these areas. As a result, finding the correct percentages to set for the top and bottom area can require some trial and error.

Plot the gap data for the last week of polling

```
# set custom color palette
colors = ['#d75c5d','#2281c4']  # red and blue
sns.set_palette(sns.color_palette(colors))

# create the plot
g = sns.catplot(data=polls_gap, x='state', y='gap', kind='bar',
                hue='advantage', dodge=False)

# format the plot
for ax in g.axes.flat:
    ax.tick_params('x', labelrotation=45)
    ax.set(title='Gap Percent One Week Before Election Day',
           xlabel='Key Swing States',
           ylabel='Percent')

# save the plot
g.fig.subplots_adjust(top=0.90)     # adjust the top to fit the title
g.fig.subplots_adjust(bottom=0.35)  # adjust the bottom to fix the y labels
g.fig.savefig('swing_state_gap_bar.png')
```

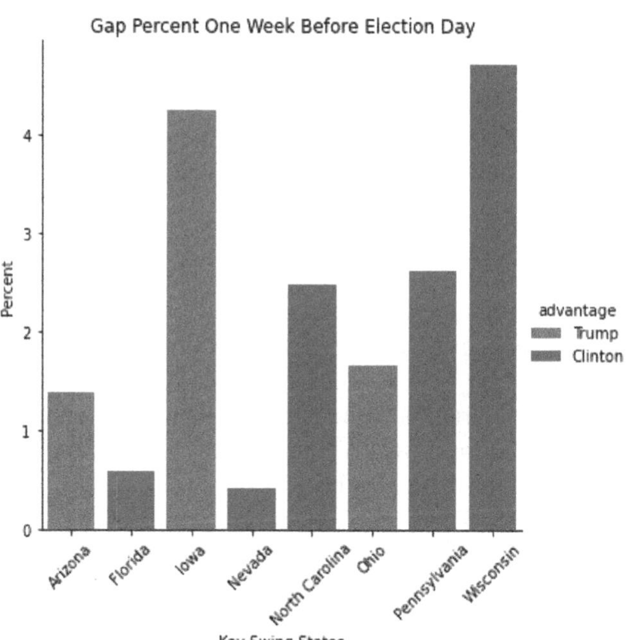

Description

- To create this plot, the catplot() method uses the dodge parameter to fix a formatting problem that causes the bars to be spaced unevenly. When you encounter a problem like that, you can usually search the Internet to find a solution for it.
- Before saving this plot, the subplots_adjust() method is used to adjust the figure so the top area that displays the title uses 10% of the figure and the bottom area that displays the labels uses 35% of the figure. This prevents the title and labels from being truncated in the PNG file that's saved.

Figure 12-5 More preparation and analysis (part 2)

Prepare the weekly gap data for the swing states

Part 3 of figure 12-5 shows how to prepare the weekly data for the swing states. To start, it creates a DataFrame named polls_heat that contains the six columns that are needed for this analysis. Then, it uses the query() method to get the rows for the swing states.

After getting the needed columns, this code adds two more columns. First, it adds a total count for Clinton and Trump in each poll by multiplying the sample size by the voting percent. Once that's done, some of the columns in the DataFrame are no longer needed, so the code selects just the four columns that are needed.

Next, this code adds a column named weekly_bins that contains weekly bins from September 1, 2016 to November 13, 2016. This is like the code presented earlier in this chapter that created monthly bins. But this time, the code uses a list comprehension with "%d %b" as the formatting code to create labels for each bin that consist of a 2-digit day of the month followed by the first three letters of the month. Also, since the first date is the starting bin edge, the list comprehension slices the dates so the labels start at the second date (index 1).

After adding the weekly bins, this code calculates the weekly gap. To do that, it groups the data by state and weekly bin and gets the total count for Clinton and Trump in each group. In other words, it sums the poll counts for each week in each state to get a total count for each candidate. Then, it uses those counts to calculate and add a gap column.

Like the gap column used earlier in this analysis, a positive value indicates that Clinton is leading in the polls and a negative value indicates that Trump is leading in the polls. To make these values easier to read, this code fills any missing values with a value of 0 and rounds all of the values to a single decimal point.

At this point, the DataFrame has a hierarchical index that was created by the groupby() function on two columns, state and weekly_bin. However, to be able to use Seaborn's heatmap() method on this data, you need to use the unstack() method to unstack the weekly_bin index. Then, you can use the droplevel() method to drop the first column level for the gap column since that level is no longer needed. If you don't do that, Seaborn automatically concatenates the two levels to get labels like gap-11-Sep, gap-18-Sep, and so on.

The result is column labels that make it easier to see how the gap column changes week by week for each state. More importantly, this prepares the DataFrame so it will work with the heatmap() method as shown in the next figure. As you'll see, this method uses the index and column information to label the columns and rows.

Prepare the weekly gap data for the swing states

Get the columns and rows for this plot

```
polls_heat = polls[['state','enddate','samplesize',
                    'clinton_pct','trump_pct','swing']].copy()
polls_heat = polls_heat.query('swing == True')

# add two columns
polls_heat['clinton_count'] = polls_heat.samplesize * polls_heat.clinton_pct
polls_heat['trump_count'] = polls_heat.samplesize * polls_heat.trump_pct

# select only the necessary columns
polls_heat = polls_heat[['state','clinton_count','trump_count','enddate']]

# create and add the weekly bins
dates = pd.date_range('09/01/2016', '11/13/2016', freq='w')
bin_labels = [dt.datetime.strftime(x, '%d %b') for x in dates[1:]]
weekly_bins = pd.cut(x=polls_heat.enddate, bins=dates, labels=bin_labels)
polls_heat['weekly_bin'] = weekly_bins
polls_heat.head(3)
```

	state	clinton_count	trump_count	enddate	weekly_bin
4223	Iowa	31200.0	36800.0	2016-11-04	06 Nov
4225	Wisconsin	57730.0	50200.0	2016-10-31	06 Nov
4226	North Carolina	35200.0	35200.0	2016-11-06	06 Nov

Calculate the weekly gap

```
# group and sum the weekly counts by state
polls_heat = polls_heat.groupby(['state','weekly_bin']).sum().fillna(0)

# add the gap column and remove all other columns
polls_heat['gap'] = ((polls_heat.clinton_count - polls_heat.trump_count) /
                  (polls_heat.clinton_count + polls_heat.trump_count)) * 100
polls_heat = polls_heat[['gap']].fillna(0).round(1)

# unstack the weekly bin level and drop level 0 (gap)
polls_heat = polls_heat.unstack(level='weekly_bin')
polls_heat = polls_heat.droplevel(level=0, axis=1)
polls_heat.head(3)
```

weekly_bin	11 Sep	18 Sep	25 Sep	02 Oct	09 Oct	16 Oct	23 Oct	30 Oct	06 Nov	13 Nov
state										
Arizona	-3.0	-4.7	-0.6	0.8	0.9	0.6	5.1	-0.3	-1.4	4.0
Colorado	5.7	2.1	1.3	7.8	6.4	9.5	7.3	7.0	4.5	7.0
Florida	-1.9	-4.3	-3.0	0.5	0.8	2.3	3.5	1.9	0.9	0.3

Figure 12-5 More preparation and analysis (part 3)

Plot the weekly gap data for the swing states

Part 4 of figure 12-5 shows how to create a heat map for the data that was prepared in part 3. To do that, you can use Seaborn's heatmap() method.

In this example, Matplotlib is used to set the figure size before the plot is created. In practice, though, you usually wouldn't add this code until you realize that the default figure size is too small for the plot. In this case, the code sets the figure to a size of 10 inches wide by 7.5 inches tall. It also stores the current Figure and Axes objects in variables named fig and ax.

After setting the figure size, the heatmap() method creates the plot. Here, the cmap parameter is set to the red and blue colors used earlier in this analysis, and the center parameter is set to 0. That way, blue is used for the numbers above 0 that correspond to a Clinton lead, and red is used for the numbers below zero that correspond to a Trump lead. Then, the annot parameter is set to True so the numbers are displayed on the heat map. The linewidths and linecolor parameters are set so they enhance the appearance of the heat map. And the cbar parameter is set to False so the color bar isn't displayed to the right of the heat map.

After creating the plot, this code adds a title and axis labels to the plot. To do that, it uses the set() method of the current Axes object. Then, this code saves the plot as a PNG file by calling the savefig() method from the Figure object that has already been created by the Matplotlib subplots() method. When you use Matplotlib to set the size of a plot, you see the results in both JupyterLab and the saved PNG file.

Plot the weekly gap data for swing states

```
# use matplotlib to set the figure size
import matplotlib.pyplot as plt
fig, ax = plt.subplots(figsize=(10,7.5))

# create the plot
sns.heatmap(polls_heat, cmap=['#d75c5d','#2281c4'], center=0,
            annot=True, linewidths=0.01, linecolor='black', cbar=False)

# format the plot
ax.set(title='Gap Percent For Swing States By Week',
       xlabel='Week', ylabel='State')

# save the figure
fig.savefig('swing_state_gap_heat_map.png')
```

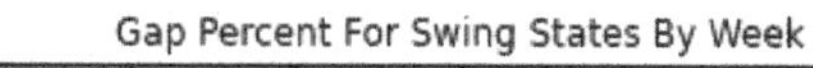

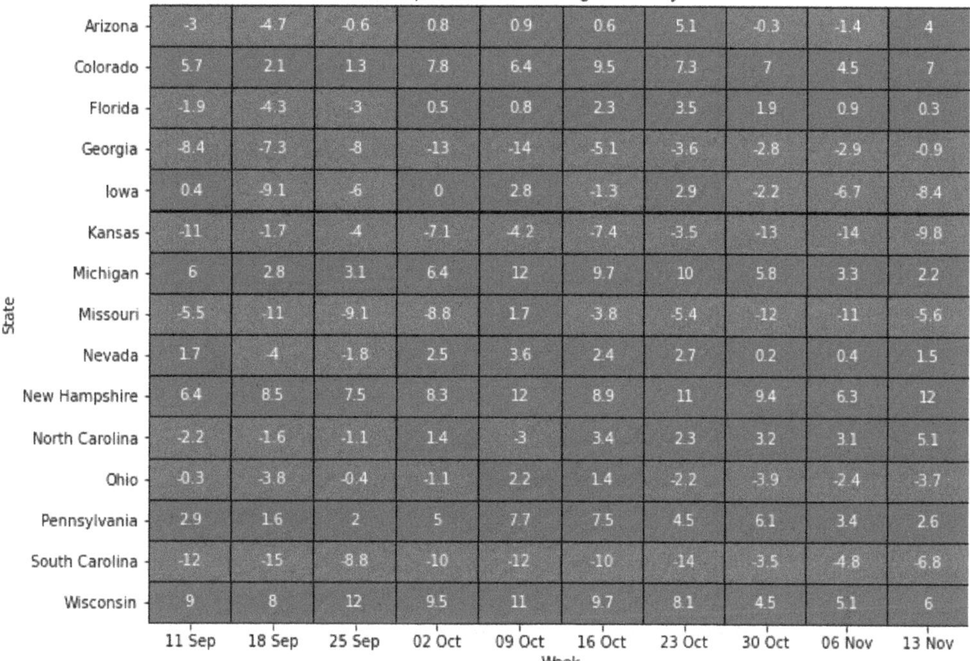

Description

- The heatmap() method sets the center parameter to 0 so the negative and positive gap values split into the correct colors. Here, the colors are set to red and blue instead of blue and red because the first row to be plotted is for the Republican.
- When the plot that's displayed is too small, you can use the Matplotlib subplots() method to increase the size. That changes the size of the plot in JupyterLab and also in the PNG file in which it's saved.

Figure 12-5 More preparation and analysis (part 4)

Perspective

This case study shows how the Pandas and Seaborn skills can be applied to a real-world analysis. As a result, it shows that cleaning the data is often a time-consuming part of an analysis. It shows that preparing and analyzing the data are closely related. And it shows that plotting, or data visualization, is a critical part of data analysis because it helps you see the trends and relationships in the data.

Exercise 12-1 Another analysis of the Polling data

This exercise guides you through another analysis of the Polling data. Before you do this analysis, you may want to run the Polling case study on your system and experiment with it to make sure you understand how it works. Also, as you do this analysis, you may want to copy and paste some code from the case study.

Get the data

1. Start JupyterLab and open the Notebook named ex_12-1_polls that should be in this folder:
   `exercises/ch12`
2. Run the first three cells in this Notebook to read the polling data into a DataFrame named polls.
3. Use the info() method to get information about this DataFrame.

Clean the data

4. Drop all columns except the columns named enddate, grade, rawpoll_clinton, rawpoll_trump, and state.
5. Drop all rows that contain missing values.
6. Add a column named type that contains a value of "national" if the poll is for the entire United States or "state" if the poll is for a specific state. To do that, you can apply a lambda expression to the state column.
7. Drop the state column.
8. Drop all rows except the ones for national polls.
9. Convert the enddate column to the datetime type.
10. Display the first five rows.

Prepare and analyze the data

11. Use the value_counts() method to display a count of each value in the grade column.
12. Use Seaborn to create a count plot to visualize this data. To enhance this plot, you can use the order parameter to order the columns from highest to lowest grade. What does this tell you about the grades for these polls?
13. Add a column named grade_letter that replaces the + and – grades with just the letter. To do that, you can apply a lambda expression to the grade column.
14. Use Seaborn to create a count plot to visualize the data in the grade_letter column. What does this tell you about the letter grades for these polls?
15. Melt the rawpoll_clinton and rawpoll_trump columns into columns named candidate and percent and assign the resulting DataFrame to a variable named pollsMelt.
16. Modify the candidate column so it stores values of "Clinton" and "Trump" instead of the old column names.
17. Display the first five rows of the pollsMelt DataFrame.

Plot the data

18. Use Seaborn to create a line plot for the pollsMelt DataFrame that shows how each candidate's average percent changed over time. When you do, display a subplot for each letter grade, and don't include a confidence interval. The result should look like this:

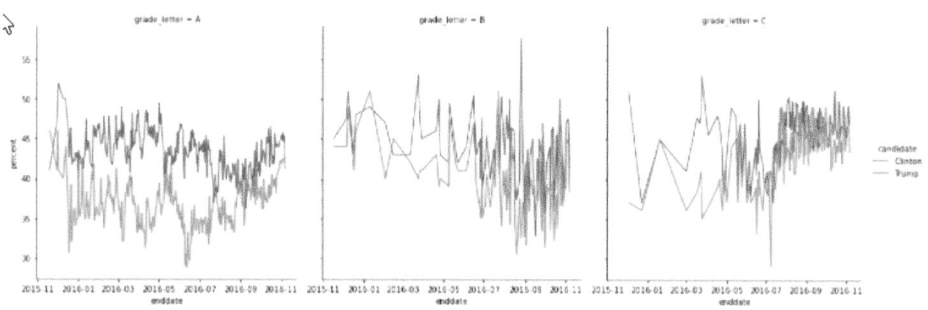

19. Make these subplots easier to read by only displaying one subplot per row and by making each subplot three times as wide.
20. Enhance the plot by setting the color for Clinton to blue and the color for Trump to red.

Chapter 13

The Forest Fires case study

The Forest Fires case study analyzes the data for forest fires in the United States from 1992 through 2015. This study gets its data from the website for the US Forest Service, which is part of the US Department of Agriculture. The data is available in several forms, but this case study gets it as a SQLite database.

To get the most from this case study, you can open the case study Notebook that's in the download for this book. Then, as you read this chapter, you can run the code in each cell to see exactly what it does. Or, if you prefer, you can read this chapter first and run the code later.

Get the data

The data for this case study is in a SQLite database that's in a zip file that you can download from the US Department of Agriculture's website. This data was compiled for the United States Forest Services.

Download and unzip the SQLite database

To get the Fires data, you start by downloading the zip file as shown in the first example in figure 13-1. To do that, you import the request module of the urllib package. Then, you use its urlretrieve() method to download the zip file.

To unzip that file, you import the ZipFile module of the zipfile package, and you use its extractall() and infolist() methods to print a list of the files that are extracted. As the second example in this figure shows, the first file in the list is the SQLite database followed by four files that provide documentation.

Connect and query the database

The third example shows how to connect to the database and create a cursor that lets you run queries against the database. Then, the fourth example uses SQL to list the tables that are available in the database, which includes the Fires table. After that, it uses SQL to list all the columns in that table. That helps you decide which columns you want to import into your DataFrame. But you can also review the four documentation files to help you decide.

Import the data into a DataFrame

The fifth example shows how to import the columns that you want from the database into a DataFrame. To do that, you first code a SQL statement that selects the columns that you want. Then, you code a Pandas read_sql_query() method with the SQL statement and the connection object as the two parameters.

In this example, only 8 columns are imported, but 1,888,465 rows are imported. As a result, it may take 30 seconds or more to import the data. That's why the sixth example saves the DataFrame as a pickle file. That way, if you mess up the DataFrame when you clean it, you can easily return to the original version.

Of course, examples 3, 4, and 5 assume that you have some knowledge of SQL and SQLite. If you don't, those are good skills to add to your skillset. But for now, you can just use the code in the Notebook to get the data and create the DataFrame.

1. Download the zip file to disk

```
fires_url = 'https://www.fs.usda.gov/rds/archive/products/RDS-2013-0009.4/'
filename = 'RDS-2013-0009.4_SQLITE.zip'
from urllib import request
request.urlretrieve(fires_url+filename, filename=filename)
```

2. Unzip and print the file info

```
from zipfile import ZipFile
with ZipFile(filename, mode='r') as zip:
    zip.extractall()
    for file in zip.infolist():
        print(file.filename, file.compress_size, file.file_size)
=================================================================
Data/FPA_FOD_20170508.sqlite 173776108 795785216
Data/ 0 0
_metadata_RDS-2013-0009.4.xml 11571 51400
Supplements/FPA_FOD_Source_List.pdf 74137 109336
Supplements/ 0 0
_fileindex_RDS-2013-0009.4.html 1098 4398
_metadata_RDS-2013-0009.4.html 13296 89005
```

3. Connect to the SQLite database and create a cursor

```
import sqlite3
fires_con = sqlite3.connect('Data/FPA_FOD_20170508.sqlite')
fires_cur = fires_con.cursor()
```

4. Check out the tables and then the columns in the Fires table

```
fires_cur.execute(
    'SELECT name FROM sqlite_master WHERE type="table"').fetchall()
fires_cur.execute('PRAGMA table_info(Fires)').fetchall()
```

5. Import the data into a DataFrame

```
fires_sql = """
            SELECT fire_name, fire_size,
                state, latitude, longitude, fire_year,
                DATETIME(discovery_date) AS discovery_date,
                DATETIME(cont_date) AS contain_date
            FROM Fires
            """
fires = pd.read_sql_query(fires_sql, fires_con)
```

6. Save the DataFrame

```
fires.to_pickle('fires_raw.pkl')
```

Description

- The Forest Fires database is part of a zip file that contains the SQLite database plus four other files that provide documentation for the database.

Figure 13-1 Get the data

Clean the data

Because you select the columns that you want to work with when you import the data into the DataFrame, you would think that you wouldn't have to do much cleaning. But real-world data is rarely clean, even if it's data from your own corporate database. So, there's usually work to do. And you start by examining the data.

Examine the data

The first group of examples in figure 13-2 shows the results of the info() method. This is where you discover that you've imported 1,880,465 rows. You can also see that all but two of the columns have non-null values in every row, which means that there are no missing values in those rows.

However, about half the rows for the other two columns (FIRE_NAME and CONTAIN_DATE) contain null values. You can also see that the two date columns have the object datatype, so they need to be converted to the datetime data type if you want to use the Python datetime methods to work with them.

The next example in this group shows how you can use the describe() method to get the scope of the numeric columns. Here, you can see that 75% of the rows have fire sizes that are 3.3 acres or less, but the largest fire (max) is 606,945 acres. That helps you decide what you want to analyze and what cleaning is required.

Improve the readability of the data

The second group of examples shows how you can improve the readability of the data. First, it shows how you can convert all of the column names to lowercase. Then, it shows how you can replace the name of the fire_size column with acres_burned, which is a more accurate description of what data the column contains.

Last, the data in the fire_name column is converted from all capital letters (all caps) to title case (only the first letters of the major words are capitalized). That will make it easier to read the names in that column.

Examine the data

With the info() method

```
fires.info(memory_usage='deep')
=============================================================
<class 'pandas.core.frame.DataFrame'>
RangeIndex: 1880465 entries, 0 to 1880464
Data columns (total 8 columns):
FIRE_NAME          923276 non-null object
FIRE_SIZE          1880465 non-null float64
STATE              1880465 non-null object
LATITUDE           1880465 non-null float64
LONGITUDE          1880465 non-null float64
FIRE_YEAR          1880465 non-null int64
discovery_date     1880465 non-null object
contain_date       988934 non-null object
dtypes: float64(3), int64(1), object(4)
memory usage: 473.8 MB
```

With the describe() method

```
fires.describe().T
```

	count	mean	std	min	25%	50%	75%	max
FIRE_SIZE	1880465.0	74.520158	2497.598180	0.000010	0.10000	1.000000	3.3000	606945.000000
LATITUDE	1880465.0	36.781213	6.139031	17.939722	32.81860	35.452500	40.8272	70.330600
LONGITUDE	1880465.0	-95.704942	16.716944	-178.802600	-110.36347	-92.043043	-82.2976	-65.256944
FIRE_YEAR	1880465.0	2003.709974	6.663099	1992.000000	1998.00000	2004.000000	2009.0000	2015.000000

Improve the readability of the data

Make the column names lowercase

```
fires.columns = fires.columns.str.lower()
fires.head(2)
```

	fire_name	acres_burned	state	latitude	longitude	fire_year	discovery_date	contain_date
0	Fountain	0.10	CA	40.036944	-121.005833	2005	2005-02-02 00:00:00	2005-02-02 00:00:00
1	Pigeon	0.25	CA	38.933056	-120.404444	2004	2004-05-12 00:00:00	2004-05-12 00:00:00

Rename the fire_size column

```
fires.rename(columns={'fire_size':'acres_burned'}, inplace=True)
```

Convert the data in the fire_name column to title case

```
fires['fire_name'] = fires.fire_name.str.title()
```

Description

- The info() method shows that all but two columns have non-null values in each row in the DataFrame, which means no missing values. In contrast, the FIRE_NAME and CONTAIN_DATE. columns have thousands of missing values.

Figure 13-2 Clean the data (part 1)

Drop unnecessary rows

Since the DataFrame contains more than a million rows for small fires and they're probably not going to enhance your analysis, it makes sense to drop the rows for fires that are smaller than some cutoff point. In this analysis, that cutoff point is 10 acres so the first example in part 2 of figure 13-2 drops the rows with fires that are smaller than that. Since that reduces the DataFrame from 473 MB to 70.6 MB, all operations will run faster once they're dropped.

Drop duplicate rows

Duplicate rows are likely whenever multiple agencies report data that's added to a database. That's why the second example in this figure uses the duplicated() method to check for them. In this case, 94 rows are detected and displayed (not shown). Then, the next statement uses the drop_duplicates() method to keep the first row in each set of duplicates, but to drop the duplicates that follow.

Convert dates to datetime objects

The third example in this figure converts the two date columns, which are object types, to datetime types. That way, you can use Python's datetime methods to work with the dates. Here, the infer_datetime_format parameter is set to True so you won't need to worry about specifying the format of the dates.

Drop unnecessary rows

Drop the rows for fires that are less than 10 acres

```
fires = fires[fires.acres_burned >= 10]
```

Check DataFrame info

```
fires.info(memory_usage='deep')
===============================================================
Int64Index: 274170 entries, 16 to 1880441
Data columns (total 8 columns):
 #   Column          Non-Null Count   Dtype
---  ------          --------------   -----
 0   fire_name       128667 non-null  object
 1   acres_burned    274170 non-null  float64
 2   state           274170 non-null  object
 3   latitude        274170 non-null  float64
 4   longitude       274170 non-null  float64
 5   fire_year       274170 non-null  int64
 6   discovery_date  274170 non-null  object
 7   contain_date    137377 non-null  object
dtypes: float64(3), int64(1), object(4)
memory usage: 70.6 MB
```

Drop duplicate rows

See if there are any duplicate rows (this returns 94 rows)

```
fires[fires.duplicated(keep=False)]
```

Drop the duplicates but keep the first duplicate in each set

```
fires = fires.drop_duplicates(keep='first')
```

Convert dates to datetime objects

```
fires.discovery_date = \
    pd.to_datetime(fires.discovery_date, infer_datetime_format=True)
fires.contain_date = \
    pd.to_datetime(fires.contain_date, infer_datetime_format=True)
```

Description

- If you're going to drop rows, you may as well do that first. That will speed up later operations.
- When data is collected from multiple sources, you should check for and drop any duplicate rows.
- If you want to use Python methods to work with dates, you need to convert the date columns from the object type to the datetime type.

Figure 13-2 Clean the data (part 2)

Check for missing contain dates

Part 3 of figure 13-2 delves into the question of why half of the rows in the contain_date column have null values. Here, the first example confirms that there are 136,747 rows that have them.

Then, the second example checks to see whether there are any missing values for fires greater than or equal to 10,000 acres...and there are. In fact, there are quite a few fires of over 100,000 acres that don't have contain dates. Here, you can see that some of them are several years old so these are probably caused by clerical errors: that is, no one ever entered the contain dates for them.

The third example examines the rows that do have contain dates to see whether the contain dates are reasonable. There, the first row shows that it took about two and one-half months to contain a fire in Alaska of more than 600,000 acres. The second row shows that it took 22 days to contain a fire in Oregon of more than 550,000 acres. The third row shows that it took about one and one-half months to contain a fire in Arizona of more than 538,000 acres. And all of those times seem to be reasonable.

With data like that, you can decide how you want to handle the missing data. The four options are given in this figure. First, if you think the data is undependable (and remember that about half the rows don't have contain dates), you can decide that you won't analyze how long it takes to contain a fire. Second, if you decide that you do want to analyze the contain times, you can analyze just the rows that have contain dates. Third, you can decide to fill the missing values with dates that you calculate based on comparable data in the rows that do have values.

Last, you can defer this decision until either the prepare or analyze phase. By then, you should have a better idea of how important the contain dates are to your analysis. And that's what this case study does.

Check for missing contain dates

In all rows

```
fires[fires.contain_date.isnull()]        # returns 136,747 rows
```

In rows for fires greater than or equal to 10,000 acres and sort them

```
fires.query('contain_date == "NaT" & acres_burned >= 10000') \
    .sort_values('acres_burned', ascending=False)
```

	fire_name	acres_burned	state	latitude	longitude	fire_year	discovery_date	contain_date
1639394	Silver	234000.0	NM	32.888889	-107.809722	2013	2013-06-07	NaT
654163	Glass	220000.0	TX	31.742160	-101.043800	2008	2008-02-25	NaT
377944	Camp Creek	175815.0	AK	64.333340	-145.166700	2004	2004-06-23	NaT
512403	Pine Ridge Complex	121687.0	MT	45.922800	-107.856100	2006	2006-07-12	NaT
350860	Moose Lake	117920.0	AK	63.591100	-152.675700	2002	2002-07-17	NaT

Analyze the rows that do have contain dates

```
fires.query('contain_date != "NaT" & acres_burned >= 100') \
    .sort_values('acres_burned', ascending=False)
```

	fire_name	acres_burned	state	latitude	longitude	fire_year	discovery_date	contain_date
211296	Inowak	606945.0	AK	61.982700	-157.085700	1997	1997-06-25	1997-09-09
1579574	Long Draw	558198.3	OR	42.391894	-117.893687	2012	2012-07-08	2012-07-30
1459664	Wallow	538049.0	AZ	33.606111	-109.449722	2011	2011-05-29	2011-07-12
305585	Boundary	537627.0	AK	65.266300	-146.885800	2004	2004-06-13	2004-09-30
1215267	Minto Flats South	517078.0	AK	64.746700	-149.504700	2009	2009-06-21	2009-09-11

Four ways to handle the missing values

- Don't consider the contain dates in your analysis because the data is incomplete.
- If you're going to include the contain dates in your analysis, only analyze the rows that have contain dates.
- Based on the contain dates in the rows that do have them, calculate appropriate values for the contain dates in the rows that have missing values.
- Defer this decision until you prepare or analyze the data. As you do that, you'll get a better idea of whether the contain dates are important to your analysis.

Save the DataFrame

```
fires.to_pickle('fires_clean.pkl')
```

Description

- About half the rows in the Fires data don't have contain dates. Then, you can either work around that or calculate appropriate contain dates for those rows.

Figure 13-2 Clean the data (part 3)

Prepare the data

When you prepare the data, you usually start by adding any columns that you're going to need when you analyze the data. Then, you consider whether the DataFrame needs any other preparation before you start your analysis.

Add fire_month and days_burning columns

The first example in figure 13-3 adds two columns to the DataFrame. First, it adds a fire_month column so the data can be summarized by month. To do that, it uses the month attribute of the datetime object for the discovery_date column.

Next, it adds a days_burning column by subtracting the discovery date from the contain date in each row. Then, it uses the days attribute of the result (note that the entire subtract operation is enclosed in parentheses) to convert the result to the number of days. At this point, those are the only new columns that seem to be needed.

Examine the contain_date and days_burning columns

Of course, the issue of missing contain dates remains, which also means that there will be missing data for the days_burning column. So, the next example in this figure gets the statistics for that column. Here, you can see that 75% of the fires burn for zero or 1 days, and the mean (or average) number of days that a fire burns is 3.25. And yet, the maximum fire length is 1,881 days...or more than 5 years!

Since that seems curious, the next example displays the data for fires of 100 or more acres, but sorted into descending sequence by days burning. Here, the first row is for the fire that took 1,881 days to contain... but it's just 120 acres. And the second row is for a fire that took 1,101 days to contain... but it's just 100 acres. At this point, you have to ask whether this data is so questionable that there's no point in trying to analyze it.

Add fire_month and days_burning columns

```
fires['fire_month'] = fires.discovery_date.dt.month
fires['days_burning'] = (fires.contain_date - fires.discovery_date).dt.days
```

Examine the data in the days_burning column

```
fires.days_burning.describe()
=============================
count    137376.000000
mean          3.254520
std          16.052833
min           0.000000
25%           0.000000
50%           0.000000
75%           1.000000
max        1881.000000
Name: days_burning, dtype: float64
```

Take a closer look at the data for fires greater than or equal to 100 acres

```
fires.query('acres_burned >= 100')[['fire_name','acres_burned', \
    'discovery_date','contain_date','days_burning']] \
    .sort_values('days_burning', ascending=False)
```

	fire_name	acres_burned	discovery_date	contain_date	days_burning
356156	Buenavista	120.0	2000-08-07	2005-10-01	1881.0
305237	Kiliovilik	100.0	2001-06-11	2004-06-16	1101.0
357487	Road 09-08 Wf	900.0	2006-03-05	2008-03-09	735.0
1324066	Jims Branch	158.0	1994-11-05	1996-11-06	732.0
1227849	30305	250.0	2003-03-25	2005-03-25	731.0
...	...	...	...	...	...
1879328	None	149.0	2013-05-28	NaT	NaN
1879498	Trabing	630.0	2008-06-20	NaT	NaN
1879564	Forty Nine	311.0	2009-08-30	NaT	NaN
1879892	Red	134.0	2015-06-21	NaT	NaN
1879968	Popcorn	3000.0	2008-06-22	NaT	NaN

54093 rows × 5 columns

Save the DataFrame

```
fires.to_pickle('fires_prepared.pkl')
```

Description

- When you prepare the data, you can start by adding any columns you might want to use in your analysis. Then, you can decide what else you need to do.
- In this case, many of the values in the contain date and days burning columns are missing or seem to be inaccurate, so you may decide not to include them in your analysis.

Figure 13-3 Prepare the data

Analyze the data

When you analyze the data, you start by trying to understand it. One way to do that is to get the statistics for the numeric columns. Another way is to plot the data in a variety of ways so you can more easily see the relationships between the data. It also makes sense to start by plotting just a portion of the data instead of all the data. That can show relationships that aren't apparent in plots for the full dataset. The figures that follow are intended to give you ideas for how the analysis might proceed.

Analyze the data for California

Part 1 of figure 13-4 starts by analyzing the data for California. Here, the first example uses the query() method to select the rows for California and the describe() method to get the statistics for the numeric columns. This shows that there's a big disparity between the fire sizes and the days burning. For instance, the mean fire size is about 882 acres, the max is over 315,000 acres, and 75% of the fires are 135 acres or less. Remember too that the fires under 10 acres in size have already been dropped from the DataFrame.

The second example in this figure plots the maximum fire size by year. Here, again, a query() method selects the rows for just California. Then, the groupby() method groups the rows by fire year. The max() method gets the maximum value of the fire size for each year. And the plot() method makes a bar chart of the maximum values in sequence by year. This chart shows that four fires have gone over 200,000 acres since 2003, and none had gone over 150,000 acres before that.

The third example is similar, but it plots the mean and median fire sizes by year. To do that, it uses an agg() method, followed by the plot() method. Here, you can see that there's an upward trend to the mean size of the fires. By contrast, the median has stayed about the same over the years, which means that hundreds of small fires are averaged in with relatively few large fires.

Analyze the data for California

Get the statistics

```
fires.query('state == "CA"')[['acres_burned','days_burning']].describe().T
```

	count	mean	std	min	25%	50%	75%	max
acres_burned	14299.0	881.934274	7342.398281	10.0	15.0	39.0	135.0	315578.8
days_burning	6733.0	5.387197	28.591571	0.0	0.0	1.0	3.0	1881.0

Plot the maximum fire size by year

```
fires.query('state == "CA"') \
    .groupby('fire_year').acres_burned.max() \
    .plot.bar(ylabel='acres_burned',
              title='Largest Fire in California by Year')
```

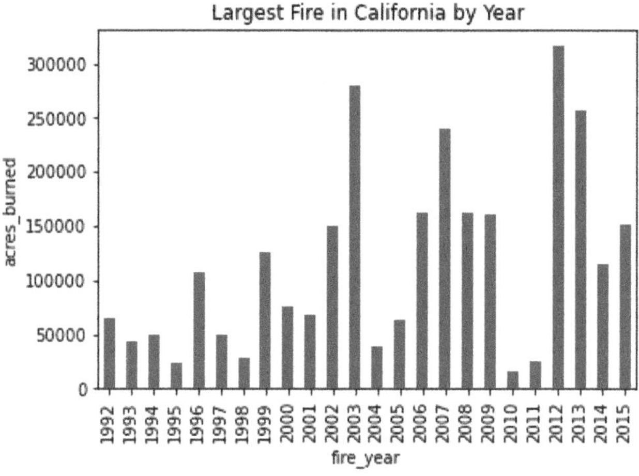

Plot the mean and median fire size by year

```
fires.query('state == "CA"') \
    .groupby('fire_year').acres_burned.agg(['mean','median']) \
    .plot(title='Mean and Median Fires Sizes in California by Year')
```

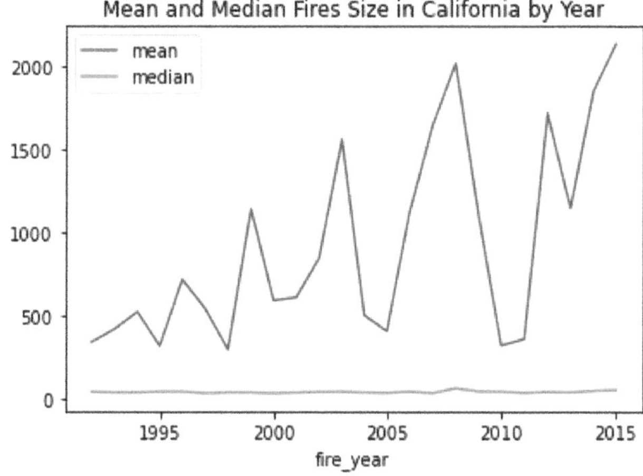

Figure 13-4 Analyze the data (part 1)

Two more plots for California fires

Part 2 of this figure keeps the California analysis going. In the first example, the fires are grouped by fire month, and the count of the fires is plotted by month. This shows that most fires start in July, and the large majority start in either June, July, or August.

Of course, it would be easy to modify this Python code to plot the mean, median, or other statistic by month. Or, if you want to plot two or more statistics at the same time, you can use an agg() method as shown in the last example in the previous figure. These plots might give a different picture of what the worst fire months are.

The second example in this figure creates a box plot for fires over 10,000 acres in each month of the year. This time, Seaborn is used to create the plot because it's easier to do with Seaborn than Pandas. This plot is revealing because it shows that 75% of the fires over 10,000 acres (the third quartile) in even the worst months are less than 50,000 acres, and the maximum sizes are less than 100,000 acres. But that's not counting the outliers, which range from the maximums to more than 300,000 acres.

Two more plots for California fires

Plot the fire count by month

```
fires.query('state == "CA"') \
    .groupby('fire_month').acres_burned.count() \
    .plot.bar(title='Number of Fires by Month in California')
```

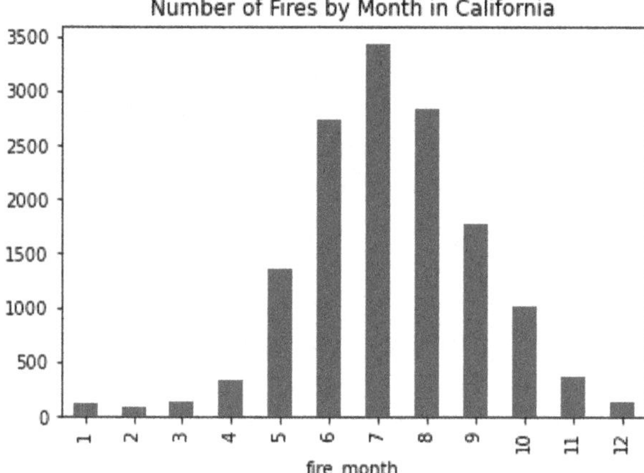

Use Seaborn to create a box plot for fires over 10,000 acres by month

```
import seaborn as sns
sns.catplot(data=fires.query('state == "CA" & acres_burned >= 10000'),
            kind='box', x='fire_month', y='acres_burned')
```

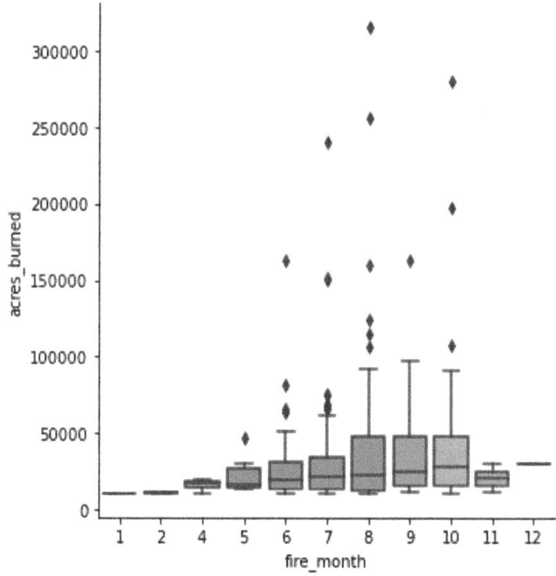

Description

- When you start an analysis, it often makes sense to work with a small portion of the data, like the data for one state, because that can make the data easier to understand.

Figure 13-4 Analyze the data (part 2)

Rank the states by total acres burned

Part 3 of figure 13-4 continues this analysis by finding the 10 states that have the largest total of fire sizes. It starts by creating a DataFrame named fires_states that contains one row for each state that contains the sum of the fire sizes. To do that, it uses the groupby(), sum(), and to_frame() methods.

Next, a state_rank column is added to the fires_states DataFrame. To do that, the code uses the rank() method to add the rank for each state in descending order. In other words, the state with the largest total is ranked 1, the state with the second largest total is ranked 2, and so on. Then, the next statement sorts the fires_states DataFrame by rank, and the head() method displays the first five rows of the DataFrame. There, you can see that Alaska has the largest sum of fires so it ranks number 1, Idaho is 2, and California is 3.

The last example in this figure plots the total acres burned for just the top 10 states. To do that, it uses the query() method to select the top 10 states and the plot method to make a bar chart from them. In the upper-left corner of the plot, you can see this code: 1e7. That refers to the exponent for the labels on the y-axis, which means that the actual value for 3.0 is 3 followed by 7 zeros, or 30,000,000. Remember, though, that this chart represents all the acres burned in each state from 1992 through 2015.

Rank the states by total acres burned

Get the sum of the fire sizes for each state

```
fires_states = fires.groupby('state').acres_burned.sum().to_frame()
```

Add the rank for each state based on its total fire acres and sort by rank

```
fires_states['state_rank'] = \
    fires_states['acres_burned'].rank(ascending=False)
fires_states.sort_values('state_rank', inplace=True)
fires_states.head()
```

state	acres_burned	state_rank
AK	3.222601e+07	1.0
ID	1.366231e+07	2.0
CA	1.261078e+07	3.0
TX	9.588463e+06	4.0
NV	9.006310e+06	5.0

Plot the total fire acres for the top 10 states

```
fires_states.query('state_rank <= 10') \
    .plot.bar(y='acres_burned', ylabel='ten millions of acreas',
              title='Total Acres Burned in the Top 10 States')
```

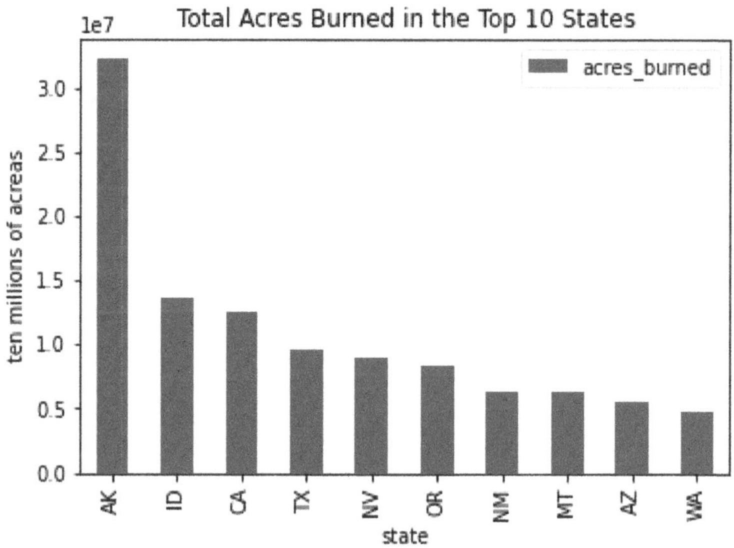

Description

- When you aggregate the sum of the fire sizes for each state and then add a ranking column, you can plot the fire sizes in order by rank.

Figure 13-4 Analyze the data (part 3)

Prepare a DataFrame for total acres burned by year within state

Now that you have seen the sum of the acres burned by state, suppose you would like to see how those sums change for each state in each year. To do that, you need to create a DataFrame that contains that data. Part 4 of figure 13-4 shows how.

Here, the first example creates a DataFrame named fires_states_years that contains the sum of the fires for each year in each state. To do that, it uses the groupby() method to group the rows by fire year within state, the sum() method to total the fire sizes, and the to_frame() method to create the DataFrame.

Then, the next example uses the join() method to join the new DataFrame with the fires_states DataFrame in the previous figure. This joins the two DataFrames based on the values in the state column. Specifically, this combines the acres burned by year column of the fires_states_years DataFrame with the total acres burned and rank columns of the fires_states DataFrame. It also uses the lsuffix and rsuffix parameters to make the names for the acres burned columns more descriptive and to prevent conflicts between columns with the same name. You can see the first four rows of the resulting DataFrame after the code.

Prepare a DataFrame for the top 4 states

Now suppose that you would like to create a plot that shows how the fire totals for the top 4 states vary by year. To do that, you can start by preparing a DataFrame for that data. This is illustrated by the last example in this figure. After the query() method selects the rows for the top 4 states, the index is reset, so the data is ready for plotting.

Prepare a DataFrame for total acres burned by year within state

Get the fire sums by year within each state

```
fires_states_years = \
    fires.groupby(['state','fire_year']).acres_burned.sum().to_frame()
fires_states_years.head(4)
```

state	fire_year	acres_burned
AK	1992	142444.7
	1993	686630.5
	1994	261604.7
	1995	43762.6

Join the fires_states_years and the fires_states DataFrames

```
fires_states_years = fires_states_years.join(fires_states,
    lsuffix='_by_year', rsuffix='_total')
fires_states_years.head(4)
```

state	fire_year	acres_burned_by_year	acres_burned_total	state_rank
AK	1992	142444.7	3.222601e+07	1.0
	1993	686630.5	3.222601e+07	1.0
	1994	261604.7	3.222601e+07	1.0
	1995	43762.6	3.222601e+07	1.0

Prepare a DataFrame for the top 4 states

```
fires_states_top4 = fires_states_years.query('state_rank <= 4')
fires_states_top4 = fires_states_top4.reset_index()
fires_states_top4.head(4)
```

	state	fire_year	acres_burned_by_year	acres_burned_total	state_rank
0	AK	1992	142444.7	3.222601e+07	1.0
1	AK	1993	686630.5	3.222601e+07	1.0
2	AK	1994	261604.7	3.222601e+07	1.0
3	AK	1995	43762.6	3.222601e+07	1.0

Description

- If you want to plot data that's obtained by two different groupings, it's sometimes easiest to join the DataFrames that contain the data.

Figure 13-4 Analyze the data (part 4)

Plot the acres burned total by year for the top 4 states

Part 5 of figure 13-4 shows how to plot the acres burned total by year for each of the top 4 states. To do that, it uses the Seaborn relplot() method. Here, the data parameter is set to the fires_states_top4 DataFrame, and the kind parameter is set to line. Then, the x-axis is set to the year and the y-axis is set to the number of acres burned. Last, because the hue and col parameters are set to state, each of the four states will have its own color and subplot.

To enhance the chart with a title and axis labels, the FacetGrid object that's returned by the relplot() method is assigned to a variable named g. Then, the fig.suptitle() method is used to set the title for the chart, and two of the Axes methods are used to set the labels for the x- and y-axis.

In the plot for this statement, you can see that there's one subplot for each of the four states in the DataFrame: Alaska, California, Idaho, and Texas. Then, if you study the subplots, you can see that Alaska had its worst fire years in the mid-2000s. You can also see that there seems to be a slight upward trend in the other three states. But that's hard to tell.

Here again, the notation in the upper-left corner of the plot tells you what the values on the y-axis represent. Since the notation is 1e6, a value of 2 means that the actual value is 2 followed by 6 zeros, or 2,000,000,

Plot the acres burned total by year for the top 4 states

```
g = sns.relplot(data=fires_states_top4, kind='line',
    x='fire_year', y='acres_burned_by_year', hue='state',
    col='state', col_wrap=2, legend=False)
g.fig.suptitle('Total Acres Burned by Year in the Top 4 States', y=1.025)
for ax in g.axes.flat:
    ax.set_xlabel('Fire Year')
    ax.set_ylabel('Millions of Acres')
```

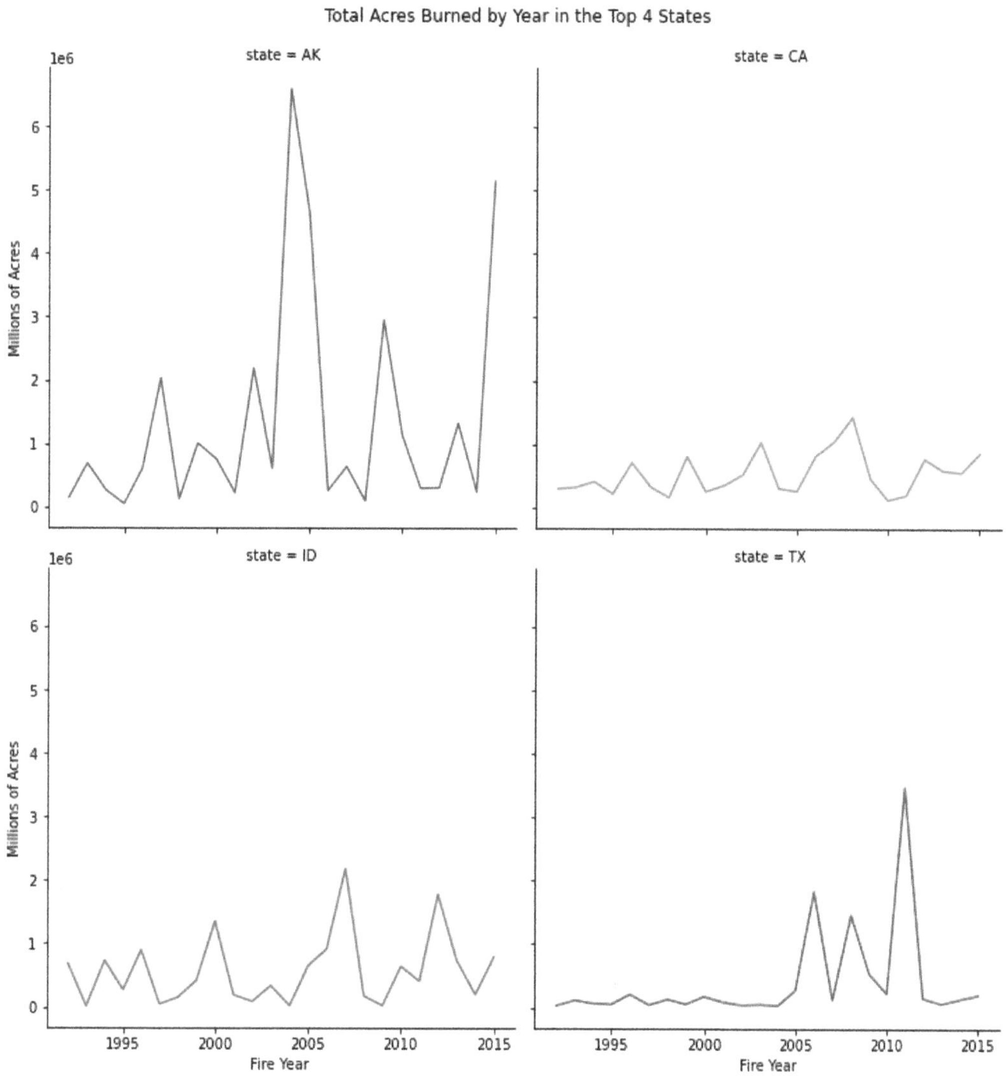

Figure 13-4 Analyze the data (part 5)

Review the 20 largest fires in California

Part 6 of figure 13-4 shows how to review the 20 largest fires in California. In the first example, the query() and nlargest() methods are used to create a DataFrame named top_fires that contains the 20 largest fires in California. Then, the fires in that DataFrame are sorted by acres burned in descending sequence, and four of the columns and ten of the rows in that DataFrame are displayed.

Here, you can see that the largest fire was in 2012, burned over 315,000 acres, and burned for 71 days. You can also see that the tenth largest fire was in 2002, burned over 150,000 acres, and burned for 38 days.

Then, the second example in this figure plots those fires with fire year on the x-axis and acres burned on the y-axis. The resulting plot shows that 4 of the 5 largest fires occurred after the year 2006, and only one occurred before 2006.

Review the 20 largest fires in California

List the fires

```
top_fires = fires.query('state == "CA"').nlargest(20, columns='acres_burned')
top_fires.sort_values('acres_burned', ascending=False)
top_fires[['fire_year','fire_name','acres_burned','days_burning']].head(10)
```

	fire_year	fire_name	acres_burned	days_burning
1572842	2012	Rush	315578.8	71.0
163770	2003	Cedar	280059.0	10.0
1641750	2013	Rim	255858.0	68.0
24834	2007	Zaca	240207.0	60.0
26363	2007	Witch	197990.0	10.0
27901	2008	Basin Complex	162818.0	36.0
14835	2006	Day	162702.0	56.0
41296	2009	Station	160371.0	27.0
1793232	2015	Rough	151623.0	98.0
152416	2002	Mcnally	150696.0	38.0

Plot the fires

```
top_fires.sort_values('fire_year').plot.bar(
    x='fire_year', y='acres_burned', title='Largest Fires in California by Year')
```

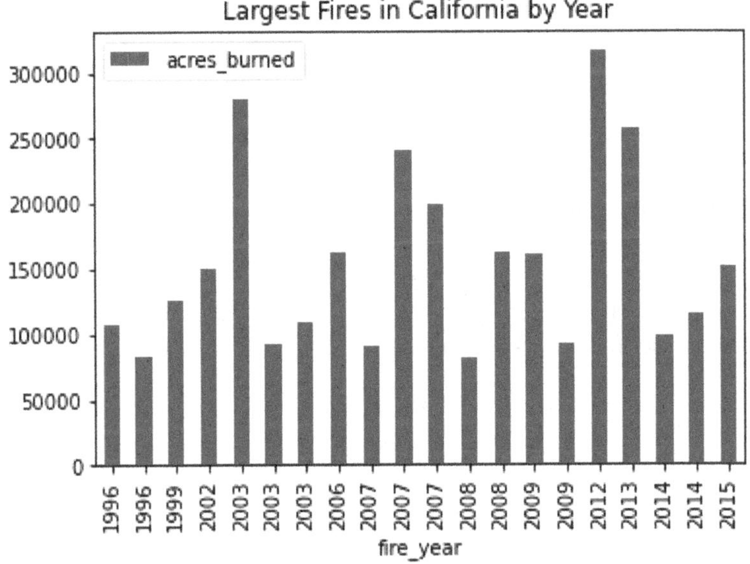

Figure 13-4 Analyze the data (part 6)

Use GeoPandas to plot the fires on a map

Of course, it would be nice to be able to plot the locations of the fires on maps of the states that they're in so you can see exactly where they are. It would also be nice to be able to plot all of the fire locations on a map of the United States. The good news is that you can do that by using a module called GeoPandas. Figure 13-5 shows how.

Before you can use GeoPandas, though, you need to install it on your computer. To do that, you can use the Anaconda prompt as shown in the appendixes of this book.

Use GeoPandas to plot the California map

To plot the locations of fires on a map, you start by creating two GeoDataFrame objects. The first one is for the fire locations. The second one is for the map.

So, the first example in this figure starts by creating a Pandas DataFrame for the California fires in 2015. Then, it creates a GeoDataFrame named fire_locations for those fires. Note here that the geometry parameter of the constructor uses the latitude and longitude columns of the DataFrame to create the geographical points for the fire locations.

The next step is to create a GeoDataFrame for the map of California, as shown by the second example in this figure. Here, the first statement uses the GeoPandas read_file() method to import all of the maps for the United States into a GeoDataFrame named usa. The data for these maps is stored in a shape file named named states.shp that's in a subfolder named Maps. This shape file is included with the download for this book, but you can find shape files for other countries or the entire world by searching the Internet.

After creating the GeoDataFrame for the United States, the second example selects the California map from that GeoDataFrame by filtering it with the STATE_ABBR column set to "CA". The result is a GeoDataFrame named ca_map.

At that point, you can use the GeoPandas plot() method to plot the California map without any data. This is illustrated by the third example. Here, the color and edgecolor parameters set the colors for the interior and border of the map.

Create a GeoDataFrame for the California fires

Create a DataFrame for the California fires in 2015

```
fires_CA_2015 = fires.query('fire_year == 2015 & state == "CA"')
```

Create a GeoDataFrame for those fires

```
import geopandas as geo
fire_locations = geo.GeoDataFrame(fires_CA_2015,
    geometry=geo.points_from_xy(fires_CA_2015.longitude, fires_CA_2015.latitude))
```

Get a California map from Geopandas

Create a GeoDataFrame for the maps of the United States

```
usa = geo.read_file('Maps/states.shp')
usa.head()
```

	STATE_NAME	DRAWSEQ	STATE_FIPS	SUB_REGION	STATE_ABBR	geometry
0	Hawaii	1	15	Pacific	HI	MULTIPOLYGON (((-160.07380 22.00418, -160.0497...
1	Washington	2	53	Pacific	WA	MULTIPOLYGON (((-122.40202 48.22522, -122.4628...
2	Montana	3	30	Mountain	MT	POLYGON ((-111.47543 44.70216, -111.48080 44.6...
3	Maine	4	23	New England	ME	MULTIPOLYGON (((-69.77728 44.07415, -69.85993 ...
4	North Dakota	5	38	West North Central	ND	POLYGON ((-98.73044 45.93827, -99.00683 45.939...

Create a GeoDataFrame for the map of California

```
ca_map = usa[usa.STATE_ABBR == 'CA']
```

Use Geopandas to plot the California map

```
ca_map.plot(color='white', edgecolor='black')
```

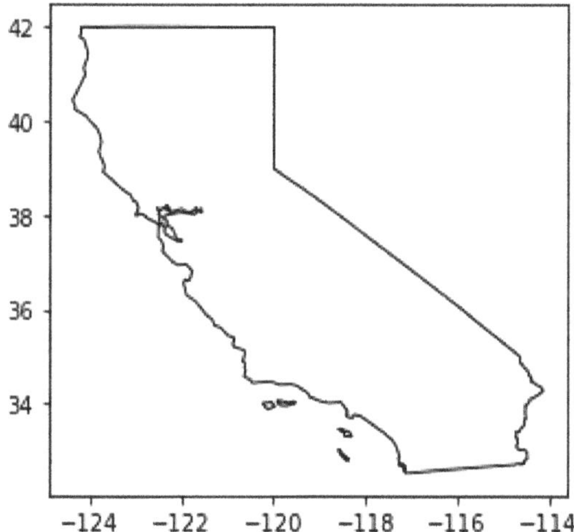

Figure 13-5 Use Geopandas to plot the fires on a map (part 1)

Use GeoPandas or Seaborn to plot the California fires on a map

At this point, you can use either GeoPandas or Seaborn to plot the fires on the map of California. So, in part 2 of figure 13-5, the first example uses GeoPandas to do that, and the second example uses Seaborn.

In the first example, the query() method selects only the fires that burned more than 500 acres from the GeoPandas DataFrame named fire_locations. Then, the GeoPandas plot() method plots the fire locations in that GeoDataFrame. In that method, the color parameter sets the dots in the plot to red, and the ax parameter plots the map of California with a white interior and a black border. This puts the scatter plot of the fires on the map of California.

Although the GeoPandas plot presents some useful information, you can create an even better plot by using Seaborn, as shown by the second example. Here, the first block uses GeoPandas to plot the map of California. Then, the Seaborn scatterplot() method plots the fires that are larger than 500 acres.

In the scatterplot() method, the size parameter is set to the acres_burned column. So, the size of each dot indicates the size of the fire: the larger the dot, the larger the fire. Similarly, the hue parameter is set to the acres_burned column. So, the color of each dot also indicates the size of the fire: the darker the color of the dot, the larger the fire.

Use Geopandas to plot the California fires over 500 acres on a map

```
fire_locations.query('acres_burned > 500').plot(color='red',
    ax=ca_map.plot(color='white', edgecolor='black'))
```

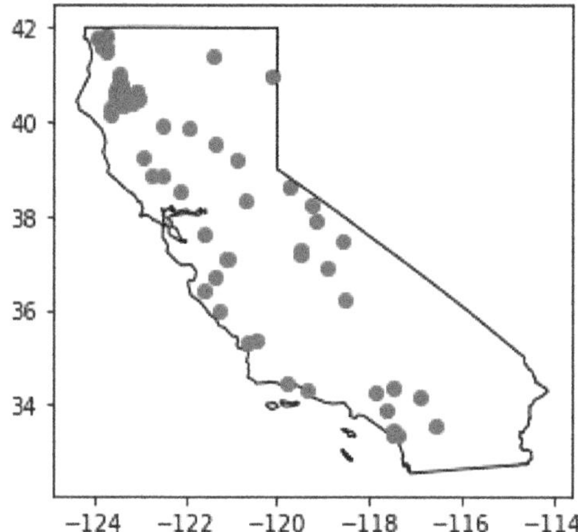

Use Geopandas and Seaborn to plot the California fires over 500 acres

Use Geopandas to plot the map of California

```
ca_map = usa[usa.STATE_ABBR == 'CA']
ca_map.plot(color='white', edgecolor='black')
```

Use Seaborn to plot the fires on the map

```
ax = sns.scatterplot(data=fires_CA_2015.query('acres_burned > 500'),
    x='longitude', y='latitude', size='acres_burned', hue='acres_burned',
    palette='flare')
ax.set(title='California fires in 2015 over 500 acres',
       ylabel=None, xlabel=None)
```

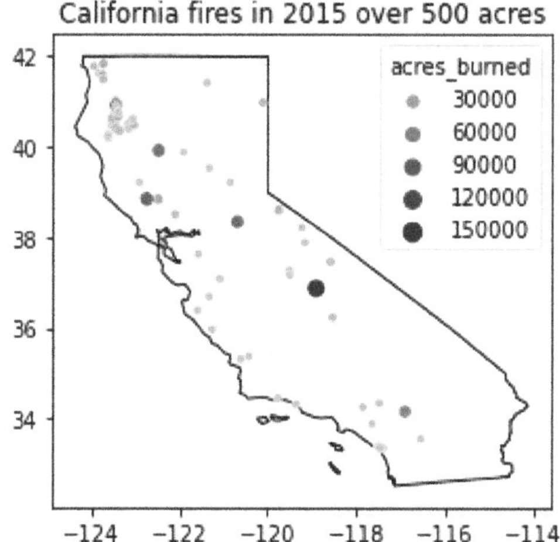

Figure 13-5 Use Geopandas to plot the fires on a map (part 2)

Plot the fires in the continental United States

Part 3 of figure 13-5 shows how to use the techniques you've just learned to plot all fires over 100,000 acres in the continental United States. As the examples in this figure show, you start by creating and plotting a GeoDataFrame for the continental United States. Then, you can use Seaborn to plot the fires on the map.

To create the GeoDataFrame for the map, you would first display the data in the GeoDataFrame named usa to learn that Hawaii has an index of 0 and Alaska has an index of 50. Then, as the first example shows, you can use the loc accessor to create a map that consists of a slice of the states with indexes from 1 to 49. You can also use the GeoPandas plot() method to plot this map.

Once the map has been created, you can use Seaborn to create a scatter plot for the fires, as shown by the second example. To make the data that's being plotted consistent with the map, the data parameter uses the query() method to filter the data so it doesn't include the data for Hawaii and Alaska. It also filters the data so only the fires of more than 100,000 acres are plotted.

In this plot() method, the size and hue parameters are the same as they were for the California plot in the previous figure. But a new parameter, the sizes parameter, is set so the dots range in size from 10 to 100. This gives more contrast to the sizes of the dots, which makes the larger fires more noticeable.

Last, the figsize parameter of the plot() method is used to make the map larger so it's easier to read. Although the dimensions set by this parameter don't always display correctly in JupyterLab, you can check them by saving the plot to a PNG file, as shown by the last example in this figure. Then, you can display that file to see whether the dimensions are the way you want them.

As this plot shows, most fires of over 100,000 acres occur in the western half of the United States. It also shows that Idaho has a high percentage of the large files, especially for the size of the state. This makes sense because, as part 3 of figure 13-4 shows, Idaho had the most acres burned in the continental United States.

Plot the fires in the continental United States

Create a GeoDataFrame for the map and plot it

```
continental_usa = usa.loc[1:49]
continental_usa.plot(color='white', edgecolor='black')
```

Use Seaborn to plot the fires over 100,000 acres on the map

```
ax = sns.scatterplot(
    data=fires.query('acres_burned > 100_000 & state not in ["AK","HI"]'),
    x='longitude', y='latitude', size='acres_burned', sizes=(10,100),
    hue='acres_burned', figsize=(12,5))

ax.set(title='Continental U.S. fires over 100,000 acres',
       ylabel=None, xlabel=None)
```

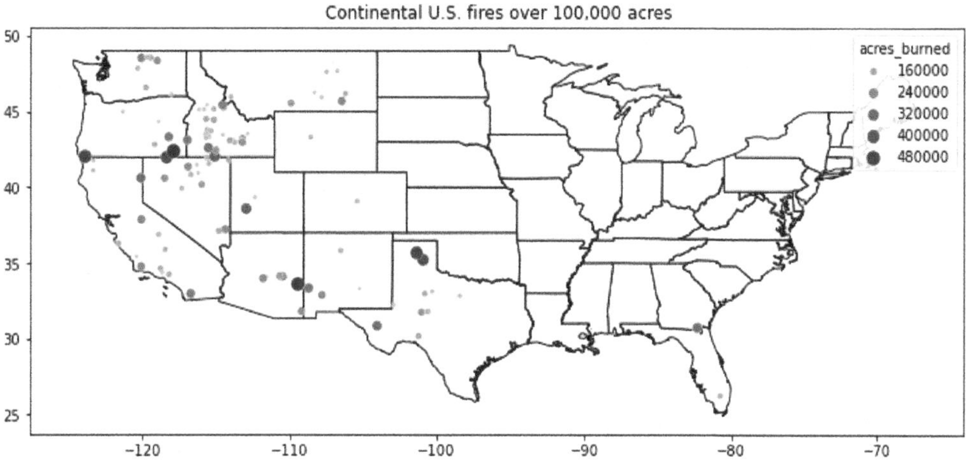

Save the plot to a PNG file

```
ax.get_figure().savefig('us_fires_map.png')
```

Description

- The sizes parameter of the Seaborn plot() method lets you set the range of dot sizes in the scatter plot. This can make it easier to distinguish large fires from smaller ones.
- The dimensions set by the figsize parameter aren't always displayed accurately by JupyterLab, but you can check them by saving the plot to a PNG file and then displaying that file.

Figure 13-5 Use Geopandas to plot the fires on a map (part 3)

Perspective

Like the Polling case study, the Fires case study shows how the Pandas and Seaborn skills can be applied to real-world data. However, because the data for the Fires case study is selected from a database before it's imported into a DataFrame, there's relatively little cleaning and preparation to do.

This case study also illustrates the use of a third-party package called GeoPandas. This is one of several packages that you can use to plot data on a map, and you can search the Internet to find others. Since GeoPandas isn't included as part of the Anaconda distribution, you need to install it before you can use it. To do that, you can follow the instructions in the appendixes of this book.

Exercise 13-1 Another analysis of the Fires data

This exercise guides you through another analysis of the Fires data. Before you do this analysis, you may want to run the Forest Fires case study on your system and experiment with it to make sure you understand how it works.

Get the data

1. Start JupyterLab and open the Notebook named ex_13-1_fires that should be in this folder:
   `exercises/ch13`
2. If you haven't already installed GeoPandas, install it now. To do that, you can use the conda install command as described in the appendixes of this book.
3. Run the first three cells in this Notebook to read the polling data into a DataFrame named fires and to view some information about this DataFrame. Note that the first cell imports the Geopandas library.

Clean and prepare the data

4. Filter the data so it only contains fires for Alaska. Hint: The two-letter abbreviation for Alaska is AK.
5. Add the days_burning column by calculating the number of days between the discovery date and the contain date.
6. Filter the data so it only contains fires that burned for at least 90 days and at least 100 acres.
7. Use the describe() method to search for outliers in the days_burning column. To do that, you can search the Internet to find out how to use the percentiles parameter to add the 90th and 95th percentiles to the output. Note the values for the 95th percentile.
8. Filter the data so it doesn't contain any fires that are outliers in the days_burning column. To do that, you can use the percentile information to choose a good cutoff point. Or, you can use a box plot to determine where the outliers start.
9. Display the first five rows.

Plot the data

10. Create a scatterplot that compares the number of acres burned to the number of days burning.
11. Enhance the scatterplot from the previous step by adding a title for the plot and labels for the x and y axes.
12. Use GeoPandas to read the shapes of the maps for the United States into a GeoDataFrame from this file:
    `data/Maps/states.shp`
13. Filter the data in the GeoDataFrame so it only contains the shape for Alaska.
14. Use the plot() method of the GeoDataFrame to display an outline for the state of Alaska.
15. Use the Seaborn scatterplot() method to display a scatterplot of all of the fires on top of the outline for the state of Alaska. To do that, you code the Seaborn plot immediate after the statement that displays the outline of Alaska and assign the Seaborn scatterplot to the ax variable.
16. Increase the size of the plot by using the figsize parameter of the plot() method that displays the outline of Alaska.
17. Modify the scatterplot to change the dot color based on the number of days the fire has been burning.
18. Modify the colors of the dots to use a redish color for the dots with a darker red for fires that have been burning for a higher number of days.
19. Modify the size of the dots with bigger dots for fires that have been burning for a higher number of days.

Chapter 14

The Social Survey case study

The Social Survey case study analyzes the responses to survey questions that were taken in the United States from 1972 to 2018. This data is available in a Stata file from the National Opinion Research Center in Chicago. The zip file for this data also includes a codebook in PDF format that provides detailed information about the data in the Stata file.

This case study shows how to get useful information from a file that consists of the answers to over 6,000 questions from over 64,000 respondents. If you want, you can open the Notebook for this case study and follow along as you read the text to make sure you understand how everything works.

Introduction to the Social Survey

The Social Survey data provides the answers to a series of survey questions that were asked in the United States over several decades. Not all of the questions were asked every year, however. In fact, most of the questions were in circulation for several years and then phased out in favor of new questions. Although a few of the questions were asked in every survey, those questions were about demographic data such as race or gender.

Download and unzip the zip file for the data

The first example in figure 14-1 shows how to import the modules for this case study and how to download the zip file for the Social Survey. Here, the urlretrieve() method of the request module is used to download the data from the specified URL and save it in a file named "gss_stata_with_codebook.zip".

The second example shows how to unzip the zip file. First, a with statement is used to open the zip file in read mode. Then, the extractall() method of the zip file object is used to extract the files from the zip file and save them in the current directory. After that, a for loop uses the infolist() method of the zip file object to extract and print the name and size of the files in the zip file.

As you can see, there were three files in the zip file: two PDFs and one Stata file (extension DTA). You can also see that the DTA file is so large (about 450MB) that you may not be able to read it into a DataFrame on your computer.

Build a DataFrame for the metadata

Remember from chapter 5, that a Stata file has two parts: the data and the metadata, and you can open either one of these parts. So, because the Stata file is so large, the third example in figure 14-1 reads just the metadata for the file. To do that, it uses the read_dta() method of the pyreadstat module to read the metadata into a DataFrame and assign it to a variable named gss_meta. Then, it prints the number_columns and number_rows items in the metadata, which shows that the Stata file has 6,110 columns and 64,814 rows!

The last example in this figure uses the DataFrame() constructor to build a DataFrame in which the index consists of the column names in the metadata (6,110 of them), and the data consists of the column labels in the metadata. As a result, each row in this DataFrame represents a different column in the dataset. If you study the descriptions in these rows, you can start to see that each column in the dataset contains the responses to a survey question.

Download the zip file for the Social Survey

```
import pandas as pd
import seaborn as sns
import pyreadstat
from urllib import request
from zipfile import ZipFile

zip_url = 'http://gss.norc.org/Documents/stata/gss_stata_with_codebook.zip'
request.urlretrieve(zip_url, filename='gss_stata_with_codebook.zip')
```

Unzip the file

```
with ZipFile('gss_stata_with_codebook.zip', mode='r') as zip:
    zip.extractall()
    for file in zip.infolist():
        print(f'{file.filename:25} - {file.file_size:15,d} Bytes')
===================================================================
Release Notes 7218.pdf    -         296,746 Bytes
GSS_Codebook.pdf          -      37,952,897 Bytes
GSS7218_R3.DTA            -     449,140,819 Bytes
```

Extract the metadata using the pyreadstat module

```
gss_empty, gss_meta = pyreadstat.read_dta('GSS7218_R3.DTA', metadataonly=True)

print('Number of columns: ', gss_meta.number_columns)
print('Number of rows: ', gss_meta.number_rows)
======================================================
Number of columns: 6110
Number of rows: 64814
```

Build a DataFrame of column names and descriptions

```
meta_cols=pd.DataFrame(data=gss_meta.column_labels,
                       index=gss_meta.column_names,
                       columns=['description'])
meta_cols
```

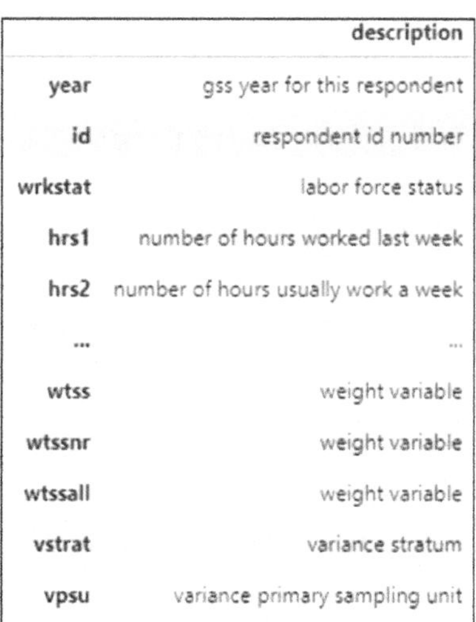

	description
year	gss year for this respondent
id	respondent id number
wrkstat	labor force status
hrs1	number of hours worked last week
hrs2	number of hours usually work a week
...	...
wtss	weight variable
wtssnr	weight variable
wtssall	weight variable
vstrat	variance stratum
vpsu	variance primary sampling unit

Figure 14-1 Download the zip file and build a DataFrame for the metadata

The employment data

The first part of this case study focuses on the employment data that is represented by the wrkstat column. This column contains the responses that were made to a question that asked the respondents about their working status.

Use the codebook and read the data that you want

When you extracted the zip file in the previous figure, one of the files that it contained was the GSS_Codebook in PDF format. This codebook is a reference manual for this dataset, and reference material like this is usually available when a dataset is large or when it consists of public or government data. A typical reference manual contains information such as what each column in the dataset represents, how the data was recorded, and how the data is organized.

When you open the codebook for the Social Survey, the first thing you will notice is that it is over 3,000 pages long. So sometimes, even the reference material is too long to process without a strategy! In that case, you can start by studying the table of contents to get an idea of what's available.

The first example in figure 14-2 shows the start of the table of contents for the Social Survey codebook. Here you see that the survey variables start on page 122. Since the DataFrame for the metadata showed that each variable or column in the codebook represents a question, this is a good place to start.

At the top of page 122, you'll find some basic information on how each question is structured. Then, you'll see the information for the wrkstat question that's shown in the second example in this figure. This summarizes the possible responses, the code for each response, and the total number of responses for each of the years in which the question was asked.

As this example shows, the codebook identifies each question in the dataset with a code that's in this format: [VAR: questionName]. So in this case, the documentation is for a question named "wrkstat" and the responses to the question are stored in the "wrkstat" column.

Once you find the column name for a question, you can use the read_stata() method to get the data for the question from the Stata file. This is illustrated by the last example in this figure. Here, the columns parameter selects the id, year, and wrkstat columns so only these columns are read into the DataFrame named workStatus. After you read the data, you can start your analysis.

The table of contents for the codebook

TABLE OF CONTENTS

The documentation for the first survey question on page 122

1. Last week were you working full time, part time, going to school, keeping house, or what?

HAND CARD A2

CIRCLE ONE CODE ONLY. IF MORE THAN ONE RESPONSE, GIVE PREFERENCE TO SMALLEST CODE NUMBER THAT APPLIES

[VAR: WRKSTAT]

RESPONSE	PUNCH	YEAR														
		1972-82	1982B	1983-87	1987B	1988-91	1993-98	2000-04	2006	2008	2010	2012	2014	2016	2018	ALL
Working full time (ASK HRS1)	1	6150	144	3662	169	2894	5612	4422	2322	1003	917	912	1230	1321	1134	31892
Working part time (ASK HRS1)	2	1174	33	811	39	648	1088	938	440	211	234	226	273	345	259	6719
With a job, but not at work because of temporary illness, vacation, strike (ASK HRS2)	3	321	2	155	2	126	199	192	90	53	33	40	40	57	53	1363
Unemployed, laid off, looking for work (GO TO OCC to COMMUTE)	4	441	25	242	11	130	273	280	148	74	145	104	104	118	84	2179
Retired (ASK EVWORK)	5	1437	38	916	49	842	1412	1221	715	336	319	357	460	574	445	9121
In school (ASK EVWORK)	6	405	11	190	11	215	289	270	140	57	93	70	90	76	81	1998
Keeping house (ASK EVWORK)	7	3507	86	1463	67	973	1264	859	496	227	235	210	263	284	242	10176
Other (SPECIFY AND ASK EVWORK)	8	191	15	103	5	79	194	211	155	60	65	54	76	89	48	1345
No answer	9	0	0	0	0	0	3	1	4	2	3	1	2	3	2	21

REMARKS: Card A2 contained responses for punches 1 through 7. Contents of WRKSTAT, punch 8 (Other, SPECIFY) available from NORC.

Load the data for the wrkstat question into a DataFrame

```
workStatus =
    pd.read_stata('GSS7218_R3.DTA', columns=['id','year','wrkstat'])
workStatus.head()
```

	id	year	wrkstat
0	1	1972	working fulltime
1	2	1972	retired
2	3	1972	working parttime
3	4	1972	working fulltime
4	5	1972	keeping house

Figure 14-2 Use the codebook and read the data that you want

Prepare the data

Suppose that the first goal for the analysis of the wrkstat data is to identify when major changes in employment status have occurred. With that goal in mind, you can think about how you need to shape the data.

Before you start shaping your data, though, you should always check the data types of your columns. So, the first example in figure 14-3 shows the results of the info() method. Here, you can see that the wrkstat column has the category data type.

You may remember from chapter 6, that this data type has index values in the column that point to the categories in a separate table. In this case, the categories are the answers to the questions. In fact, all of the columns that contain answers to multiple-choice questions have the category data type. Although this data type saves a lot of memory, it also presents some complications.

Remember too that the DataFrame currently has a row for every response to a survey question. That means that each row contains the year of the response as well as the index value of the response. So, one of the first things you may want to do is get the total number of responses for each work status. To do that, you can use the value_counts() method with the dropna parameter set to False, as in the second example in this figure.

As you can see, most people either work fulltime, keep house, are retired, or work parttime. You can also see that there are only 21 missing values. As a result, you can safely ignore the rows with those values since there are so few relative to the total number of responses.

The third example in this figure shows how you use the groupby() method to create a DataFrame named statusCounts that summarizes the wrkstat responses by year. In this case, the as_index parameter is set to False because an index will just get in the way when you plot the data. After the data is grouped, the count() method gets the count of each type of response for each year. Last, the column names are set to year, wrkstat, and counts, and the head() method shows what the data looks like now.

View the data types of the columns

```
workStatus.info()
======================================
Data columns (total 3 columns):
 #   Column   Non-Null Count  Dtype
---  ------   --------------  -----
 0   id       64814 non-null  int16
 1   year     64814 non-null  int16
 2   wrkstat  64793 non-null  category
dtypes: category(1), int16(2)
memory usage: 823.2 KB
```

Check the work status data for missing responses

```
workStatus['wrkstat'].value_counts(dropna=False)
================================================
working fulltime    31892
keeping house       10176
retired              9121
working parttime     6719
unempl, laid off     2179
school               1998
temp not working     1363
other                1345
NaN                    21
Name: wrkstat, dtype: int64
```

Add counts by year

```
statusCounts = workStatus.groupby(
    by=['year','wrkstat'], as_index=False).count()
statusCounts.columns = ['year', 'wrkstat', 'counts']
statusCounts.head()
```

	year	wrkstat	counts
0	1972	working fulltime	750
1	1972	working parttime	121
2	1972	temp not working	38
3	1972	unempl, laid off	46
4	1972	retired	144

Figure 14-3 Prepare the wrkstat data

Plot the data and reduce the number of categories

The first example in figure 14-4 shows how to plot the prepared data with the relplot() method. As you can see, the x parameter is the year the survey was taken and the y parameter is the counts for each response. Then, the hue parameter plots each response in a separate line.

Although this plot presents some useful information, the plot lines at the bottom of the chart run together, so the plot is difficult to read. One way to fix that problem is to narrow down the data to just three or four of the categories.

So, the second example in this figure uses the query() method to filter the data to just four categories: working fulltime, working parttime, retired, and unemployed or laid off. Then, this data is stored in a new DataFrame named topCounts.

Recall from the previous figure, though, that the wrkstat column has the category data type. But when you filter categorical data, the categories remain even if there are no values for them. In fact, if you call the value_counts() method as shown in the third example, you will see that all of the categories are still there, even though there are zeros for the four that have been dropped.

The trouble is that these empty categories will be plotted if you don't remove them. That's why the fourth example shows how to remove them. It uses the cat accessor to call the remove_unused_categories() method, which drops any categories that have no values.

Once the data has been filtered and the unused categories have been removed, the plot will be easier to read. But before you plot the data, take a look at the plot in this figure and see whether you notice some strange patterns. For instance, all categories fell in 2009. Since a recession started in 2008, that makes sense for the people working fulltime or parttime. But why would the unemployed and retired counts go down when you would expect them to go up? In the next figure, you'll try to figure out why.

Plot the wrkstat data

```
sns.relplot(data=statusCounts, x='year', y='counts', hue='wrkstat',
            kind='line')
```

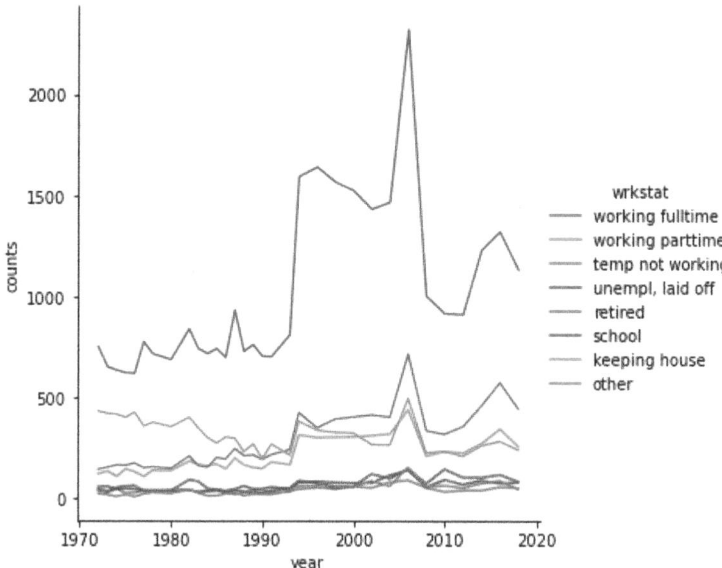

Reduce the number of plotted categories

```
statusCountsTop = statusCounts.query(
    'wrkstat in ["working fulltime", "working parttime", "retired", \
    "unempl, laid off"]').copy()
```

The categories after filtering

```
statusCountsTop.wrkstat.value_counts()
======================================
retired             32
unempl, laid off    32
working parttime    32
working fulltime    32
other                0
keeping house        0
school               0
temp not working     0
Name: wrkstat, dtype: int64
```

Remove unused categories

```
statusCountsTop.wrkstat = statusCountsTop.wrkstat.cat.remove_unused_categories()
statusCountsTop.wrkstat.value_counts()
======================================
retired             32
unempl, laid off    32
working parttime    32
working fulltime    32
Name: wrkstat, dtype: int64
```

Figure 14-4 Plot the data and reduce the number of categories

Plot the total counts of the responses

When surveys are repeated year after year, the number of yearly responses often fluctuates. But this fluctuation can cause problems if the trendlines represent the change in the total count more than the change in the ratio between the responses. That's probably what caused the strange pattern in the chart in the previous figure.

One way to confirm this suspicion is to plot the total counts of the responses by year. Before you can do that, though, you need to add a new column to the DataFrame that represents the total counts. So, the first example in 14-5 shows how to do that. It uses the groupby() and sum() methods to get the total count of the responses by year. The result is stored in a new DataFrame named topCountsByYear.

Then, the second example uses the merge() method to combine the original and new DataFrames into a DataFrame named topCounts. Here, the on parameter is set to year, so the two DataFrames will be merged on that column. In addition, the suffixes parameter is set so the name of the counts column in the topCounts DataFrame will stay the same (an empty string is added to it). But the name of the counts column in the countsByYear DataFrame will be changed to countsTotal ("Total" is added to it).

After the countsByYearPercents DataFrame is prepared, the last example plots the countsTotal column by year. But now, the lines for all four categories overlap because they're the same. And if you compare this plot with the one in figure 14-4, you'll see that the lines in that plot have the same general movement as the countsTotal line. This means that the trends of the lines in figure 14-4 are due more to the changes in the total number of respondents than to the changes in the responses to the question. In the next figure, you will learn how to address this problem.

Count the total number of responses by year

```
topCountsByYear = topCounts.groupby(by=['year'], as_index=False).sum()
topCountsByYear.head()
```

	year	counts
0	1972	1061
1	1973	974
2	1974	964
3	1975	993
4	1976	989

Merge the topCountsByYear DataFrame with the topCounts DataFrame

```
topCounts = topCounts.merge(topCountsByYear, on='year', suffixes=('','Total'))
topCounts.head()
```

	year	wrkstat	counts	countsTotal
0	1972	working fulltime	750	1061
1	1972	working parttime	121	1061
2	1972	unempl, laid off	46	1061
3	1972	retired	144	1061
4	1973	working fulltime	651	974

Plot the data

```
sns.relplot(data=topCounts, x='year', y='countsTotal',
            kind='line')
```

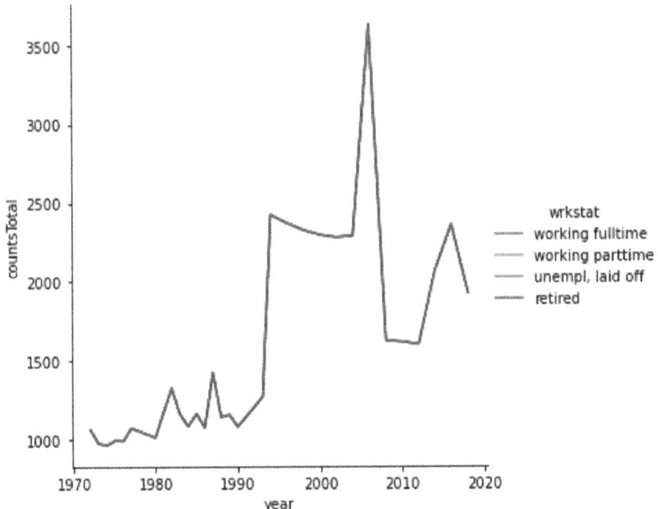

Figure 14-5 Plot the total counts of the responses

Convert the counts to percents and plot them

In the previous figure, you saw the total response counts change so much from year to year that you can't tell whether a change in a work status count is due to the difference in the number of responses or an actual change in the status count.

To better understand that, assume that you want to compare the working status data for two years: one with 100 responses and one with 200. Also, assume that 80 people say they're working fulltime the first year, and 160 people say that the second year. If you compare those numbers directly, the second year has a higher count. But if you look at the counts as a percentage of the total, both are 80%, which means that there was no change.

Figure 14-6 shows how to apply this logic to the wrkstat data. In the first example, a new column named percent is added to the DataFrame. This column treats each response value as a percent of the total count for the year.

Then, the second example plots the percentages instead of the counts. If you compare this plot with the one in figure 14-4, you will see that the new plot accurately identifies some trends. First, the percent of people working fulltime has been declining. Second, the percent of retired people has been rising. Third, the percent of people who are unemployed, laid off, or working parttime has stayed about the same.

Convert each measurement to a percentage of the total

```
topCounts['percent'] = topCounts.counts / topCounts.countsTotal
topCounts.head()
```

	year	wrkstat	counts	countsTotal	percent
0	1972	working fulltime	750	1061	0.706880
1	1972	working parttime	121	1061	0.114043
2	1972	unempl, laid off	46	1061	0.043355
3	1972	retired	144	1061	0.135721
4	1973	working fulltime	651	974	0.668378

Plot the percentage data

```
sns.relplot(data=topCounts, x='year', y='percent', kind='line',
            hue='wrkstat', palette='colorblind')
```

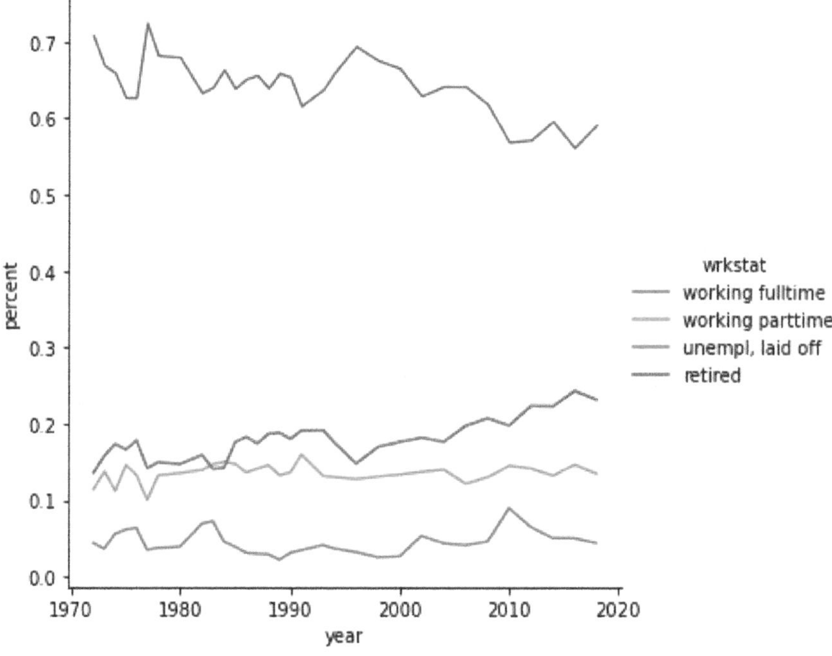

Description

- When plotting data over time, you need to be sure that the sample size for each measurement doesn't fluctuate. If it does, convert each measurement to a percentage of the total number of measurements and plot that number

Figure 14-6 Convert the wrkstat counts to percents and plot them

The work-life balance data

The analysis that you just reviewed identified some trends in the responses to a single question. By contrast, this next analysis tries to get useful information from the responses to several related questions that deal with the balance of work and life.

Search the codebook for small question sets

To find an interesting set of questions, you need to return to the codebook. At first, you may want to analyze the data in small sets of questions because that's easier to do. So to start, you can search the table of contents for question sets that take only a few pages.

To illustrate, the first example in figure 14-7 shows a portion of the table of contents. There, you can see that the Civil Liberties questions take up just 3 pages, from page 2673 to 2676, but the Suicide questions take up 9 pages, from page 2706 to 2715. And if you were to continue down the table of contents, you would see that the Work and Relationships questions take just 2 pages, from 3103 to 3104.

Then, if you go to page 3103 in the codebook, you'll see that there are only three questions in this set. The documentation for the first two are shown in the second example in this figure. Here, the first question is the wkcontct question. This question asks the respondents how often they are contacted for work matters outside of working hours. You can see the wording of this question at the top of the codebook entry.

The other two questions are the talkspvs and effctsup questions. The talkspvs question asks the respondents how comfortable they are with talking to their supervisors about conflicts between their work and personal lives. The effctsup question asks how effective their supervisors are in helping to solve these conflicts.

If you look at the yearly response counts in the codebook, you can see that these questions were only asked in the year 2014. You can also see the counts for each of the responses to the questions. Those are the counts that you'll be analyzing.

Search the table of contents for small question sets

Additional GSS Modules

The first two questions in the Work and Relationships set

Page 3103

WORK AND RELATIONSHIPS
(WKCONTCT-EFFCTSUP)

2056. Some workers must respond to coworkers, supervisors, managers, customers, or clients about work-related matters when they are not working. These contacts may be by phone, text, instant message, email, etc. How often are you contacted about work-related matters when you are not working?

[VAR: WKCONTCT]

RESPONSE	PUNCH	1972-82	1982B	1983-87	1987B	1988-91	1993-98	2000-04	2006	2008	2010	2012	2014	2016	2018	ALL
		YEAR														
Never	1	0	0	0	0	0	0	0	0	0	0	0	401	0	0	401
Less than once a month	2	0	0	0	0	0	0	0	0	0	0	0	214	0	0	214
Once or twice a month	3	0	0	0	0	0	0	0	0	0	0	0	194	0	0	194
Once a week	4	0	0	0	0	0	0	0	0	0	0	0	119	0	0	119
Several times a week	5	0	0	0	0	0	0	0	0	0	0	0	202	0	0	202
Once a day	6	0	0	0	0	0	0	0	0	0	0	0	42	0	0	42
Two or more times a day	7	0	0	0	0	0	0	0	0	0	0	0	65	0	0	65
Don't know	DK	0	0	0	0	0	0	0	0	0	0	0	7	0	0	7
No answer	REF	0	0	0	0	0	0	0	0	0	0	0	2	0	0	2
Not applicable	0	13626	354	7542	353	5907	10334	8394	4510	2023	2044	1974	1292	2867	2348	63568

2057. How comfortable are you talking with your supervisor about conflicts between work and personal or family life

[VAR: TALKSPVS]

RESPONSE	PUNCH	1972-82	1982B	1983-87	1987B	1988-91	1993-98	2000-04	2006	2008	2010	2012	2014	2016	2018	ALL
		YEAR														
Not at all comfortable	1	0	0	0	0	0	0	0	0	0	0	0	139	0	0	139
A little	2	0	0	0	0	0	0	0	0	0	0	0	119	0	0	119
Somewhat	3	0	0	0	0	0	0	0	0	0	0	0	262	0	0	262
Very	4	0	0	0	0	0	0	0	0	0	0	0	337	0	0	337
Extremely	5	0	0	0	0	0	0	0	0	0	0	0	166	0	0	166
Don't know	DK	0	0	0	0	0	0	0	0	0	0	0	5	0	0	5
No answer	REF	0	0	0	0	0	0	0	0	0	0	0	5	0	0	5
Not applicable	0	13626	354	7542	353	5907	10334	8394	4510	2023	2044	1974	1505	2867	2348	63761

Description

- There are three questions in this set that are represented by the wkcontct, talkspvs, and effctsup variables. Each of these questions is about the respondent's work-life relationship.
- This set of questions was only asked in 2014.

Figure 14-7 Search the codebook for small question sets

Read and review the work-life data

The first example in figure 14-8 shows how to read the data for the work-life questions into a DataFrame. Here, the names of the three question columns (wkcontct, talkspvs, and effctsup) are saved in a list. Then, that list is used in the columns parameter of the read_stata() method so only the three columns are read.

But note that the dropna() method is chained to the read_stata() method so any rows with missing values in the three columns aren't included. That's necessary because these questions were only asked in 2014. As a result, there will be rows with missing values for all the other years if you don't drop them. Instead, 1,000 rows are read and all of them have valid responses.

If you study the data, you can see that each response is one of the categories for that column. Then, if you look back to the codebook, you can see that these categories match up with the response values. Remember, though, that these columns have the category data type so the actual values in the columns are index values that point to the categories.

In the second example in this figure, you can see the categories for each question and the distribution of the responses. At this point, this data is ready for plotting.

Read the work-life balance data

```
wlBalanceCols = ['wkcontct','talkspvs','effctsup']
wlBalance = pd.read_stata('GSS7218_R3.DTA', columns=wlBalanceCols).dropna()
wlBalance
```

	wkcontct	talkspvs	effctsup
57062	once or twice a month	very	very
57064	never	very	very
57074	never	very	somewhat
57079	never	somewhat	very
57081	never	very	very
...	...	...	...
59591	once or twice a month	somewhat	somewhat
59595	less than once a month	very	very
59596	never	somewhat	somewhat
59597	once or twice a month	a little	somewhat
59598	never	extremely	very

1000 rows × 3 columns

Identify the response values for each question

```
wlBalance.wkcontct.value_counts()
=================================
never                       329
less than once a month      187
once or twice a month       170
several times a week        145
once a week                  98
two or more times a day      42
once a day                   29
Name: wkcontct, dtype: int64

wlBalance.talkspvs.value_counts()
=================================
very                      333
somewhat                  259
extremely                 165
not at all comfortable    127
a little                  116
Name: talkspvs, dtype: int64

wlBalance.effctsup.value_counts()
=================================
very                    338
somewhat                287
a little                158
extremely               125
not at all effective     92
Name: effctsup, dtype: int64
```

Figure 14-8 Read and review the work-life data

Plot the responses for the first question

Since both the talkspvs and the effctsup columns have five category values that are almost the same, these columns can be plotted together. By contrast, you have to plot the wkcontct column on its own since its category values are different.

The first example in figure 14-9 shows how to prepare the data for the wkcontct column so it can be plotted. First, you use the value_counts() method to count how many times each response occurs. But remember that this method returns a Series so you need to chain the to_frame() method to it if you want to create a DataFrame for the data. Also, because the to_frame() method automatically creates an index for each category, you should chain the reset_index() method to the to_frame() method.

Once the DataFrame has been created, you can use the columns attribute of the new DataFrame to assign new names to the columns. As the DataFrame in this first example shows, the new columns are named "answer" and "count". These names will become the axis labels when you chart the data.

The second example in this figure shows how to create a horizontal bar chart for the wkcontct column. Here, the x-axis shows the counts of the responses to the questions, and the y-axis shows what those responses were. This shows that a relatively low number of people are contacted about work more than once a week when they aren't on the job.

Prepare the data for the wkcontct question

```
workContact = wlBalance.wkcontct.value_counts().to_frame().reset_index()
workContact.columns = ['answer','count']
workContact
```

	answer	count
0	never	329
1	less than once a month	187
2	once or twice a month	170
3	several times a week	145
4	once a week	98
5	two or more times a day	42
6	once a day	29

Plot the data for the wkcontct question

```
g = sns.catplot(data=workContact, x='count', y='answer',
                kind='bar', orient='h', aspect=1.25)

g.set(title="How often are you contacted about work\n" +
            "when you aren't on the job?")
```

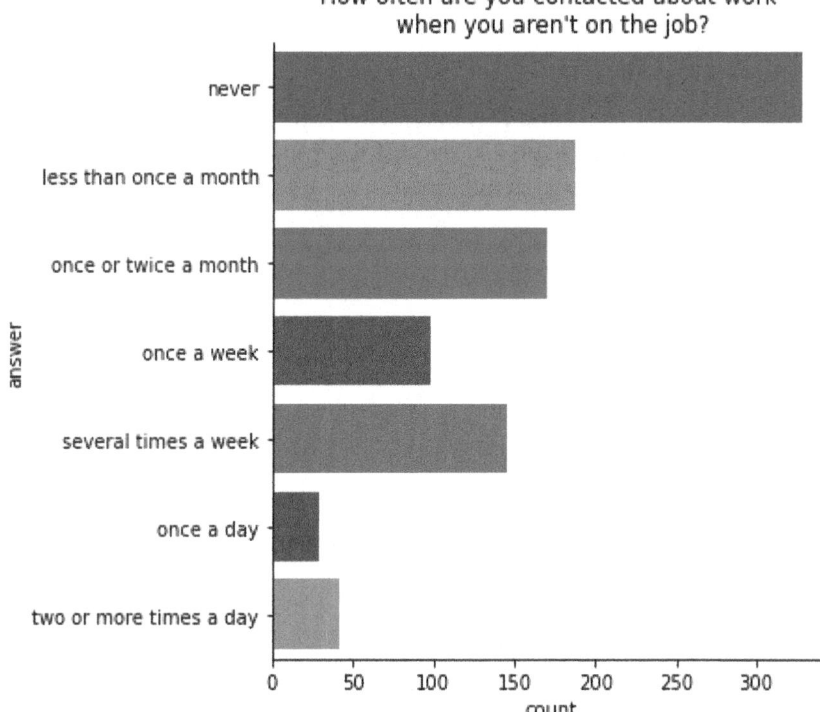

Figure 14-9 Plot the work-life responses for the first question

Plot the responses for the second and third questions

Figure 14-10 shows how to plot the responses for the talkspvs and the effctsup questions. Since both of these questions have the same responses, you can plot them together.

To prepare the data for the plotting, the value_counts() and to_frame() methods are used to create a DataFrame for each question (or column). Since these columns have the category data type, the index for each of the new DataFrames consists of the five valid responses to the question. Then, the index attribute of each DataFrame is used to shorten one of the index values to "not at all", which means that the responses for both questions are now the same.

Next, the two DataFrames are joined to create a new DataFrame named supervisorData based on their indexes, which are the same. But chained to this method is the reset_index() method so the categories aren't used as the index. As you can see, the resulting DataFrame has just 5 rows.

To complete the preparation of the data, you need to use the melt() method to melt the talkspvs and effctsup columns into a single column. That way, you'll be able to plot both questions in a single plot. The melt() method is followed by a statement that uses the columns attribute of the DataFrame to set the names for the three columns. The resulting DataFrame has 10 rows and 3 columns.

Once the data has been prepared, you can plot it as shown in the last example in this figure. Here, the col parameter divides the plot into two subplots, one for each question. And the set_title() method sets the title for each subplot to the question that it answers.

These subplots show that most employees are at least "somewhat" comfortable with their supervisors and feel that their supervisors are at least "somewhat" effective in helping them solve work-life conflicts. But even then, some employees don't feel that way "at all".

Prepare the data for plotting

Create DataFrames for the second and third questions

```
df1 = wlBalance.talkspvs.value_counts().to_frame()
df1 = df1.rename(index={'not at all comfortable':'not at all'})

df2 = wlBalance.effctsup.value_counts().to_frame()
df2 = df2.rename(index={'not at all effective':'not at all'})
```

Join the DataFrames

```
supervisorData = df1.join(df2).reset_index()
supervisorData.head()
```

	index	talkspvs	effctsup
0	very	333	338
1	somewhat	259	287
2	extremely	165	125
3	not at all	127	92
4	a little	116	158

Melt the data in the combined DataFrame

```
supervisorData = pd.melt(supervisorData, id_vars='index',
                         value_vars=['talkspvs', 'effctsup'])
supervisorData.columns = ['answer','question','responseCount']
```

Plot the data for the questions

```
g = sns.catplot(data=supervisorData, x='answer', y='responseCount',
                kind='bar', col='question', aspect=1.25, col_wrap=2)
titles = ['How comfortable are you talking with your supervisor?',
          'How helpful is your supervisor at resolving work-life conflicts?']
for i, ax in enumerate(g.axes.flat):
    ax.tick_params('x',labelrotation=45)
    ax.set_title(titles[i])
```

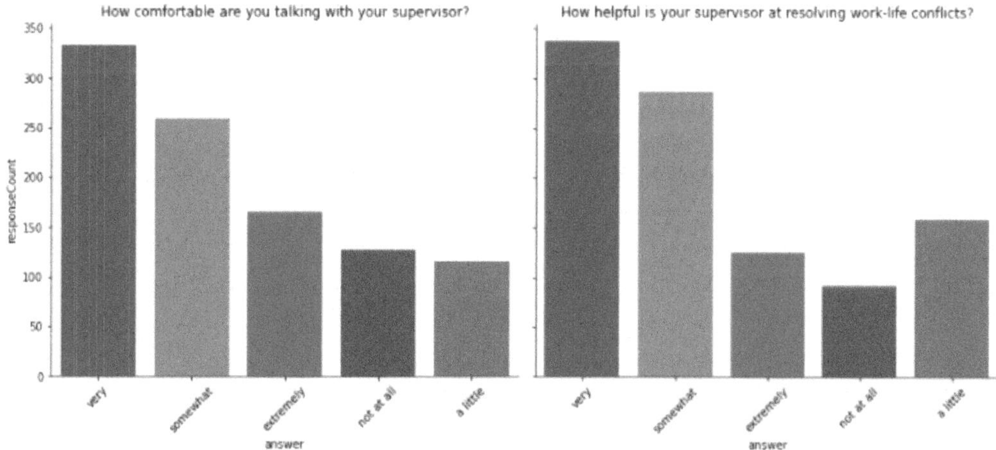

Figure 14-10 Plot the responses for the second and third questions

How to expand the scope of the analysis

So far, you have seen how to analyze the data for single questions as well as the data for a small set of related questions. Now, you'll learn how to expand the scope of your analyses by combining survey data with *demographic data* like gender, race, and location. Typically, demographic questions are asked of every respondent along with rotating question sets.

Use the codebook to find related columns

Since the demographic questions are asked of every respondent, one way to find them is to look for columns with no missing values. The first example in figure 14-11 shows how to do that. To start, it reads the entire Stata file. Then, it uses the dropna() method to drop all columns (axis=1) that have missing values.

This shows that there are only 16 columns in the entire Stata file with no missing values, and you can guess the content of most of them. For instance, year, sex, and region clearly provide demographic data. For the columns that aren't obvious, like the xnorcsiz column, you can search the codebook for more information. To illustrate, the second example in this figure shows the results of a search for the region column.

Before you try reading the entire Stata file, though, be warned! This file is so large that reading it requires about 3 gigabytes of memory. As a result, many personal computers won't be able to read it, and JupyterLab may crash if you try to read it.

Even if you can't read the entire Stata file and you don't have the data that's shown in the table in this figure, you can still use the codebook to find the questions that you want to analyze. And you can include the demographic questions in the data for your analysis along with the other questions.

Read the entire dataset and find the columns with no missing values

```
allData = pd.read_stata('GSS7218_R3.DTA')
allData.dropna(axis=1)
```

	year	id	sex	race	reg16	region	xnorcsiz	srcbelt	size	pres16	formwt	sample	oversamp	wtss	wtssnr	wtssall
0	1972	1	2	1	2	3	3	3	72	0	1.0	1	1.0	1.000000	1.000000	0.444600
1	1972	2	1	1	3	3	3	3	72	0	1.0	1	1.0	1.000000	1.000000	0.889300
2	1972	3	2	1	3	3	3	3	72	0	1.0	1	1.0	1.000000	1.000000	0.889300
3	1972	4	2	1	0	3	3	3	72	0	1.0	1	1.0	1.000000	1.000000	0.889300
4	1972	5	2	1	3	3	3	3	72	0	1.0	1	1.0	1.000000	1.000000	0.889300
...	...	...	...	...	...	...	...	...	...	...	...	...	...	...	...	...
64809	2018	2344	2	1	3	1	10	6	1	0	1.0	10	1.0	0.471499	0.482425	0.471499
64810	2018	2345	2	1	1	1	10	6	1	2	1.0	10	1.0	0.942997	0.964850	0.942997
64811	2018	2346	2	1	1	1	10	6	1	3	1.0	10	1.0	0.942997	0.964850	0.942997
64812	2018	2347	1	1	2	1	10	6	1	2	1.0	10	1.0	0.942997	0.964850	0.942997
64813	2018	2348	2	1	1	1	10	6	1	0	1.0	10	1.0	0.471499	0.482425	0.471499

64814 rows × 16 columns

Search for the columns in the codebook

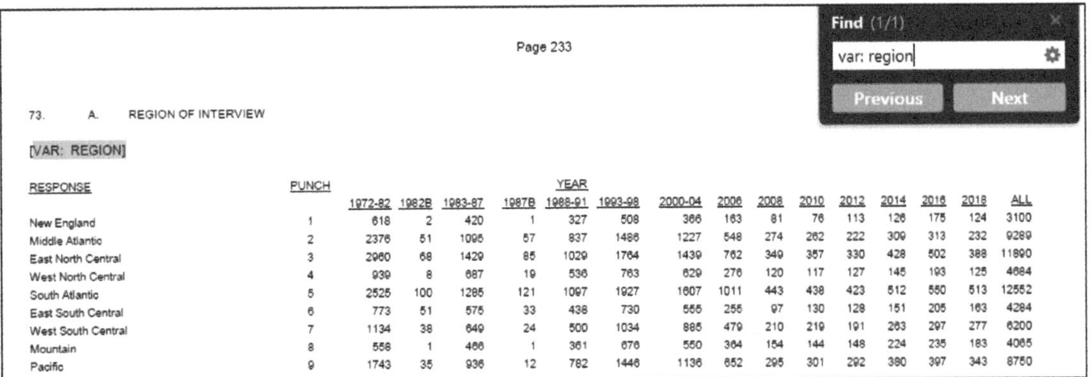

Page 233

73. A. REGION OF INTERVIEW

[VAR: REGION]

RESPONSE	PUNCH	YEAR 1972-82	1982B	1983-87	1987B	1988-91	1993-98	2000-04	2006	2008	2010	2012	2014	2016	2018	ALL
New England	1	618	2	420	1	327	508	366	163	81	76	113	126	175	124	3100
Middle Atlantic	2	2376	51	1095	57	837	1486	1227	548	274	262	222	309	313	232	9289
East North Central	3	2960	68	1429	85	1029	1764	1439	762	349	357	330	428	502	388	11890
West North Central	4	939	8	687	19	536	763	629	276	120	117	127	145	193	125	4684
South Atlantic	5	2525	100	1285	121	1097	1927	1607	1011	443	438	423	512	550	513	12552
East South Central	6	773	51	575	33	438	730	565	255	97	130	128	151	205	163	4284
West South Central	7	1134	38	649	24	500	1034	885	479	210	219	191	263	297	277	6200
Mountain	8	558	1	466	1	361	676	550	364	154	144	148	224	235	183	4065
Pacific	9	1743	35	936	12	782	1446	1136	652	295	301	292	380	397	343	8750

Description

- Reading the entire Social Survey dataset requires about 3 gigabytes of memory. Because of that, some computers won't be able to read it.
- Reading the dataset and finding the columns that don't have any null values shows that only the 16 columns shown above don't have any null values.
- Once you know which columns don't have any null values, you can search the codebook to determine what each column represents and whether it will be useful for your analysis.
- It often makes sense to combine the *demographic data* (like gender, race, and region) with the data for the other types of questions.

Figure 14-11 Use the codebook to find related columns

Use the codebook to find follow-up questions

Some of the questions in the codebook suggest follow-up questions that the surveyor can ask. This is illustrated in the first example in figure 14-12, which shows the documentation for the WRKSTAT question. Here, you can see that many of the responses suggest follow-up questions. For instance, the "working full time" response suggests "ASK HRS1". And the "retired" response suggests "ASK EVWORK".

The second example in this figure shows the documentation for the HRS1 question. Here, you can see that the answers correspond to the different numbers of hours that people may work.

The WRKSTAT question

1. Last week were you working full time, part time, going to school, keeping house, or what?

HAND CARD A2

CIRCLE ONE CODE ONLY. IF MORE THAN ONE RESPONSE, GIVE PREFERENCE TO SMALLEST CODE NUMBER THAT APPLIES

[VAR: WRKSTAT]

RESPONSE	PUNCH	YEAR									
		1972-82	1982B	1983-87	1987B	1988-91	1993-98	2000-04	2006	2008	20
Working full time (ASK HRS1)	1	6150	144	3662	169	2894	5612	4422	2322	1003	9
Working part time (ASK HRS1)	2	1174	33	811	39	648	1088	938	440	211	2
With a job, but not at work because of temporary illness, vacation, strike (ASK HRS2)	3	321	2	155	2	126	199	192	90	53	
Unemployed, laid off, looking for work (GO TO OCC to COMMUTE)	4	441	25	242	11	130	273	280	148	74	1
Retired (ASK EVWORK)	5	1437	38	916	49	842	1412	1221	715	336	3
In school (ASK EVWORK)	6	405	11	190	11	215	289	270	140	57	
Keeping house (ASK EVWORK)	7	3507	86	1463	67	973	1264	859	496	227	2
Other (SPECIFY AND ASK EVWORK)	8	191	15	103	5	79	194	211	155	60	
No answer	9	0	0	0	0	0	3	1	4	2	

REMARKS: Card A2 contained responses for punches 1 through 7. Contents of WRKSTAT, punch 8 (Other, SPECIFY) available from NORC.

The HRS1 follow-up question

A. IF WORKING, FULL OR PART TIME: How many hours did you work last week, at all jobs?

[VAR: HRS1]

RESPONSE	PUNCH	YEAR							
		1972-82	1982B	1983-87	1987B	1988-91	1993-98	2000-04	200
0-9 hours	0	125	2	104	4	88	130	89	5
10-19 hours	1	353	12	200	9	173	281	229	11
20-29 hours	2	471	19	363	20	285	513	415	20
30-39 hours	3	909	29	614	37	460	843	690	35
40-49 hours	4	3422	97	2172	106	1662	3111	2502	126
50-59 hours	5	598	8	498	16	459	946	716	40
60-69 hours	6	337	6	301	8	265	544	413	21
70-79 hours	7	117	0	106	4	76	164	127	7
80 or more hours	8	104	4	97	3	59	127	129	6
Don't know	9	5	0	5	0	4	5	8	
No answer	10	12	0	13	1	11	39	43	1
Not applicable (Punches 3 to 8 in WRKSTAT)	-1	7173	177	3069	145	2365	3631	3033	174

Description

- Each of the responses to a primary question in the codebook points to a follow-up question.

Figure 14-12 Use the codebook to find follow-up questions

Select the columns for an expanded DataFrame

When you finish your review of the questions and follow-up questions, you're ready to create a DataFrame for the questions that you want to include in your next analysis. The first example in figure 14-13 shows how. Here, the read_stata() method is used to read eight of the columns in the Stata file.

Once the data has been read, the dropna() method is used to drop any rows (axis=0) that have missing values, and the index is reset. Dropping the rows with missing values is important because you don't want to have gaps in the data because certain questions weren't asked in some of the years.

After you create the DataFrame, it's good to review it to make sure that it contains the right data for your analysis. If you look at the year column, for example, you can see that only the year 2014 is shown. Then, to confirm that, you can run the value_counts() method on the year column, as shown in the second example in this figure. This shows that the only value in the year column is 2014.

Now, remember that the wkcontct, talkspvs, and effctsup questions were only asked in 2014. That means that there were missing responses for all other years. So when the dropna() method was called after the DataFrame was created, only the responses for 2014 were kept.

Another issue that you may need to address is that the hrs1 column doesn't appear to be binned, even though the codebook shows it should be. To check that, the third example in this figure displays the first five rows in the hrs1 column. Here, you can see that this column has the category data type. But you can also see that there's a category for each integer from 0 through 88, plus a category for the string "89+ hrs". Since that isn't what you want, you have to do your own binning as shown the next figure.

The expanded work dataset

```
workCols = ['year', 'sex', 'region', 'wrkstat', 'hrs1', 'wkcontct',
    'talkspvs', 'effctsup']
workData = pd.read_stata('GSS7218_R3.DTA', columns=workCols) \
    .dropna(axis=0).reset_index(drop=True)
workData
```

	year	sex	region	wrkstat	hrs1	wkcontct	talkspvs	effctsup
0	2014	female	new england	working fulltime	40	once or twice a month	very	very
1	2014	female	new england	working parttime	20	never	very	very
2	2014	female	middle atlantic	working fulltime	37	never	very	somewhat
3	2014	male	new england	working fulltime	50	never	somewhat	very
4	2014	female	new england	working fulltime	38	never	very	very
...	...	...	...	...	...	...	...	...
965	2014	male	new england	working fulltime	48	once or twice a month	somewhat	somewhat
966	2014	male	new england	working fulltime	46	less than once a month	very	very
967	2014	male	new england	working fulltime	40	never	somewhat	somewhat
968	2014	male	new england	working fulltime	40	once or twice a month	a little	somewhat
969	2014	female	new england	working parttime	48	never	extremely	very

970 rows × 8 columns

Identify missing data

```
workData.year.value_counts()
============================
2014    970
Name: year, dtype: int64
```

Find discrepancies between the codebook and the data

```
workData.hrs1.head()
====================
0    40
1    20
2    37
3    50
4    38
Name: hrs1, dtype: category
Categories (90, object): [0 < 1 < 2 < 3 ... 86 < 87 < 88 < '89+ hrs']
```

Description

- The data for the expanded analysis will consist of two demographic columns and five question columns, four of which you have already seen.
- After you create the DataFrame for an analysis, you should review it to make sure that it contains the right data.

Figure 14-13 Select the columns for an expanded DataFrame

Bin the data for a column

Figure 14-14 shows how to bin the data for the hrs1 column in the DataFrame for the expanded analysis. To start, you need to convert the data in that column to the float data type. The first example shows how.

Because the hrs1 column has the category data type, you need to start by using the astype() method to convert it to the string data type. Then, you need to use the replace() method to replace the "89+ hrs" values in that column with 89 because "89+ hrs" can't be converted to a float data type. Last, you can use the astype() method again to convert the column to the float data type.

The second example in this figure shows how to create the bin labels that you want to use for the bins that you're going to create. Here, a formatted string literal (or f-string) is used within a list comprehension. If you refer back to the codebook in figure 14-12, you can see that all but the last of these labels match up with the values in the codebook.

The third example in this figure shows how you can use these labels to bin the data with the cut() method. Here, the bins parameter specifies a list of bin edges. Then, since the right parameter is set to False, the right bin edge won't be included. So, the values 0-9 will be in the first bin, 10-19 will be in the second bin, and so on. Last, the labels parameter passes the labels that were created in the previous example. The result is an hrs1 column that is properly binned.

Prepare the data for binning

```
workData.hrs1. = workData.hrs1.astype(str).replace('89+ hrs','89').astype(float)
workData.hrs1.head()
================================================================================
0    40.0
1    20.0
2    37.0
3    50.0
4    38.0
Name: hrs1, dtype: float64
```

Create the bin labels

```
binLabels = [f'{i}-{i+9} hours' for i in range(0,90,10)]
binLabels
========================================================
['0-9 hours',
 '10-19 hours',
 '20-29 hours',
 '30-39 hours',
 '40-49 hours',
 '50-59 hours',
 '60-69 hours',
 '70-79 hours',
 '80-89 hours']
```

Bin the data

```
workData.hrs1 = pd.cut(workData.hrs1,
                       bins=[0,10,20,30,40,50,60,70,80,90], right=False,
                       labels=binLabels)
workData.head()
```

	year	sex	region	wrkstat	hrs1	wkcontct	talkspvs	effctsup
0	2014	female	new england	working fulltime	40-49 hours	once or twice a month	very	very
1	2014	female	new england	working parttime	20-29 hours	never	very	very
2	2014	female	middle atlantic	working fulltime	30-39 hours	never	very	somewhat
3	2014	male	new england	working fulltime	50-59 hours	never	somewhat	very
4	2014	female	new england	working fulltime	30-39 hours	never	very	very

Figure 14-14 Bin the data for the hrs1 column

How to use a hypothesis to guide your analysis

A *hypothesis* is an educated guess that you make about what your data may show. You should be able to state this hypothesis in one sentence and determine whether or not it is supported by the data. Hypotheses can help guide your analyses because they provide clear objectives. The figures that follow show how to use three hypotheses as you analyze the data in the expanded DataFrame for the Social Survey data. These figures don't use statistics to test and judge each hypothesis. Instead, each one displays a plot that gives a good indication of whether the hypothesis is supported by the data.

Develop and test a first hypothesis

Every hypothesis that you create should have the four characteristics shown at the top of figure 14-15. A hypothesis is specific if it contains all of the relevant variables in the study. A hypothesis is clearly stated if it is written in clear and concise language. A hypothesis is testable if you can make observations that agree or disagree with it. A hypothesis is educated if it is made with respect to some body of knowledge.

With that as background, take the time to read the hypothesis in this figure. Then, observe whether it can be tested with the expanded DataFrame.

Before you can test this hypothesis, you need to make sure the DataFrame contains an equal number of male and female respondents. To do that, you can use the value_counts() method on the sex column as in the first example. Then, if the number of respondents isn't equal, you can drop some of the respondents to make the number of male and female respondents equal. Or, you can add columns to the DataFrame that allow you to calculate the percentages for men and women when you plot the data.

The second example shows how you can test this hypothesis by creating a count plot. Since this hypothesis is only concerned with what happens "on a daily basis," you only need to look at the "once a day" and "several times a day" responses. This example implements that by storing those response values in a list called responses and using that list to query the DataFrame with the result saved in a new DataFrame named df.

Remember, though, that the wrkcontct column has the category data type. As a result, the other categories will still be there, even if they aren't used. That's why the next statement removes the unused categories.

At that point, you can plot the data with the sex column as the x-axis and the wkcontct column as the col parameter. The result is one subplot for each response value: "once a day" or "two or more times a day." And this does show that men are contacted more outside of working hours.

When you finish testing a hypothesis, it's a good practice to write a conclusion like the one at the bottom of this figure. When you do that, you should restate the hypothesis and state whether or not the results support the hypothesis.

Characteristics of a good hypothesis

Specific Clearly stated Testable Educated

The first hypothesis

- Men are contacted on a daily basis for work reasons outside of working hours more often than women are.

Prepare the data

```
workData.sex.value_counts()
===========================
female    514
male      456

# drop 58 female respondents to get an equal number of male and female respondents
workData = workData.sort_values('sex', ascending=False).iloc[58:]
```

Test the first hypothesis

```
responses = ['once a day','two or more times a day']
df = workData.query('wkcontct in @responses').copy()
df.wkcontct = df.wkcontct.cat.remove_unused_categories()

g = sns.catplot(data=df, x='sex', col='wkcontct', kind='count')
g.fig.suptitle('Are men contacted more on a daily basis in non-working hours?',
               y=1.035)
```

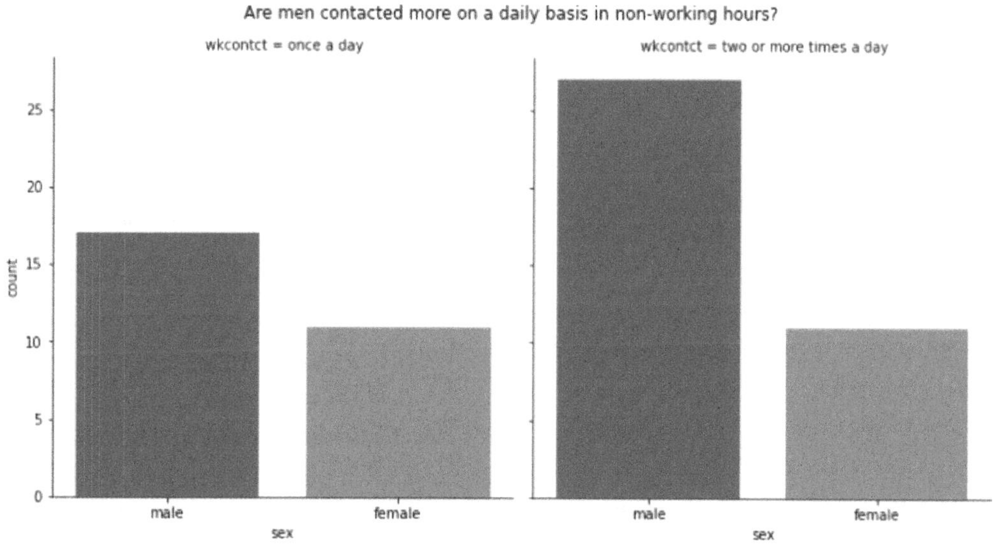

Conclusion for the first hypothesis

- The results support the hypothesis. Men are contacted on a daily basis for work reasons outside of working hours more often than women are.

Figure 14-15 Develop and test a first hypothesis

Develop and test a second hypothesis

Figure 14-16 starts with the second hypothesis. Here again, take the time to read the hypothesis. It suggests that workers who are uncomfortable talking with their supervisors will work more hours than those who are comfortable talking with their supervisors.

Because this hypothesis deals with several variables, a heatmap is going to work better than a bar plot to show the responses for each variable. This is illustrated by the heatmap in this figure.

To create this heatmap, the pivot_table() method is used to shape the data for the plot. In this pivot table, the columns are the values in the hrs1 column. The index is the values in the talkspvs column. And the aggregate function is the count() method. This creates a pivot table that has two column levels where the first column level is for the year column. Since this column isn't needed and makes the plot labels longer and more difficult to read, you can drop this column level before plotting the heatmap.

If this hypothesis were true, you would expect to see a higher number of hours worked for the "not at all comfortable" and "a little" responses. But since this heatmap doesn't show that, the hypothesis isn't supported by the data, and the conclusion states that.

The second hypothesis

- Respondents who are uncomfortable talking with their supervisors about conflicts between their work and their personal lives will work more hours than respondents who are comfortable with talking to their supervisors about conflicts between their work and their personal lives.

Test the second hypothesis

```
# create pivot table
workPivot = workData[['year','hrs1','talkspvs']].pivot_table(
    columns='hrs1', index='talkspvs', aggfunc='count')
workPivot = workPivot.droplevel(0, axis=1)   # the top column level isn't needed

# create heatmap for pivot table
ax = sns.heatmap(workPivot, cmap='Blues', annot=True, fmt='.3g')
ax.set_title(
    "Do those who don't like to talk with their supervisors work more hours?\n")
ax.set(xlabel='', ylabel='How comfortable talking with supervisor?')
```

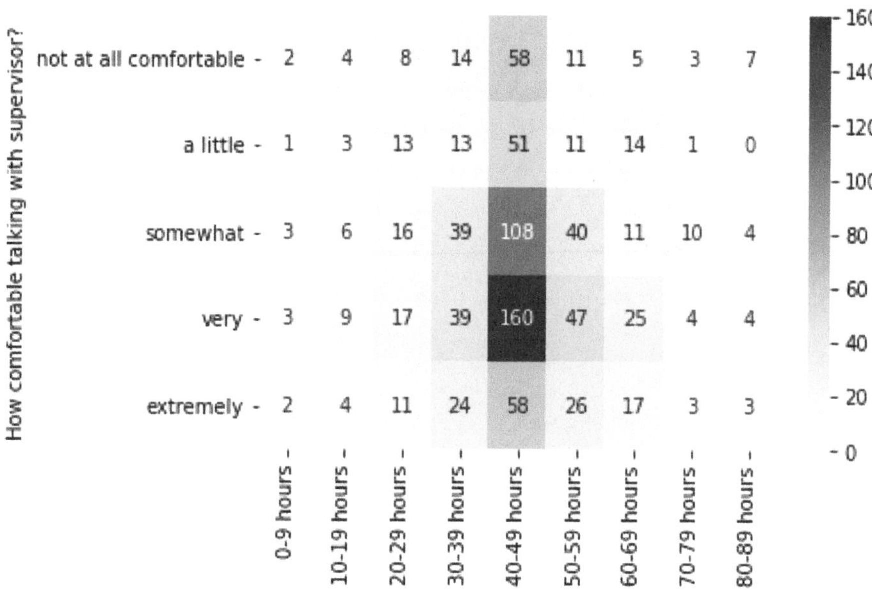

Conclusion for the second hypothesis

- The data doesn't support the hypothesis. The comfort level of the respondents when talking with their supervisors about work-life conflicts doesn't have a significant effect on their weekly number of hours worked.

Figure 14-16 Develop and test a second hypothesis

Develop and test a third hypothesis

Figure 14-17 starts with a third hypothesis. When you read it, you can see that it deals with how the male and female responses are distributed. So here again, you can use a count plot to test the hypothesis.

To get the data for the plot, a DataFrame is created for three of the responses in the effctsup column. Next, the unused categories in this column are removed. At that point, the data is ready for plotting.

Then, the catplot() method is used to plot the data with sex on the x-axis and one subplot for each response in the effctsup column. As you can see, the data doesn't support the hypothesis since the results are mixed between the three responses.

The third hypothesis

- More women than men think their supervisors are effective when helping them resolve work-life conflicts.

Test the third hypothesis

```
responses = ['very','somewhat','extremely']
df = workData.query('effctsup in @responses').copy()
df.effctsup = df.effctsup.cat.remove_unused_categories()

g = sns.catplot(data=df, x='sex', col='effctsup', kind='count', col_wrap=2)
g.fig.suptitle('How effective is your supervisor at helping you resolve ' +
               'work-life conflicts?', y=1.025)
```

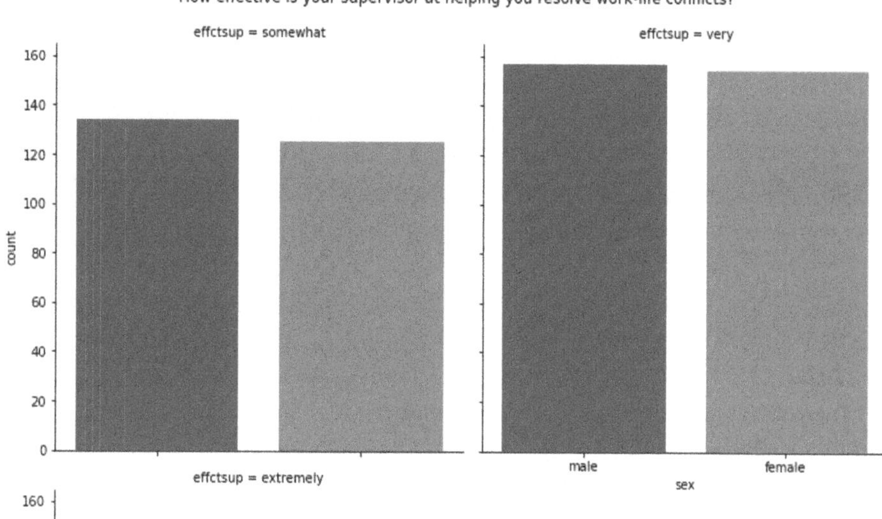

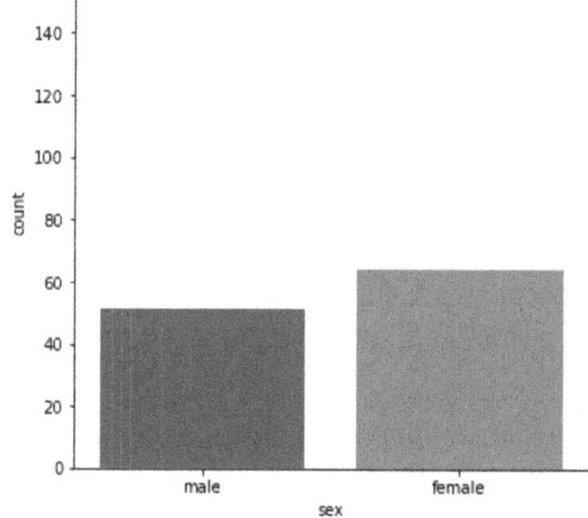

Conclusion for the third hypothesis

- The data does not support the hypothesis. It is not clear that more women than men think their supervisors are effective when helping them resolve work-life conflicts.

Figure 14-17 Develop and test a third hypothesis

Perspective

The case study presented in this chapter shows how you can extract useful information from a large dataset of survey questions and answers. When you work with large datasets like this, you need to use whatever documentation is available to help you navigate the dataset.

Later, if you plot the responses to the survey questions by year, you need to be sure that the results aren't affected by a varying number of responses in each year. If they are, you need to plot the percentages of the responses, not the counts.

Then, to expand your analysis of the data in the survey, you can combine demographic data with the responses to survey questions. You can also develop a hypothesis before you start to analyze the data. That hypothesis should provide the objective for your analysis.

Exercise 14-1 More analysis of the Social Survey data

This exercise guides you through more analysis of the Social Survey data, including helping you to test a hypothesis. Before you do this analysis, you may want to run the Social Survey case study on your system and experiment with it to make sure you understand how it works.

Get the data

1. Start JupyterLab and open the Notebook named ex_14-1_social that should be in this folder:

   `exercises/ch14`

2. If you haven't already installed pyreadstat, install it now. To do that, you can use the conda install command as described in the appendixes.
3. Run the first cell to import all of the modules that you'll use.
4. Open the PDF file for the code book. This PDF file should be in the python_analysis/data folder. If it isn't, open the notebook named download_more_data, and run all of its cells.
5. Read through the question sets that start on pages 2,715 and 2,768. To find these pages, you can search the code book for "page 2715" and "page 2768".
6. Run the cells that get the data for the DataFrames named socialMedia and mentalHealth. This dataset is large, so this may take a while.
7. For both DataFrames, drop all rows that have missing values, and set an index on the id column.
8. Use an inner join to join the two DataFrames, and assign the new DataFrame to a variable named socialHealth.

9. Display the first five rows of the socialHealth DataFrame.
10. Use the info() method to view the data types for each column. Note that all columns are of the category type.

Clean and prepare the data

11. Run the cell to rename the columns to make them more readable.
12. View the value counts for the weekdayMinutes and weekendMinutes columns.
13. Remove any rows that don't have values of 0, 15, 30, or 45 in these columns.
14. Convert the first five columns from the category type to the int type.
15. Modify the weekdayHours and weekendHours columns so they store the combined hours and minutes. To do that, you'll need to divide the minutes data by 60 and add it to the hours.
16. Drop the weekdayMinutes and weekendMinutes columns since you don't need them anymore.
17. Display the first five rows.

Form and test a hypothesis

18. Read the hypothesis that's displayed in the Notebook.
19. Use Seaborn to create a box plot for the restlessSleep and weekdayHours columns.
20. Use the cut() method to bin the weekdayHours column into five 3-hour groups (0-3 hours, 3-6 hours, etc.). Use the labels parameter to create intuitive labels for your groups. Assign the bins to a new column called weekdayHoursBin.
21. Display the value counts for all combinations of the weekdayHoursBin and restlessSleep columns.
22. Use Seaborn to create a count plot that shows the count of the restlessSleep values for each time bin.
23. Group the DataFrame by the weekdayHoursBin column. Then, call the value_counts() method from the restlessSleep column with the normalize parameter set to True. Convert the results to a DataFrame and assign it to a new variable named hoursGrouped.
24. Rename the column for the hoursGrouped DataFrame to percentage and reset the index.
25. Use Seaborn to create a bar plot that displays the percentage on the y-axis and the weekdayHoursBin column on the x-axis. In addition, this plot should use colors to identify the restlessSleep column.
26. Write a conclusion statement for the hypothesis.
27. Develop and test your own hypothesis for the data.

Chapter 15

The Sports Analytics case study

Sports analytics is a broad field that applies data analysis to sports data. In this case study, you'll analyze the basketball game data for Stephen Curry of the Golden State Warriors. This study gets the data from NBA stats, and the data includes the shot location for every missed and made shot in every game that Curry played in from 2009 to 2019.

Get the data and build the DataFrame

Because the Curry data is stored in a JSON file that's several levels deep, you can't just import the data into a DataFrame. Instead, you need to get the JSON data, convert it to a dictionary, and then build a DataFrame from the right levels of the dictionary.

Get the data

Figure 15-1 gives a quick review of how you can get the data for this analysis. Here, the first example shows how to import the modules that you will need for this case study.

Then, the second example shows how to get the Curry data and load it into a dictionary. Here, step 1 downloads the JSON file to disk and stores it in the same directory as the Notebook for the case study. Then, step 2 opens the JSON file and uses the load() method of the json module to convert the JSON data to a dictionary.

However, since this dictionary has more than two levels, you can't just read it into a DataFrame. Instead, you need to figure out what data you want to analyze, and then build a DataFrame from it. To figure that out, you can use JupyterLab to drill down into the data, as shown in figure 5-10 of chapter 5. That will show you that the relevant parts of the dictionary are in the resultSets key.

Build the DataFrame

The third example in this figure shows how to build the DataFrame for the Curry shot data once you know which parts of the dictionary you want to use. In this case, those parts are in the resultSets key.

So, step 1 gets the headers in the resultSets key that contain the column names for the DataFrame and assigns them to the columnHeaders variable. Then, it uses a list comprehension to convert each column name in this variable to all lowercase letters.

Next, step 2 gets the rows in the resultSets key and assigns them to the rows variable. And step 3 uses the DataFrame constructor to build a DataFrame from the data in the columnHeaders and rows variables. The resulting DataFrame has 24 columns, and 11,846 rows, one for each shot Curry took during the ten seasons that are included in the data.

Import the modules for this case study

```
import pandas as pd
import seaborn as sns
import json
from urllib import request
```

Get the Stephen Curry data

Step 1: Download the JSON file for the Curry shots data

```
shots_url = 'https://www.murach.com/python_analysis/shots.json'
shots = request.urlretrieve(shots_url, filename='shots.json')
```

Step 2: Load the Curry shots data into a dictionary

```
with open('shots.json') as jsonData:
    shots = json.load(jsonData)
shots.keys()
====================================================
dict_keys(['resource', 'parameters', 'resultSets'])
```

Build the DataFrame for the Curry data

Step 1: Get the column headers

```
columnHeaders = shots['resultSets'][0]['headers']
columnHeaders = [x.lower() for x in columnHeaders]
columnHeaders
=======================================================
['grid_type',
 'game_id',
 'game_event_id',
 'player_id',
 ...
 'vtm']
```

Step 2: Get the rows data

```
rows = shots['resultSets'][0]['rowSet']
```

Step 3: Build the dataframe

```
shots = pd.DataFrame(data=rows, columns=columnHeaders)
shots.head(4)
```

	grid_type	game_id	game_event_id	player_id	player_name	team_id	team_name	period	minutes_remaining	seconds_remaining	...
0	Shot Chart Detail	0020900015	4	201939	Stephen Curry	1610612744	Golden State Warriors	1	11	25	...
1	Shot Chart Detail	0020900015	17	201939	Stephen Curry	1610612744	Golden State Warriors	1	9	31	...
2	Shot Chart Detail	0020900015	53	201939	Stephen Curry	1610612744	Golden State Warriors	1	6	2	...
3	Shot Chart Detail	0020900015	141	201939	Stephen Curry	1610612744	Golden State Warriors	2	9	49	...

Figure 15-1 Get the data and build the DataFrame

Clean the data

When you clean the data for this analysis, you start by examining the data to see whether you can drop any rows or columns that you won't need for your analysis.

Locate and drop unneeded rows

The first example in figure 15-2 shows how you can find and delete unneeded rows. There, the unique() method shows the data in the "periods" column. As you can see, it consists of the numbers 1 through 6, which means that the data includes the rows for two overtime periods. But since they aren't needed for the goals of this analysis, the rows for those periods are dropped by assigning the rows for all the other periods to the DataFrame named shots.

Locate and drop unneeded columns

The second example in this figure starts by showing the number of unique values in each column. That will help you determine which columns can be dropped. For example, you can drop id columns like game_event_id because you won't use that data in your analysis.

You can also drop columns that provide redundant information like the shot_zone_range and the shot_attempted_flag columns. In this case, the shot_zone_range column is redundant because it provides the same information as the shot_distance column, although with less detail. And the shot_attempted_flag column is redundant because you can get the same data by using the shot_made_flag column.

If you decide that your analysis will focus on numeric data, you can drop categorical columns like shot_zone_basic, shot_zone_area, event_type, and action_type. And since you know that this data only applies to Stephen Curry, you can drop columns like player_id and player_name.

Last, after you've decided on the other columns, you need to decide whether you want to include columns that deal with time, including the period, minutes_remaining, and seconds_remaining columns. For this case study, those columns are dropped too.

Convert the game_date column to datetime data

The third example in this figure converts the game_date column to the datetime data type. That way, you can use the datetime methods to work with this data. Then, the fourth example uses the info() method to summarize the 6 columns and 11,753 rows that remain in the DataFrame.

View the data for the periods column

```
shots.period.unique()
================================
array([1., 2., 4., 3., 5., 6.])
```

Drop the rows for periods 5 and 6

```
shots = shots.query('period < 5.0')
```

Locate unneeded columns

```
shots.nunique(dropna=False)
=========================
grid_type               1
game_id               692
game_event_id         692
player_id               1
player_name             1
team_id                 1
team_name               1
period                  4
minutes_remaining      12
...
shot_distance          71
loc_x                 489
loc_y                 437
shot_attempted_flag     1
shot_made_flag          2
game_date             692
htm                    32
vtm                    32
```

Drop the unneeded columns

```
shots = shots.drop(columns=['grid_type','game_event_id','team_id',
    'team_name','player_id','shot_zone_range','shot_zone_basic',
    'shot_zone_area','event_type','action_type','minutes_remaining',
    'seconds_remaining','shot_distance','player_name','period','htm',
    'vtm','shot_attempted_flag'])
```

Convert the game_date column to datetime data

```
shots.game_date = pd.to_datetime(shots.game_date)
```

Get the info for the columns that remain

```
shots.info()
====================================================
Int64Index: 11753 entries, 0 to 11845
#   Column          Non-Null Count  Dtype
---  ------          --------------  -----
 0   game_id         11753 non-null  object
 1   shot_type       11753 non-null  object
 2   loc_x           11753 non-null  int64
 3   loc_y           11753 non-null  int64
 4   shot_made_flag  11753 non-null  int64
 5   game_date       11753 non-null  datetime64[ns]
```

Figure 15-2 Clean the data

Prepare the data

When you prepare the data for an analysis, you add any new columns that will help you analyze or plot the data. For this case study, figure 15-3 shows how to add six new columns.

Add a column for the season

The first example in this figure shows what the DataFrame looks like after the cleaning process. As you can see, most of the original columns have been dropped and the remaining columns deal with the game and shot data.

Then, the second example starts the preparation process by setting an index on the game_id column. This helps organize the data by game.

When you analyze this data, you will probably want to look at it on a season-by-season basis. However, since a basketball season starts in the fall and goes into the spring, games from a single season take place in two calendar years. So, to help you analyze the data by season, you can create a column that identifies the season. The third example shows how.

In this example, a function named get_season() takes a row as a parameter. Then, this function looks at the month that a game was played in to determine which season it belongs to. The logic is this: if the game took place after June of the current calendar year, you know that the season for this game must go from the current year into the next year. And if it took place before June, it must be that the season started in the previous year and is extending into the current year.

The function in this example uses this logic to return a string that represents the season for the row. Then, the apply() method calls this function with the axis parameter set to 1 so the function is applied to each row, and the returned values are assigned to a new column called "season".

Add a column for the shot result

The fourth example in this figure shows how you can use the replace() method to create labels based on the shot_made_flag column and assign them to a new column named "shot_result". Here, 0 in the shot_made_flag column represents a missed shot and 1 represents a made shot, and the replace() method replaces each integer with a string. Note, however, that a new column is created instead of just replacing the integer in the shot_made_flag column because that column will be needed later on.

The shots DataFrame

```
shots.head(3)
```

	game_id	shot_type	loc_x	loc_y	shot_made_flag	game_date
0	0020900015	3PT Field Goal	99	249	0	2009-10-28
1	0020900015	2PT Field Goal	-122	145	1	2009-10-28
2	0020900015	2PT Field Goal	-60	129	0	2009-10-28

Set an index on the game_id

```
shots.set_index('game_id', inplace=True)
```

Add a column for the season

```
def get_season(row):
    if row.game_date.month > 6:
        season = f'{row.game_date.year}-{row.game_date.year + 1}'
    else:
        season = f'{row.game_date.year - 1}-{row.game_date.year}'
    return season

shots['season'] = shots.apply(get_season, axis=1)
shots.head()
```

	shot_type	loc_x	loc_y	shot_made_flag	game_date	season
game_id						
0020900015	3PT Field Goal	99	249	0	2009-10-28	2009-2010
0020900015	2PT Field Goal	-122	145	1	2009-10-28	2009-2010
0020900015	2PT Field Goal	-60	129	0	2009-10-28	2009-2010
0020900015	2PT Field Goal	-172	82	0	2009-10-28	2009-2010
0020900015	2PT Field Goal	-68	148	0	2009-10-28	2009-2010

Add a string column for the shot result

```
shots['shot_result'] = shots.shot_made_flag.replace({0:'Missed', 1:'Made'})
shots.head()
```

	shot_type	loc_x	loc_y	shot_made_flag	game_date	season	shot_result
game_id							
0020900015	3PT Field Goal	99	249	0	2009-10-28	2009-2010	Missed
0020900015	2PT Field Goal	-122	145	1	2009-10-28	2009-2010	Made
0020900015	2PT Field Goal	-60	129	0	2009-10-28	2009-2010	Missed
0020900015	2PT Field Goal	-172	82	0	2009-10-28	2009-2010	Missed
0020900015	2PT Field Goal	-68	148	0	2009-10-28	2009-2010	Missed

Figure 15-3 Prepare the data (part 1)

Add a column for points made for each shot

There are two types of shots in the current DataFrame: 3-point field goals are shots made from behind the 3-point line and count for 3 points, and 2-point field goals are shots made inside the 3-point line and count for 2 points. There are also free throws that count for 1 point, but those aren't included in this dataset so you don't need to worry about them.

The first example in part 2 of figure 15-3 shows how you can use the shot_type and shot_made_flag columns to calculate how many points were made for each shot. First, the unique() method is used see what the values are in the shot_type column. Then, to perform the calculation, the apply() method applies a lambda expression.

The lambda expression first checks if the shot was missed. If so, 0 is returned. Otherwise, the lambda checks if it was a 2-point shot or a 3-point shot and returns the appropriate value. Here again, 1 is used for the axis parameter because this expression needs to operate on the rows rather than the columns. The results are assigned to a new column named points_made.

Add three summary columns

The second example in this figure shows how to add three more columns to the DataFrame: points_made_game, shots_attempted, and shots_made. These columns represent the points made, shots attempted, and shots made for the entire game.

To add each of these columns, the groupby() method groups the rows by game_id, and the transform() method applies an aggregate method to the grouped data. In this case, the sum function is used for the points_made_game and shots_made columns, but the count() method is used for the shots_attempted column. That works because each row represents a shot taken so if you count the rows for each game, you know how many shots were taken for that game.

The DataFrame for this second example shows the results of the column additions. At this point, you can consider adding other columns like shots missed per game or percent made per game. But for this analysis, the three summary columns are enough.

Add a column for points made for each shot

Check the shot types

```
shots['shot_type'].unique()
===========================
array(['3PT Field Goal', '2PT Field Goal'], dtype=object)
```

Add the points_made column

```
shots['points_made'] = shots.apply(lambda x: 0 if x.shot_result == 'Missed' else
                          (3 if x.shot_type == '3PT Field Goal' else 2), axis=1)
shots.head()
```

	shot_type	loc_x	loc_y	shot_made_flag	game_date	season	shot_result	points_made
game_id								
0020900015	3PT Field Goal	99	249	0	2009-10-28	2009-2010	Missed	0
0020900015	2PT Field Goal	-122	145	1	2009-10-28	2009-2010	Made	2
0020900015	2PT Field Goal	-60	129	0	2009-10-28	2009-2010	Missed	0
0020900015	2PT Field Goal	-172	82	0	2009-10-28	2009-2010	Missed	0
0020900015	2PT Field Goal	-68	148	0	2009-10-28	2009-2010	Missed	0

Add summary columns for points, shots attempted, and shots made

```
shots['points_made_game'] = shots.groupby('game_id').points_made.transform('sum')
shots['shots_attempted'] = shots.groupby('game_id').shot_made_flag.transform('count')
shots['shots_made'] = shots.groupby('game_id').shot_made_flag.transform('sum')

shots[['shot_type','points_made','points_made_game','shots_attempted','shots_made']]
```

	shot_type	points_made	points_made_game	shots_attempted	shots_made
game_id					
0020900015	3PT Field Goal	0	14	12	7
0020900015	2PT Field Goal	2	14	12	7
0020900015	2PT Field Goal	0	14	12	7
0020900015	2PT Field Goal	0	14	12	7
0020900015	2PT Field Goal	0	14	12	7
...	...	...	...	...	...
0021801205	3PT Field Goal	3	25	20	11
0021801215	2PT Field Goal	0	5	4	2
0021801215	3PT Field Goal	3	5	4	2
0021801215	3PT Field Goal	0	5	4	2
0021801215	2PT Field Goal	2	5	4	2

11753 rows × 5 columns

Figure 15-3 Prepare the data (part 2)

Plot the summary data

Figure 15-4 shows two examples of how you can plot the summary data. Those plots give the first indication of whether a player's performance is improving from year to year.

Plot the points per game by season

The first example in this figure plots the points per game by season. First, it gets just the columns that are needed for the plot and stores them in a DataFrame named shotsSeason. This data includes the season and game_date columns plus the three summary columns. But note that the drop_duplicates() method drops all the duplicates, which means that only one row remains for each game in each season, a total of 692 rows.

Then, the Seaborn catplot() method is used to make a box plot of Curry's points per game for each season. Here, you can see that in terms of scoring the 2015-2016 season was one of his best and much better than his first two seasons.

Plot the averages of shots, shots made, and points per game by season

The second example in this figure shows how to make a line plot for the average number of shots, shots made, and points per game in each season. To start, the groupby() method groups the data in the shotsSeason DataFrame by season, the mean() method gets the average for each column in each group, and the index is reset. Then, the result is assigned to a new DataFrame named shotsSeasonAvg.

Once the DataFrame is created, the Pandas plot() method is used to make a line plot of the three summary columns by season. This method is used instead of a Seaborn method because Pandas lets you assign more than one column to the y parameter. To get the same results with Seaborn, you would have to melt the columns into one column before you could create the line plot.

The resulting line plot gives you another view of the data. Here, you can see that all three lines peak in the 2015-2016 season: points made, shots made, and shots attempted. In fact, that was one of the seasons in which Stephen Curry won the Most Valuable Player award.

If you look at the code for this plot() method, you can see how the color parameter is used to assign colors to each of the lines in the plot. You can also see how the ylim parameter is used to set the range of the y-axis from zero to 30. If you don't do that, the range is from 5 to 25, which misrepresents the data by making the shots_made line seem lower than it is.

Plot the points per game by season

Get the data for the seasons

```
shotsSeason = shots[['season','game_date','points_made_game','shots_made',
                     'shots_attempted']].drop_duplicates()
```

Plot the points per game by season

```
sns.catplot(data=shotsSeason, kind='box', x='season', y='points_made_game',
            aspect=2.5, palette='deep')
```

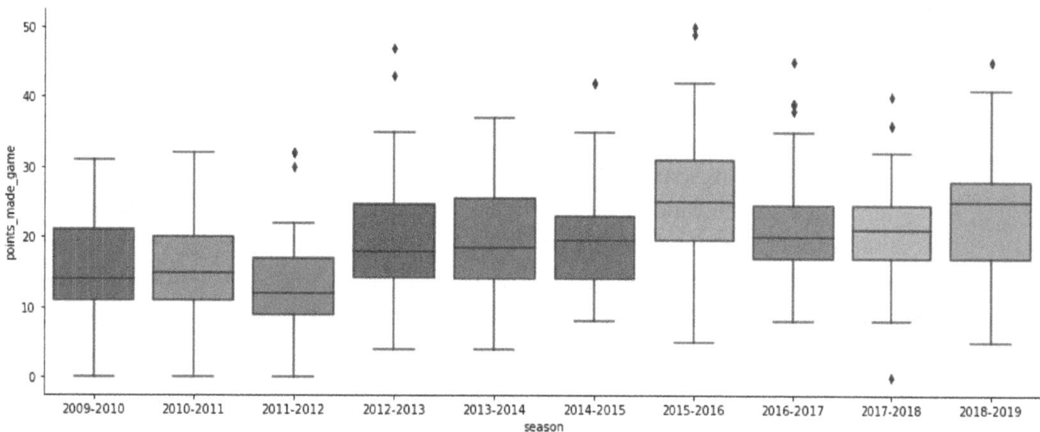

Plot the averages of shots, shots made, and points per game by season

Group the data

```
shotsSeasonAvg = shotsSeason.groupby('season').mean().reset_index()
```

Plot the data with the Pandas plot() method

```
shotsSeasonAvg.plot(
    x='season', y=['points_made_game','shots_made','shots_attempted'],
    color={'points_made_game':'red','shots_made':'blue','shots_attempted':'green'},
    figsize=(8,5), ylim=(0,30))
```

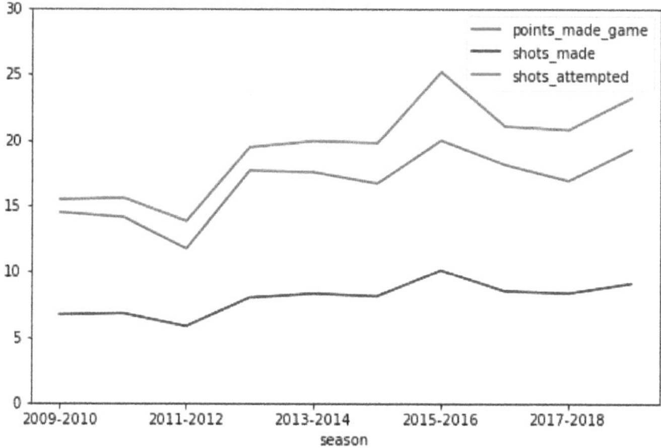

Figure 15-4 Plot the summary data

Plot the shot locations

Another way to analyze the Curry data is to plot the shot locations for the missed and made shots. As you will see, that can be revealing.

Plot the shot locations for two games

Figure 15-5 shows how to plot the shot locations for two games. Here, the first example creates a list of the IDs for the two games. There's nothing special about these games, they just happen to be games in which Curry took a lot of shots. As a result, they do a good job of showing how the shot locations look when they're plotted.

After the two games are put into the list, the Seaborn relplot() method makes a scatterplot of the shot locations for the two games. Here, the hue parameter colors the shots based on the shot_result column, and the col parameter makes a separate subplot for each game. Although this is a good start, you really can't tell where the shots are being taken from without drawing a basketball court on the scatterplot.

So, the second example shows how to use the draw_court() method to overlay the court lines on the scatterplot. This draw_court() method makes extensive use of Matplotlib methods so it won't be explained in this book. But if you're interested, the code is available in the Notebook for this chapter.

This second example starts by plotting the data with the relplot() method in the same way that it was in the first example. Then, all of the Axes objects are looped through using the g.axes.flat accessor. Within each loop, the draw_court() method is called to overlay the court lines on the scatterplot. Then, the x-axis and y-axis limits are set.

In the resulting scatterplot, it's easy to tell where Curry took his shots, where he missed, and where he made. But that's just for two games. Wouldn't this be more telling if the plot covered the shots for an entire season?

Plot the shot locations for two games

```
gameIDs = ['0021800923','0021800642']
g = sns.relplot(data=shots.query('game_id in @gameIDs'), kind='scatter',
    x='loc_x', y='loc_y', hue='shot_result', col='game_id')
```

Plot the shots and draw the court with the draw_court() method

```
g = sns.relplot(data=shots.query('game_id in @gameIDs'), kind='scatter',
    x='loc_x', y='loc_y', hue='shot_made_flag', col='game_id', s=50)

for i, ax in enumerate(g.axes.flat):
    ax = draw_court(ax, outer_lines=True)
    ax.set_xlim(-300, 300)
    ax.set_ylim(-100, 500)
```

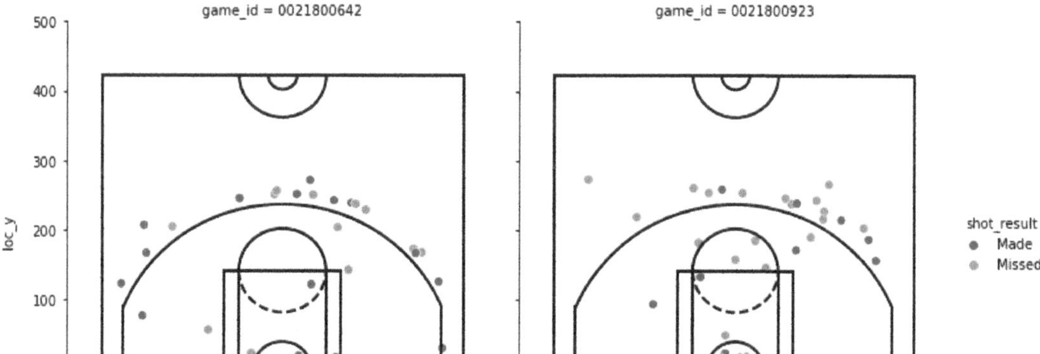

Figure 15-5 Plot the shot locations for two games

Plot the shot locations for two seasons

The example in figure 15-6 plots the shot locations for every shot that Stephen Curry took in his rookie season and in his first MVP season (2015-2016). The code for this example is like the code in the previous figure, but the col parameter is set to season and the col_wrap parameter is set to 1. In addition, the color palette is set so the made shots are blue and the missed shots are red.

If you study these subplots, you can see some significant differences. In particular, the shots for the 2015-2016 season are tightly clustered behind the three-point line and near the basket. By contrast, the shots for the 2009-2010 are more evenly distributed throughout the court. Could that be the reason that Curry's scoring average went up?

Although this data is somewhat revealing, there are so many datapoints that there aren't any obvious "hot spots" of shot activity. That's one of the problems that you encounter when you use scatterplots for high-density datasets. So in the next figure, you will see how distribution plots can be used to make more sense of data like this.

Plot the shot locations for two seasons

```
colors = ['#FF0B04','#4374B3'] # blue and red
sns.set_palette(sns.color_palette(colors))

seasons = ['2009-2010','2015-2016']
g = sns.relplot(data=shots.query('season in @seasons'), kind='scatter',
    x='loc_x', y='loc_y', hue='shot_result', col='season', col_wrap=1)

for ax in g.axes.flat:
    ax = draw_court(ax, outer_lines=True)
    ax.set_xlim(-300, 300)
    ax.set_ylim(-100, 500)
```

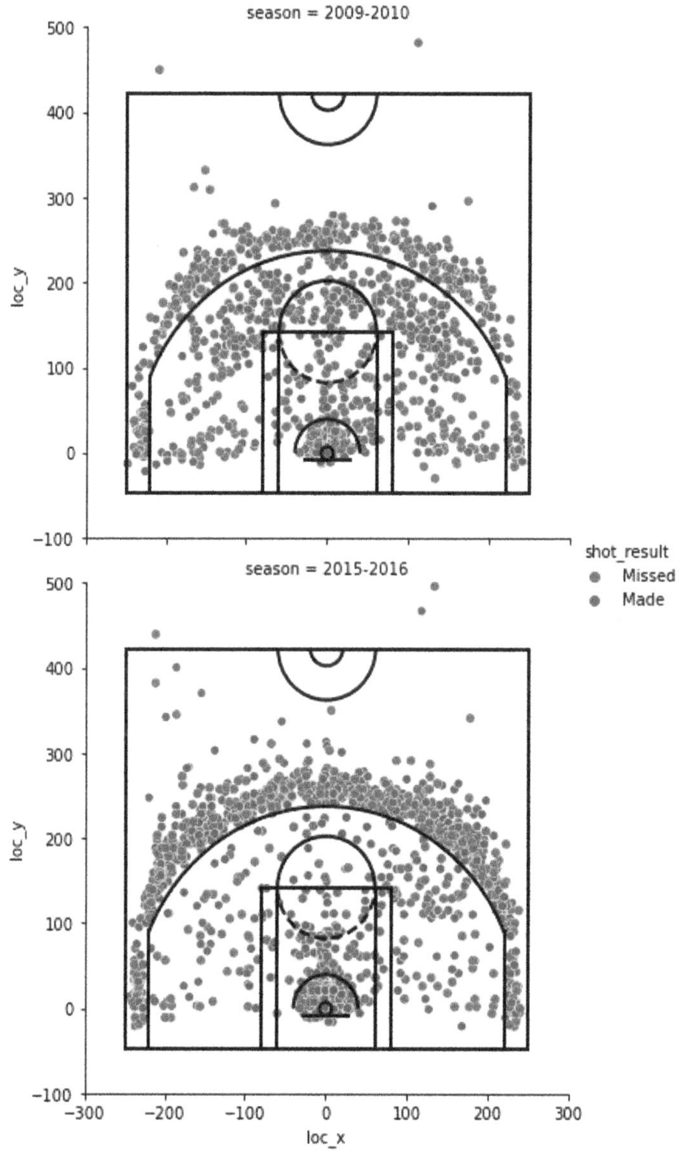

Figure 15-6 Plot the shot locations for two seasons

Plot the shot density for one season

The example in figure 15-6 shows how to plot the data for the 2015-2016 season that was used in the last figure, but with a density plot instead of a scatterplot. Here, the Seaborn displot() method is used instead of the relplot() method, and the kind parameter is set to "kde" so the plot is a kernel density plot, or just density plot.

For geographic data, a density plot is similar to a topographic map. If the lines are closer together, the data is denser, and if the lines are farther apart, the data is less dense.

As a result, these plots show that Curry shoots in two distinct zones. The first zone is in an arc just above the three-point line. The second zone is in the key near the basket. You should also note that the symmetry between the shot made and shot attempted charts indicates that there is no obvious zone in which Curry is more or less likely to make the shot.

One other thing to note in this example is that the color palette is reset at the start of the code, so the red and blue colors are in the reverse sequence of what they were in in the previous figure. That's done because the first color is assigned to the first value that's plotted, and a missed shot came up first. So, in order to keep blue for made shots and red for missed shots, the palette colors had to be reversed.

Plot the shot density for one season

```
colors = ['#4374B3','#FF0B04'] # red and blue
sns.set_palette(sns.color_palette(colors))

g = sns.displot(data=shots.query('season == "2015-2016"'), kind='kde', legend=False,
    x='loc_x', y='loc_y', col='shot_result', hue='shot_result', col_wrap=1)

for ax in g.axes.flat:
    ax = draw_court(ax, outer_lines=True)
    ax.set_xlim(-300, 300)
    ax.set_ylim(-100, 500)
```

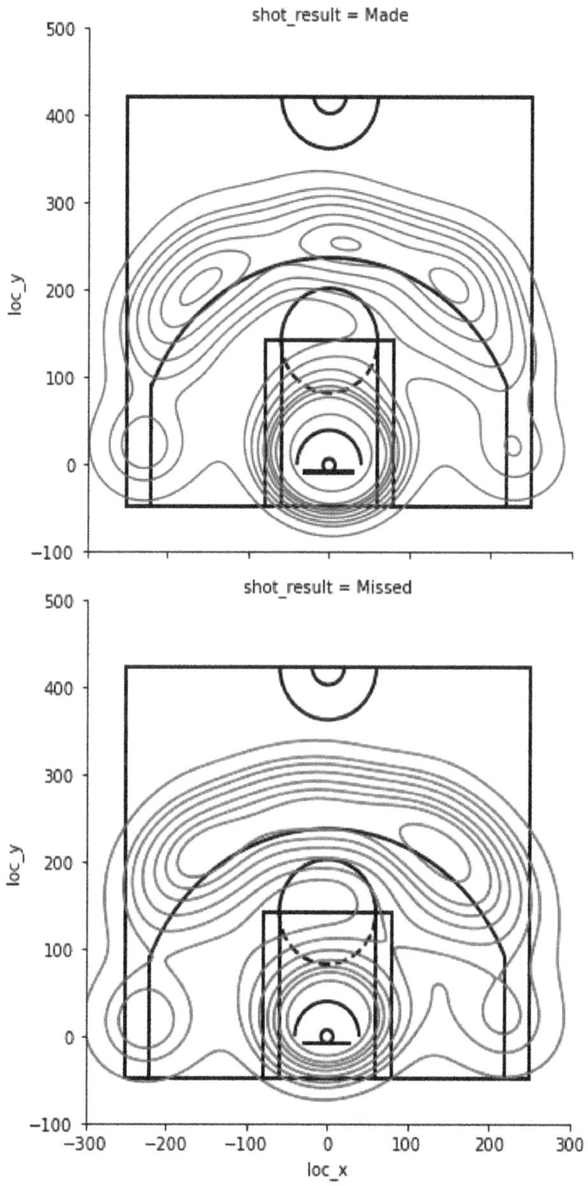

Figure 15-7 Plot the shot density for one season

Plot the shot density for two seasons

Just for fun, figure 15-8 plots the density for two seasons, Curry's rookie season and his first MVP season. There's nothing much new here, but the plots are interesting. Here again, the color palette is switched so the missed plots are red and the made plots are blue.

If you compare this plot with the one in figure 15-6, you can see how a density plot can be easier to interpret than a scatterplot. Here, the density plot gives you a much better idea of how Curry's shot locations changed from his rookie to his first MVP season. For the 2015-2016 season, the density lines outside the 3-point circle are much closer together than they were for his 2009-2010 season. That's also true for the lines under the basket.

Plot the shot density for two seasons

```
colors colors = ['#FF0B04','#4374B3'] # blue and red
sns.set_palette(sns.color_palette(colors))

seasons = ['2009-2010','2015-2016']
g = sns.displot(data=shots.query('season in @seasons'), kind='kde',
                x='loc_x', y='loc_y', row='shot_result', col='season',
                hue='shot_result', legend=False)
for ax in g.axes.flat:
    ax = draw_court(ax, outer_lines=True)
    ax.set_xlim(-300, 300)
    ax.set_ylim(-100, 500)
```

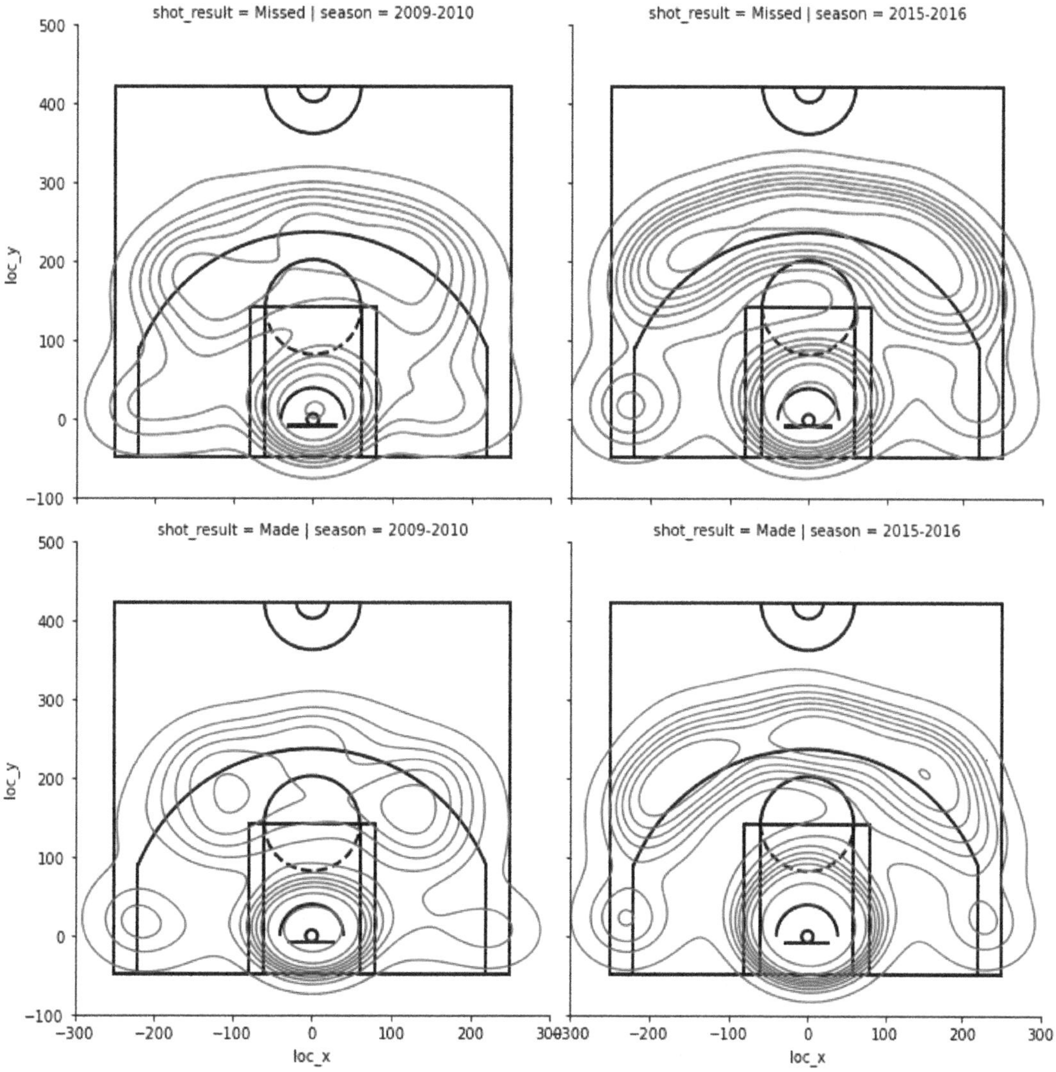

Figure 15-8 Plot the shot density for two seasons

Perspective

This case study shows that the data analysis skills that you apply to business, political, environmental, or social data can also be applied to sports. In fact, sports analytics has changed the way that many sports are coached and played.

Exercise 15-1 More analysis of the Curry data

This exercise guides you through more analysis of the data for Stephen Curry's shots. Before you do this analysis, you may want to run the case study.

Get the data

1. Start JupyterLab and open the Notebook named ex_15-1_curry that should be in this folder:
   `python_analysis/exercises/ch15`
2. Run the first cell to import all of the modules that you'll use.
3. Run the second cell to load the json data into a dictionary and build a DataFrame named shots.
4. Display the first five rows.

Clean the data

5. Run the cell that drops some of the unneeded columns.
6. Display the first five rows of the shots DataFrame.
7. Display the value counts for the period column. Then, drop the rows for periods 5 and 6.

Prepare and analyze the data

8. Display the number of unique values for the action_type column. Then, display the value counts for the action_type column.
9. Add substrings such as "Jump" and "Layup" to the list of common substrings that identify each action type. Then, continue to add substrings and to test this code until you're sure that it provides all the values for the action_type column.
10. Define a function named get_label() that takes a row as input and loops through the common substrings list. In the loop, check if the substring is in the row's action_type column. If so, return the substring.
11. Apply this function to every row in the shots DataFrame and assign the result to the shot_type column.

Plot the data

12. Use Seaborn to create a count plot that shows the counts for each shot type.
13. Use the draw_court() function and the Seaborn displot() method to create a KDE plot with subplots for the "Jump" and "Layup" types.

Appendix A

How to set up Windows for this book

This appendix shows how to install the Anaconda distribution of Python. This distribution includes the Pandas and Seaborn libraries described in this book as well as JupyterLab, which is the Integrated Development Environment (IDE) that you'll be using throughout this book. This IDE lets you keep the code for each analysis in a Jupyter Notebook that consists of cells that contain the headings and code for the analysis.

This appendix also shows how to download and install the Notebooks for this book. That includes the Notebooks for the examples in chapters 1-11, the case studies in chapters 12-15, and the exercises at the ends of chapters 1-15.

How to install and use Anaconda

Before you can learn how to use Python for data analysis, you need to install the Anaconda distribution of Python, and you need to know how to use the Anaconda Prompt and the Anaconda Navigator. The first two figures show how.

How to install Anaconda

Figure A-1 shows how to install a Python environment for data analysis on your own computer. Specifically, it shows you how to install Anaconda, which is the most popular Python distribution for data analysis and visualization.

This is a typical installation that shouldn't give you any trouble. For this book, you should install the latest release, which is 3.8 at this writing. If you're like most users, you can accept all of the defaults.

If you're an experienced user, though, and you want to add Anaconda to your system path, you can change the option in that dialog box. In that case, you'll be able to run "conda" commands from the regular Windows Command Prompt rather than by opening a command prompt within an Anaconda environment.

When the installation program is finished, you should be able to use your Windows start menu to display a drop-down menu for Anaconda like the one that's shown in this figure. Then, you can use that menu to start components like the Anaconda Prompt and the Anaconda Navigator.

The URL for Anaconda's download page

www.anaconda.com/products/individual

How to install Anaconda

1. Go to the URL shown above. This displays the download page for the Individual Edition of the Anaconda distribution. You can also find this page by searching the Internet for "anaconda download".
2. Click the Download button to download an exe file.
3. Open the file after it is downloaded or find it the Downloads folder of Windows Explorer and double-click on it. That will start the Python installer for Windows.
4. Respond to the dialog boxes that are displayed while the installer runs. When in doubt, accept the default options.

The drop-down menu for Anaconda on the Windows start menu

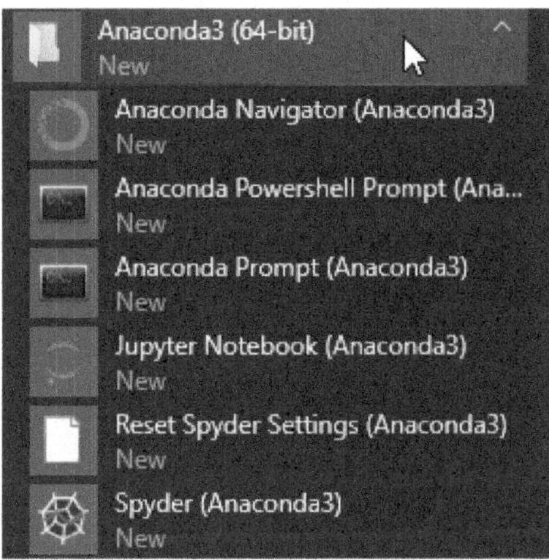

Description

- After the Anaconda distribution has been installed, its components are available from a drop-down menu like the one shown above.

Figure A-1 How to install Anaconda

How to use the Anaconda Prompt

The Anaconda Prompt can be used to run commands like updating Anaconda to the latest release or installing a Python package or module that isn't included in the Anaconda distribution. Figure A-2 illustrates this prompt as well as commands for updating the distribution and installing packages that are used by the code presented in this book but aren't included in the Anaconda distribution.

How to use the Anaconda Navigator

When you launch Anaconda Navigator, it displays a Home tab like the one shown in figure A-2. This tab shows the installed and available applications for your base environment. An *environment* is one version of Python that's configured with a specific group of settings, packages, and related applications.

As the Home tab shows, the Anaconda base installation includes components like JupyterLab, the IDE that you'll use for this book. To start this component, you just click on its Launch button.

However, the Navigator has more to offer than just that. For instance, you can use the Environments tab to browse an index of all the installed packages in your current environment. There, you can update, install, and delete packages.

Similarly, you can use the Learning tab to get access to all sorts of information that will help you learn how to use Python for data analysis. That includes documentation, demonstrations, tutorials, and more. Of course, all of that will make more sense and be more useful to you after you read this book.

The Anaconda Prompt with a command running

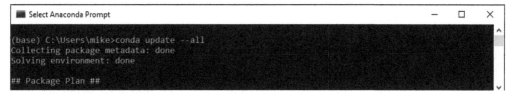

The command for updating Anaconda to the latest release

```
conda update --all
```

Commands for installing two packages that aren't included with Anaconda

```
conda install pyreadstat --channel conda-forge --yes
conda install geopandas --channel conda-forge
```

The Anaconda Navigator with the Home tab displayed

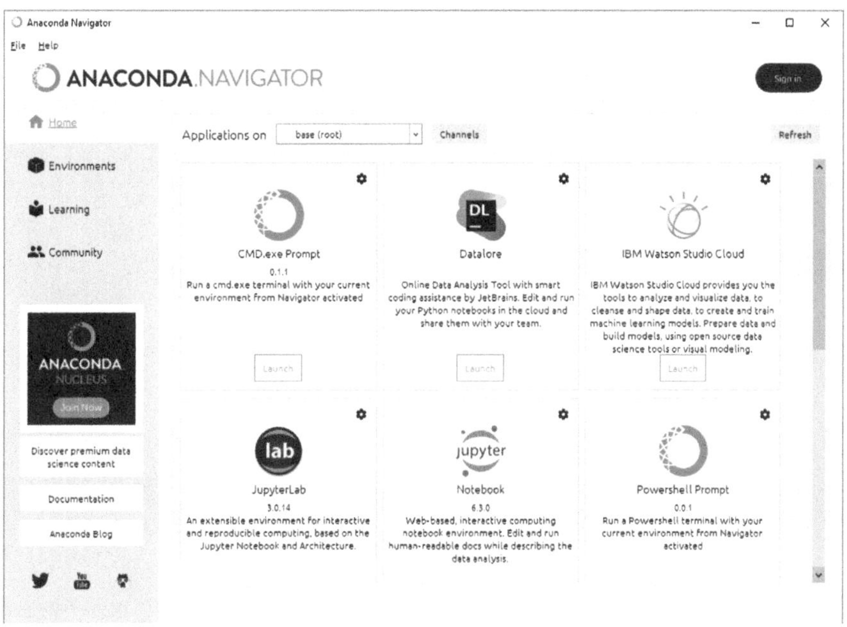

Description

- You can use the Anaconda *prompt* (or *console*) to run commands that update the Anaconda release or to install packages that aren't included in the Anaconda distribution.
- You can use the Home tab of Anaconda Navigator to launch the components that are included in the distribution and to install other components.
- You can use the Environments tab of Anaconda Navigator to browse, update, install, and delete packages in your current environment.
- You can use the Learning tab of Anaconda Navigator to access documentation, demonstrations, and tutorials on all aspects of Python data analysis.

Figure A-2 How to use the Anaconda Prompt and Navigator

How to install and use the files for this book

To help you get the most from this book, all of the files that you need for doing that are included in the download for this book. The two figures that follow show how to install them as well as how to use them to test your Anaconda installation and to download the large files for this book.

How to install the files for this book

Figure A-3 shows how to install the Notebooks and data files that you need for this book. This includes the Notebooks for all of the book examples and case studies presented in this book as well as the Notebooks that you'll need for doing the exercises at the end of each chapter.

When you finish the procedure in this figure, the Notebooks for this book will be in the folders shown in this figure. Then, you can open these Notebooks, review the code, run the code, do the exercises, and experiment on your own.

The Murach website

`www.murach.com`

The folder for the book examples, case studies, and exercises

`\Documents\python_analysis`

The subfolders

Folder	Description
`case_studies`	The case studies presented in chapters 12-15 of this book.
`data`	Some of the data files that are used by this book.
`examples`	The examples presented in chapters 1-11 of this book.
`exercises`	The starting points for the exercises presented at the end of each chapter.
`solutions`	The solutions to the exercises.

How to download and install the files for this book

1. Go to www.murach.com.
2. Find the page for *Murach's Python for Data Analysis.*
3. If necessary, scroll down to the FREE downloads tab.
4. Click the FREE downloads tab.
5. Click the Download Now button for the zip file. This should download a file named dap1_allfiles.zip.
6. Find the zip file on your computer and double-click on it. This should extract the files for this book into a folder named python_analysis.
7. Use Explorer to move the python_analysis folder into your Documents folder.

Description

- You can download the folders and files that contain the Jupyter Notebooks for this book from our website.
- After you install the folders and files on your computer, you can move or copy them to another device or another location.
- You may also want to make a second copy of the exercises folder as a backup. Then, if you want to go back to the original version of the starting code for an exercise, you'll have it.

Figure A-3 How to install the files for this book

How to make sure Anaconda is installed correctly

Figure A-4 begins by showing how to make sure Anaconda is installed correctly. To do that, you can start JupyterLab, open the Notebook file named test_anaconda, and run all of the cells in this Notebook. These cells use Pandas to display a table and Seaborn to display a plot. As a result, if these cells run correctly, Anaconda is installed correctly on your system.

How to download the large data files for this book

This figure also shows how to download three large data files that aren't included in the download for this book. To do that, you use JupyterLab to open the Notebook file named download_more_data. Then, you run all of the cells in this notebook. If these cells run successfully, you have downloaded and unzipped the large data files needed for this book. Since these files are approximately 300MB, it may take several minutes or more to download them.

The folder that contains the data files for this book

`\Documents\python_analysis\data`

JupyterLab with the Notebook named test_anaconda open

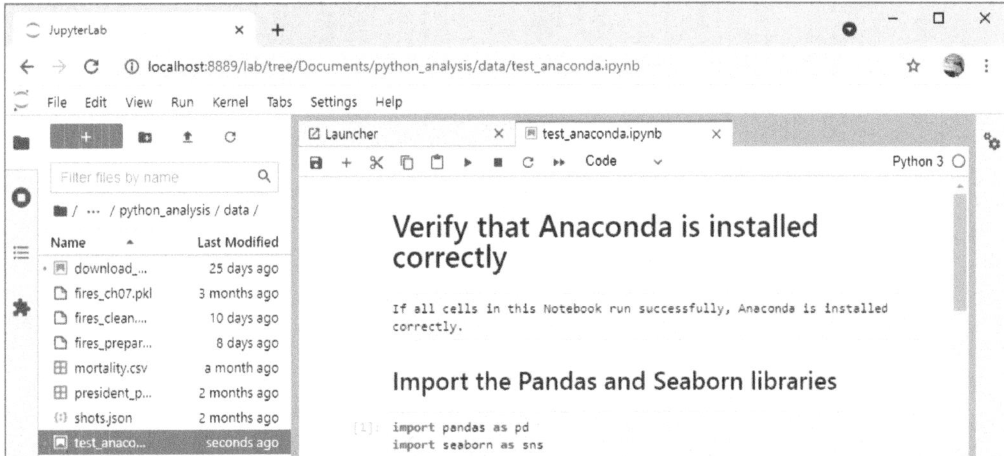

How to test Anaconda to make sure it's installed correctly

1. Start Anaconda Navigator.
2. Start JupyterLab.
3. Use JupyterLab to navigate to the data folder shown above.
4. Double-click on the Notebook file named test_anaconda to open it.
5. From the Kernel menu, select "Restart Kernel and Run All Cells". When you do, the cells in this Notebook should read some data from a CSV file and display that data in a table and a plot.

How to download the large data files for this book

1. Open the Notebook file named download_more_data.
2. From the Kernel menu, select "Restart Kernel and Run All Cells". This should download and unzip the large data files needed for this book. This may take several minutes or more to run, so be patient.

Description

- The download for this book contains most of the data files that are used by this book. However, some of the files are too large to include in the download for this book. To get these files, you can run the Notebook named download_more_data that's in the python_analysis\data folder.
- The cells in the download_more_data Notebook download and unzip files that are approximately 300MB. As a result, they may take several minutes or more to run.

Figure A-4 How to test Anaconda and download the large data files

Appendix B

How to set up macOS for this book

This appendix shows how to install the Anaconda distribution of Python. This distribution includes the Pandas and Seaborn libraries described in this book as well as JupyterLab, which is the Integrated Development Environment (IDE) that you'll be using throughout this book. This IDE lets you keep the code for each analysis in a Jupyter Notebook that consists of cells that contain the headings and code for the analysis.

This appendix also shows how to download and install the Notebooks for this book. That includes the Notebooks for the examples in chapters 1-11, the case studies in chapters 12-15, and the exercises at the ends of chapters 1-15.

How to install and use Anaconda

Before you can learn how to use Python for data analysis, you need to install the Anaconda distribution of Python, and you need to know how to use the Anaconda Prompt and the Anaconda Navigator. The first two figures show how.

How to install Anaconda

Figure B-1 shows how to install a Python environment for data analysis on your own computer. Specifically, it shows you how to install Anaconda, which is the most popular distribution for data analysis and visualization.

This is a typical installation that shouldn't give you any trouble. For this book, you should install the latest release, which is 3.8 at this writing. If you're like most users, you can accept all of the defaults.

When the installation program is finished, you should be able to use Finder to start Anaconda Navigator as described in this figure. In addition, you should be able to start Terminal.

The URL for Anaconda's download page

www.anaconda.com/products/individual

How to install Anaconda

1. Go to the URL shown above. This displays the download page for the Individual Edition of the Anaconda distribution.
2. Click the Download button. This should download the Python 3.8 installer file for macOS.
3. Run the installer and respond to the resulting dialog boxes. When in doubt, accept the default options.

How to start Anaconda Navigator

1. Start Finder and select Applications.
2. Double-click on Anaconda-Navigator.

How to start Terminal

1. Start Finder and select Applications.
2. Expand Utilities.
3. Double-click on Terminal.

Description

- After the Anaconda distribution has been installed, you can start Anaconda Navigator and Terminal, and you can use them as described in the next figure.

Figure B-1 How to install Anaconda

How to run conda commands

The Terminal application can be used to run conda commands that update Anaconda to the latest release or install a Python package or module that isn't included in the Anaconda distribution. Figure B-2 shows Terminal as well as the commands for updating Anaconda and installing packages that aren't in the Anaconda distribution that are used by this book.

How to use the Anaconda Navigator

When you launch Anaconda Navigator, it displays a Home tab like the one shown in figure B-2. This tab shows the installed and available applications for your base environment. An *environment* is one version of Python that's configured with a specific group of settings, packages, and related applications.

As the Home tab shows, the Anaconda base installation includes components like JupyterLab, the IDE that you'll use for this book. Then, to start this component, you just click on its Launch button.

However, the Navigator has more to offer than just that. For instance, you can use the Environments tab to browse an index of all the installed packages in your current environment. There, you can update, install, and delete packages.

Similarly, you can use the Learning tab to get access to all sorts of information that will help you learn how to use Python for data analysis. That includes documentation, demonstrations, tutorials, and more. Of course, all of that will make more sense and be more useful to you after you read this book.

Terminal with a command running

```
joelmurach — conda update --all — 80×24
Last login: Mon May  3 22:34:27 on ttys001
(base) Joels-MacBook-Air:~ joelmurach$ conda update --all
Collecting package metadata (current_repodata.json): done
Solving environment: -
```

The command for updating Anaconda to the latest release

```
conda update --all
```

Commands for installing two packages that aren't included with Anaconda

```
conda install pyreadstat --channel conda-forge --yes
conda install geopandas --channel conda-forge
```

The Home tab of the Anaconda Navigator

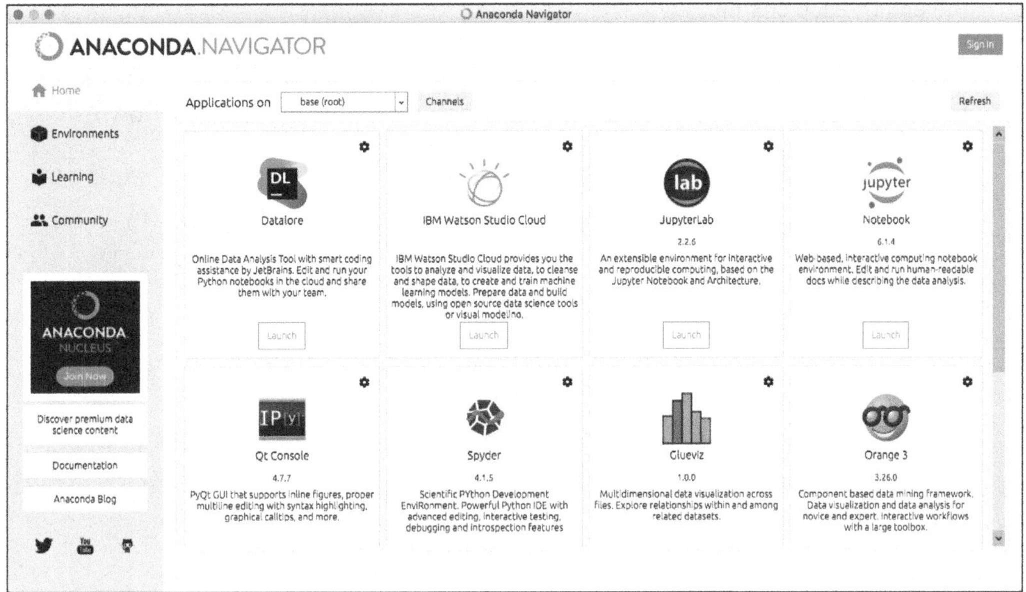

Description

- You can use Terminal to run conda commands that update the Anaconda release or to install packages that aren't included in the Anaconda distribution.
- You can use the Home tab of Anaconda Navigator to launch the components that are included in the distribution and to install other components.
- You can use the Environments tab of Anaconda Navigator to browse, update, install, and delete packages in your current environment.
- You can use the Learning tab of Anaconda Navigator to access documentation, demonstrations, and tutorials on all aspects of Python data analysis.

Figure B-2 How to run conda commands and use the Anaconda Navigator

How to install and use the files for this book

To help you get the most from this book, all of the files that you need for doing that are included in the download for this book. The two figures that follow show how to install them as well as how to use them to test your Anaconda installation and to download the large files for this book.

How to install the files for this book

Figure B-3 shows how to install the Notebooks that you need for this book. This includes the Notebooks for all of the book examples and case studies presented in this book as well as the Notebooks that you'll need for doing the exercises at the end of each chapter.

When you finish the procedure in this figure, the Notebooks for this book will be in the folders shown in this figure. Then, you can open these Notebooks, review the code, test the code, do the exercises, and experiment on your own.

The Murach website

`www.murach.com`

The folder for the book examples, case studies, and exercises

`\Documents\python_analysis`

The subfolders

Folder	Description
`case_studies`	The case studies presented in chapters 12-15 of this book.
`data`	Some of the data files that are used by this book.
`examples`	The examples presented in chapters 1-11 of this book.
`exercises`	The starting points for the exercises presented at the end of each chapter.
`solutions`	The solutions to the exercises.

How to download and install the files for this book

1. Go to www.murach.com.
2. Find the page for *Murach's Python for Data Analysis.*
3. If necessary, scroll down to the FREE downloads tab.
4. Click the FREE downloads tab.
5. Click the Download Now button for the zip file. This should download a file named dap1_allfiles.zip.
6. Find the zip file on your computer and double-click on it. This should extract the files for this book into a folder named python_analysis.
7. Use Finder to move the python_analysis folder into your Documents folder.

Description

- You can download the folders and files that contain the Jupyter Notebooks for this book from our website.
- After you install the folders and files on your computer, you can move or copy them to another device or another location.
- You may also want to make a second copy of the exercises folder as a backup. Then, if you want to go back to the original version of the starting code for an exercise, you'll have it.

Figure B-3 How to install the files for this book

How to make sure Anaconda is installed correctly

Figure B-4 begins by showing how to make sure Anaconda is installed correctly. To do that, you can start JupyterLab, open the Notebook file named test_anaconda, and run all of the cells in this notebook. These cells use Pandas to display a table and Seaborn to display a plot. As a result, if these cells run correctly, Anaconda is installed correctly on your system.

How to download the large data files for this book

This figure also shows how to download three large data files there weren't included in the download for this book. To do that, you use JupyterLab to open the Notebook file named download_more_data. Then, you run all of the cells in this notebook. If these cells run successfully, you have downloaded and unzipped the large data files needed for this book. Since these files are approximately 300MB, it may take several minutes or more to download them.

The folder that contains the data files for this book

```
\Documents\python_analysis\data
```

JupyterLab with the Notebook named test_anaconda open

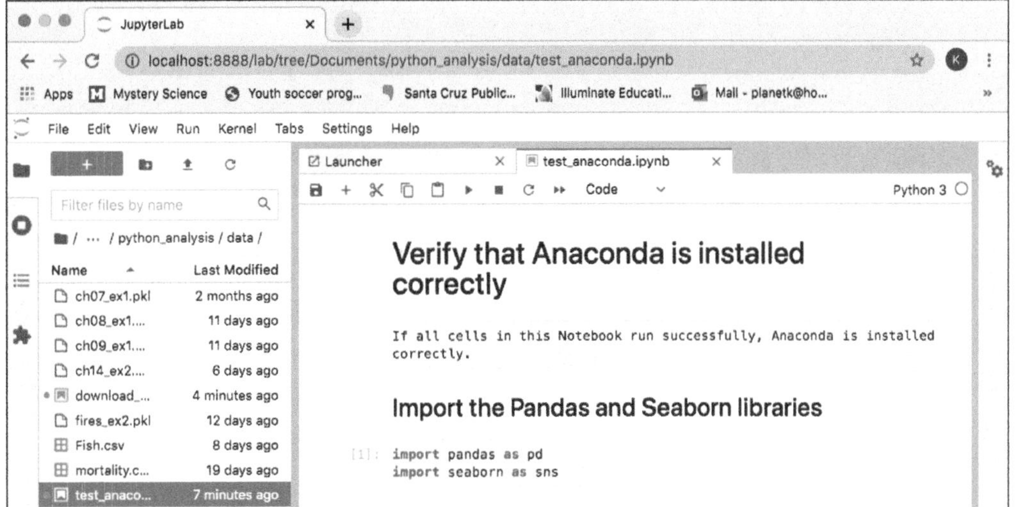

How to test Anaconda to make sure it's installed correctly

1. Start Anaconda Navigator.
2. Start JupyterLab.
3. Use JupyterLab to navigate to the data folder shown above.
4. Double-click on the Notebook file named test_anaconda to open it.
5. From the Kernel menu, select "Restart Kernel and Run All Cells". When you do, the cells in this Notebook should read some data from a CSV file and display that data in a table and a plot.

How to download the large data files for this book

1. Open the Notebook file named download_more_data.
2. From the Kernel menu, select "Restart Kernel and Run All Cells". This should download and unzip the large data files needed for this book.

Description

- The download for this book contains most of the data files that are used by this book. However, some of the files were too large to include in the download for this book. To get these files, you can run the Notebook named download_more_data that's in the python_analysis\data folder.
- The cells in the download_more_data Notebook download and unzip files that are approximately 300MB. As a result, they may take several minutes or more to run.

Figure B-4 How to test Anaconda and download the large data files

Index

D

E

F

G

H

I

J

K

L

M

N

O

P

Q

R

S

T

U

V

W

XYZ

100% Guarantee

When you order directly from us, you must be satisfied. Try our books for 30 days or our eBooks for 14 days. They must work better than any other programming training you've ever used, or you can return them for a prompt refund. No questions asked!

Mike Murach, Publisher   *Ben Murach, President*

Have you mastered Python?

Python is everywhere today! So if you know only enough to get by, let our Python book build up your skills and your options, using the same practical approach, paired pages, and real-world examples that have turned you into a data analyst.

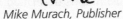

Programming language books

Murach's Python Programming (2nd Ed.)	$59.50
Murach's C# (7th Ed.)	59.50
Murach's C++ Programming	59.50
Murach's Java Programming (5th Ed.)	59.50

Data analysis and SQL books

Murach's Python for Data Analysis	$59.50
Murach's MySQL (3rd Ed.)	$57.50
Murach's Oracle SQL and PL/SQL for Developers (2nd Ed.)	54.50
Murach's SQL Server 2019 for Developers	59.50

Web development books

Murach's JavaScript and jQuery (4th Ed.)	$59.50
Murach's PHP and MySQL (3rd Ed.)	57.50
Murach's ASP.NET Core MVC	59.50
Murach's ASP.NET 4.6 Web Programming with C# 2015	59.50
Murach's Java Servlets and JSP (3rd Ed.)	57.50

**Prices and availability are subject to change. Please visit our website or call for current information.*

We want to hear from you

Do you have any comments, questions, or compliments to pass on to us? It would be great to hear from you! Please share your feedback in whatever way works best.

 www.murach.com

 1-800-221-5528
(Weekdays, 8 am to 4 pm Pacific Time)

 murachbooks@murach.com

 twitter.com/murachbooks

 facebook.com/murachbooks

 linkedin.com/company/mike-murach-&-associates

 instagram.com/murachbooks

What software you need for this book

- The Anaconda distribution of Python and the JupyterLab development environment that comes with it.
- You can download this software for free and install it as described in appendix A (Windows) or appendix B (macOS).

The downloadable files for this book

- JupyterLab Notebook files that contain the code examples that are presented in chapters 1-11.
- JupyterLab Notebook files that contain the four case studies that are presented in chapters 12-15.
- JupyterLab Notebook files for the starting points for the exercises presented at the end of each chapter.
- JupyterLab Notebook files for the solutions to the exercises.

How to download the programs and files

1. Go to www.murach.com.
2. Find the page for ***Murach's Python for Data Analysis.***
3. If necessary, scroll down to the FREE downloads tab.
4. Click the FREE downloads tab.
5. Click the Download Now button for the zip file. This should download a file named dap1_allfiles.zip.
6. Find the zip file on your computer and double-click on it. This should extract the files for this book into a folder named python_analysis.
7. Move the python_analysis folder into your Documents folder.

   For more information, please see appendix A (Windows) or B (macOS).